Dictionary
of
Pronunciation

Also by Abraham Lass

THE WAY TO WRITE (with Rudolf Flesch)
BUSINESS SPELLING AND WORD POWER

Dictionary
of
Pronunciation

Abraham and Betty Lass

Quadrangle/The New York Times Book Co.

Copyright © 1976 by Abraham and Betty Lass

All rights reserved, including the right to reproduce
this book or portions thereof in any form.

For information, address:
Quadrangle/The New York Times Book Co., Inc.
10 East 53 Street, New York, New York 10022.

Manufactured in the United States of America.
Published simultaneously in Canada by
Fitzhenry & Whiteside, Ltd., Toronto.

Designed by Beth Tondreau

Second printing, November 1978

Library of Congress Cataloging in Publication Data

Lass, Abraham Harold, 1907–
    Dictionary of pronunciation.

    1. English language—Pronunciation.
2. English language—Dictionaries. I. Lass, Betty,
joint author. II. Title.
PE1137.L38   428′.1   75–36252
ISBN 0–8129–0614–4

to
Janet, Paul, and Miranda

Acknowledgments

Our thanks—
At Quadrangle/The New York Times Book Company
 To Herbert Nagourney, President, for his encouragement and his many kindnesses.
 To Roger Jellinek, Editor-in-Chief, for his patience, wit, and resourcefulness.
 To Edward McLeroy, Editor, for his unflappably meticulous attention to everything.
 To Addie Sneider for her gracious, unfailing helpfulness.
To Victor Weidman, Vice-President, G. & C. Merriam Company, publishers of the *Merriam-Webster Dictionaries,* for making available to us his staff's scholarship and expertise.
To John K. Bollard, Assistant Editor, G. & C. Merriam Company, for his valuable insights and incisive comments.
To David R. Replogle, Director of the *American Heritage Dictionary of the English Language,* and to Ms. Leonore C. Hauck, Managing Editor, *Random House Dictionaries,* for their full and informative responses to our many queries.
We are especially grateful to David B. Guralnik, Editor-in-Chief, *Webster's New World Dictionary,* for his professional suggestions and assistance, and for his personal warmth and generosity.

A.L.
B.L.

Dictionary
of
Pronunciation

Introduction

The following forty words appeared in four pages of *The New York Times* of August 6, 1975. Some have only one correct pronunciation; others have three or more. How do you pronounce them?

either	schizophrenia	penal
vanilla	economics	municipal
corral	bubonic	surveillance
raspberry	divorcee	chocolate
hierarchy	barbiturate	abdomen
clique	temperature	adult
era	amateur	haphazard
advertisement	aerial	inherent
patronage	subsidiary	punitive
conglomerate	deteriorate	priority
primordial	grandeur	jeopardy
decolletage	chaise longue	squander
binoculars	environment	milieu
taut		

Now try pronouncing the underlined words in the following tales: *The Sheriff's Dilemma* and *An Orthoepic Mélange.**

*Used by permission of G. & C. Merriam Company, publishers of the Merriam-Webster Dictionaries. When first published, these two tales were widely used in American colleges and universities to pique students' interest in pronunciation. They were designed to be both amusing and instructive.

The Sheriff's Dilemma

"Form a posse!" shouted the robust sheriff. "A most formidable brigand is at large."

"Is where?" asked the comptroller, lying on an exquisite divan. He was enjoying a respite from the worries of finance.

"You chimpanzee," replied the sheriff, gnashing his teeth, "your ignorance is lamentable—and grievous, and—"

"Irremediable," supplied his incomparable deputy, who hated the comptroller for divers causes. With an admirable twist to his mustache, he continued, "Unless I err, the gibbet, an elephantine tripod, is ready, sheriff. Let's end this longevity of our barbarous brigand."

"He means levity," roared the comptroller. But they had left, carrying with great travail a tarpaulin and a tepee.

After passing a commandant and his corps, who offered means of condign punishment—but no help or victuals—they halted their excursion, for culinary purposes, albeit they had only one vegetable, some pecans, a salmon, and little venison.

"We must wrestle with this further," bade the sheriff in his address.

"Aye," responded a mischievous adult, chewing in bestial fashion, "although genuine venison would be preferable. In zoology, I remember, viscera were not—"

"I reckon," calmly interrupted the incomparable deputy, gnawing, "we'd better reconnoiter. Our infamous, despicable combatant—"

"Competent," corrected the agile comptroller, who, completing his chores, had arrived. "Your orthoepy is—"

"Admirable," finished the sheriff, all roiled. "Let's cross this bayou."

"Chaos and mortgages!" shouted the comptroller, scratching himself as they forded the creek. The water had rinsed off his medicinal preparation for eczema.

"The curse of the brigand!" was the cry, and they seized him. An epistle and a coupon disclosed his cognomen. Mounting a natural dais near a crevasse, he gave, somewhat awry, his version of his biography.

While erecting the caryatides on the façade of a cathedral, he fell into the slough of despond because of conjugal difficulties. His courtierlike attitude was short-lived, and he married a geisha who had a penchant for buying perukes all the livelong day.

"Impious," muttered the sheriff, looking askance at him, "but explicable. Now, an autopsy will—"

"No alibi," went on the brigand, now docile enough, "will condone my debut into crime. Hospitable, subtle, I could have been—" He daubed his eyes. The incomparable deputy, discomfited, plucked a gladiolus and burst into a ribald song. Becoming anecdotal, the brigand told of a gala orgy in an occult chasm, the story almost causing a schism in the group.

Failing to soften the jury, he was indicted as a sleek villain, as the epitome of all criminal debris. To his valet he bequeathed his broken, though reparable, yacht. Deaf to all, he drank naphtha to cure his ague and diphtheria. Finally, bitten by remorse, already clad in cerements, he contracted rabies, and, muttering diphthongs, burst his jugular vein. With great clangor, his demise was announced. A psalm was sung as a requiem by the posse, which made up the cortege.

An Orthoepic Mélange

Not long since, a robust collegian, his clothes of the latest Pall Mall cut, his carmine bifurcated necktie ornamented with a solitaire, his hair dressed with oleomargarine and perfumed with ambergris, his face innocent of hirsute adornment, but his mouth guilty of nicotine, informed a senile, splenetic lawyer that he did not pronounce according to the dictionary.

"For," observed the young man, with an air of research, "in your Tuesday's address you said that the sight of cerements sufficed to enervate an attorney; that a salamander treated for obesity with prussic acid and pomegranate rind was disinclined to serpentine movements; that in an Aldine edition of a legal work you read of a lugubrious man afflicted with virulent bronchitis, for which a jocund allopathist injected iodine and cayenne pepper with a syringe warmed in a caldron of tepid sirup—a malpractice suit being the result. By the way, you have a dictionary?"

"Dictionary?" replied the lawyer; "pugh! It is a granary from which the pronunciation fiend fills his commissariat with orthoepic romances and vagaries which, to him, grow into a fetish; and this fetishism finds outward expression in a supercilious ostentation of erudite vacuity."

Nothing daunted, the young man continued: "You said, 'According to precedent it was obligatory upon him to plait his hair as his Nomad parents had done, but instead he, precedent to stepping under the mistletoe, indulged in fulsome praise of himself, hoping thereby to induce a favorite girl to join him. But she, being averse to undergo an ordeal so embarrassing, refused; whereupon his features became immobile with chagrin.' This is a verbatim quotation. You sometimes consult a dictionary?"

"Young man," retorted the lawyer, his aquiline nose quivering with derisive disdain, "I have no use for a dictionary."

"Pardon me, your pronunciation indicates the contrary; thus, in your peroration this occurs: 'An incognito communist, being commandant on the frontier, in one of his hunting expeditions came upon an Indian, who, to the accompaniment of the soughing wind, was softly playing a flageolet, for the purpose of quieting a wounded hydrophobic tiger, which, penned up in a hovel, was making hideous grimaces.

" 'The Colonel's companion, comely but truculent, acting as seneschal suggested giving the rampant animal some <u>dynamite</u>, <u>morphine</u>, and <u>saline</u> yeast.

" 'A <u>noose</u> was adjusted, and the <u>nauseous</u> dose administered, whereupon the <u>combative</u> tiger, thus <u>harassed</u>, coming in premature contact with a <u>dilapidated divan bade adieu</u> to things <u>sublunary</u>.' You have a dictionary?"

The old man, angered at the <u>raillery</u> of this question, and at the <u>cherubic</u> smile of superiority with which it was asked, launched forth in a tirade.

There are many more than 194 acceptable pronunciations for these 194 underlined words. A good number are correctly pronounced more than one way. And a good number are regularly mispronounced.

The following statements probably describe how you felt or what you thought as you tried to pronounce the words from *The New York Times, The Sheriff's Dilemma,* and *An Orthoepic Mélange.*

• Some of these words you were absolutely sure you were pronouncing correctly.

• Some words were not quite so familiar to you. You had pronounced them occasionally or had heard them pronounced by others. But you were no longer certain about how to pronounce them. So you hesitated a few moments, considered a few alternative pronunciations, and then just guessed at what you thought you remembered.

• While you understood what these words meant, you had not the faintest idea how to pronounce them—so you didn't even try to pronounce them.

• You thought there was only one acceptable pronunciation for each word.

• You may have discovered that you were actually mispronouncing words you had thought you always pronounced correctly.

So these 234 words left you feeling a little less confident about how acceptable your pronunciation really is.

If you are like most of us, you are embarrassed when you mispronounce a word. You feel that mispronouncing common, or even uncommon, words marks you as not quite educated. And you are right. True, every day some radio and television announcers, prominent public figures, and others who should know better commit many common or rare or inventive or outrageous pronunciation errors like

substantuate for *substantiate*
(the venerable Senator Sam Ervin during the Watergate hearings)

grievious for *grievous*
(former Attorney-General John Mitchell at the Watergate hearings)

nucular for *nuclear*
(a former President of the United States)

surrupchoous for *surreptitious*
(an anchor man on a television program)

archeepelaygo for *archipelago*
(a prominent Hollywood commentator).

And here are a few more that make their perpetrators sound at least a trifle uneducated:

jewlery for *jewelry*
anticlimatic for *anticlimactic*
shamelon for *chameleon*
deteriate for *deteriorate*
irrevelant for *irrelevant*
mischeevious for *mischievous*
athalete for *athlete*
heighth for *height*
perculator for *percolator*

Though many of these (and other) mispronunciations are fairly common, the educated community does not regard them as anything to be proud of. Of course, you can still make a million, have friends, influence people, be admired for your good sense, be loved for your good heart, send your children to the best colleges, become President of the United States even if your pronunciation is not what it should be. But you will still be judged by the words you mispronounce. And you may not be judged kindly.

Can you acquire a pronunciation vocabulary that will not embarrass you? Yes, you can, with the aid of this *Dictionary of Pronunciation,* which we have designed to enable you quickly and easily to check your pronunciation with the country's foremost authorities on the English language.

First we drew up a list of over 8000 words that pose various kinds of pronunciation problems for all sorts of people—for the elementary school, or high school, or college graduate, the doctor, the lawyer, the radio and TV announcer, the college professor. At one time or another, these words confuse and embarrass most people. Some of these words you see, hear, and use frequently. Some you recognize immediately. You know what they mean, but you don't use them often in your speech, and you don't often hear them spoken. Others you may run into infrequently or not at all.

We compiled this list of words from various sources: tested "word lists" which indicate how frequently you are likely to meet them in your reading, scholarly pronouncing dictionaries, source books of words frequently mispronounced, and our own and our friends' experiences with the fascinating unpredictabilities of American pronunciation of the English language.

Then, for each of these 8000 and more words, we set down the pronunciations recorded in each of four major American desk dictionaries: *Webster's New World Dictionary, American Heritage Dictionary of the English Language, Webster's New Collegiate Dictionary,* and the *Random House College Dictionary.* We chose the desk dictionaries rather than the unabridged dictionaries because most people own and use desk dictionaries, and because they are authoritative without being overwhelming.

A great many words have more than one acceptable pronunciation; all the dictionaries, however, do not list the same number of acceptable pronunciations. So we compiled a "box score" for each acceptable pronunciation of each word, and next to each pronunciation we placed a figure that tells you how many of our four desk dictionaries record that specific pronunciation. For example, the figure 4 at the right of the pronunciation tells you that all of the four desk dictionaries recognize this pronunciation as heard among educated speakers, and hence record it as acceptable. The figure 3 at the right of the pronunciation tells you that only three of the four desk dictionaries find this pronunciation acceptable.

The desk dictionaries do not list all the pronunciations (called "variants") that their experts have recorded for each of our 8000-plus words. They list only those that they believe are the most frequently used and heard. As our box score makes clear, the dictionaries do not always agree, though many variants seem to differ only very slightly from each other. If you hear one of the less frequent variants used among educated people in your part of our country, you should feel perfectly comfortable in using it, no matter how it rates on our box score—4, 3, 2, or 1. We have not listed all the variant pronunciations recorded by the four desk dictionaries for to have done so would have made this book impossibly long.

The variant pronunciations we have listed are characterized by the dictionaries as "acceptable," "standard," "used by the greatest numbers of cultivated speakers," "those of educated speech." (See below for a fuller description of how dictionary makers arrive at these conclusions.) Earlier dictionaries used to indicate which variant pronunciation they preferred. Modern dictionaries avoid indicating any preference among pronunciations. They simply record the pronunciations they hear most often among educated people.

We have placed an asterisk (*) next to our preferred pronunciations.
Here are some reasons for our preferences:
• This is the way our elementary school teachers first taught us to say the word. They taught us pronunciation with the same kind of zeal and thoroughness they taught us everything else.
• This is how we first heard the words pronounced. This is how we have always pronounced them. So they sound right and feel right to us.
• This is how we have heard educated people in our part and other parts of our country pronounce these words.
• We prefer our pronunciations because we have lived with them all our lives.
The words we have listed are not the only English words frequently mispronounced. There are obviously many we have not included. But our list, we feel, represents a wide range of common words that spell pronunciation trouble for many people. We have also included some less common words for their intrinsic pronunciation interest. We have omitted many foreign words we had hoped to include because the dictionaries could not reach a reasonable agreement about how these words should be pronounced in *English*. Finally, where the *total* box score for any word adds up to only 3, this indicates that one of our dictionaries did not list that word.

Who decides which pronunciations are "correct" or "standard"?
Offhand you would say, "the dictionaries." But you would be wrong. Today's dictionaries do not really decide. They do not tell you what to say or how to say it. Here is how they see themselves (italics ours):
"Dictionaries are not lawmakers. They are merely *law recorders.* A pronunciation is not 'correct' or standard because it is given in a dictionary; rather it should be found in a good dictionary because *good usage has already made it standard.* There is no single hypothetically 'correct' standard for all speakers of American English (in the sense that Received English is the guide for British English) since *the usage*

of cultivated speakers in any region or locality constitutes a standard for that area. Hence, since the scope of a desk dictionary prohibits inclusion of every possible acceptable variant, the editors of such a dictionary are justified in recording *those pronunciations used by the greatest numbers of cultivated speakers. . . .* The reader can be assured that although no single standard exists for the whole nation, the kind of pronunciation here indicated is acceptable anywhere in the United States. . . . The pronunciations recorded in this dictionary are those used by cultivated speakers in normal, relaxed conversation." *(Webster's New World Dictionary)*

"The pronunciations recorded in the Dictionary are *exclusively* those of educated speech. No pronunciation is given that would be regarded by any large group as a mispronunciation. . . . In every community, educated speech is accepted and understood by everyone, including those who do not use it." *(American Heritage Dictionary of the English Language)*

"The function of a pronouncing dictionary is to record as far as possible the pronunciations prevailing in the best present usage rather than to attempt to dictate what that usage should be. Insofar as a dictionary may be known and acknowledged as a faithful recorder and interpreter of such usage, so far and no farther may it be appealed to as an authority. In the case of diverse usages of extensive prevalence, the dictionary must recognize each of them." *(Webster's New Collegiate Dictionary)*

". . . any pronunciation shown is common to many educated speakers of the language." *(Random House College Dictionary)*

We asked the editors of the desk dictionaries we used how they decided which pronunciations to list. We are very grateful indeed for their sharing with us and our readers a description of their problems and procedures. We believe that this is the first time that such an insider's look into the intricate process of dictionary-making has appeared in a book of this kind.

Dr. David B. Guralnik, Editor-in-Chief of *Webster's New World Dictionary,* tells us how he and his staff reach their decisions on which pronunciations to record:

> Our decisions are based on 1) an oral citation file collected and maintained by our phonologist, Dr. William Chisholm, and other members of the staff (inadequate, to be sure, but so any such file would be unless it consisted of tapes collected by hundreds of field workers distributed throughout the country, recording continually on the wing); 2) the collective judgments of a staff of linguistically sensitive lexicographers; 3) the responses to polls taken among a group of geographically distributed informants; 4) for technical terms in the special disciplines, the judgments of our special editors, fortified by polls taken by them among colleagues; 5) for names of places and persons, the responses to our queries from the persons bearing the names or from officials in the places. . . .
>
> Where two or more pronunciations for a single word are given, the order in which they are entered does not necessarily mean that the first is preferred to or more correct than the one or ones that follow. In most cases, the order indicates that on the basis of available information, the form given first is the one most frequent in general cultivated use. Where usage is about evenly divided, the editors' preference generally prevails. Unless a variant is qualified by *now rarely* or *occasionally* or some such note, it is understood that any pronunciation here entered represents standard use.

Here is how John K. Bollard, assistant editor of G. & C. Merriam Company (publishers of *Webster's New Collegiate Dictionary*) and his staff decide which pronunciations to list in their dictionaries:

> Many words in English have two, three, or even more different pronunciations, all of which are perfectly acceptable. *In our dictionaries the pronunciations represented are determined by the files we have built up over the years of actual pronunciations used by educated speakers of English* [italics ours]. We have spent thousands of hours over the past forty years listening to and transcribing live speech and radio and television broadcasts and have built up a unique and extensive set of pronunciation files which provide the evidence on which our decisions are based. (Naturally, our pronunciation editors also do their best to keep up with developments in linguistic theory, with publications in journals devoted to language, and with the progress of the various projects throughout the country relating to the Linguistic Atlas of the United States and Canada.) When it comes time to transcribe the pronunciation in a dictionary entry, we examine the files for that word and we include the variants which appear frequently enough to show that they are widely used. In general the variants which appear most frequently are entered first, followed by less frequent, but still acceptable, variants. With many words, however, two or more variants are so widely used that no one can be said to be more frequent than another; but of course one of them has to be printed first and another last. Thus the order of variants does not necessarily indicate significant difference in frequency or preference. A variant that is noticeably less common is prefixed by *also,* as at the entry *rabid* in Webster's New Collegiate Dictionary. These less common variants are still acceptable and are used by many educated speakers, but not as many as use the preceding variants. Occasionally regional labels are used to indicate the geographic restriction of a variant pronunciation if that variant differs significantly from other variants and if its distribution may be described succinctly, as at *dahlia* and *great* in the New Collegiate. *We recommend that the dictionary consultant adopt whichever variant seems most natural to him and most suitable to the dialect spoken in his own region; we do not feel that we should prescribe usage or pronunciation when millions of educated English speakers can be heard to use so many variant pronunciations. Pronunciations of a given word in various dictionaries edited at different times may not always agree, but for our part we do our best to describe the pronunciation of present-day English as accurately and as objectively as possible* [italics ours].

Mr. Bollard comments further: "... I would like to stress that we consider all the elements contained in that (the above) paragraph to be important factors in our understanding and evaluation of modern American pronunciation. As lexicographers, we can only describe the language as we find it is spoken and written; it is not our role to prescribe or dictate usage in any sense."*

*The publishers of *Webster's New Collegiate Dictionary,* copyright 1975, G. & C. Merriam Co., are in no way responsible for the interpretations and retranscriptions in this book. The information represented by the pronunciation system in *Webster's New Collegiate Dictionary* is best obtained by direct reference to the dictionary itself, especially to the explanatory notes on pages 11a-12a and the chart of pronunciation symbols on page 32a.

Speaking for the *Random House College Dictionary*, Ms. Leonore C. Hauck, Managing Editor, Random House Dictionaries, writes:

Here is a general picture of our own procedures: We had a number of editors assigned fully to pronunciations, directed on policy primarily by Professor Arthur Bronstein. In their work they were guided by available publications (popular and scholarly), by taped and transcribed citations, by inquiries addressed to selected authorities, and by staff discussions. The decisions as to which pronunciations to include and which to restrict by usage labels were reached by the above techniques, subject to review by the general supervisory editors.

With regard to the frequency of pronunciations: The first pronunciation shown is generally the one considered to be in most frequent use, although there may be very little difference in usage between any two consecutive pronunciations. Occasionally, when there is some disagreement about how widespread a certain pronunciation is among educated speakers, that pronunciation may be preceded by a qualifying label, as 'often' or 'sometimes.' To amplify this with respect to your specific queries, we would say that while the above was the general aim, and it is therefore valid to say that the first pronunciation shown was determined in general to be the most frequent, *it is not possible to infer any real distinction from the position of subsequent variants, which often are equally frequent and there is no way of showing this.* In fact, it is even conceivable that there may be cases where the first pronunciation and the first variant are equally frequent.

According to David R. Replogle, consultant to the *American Heritage Dictionary of the English Language,* this is the approach to pronunciation adopted by that dictionary's staff:

The American Heritage Dictionary was conceived and developed with the intention of providing the user with superior usage guidance comparable to that which is available in strictly citational based, "descriptive" styled dictionaries. This concept applies to pronunciation as well as word usage. To accomplish this, the opinion of experts was sought, i.e., the Usage Panel and experienced pronunciation editors.

The direction relative to pronunciation has simply been to list standard, conservative, widely acceptable pronunciation for each entry word. Variants in pronunciation are treated by listing the most common formal standard form first with more informal usage variants given thereafter as appropriate.

Heritage did not do extensive "listening" citational work for pronunciations. Expert opinion was directly called upon and there was a dependence on information from technical works and specialized dictionaries.

Here, then, in brief, is what the four major desk dictionaries we have consulted agree upon when they record their pronunciations:
• They "reflect the pronunciations of cultivated speakers" all over the country as accurately as they can determine these with their present instruments and techniques. They do not know how many cultivated speakers are employing their pronunciations. At best theirs is an informed guess.

• There is no single standard American pronunciation. There are a number of regional pronunciations used in different areas of our country. These differ from each other in some respects. But individuals from one region have no difficulty understanding the pronunciations of cultivated individuals from other regions. "It is accepted here that cultivated speech can and does exist in all regions . . ." *(Random House College Dictionary)*

• All living languages change. In the last two generations our language has undergone many changes. These changes have been set in motion and accelerated by two World Wars, vast population shifts in our country, the pervasive influence of the mass media (the press, radio, television, movies, etc.). Our dictionaries have tried to reflect the way educated people all over America use our language today.

As Philip Gove, the late editor-in-chief of the Merriam-Webster Dictionaries put it in a letter to *The New York Times* (November 5, 1961), "Whether you or I or others who fixed our linguistic notions several decades ago like it or not, the contemporary English language . . . the language we have to live with, the only language we have to survive with, is not the language of the Nineteen Twenties and Thirties."

• Today's dictionary-makers derive their "acceptable" pronunciations from a vast number of recordings of radio, TV, public addresses, transcriptions of interviews, etc. These provide them with a record of actual pronunciations in a natural context—"the only sound basis for determining pronunciation." No dictionary records every pronunciation used by educated speakers for each word it lists. Those they do list you can use with confidence. "An omitted pronunciation does not necessarily imply its absence in the educated community." *(Random House College Dictionary)*

HOW TO USE THIS DICTIONARY

The following Pronunciation Key appears on every right hand page of this book.

The Symbols (letters) in the first column represent all the important sounds in English. There is one symbol (letter or letters) for each sound.

The Key Words illustrate how each symbol (letter or letters) sounds when it appears in a word.

When you want to find the pronunciation of any word, you simply match the letters of the word you are looking up with the symbols listed in the Pronunciation Key, and then, with the examples given in the Key Words, pronounce the letters in your word just as you pronounce them in the Key Words.

The Pronunciation Key and the Key Words are so put together that when you pronounce the Key Words for each symbol you will almost automatically pronounce your word in a way that is consistent with educated speech in your community or region of the country.

PRONUNCIATION KEY

Symbol	Key words	Symbol	Key words	Symbol	Key words
a	asp, fat, parrot	†ə	a in ago	r	red, port, dear
ā	ape, date, play		e in agent	s	sell, castle, pass
†ä	ah, car, father		i in sanity	t	top, cattle, hat
e	elf, ten, berry		o in comply	v	vat, hovel, have
ē	even, meet, money		u in focus	w	will, always, swear
i	is, hit, mirror	ər	perhaps, murder	y	yet, onion, yard
ī	ice, bite, high	b	bed, fable, dub	z	zebra, dazzle, haze
ō	open, tone, go	d	dip, beadle, had	ch	chin, catcher, arch
ô	all, horn, law	f	fall, after, off	sh	she, cushion, dash
o͞o	ooze, tool, crew	g	get, haggle, dog	th	thin, nothing, truth
oo	look, pull, moor	h	he, ahead, hotel	th	then, father, lathe
yo͞o	use, cute, few	j	joy, agile, badge	zh	azure, leisure
yoo	united, cure, globule	k	kill, tackle, bake	ŋ	ring, anger, drink
oi	oil, point, toy	l	let, yellow, ball	ʹʹ	see p. 15.
ou	out, crowd, plow	m	met, camel, trim	✓	see p. 15.
u	up, cut, color	n	not, flannel, ton	+	see p. 14.
ur	urn, fur, deter	p	put, apple, tap	ʹ	see p. 15.
†See p. 14.		†See p. 16.		○	see p. 14.

Dictionary makers have not been able to agree on a universally accepted set of pronunciation symbols. But they do agree about the sounds they want to present. To simplify, we have, with the permission of the publisher, adopted the Pronunciation Guide and Key Words used by *Webster's New World Dictionary* (Copyright © 1974 by Collins & World Publishing Co.). We have "translated" or "transcribed" the pronunciations recorded by the other dictionaries into the equivalent symbols used in *Webster's New World Dictionary*. In each instance, using our one set of *Webster's New World Dictionary* symbols, we have presented the pronunciations as the other three individual dictionaries have recorded them. We have also added some symbols for the special purposes of this book, as is explained below. These dictionaries *(Webster's New Collegiate Dictionary, Random House College Dictionary,*

American Heritage Dictionary of the English Language) are, of course, in no way responsible for our interpretations and retranscriptions.

Explanatory Notes

+   **ä**   This symbol essentially represents the sound of *a* in c*a*r and f*a*ther. We also show certain words, like

alms

hot

rod

with the ä symbol, like this:

ämz

hät

räd.

Many educated people pronounce these words in various ways, ranging all the way to

ômz

hôt

rôd.

We do not record all of these pronunciations. But you may assume that they exist and that they are quite acceptable.

Where this range of pronunciations is to be found, the + symbol is placed next to the word to alert you to the fact that here *ä* sounds like the *a* in father, but it also represents a variety or gradation of other acceptable sounds. When you pronounce the word, you will pronounce the *a* sound in a way that is natural and native to you.

○   **ir**   This symbol is used to represent the vowel sound in d*ea*r. We would show this word like this: *dir*. This is how it is most frequently pronounced. But many educated people in parts of the United States pronounce *dear* in various other ways:

dē' ər

di' ər

di' ə.

We do not record all of the different ways *dear* and similar words are pronounced. But you may assume that other pronunciations exist in various educated circles and that they are hence quite acceptable. Where this range of pronunciations is to be found, we have placed the symbol ○ next to the word to alert you to the fact that *i* followed by *r (ir)* represents a variety or gradation of acceptable pronunciations. When you pronounce the word, you will make the *ir* sound in a way that is natural and native to you.

√   **er**   This symbol is used to represent the vowel sound in words like c*are*. We show the word like this: *ker.* This is how it is most frequently pronounced. But many educated people in parts of the United States pronounce *care* in various other ways:

kār

kā′ ə

kā′ ər

kar.

We do not record all the different ways *care* and similar words are pronounced. But you may assume that these pronunciations exist in various educated circles and that they are therefore quite acceptable. Where this range of pronunciations is to be found, we have placed the symbol √ next to the word to alert you to the fact that here *e* followed by *r (er)* represents a variety or gradation of acceptable pronunciations. When you pronounce the word, you will do so in a way that is natural, native to you, and acceptable.

(')   When the apostrophe (') comes before *l, m,* or *n,* this shows that the pronunciation of the *l, m,* or *n* is merged with or made part of a syllable that has practically no vowel sound. We can best illustrate this with the word *apple.* In normal, easy conversation, most people pronounce *apple* like this: *ap′ 'l,* almost as if it were a one-syllable word.

When you pronounce the *'l* you create only the slightest trace of a vowel sound. What you say and what the listener hears is the *ap* syllable and *'l* becoming virtually one syllable, without any easily distinguishable sound where (') appears. Of course, you are making *some* kind of sound, but it is not a full vowel. The same holds true of words like *happen (hap′ 'n)* and *rhythm (rith′ 'm).*

Some dictionaries record a fuller sound that we would normally hear if the word were spoken just as a word, not part of any sentence. These dictionaries record *apple* as *ap′ əl.*

In our listing, we have set down both *'l* and *əl; 'm* and *əm; 'n* and *ən* wherever the individual dictionaries indicate this is what their experts say they hear among educated speakers. Actually, the difference between *'l* and *əl* is very slight indeed. But, in the interest of precise reporting, we have entered both forms. You would be speaking correctly and acceptably using either.

′ ′   These two signs show which syllable in a word receives the *primary* (or strong) stress, and which syllable receives the *secondary* (or weak) stress. The primary stress is shown by a heavy, dark stroke (′). The secondary stress by a lighter stroke (′). The stress mark follows the stressed syllable.

The word *biochemistry* contains five syllables, transcribed in the dictionary like this: bī′ ō kem′ is trē. The primary stress falls on the syllable *kem′*. The secondary stress falls on the syllable *bī′*. The three other syllables (*ō, is, trē*) receive no appreciable stress.

ə   This symbol is called the *schwa*. According to Professor Arthur Bronstein, a recognized authority on American pronunciation, "ə (schwa) is the most commonly used vowel sound for completely unstressed syllables in our language."

Webster's New World Dictionary defines the *schwa* this way: "It represents the relaxed vowel of neutral coloration heard in the *unstressed* [italics ours] syllables of

> *a* in *a*go
>
> *e* in ag*e*nt
>
> *i* in san*i*ty
>
> *o* in c*o*mply
>
> *u* in foc*u*s."

The *schwa* does not represent a single exact vowel sound. Its pronunciation varies from word to word and from speaker to speaker. In many contexts, *Webster's New World Dictionary* notes, "as for *itis* (īt′ əs), the vowel is often raised to i (īt′ is). Such variants, when not shown, may be inferred."

When you are pronouncing a syllable with ə, use the Key Word in the Pronunciation Key as your guide, and pronounce the ə as you would in your everyday conversation.

Syllabification

One problem we had to confront in preparing this book concerns the division of the transcriptions into syllables. The dictionaries do not always agree on where to divide a word, even when the pronunciation being transcribed is in other respects the same in all the books. In normal speech, we do not usually make a sharp break between syllables, but the final sound of one syllable tends to merge into the next sound, often even into the first sound of the next word. Some pronouncing dictionaries do not attempt to indicate any syllable division, simply showing a continuous line of symbols with stress marks where they occur. Most general dictionaries, recognizing how difficult it often is to read a transcription, especially of a lengthy word, unless the weary reader is given a chance to rest his eyes from time to time, show breaks at what must be called arbitrary stop points. Even though the boundaries are not always the same in all dictionaries, a case can generally be made for any such division, and, even more important, such variant transcriptions almost always sound alike.

Since a pronunciation is not really affected by the placement of syllabic breaks, and since we did not wish to burden the user of this book with variant transcriptions of the same pronunciation, we have arbitrarily shown only one syllable division in all such cases. It should be understood, however, that one or more of the dictionaries may show different breaks for the same pronunciation.

AARDVARK
ärd′ värk′ 4

ABACUS
ab′ ə kəs 4*
ə bak′ əs 3

ABALONE
ab′ ə lō′ nē 4

ABANDON
ə ban′ dən 4

ABATTOIR
ab′ ə twär′ 4*
ab′ ə twär′ 1

ABBÉ
a′ bā 4*
a bā′ 3

ABBESS
ab′ əs 2*
ab′ is 2

ABBEY
ab′ ē 4

ABBOTT
ab′ ət 4

ABBREVIATE
ə brē′ vē āt′ 4

ABDOMEN
ab′ də mən 4*
ab dō′ mən 4

ABDOMINAL +
ab dä′ mə n′l 3*
ab dä′ mə nəl 1

ABECEDARIAN ✓
ā′ bē sē der′ ē ən 4

ABERRANT
a ber′ ənt 3*
ə ber′ ənt 2
ab′ ər ənt 1

ABERRATION
ab′ ə rā′ shən 4

ABET
ə bet 4

ABEYANCE
ə bā′ əns 4

ABHOR
ab hôr′ 4*
əb hôr′ 2

ABHORRENT +
ab här′ ənt 3*
ab hôr′ ənt 3
əb hôr′ ənt 2
əb här′ ənt 2

AB INITIO
ab′ in ish′ ē ō 1*
ab′ in ish′ ē ō′ 1
ab′ ən ish′ ē ō′ 1
äb in it′ ē ō′ 1

ABJECT
ab jekt′ 4
ab′ jekt 3*

ABJURE
ab joor′ 4*
əb joor′ 1
ab joo′ ər 1

ABLATIVE
ab′ lə tiv 4

ABLUTION
ab loo′ shən 4*
əb loo′ shən 3

ABNEGATE
ab′ nə gāt′ 2*
ab′ ni gāt′ 2

ABODE
ə bōd'   4

ABOLITION
ab' ə lish' ən   4

ABOMINABLE   +
ə bäm' ə nə bəl   3*
ə bäm' nə bəl   1

ABOMINATION   +
ə bäm' ə nā' shən   4

ABORIGINE
ab' ə rij' ə nē'   4

ABORT
ə bôrt   4

ABRACADABRA
ab' rə kə dab' rə   4

ABRASION
ə brā' zhən   4

ABRASIVE
ə brā' siv   4*
ə brā' ziv   3

ABROGATE
ab' rə gāt'   3*
ab' rō gāt'   1

ABSCESS
ab' ses   4

ABSCOND   +
ab skänd'   4*
əb skänd'   1

ABSENT (v)
ab sent'   4

ABSENT (adj)
ab' sent   3
ab' s'nt   1*

ABSENTEE
ab' sən tē'   4

ABSINTHE (ABSINTH)
ab' sinth   3*
ab' sinth'   1

ABSOLUTE
ab' sə loōt'   4*
ab' sə loōt'   1

ABSOLUTION
ab' sə loō' shən   4

ABSOLVE   +
ab zälv'   3*
ab sälv'   3
əb sälv'   2
əb zôlv'   2
əb sôlv'   1

ABSORB
ab sôrb'   3*
ab zôrb'   3
əb sôrb'   2
əb zôrb'   2

ABSTEMIOUS
ab stē' mē əs   3*
əb stē' mē əs   1

ABSTINENCE
ab' stə nəns   4

ABSTRACT (adj)
ab' strakt   4*
ab strakt'   4

ABSTRACT (n)
ab' strakt   4

ABSTRACT (v)
ab strakt'   4*
ab' strakt   1

ABSTRUSE
ab stroōs'   4*
əb stroōs'   2

ABSURD
ab surd'   3*
ab zurd'   3
əb surd'   2
əb zurd'   2

ABUSE (n)
ə byoōs'   4

ABUSE (v)
ə byoōz'   4

ABUSIVE
ə byoō' siv   4*
ə byoō' ziv   2

ABYSMAL
ə biz' məl   4*
ə biz' m'l   1

ABYSS
ə bis'   4

ACADEME
ak' ə dēm'   4*
ak' ə dēm'   1

ACADEMIC
ak' ə dem' ik   4

ACADEMICIAN
ə kad' ə mish' ən   3*
ak' ə də mish' ən   3

A CAPPELLA
ä kə pel' ə   3*
ä' kə pel' ə   1

ACCEDE
ak sēd'   4

ACCELERATE
ak sel' ə rāt'   4*
ik sel' ə rāt'   1
ək sel' ə rāt'   1

ACCELERATION
ak sel' ə rā' shən   4*
ik sel' ə rā' shən   2

ACCELERATOR
ak sel′ ə rāt′ ər   4*
ək sel′ ə rāt′ ər   1
ik sel′ ə rāt′ ər   1

ACCENT (n)
ak′ sent′   4*
ak′ s'nt   1

ACCENT (v)
ak′ sent   4
ak sent′   3*

ACCESSION
ak sesh′ ən   4*
ək sesh′ ən   1

ACCESSORY
ak ses′ ər ē   4*
ək ses′ ər ē   1
ik ses′ rē   1
ik ses′ ər ē   1

ACCENTUATE
ak sen′ choo āt′   3*
ək sen′ choo āt′   1
ak sen′ chə′ wāt   1

ACCEPT
ak sept′   4*
ək sept′   2

ACCESS
ak′ ses   4

ACCLAMATION
ak′ lə mā′ shən   4

ACCLIMATE
ə klī′ mət   4*
ak′ lə māt′   4

ACCLIMATIZE
ə klī′ mə tīz′   4

ACCOLADE
ak′ ə lād′   4*
ak′ ə lād′   2
ak′ ə läd′   1

ACCOMPANIMENT
ə kum′ pə nē mənt   4*
ə kump′ nē mənt   3
ə kump′ ni mənt   1

ACCOMPANIST
ə kum′ pə nist   3*
ə kump′ nist   2

ACCOMPANY
ə kum′ pə nē   4*
ə kump′ nē   3

ACCOMPLICE   +
ə käm′ pləs   4*
ə kum′ pləs   1

ACCORDION
ə kôr′ dē ən   4

ACCOST   +
ə käst′   4*
ə kôst′   4

ACCOUTERMENT
ə koot′ ər mənt   4

ACCOUTREMENT
ə koo′ trə mənt   4

ACCRUAL
ə kroo′ əl   4

PRONUNCIATION KEY

Symbol	Key words	Symbol	Key words	Symbol	Key words
a	asp, fat, parrot	†ə	a in ago	r	red, port, dear
ā	ape, date, play		e in agent	s	sell, castle, pass
†ä	ah, car, father		i in sanity	t	top, cattle, hat
e	elf, ten, berry		o in comply	v	vat, hovel, have
ē	even, meet, money		u in focus	w	will, always, swear
i	is, hit, mirror	ər	perhaps, murder	y	yet, onion, yard
ī	ice, bite, high	b	bed, fable, dub	z	zebra, dazzle, haze
ō	open, tone, go	d	dip, beadle, had	ch	chin, catcher, arch
ô	all, horn, law	f	fall, after, off	sh	she, cushion, dash
oo	ooze, tool, crew	g	get, haggle, dog	th	thin, nothing, truth
oo	look, pull, moor	h	he, ahead, hotel	th	then, father, lathe
yoo	use, cute, few	j	joy, agile, badge	zh	azure, leisure
yoo	united, cure, globule	k	kill, tackle, bake	ŋ	ring, anger, drink
oi	oil, point, toy	l	let, yellow, ball	′′	see p. 15.
ou	out, crowd, plow	m	met, camel, trim	✓	see p. 15.
u	up, cut, color	n	not, flannel, ton	+	see p. 14.
ur	urn, fur, deter	p	put, apple, tap	′	see p. 15.
†See p. 14.		†See p. 16.		○	see p. 14.

ACCRUE
ə krōō′ 4

ACCUMULATE
ə kyōōm′ yə lāt′ 4

ACCURACY
ak′ yər ə sē 4

ACCURATE
ak′ yər it 3*
ak′ yər ət 1

ACCURSED
ə kʉr′ sid 4*
ə kʉrst′ 4

ACCUSATORY
ə kyōō′ zə tôr′ ē 4*
ə kyōō′ zə tōr′ ē 3

ACERB
ə sʉrb′ 4*
a sʉrb′ 1

ACETATE
as′ ə tāt′ 3*
as′ i tāt′ 1

ACETIC
ə sēt′ ik 4*
ə set′ ik 2

ACETYLENE
ə set′ ′l ēn′ 4*
ə set′ ′l ən 2
ə set′ ′l in 1

ACIDULOUS
ə sij′ ə ləs 2*
ə sij′ oo ləs 1
ə sij′ ōō ləs 1
ə sid′ yə ləs 1

ACME
ak′ mē 4

ACNE
ak′ nē 4

ACOLYTE
ak′ ə līt′ 4

ACOUSTICS
ə kōō′ stiks 4

ACQUIESCE
ak′ wē es′ 4

ACQUIESCENCE
ak′ wē es′ əns 3*
ak′ wē es′ ′nts 1
ak′ wē es′ ′ns 1

ACQUISITIVE
ə kwiz′ ə tiv 3*
ə kwiz′ i tiv 1

ACQUITTAL
ə kwit′ ′l 4

ACREAGE
āk′ ər ij 4*
ā′ krij 3

ACRID
ak′ rid 3*
ak′ rəd 1

ACRIMONIOUS
ak′ rə mō′ nē əs 4

ACRIMONY
ak′ rə mō′ nē 4

ACROMEGALY
ak′ rō meg′ ə lē 3*
ak′ rə meg′ ə lē 1

ACRONYM
ak′ rə nim 3*
ak′ rə nim′ 1

ACROSTIC   +
ə krôs′ tik 4
ə kräs′ tik 2*

ACRYLIC
ə kril′ ik 4

ACTINIC
ak tin′ ik 4

ACTUALLY
ak′ chə lē 2
ak′ chōō əl ē 1*
ak′ choo wəl ē 1
ak′ shoo wəl ē 1
ak′ chə wə lē 1

ACTUARIAL ✓
ak′ chōō wer′ ē əl 1*
ak′ chōō er′ ē el 1
ak′ chə wer′ ē əl 1

ACTUARY
ak′ chōō er′ ē 2*
ak′ chōō wer′ ē 1
ak′ chə wer′ ē 1

ACUITY
ə kyōō′ ə tē 3*
ə kyōō′ i tē 1

ACUMEN
ə kyōō′ mən 4*
ak′ yoo mən 1
ak′ yə mən 1

ACUPUNCTURE
ak′ yoo puŋk′ chər 4

ADAGE
ad′ ij 4

ADAGIO
ə dä′ jō 4
ə dä′ jē ō′ 3
ə dä′ zhē ō′ 3
ə dä′ zhō 2*

ADAMANT
ad′ ə mənt 4*
ad′ ə mənt′ 4

ADAMANTINE
ad′ ə man′ tēn 3*
ad′ ə man′ tīn 3
ad′ ə man′ tin 3

ADDITIVE
ad′ ə tiv   3*
ad′ i tiv   1

ADENOIDS
ad′ ′n oidz′   4

ADDENDUM
ə den′ dəm   4

ADDICT (n)
ad′ ikt   4

ADDICT (v)
ə dikt′   4

ADDRESS (v)
ə dres′   4

ADDRESS (n)
ə dres′   4*
ad′ res   3
ad′ res′   1

ADHESION
ad hē′ zhən   4*
əd hē′ zhən   2

ADHESIVE
ad hes′ iv   4*
ad hēz′ iv   3
əd hes′ iv   1
əd hēz′ iv   1

AD HOC   +
ad häk′   3*
ad′ häk′   1

AD HOMINEM   +
ad′ hä′ mə nem   1*
ad′ hä′ mə nəm′   1
ad hä′ mi nem   1
ad hä′ mə nəm′   1

ADIEU
ə dyo͞o′   4*
ə do͞o′   4

AD INFINITUM
ad in′ fə nīt′ əm   3*
ad′ in′ fə nīt′ əm   1

ADIOS
ä dē ōs′   3*
a dē ōs′   2
ad′ ē ōs′   2
äd′ ē ōs′   1

ADIPOSE
ad′ ə pōs′   4

ADJACENT
ə jās′ ənt   3*
ə jās′ ′nt   1

ADJOIN
ə join′   4

ADJOURN
ə jʉrn   4

ADJUDICATE
ə jo͞o′ di kāt′   3*
ə joo′ də kāt′   1

ADJUNCT
aj′ uŋkt   4

ADJUTANT
aj′ ə tənt   3*
aj′ o͞o tənt   1

ADMIRABLE
ad′ mə rə bəl   3*
ad′ mə rə b′l   1
ad′ mrə bəl   1

PRONUNCIATION KEY

Symbol	Key words	Symbol	Key words	Symbol	Key words
a	asp, fat, parrot	†ə	a in ago	r	red, port, dear
ā	ape, date, play		e in agent	s	sell, castle, pass
†ä	ah, car, father		i in sanity	t	top, cattle, hat
e	elf, ten, berry		o in comply	v	vat, hovel, have
ē	even, meet, money		u in focus	w	will, always, swear
i	is, hit, mirror	ər	perhaps, murder	y	yet, onion, yard
ī	ice, bite, high	b	bed, fable, dub	z	zebra, dazzle, haze
ō	open, tone, go	d	dip, beadle, had	ch	chin, catcher, arch
ô	all, horn, law	f	fall, after, off	sh	she, cushion, dash
o͞o	ooze, tool, crew	g	get, haggle, dog	th	thin, nothing, truth
oo	look, pull, moor	h	he, ahead, hotel	th	then, father, lathe
yo͞o	use, cute, few	j	joy, agile, badge	zh	azure, leisure
yoo	united, cure, globule	k	kill, tackle, bake	ŋ	ring, anger, drink
oi	oil, point, toy	l	let, yellow, ball	′′	see p. 15.
ou	out, crowd, plow	m	met, camel, trim	✓	see p. 15.
u	up, cut, color	n	not, flannel, ton	+	see p. 14.
ʉr	urn, fur, deter	p	put, apple, tap	′	see p. 15.
†See p. 14.		†See p. 16.		○	see p. 14.

ADMIRALTY
ad′ mər əl tē   4*
ad′ mrəl tē   1

ADMONITION
ad′ mə nish′ ən   4

ADO
ə dōō′   4

ADOBE
ə dō′ bē   4

ADOLESCENT
ad′l es′ ′nt   2*
ad′l es′ ənt   2

ADONIS   +
ə dän′ is   3*
ə dō′ nis   3
ə dän′ əs   1
ə dō′ nəs   1

ADRENAL
ə drē′ n′l   3*
ə drē′ nəl   1

ADRENALIN
ə dren′ ′l in   2*
ə dren′ ′l ən   1
ə dren′ əl in   1
ə dren′ ′l ēn′   1

ADROIT
ə droit′   4

ADULATION
aj′ ə lā′ shən   3*
aj′ oo lā′ shən   1

ADULT
ə dult′   4*
ad′ ult   3

ADULTERANT
ə dul′ tər ənt   4*
ə dul′ trənt   1

ADULTERY
ə dul′ tə rē   4*
ə dul′ trē   1

AD VALOREM
ad və lôr′ əm   2*
ad və lōr′ əm   2
ad′ və lôr′ əm   2
ad′ və lōr′ əm   1

ADVANTAGEOUS
ad′ vən tā′ jəs   4*
ad′ van tā′ jəs   2

ADVENT
ad′ vent   3*
ad′ vent′   1

ADVENTITIOUS
ad′ vən tish′ əs   3*
ad′ ven tish′ əs   1

ADVENTURE
əd ven′ chər   2*
ad ven′ chər   2

ADVERSARY ✓
ad′ vər ser′ ē   4*
ad′ və ser′ ē   1

ADVERSE
ad vurs′   4*
ad′ vurs   3
əd vurs′   1

ADVERSITY
ad vur′ sə tē   3*
əd vur′ sə tē   1
ad vur′ si tē   1

ADVERTISE
ad′ vər tīz′   3*
ad′ vər tīz   1

ADVERTISEMENT
ad′ vər tīz′ mənt   4
ad vur′ tiz mənt   2*
ad vur′ tis mənt   2

ADVICE
əd vīs′   2*
ad vīs′   2

ADVISE
əd vīz′   2*
ad vīz′   2

ADVISEDLY
əd vī′ zid lē   3*
əd vī′ zəd lē   1

ADVOCACY
ad′ və kə sē   4

ADVOCATE (n)
ad′ və kāt′   4
ad′ və kit   3*
ad′ və kət   1

ADVOCATE (v)
ad′ və kāt′   4

ADZE
adz   4

AEGIS
ē′ jis   3*
ē′ jəs   1

AEON (see eon)   +
ē′ ən   4
ē′ än   2*
ē′ än′   2

AERATE ✓
ā′ ər āt′   3*
er′ āt   2
er′ āt′   2
ār′ āt′   1

AERIAL ✓ ○
er′ ē əl   4*
ā ir′ ē əl   4
ar′ ē əl   1

AERIE ✓ ○
ir′ ē 4
er′ ē 3*
ar′ ē 2
ā′ rē 1

AERONAUT ✓ +
er′ ə nôt′ 4*
er′ ə nät′ 4

AEROSOL ✓ +
er′ ə säl′ 4
er′ ə sôl′ 4
er′ ə sōl′ 3*

AESTHETE
es′ thēt′ 3*
es′ thēt 1

AESTHETIC
es thet′ ik 4

AESTIVATE
es′ tə vāt′ 4

AFICIONADO
ə fis′ ē ə nä′ dō 3
ə fēs′ ē ə nä′ dō 3
ə fish′ ə nä′ dō 2*
ə fēsh ə nä′ dō 2
ə fish′ yə nä′ dō 1

AFFIDAVIT
af′ ə dā′ vit 2*
af′ i dā′ vit 1
af′ ə dā′ vət 1

AFFILIATE (n)
ə fil′ ē it 3*
ə fil′ ē ət 1
ə fil′ ē āt′ 1

AFFILIATE (v)
ə fil′ ə āt′ 4

AFFINITY
ə fin′ ə tē 3*
ə fin′ i tē 1

AFFIRMATION
af′ ər mā′ shən 4

AFFIRMATIVE
ə fur′ mə tiv 4

AFFLATUS
ə flāt′ əs 4*
a flāt′ əs 1

AFFLUENT
af′ lōō ənt 3*
af′ loo wənt 1
af′ lə wənt 1
af lōō′ wənt 1

AFFRONT
ə frunt′ 4

AFGHAN
af′ gan 4*
af′ gən 4

AFTERMATH
af′ tər math′ 4*
äf′ tər math′ 3

AGA
ä′ gə 3

AGAPE
ə gāp′ 4*
ə gap′ 3

PRONUNCIATION KEY

Symbol	Key words	Symbol	Key words	Symbol	Key words
a	asp, fat, parrot	†ə a in ago		r	red, port, dear
ā	ape, date, play	e in agent		s	sell, castle, pass
†ä	ah, car, father	i in sanity		t	top, cattle, hat
e	elf, ten, berry	o in comply		v	vat, hovel, have
ē	even, meet, money	u in focus		w	will, always, swear
i	is, hit, mirror	ər	perhaps, murder	y	yet, onion, yard
ī	ice, bite, high	b	bed, fable, dub	z	zebra, dazzle, haze
ō	open, tone, go	d	dip, beadle, had	ch	chin, catcher, arch
ô	all, horn, law	f	fall, after, off	sh	she, cushion, dash
ōō	ooze, tool, crew	g	get, haggle, dog	th	thin, nothing, truth
oo	look, pull, moor	h	he, ahead, hotel	th	then, father, lathe
yōō	use, cute, few	j	joy, agile, badge	zh	azure, leisure
yoo	united, cure, globule	k	kill, tackle, bake	ŋ	ring, anger, drink
oi	oil, point, toy	l	let, yellow, ball	′′	see p. 15.
ou	out, crowd, plow	m	met, camel, trim	✓	see p. 15.
u	up, cut, color	n	not, flannel, ton	+	see p. 14.
ur	urn, fur, deter	p	put, apple, tap	′	see p. 15.
†See p. 14.		†See p. 16.		○	see p. 14.

AGATE
ag′ ət 2*
ag′ it 2

AGED
ā′ jid 3*
ā′ jəd 1

AGED
  (improved by aging)
ājd 4

AGENDA
ə jen′ də 4

AGGLUTINATE (v)
ə glо̄о̄t′ 'n āt 4

AGGRANDIZE
ə grān′ dīz′ 4*
ag′ rən dīz′ 4

AGGRANDIZEMENT
ə gran′ diz mənt 3*
ə gran′ dīz′ mənt 2
ə gran′ dəz mənt 1
ag′ rən dīz′ mənt 1

AGGRAVATE
ag′ rə vāt′ 4

AGGREGATE (adj)
ag′ rə gət 1*
ag′ ri gət 1
ag′ rə git 1
ag′ rə git′ 1

AGGREGATE (n)
ag′ rə gət 2*
ag′ rə git 2
ag′ rə gāt′ 1

AGHAST
ə gast′ 4*
ə gäst′ 3

AGILE
aj′ əl 3*
aj′ il 1

AGILITY
ə jil′ ə tē 3*
ə jil′ i tē 1

AGITATE
aj′ ə tāt′ 3*
aj′ i tāt′ 1

AGITATO
ä jē tä′ tо̄ 2*
a ji′ tä′ tо̄ 1
aj′ ə tä′ tо̄ 1

AGNOSTIC   +
ag näs′ tik 4*
ag nôs′ tik 1

AGORA
ag′ ə rə 4

AGRARIAN ✓
ə grer′ ē ən 3*
ə grar′ ē ən 1

AGUE
a′ gyо̄о̄ 4

AIDE
ād 4

AIGRETTE
ā gret′ 4
ā′ gret 3*

AILERON   +
ā′ lə rän′ 4

AISLE
īl 4

AKIMBO
ə kim′ bо̄ 4*
ə kim′ bо̄′ 1

AKIN
ə kin′ 4

AKVAVIT
äk′ wə vēt′ 2
äk′ vä vēt′ 2
ak′ və vēt′ 1*
äk′ və vēt′ 1

À LA
ä′ lä 4*
ä′ lə 4
al′ ə 3

ALABASTER
al′ ə bas′ tər 4*
al′ ə bä stər 1

À LA CARTE
al′ ə kärt′ 4*
a′ lə kärt′ 2
ä′ lä kärt′ 1

ALACRITY
ə lak′ rə tē 3*
ə lak′ ri tē 1

À LA MODE
al′ ə mо̄d′ 4*
ä′ lə mо̄d′ 2

ALBATROSS   +
al′ bə träs′ 4*
al′ bə trôs′ 4

ALBEIT
ôl bē′ it 3*
al bē′ it 3
ôl bē′ ət 1
al bē′ ət 1

ALBINO
al bī′ nо̄ 4

ALBUMEN
al byо̄о̄′ mən 4*
al′ byə mən 1

ALCHEMIST
al′ kə mist 3*
al′ kə məst 1

ALCHEMY
al′ kə mē   4

ALCOVE
al′ kōv   3*
al′ kōv′   1

ALEATORY
ā′ lē ə tôr′ ē   4*
ā′ lē ə tōr′ ē   3

ALEMBIC
ə lem′ bik   4

ALFALFA
al fal′ fə   4

AL FRESCO
al fres′ kō   4

ALGAE
al′ jē   4

ALGEBRAIC
al′ jə brā′ ik   4

ALIAS
ā′ lē əs   4*
āl′ yəs   3

ALIBI
al′ ə bī′   4

ALIEN
āl′ yən   4*
ā′ lē ən   3

ALIENATE
āl′ yən āt′   4*
ā′ lē ən āt′   4

ALIGN
ə līn′   4

ALIMENTARY
al′ ə men′ tər ē   4*
al′ ə men′ trē   3

ALIMONY
al′ ə mō′ nē   4

ALKALI
al′ kə lī′   4

ALKALINE
al′ kə līn′   4*
al′ kə lin   3
al′ kə lən   1

ALLAY
ə lā′   4

ALLEGE
ə lej′   4

ALLEGIANCE
ə lē′ jəns   4

ALLEGORICAL   +
al′ ə gôr′ i kəl   4
al′ ə gär′ i kəl   2*

ALLEGORY
al′ ə gôr′ ē   4*
al′ ə gōr′ ē   3

ALLEGRO
ə leg′ rō   4*
ə lā′ grō   4

ALLEGRETTO
al′ ə gret′ ō   4*
äl ə gret′ ō   1

PRONUNCIATION KEY

Symbol	Key words	Symbol	Key words	Symbol	Key words
a	asp, fat, parrot	†ə	a in ago	r	red, port, dear
ā	ape, date, play		e in agent	s	sell, castle, pass
†ä	ah, car, father		i in sanity	t	top, cattle, hat
e	elf, ten, berry		o in comply	v	vat, hovel, have
ē	even, meet, money		u in focus	w	will, always, swear
i	is, hit, mirror	ər	perhaps, murder	y	yet, onion, yard
ī	ice, bite, high	b	bed, fable, dub	z	zebra, dazzle, haze
ō	open, tone, go	d	dip, beadle, had	ch	chin, catcher, arch
ô	all, horn, law	f	fall, after, off	sh	she, cushion, dash
ōō	ooze, tool, crew	g	get, haggle, dog	th	thin, nothing, truth
oo	look, pull, moor	h	he, ahead, hotel	th	then, father, lathe
yōō	use, cute, few	j	joy, agile, badge	zh	azure, leisure
yoo	united, cure, globule	k	kill, tackle, bake	ŋ	ring, anger, drink
oi	oil, point, toy	l	let, yellow, ball	″	see p. 15.
ou	out, crowd, plow	m	met, camel, trim	✓	see p. 15.
u	up, cut, color	n	not, flannel, ton	+	see p. 14.
ʉr	urn, fur, deter	p	put, apple, tap	′	see p. 15.
†See p. 14.		†See p. 16.		○	see p. 14.

ALLEMANDE
al′ ə mand′   3*
al′ ə mand′   3
al′ ə mänd′   1
al′ ə mänd′   1
al′ ə man   1

ALLERGEN
al′ ər jən   3*
al′ ər jən′   1

ALLERGIC
ə lʉr′ jik   4

ALLEVIATE
ə lē′ vē āt′   4

ALLIED
ə līd′   4*
al′ īd′   3
al′ īd   1

ALLIGATOR
al′ ə gā′ tər   4

ALLITERATION
ə lit′ ə rā′ shən   4

ALLOCATE
al′ ə kāt′   4*
al′ ō kāt′   1

ALLOT   +
ə lät′   4

ALLOY (n)
al′ oi   4*
ə loi′   3

ALLOY (v)
ə loi′   4*
al′ oi′   2

ALLUDE
ə lood′   4

ALLURE
ə loor′   4*
ə loo′ ər   1

ALLUSION
ə loo′ zhən   4*
a loo′ zhən   1

ALLUVIAL
ə loo′ vē əl   4

ALLY (n)
ə lī′   4*
al′ ī   2

ALLY (v)
ə lī′   4*
al′ ī′   2

ALMA MATER
al′ mə mät′ ər   4*
al′ mə māt′ ər   2
äl′ mə mät′ ər   2

ALMANAC
ôl′ mə nak′   4*
al′ mə nak′   3

ALMOND
ä′ mənd   4*
am′ ənd   4
al′ mənd   3
äl′ mənd   1

ALMONER
al′ mən ər   4*
ä′ mən ər   4

ALMS
ämz   4*
älmz   1

ALOE
al′ ō   4

ALOHA
ə lō′ ə   3*
ä lō′ hä′   2

ALOOF
ə loof′   4

ALPACA
al pak′ ə   4

ALTAR
ôl′ tər   4

ALTERCATION
ôl′ tər kā′ shən   4*
al′ tər kā′ shən   2

ALTER EGO
ôl′ tər ē′ gō   4*
ôl′ tər eg′ ō   2
al′ tər ē′ gō   2
al′ tər eg′ ō   2

ALTERNATE (v)
ôl′ tər nāt′   4*
al′ tər nāt′   1

ALTERNATE (n)
ôl′ tər nit   3*
al′ tər nit   3
ôl′ tər nət   1
al′ tər nət   1

ALTERNATIVE (n)
ôl tʉr′ nə tiv   4*
al tʉr′ nə tiv   4

ALTIMETER
al tim′ ə tər   3*
al′ tə mēt′ ər   2

ALTO
al′ tō   4

ALTRUISM
al′ troo iz′ əm   3*
al′ troo iz′ əm   1

ALTRUISTIC
al′ troo is′ tik   3*
al′ troo is′ tik   1

ALUM
al′ əm   4

ALUMNA
ə lum′ nə   4

ALUMNAE
ə lum′ nē   4

ALUMNI
ə lum′ nī   4

ALUMNUS
ə lum′ nəs   4

AMALGAM
ə mal′ gəm   4

AMALGAMATE
ə mal′ gə mat′   4

AMANUENSIS
ə man′ yo͞o en′ sis   2*
ə man′ yoo wen′ sis   1
ə man′ yə wen′ səs   1

AMATEUR
am′ ə tʉr′   2*
am′ ə chər   2
am′ ə tər   2
am′ ə toor   2
am′ ə tyoor   2
am′ ə tyo͞or′   2
am′ ə choor′   2
am′ ə cho͞or′   1

AMAZON   +
am′ ə zän′   4*
am′ ə zən   4

AMBERGRIS
am′ bər gris′   4*
am′ bər grēs′   4

AMBIANCE
am′ bē əns   4

AMBIDEXTROUS
am′ bi dek′ strəs   3*
am′ bə dek′ strəs   1

AMBIGUITY
am′ bi gyo͞o′ ə tē   2*
am′ bə gyo͞o′ i tē   1
am′ bə gyo͞o′ ə tē   1

AMBIGUOUS
am big′ yo͞o əs   2*
am big′ yoo wəs   1
am big′ yə wəs   1

AMBIVALENCE
am biv′ ə ləns   4

AMBROSIA
am brō′ zhə   4*
am brō′ zhē ə   3

AMBULATORY
am′ byə lə tôr′ ē   4*
am′ byə lə tōr′ ē   3

AMBUSH
am′ boosh′   4

AMELIORATE
ə mēl′ yə rāt′   4*
ə mē′ lē ə rāt′   1

AMEN
ā′ men′   2*
ä′ men′   2
ā′ men′   2
ä′ men′   2
ā men′   1
ä men′   1

AMENABLE
ə mē′ nə bəl   3*
ə men′ ə bəl   3
ə mē′ nə b'l   1
ə men′ ə b'l   1

PRONUNCIATION KEY

Symbol	Key words		Symbol	Key words		Symbol	Key words
a	asp, fat, parrot		†ə	a in ago		r	red, port, dear
ā	ape, date, play			e in agent		s	sell, castle, pass
†ä	ah, car, father			i in sanity		t	top, cattle, hat
e	elf, ten, berry			o in comply		v	vat, hovel, have
ē	even, meet, money			u in focus		w	will, always, swear
i	is, hit, mirror		ər	perhaps, murder		y	yet, onion, yard
ī	ice, bite, high		b	bed, fable, dub		z	zebra, dazzle, haze
ō	open, tone, go		d	dip, beadle, had		ch	chin, catcher, arch
ô	all, horn, law		f	fall, after, off		sh	she, cushion, dash
o͞o	ooze, tool, crew		g	get, haggle, dog		th	thin, nothing, truth
oo	look, pull, moor		h	he, ahead, hotel		th	then, father, lathe
yo͞o	use, cute, few		j	joy, agile, badge		zh	azure, leisure
yoo	united, cure, globule		k	kill, tackle, bake		ŋ	ring, anger, drink
oi	oil, point, toy		l	let, yellow, ball		″	see p. 15.
ou	out, crowd, plow		m	met, camel, trim		✓	see p. 15.
u	up, cut, color		n	not, flannel, ton		+	see p. 14.
ʉr	urn, fur, deter		p	put, apple, tap		′	see p. 15.
†See p. 14.			†See p. 16.			○	see p. 14.

AMENITY
ə men′ ə tē   3*
ə mē′ nə tē   3
ə men′ i tē   1
ə mē′ ni tē   1

AMIABLE
ā′ mē ə bəl   3*
ām′ yə b'l   1

AMICABLE
am′ i kə bəl   2*
am′ ə kə bəl   1
am′ i kə b'l   1

AMICUS CURIAE
ə mē′ kəs kyoor′ ē ī′   3*
ə mī′ kəs kyoor′ i ē′   1
ə mī′ kəs kyoor′ ē ē′   1
ə mē′ kəs koor′ ē ī′   1

AMIGO
ə mē′ gō   4*
ä mē′ gō   2

AMINO
ə mē′ nō   4*
am′ ə nō′   4

AMITY
am′ ə tē   3*
am i tē   1

AMMONIA
ə mōn′ yə   4*
ə mō′ nē ə   1

AMNESIA
am nē′ zhə   4*
am nē′ zhē ə   1

AMNESTY
am′ nəs tē   3*
am′ nis tē   1

AMOEBA
ə mē′ bə   4

AMOK   +
ə muk′   4*
ə mäk′   2

AMORAL   +
ā mär′ əl   4*
ā môr′ əl   4
a môr′ əl   2
a mär′ əl   2

AMOROUS
am′ ər əs   3*
am′ rəs   1

AMORPHOUS
ə môr′ fəs   4

AMORTISE
am′ ər tīz′   4*
ə môr′ tīz′   3

AMOUR
ə moor′   3*
ə moor′   3
a moor′   1
ä moor′   1

AMPERE ○
am′ pir   3*
am′ pir′   1
am pir′   1

AMPHETAMINE
am fet′ ə mēn′   4*
am fet′ ə min   3

AMPHIBIAN
am fib′ ē ən   4

AMPHITHEATER
am′ fə thē′ ə tər   4

AMPULE
am′ pyool   3
am′ pool   2
am′ pyool   1*

AMULET
am′ yə lit   3*
am′ yə lət   1

ANABASIS
ə nab′ ə sis   3*
ə nab′ ə səs   1

ANACHRONISM
ə nak′ rə niz′ əm   3*
ə nak′ rə niz′ 'm   1

ANACONDA   +
an′ ə kän′ də   4

ANAEMIA (see ANEMIA)

ANAESTHESIA
  (see ANESTHESIA)

ANAL
ān′ 'l   3*
ān′ əl   1

ANALGESIA
an′ 'l jē′ zē ə   3*
an′ 'l jē′ sē ə   2
an′ əl jē′ zē ə   1
an′ əl jē′ zhə   1
an′ 'l jē′ zhə   1

ANALGESIC
an′ 'l jē′ zik   3*
an′ 'l jē′ sik   3
an′ əl jē′ zik   1
an′ əl jē′ sik   1

ANALOGY
ə nal′ ə jē   4

ANALYSIS
ə nal′ ə sis   2*
ə nal′ i sis   1
ə nal′ ə səs   1

ANALOGOUS
ə nal′ ə gəs   4

ANALYST
an' ə list   2*
an' 'l ist   1
an' 'l əst   1

ANARCHIC
an är' kik   4*
ə när' kik   1

ANARCHISM
an' ər kiz' əm   3*
an' ər kiz' 'm   1

ANARCHY
an' ər kē   4

ANATHEMA
ə nath' ə mə   4

ANATHEMATIZE
ə nath' ə mə tīz'   4

ANATOMICAL   +
an' ə täm' i kəl   3*
an' ə täm' i k'l   1

ANATOMY
ə nat' ə mē   4

ANCESTOR
an' ses' tər   3*
an' ses tər   1
an' səs tər   1

ANCESTRAL
an ses' trəl   4

ANCHORITE
aŋ' kə rīt'   4

ANCHOVY
an' chō' vē   3*
an' chə vē   2
an' chō' vē   2

ANCIENT
ān' shənt   4*
ān' chənt   1

ANCILLARY   ✓
an' sə ler' ē   4

ANDANTE
än dän' tā   4*
an dan' tē   3

ANDIRON
an' dī' ərn   4*
an' dīrn   1

ANDROGYNOUS   +
an dräj' ə nəs   4

ANECDOTAL
an' ik dōt' 'l   3*
an' ik dōt' 'l   1
an' ik dōt 'l   1

ANEMIA
ə nē' mē ə   4*
ə nē myə   1

ANEMOMETER   +
an' ə mäm' ə tər   3*
an' ə mäm' i tər   1

ANEMONE
ə nem' ə nē   2*
ə nem' ə nē'   2

ANESTHESIA
an' is thē' zhə   2*
an' əs thē' zhə   2
an' əs thē' zhē ə   1
an' əs thē' zē ə   1

PRONUNCIATION KEY

Symbol	Key words	Symbol	Key words	Symbol	Key words
a	asp, fat, parrot	†ə	a in ago	r	red, port, dear
ā	ape, date, play		e in agent	s	sell, castle, pass
†ä	ah, car, father		i in sanity	t	top, cattle, hat
e	elf, ten, berry		o in comply	v	vat, hovel, have
ē	even, meet, money		u in focus	w	will, always, swear
i	is, hit, mirror	ər	perhaps, murder	y	yet, onion, yard
ī	ice, bite, high	b	bed, fable, dub	z	zebra, dazzle, haze
ō	open, tone, go	d	dip, beadle, had	ch	chin, catcher, arch
ô	all, horn, law	f	fall, after, off	sh	she, cushion, dash
o͞o	ooze, tool, crew	g	get, haggle, dog	th	thin, nothing, truth
oo	look, pull, moor	h	he, ahead, hotel	th	then, father, lathe
yo͞o	use, cute, few	j	joy, agile, badge	zh	azure, leisure
yoo	united, cure, globule	k	kill, tackle, bake	ŋ	ring, anger, drink
oi	oil, point, toy	l	let, yellow, ball	"	see p. 15.
ou	out, crowd, plow	m	met, camel, trim	✓	see p. 15.
u	up, cut, color	n	not, flannel, ton	+	see p. 14.
ur	urn, fur, deter	p	put, apple, tap	'	see p. 15.
†See p. 14.		†See p. 16.		○	see p. 14.

ANESTHETIC
an′ is t**h**et′ ik   3*
an′ əs t**h**et′ ik   1

ANESTHETIST
ə nes′ t**h**ə tist   2*
ə nes′ t**h**i tist   1
ə nes′ t**h**ə təst   1

ANEURYSM
an′ yə riz′ əm   3*
an′ yə riz′m   1

ANGELIC
an jel′ ik   4

ANGINA
an jī′ nə   4*
an′ jə nə   2

ANGLOPHILE
aŋ′ glə fīl   2*
aŋ′ glə fīl′   2
aŋ′ glə fil   1

ANGLOPHOBE
aŋ′ glə fōb′   4

ANGORA
aŋ gôr′ ə   4*
an gôr′ ə   3
an gōr′ ə   2

ANGOSTURA
aŋ′ gəs toor′ ə   3*
aŋ′ gəs tyoor′ ə   3
an′ gəs toor′ ə   1
an′ gəs tyoor′ ə   1

ANGST
äŋst   3

ANGUISH
aŋ′ gwis**h**   4

AVUNCULAR
ə vuŋ′ kyə lər   4

ANILINE
an′ ′l in   2*
an′ ′l īn′   2
an′ ′l ēn′   1
an′ ′l ən   1
an′ ə lin   1

ANIMADVERSION
an′ ə mad vʉr′ s**h**ən   4
an′ ə mad vʉr′ z**h**ən   3*

ANIMALCULE
an′ ə mal′ kyo͞ol   3*
an′ ə mal′ kyo·ol   1
an′ ə mal′ kyo͞o əl   1

ANIMATE (v)
an′ ə māt′   4

ANIMATE (adj)
an′ ə mit   3*
an′ ə mət   1

ANIMOSITY   +
an′ ə mäs′ ə tē   3*
an′ ə mäs′ i tē   1

ANIMUS
an′ ə məs   4

ANUS
an′ is   3*
an′ əs   1

ANISETTE
an′ ə set′   3
an′ ə zet′   3*
an′ i set′   1
an′ i zet′   1

ANNALS
an′ ′lz   3*
an′ əlz   1

ANNEX (v)
ə neks′   4*
an′ eks′   2

ANNEX (n)
an′ eks′   3*
an′ iks   2
an′ eks   1

ANNIHILATE
ə nī′ ə lāt′   4

ANNO DOMINI   +
an′ ō däm′ ə nī′   4
an′ ō däm′ ə nē   2
an′ ō dō′ mə nē   2
an′ ō däm′ ə nē   2
än′ ō dō′ mə nē   1*

ANNUITY
ə no͞o′ ə tē   4*
ə nyo͞o′ ə tē   4

ANNUL
ə nul′   4

ANNUNCIATION
ə nun′ sē ā′ s**h**ən   4*
ə nun′ s**h**ē ā′ s**h**ən   2
ə nunt′ sē ā′ s**h**ən   1

ANODE
an′ ōd   2*
an′ ōd′   2

ANODYNE
an′ ə dīn′   4

ANOINT
ə noint′   4

ANOMALOUS   +
ə näm ə ləs   4

ANOMALY   +
ə näm′ ə lē   4

ANOMIE
an′ ə mē   3*
an′ ə mē′   1

ANON   +
ə nän′   4

ANONYMITY
an′ ə nim′ ə tē　3*
an′ ə nim′ i tē　1

ANONYMOUS　+
ə nän′ ə məs　4

ANOPHELES
ə näf′ ə lēz′　4

ANTARCTIC
ant ärk′ tik　4*
ant är′ tik　4

ANTAGONIST
an tag′ ə nist　3*
an tag′ ə nəst　1

ANTE (poker)(n)
an′ tē　4

ANTE BELLUM
an′ ti bel′ əm　2
an′ tē bel′ əm　1*
an′ tē bel′ əm　1

ANTECEDENT
an′ tə sēd′ ′nt　2*
an′ tə sēd′ ənt　1
an′ ti sēd′ ′nt　1

ANTEDILUVIAN
an′ ti də lōō′ vē ən　3*
an′ tē di lōō′ vē ən　1

ANTELOPE
an′ tə lōp′　4

ANTENNA
an ten′ ə　4

ANTENNAE
an ten′ ē　3*
an ten′ ē′　1

ANTHOLOGY　+
an thäl′ ə gē　4

ANTHRACITE
an′ thrə sīt′　4

ANTHROPOID
an′ thrə poid′　4*
ant′ thrə poid′　1

ANTHROPOLOGY　+
an′ thrə päl′ ə jē　4*
ant′ thrə päl′ ə jē　1

ANTHROPOMORPHIC
an′ thrə pō môr′ fik　3
an′ thre pə môr′ fik　2*
ant′ thrə pə môr′ fik　1

ANTIBIOTIC　+
an′ ti bī ät′ ik　2*
an′ tī bī ät′ ik　2
an′ ti bē ät′ ik　2
an′ tē bī ät′ ik　1
an′ tē bē ät′ ik　1

ANTIBODY　+
an′ ti bäd′ ē　4*
an′ tē bäd′ ē　1

ANTICIPATORY
an tis′ ə pə tôr′ ē　4*
an tis′ ə pə tōr′ ē　3

ANTICLIMACTIC
an′ ti klī mak′ tik　4

PRONUNCIATION KEY

Symbol	Key words	Symbol	Key words	Symbol	Key words
a	asp, fat, parrot	†ə	a in ago	r	red, port, dear
ā	ape, date, play		e in agent	s	sell, castle, pass
†ä	ah, car, father		i in sanity	t	top, cattle, hat
e	elf, ten, berry		o in comply	v	vat, hovel, have
ē	even, meet, money		u in focus	w	will, always, swear
i	is, hit, mirror	ər	perhaps, murder	y	yet, onion, yard
ī	ice, bite, high	b	bed, fable, dub	z	zebra, dazzle, haze
ō	open, tone, go	d	dip, beadle, had	ch	chin, catcher, arch
ô	all, horn, law	f	fall, after, off	sh	she, cushion, dash
ōō	ooze, tool, crew	g	get, haggle, dog	th	thin, nothing, truth
oo	look, pull, moor	h	he, ahead, hotel	th	then, father, lathe
yōō	use, cute, few	j	joy, agile, badge	zh	azure, leisure
yoo	united, cure, globule	k	kill, tackle, bake	ŋ	ring, anger, drink
oi	oil, point, toy	l	let, yellow, ball	′′	see p. 15.
ou	out, crowd, plow	m	met, camel, trim	✓	see p. 15.
u	up, cut, color	n	not, flannel, ton	+	see p. 14.
ur	urn, fur, deter	p	put, apple, tap	′	see p. 15.
†See p. 14.		†See p. 16.		○	see p. 14.

ANTIDOTE
an' ti dōt'   3*
an' tə dōt'   1

ANTIHISTAMINE
an' ti his' tə mēn'   3
an' ti his' tə min   2
an tē his' tə mən   1*
an' tī his' tə mēn'   1
an ti his' tə mēn'   1

ANTIMACASSAR
an' ti mə kas' ər   4*
an tī mə kas' ər   1
an tē mə kas' ər   1

ANTIPASTO
an' ti pas' tō   3
an' ti päs' tō   2*
än' tē päs' tō   1

ANTIPATHY
an tip' ə thē   4

ANTIPERSPIRANT
an' ti pur' spər ənt   2*
an' tī pur' spər ənt   1
an' tē pur' spər ənt   1
an' ti pur' sprənt   1

ANTIPHONAL
an tif' ə n'l   3*
an tif' ə nəl   1

ANTIPODAL
an tip' ə dəl   2*
an tip' ə d'l   2

ANTIPODES
an tip' ə dēz'   4

ANTIQUARY ✓
an' tə kwer' ē   4

ANTIQUARIAN ✓
an' tə kwer' ē ən   3*
an' ti kwer' ē ən   1

ANTIQUATED
an' tə kwāt' id   4

ANTIQUE
an tēk'   4

ANTIQUITY
an tik' wə tē   3*
an tik' wi tē   1

ANTI - SEMITE
an' ti sem' īt'   2
an' tē sem' īt   1*
an' ti sem' īt   1
an' tī sem' īt   1

ANTI - SEMITIC
an' ti sə mit' ik   3
an' tē sə mit' ik   1*
an' tī sə mit' ik   1

ANTI - SEMITISM
an' tē sem' i tiz' əm   1*
an' ti sem' ə tiz' 'm   1
an' ti sem' ə tiz' əm   1
an' tī sem' i tiz' əm   1

ANTITHESIS
an tith' ə sis   2*
an tith' i sis   1
an tith' ə səs   1

ANTITOXIN   +
an' ti täk' sin   3*
an' tē täk' sin   2
an' tī täk' sin   1
an' ti täk' sən   1

ANUS
ā' nəs   4

ANXIETY
aŋ zī' ə tē   3*
aŋ zī' i tē   1

ANXIOUS
aŋk' shəs   4*
aŋ' shəs   4

AORTA
ā ôr' tə   4

APACHE
ə pash'   4*
ə päsh'   3

APACHE (Indian)
ə pach' ē   4

APARTHEID
ə pärt' hāt   2
ə pärt' hīt   2
ə pär' tīt'   1*
ə pär' tāt'   1

APATHETIC
ap' ə thet' ik   4

APATHY
ap' ə thē   4

APÉRITIF
ə per' ə tēf'   1*
ä per' ə tēf'   1
ä per' i tēf'   1
ä' pā rə tēf'   1

APERTURE
ap' ər chər   4*
ap' ər choor   1
ap' ə choor   1
ap' ər choor   1
ap' ə chər   1
ap' ər toor   1
ap' ə tyoor   1

APEX
ā' peks   3*
ā' peks'   1

APHASIA
ə fā' zhə   4*
ə fā' zhē ə   2

APHID
ā' fid   3*
af' id   3
ā' fəd   1
af' əd   1

APHORISM
af′ ə riz′ əm   3*
af′ ə riz ′m   1

APHRODISIAC
af′ rə diz′ ē ak′   4

APIARY ✓
ā′ pē er′ ē   4

APLOMB +
ə pläm′   4*
ə plum′   4
ə plôm   1

APOCALYPSE +
ə päk′ ə lips′   3*
ə päk′ ə lips   1

APOCALYPTIC +
ə päk′ ə lip′ tik   4

APOCRYPHAL +
ə päk′ rə fəl   3*
ə päk′ rə f′l   1

APOGEE
ap′ ə jē′   3*
ap′ ə jē   2

APOLOGETIC +
ə päl′ ə jet′ ik   4

APOLOGY +
ə päl′ ə jē   4

APOPLECTIC
ap′ ə plek′ tik   4

APOSTASY +
ə päs′ tə sē   4

APOSTATE +
ə päs′ tit   4
ə päs′ tāt   2*
ə päs′ tāt′   2
ə päs′ tət   1

APOSTLE +
ə päs′ əl   3*
ə päs′ ′l   1

APOSTOLIC +
ap′ ə stäl′ ik   4

APOSTROPHE +
ə päs′ trə fē   4*
ə päs′ trə fē′   1

APOTHECARY + ✓
ə pä*th*′ ə ker′ ē   4

APOTHEGM
ap′ ə *th*em′   4

APOTHEOSIS +
ap′ ə *th*ē′ ə sis   3*
ə pä*th*′ ē ō′ sis   2
ap′ ə *th*ē′ ə səs   1
ə pä*th* ē ō′ səs   1

APOTHEOSIZE +
ap′ ə *th*ē′ ə siz′   4*
ə pä*th*′ ē ə siz′   4

APPALL
ə pôl′   4

APPARATUS
ap′ ə rāt′ əs   4*
ap′ ə rat′ əs   4

APPAREL ✓
ə par′ əl   4*
ə per′ əl   1

PRONUNCIATION KEY

Symbol	Key words	Symbol	Key words	Symbol	Key words
a	asp, fat, parrot	†ə	a in ago	r	red, port, dear
ā	ape, date, play		e in agent	s	sell, castle, pass
†ä	ah, car, father		i in sanity	t	top, cattle, hat
e	elf, ten, berry		o in comply	v	vat, hovel, have
ē	even, meet, money		u in focus	w	will, always, swear
i	is, hit, mirror	ər	perhaps, murder	y	yet, onion, yard
ī	ice, bite, high	b	bed, fable, dub	z	zebra, dazzle, haze
ō	open, tone, go	d	dip, beadle, had	ch	chin, catcher, arch
ô	all, horn, law	f	fall, after, off	sh	she, cushion, dash
ōō	ooze, tool, crew	g	get, haggle, dog	th	thin, nothing, truth
oo	look, pull, moor	h	he, ahead, hotel	th	then, father, lathe
yōō	use, cute, few	j	joy, agile, badge	zh	azure, leisure
yoo	united, cure, globule	k	kill, tackle, bake	ŋ	ring, anger, drink
oi	oil, point, toy	l	let, yellow, ball	″	see p. 15.
ou	out, crowd, plow	m	met, camel, trim	✓	see p. 15.
u	up, cut, color	n	not, flannel, ton	+	see p. 14.
ur	urn, fur, deter	p	put, apple, tap	′	see p. 15.
†See p. 14.		†See p. 16.		○	see p. 14.

APPARENT ✓
ə par′ ənt 4*
ə per′ ənt 4

APPARITION
ap′ ə rish′ ən 4

APPELLANT
ə pel′ ənt 4

APPELLATE
ə pel′ it 3*
ə pel′ ət 1

APPENDAGE
ə pen′ dij 4

APPENDECTOMY
ap′ ən dek′ tə mē 4

APPENDICES
ə pen′ də sēz′ 2*
ə pen′ di sēz′ 2

APPENDICITIS
ə pen′ də sī′ tis 3*
ə pen′ di sī′ tis 1

APPLIANCE
ə plī′ əns 4*
ə plī′ ənts 1

APPLICABLE
ap′ li kə bəl 3*
ə plik′ ə bəl 2
ap′ lə kə bəl 1

APPLICANT
ap′ li kənt 3*
ap′ lə kənt 1

APPLIQUÉ
ap′ lə kā′ 3*
ap′ li kā′ 1

APPOSITE +
ap′ ə zit 3*
ap′ ə zət 1
ə päz′ it 1

APPRECIABLE
ə prē′ shə bəl 4
ə prē′ shē ə bəl 2*

APPRECIATE
ə prē′ shē āt′ 4

APPREHEND
ap′ ri hend′ 3
ap′ rə hend′ 1*

APPRENTICE
ə pren′ tis 3*
ə pren′ təs 1

APPRISE
ə prīz′ 4

APPROBATION
ap′ rə bā′ shən 4

APPROPRIATE (adj)
ə prō′ prē it 3*
ə prō′ prē ət 1

APPROPRIATE (v)
ə prō′ prē āt′

APPROXIMATE + (adj)
ə präk′ sə mit 3*
ə präk′ sə mət 1

APPROXIMATE + (v)
ə präk′ sə māt′ 4

APPURTENANCE
ə pur′ t′n əns 4*
ə purt′ nəns 1

APRICOT +
ā′ prə kät′ 3*
ap′ rə kät′ 3
ā′ pri kät′ 1
ap′ ri kät′ 1

A PRIORI
ä′ prē ôr′ ē 4*
ä′ prī ôr′ ē 3
ā′ prē ōr′ ē 3
ā′ prī ōr′ ī′ 2
ā′ prī ôr′ ē 1
a′ prē ôr′ ē 1
a′ prē ōr′ ē 1

APROPOS
ap′ rə pō′ 4*
ap′ rə pō′ 1

APSE
aps 4

AQUA
äk′ wə 4*
ak′ wə 3
āk′ wə 1

AQUARIUM ✓
ə kwer′ ē əm 4

AQUARIUS ✓
ə kwer′ ē əs 4*
ə kwar′ ē əs 1

AQUATIC
ə kwat′ ik 4*
ə kwät′ ik 4

AQUAVIT
äk′ wə vēt′ 3*
ak′ wə vēt′ 3

AQUEDUCT
ak′ wə dukt′ 3*
ak′ wi dukt′ 1

AQUEOUS
ā′ kwē əs 4*
ak′ wē əs 4

AQUILINE
ak′ wə līn′ 4*
ak′ wə lin 2
ak′ wə lən 2

ARABESQUE ✓
ar' ə besk' 4*
er' ə besk' 1

ARABLE ✓
ar' ə bəl 3*
ar' ə b'l 1
er' ə b'l 1

ARACHNID
ə rak' nid 3*
ə rak' nəd 1

ARBITER
är' bə tər 3*
är' bi tər 1

ARBITRARY ✓
är' bə trer' ē 3*
är' bi trer' ē 1

ARBOREAL
är bôr' ē əl 4*
är bōr' ē əl 3

ARBORETUM
är' bə rēt' əm 4

ARBUTUS
är byōō' təs 4

ARCANE
är kān' 4

ARCANUM
är kā' nəm 4

ARCHAEOLOGY +
är' kē äl' ə jē 4

ARCHAIC
är kā' ik 4

ARCHANGEL
ärk' ān' jəl 3*
ärk' ān' j'l 1

ARCHER
är' chər 4

ARCHETYPAL
är' kə tīp' əl 2*
är' ki tīp' əl 2

ARCHETYPE
är' kə tīp' 2*
är' ki tīp' 2

ARCHIPELAGO
är' kə pel' ə gō 3*
är' chə pel' ə gō 1
är' kə pel' ə gō' 1

ARCHITECT
är' kə tekt' 3*
är' ki tekt' 1

ARCHITECTURE
är' kə tek' chər 3*
är' ki tek' chər

ARCHIVES
är' kīvz 2*
är' kīvz' 2

ARCHIVIST
är' kə vist 3*
är' kī' vist 2
är' kə vəst 1

ARCTIC
ärk' tik 4*
är' tik 4

ARDENT
är' d'nt 3*
är' dənt 1

PRONUNCIATION KEY

Symbol	Key words	Symbol	Key words	Symbol	Key words
a	asp, fat, parrot	†ə	a in ago	r	red, port, dear
ā	ape, date, play		e in agent	s	sell, castle, pass
†ä	ah, car, father		i in sanity	t	top, cattle, hat
e	elf, ten, berry		o in comply	v	vat, hovel, have
ē	even, meet, money		u in focus	w	will, always, swear
i	is, hit, mirror	ər	perhaps, murder	y	yet, onion, yard
ī	ice, bite, high	b	bed, fable, dub	z	zebra, dazzle, haze
ō	open, tone, go	d	dip, beadle, had	ch	chin, catcher, arch
ô	all, horn, law	f	fall, after, off	sh	she, cushion, dash
ōō	ooze, tool, crew	g	get, haggle, dog	th	thin, nothing, truth
oo	look, pull, moor	h	he, ahead, hotel	th	then, father, lathe
yōō	use, cute, few	j	joy, agile, badge	zh	azure, leisure
yoo	united, cure, globule	k	kill, tackle, bake	ŋ	ring, anger, drink
oi	oil, point, toy	l	let, yellow, ball	″	see p. 15.
ou	out, crowd, plow	m	met, camel, trim	✓	see p. 15.
u	up, cut, color	n	not, flannel, ton	+	see p. 14.
ʉr	urn, fur, deter	p	put, apple, tap	'	see p. 15.
†See p. 14.		†See p. 16.		○	see p. 14.

ARDOR
är′ dər 4

ARDUOUS
är′ jo͞o əs 2*
är′ joo wəs 1
ärj′ wəs 1
är′ jə wəs 1

AREA ✓
er′ ē ə 4

ARENA
ə rē′ nə 4

ARGOSY
är′ gə sē 4

ARGOT
är′ gō 4*
är′ gət 4

ARGYLE (ARGYLL)
är′ gīl 3*
är′ gīl′ 1

ARIA ✓
ä′ rē ə 4*
er′ ē ə 2

ARID
ar′ id 3*
ar′ əd 1
er′ id 1

ARIES ✓
er′ ēz 3*
er′ ē ēz′ 3
ar′ ē ēz′ 1
ar′ ēz 1

ARISTOCRACY ✓ +
ar′ ə stä′ krə sē 2*
ar′ i stä′ krə sē 2
er′ ə stä′ krə sē 1

ARISTOCRAT
ə ris′ tə krat′ 4*
ar′ is tə krat′ 3
a ris′ tə krat′ 1

ARMADA
är mä′ də 4*
är mā′ də 4

ARMAGEDDON
är′ mə ged′ ′n 3*
är mə ged′ ən 1

ARMAMENT
är′ mə mənt 4

ARMATURE
är′ mə chər 3*
är′ mə choor′ 1
är′ mə cho͞or 1
är′ mə tyo͞or′ 1
är′ mə to͞or′ 1

ARMISTICE
är′ mə stis 2*
är′ mi stis 1
är′ mə stəs 1

ARMOIRE
är mwär′ 4*
är′ mər 2

ARMOR
är′ mər 4

AROMA
ə rō′ mə 4

AROMATIC ✓
ar′ ə mat′ ik 4*
er′ ə mat′ ik 1

ARPEGGIO
är pej′ ō 4
är pej′ ē ō′ 3*

ARRAIGN
ə rān′ 4

ARRANT ✓
ar′ ənt 4*
er′ ənt 1

ARRAS ✓
ar′ əs 4*
er′ əs 1

ARRAY
ə rā′ 4

ARRIVISTE
ar′ ē vēst′ 2*
ar′ i vēst′ 1

ARROGANCE ✓
ar′ ə gəns 4*
er′ ə gəns 1
ar′ ə gənts 1

ARROGATE
ar′ ə gāt 2*
ar′ ə gāt′ 2

ARROYO
ə roi′ ō 4*
ə roi′ ə 2

ARSENAL
är′ s′n əl 2*
är′ snəl 2
är′ sə nəl 1

ARSENIC
ärs′ nik 3
är′ sə nik 2*
är′ s′n ik 1

ARSON
är′ s′n 3*
är′ sən 2

ARTERIAL ○
är tir′ ē əl 4

ARTERIOSCLEROSIS ○
är tir′ ē ō sklə rō′ sis 4

ARTERY
är′ tər ē 4

ARTESIAN
är tē′ zhən 4

ARTHRITIS
är thrī tis 4

ARTICULATE (adj)
är tik′ yə lit 3*
är tik′ yə lət 1

ARTICULATE (v)
är tik′ yə lāt′ 4

ARTIFACT
är′ tə fakt′ 4

ARTIFICE
är′ tə fis 3*
är′ tə fəs 1

ARTIFICER
är tif′ ə sər 3*
är tif′ i sər 1
ärt′ ə fə sər 1

ARTIFICIAL
är′ tə fish′ əl 4

ARTILLERY
är til′ ər ē 4*
är til′ rē 1

ARTISAN
är′ tə zən 2*
är′ tə sən 2
är′ ti zən 1
är′ tə z′n 1
är′ tə s′n 1

ARTISTE
är tēst′ 4

ART NOUVEAU
ärt′ n<u>oo</u> vō′ 3*
är′ n<u>oo</u> vō′ 2

ASBESTOS
as bes′ təs 4*
az bes′ təs 4

ASCEND
ə send′ 4

ASCENDANT
ə sen′ dənt 4

ASCERTAIN
as′ ər tān′ 4

ASCETIC
ə set′ ik 4

ASCETICISM
ə set′ ə siz′ əm 2*
ə set′ i siz′ əm 1
ə set′ ə siz′m 1

ASCOT   +
as′ kət 4*
as′ kät′ 3

ASEPTIC
ā sep′ tik 4*
ə sep′ tik 3

ASININE
as′ ə nīn′ 3*
as′ ′n īn′ 1

ASK
ask 4*
äsk 3

ASKANCE
ə skans′ 4*
ə skants′ 1

ASPARAGUS ✓
ə spar′ ə gəs 3*
ə sper′ ə gəs 2

PRONUNCIATION KEY

Symbol	Key words	Symbol	Key words	Symbol	Key words
a	asp, fat, parrot	†ə	a in ago	r	red, port, dear
ā	ape, date, play		e in agent	s	sell, castle, pass
†ä	ah, car, father		i in sanity	t	top, cattle, hat
e	elf, ten, berry		o in comply	v	vat, hovel, have
ē	even, meet, money		u in focus	w	will, always, swear
i	is, hit, mirror	ər	perhaps, murder	y	yet, onion, yard
ī	ice, bite, high	b	bed, fable, dub	z	zebra, dazzle, haze
ō	open, tone, go	d	dip, beadle, had	ch	chin, catcher, arch
ô	all, horn, law	f	fall, after, off	sh	she, cushion, dash
<u>oo</u>	ooze, tool, crew	g	get, haggle, dog	th	thin, nothing, truth
oo	look, pull, moor	h	he, ahead, hotel	th	then, father, lathe
y<u>oo</u>	use, cute, few	j	joy, agile, badge	zh	azure, leisure
yoo	united, cure, globule	k	kill, tackle, bake	ŋ	ring, anger, drink
oi	oil, point, toy	l	let, yellow, ball	″	see p. 15.
ou	out, crowd, plow	m	met, camel, trim	✓	see p. 15.
u	up, cut, color	n	not, flannel, ton	+	see p. 14.
ur	urn, fur, deter	p	put, apple, tap	′	see p. 15.
†See p. 14.		†See p. 16.		○	see p. 14.

ASPECT
as′ pekt′   2*
as′ pekt   2

ASPERITY
as per′ ə tē   3*
əs per′ i tē   1
əs per′ ə tē   1

ASPERSION
ə spʉr′ zhən   4*
ə spʉr′ shən   4

ASPHALT
as′ fôlt   2*
as′ fôlt′   2
as′ falt   1

ASPHODEL
as′ fə del   4*
as′ fə dəl′   1

ASPHYXIA
as fik′ sē ə   4*
əs fik′ sē ə   1

ASPHYXIATE
as fik′ sē āt′   4

ASPIC
as′ pik   4

ASPIRANT
as′ pər ənt   3
ə spīr′ ənt   2*
as′ prənt   1

ASPIRATE (v)
as′ pə rāt′   4

ASSASSIN
ə sas′ in   2*
ə sas′ ′n   2

ASSAULT
ə sôlt   4

ASSAY (n)
a sā′   3
as′ ā   2*
ə sā′   1

ASSAY (v)
a sā′   3
ə sā′   2*
as′ ā′   2

ASSENT
ə sent   4

ASSERT
ə sʉrt′   4

ASSESS
ə ses′   4

ASSET
as′ et   3*
as′ et′   1

ASSEVERATE
ə sev′ ə rāt′   4

ASSIDUITY
as′ ə dyŏŏ′ ə tē   3*
as′ ə dŏŏ′ ə tē   3
as′ i dŏŏ′ i tē   1
as′ i dyŏŏ′ i tē   1

ASSIDUOUS
ə sij′ ŏŏ əs   2*
ə sij′ oo wəs   1
ə sij′ wəs   1

ASSIGN
ə sīn′   4

ASSIGNATION
as′ ig nā′ shən   4

ASSIGNEE
ə sī′ nē′   4*
as′ ə nē′   2
as′ i nē′   1

ASSIMILATE
ə sim′ ə lāt′   4

ASSIMILATION
ə sim′ ə lā′ shən   4

ASSIZE
ə sīz′   4

ASSOCIATE (n, adj)
ə sō′ shē it   3*
ə sō′ sē it   3
ə sō′ shē āt′   3
ə sō′ sē āt′   3
ə sō′ shē ət   1
ə sō′ shət   1

ASSOCIATION
ə sō′ shē ā′ shən   4
ə sō′ sē ā′ shən   4*

ASSONANCE
as′ ə nəns   4*
as′ ə nənts   1

ASSUAGE
ə swāj′   4

ASSURE
ə shoor′   4*
ə shoo′ ʉr   1

ASTERISK
as′ tə risk   2*
as′ tə risk′   2

ASTEROID
as′ tə roid′   4

ASTHMA
az′ mə   4*
as′ mə   1

ASTIGMATISM
ə stig′ mə tiz′ əm   3*
ə stig′ mə tiz′m   1

ASTIR
ə stʉr′   4

ASTRAL
as′ trəl   4

ASTRINGENT
ə strin' jənt   4

ASTROLOGY   +
ə sträl ə jē   4

ASTRONOMY   +
ə strän' ə mē   4

ASTUTE
ə sty$\overline{oo}$t'   4*
ə st$\overline{oo}$t'   4
a st$\overline{oo}$t'   1
a sty$\overline{oo}$t'   1

ASYLUM
ə sī' ləm   4

ASYMMETRIC
ā' sə met' rik   3*
ā' si met' rik   1
a' sə met' rik   1

ASYMMETRY
ā sim' ə trē   3*
ā sim' i trē   1

ATAVISM
at' ə viz' əm   3*
at' ə viz'm   1

ATAXIA
ə tak' sē ə   4

ATELIER
at'l yā'   2*
at' 'l yā'   2

ATHEIST
ā' thē ist   3*
ā' thē əst   1

ATHEROSCLEROSIS
ath' ər ō sklə rō' sis   3*
ath' ər ō sklə rō' səs   1

ATHLETE
ath' lēt   3*
ath' lēt'   1

ATHLETIC
ath let' ik   4

ATLAS
at' ləs   4

ATMOSPHERIC   ○
at məs' fer' ik   4*
at məs' fir' ik   3

ATOLL   +
a' tôl   3*
a' täl   3
ā' tôl   2
ā' täl   2
ā' tōl   2
ə tôl'   1
ə täl'   1
ə tōl'   1

ATOM
at' əm   4

ATOMIC   +
ə täm' ik   4

ATONAL
ā tōn' 'l   3*
ā tōn' əl   1

ATONE
ə tōn'   4

ATRIUM
ā' trē əm   4

PRONUNCIATION KEY

Symbol	Key words	Symbol	Key words	Symbol	Key words
a	asp, fat, parrot	†ə	a in ago	r	red, port, dear
ā	ape, date, play		e in agent	s	sell, castle, pass
†ä	ah, car, father		i in sanity	t	top, cattle, hat
e	elf, ten, berry		o in comply	v	vat, hovel, have
ē	even, meet, money		u in focus	w	will, always, swear
i	is, hit, mirror	ər	perhaps, murder	y	yet, onion, yard
ī	ice, bite, high	b	bed, fable, dub	z	zebra, dazzle, haze
ō	open, tone, go	d	dip, beadle, had	ch	chin, catcher, arch
ô	all, horn, law	f	fall, after, off	sh	she, cushion, dash
$\overline{oo}$	ooze, tool, crew	g	get, haggle, dog	th	thin, nothing, truth
oo	look, pull, moor	h	he, ahead, hotel	th	then, father, lathe
y$\overline{oo}$	use, cute, few	j	joy, agile, badge	zh	azure, leisure
yoo	united, cure, globule	k	kill, tackle, bake	ŋ	ring, anger, drink
oi	oil, point, toy	l	let, yellow, ball	''	see p. 15.
ou	out, crowd, plow	m	met, camel, trim	✓	see p. 15.
u	up, cut, color	n	not, flannel, ton	+	see p. 14.
ʉr	urn, fur, deter	p	put, apple, tap	'	see p. 15.
†See p. 14.		†See p. 16.		○	see p. 14.

ATROCIOUS
ə trō′ shəs 4

ATROCITY   +
ə träs′ ə tē 3*
ə träs′ i tē 1

ATROPHY
at′ rə fē 4

ATTACHÉ
at′ ə shā′ 4

ATTENUATE
ə ten′ yo͞o āt′ 2*
ə ten′ yoo wāt′ 1
ə ten′ yə wāt′ 1

ATTAR
at′ ər 4*
at′ är′ 1

ATTEST
ə test′ 4

ATTORNEY
ə tʉr′ nē 4

ATTRIBUTE (n)
a′ trə byo͞ot′ 4

ATTRIBUTE (v)
ə trib′ yo͞ot 3*
ə trib′ yət 1

ATTRITION
ə trish′ ən 4

ATYPICAL
ā tip′ i kəl 4*
ā′ tip′ i kəl 1

AUBURN
ô′ bərn 4

AUCTION
ôk′ shən 4

AUDACIOUS
ô dā′ shəs 4

AUDACITY
ô das′ ə tē 3*
ô das′ i tē 1

AUDIBLE
ô′ də bəl 3
ô′ də b′l 1*

AUDIO
ô′ dē ō 2*
ô′ dē ō′ 2

AUDIT
ô′ dit 3*
ô′ dət 1

AUDITION
ô dish′ ən 4

AUDITOR
ô′ də tər 3*
ô′ di tər 1

AUF WIEDERSEHEN
ouf vē′ dər zā′ ən 3*
ouf vē′ dər zān′ 1

AUGER
ô′ gər 4

AUGHT
ôt 4*
ät 1

AUGMENT
ôg ment′ 4

AU GRATIN
ō grat′ ’n 4*
ō grät′ ’n 4
ô grät′ ’n 3
ô grat′ ’n 3

AUGUR
ô′ gər 4

AUGURY
ô′ gyər ē 4*
ô′ gə rē 1

AUGUST (adj)
ô gust′ 4

AURA
ôr′ ə 4

AURAL
ôr′ əl 4

AUREOLE
ôr′ ē ōl′ 4

AURICLE
ôr′ i kəl 3
ôr′ i k′l 1*

AURICULAR
ô rik′ yə lər 3*
ô rik′ yo͞o lər 1

AURORA
ô rôr′ ə 4*
ə rôr′ ə 4
ô rōr′ ə 3
ə rōr′ ə 2

AUSPICES
ôs′ pə sēz′ 3*
ôs′ pə səz 1
ôs′ pi siz 1

AUSPICIOUS
ôs pish′ əs 4

AUSTERE ○
ô stir′ 4

AUSTERITY
ô ster′ ə tē 3*
ô ster′ i tē 1

AUTARCHY
ô′ tär kē 3*
ô′ tär′ kē 1

AUTHENTIC
ô then′ tik 4*
ə then′ tik 1

AUTHENTICITY
ô′ then tis′ ə tē   3*
ô′ thin tis′ i tē   1
ô′ then tis′ i tē   1

AUTHORITARIAN ✓ +
ə thär′ ə ter′ ē ən   3*
ə thôr′ ə ter′ ē ən   3
ô thôr′ ə ter′ ē ən   3
ô thär′ ə ter′ ē ən   2

AUTHORITATIVE   +
ə thär′ ə tāt′ iv   3*
ə thôr′ ə tāt′ iv   3
ô thôr′ ə tāt′ iv   3
ô thär′ ə tāt′ iv   3
ə thôr′ i tāt′ iv   1
ə thär′ i tāt′ iv   1

AUTHORITY   +
ə thär′ ə tē   3*
ə thôr′ ə tē   3
ô thôr′ ə tē   2
ô thär′ ə tē   2
ə thôr′ i tē   1
ə thär′ i tē   1

AUTISTIC
ô tis′ tik   4

AUTOBAHN
ou′ tō bän′   3*
ôt′ ō bän′   1

AUTOCRACY   +
ô tä′ krə s̬ē   4

AUTOCRAT
ô′ tə krat′   4

AUTO-DA-FÉ
ôt′ ō də fā′   4*
out′ ō də fā′   2

AUTOMATA   +
ô täm′ ə tə   4*
ô täm′ ə tä′   1

AUTOMATE
ôt′ ə māt′   4

AUTOMATIC
ôt ə mat′ ik   2*
ôt′ ə mat′ ik   2

AUTOMATION
ôt′ ə mā′ shən   4

AUTOMATON   +
ô täm′ ə tän′   3*
ô täm′ ə tən   3

AUTONOMOUS   +
ô tän′ ə məs   4

AUTONOMY   +
ô tän′ ə mē   4

AUTOPSY   +
ô′ täp′ sē   3*
ô′ təp sē   2

AUTUMN
ôt′ əm   4

AUTUMNAL
ô tum′ nəl   2*
ô tum′ n′l   2

AUXILIARY
ôg zil′ yər ē   4*
ôg zil′ ər ē   4
ôg zil′ rē   1

AVALANCHE
av′ ə lanch′   4*
av′ ə länch′   3

PRONUNCIATION KEY

Symbol	Key words	Symbol	Key words	Symbol	Key words
a	asp, fat, parrot	†ə	a in ago	r	red, port, dear
ā	ape, date, play		e in agent	s	sell, castle, pass
†ä	ah, car, father		i in sanity	t	top, cattle, hat
e	elf, ten, berry		o in comply	v	vat, hovel, have
ē	even, meet, money		u in focus	w	will, always, swear
i	is, hit, mirror	ər	perhaps, murder	y	yet, onion, yard
ī	ice, bite, high	b	bed, fable, dub	z	zebra, dazzle, haze
ō	open, tone, go	d	dip, beadle, had	ch	chin, catcher, arch
ô	all, horn, law	f	fall, after, off	sh	she, cushion, dash
ōo	ooze, tool, crew	g	get, haggle, dog	th	thin, nothing, truth
oo	look, pull, moor	h	he, ahead, hotel	th	then, father, lathe
yōo	use, cute, few	j	joy, agile, badge	zh	azure, leisure
yoo	united, cure, globule	k	kill, tackle, bake	ŋ	ring, anger, drink
oi	oil, point, toy	l	let, yellow, ball	″	see p. 15.
ou	out, crowd, plow	m	met, camel, trim	✓	see p. 15.
u	up, cut, color	n	not, flannel, ton	+	see p. 14.
ur	urn, fur, deter	p	put, apple, tap	′	see p. 15.
†See p. 14.		†See p. 16.		○	see p. 14.

AVANT GARDE
ä′ vän′ gärd′ 1*
ä vänt′ gärd′ 1
ä′ vänt′ gärd′ 1
ə vänt′ gärd′ 1
ə vant′ gärd′ 1
ä′ vänt′ gärd′ 1

AVARICE
av′ ər is 3*
av′ rəs 1

AVARICIOUS
av′ ə rish′ əs 4

AVATAR
av′ ə tär 4

AVE MARIA
ä′ vä mə rē′ ə 2*
ä′ vē mə rē′ ə 1
ä vä mə rē′ ə 1
ä vē mə rē′ ə 1

AVENUE
av′ ə nyōō′ 4*
av′ ə nōō′ 4

AVER
ə vʉr′ 4

AVIAN
ā′ vē ən 4

AVIARY ✓
ā′ vē er′ ē 4

AVIATION
ā′ vē ā′ shən 4*
av′ ē ā′ shən 4

AVIATOR
ā′ vē āt′ ər 4*
av′ ē āt′ ər 4

AVID
av′ id 3*
av′ əd 1

AVIDITY
ə vid′ ə tē 3*
ə vid′ i tē 1
a vid′ ə tē 1

AVOCADO
av′ ə kä′ dō 4*
ä′ və kä′ dō 2

AVOIRDUPOIS
av′ ər də poiz′ 4*
av′ ər də poiz′ 1

AVOUCH
ə vouch′ 4

AVOW
ə vou′ 4

AVUNCULAR
ə vuŋ′ kyə lər 4

AWE
ô 4

AWRY
ə rī′ 4

AXIAL
ak′ sē əl 4

AXIOM
ak′ sē əm 4

AYE (yes)
ī 4

AZALEA
ə zāl′ yə 4

AZIMUTH
az′ ə məth 4*
az′ məth 1

AZURE
azh′ ər 4

BABEL
bā′ bəl 3*
bab′ əl 3

BABOON
ba bōōn′ 4*
bə bōōn′ 1

BABUSHKA
bə boosh′ kə 4*
bə bōōsh′ kə 2

BACCALAUREATE
bak′ ə lôr′ ē it 3*
bak′ ə lôr′ ē ət 1
bak′ ə lär′ ē ət 1

BACCARAT
bak′ ə rä′ 4*
bäk′ ə rä′ 4
bak′ ə rä′ 2
bäk′ ə rä′ 1

BACCHANAL
bak′ ə nal′ 2*
bak′ ə nəl 2
bak′ ə n′l 2
bak′ ə näl′ 2
bak′ ə nal′ 1

BACCHANTE
bə kan′ tē 4
bə kän′ te 3*
bə kant′ 4
bə känt′ 2
bak′ ənt 1

BACILLI
bə sil′ ī 3*
bə sil′ ī′ 1
bə sil′ ē 1

BACILLUS
bə sil′ əs 4

BACTERIA ✓ ○
bak tir′ ē ə 4

BADE
bad 4*
bād 2

BADINAGE
bad′ ə näzh′ 4*
bad′ ′n ij 2

BADMINTON
bad′ min t′n 3*
bad′ min tən 1

BAGATELLE
bag′ ə tel′ 4

BAGEL
bā′ gəl 3
bā′ g′l 1*

BAGUETTE
ba get′ 4

BAILIFF
bā′ lif 3*
bā′ ləf 1

BAILIWICK
bā′ li wik′ 2*
bā′ lə wik 2

BAIRN ✓
bern 4

BAKLAVA
bäk′ lə vä′ 2*
bäk′ lə vä′ 2

BAKSHEESH
bak′ shēsh 3*
bak shēsh′ 2

BALALAIKA
bal′ ə līk′ ə 4

BALBRIGGAN
bal brig′ ən 4

BALCONY
bal' kə nē 4

BALDERDASH
bôl' dər dash 4

BALEEN
bə lēn' 4

BALK
bôk 4

BALLAD
bal' əd 4

BALLADE
bə läd' 4*
ba läd' 3

BALLAST
bal' əst 4

BALLERINA
bal' ə rē' nə 4

BALLET
ba lā' 4
bal' ā 3*

BALLETOMANE
ba let' ə mān' 4*
bə let' ə mān' 1

BALLISTIC
bə lis' tik 4

BALM
bäm 4*
bälm 2

BALMACAAN
bal' mə kan' 3*
bal' mə kän' 2

BALSA
bôl' sə 4*
bäl' sə 1

BALSAM
bôl' səm 4

BALUSTRADE
bal' ə strād' 4*
bal' ə strād' 1

BAMBOO
bam boo' 4

BANAL
bə näl' 4
bə nal' 4
bān' 'l 3*
ba nal' 1

BANDOLEER ○
ban' də lir' 4

BANKRUPTCY
baŋk' rəp sē 3*
baŋk' rupt' sē 3
baŋk' rəpt sē 2

BANQUET
baŋ' kwit 3*
ban' kwit 1
baŋ' kwət 1
ban' kwət 1

BANQUETTE
baŋ ket' 4*
ban ket' 1

BANSHEE
ban' shē 4*
ban shē' 2
ban' shē' 1

BANTAM
ban' təm 4

BANYAN
ban' yən 4

BANZAI
bän' zī' 3*
bän' zī' 3

BAPTISM
bap' tiz' əm 3*
bap' tiz 'm 1

BAPTISMAL
bap tiz' məl 3*
bap tiz' m'l 1

BAPTIZE
bap tīz' 4
bap' tīz 2*
bap' tīz' 2

BARBARIAN ✓
bär ber' ē ən 4*
bär bar' ē ən 1

BARBARIC ✓
bär bar' ik 3*
bär ber' ik 1

BARBARISM
bär' bər iz' əm 3*
bär' bər iz 'm 1

BARBARITY ✓
bär bar' ə tē 2*
bär ber' ə tē 1
bär bar' i tē 1

BARBAROUS
bär' bər əs 4*
bär' brəs 1

BARBECUE
bär' bi kyoo' 2*
bär' bə kyoo' 2

BARBITURATE
bär bich' ə rāt' 4
bär bich' ər it 3*
bär' bə toor' āt' 3
bär' bə tyoor' it 3
bär' bə toor' it 1
bär bich' ər ət 1

BARCAROLE
bär' kə rōl' 4

BARITONE ✓
bar' ə tōn' 3*
ber' ə tōn' 1
bar' i tōn' 1

BAR MITZVAH
bär mits′ və   4

BARNACLE
bär′ nə kəl   2*
bär′ ni k′l   1
bär′ ni kəl   1

BAROMETER   +
bə räm′ ə tər   3*
bə ram′ i tər   1

BAROMETRIC
bar′ ə met′ rik   4

BARON   ✓
bar′ ən   4*
ber′ ən   1

BARONESS   ✓
bar′ ə nis   3*
bar′ ə nəs   1
ber′ ə nis   1

BARONET
bar′ ə nit   3*
bar′ ə net′   2
bar′ ə net′   2
bar′ ə nət   1

BARONIAL
bə rō′ nē əl   4

BARONY   ✓
bar′ ə nē   4*
ber′ ə nē   1

BAROQUE   +
bə rōk′   4*
ba rōk′   1
bə räk′   1

BARRACUDA   ✓
bar′ ə kōō′ də   4*
ber′ ə kōō′ də   1

BARRAGE
bə räzh′   4*
bə räj′   2

BARREN   ✓
bar′ ən   4*
ber′ ən   1

BARRETTE
bə ret′   4*
bä ret′   3

BARRICADE   ✓
bar′ ə kād′   4*
bar′ ə kād′   4
ber′ ə kād′   1

BARRIER   ✓
bar′ ē ər   4*
ber′ ē ər   1

BARRIO
bar′ ē ō′   1*
bär′ ē ō   1
bä′ ryō   1

BARRISTER   ✓
bar′ is tər   3*
bar′ əs tər   1
ber′ is tər   1

BASAL
bā′ zəl   3*
bā′ səl   3

BASALT
bə sôlt′   4
bā′ sôlt   2*
bā′ sôlt′   2

PRONUNCIATION KEY

Symbol	Key words		Symbol	Key words		Symbol	Key words
a	asp, fat, parrot		†ə	a in ago		r	red, port, dear
ā	ape, date, play			e in agent		s	sell, castle, pass
†ä	ah, car, father			i in sanity		t	top, cattle, hat
e	elf, ten, berry			o in comply		v	vat, hovel, have
ē	even, meet, money			u in focus		w	will, always, swear
i	is, hit, mirror		ər	perhaps, murder		y	yet, onion, yard
ī	ice, bite, high		b	bed, fable, dub		z	zebra, dazzle, haze
ō	open, tone, go		d	dip, beadle, had		ch	chin, catcher, arch
ô	all, horn, law		f	fall, after, off		sh	she, cushion, dash
ōō	ooze, tool, crew		g	get, haggle, dog		th	thin, nothing, truth
oo	look, pull, moor		h	he, ahead, hotel		th	then, father, lathe
yōō	use, cute, few		j	joy, agile, badge		zh	azure, leisure
yoo	united, cure, globule		k	kill, tackle, bake		ŋ	ring, anger, drink
oi	oil, point, toy		l	let, yellow, ball		″	see p. 15.
ou	out, crowd, plow		m	met, camel, trim		✓	see p. 15.
u	up, cut, color		n	not, flannel, ton		+	see p. 14.
ur	urn, fur, deter		p	put, apple, tap		′	see p. 15.
†See p. 14.			†See p. 16.			◯	see p. 14.

BASES
bā′ sēz   4

BASIL
baz′ əl   3
bāz′ əl   2*
baz′ ′l   1
bās′ əl   1
bas′ əl   1

BASILICA
bə sil′ i kə   4*
bə zil′ i kə   1

BASILISK
bas′ ə lisk′   3*
baz′ ə lisk′   2
bas′ ə lisk   1
baz′ ə lisk   1

BASIS
bā′ sis   3*
bā′ səs   1

BAS RELIEF
bä′ ri lēf′   3*
bas′ ri lef′   1
bä′ ri lēf′   1
bas′ ri lēf′   1
bä rə lēf′   1
bas rə lēf′   1

BASS (fish)
bas   4

BASS (music)
bās   4

BASSET
bas′ it   3*
bas′ ət   1

BASSO
bäs′ ō   3*
bas′ ō   1

BASSOON
bə sōōn′   4*
ba sōōn′   4

BASTARD
bas′ tərd   4

BASTE
bāst   4

BASTILLE
bas tēl′   4

BASTINADO
bas′ tə nā′ dō   4
bas′ tə nä′ dō   3*

BASTION
bas′ chən   4*
bas′ tē ən   3

BATH
bath   4*
bäth   3

BATHE
bāth   4

BATHOS   +
bā′ thäs   2*
bā′ thäs′   2
bā′ thôs   1

BATHYSCAPHE
bath′ i skāf′   3*
bath′ i skaf′   3

BATHYSPHERE   ○
bath′ i sfir′   4*
bath′ i sfiər′   1

BATIK
bə tēk′   4*
bat′ ik   4

BATISTE
bə tēst′   4*
ba tēst′   4

BATON   +
bə tän′   4*
bat′ ′n   3
ba tän′   3

BATTALION
bə tal′ yən   4

BAUBLE
bô′ bəl   3*
bô′ b′l   1

BAUXITE
bôk′ sīt   2*
bō′ zīt   2
bôk′ sīt′   2
bäk′ sīt′   1

BAWDY
bô′ dē   4

BAYONET
bā′ ə net′   4*
bā′ ə net′   4
bā′ ə nit   3
bā′ ə nət   1

BAYOU
bī′ ōō   4*
bī′ ō   4
bī′ ə   1
bī′ yə   1

BAZAAR
bə zär′   4

BAZOOKA
bə zōō′ kə   4

BEATIFIC
bē′ ə tif′ ik   4

BEATIFICATION
bē at′ ə fi kā′ shən   2*
bē at′ ə fə kā′ shən   2

BEATITUDE
bē at′ ə tōōd′   4*
bē at′ ə tyōōd′   4

BEAU
bō   4

BEAUTIFUL
byōō′ tə fəl   4

BEAUX ARTS
bō zär′ 3*
bō zärt′ 1

BEBOP +
bē′ bäp′ 4

BECOME
bi kum′ 4

BEDIZEN
bi dīz′ 'n 2*
bi diz′ 'n 2
bi dīz′ ən 1
bi diz′ ən 1

BEDLAM
bed′ ləm 4

BEDOUIN
bed′ o͞o in 2*
bed′ oo win 1
bed′ win 1
bed′ ə wən 1
bed′ wən 1

BEELZEBUB
bē el′ zə bub′ 2*
bē el′ zi bub′ 2
bēl′ zi bub′ 1

BEGONIA
bi gōn′ yə 4*
bi gō′ nē ə 1

BEGUILE
bi gīl′ 4*
bi gī əl′ 1

BEGUINE
bi gēn′ 4

BEGUM
bē′ gəm 4

BEHEMOTH
bi hē′ məth 4*
bē′ ə məth 2
bē′ ə môth 2

BEIGE
bāzh 4

BEL CANTO
bel kän′ tō 2*
bel′ kän′ tō 1
bel kän′ tō′ 1

BELEAGUER
bi lē′ gər 4

BELIE
bi lī′ 4

BELLE
bel 4

BELLES LETTRES
bel let′ rə 4

BELLICOSE
bel′ i kōs 2*
bel′ ə kōs′ 2

BELLIGERENT
bə lij′ ər ənt 3*
bə lij′ rənt 1

BELOVED
bi luvd′ 4
bi luv′ id 3*
bi luv′ əd 1

BEMA
bē′ mə 4

BENEDICT
ben′ ə dikt′ 3*
ben′ i dikt 1

PRONUNCIATION KEY

Symbol	Key words	Symbol	Key words	Symbol	Key words
a	asp, fat, parrot	†ə	a in ago	r	red, port, dear
ā	ape, date, play		e in agent	s	sell, castle, pass
†ä	ah, car, father		i in sanity	t	top, cattle, hat
e	elf, ten, berry		o in comply	v	vat, hovel, have
ē	even, meet, money		u in focus	w	will, always, swear
i	is, hit, mirror	ər	perhaps, murder	y	yet, onion, yard
ī	ice, bite, high	b	bed, fable, dub	z	zebra, dazzle, haze
ō	open, tone, go	d	dip, beadle, had	ch	chin, catcher, arch
ô	all, horn, law	f	fall, after, off	sh	she, cushion, dash
o͞o	ooze, tool, crew	g	get, haggle, dog	th	thin, nothing, truth
oo	look, pull, moor	h	he, ahead, hotel	th	then, father, lathe
yo͞o	use, cute, few	j	joy, agile, badge	zh	azure, leisure
yoo	united, cure, globule	k	kill, tackle, bake	ŋ	ring, anger, drink
oi	oil, point, toy	l	let, yellow, ball	″	see p. 15.
ou	out, crowd, plow	m	met, camel, trim	✓	see p. 15.
u	up, cut, color	n	not, flannel, ton	+	see p. 14.
ur	urn, fur, deter	p	put, apple, tap	′	see p. 15.
†See p. 14.		†See p. 16.		◯	see p. 14.

BENEDICTION
ben′ ə dik′ shən 3*
ben′ i dik′ shən 1

BENEFICE
ben′ ə fis 3*
ben′ ə fəs 1

BENEFICENT
bə nef′ ə sənt 2*
bə nef′ i sənt 1
bə nef′ ə s′nt 1

BENEFICIAL
ben′ ə fish′ əl 4

BENEFICIARY ✓
ben′ ə fish′ ē er′ ē 4*
ben′ ə fish′ ə rē 3
ben′ ə fish′ rē 1

BENEVOLENT
bə nev′ ə lənt 4*
bə nev′ lənt 1

BENIGHTED
bi nī′ tid 3*
bi nī′ təd 1

BENIGN
bi nīn′ 4

BENIGNANT
bi nig′ nənt 4

BENISON
ben′ ə sən 2
ben′ ə zən 2
ben′ i sən 1*
ben′ i zən 1
ben′ ə z′n 1
ben′ ə s′n 1

BENZOATE
ben′ zō āt′ 3*
ben′ zə wāt′ 1

BEQUEATH
bi kwēth 4*
bi kwēth′ 4

BERET
bə rā′ 4*
ber′ ā 1

BERGAMOT
bur′ gə mät′ 4

BERIBERI
ber′ ē ber′ ē 2*
ber′ ē ber′ ē 1
ber′ ē ber′ ē 1

BERSERK
bər surk′ 4*
bər zurk′ 4
bə surk′ 1

BESOM
bē′ zəm 4

BESTIAL
bes′ chəl 4*
bēs′ chəl 3
best′ yəl 2

BESTIALITY
bes′ chē al′ ə tē 4*
bes′ tē al′ ə tē 3
bes′ chē al′ i tē 1
bes′ tē al′ i tē 1
bēs′ chē al′ i tē 1
bēs′ chē al′ ə tē 1

BETA
bāt′ ə 4*
bēt′ ə 3

BETEL
bēt′ ′l 4

BÊTE NOIRE
bet′ nə wär′ 1
bāt′ nə wär′ 1
bet nwär′ 1*
bāt′ nwär′ 1

BETRAY
bi trā′ 4

BETROTH +
bi trôth′ 4
bi trōth′ 4*
bi trôth′ 1
bi träth 1
bi träth 1

BETROTHAL +
bi trō′ thəl 4*
bi trô′ thəl 4
bi trō′ thəl 1

BEVEL
bev′ əl 3*
bev′ ′l 1

BEVY
bev′ ē 4

BEY
bā 4

BIAS
bī′ əs 4

BIBELOT
bib′ lō 3*
bib′ ə lō′ 1
bē′ bə lō′ 1

BIBLICAL
bib′ li kəl 3
bib′ li k′l 1

BIBLIOGRAPHY +
bib′ lē äg′ rə fē 4

BIBLIOPHILE
bib′ lē ə fīl′ 4
bib′ lē ə fil 1

BIBULOUS
bib′ yə ləs 3*
bib′ yoo ləs 1

BICAMERAL
bī kam′ ər əl 4*
bī kam′ rəl 2
bī′ kam′ ər əl 1

BICARBONATE
bī kär′ bə nāt′ 3
bī kär′ bə nit 2*

BICENTENNIAL
bī′ sen ten′ ē əl 4

BICEPS
bī′ seps 3*
bī′ seps′ 1

BICUSPID
bī kus′ pid 4*

BICYCLE
bī′ si k′l 4*
bī′ si kəl 2

BIDET
bē dā′ 2*
bi dā′ 1
bi det′ 1

BIENNIAL
bī en′ ē əl 4*
bī′ en′ ē əl 1

BIER ○
bir 4
bi ər 1

BIFOCAL
bī fō′ kəl 3*
bī fō′ k′l 1
bī′ fō kəl 1

BIFURCATE
bī′ fər kāt′ 4*
bī fur′ kāt 4

BIGAMY
big′ ə mē 4

BIGOT
big′ ət 4

BIGOTRY
big′ ə trē 4

BIJOU
bē′ zhoo 3*
bi zhoo′ 2

BIKINI
bi kē′ nē 4

BILGE
bilj 4

BILINGUAL
bī liŋ′ gwəl 4

BILIOUS
bil′ yəs 4

BILLET
bil′ it 3*
bil′ ət 1

BILLET DOUX
bil′ ē doo′ 2*
bil′ ā doo′ 2
bil′ ē doo′ 1
bil′ ā doo′ 1

BILLIARDS
bil′ yərdz 4

BINARY
bī′ nər ē 4

PRONUNCIATION KEY

Symbol	Key words	Symbol	Key words	Symbol	Key words
a	asp, fat, parrot	†ə	a in ago	r	red, port, dear
ā	ape, date, play		e in agent	s	sell, castle, pass
†ä	ah, car, father		i in sanity	t	top, cattle, hat
e	elf, ten, berry		o in comply	v	vat, hovel, have
ē	even, meet, money		u in focus	w	will, always, swear
i	is, hit, mirror	ər	perhaps, murder	y	yet, onion, yard
ī	ice, bite, high	b	bed, fable, dub	z	zebra, dazzle, haze
ō	open, tone, go	d	dip, beadle, had	ch	chin, catcher, arch
ô	all, horn, law	f	fall, after, off	sh	she, cushion, dash
oo	ooze, tool, crew	g	get, haggle, dog	th	thin, nothing, truth
oo	look, pull, moor	h	he, ahead, hotel	th	then, father, lathe
yoo	use, cute, few	j	joy, agile, badge	zh	azure, leisure
yoo	united, cure, globule	k	kill, tackle, bake	ŋ	ring, anger, drink
oi	oil, point, toy	l	let, yellow, ball	″	see p. 15.
ou	out, crowd, plow	m	met, camel, trim	✓	see p. 15.
u	up, cut, color	n	not, flannel, ton	+	see p. 14.
ur	urn, fur, deter	p	put, apple, tap	′	see p. 15.
†See p. 14.		†See p. 16.		○	see p. 14.

BINAURAL
bī nôr′ əl   4*
bi nôr′ əl   4

BINNACLE
bin′ ə kəl   2*
bin′ i kəl   1
bin′ i k′l   1

BINOCULAR   +
bī näk′ yə lər   4
bə näk′ yə lər   2*
bi näk′ yə lər   1

BINOMIAL
bī nō′ mē əl   4

BIMODAL
bī mōd′ ′l   4*
bī′ mōd′ ′l   1

BIODEGRADABLE
bī′ ō di grā′ də bəl   4

BIOPSY   +
bī′ äp sē   3*
bī′ äp′ sē   1

BIPARTISAN
bī pär′ tə zən   2*
bī pär′ tə z′n   1
bī pär′ ti zən   1
bī pär′ tə sən   1

BIPED
bī′ ped′   2*
bī′ ped   2

BIREME
bī′ rēm′   2*
bī′ rēm   2

BIRETTA
bə ret′ ə   4

BISCUIT
bis′ kit   3*
bis′ kət   1

BISON
bī′ s′n   2*
bī′ z′n   2
bī′ sən   2
bī′ zən   2

BISQUE
bisk   4

BISTRO
bis′ trō   4
bēs′ trō   2*

BITUMINOUS
bi tōō′ mə nəs   4*
bi tyōō′ mə nəs   4
bi tōō′ mə nəs   3
bi tyōō′ mə nəs   3

BIVALVE
bī′ valv′   4

BIVOUAC
biv′ wak   3
biv′ ōō ak   1*
biv′ ōō ak′   1
biv′ oo wak′   1
biv′ ə wak′   1
biv′ wak′   1

BIZARRE
bi zär′   4

BLACKGUARD
blag′ ərd   4*
blag′ ärd   2
blak′ gärd′   1

BLANC MANGE
blə mänzh′   3*
blə mänj′   3

BLASÉ
blä zā′   4*
blä′ zā   3

BLASPHEME
blas fēm′   4*
blas′ fēm   3

BLASPHEMOUS
blas′ fə məs   4

BLASPHEMY
blas′ fə mē   4

BLATANT
blā′ t′nt   3*
blāt′ ənt   1

BLAZON
blā′ z′n   2*
blā′ zən   2

BLESSED (adj)
bles′ id   3*
blest   3
bles′ əd   1

BLESSED (v)
blest   4

BLOUSE
blous   4*
blouz   4

BLITHE
blīth   4*
blīth   4

BLITZKRIEG
blits′ krēg′   4

BLUCHER
blōō′ chər   4*
blōō′ kər   4

BLUDGEON
bluj′ ən   3*
bluj′ ′n   1

BOA
bō′ ə   4

BOATSWAIN
bō′ sən   2*
bō′ s′n   2

BOCCIE   ○
bäch′ ē   3

BODICE
bäd′ is 4

BODING
bō′ diŋ 4

BOGEY (golf)
bō′ gē 4

BOGIE
bō′ gē 4

BOGUS
bō′ gəs 4

BOHEMIAN
bō hē′ mē ən 4*
bō hēm′ yən 1

BOISTEROUS
boi′ strəs 3*
bois′ tər əs 3

BOLERO ✓
bə ler′ ō 3*
bō ler′ ō 3
bə le′ ər ō 1
bə ler′ ō′ 1
bə le′ ər ō′ 1

BOLL
bōl 4

BOLSTER
bōl′ stər 4

BOLT
bōlt 4

BOLUS
bō′ ləs 4

BOMBARD +
bäm bärd′ 4*
bəm bärd′ 2

BOMBARDIER ✓ +
bäm′ bə dir′ 2*
bäm′ bər di′ ər 2
bäm′ bər dir′ 2

BOMBAST +
bäm bast′ 2*
bäm′ bast 2

BONA FIDE +
bän′ ə fīd′ 4*
bō′ nə fīd′ 4
bō′ nə fī′ dē 3

BONANZA
bə nan′ zə 4*
bō nan′ zə 2

BONBON +
bän′ bän′ 4

BONIFACE +
bän′ ə fās′ 4*
bän′ ə fis 1
bän′ ə fəs 1

BONITO
bə nē′ tō 4*
bə nē′ tə 1

BONSAI +
bōn sī′ 2
bōn′ sī 2
bän′ sī 1*
bän sī′ 1

BONUS
bō′ nəs 4

BOOMERANG
boo′ mə rang′ 4

PRONUNCIATION KEY

Symbol	Key words	Symbol	Key words	Symbol	Key words
a	asp, fat, parrot	†ə	a in ago	r	red, port, dear
ā	ape, date, play		e in agent	s	sell, castle, pass
†ä	ah, car, father		i in sanity	t	top, cattle, hat
e	elf, ten, berry		o in comply	v	vat, hovel, have
ē	even, meet, money		u in focus	w	will, always, swear
i	is, hit, mirror	ər	perhaps, murder	y	yet, onion, yard
ī	ice, bite, high	b	bed, fable, dub	z	zebra, dazzle, haze
ō	open, tone, go	d	dip, beadle, had	ch	chin, catcher, arch
ô	all, horn, law	f	fall, after, off	sh	she, cushion, dash
oo	ooze, tool, crew	g	get, haggle, dog	th	thin, nothing, truth
oo	look, pull, moor	h	he, ahead, hotel	th	then, father, lathe
yoo	use, cute, few	j	joy, agile, badge	zh	azure, leisure
yoo	united, cure, globule	k	kill, tackle, bake	ŋ	ring, anger, drink
oi	oil, point, toy	l	let, yellow, ball	ʺ	see p. 15.
ou	out, crowd, plow	m	met, camel, trim	✓	see p. 15.
u	up, cut, color	n	not, flannel, ton	+	see p. 14.
ur	urn, fur, deter	p	put, apple, tap	′	see p. 15.
†See p. 14.		†See p. 16.		○	see p. 14.

BOONDOGGLE +
bo͞on′ däg′ əl 3*
bo͞on′ dôg′ əl 2
bo͞on′ dôg′l 1
bo͞on′ däg′l 1

BOOR
boor 4*
boo ər 1

BOUQUET (fragrance of wine or liqueur)
bo͞o kā′ 4*
bō kā′ 1

BOUQUET (nosegay; compliment)
bo͞o kā′ 4*
bō kā′ 4

BORDELLO
bôr del′ ō 4*
bôr del′ ō′ 1

BORZOI
bôr′ zoi 3*
bôr′ zoi′ 1

BOSCAGE +
bäs′ kij 4

BOSOM
booz′ əm 4*
bo͞o′ zəm 3

BOTANICAL
be tan′ i kəl 3*
bə tan′ i k′l 1

BOTANY +
bät′ 'n ē 4*
bät′ nē 2

BOTULISM +
bäch′ ə liz′ əm 1*
bäch′ oo liz′ əm 1
bäch′ ə liz əm 1
bäch′ ə liz′m 1

BOUCLÉ
bo͞o klā′ 4

BOUDOIR
bo͞od′ wôr′ 3
bo͞od′ wär 2*
bo͞od′ wär′ 2
bo͞o dwär′ 1
boo dwär′ 1

BOUFFANT
bo͞o fänt′ 4

BOUGAINVILLEA
bo͞o′ gən vil′ ē ə 3
bo͞o′ gən vil′ yə 2*
bo͞o′ gən vē′ ə 1
bō′ gən vil′ yə 1
bō′ gən vē′ yə 1
boo′ gən vil′ yə 1
boo′ gən vē′ yə 1

BOUGH
bou 4

BOUILLABAISSE
bo͞ol′ yə bäs′ 2*
bo͞o′ yə bäs′ 2
bo͞ol′ yə bäs′ 1
bo͞o′ lə bäs′ 1

BOUILLON +
bool′ yän 4*
bool′ yən 3
bo͞o′ yän′ 2
bo͞o′ yən 1
bo͞ol′ yən 1

BOULDER
bōl′ dər 4

BOULEVARD
bool′ ə värd′ 4*
bo͞ol′ ə värd′ 3

BOURBON
bʉr′ bən 4*
boor′ bən 3
bo͞or′ bən 2
bōr′ bən 1
bôr′ bən 1

BOURGEOIS
boor zhwä′ 4*
bo͞or′ zhwä′ 3
boor′ zhwä′ 1

BOURGEOISIE
boor′ zhwä zē′ 2*
boor′ zhwä zē′ 2

BOURSE
boors 4

BOUTIQUE
bo͞o tēk′ 4

BOUTONNIERE ○ ✓
bo͞ot′ 'n ir′ 3*
bo͞ot′ 'n yer 2
bo͞ot′ ən yer 2
bo͞ot′ ə nir 1

BOVINE
bō′ vīn 2*
bō′ vin 2
bō′ vēn 2

BOW (prow; nod)
bou 4

BOW (weapon; curve; knot)
bō 4

BOWDLERIZE
boud′ lə rīz′ 4*
bōd′ lə rīz′ 4

BOWER
bou′ ər 4*
bour 1

BOWIE (knife)
bo͞o′ ē 4*
bō′ ē 4

BOWLINE
bō′ lin′ 4*
bō′ lin 3
bō′ lən 1

BRACERO ✓
brə ser′ ō 4

BRAE
brā 4*
brē 1

BRAGGADOCIO
brag′ ə dō′ shē ō 2*
brag′ ə dō′ shē ō′ 2
brag′ ə dō′ shō 1
brag′ ə dō′ shō′ 1
brag′ ə dō′ sē ō 1
brag′ ə dō′ sē ō′ 1

BRAISE
brāz 4

BRASSIERE ○
brə zir′ 4

BRAVADO
brə vä′ dō 4

BRAVO
brä′ vō 3*
brä vō′ 2

BRAVURA
brə vyoor′ ə 4*
brə voor′ ə 1

BRAZIER
brā′ zhər 4

BREECHES
brich′ iz 4

BREVET
brə vet′ 3*
bri vet′ 1

BREVIARY ✓
brē′ vē er′ ē 3*
brev′ ē er ē 2
brē′ və rē 1

BREVITY
brev′ ə tē 3
brev′ i tē 1*

BRIAR (BRIER)
brī′ ər 4*
brīr 1

BRIDLE
brīd′ ′l 4

BRIGADE
bri gād′ 4

BRIGADIER ○
brig′ ə dir 4

BRIGAND
brig′ ənd 4

BRIGANTINE
brig′ ən tēn′ 4*
brig′ ən tīn′ 1

BRILLIANT
bril′ yənt 4

BRILLIANTINE
bril′ yən tēn′ 4

BRIQUETTE
bri ket′ 4

PRONUNCIATION KEY

Symbol	Key words	Symbol	Key words	Symbol	Key words
a	asp, fat, parrot	†ə	a in ago	r	red, port, dear
ā	ape, date, play		e in agent	s	sell, castle, pass
†ä	ah, car, father		i in sanity	t	top, cattle, hat
e	elf, ten, berry		o in comply	v	vat, hovel, have
ē	even, meet, money		u in focus	w	will, always, swear
i	is, hit, mirror	ər	perhaps, murder	y	yet, onion, yard
ī	ice, bite, high	b	bed, fable, dub	z	zebra, dazzle, haze
ō	open, tone, go	d	dip, beadle, had	ch	chin, catcher, arch
ô	all, horn, law	f	fall, after, off	sh	she, cushion, dash
o͞o	ooze, tool, crew	g	get, haggle, dog	th	thin, nothing, truth
oo	look, pull, moor	h	he, ahead, hotel	th	then, father, lathe
yo͞o	use, cute, few	j	joy, agile, badge	zh	azure, leisure
yoo	united, cure, globule	k	kill, tackle, bake	ŋ	ring, anger, drink
oi	oil, point, toy	l	let, yellow, ball	″	see p. 15.
ou	out, crowd, plow	m	met, camel, trim	✓	see p. 15.
u	up, cut, color	n	not, flannel, ton	+	see p. 14.
ur	urn, fur, deter	p	put, apple, tap	′	see p. 15.
†See p. 14.		†See p. 16.		○	see p. 14.

BRISTLE
bris' əl 3*
bris' 'l 1

BRITICISM
brit' ə siz' əm 2*
brit' i siz' əm 1
brit' ə siz'm 1

BROCCOLI +
bräk' ə lē 4*
bräk' lē 1

BROCHETTE
brō s̶het' 4

BROCHURE
brō s̶hoor' 4*
brō s̶hyoor' 1

BROGAN
brō' gən 3*
brō gan' 1
brō' gan' 1
brō' g'n 1

BROGUE
brōg 4

BROMIDE
brō' mīd' 4*
brō' mid 1

BRONCHIAL +
bräŋ' kē əl 4

BRONCHITIS +
bräŋ kīt' is 3*
bräŋ kīt' əs 1
brän kīt' əs 1

BROOCH
brōc̶h 4*
brōōc̶h 4

BROTHEL +
bräth' əl 4*
brôth' əl 4
bräth' əl 2
brôth' əl 2

BROUGHAM
brōōm 4*
brōō' əm 4
brō' əm 4

BRUIN
brōō' in 2*
brōō' ən 2

BRUIT
brōōt 4

BRUMMAGEM
brum' ə jəm 3*
brum' i jəm 1

BRUNET (TE)
brōō net' 4

BRUT
brōōt 4

BUBONIC +
byōō bän' ik 4*
bōō bän' ik 4

BUCCANEER ○
buk' ə nir' 4*
buk' ə niər' 1

BUCOLIC +
byōō käl' ik 4

BUDDHISM
bōō' diz' əm 2*
bood' iz' əm 2
bōō' diz əm 1
bood' iz əm 1
bōō' diz 'm 1
bood' iz 'm 1

BUFFET (n.v. blow)
buf' it 3*
buf' ət 1

BUFFET (n)
bə fā' 4*
boo fā' 3
bōō fā' 1

BUFFOON
bə fōōn' 4

BUGLE
byōō' gəl 3*
byōō g'l 1

BULLION
bool' yən 4

BULWARK
bool' wərk 4*
bul' wərk 4
bool' wôrk' 2

BUMPTIOUS
bump' s̶həs 4*
bum' s̶həs 1

BUOY
boi 4*
bōō' ē 4

BUOYANT
boi' ənt 4*
bōō' yənt 4

BUREAU
byoor' ō 4

BUREAUCRACY +
byoo räk' rə sē 4

BURGEON
bur' jən 4

BURGHER
bʉr' gər 4

BURIAL
ber' ē əl 4

BURLESQUE
bər lesk' 4

BURNOOSE
bər nōōs' 3*
bʉr nōōs' 2
bʉr' nōōs' 1

BURRO
boor′ ō 4*
bʉr′ ō 3
bur′ ō 2

BURSAR
bʉr′ sər 4*
bʉr′ sär′ 3

BURSITIS
bər sī′ tis 3
bər sī′ təs 1*

BUSBY
buz bē 4

BUTANE
byo͞o′ tān 3*
byo͞o tān′ 2
byo͞o′ tān′ 1

BUXOM
buk′ səm 4

BYZANTINE
bi zan′ tin 3
biz′ ən tīn 2*
biz′ ən tēn′ 2
biz′n′ tēn′ 2
biz′n′ tīn 2

PRONUNCIATION KEY

Symbol	Key words	Symbol	Key words	Symbol	Key words
a	asp, fat, parrot	†ə a in ago		r	red, port, dear
ā	ape, date, play	e in agent		s	sell, castle, pass
†ä	ah, car, father	i in sanity		t	top, cattle, hat
e	elf, ten, berry	o in comply		v	vat, hovel, have
ē	even, meet, money	u in focus		w	will, always, swear
i	is, hit, mirror	ər	perhaps, murder	y	yet, onion, yard
ī	ice, bite, high	b	bed, fable, dub	z	zebra, dazzle, haze
ō	open, tone, go	d	dip, beadle, had	ch	chin, catcher, arch
ô	all, horn, law	f	fall, after, off	sh	she, cushion, dash
o͞o	ooze, tool, crew	g	get, haggle, dog	th	thin, nothing, truth
oo	look, pull, moor	h	he, ahead, hotel	th	then, father, lathe
yo͞o	use, cute, few	j	joy, agile, badge	zh	azure, leisure
yoo	united, cure, globule	k	kill, tackle, bake	ŋ	ring, anger, drink
oi	oil, point, toy	l	let, yellow, ball	″	see p. 15.
ou	out, crowd, plow	m	met, camel, trim	✓	see p. 15.
u	up, cut, color	n	not, flannel, ton	+	see p. 14.
ʉr	urn, fur, deter	p	put, apple, tap	′	see p. 15.
†See p. 14.		†See p. 16.		○	see p. 14.

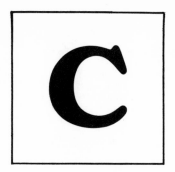

CABAL
kə bal' 4

CABALA
kə bäl' ə 4*
kab' ə lə 4

CABALLERO
kab' ə ler' ō 4*
kab' əl yer' ō 3
kab' ə ler' ō' 1
kab' ə yer' ō' 1

CABANA
kə ban' yə 4
kə ban' yə 3*
kə bän' ə 2
kə bän' yə 2

CABARET
kab' ə rā' 4*
kab' ə rā' 1

CABOCHON   +
kab' ə shän' 4

CABRIOLE
kab' rē ōl' 4

CABRIOLET
kab' rē ə lā' 4*
kab' rē ə let' 1

CACAO
kə kā' ō 4*
kə kä' ō 3
kə kou' 2

CACHE
kash 4

CACHET
ka shā' 4*
kash' ā 2

CACHINNATE
kak' ə nāt' 4

CACOETHES
kak' ō ē' thēz 3*
kak' ə wē' thēz 1
kak' ə wē' thēz' 1

CACOPHONOUS   +
kə käf' ə nəs 2*
ka käf' ə nəs 2

CADAVER
kə dav' ər 4*
kə dā' vər 1

CADAVEROUS
kə dav' ər əs 3*
kə dav' rəs 1

CADENCE
kād' 'ns 3*
kād' əns 1
kād' 'nts 1

CADENZA
kə den' zə 4

CADET
kə det' 4

CAESAREAN   ✓
(operation)
si zer' ē ən 4*
si zar' ē ən 1

CAESURA
si zhoor' ə 4*
si zoor' ə 3
si zyoor' ə 2
si zyoor' ə 1

CADRE
kad' rē 4*
kä' drə 1

CADUCEUS
kə dōō' sē əs 4*
kə dyōō' sē əs 4

CAFE
ka fā′ 4*
kə fā′ 4

CAFETERIA ○
kaf′ ə tir′ ē ə 3*
kaf′ i tir′ ē ə 1

CAFFEINE
ka fēn′ 4
kaf′ ē in 3
kaf′ ēn 2*

CAFTAN
kaf′ tən 4*
kaf tan′ 3
käf tän′ 2
kaf′ tan 1

CAIRN ✓
kern 3*
ke ərn 2

CAISSON +
kā′ sän 2*
kā′ sän′ 2
kā′ sən 2
kās′ ’n 2

CAJOLE
kə jōl′ 4

CALAMITOUS
kə lam′ ə təs 3*
kə lam′ i təs 1

CALCIFY
kal′ sə fī′ 4

CALCIMINE
kal′ sə mīn′ 4*
kal′ sə min 2

CALCIUM
kal′ sē əm 4

CALCULATE
kal′ kyə lāt′ 4

CALCULUS
kal′ kyə ləs 4

CALDRON
kôl′ drən 4

CALECHE (CALÈCHE)
kə lesh′ 3*
ka ləsh′ 1

CALF
kaf 4*
käf 3

CALIPER
kal′ ə pər 4

CALIPH
kā′ lif 3*
kal′ if 3
kā′ ləf 1
kal′ əf 1

CALISTHENICS
kal′ əs then′ iks 3*
kal′ is then′ iks 1

CALK
kôk 4

CALLIGRAPHY
kə lig′ rə fē 4

CALLIOPE
kə lī′ ə pē′ 4*
kal′ ē ōp′ 2

CALLOUS
kal′ əs 4

CALLUS
kal′ əs 4

CALM
käm 4*
kälm 2

CALOMEL
kal′ ə mel′ 4*
kal′ ə məl 4

CALORIC +
kə lôr′ ik 4*
kə lär′ ik 4
kə lōr′ ik 1
kal′ ə rik 1

CALORIE
kal′ ə rē 4*
kal′ rē 1

CALUMET
kal′ yə met′ 4*
kal′ yə met′ 3
kal′ yə mət 2
kal′ yə mit 1

CALUMNY
kal′ əm nē 4

CALVARY
kal′ vər ē 4*
kalv′ rē 1

CALYPSO
kə lip′ sō 4*
kə lip′ sō′ 1

CAMARADERIE
käm′ ə räd′ ə rē 4
kam′ ə räd′ ə rē 4*
käm′ räd′ rē 1
kam′ räd′ rē 1

CAMBRIC
kām′ brik 4

CAMELLIA
kə mēl′ yə 4*
kə mē′ lē yə 2

CAMEMBERT ✓
kam′ əm ber′ 4

CAMEO
kam′ ē ō′ 4*
kam′ yō 1

CAMERA
kam′ rə 4*
kam′ ər ə 4

CAMOMILE
(CHAMOMILE)
kam′ ə mīl′ 4*
kam′ ə mēl′ 2

CAMOUFLAGE
kam′ ə fläzh′ 4*
kam′ ə fläj′ 3

CAMPANILE
kam′ pə nē′ lē 4

CANAILLE
kə nāl′ 4
kə nī′ 2*

CANAPÉ
kan′ ə pā′ 4*
kan′ ə pē 4

CANARD
kə närd′ 4

CANCER
kan′ sər 4

CANDELABRUM
kan′ də lä′ brəm 3*
kan′ də lā′ brəm 3
kan′ də lab′ rəm 3
kan′ d'lä′ brəm 1
kan′ d'lā′ brəm 1

CANDIDACY
kan′ də də sē 3*
kan′ di də sē 1
kan′ əd ə sē 1

CANDIDATE
kan′ də dāt′ 3*
kan′ di dāt′ 2
kan′ di dit 1
kan′ ə dāt′ 1
kan′ ə dət 1
kan′ də dət 1

CANINE
kā′ nīn′ 2*
kā′ nīn 2
kə nīn′ 1

CANKER
kaŋ′ kər 4

CANNABIS
kan′ ə bis 3*
kan′ ə bəs 1

CANNEL
kan′ 'l 4

CANON
kan′ ən 4

CAÑON
kan′ yən 4

CANONICAL +
kə nän′ i k'l 2*
kə nän′ i kəl 2

CANOPY
kan′ ə pē 4

CANTALOUP (E)
kan′ tə lōp′ 2*
kan′ t'l ōp′ 1
kan′ t'l ōp 1

CANTANKEROUS
kan taŋ′ kər əs 3*
kan taŋ′ krəs 1
kən taŋ′ krəs 1

PRONUNCIATION KEY

Symbol	Key words		Symbol	Key words		Symbol	Key words
a	asp, fat, parrot		†ə	a in ago		r	red, port, dear
ā	ape, date, play			e in agent		s	sell, castle, pass
†ä	ah, car, father			i in sanity		t	top, cattle, hat
e	elf, ten, berry			o in comply		v	vat, hovel, have
ē	even, meet, money			u in focus		w	will, always, swear
i	is, hit, mirror		ər	perhaps, murder		y	yet, onion, yard
ī	ice, bite, high		b	bed, fable, dub		z	zebra, dazzle, haze
ō	open, tone, go		d	dip, beadle, had		ch	chin, catcher, arch
ô	all, horn, law		f	fall, after, off		sh	she, cushion, dash
ōō	ooze, tool, crew		g	get, haggle, dog		th	thin, nothing, truth
oo	look, pull, moor		h	he, ahead, hotel		th	then, father, lathe
yōō	use, cute, few		j	joy, agile, badge		zh	azure, leisure
yoo	united, cure, globule		k	kill, tackle, bake		ŋ	ring, anger, drink
oi	oil, point, toy		l	let, yellow, ball		″	see p. 15.
ou	out, crowd, plow		m	met, camel, trim		✓	see p. 15.
u	up, cut, color		n	not, flannel, ton		+	see p. 14.
ur	urn, fur, deter		p	put, apple, tap		′	see p. 15.
†See p. 14.			†See p. 16.			◯	see p. 14.

CANTATA
kən tä′ tə   4

CANTEEN
kan tēn′   4

CANTHARIDES
kan t̸har′ ə dēz′   3*
kan t̸har′ i dēz′   1

CANTICLE
kan′ ti kəl   3*
kan′ ti k'l   1

CANTILEVER
kan′ t'l ē vər   3
kan′ tə lē′ vər   1*
kan′ t'l ev′ ər   1
kan′ tə lev′ ər   1

CANTO
kan′ tō   4*
kan′ tō′   1

CANTON   +
kan′ tän′   3*
kan′ tən   3
kan′ t'n   2
kan tän′   2

CANTONMENT   +
kan tōn′ mənt   4*
kan tän′ mənt   4

CAOUTCHOUC
kou chook′   3*
kou chook′   2
koo′ chook   1
kou chook′   1
kou′ choo′   1

CAPACIOUS
kə pā′ shəs   4

CAPARISON
kə par′ ə sən   2*
kə par′ i sən   1
kə par′ ə s'n   1

CAPILLARY   ○
kap′ ə ler′ ē   4

CAPON   +
kā′ pən   4
kā′ pän   3*
kā′ pän′   1

CAPRICE
kə prēs′   4

CAPRICIOUS
kə prish′ əs   4*
kə prē′ shəs   3

CAPRICORN
kap′ ri kôrn′   2*
kap′ rə kôrn′   2

CAPSULE
kap′ səl   3
kap′ syool   2*
kap′ sool   1

CAPTIOUS
kap′ shəs   4

CAPTURE
kap′ chər   4

CARACUL
kar′ ə kəl   4

CARAFE
kə raf′   4*
kə räf′   2

CARAMEL
kar′ ə mel   2*
kar′ ə məl   2
kär′ məl   2

CARAT
kar′ ət   4

CARAVAN
kar′ ə van′   4

CARAVANSARY
kar′ ə van′ sə rē   4*
kar′ ə vant′ sə rē   1

CARAVEL
kar′ ə vel′   4*
kar′ ə vel   1

CARAWAY
kar′ ə wā′   4

CARBINE
kär′ bīn   3*
kär′ bēn   2
kär′ bīn′   2
kär′ bēn′   1

CARBOHYDRATE
kär′ bō hī′ drāt′   2*
kär′ bə hī′ drāt   2
kär′ bō hī′ drāt   1
kär′ bō hī′ drət   1

CARBURETOR
kär′ bə rā′ tər   4
kär′ byə rā′ tər   3*
kär′ byoo rā′ tər   1

CARCASS
kär′ kəs   4

CARCINOGEN
kär sin′ ə jən   4
kär′ sin ə jən′   2*

CARCINOMA
kär′ sə nō′ mə   3*
kär′ s'n ō′ mə   1

CARDIAC
kär′ dē ak′   4

CARDIGAN
kär′ di gən   2*
kär′ də gən   2

CARESS
kə res′   4

CARET   ✓
kar′ it   3*
kar′ ət   1
ker′ it   1

CARIBOU
kar′ ə bōō′ 4

CARICATURE
kar′ i kə choor′ 2*
kar′ ə kə chər 2
kar′ ə kə choor 2
kar′ i kə toor′ 1

CARIES ✓
ker′ ēz 3*
ker′ ē ēz′ 1
kar′ ēz 1

CARILLON +
kar′ ə län′ 4*
kə ril′ yən 2
kar′ ə lən 1

CARMINATIVE
kär′ mə nāt′ iv 4*
kär min′ ə tiv 4

CARMINE
kär′ min 3
kär′ mīn 2*
kär′ mən 1

CARNAGE
kär′ nij 4

CARNAL
kär′ n′l 3*
kär′ nəl 1

CARNELIAN
kär nēl′ yən 4

CARNIVORE
kär′ nə vôr′ 4*
kär′ nə vōr′ 3

CARNIVOROUS
kär niv′ ə rəs 4*
kär niv′ rəs 1

CAROL
kar′ əl 4

CAROM
kar′ əm 4

CAROTID +
kə rät′ id 3*
kə rät′ əd 1

CAROUSAL
kə rou′ zəl 4

CAROUSE
kə rouz′ 4

CAROUSEL
kar′ ə sel′ 4*
kar′ ə zel′ 4

CARREL
kar′ əl 4

CARRION
kar′ ē ən 4

CARTE BLANCHE
kärt′ blänch′ 3*
kärt′ blänsh′ 1
kärt′ blanch′ 1

CARTEL
kär tel′ 4*
kär′ t′l 1

CARTILAGE
kärt′ ′l ij 3*
kärt′ lij 2
kärt′ ə lij 1

PRONUNCIATION KEY

Symbol	Key words	Symbol	Key words	Symbol	Key words
a	asp, fat, parrot	†ə a in ago		r	red, port, dear
ā	ape, date, play	e in agent		s	sell, castle, pass
†ä	ah, car, father	i in sanity		t	top, cattle, hat
e	elf, ten, berry	o in comply		v	vat, hovel, have
ē	even, meet, money	u in focus		w	will, always, swear
i	is, hit, mirror	ər	perhaps, murder	y	yet, onion, yard
ī	ice, bite, high	b	bed, fable, dub	z	zebra, dazzle, haze
ō	open, tone, go	d	dip, beadle, had	ch	chin, catcher, arch
ô	all, horn, law	f	fall, after, off	sh	she, cushion, dash
ōō	ooze, tool, crew	g	get, haggle, dog	th	thin, nothing, truth
oo	look, pull, moor	h	he, ahead, hotel	th	then, father, lathe
yōō	use, cute, few	j	joy, agile, badge	zh	azure, leisure
yoo	united, cure, globule	k	kill, tackle, bake	ŋ	ring, anger, drink
oi	oil, point, toy	l	let, yellow, ball	″	see p. 15.
ou	out, crowd, plow	m	met, camel, trim	✓	see p. 15.
u	up, cut, color	n	not, flannel, ton	+	see p. 14.
ur	urn, fur, deter	p	put, apple, tap	′	see p. 15.
†See p. 14.		†See p. 16.		○	see p. 14.

CARTILAGINOUS
kärt′ ′l aj′ ə nəs 3*
kärt′ əl aj′ ə nəs 1

CARTON
kärt′ ′n 4

CARTOON
kär tōōn′ 4

CARTOUCHE
kar tōōsh′ 4

CARYATID
kar′ ē at′ id 3*
kar′ ē at′ əd 1

CARYATIDES
kar′ ē at′ ə dēz 2*
kar′ ē at′ i dēz′ 1
kar′ ē at′ ə dēz′ 1

CASABA
kə sä′ bə 4

CASBAH
käz′ bä 4*
kaz′ bä 3
kas′ bä 1
kaz′ bə 1

CASEIN
kā′ sēn 3*
kā′ sē in 3
kā sēn′ 2
kā′ sē ən 1

CASHEW
kash′ ōō 4*
kə shōō′ 2

CASHIER ○
ka shir′ 4*
kə shir′ 1

CASHMERE ○
kash′ mir 4*
kaʒh′ mir 3

CASINO
kə sē′ nō 4*
kə sē′ nō′ 1

CASKET
kas′ kit 3*
käs′ kit 2
kas′ kət 1

CASQUE
kask 4

CASSEROLE
kas′ ə rōl′ 4*
kaz′ ə rōl′ 1

CASSETTE
ka set′ 4*
kə set′ 3

CASSOCK
kas′ ək 4

CASSOWARY ✓
kas′ ə wer′ ē 4

CASTANET
kas′ tə net′ 4

CASTE
kast 4*
käst 3

CASTIGATE
kas′ tə gāt′ 4

CASUAL
kaʒh′ ōō əl 2*
kaʒh′ oo wəl 1
kaʒh′ wəl 1
kaʒh′ ə wəl 1
kaʒh′ əl 1

CASUALTY
kaʒh′ ōō əl tē 2*
kaʒh′ əl tē 2
kaʒh′ oo wəl tē 1
kaʒh′ wəl tē 1

CASUISTRY
kaʒh′ ōō is trē 2*
kaʒh′ oo wis trē 1
kaʒh′ wəs trē 1

CATACLYSM
kat′ ə kliz′ əm 3*
kat′ ə kliz′ ′m 1

CATACOMB
kat′ ə kōm′ 4

CATAFALQUE
kat′ ə fôlk′ 4*
kat′ ə falk′ 4
kat′ ə fôk′ 3

CATALOG (UE) +
kat′l′ äg′ 4*
kat′l′ ôg′ 4

CATALYST
kat′l′ ist 3*
kat′l′ əst 1

CATALYTIC
kat′l it′ ik 4

CATAMARAN
kat′ ə mə ran′ 4

CATAPULT
kat′ ə pult′ 4*
kat′ ə pōolt′ 3

CATARRH
kə tär′ 4

CATASTROPHE
kə tas′ trə fē 4*
kə tas′ trə fē′ 1

CATASTROPHIC +
kat′ ə sträf′ ik 4

CATATONIA
kat′ ə tō′ nē ə 4

CATATONIC +
kat′ ə tän′ ik 4

CATECHISM
kat' ə kiz' əm   3*
kat' ə kiz' 'm   1

CATECHUMEN
kat' ə kyoo' mən   4

CATEGORICAL   +
kat' ə gôr' i kəl   3
kat' ə gär' i kəl   2*
kat' ə gōr' i kəl   1
kat' ə gôr' ə k'l   1
kat' ə gär' ə k'l   1

CATEGORIZE
kat' ə gə rīz'   3*
kat' i gə rīz'   1

CATEGORY
kat' ə gôr' ē   4*
kat' ə gōr' ē   3

CATERPILLAR
kat' ər pil' ər   4*
kat' ə pil' ər   4

CATERWAUL
kat' ər wôl'   4

CATHARSIS
kə thär' sis   3*
kə thär' səs   1

CATHARTIC
kə thär' tik   4

CATHEDRAL
kə thē' dral   4

CATHETER
kath' ə tər   3*
kath' i tər   1
kath' tər   1

CATHODE
kath' ōd   3*
kath' ōd'   1

CATHOLIC
kath' ə lik   4*
kath' lik   4

CATHOLICITY
kath' ə lis' ə tē   3*
kath' ə lis' i tē   1

CAUCASIAN
kô kā' zhən   4*
kô kā' shən   2
kô ka' zhən   1
kô ka' shən   1

CAUCUS
kôk' əs   4

CAUL
kôl   4

CAULIFLOWER   +
kôl' ə flou' ər   2
käl' ə flou' ər   2
kôl' i flou' ər   2
käl' i flou' ər   2
käl' ē flou' ər   1
kôl' ē flou' ər   1*
kôl' i flour'   1
käl' i flour'   1

CAULK
kôk   4

CAUSAL
kô' zəl   3*
kô' z'l   1

PRONUNCIATION KEY

Symbol	Key words	Symbol	Key words	Symbol	Key words
a	asp, fat, parrot	†ə	a in ago	r	red, port, dear
ā	ape, date, play		e in agent	s	sell, castle, pass
†ä	ah, car, father		i in sanity	t	top, cattle, hat
e	elf, ten, berry		o in comply	v	vat, hovel, have
ē	even, meet, money		u in focus	w	will, always, swear
i	is, hit, mirror	ər	perhaps, murder	y	yet, onion, yard
ī	ice, bite, high	b	bed, fable, dub	z	zebra, dazzle, haze
ō	open, tone, go	d	dip, beadle, had	ch	chin, catcher, arch
ô	all, horn, law	f	fall, after, off	sh	she, cushion, dash
oo	ooze, tool, crew	g	get, haggle, dog	th	thin, nothing, truth
oo	look, pull, moor	h	he, ahead, hotel	th	then, father, lathe
yoo	use, cute, few	j	joy, agile, badge	zh	azure, leisure
yoo	united, cure, globule	k	kill, tackle, bake	ŋ	ring, anger, drink
oi	oil, point, toy	l	let, yellow, ball	"	see p. 15.
ou	out, crowd, plow	m	met, camel, trim	✓	see p. 15.
u	up, cut, color	n	not, flannel, ton	+	see p. 14.
ʉr	urn, fur, deter	p	put, apple, tap	'	see p. 15.
†See p. 14.		†See p. 16.		○	see p. 14.

CAUSALITY
kô zal′ ə tē   3*
kô zal′ i tē   1

CAUSERIE
kō′ zə rē′   2*
kōz rē′   2
kô′ zə rē′   1

CAUSTIC
kôs′ tik   4

CAUTERIZE
kô′ tə rīz′   4

CAUTERY
kôt′ ər ē   4

CAVALCADE
kav′ əl kād′   3*
kav′ əl kād′   3
kav″l kād   1
kav″l kād′   1

CAVALIER ○
kav′ ə lir′   4

CAVALRY
kav′ əl rē   3*
kav′ ′l rē   1

CAVEAT
kā′ vē at′   4
kav′ ē at′   3*
kā′ vē ət   1
kav′ ē ət   1
käv′ ē ät′   1

CAVERNOUS
kav′ ər nəs   4

CAVIAR
kav′ ē är′   3
kav′ ē är′   2*
käv′ ē är′   2

CAVIL
kav′ əl   3
kav′ ′l   1*

CAYENNE
kī en′   4*
kā en′   4

CEDILLA
si dil′ ə   4

CELEBRANT
sel′ ə brənt   4

CELEBRITY
sə leb′ rə tē   3*
sə leb′ ri tē   1

CELERIAC ○
sə lir′ ē ak′   3*
sə ler′ ē ak′   3
si ler′ ē ak′   1

CELERITY
sə ler′ ə tē   3*
sə ler′ i tē   1

CELESTA
sə les′ tə   4

CELESTIAL
sə les′ chəl   4*
sə lesh′ chəl   1

CELIAC
sē′ lē ak′   4

CELIBACY
sel′ ə bə sē   4

CELIBATE
sel′ ə bət   2*
sel′ ə bāt′   2
sel′ ə bit   2

CELLO
chel′ ō   4*
chel′ ō′   1

CELLOPHANE
sel′ ə fān′   4

CELLULOSE
sel′ yə lōs′   3*
sel′ yə lōz′   2
sel′ yoo lōs′   1

CEMENT
si ment′   4

CENOBITE
sen′ ə bīt′   4*
sē′ nə bīt′   3

CENOTAPH
sen′ ə taf′   4*
sen′ ə täf′   2

CENSER
sen′ sər   4

CENSOR
sen′ sər   4*
sent′ sər   1

CENSURE
sen′ shər   3*
sen′ chər   1

CENTAUR
sen′ tôr   3*
sen′ tôr′   1

CENTAVO
sen tä′ vō   4

CENTENARY ✓
sen ten′ ə rē   3
sen′ tə ner′ ē   3*

CENTENNIAL
sen ten′ ē əl   4

CENTIGRADE
sen′ tə grād′   3*
sen′ ti grād′   1
sän′ tə grād′   1

CENTIMETER
sen′ tə mē′ tər   4*
sän′ tə mē′ tər   2

CENTIPEDE
sen' tə pēd' 4

CENTRIFUGAL
sen trif' yə gəl 4*
sen trif' ə gəl 3

CENTRIFUGE
sen' trə fyōōj' 4*
sän' trə fyōōj' 1

CENTRIPETAL
sen trip' ət 'l 2*
sen trip' it 'l 1
sen trip' ət əl 1

CENTURION
sen tyoor' ē ən 4
sen toor' ē ən 4*

CERAMIC
sə ram' ik 4

CERAMIST
sə ram' ist 3
ser' ə mist 2*
sə ram' əst 1

CEREBELLUM
ser' ə bel' əm 4

CEREBRAL
ser' ə brəl 4*
sə rē' brəl 4

CEREBRUM
ser' ə brəm 4*
se rē' brəm 4

CEREMENT ○
sir' mənt 4
ser' ə mənt 2*

CEREMONIAL
ser' ə mō' nē əl 4*
ser' ə mō' nyəl 1

CEREMONY
ser' ə mō' nē 4

CERISE
sə rēs' 4*
sə rēz' 4

CERTIORARI ✓
sʉr' shē ə rer' ē 3*
sʉr' shē ə rär' ē 3
sʉr' shē ə rar' ē 1
sʉr' shə rar' ē 1

CERULEAN
sə rōō' lē ən 4

CERVIX
sʉr' viks 4

CHAGRIN
shə grin' 4

CHAISE LONGUE
shāz' lôŋ' 3*
chāz' lôŋ' 1
shāz lôŋ 1

CHALCEDONY
kal sed' 'n ē 4*
kal' sə dō' nē 2

CHALET
sha lā' 4*
shal' ē 1
shal' ā 1

PRONUNCIATION KEY

Symbol	Key words	Symbol	Key words	Symbol	Key words
a	asp, fat, parrot	†ə	a in ago	r	red, port, dear
ā	ape, date, play		e in agent	s	sell, castle, pass
†ä	ah, car, father		i in sanity	t	top, cattle, hat
e	elf, ten, berry		o in comply	v	vat, hovel, have
ē	even, meet, money		u in focus	w	will, always, swear
i	is, hit, mirror	ər	perhaps, murder	y	yet, onion, yard
ī	ice, bite, high	b	bed, fable, dub	z	zebra, dazzle, haze
ō	open, tone, go	d	dip, beadle, had	ch	chin, catcher, arch
ô	all, horn, law	f	fall, after, off	sh	she, cushion, dash
ōō	ooze, tool, crew	g	get, haggle, dog	th	thin, nothing, truth
oo	look, pull, moor	h	he, ahead, hotel	th	then, father, lathe
yōō	use, cute, few	j	joy, agile, badge	zh	azure, leisure
yoo	united, cure, globule	k	kill, tackle, bake	ŋ	ring, anger, drink
oi	oil, point, toy	l	let, yellow, ball	''	see p. 15.
ou	out, crowd, plow	m	met, camel, trim	✓	see p. 15.
u	up, cut, color	n	not, flannel, ton	+	see p. 14.
ʉr	urn, fur, deter	p	put, apple, tap	'	see p. 15.
†See p. 14.		†See p. 16.		○	see p. 14.

CHALICE
chal′ is   3*
chal′ əs   1

CHALLIS
shal′ ē   4

CHAMBERLAIN
chām′ bər lin   3*
chām′ bər lən   1

CHAMBRAY
sham′ brā′   4

CHAMELEON
kə mē′ lē ən   4*
kə mēl′ yən   4

CHAMOIS
sham′ ē   4

CHAMOMILE
kam′ ə mīl′   4*
kam′ ə mēl′   3

CHAMPAGNE
sham pān   4

CHAMPION
cham′ pē ən   4

CHANCEL
chan′ səl   3*
chän′ səl   2

CHANCELLOR
chan′ sə lər   3*
chan′ slər   3
chän′ sə lər   3
chän′ slər   2

CHANCERY
chan′ sər ē   3*
chän′ sər ē   3
chans′ rē   1

CHANCRE
shaŋ′ kər   4

CHANDELIER ○
shan′ də lir′   4

CHANTEUSE
shan tooz′   1*
shan tōōs′   1
shan tōōz′   1

CHANTEY
shan′ tē   4*
chan′ tē   4

CHANTICLEER ○
chan′ tə klir   2*
shan′ tə klir′   1
chan′ tə klir′   1
shan′ tə klir′   1

CHAOS   +
kā′ äs   2*
kā′ äs′   2

CHAOTIC   +
kā ät′ ik   4

CHAPARRAL
shap′ ə ral′   3*
chap′ ə ral′   2
shap′ ə rel′   1

CHAPEAU
sha pō′   4

CHAPERON (E)
shap′ ə rōn′   4

CHAPLAIN
chap′ lin   2*
chap′ lən   2

CHARADE
shə rād′   4

CHARGÉ D'AFFAIRES ✓
shär zhā′ də fer′   3*
shär′ zhā də fer′   1
shär zhā′ də far′   1

CHARISMA
kə riz′ mə   4

CHARISMATIC
kar′ iz mat′ ik   3*
kar′ əz mat′ ik   1

CHARIVARI
shiv ə rē′   4*
shiv′ ə rē   3
shə riv′ ə rē′   2

CHARLATAN
shär′ lə tən   2*
shär′ lə t'n   2

CHARLOTTE RUSSE
shär′ lət rōōs′   2*
shär′ lət rōōs′   2

CHARNEL
chär′ n'l   3*
chär′ nəl   1

CHARTREUSE
shär trōōz′   4
shär trōōs′   3*

CHARY ✓
cher′ ē   3*
char′ ē   2

CHASM
kaz′ əm   3*
kaz′ 'm   1

CHASSIS
chas′ ē   4*
shas′ ē   4
shas′ is   1

CHASTE
chāst   4

CHASTEN
chā′ sən   2*
chās′ 'n   2

CHASTISE
chas tīz′   4
chas′ tīz   2*

CHASTITY
chas' tə tē 3*
chas' ti tē 1

CHASUBLE
chas' yə bəl 2*
chaz' yə bəl 2
chaz' ə bəl 2
chaz' yoo b'l 1
chas' yoo b'l 1

CHATEAU
sha tō' 4

CHATELAINE
shat' 'l ān' 2
shat' ə lān' 1*
shat' 'l ān 1

CHATTEL
chat' 'l 4

CHAUFFEUR
shō' fər 4*
shō fur' 4

CHAUTAUQUA
shə tô' kwə 4*
chə tô' kwə 1

CHAUVINIST
shō' vin ist 2*
shō' vən əst 1
shō' vən ist 1

CHEETAH
chēt' ə 4

CHEF
shef 4

CHEMISE
shə mēz' 4

CHEMOTHERAPY
kem' ō ther' ə pē 3
kē' mō ther' ə pē 1*
kem' ə ther' ə pē 1

CHENILLE
shə nēl' 4*
shə nē əl' 1

CHEROOT
shə rōōt' 4*
chə rōōt' 2

CHERUB
cher' əb 4

CHERUBIC
chə rōō' bik 4

CHERUBIM
cher' ə bim 2*
cher' ə bim' 2
cher' yə bim 2
cher' yōō bim 1

CHESTNUT
ches' nut' 4*
ches' nət 4

CHEVALIER ○
shev' ə lir 4
shə val' yā 3*
shə väl' yā 1

CHEVIOT (FABRIC)
shev' ē ət 4

CHEVRON
shev' rən 4

CHIANTI
kē än' tē 4*
kē an' tē 4

CHIAROSCURO
kē är′ ə skyoor′ ō   4*
kē är′ ə skoor′ ō   2

CHIC
shēk   4*
shik   1

CHICANERY
shi kān′ ə rē   3*
shi kān′ rē   1

CHICLE
chik′ əl   3*
chik′l   1
chik′ lē   1

CHICORY
chik′ ə rē   4*
chik′ rē   1

CHIEFTAIN
chēf tən   4*
chēf tin   1

CHIFFON   +
shi fän′   4*
shif′ än   2

CHIFFONIER   ○
shif′ ə nir   4

CHIGNON   +
shēn′ yän′   3*
shēn yun′   1

CHIHUAHUA
chi wä′ wä   3*
chi wä′ wə   2
chə wä′ wä   1
shə wä′ wä   1

CHILBLAIN
chil′ blān′   4

CHILE CON CARNE   +
chil′ ē kän kär′ nē   2
chil′ ē kən kär′ nē   1*
chil′ ē kän′ kär′ nē   1
chil′ ē kən kär′ nē   1

CHIMERA   ○
kī mir′ ə   4
ki mir′ ə   2*
kə mir′ ə   2

CHIMERICAL   ○
kī mir′ i kəl   4
kī mer′ i kəl   3
ki mer′ i kəl   2*
kə mer′ i kəl   2
kə mir′ i kəl   2
ki mir′ i kəl   1

CHIMNEY
chim′ nē   4

CHIMPANZEE
chim′ pan zē′   4*
chim pan′ zē   4
chim′ pan′ zē′   1
shim′ pan′ zē′   1
shim′ pan zē′   1
shim pan′ zē   1

CHINO
chē′ nō   4*
shē′ nō   3

CHIROMANCY
kī′ rə man′ sē   4

CHIROPODIST   +
kə räp′ ə dist   2*
kī räp′ ə dist   2
shə räp′ ə dist   2
kə räp′ ə dəst   1
kī räp′ ə dəst   1

CHIROPRACTOR
kī′ rə prak′ tər   4

CHITTERLINGS
chit′ linz   2*
chit′ lənz   2
chit′ ər liŋz   1

CHIVALROUS
shiv′ əl rəs   3*
shiv′l′ rəs   1

CHIVALRY
shiv′ əl rē   3*
shiv′l′ rē   1

CHIVY
chiv′ ē   4

CHLORINE
klôr′ in   3
klôr′ ēn′   2*
klōr′ ēn′   2
klōr′ in   2
klôr′ ēn   2
klōr′ ēn   1
klôr′ ən   1
klōr′ ən   1

CHLOROPHYLL
klôr′ ə fil   3*
klōr′ ə fil   2
klôr′ ə fil′   1
klōr′ ə fil′   1
klôr′ ə fəl   1
klōr′ ə fəl   1

CHOCOLATE   +
chäk′ lit   2*
chôk′ lət   2
chäk′ lət   2
chôk′ ə lət   2
chäk′ ə lət   2
chôk′ lit   2

CHOIR
kwīr   3*
kwī′ ər   2

CHOLERA   +
käl′ ər ə   4

CHOLERIC   +
kə ler′ ik   4*
käl′ ər ik   4

CHOLESTEROL   +
kə les′ tə rōl′   4*
kə les′ tə rôl′   3
kə les′ tə räl′   1

CHORAL
kôr′ əl 4*
kōr′ əl 3

CHORALE
kə ral′ 4*
kə räl′ 3
kô ral′ 2
kō ral′ 1
kōr′ əl 1
kôr′ əl 1

CHOREA
kô rē′ ə 3*
kō rē′ ə 2
kə rē′ ə 2

CHOREOGRAPHY +
kôr′ ē äg′ rə fē 4*
kōr′ ē äg′ rə fē 3

CHORE
chôr 4*
chōr 3

CHORISTER +
kôr′ is tər 3*
kär′ is tər 2
kôr′ əs tər 1
kōr′ is tər 1
kōr′ əs tər 1
kär′ əs tər 1

CHORTLE
chor′ t′l 4

CHRESTOMATHY +
kres täm′ ə thē 4

CHRISTEN
kris′ ən 2*
kris′ ′n 2

CHROMATIC
krō mat′ ik 4

CHROMIUM
krō′ mē əm 4

CHROMOSOME
krō′ mə sōm′ 4*
krō′ mə zōm′ 1

CHRONIC +
krän′ ik 4

CHRONICLE + ○
krän′ i kəl 3*
krän′ i k′l 1

CHRONOLOGY +
krə näl′ ə jē 4

CHRYSALIS
kris′ ə lis 2*
kris′l′ əs 1
kris′ ə ləs 1

CHRYSANTHEMUM
kri san′ thə məm 4

CHRYSOPRASE
kris′ ə prāz′ 4

CHUKKA
chuk′ ə 4

CHURLISH
churl′ ish 4

CHUTNEY
chut′ nē 4

PRONUNCIATION KEY

Symbol	Key words	Symbol	Key words	Symbol	Key words
a	asp, fat, parrot	†ə	a in ago	r	red, port, dear
ā	ape, date, play		e in agent	s	sell, castle, pass
†ä	ah, car, father		i in sanity	t	top, cattle, hat
e	elf, ten, berry		o in comply	v	vat, hovel, have
ē	even, meet, money		u in focus	w	will, always, swear
i	is, hit, mirror	ər	perhaps, murder	y	yet, onion, yard
ī	ice, bite, high	b	bed, fable, dub	z	zebra, dazzle, haze
ō	open, tone, go	d	dip, beadle, had	ch	chin, catcher, arch
ô	all, horn, law	f	fall, after, off	sh	she, cushion, dash
o͞o	ooze, tool, crew	g	get, haggle, dog	th	thin, nothing, truth
oo	look, pull, moor	h	he, ahead, hotel	th	then, father, lathe
yo͞o	use, cute, few	j	joy, agile, badge	zh	azure, leisure
yoo	united, cure, globule	k	kill, tackle, bake	ŋ	ring, anger, drink
oi	oil, point, toy	l	let, yellow, ball	″	see p. 15.
ou	out, crowd, plow	m	met, camel, trim	✓	see p. 15.
u	up, cut, color	n	not, flannel, ton	+	see p. 14.
ur	urn, fur, deter	p	put, apple, tap	′	see p. 15.
†See p. 14.		†See p. 16.		○	see p. 14.

CICADA
si kā′ də   4*
si kä′ də   4
sə kā′ də   1
sə kä′ də   1

CICATRIX
sik′ ə triks   4*
si kā′ triks   3

CICERONE
sis′ ə rō′ nē   4*
chich′ ə rō′ nē   2

CIGARETTE
sig′ ə ret′   4*
sig′ ə ret′   4

CILIA
sil′ ē ə   4

CINCHONA
siŋ kō′ nə   3*
sin chō′ nə   2
sin kō′ nə   2

CINCTURE
siŋk′ chər   4*
siŋ′ chər   1

CINEMA
sin′ ə mə   4

CINEMATOGRAPHY   +
sin′ ə mə täg′ rə fē   4

CIRCA
sʉr′ kə   4*
kir′ kä   2
kir′ kä′   2

CIRCADIAN
sər kā′ dē ən   3*
sʉr kə dē′ ən   2
sər kad′ ē ən   1
sər kə dī′ ən   1

CIRCUIT
sʉr′ kit   3*
sʉr′ kət   1

CIRCUITOUS
sər kyo͞o′ ə təs   3*
sər kyo͞o′ i təs   1

CIRCUMCISION
sʉr′ kəm sizh′ ən   4

CIRCUMFERENCE
sər kum′ fər əns   3*
sər kum′ frəns   1
sə kum′ fərns   1
sər kump′ fərnts   1

CIRCUMSTANCE
sʉr′ kəm stans′   4*
sʉr′ kəm stəns   2
sʉr′ kəm stants′   1

CIRRHOSIS
si rō′ sis   3*
sə rō′ səs   1

CIRRUS
sir′ əs   4

CISTERN
sis′ tərn   4

CITADEL
sit′ ə del′   4*
sit′ ə d'l   3

CITRON
si′ trən   4

CITRUS
si′ trəs   4

CIVET
siv′ it   3*
siv′ ət   1

CIVIL
siv′ əl   3*
siv′ 'l   1

CIVILIAN
sə vil′ yən   2*
si vil′ yən   2

CLAIRVOYANCE   ✓
kler voi′ əns   3*
klar voi′ əns   1

CLAMBER
klam′ bər   4*
klam′ ər   3

CLAMOR
klam′ ər   4

CLANDESTINE
klan des′ tən   3*
klan des′ tin   1
klan des′ tīn′   1
klan des′ tēn′   1
klan′ dəs tən   1
klan′ dəs tīn′   1
klan′ dəs tēn′   1

CLANGOR
klaŋ′ ər   4
klaŋg′ gər   3*

CLAPBOARD
klab′ ərd   4*
klap′ bôrd′   3
klap′ bōrd′   3
kla′ bōrd   1
kla′ bôrd   1

CLAQUE
klak   4

CLARET
klar′ ət   2*
klar′ it   2

CLARION
klar′ ē ən   4

CLAUSTROPHOBIA
klôs′ trə fō′ bē ə   2*
klôs trə fō′ bē ə   2

CLAVICHORD
klav′ ə kôrd′   3*
klav′ i kôrd′   1

CLAVICLE
klav′ i kəl 2
klav′ ə k'l 1*
klav′ ə kəl 1

CLAVIER ○
klə vir′ 4*
klā′ vē ər 2
klä′ vē ər 1

CLEANLY (adj)
klen′ lē 4

CLEANLY (adv)
klēn′ lē 4

CLEANSE
klenz 4

CLEMENCY
klem′ ən sē 4

CLEMENT
klem′ ənt 4

CLERGY
klʉr′ jē 4

CLERESTORY ○
klir′ stôr′ ē 4*
klir′ stōr′ ē 4

CLERIC
kler′ ik 4

CLERIHEW ✓
kler′ i hyōō′ 2*
kler′ ə hyōō′ 2

CLICHÉ
klē shā′ 3*
kli shā′ 2

CLIENT
klī′ ənt 4

CLIENTELE
klī′ ən tel′ 4*
klē′ ən tel′ 1

CLIMACTERIC
klī mak ter′ ik 4*
klī mak′ tər ik 4

CLIMACTIC
klī mak′ tik 4

CLINICIAN
kli nish′ ən 4

CLIQUE
klēk 4*
klik 4

CLITORIS
klit′ ə ris 3*
klīt′ ə ris 3
klit′ ə rəs 1
klīt′ ə rəs 1

CLOACA
klō ā′ kə 4

CLOCHE
klōsh 4*
klôsh 1

CLOISSONÉ
kloi zə nā′ 2*
kloi′ zə nā′ 1
kloi′ z'n ā 1

CLOSE (n)
klōz (conclusion) 4
klōs (enclosure) 4

PRONUNCIATION KEY

Symbol	Key words	Symbol	Key words	Symbol	Key words
a	asp, fat, parrot	†ə	a in ago	r	red, port, dear
ā	ape, date, play		e in agent	s	sell, castle, pass
†ä	ah, car, father		i in sanity	t	top, cattle, hat
e	elf, ten, berry		o in comply	v	vat, hovel, have
ē	even, meet, money		u in focus	w	will, always, swear
i	is, hit, mirror	ər	perhaps, murder	y	yet, onion, yard
ī	ice, bite, high	b	bed, fable, dub	z	zebra, dazzle, haze
ō	open, tone, go	d	dip, beadle, had	ch	chin, catcher, arch
ô	all, horn, law	f	fall, after, off	sh	she, cushion, dash
ōō	ooze, tool, crew	g	get, haggle, dog	th	thin, nothing, truth
oo	look, pull, moor	h	he, ahead, hotel	th	then, father, lathe
yōō	use, cute, few	j	joy, agile, badge	zh	azure, leisure
yoo	united, cure, globule	k	kill, tackle, bake	ŋ	ring, anger, drink
oi	oil, point, toy	l	let, yellow, ball	″	see p. 15.
ou	out, crowd, plow	m	met, camel, trim	✓	see p. 15.
u	up, cut, color	n	not, flannel, ton	+	see p. 14.
ʉr	urn, fur, deter	p	put, apple, tap	′	see p. 15.
†See p. 14.		†See p. 16.		○	see p. 14.

CLOSE (v.)
klōz 4

CLOSE (adj)
klōs 4

CLOSURE
klō' zhər 4

CLOTH
klôth 4*
kläth 3

CLOTHE
klōth 4

CLOTHIER
klō' thē ər 4*
klōth' yər 4

CLOTURE
klō' chər 4

COADJUTOR
kō' ə jōōt' ər 4*
kō aj' ə tər 4

COAGULATE
kō ag' yə lāt' 4

COALESCE
kō' ə les' 4

COALITION
kō' ə lish' ən 4

COAXIAL
kō ak' sē əl 4

COBALT
kō' bôlt' 2*
kō' bôlt 2

COBRA
kō' brə 4

COCAINE
kō kān' 4*
kō' kān' 3
kō' kān 1

COCCI +
käk' sī 2*
käk' ī 1
käk' ī' 1
käk' ē' 1
käk' sē' 1

COCCUS +
käk' əs 4

COCCYX +
käk' siks 4

COCHINEAL +
käch' ə nēl' 4*
käch' ə nēl' 4
kō' chə nēl' 1

COCKATRICE +
käk' ə tris 2*
käk' ə trīs' 2
käk' ə tris' 1
käk' ə trəs 1

COCOON
kə kōōn' 4

CODA
kō' də 4

CODEINE
kō' dēn 2*
kō' dē in 2
kō' dēn' 2

CODICIL +
käd' ə sil 1*
käd' i səl 1
käd' i s'l 1
käd' i sil 1
käd' ə səl 1
käd' ə sil' 1

CODIFY +
käd' ə fī' 3*
kō' də fī 3
käd' ə fī 1

COEFFICIENT
kō' ə fish' ənt 4

COELACANTH
sē' lə kanth' 4*
sē' lə kantth' 1

COERCE
kō urs' 4

COERCION
kō ur' shən 4*
kō ur' zhən 2

COEVAL
kō ē' vəl 3*
kō ē' v'l 1

COFFEE +
kôf' ē 4*
käf' ē 4

COFFER +
käf' ər 4*
kôf' ər 4

COFFIN +
kôf' in 2*
käf' in 2
kôf' ən 2

COGENT
kō' jənt 4

COGITATE +
käj' ə tāt' 3*
käj' i tāt' 1

COGNAC +
kōn' yak 3*
kän' yak 3
kôn' yak 2
kōn' yak' 1

COGNATE +
käg' nāt' 3*
käg' nāt 1

COGNIZANT +
käg' nə zənt 2*
käg' ni zənt 1
kän' i zənt 1

COGNOMEN   +
käg nō′ mən   4

COGNOSCENTI   +
käg′ nə shent′ ē   2*
kän′ yō shent′ ē   1
kōn′ yō shent′ ē   1
kän′ ə shent′ ē   1
kän′ yə shent′ ē   1

COHERENT   ○
kō hir′ ənt   4*
kō her′ ənt   2

COHESION
kō hē′ zhən   4

COHORT
kō′ hôrt′   2*
kō′ hôrt   2

COIFFURE
kwä fyoor′   4*
kwä fyʉr′   1

COINCIDE
kō′ in sīd′   3*
kō′ ən sīd′   1
kō′ ən sīd′   1

COINCIDENCE
kō in′ sə dəns   3*
kō in′ si dəns   1
kō in′ sə dens   1

COITUS
kō′ it əs   2
kō′ ət əs   2
kō ēt′ əs   1*

COLANDER   +
käl′ ən dər   4*
kul′ ən dər   3

COLE SLAW
kōl′ slô′   4

COLIC   +
käl′ ik   4

COLIFORM   +
käl′ ə fôrm′   4*
kō′ lə fôrm′   4

COLISEUM
(COLOSSEUM)   +
käl′ ə sē′ əm   3*
käl′ i sē′ əm   1

COLITIS
kō lī′ tis   3
kə lī′ tis   1*
kō lī′ təs   1

COLLABORATE
kə lab′ ə rāt′   4

COLLAGE
kə läzh′   3*
kō läzh′   2

COLLARD
käl′ ərd   4

COLLATE   +
kə lāt′   4
kō′ lāt   2*
kä lāt′   2

COLLATERAL
kə lat′ ər əl   4*
kə lat′ rəl   1

COLLATION   +
kə lā′ shən   4*
kä lā′ shən   4
kō lā′ shən   3

PRONUNCIATION KEY

Symbol	Key words	Symbol	Key words	Symbol	Key words
a	asp, fat, parrot	†ə	a in ago	r	red, port, dear
ā	ape, date, play		e in agent	s	sell, castle, pass
†ä	ah, car, father		i in sanity	t	top, cattle, hat
e	elf, ten, berry		o in comply	v	vat, hovel, have
ē	even, meet, money		u in focus	w	will, always, swear
i	is, hit, mirror	ər	perhaps, murder	y	yet, onion, yard
ī	ice, bite, high	b	bed, fable, dub	z	zebra, dazzle, haze
ō	open, tone, go	d	dip, beadle, had	ch	chin, catcher, arch
ô	all, horn, law	f	fall, after, off	sh	she, cushion, dash
ōō	ooze, tool, crew	g	get, haggle, dog	th	thin, nothing, truth
oo	look, pull, moor	h	he, ahead, hotel	th	then, father, lathe
yōo	use, cute, few	j	joy, agile, badge	zh	azure, leisure
yoo	united, cure, globule	k	kill, tackle, bake	ŋ	ring, anger, drink
oi	oil, point, toy	l	let, yellow, ball	″	see p. 15.
ou	out, crowd, plow	m	met, camel, trim	✓	see p. 15.
u	up, cut, color	n	not, flannel, ton	+	see p. 14.
ʉr	urn, fur, deter	p	put, apple, tap	′	see p. 15.
†See p. 14.		†See p. 16.		○	see p. 14.

COLLEAGUE   +
käl′ ēg′ 2*
käl′ ēg 2
käl′ ig 1

COLLECT (n)   +
käl′ ekt′ 2*
käl′ ikt 2
käl′ ekt 2

COLLECT (v)
kə lekt′ 4

COLLEEN   +
kä lēn′ 3
käl′ ēn 2*
kə lēn′ 1

COLLEGIATE
kə lē′ jit 2*
kə lē′ jət 2
kə lē′ jē ət 2
kə lē′ jē it 2

COLLIERY   +
käl′ yər ē 4

COLLOQUIAL
kə lō′ kwē əl 4

COLLOQUY   +
käl′ ə kwē 4

COLLUSION
kə loo′ zhən 4

COLOGNE
kə lōn′ 4

COLONEL
kʉr′ n′l 3*
kʉr′ nəl 1

COLON
kō′ lən 4

COLONNADE   +
käl′ ə nād′ 4

COLOPHON   +
käl′ ə fän′ 4
käl′ ə fən 4

COLORATURA   +
kul′ ər ə toor′ ə 4*
kul′ ər ə tyoor′ ə 4
käl′ ər ə toor′ ə 1
käl′ ər ə tyoor′ ə 1

COLOSSAL   +
kə läs′ əl 3*
kə läs′ ′l 1

COLOSSUS   +
kə läs′ əs 4

COLOSTOMY   +
kə läs′ tə mē 4

COLT
kōlt 4

COLUMBINE   +
käl′ əm bīn′ 4

COLUMNIST   +
käl′ əm nist 3*
käl′ ə mist 3
käl′ ə məst 1
käl′ əm nəst 1
käl′ yəm ist 1
käl′ yəm əst 1

COMA
kō mə 4

COMATOSE   +
kō′ mə tōs′ 4*
käm′ ə tōs′ 4

COMBAT (n)   +
käm′ bat′ 2*
käm′ bat 2
kum′ bat 2

COMBAT (v)   +
kəm bat′ 4*
käm′ bat′ 2
käm′ bat 2
kum′ bat 1

COMBATANT   +
käm′ bə tənt 3*
kəm bat′ ′nt 3
kəm bat′ ənt 1

COMBATIVE   +
kəm bat′ iv 4
käm′ bə tiv 2*
kum′ bə tiv 1

COMBINE (n)   +
käm′ bīn 2*
käm′ bīn′ 2

COMBINE (v)   +
kəm bīn′ 4*
käm′ bīn′ 1

COMEDIC
kə mē′ dik 3*
kə med′ ik 3

COMEDIENNE
kə mē′ dē en′ 4*
kə mā′ dē en′ 1

COMELY
kum′ lē 4

COMESTIBLE
kə mes′ tə bəl 3*
kə mes′ tə b′l 1

COMFORTABLE
kum′ fər tə bəl 4*
kumf′ tər bəl 3
kumf′ tə bəl 2

COMFORTER
kum′ fər tər 4*
kum′ fə tər 2

COMITY   +
käm′ ə tē   4*
kōm′ ə tē   1

COMMA   +
käm′ ə   4

COMMANDANT   +
käm′ ən dänt′   2*
käm′ ən dant′   2
käm′ ən dant′   2
käm′ ən dänt′   2

COMMANDEER   +   ○
käm ən dir′   2*
käm′ ən dir′   2

COMMANDO
kə man′ dō   4*
kə män′ dō   3

COMMEMORATE
kə mem′ ə rāt′   4

COMMEMORATIVE
kə mem′ ər ə tiv   4*
kē mem′ e rāt′ iv   4
kə mem′ rə tiv   1

COMMEND
kə mend′   4

COMMENDATION   +
käm′ ən dā′ shən   4*
käm′ en′ dā′ shən   1

COMMENSURATE
kə men′ shər it   3*
kə men′ sər it   3
kə mens′ rət   1

COMMENT   +
käm′ ənt   2*
käm′ ent′   1
käm′ ent   1

COMMENTARY   +✓
käm′ ən ter′ ē   4

COMMISSAR   +
käm′ ə sär′   3*
käm′ i sär′   1
käm′ i sär′   1

COMMISSARIAT   +✓
käm′ ə ser′ ē ət   2*
käm′ ə ser′ ē it   1
käm′ i ser′ ē ət   1
käm′ ə sar′ ē ət   1

COMMISSARY   +✓
käm′ ə ser′ ē   3
käm′ i ser′ ē   1

COMMISERATE
kə miz′ ə rāt′   4

COMMODE
kə mōd′   4

COMMODIOUS
kə mō′ dē əs   4

COMMODITY   +
kə mäd′ ə tē   3*
kə mäd′ i tē   1

COMMODORE   +
käm′ ə dôr′   4*
käm′ ə dōr′   3
käm′ ə dōər′   1

PRONUNCIATION KEY

Symbol	Key words	Symbol	Key words	Symbol	Key words
a	asp, fat, parrot	†ə	a in ago	r	red, port, dear
ā	ape, date, play		e in agent	s	sell, castle, pass
†ä	ah, car, father		i in sanity	t	top, cattle, hat
e	elf, ten, berry		o in comply	v	vat, hovel, have
ē	even, meet, money		u in focus	w	will, always, swear
i	is, hit, mirror	ər	perhaps, murder	y	yet, onion, yard
ī	ice, bite, high	b	bed, fable, dub	z	zebra, dazzle, haze
ō	open, tone, go	d	dip, beadle, had	ch	chin, catcher, arch
ô	all, horn, law	f	fall, after, off	sh	she, cushion, dash
o͞o	ooze, tool, crew	g	get, haggle, dog	th	thin, nothing, truth
oo	look, pull, moor	h	he, ahead, hotel	th	then, father, lathe
yo͞o	use, cute, few	j	joy, agile, badge	zh	azure, leisure
yoo	united, cure, globule	k	kill, tackle, bake	ŋ	ring, anger, drink
oi	oil, point, toy	l	let, yellow, ball	′′	see p. 15.
ou	out, crowd, plow	m	met, camel, trim	✓	see p. 15.
u	up, cut, color	n	not, flannel, ton	+	see p. 14.
ur	urn, fur, deter	p	put, apple, tap	′	see p. 15.
†See p. 14.		†See p. 16.		○	see p. 14.

COMMUNAL   +
kə my$\overline{oo}$n′ ′l   3*
käm′ yən ′l   2
käm′ yoon ′l   1

COMMUNE (v)
kə my$\overline{oo}$n′   4

COMMUNE (n)   +
käm′ y$\overline{oo}$n′   2*
käm′ y$\overline{oo}$n   2
kə my$\overline{oo}$n′   1

COMMUNICABLE
kə my$\overline{oo}$′ ni kə bəl   2*
kə my$\overline{oo}$′ nə kə bəl   1
kə my$\overline{oo}$′ ni kə b′l   1

COMMUNION
kə my$\overline{oo}$n′ yən   4

COMMUNIQUÉ
kə my$\overline{oo}$′ nə kā′   4*
kə my$\overline{oo}$′ nə kā′   3

COMMUTE
kə my$\overline{oo}$t′   4

COMPACT (n)   +
käm′ pakt   2*
käm′ pakt′   2

COMPACT   + (adj)
kəm pakt′   3*
käm pakt′   2
käm′ pakt′   2
käm′ pakt   1

COMPACT (v)   +
kəm pakt′   4*
käm pakt′   1
käm′ pakt′   1

COMPARABLE   +
käm′ pər ə bəl   4*
käm′ prə bəl   1

COMPARATIVE
kəm par′ ə tiv   4

COMPASS   +
kum′ pəs   4*
käm′ pəs   2

COMPATIBLE
kəm pat′ ə bəl   3*
kəm pat′ ə b′l   1

COMPATRIOT   +
kəm pā′ trē ət   4*
käm pā′ trē ət   1
käm pā′ trē ät′   2

COMPENDIUM
kəm pen′ dē əm   4

COMPENSATE   +
käm′ pən sāt′   4

COMPETENT   +
käm′ pə tənt   3*
käm′ pi t′nt   1

COMPETITIVE
kəm pet′ ə tiv   3*
kəm pet′ i tiv   1

COMPILATION   +
käm′ pə lā′ shən   4*
käm′ pī lā′ shən   1

COMPLACENT
kəm plā′ sənt   2*
kəm plā′ s′nt   2

COMPLAINANT
kəm plān′ ənt   4

COMPLEMENT (n)   +
käm′ plə mənt   4

COMPLEMENT (v)   +
käm′ plə mənt′   2*
käm′ plə ment′   2

COMPLEX (n)   +
käm′ pleks   2*
käm′ pleks′   2

COMPLEX (adj)   +
kəm pleks′   4*
käm′ pleks   3
käm′ pleks′   2

COMPLIANT
kəm plī′ ənt   4

COMPLICITY
kəm plis′ ə tē   3*
kəm plis′ i tē   1

COMPLIMENT (n)   +
käm′ plə mənt   4

COMPLIMENT (v)   +
käm′ plə ment′   3*
käm′ plə ment   1

COMPLIMENTARY
käm′ plə men′ tər $\overline{e}$ 4*
käm′ plə men′ trē   2

COMPONENT
kəm p$\overline{o}$′ nənt   4

COMPORT
kəm pôrt′   4*
kəm p$\overline{o}$rt′   2

COMPOSITE   +
kəm päz′ it   3
käm päz′ ət   1*
kəm päz′ ət   1

COMPOSITOR   +
kəm päz′ ə tər   3*
kəm päz′ i tər   1

COMPOST   +
käm′ p$\overline{o}$st   3
käm′ p$\overline{o}$st′   1

COMPOSURE
kəm p$\overline{o}$′ zhər   4

COMPOTE   +
käm′ p$\overline{o}$t   3*
käm′ p$\overline{o}$t′   1

COMPOUND (n)   +
käm′ pound 3*
käm′ pound′ 1

COMPOUND (adj)   +
käm′ pound 3*
käm pound′ 3
kəm pound′ 1

COMPOUND (v)
kəm pound′ 4*
käm pound′ 3
käm′ pound′ 1

COMPRESS (n)   +
käm′ pres′ 3*
käm′ pres 1

COMPRESS (v)
kəm pres′ 4

COMPRISE
kəm prīz′ 4

COMPTROLLER
    (see CONTROLLER)

CONCAVE   +
kän kāv′ 4*
kän′ kāv 3

CONCENTRIC   +
kən sen′ trik 4*
kän′ sen′ trik 1
kän sen′ trik 1

CONCERTED
kən sur′ tid 3*
kən sur′ təd 1

CONCERTINA   +
kän′ sər tē′ nə 4*
känt′ sər tē′ nə 1

CONCERTO
kən cher′ tō 4

CONCH   +
känch 4*
käŋk 4
kôŋk 1

CONCIERGE   +
kän′ sē erzh′ 1*
kän′ sē urzh′ 1
kän′ sē urzh 1

CONCILIATE
kən sil′ ē āt′ 4

CONCISE
kən sīs′ 4

CONCLAVE   +
kän′ klāv 3*
käŋ klāv 3
kän′ klāv′ 1

CONCOCT   +
kən käkt′ 4*
kän käkt′ 2

CONCOMITANT   +
kən käm′ ə tənt 3*
kän käm′ i t′nt 1

CONCORD   +
kän′ kôrd 3*
käŋ′ kôrd 3
kän′ kôrd′ 1
käŋ′ kôrd′ 1

CONCORDANCE   +
kän kôr′ d′ns 3*
kən kôr′ d′ns 3
kən kôr′ dəns 1

PRONUNCIATION KEY

Symbol	Key words	Symbol	Key words	Symbol	Key words
a	asp, fat, parrot	†ə	a in ago	r	red, port, dear
ā	ape, date, play		e in agent	s	sell, castle, pass
†ä	ah, car, father		i in sanity	t	top, cattle, hat
e	elf, ten, berry		o in comply	v	vat, hovel, have
ē	even, meet, money		u in focus	w	will, always, swear
i	is, hit, mirror	ər	perhaps, murder	y	yet, onion, yard
ī	ice, bite, high	b	bed, fable, dub	z	zebra, dazzle, haze
ō	open, tone, go	d	dip, beadle, had	ch	chin, catcher, arch
ô	all, horn, law	f	fall, after, off	sh	she, cushion, dash
o͞o	ooze, tool, crew	g	get, haggle, dog	th	thin, nothing, truth
o͝o	look, pull, moor	h	he, ahead, hotel	th	then, father, lathe
yo͞o	use, cute, few	j	joy, agile, badge	zh	azure, leisure
yo͝o	united, cure, globule	k	kill, tackle, bake	ŋ	ring, anger, drink
ơi	oil, point, toy	l	let, yellow, ball	′′	see p. 15.
ơu	out, crowd, plow	m	met, camel, trim	✓	see p. 15.
u	up, cut, color	n	not, flannel, ton	+	see p. 14.
ur	urn, fur, deter	p	put, apple, tap	′	see p. 15.
†See p. 14.		†See p. 16.		◯	see p. 14.

CONCORDAT +
kən kôr′ dat′ 3*
kän kôr′ dat 2

CONCOURSE +
kän′ kôrs 3*
kän′ kōrs 3
käŋ′ kôrs 3
käŋ′ kōrs 3
kän′ kôrs′ 1
kän′ kōrs′ 1
käŋ′ kôrs′ 1
käŋ′ kōrs′ 1

CONCUBINE +
käŋ′ kyə bīn′ 3*
kän′ kyə bīn′ 3
käŋ′ kyoo bīn′ 1
kän′ kyoo bīn′ 1

CONCUPISCENCE +
kän kyo͞op′ ə səns 2
kän kyo͞op′ i səns 1*
kän kyo͞op′ ə s′ns 1

CONDIGN +
kən dīn′ 4*
kän′ dīn 1

CONDIMENT +
kän′ də mənt 4

CONDOLENCE +
kən dō′ ləns 4*
kän′ də ləns 1
kən dō′ lənts 1

CONDOMINIUM +
kän′ də min′ ē əm 4

CONDONE
kən dōn′ 4

CONDOR +
kän′ dər 4
kän′ dôr′ 1*
kän′ dôr 1

CONDUCT (n) +
kän′ dukt 2*
kän′ dəkt 2
kän′ dukt′ 1
kän′ dəkt′ 1

CONDUCT (v)
kən dukt′ 4

CONDUIT +
kän′ dit 3
kän′ do͞o it 2*
kän′ doo ət 1
kän′ dwit 1
kän′ dyo͞o it 1

CONEY
kō′ nē 4*
kun′ ē 2

CONFEDERACY
kən fed′ ər ə sē 4*
kən fed′ rə se 4

CONFEREE +
kän′ fə rē′ 2*
kän fə rē′ 2

CONFIDANT (E) +
kän′ fə dänt′ 3*
kän′ fə dant′ 3
kän′ fə dant′ 2
kän′ fə dänt′ 2
kän′ fə dant 1
kän′ fə dänt 1
kän′ fi dant′ 1
kän′ fi dänt′ 1
kän′ fi dant′ 1
kän′ fi dänt′ 1

CONFIDENT +
kän′ fə dənt 3*
kän′ fi dənt 1

CONFIDENTIAL +
kän′ fə den′ sħəl 2
kän′ fə den′ cħəl 2
kän′ fi den′ sħəl 1*

CONFINE (n) +
kän′ fīn′ 3*
kən fīn′ 2
kän′ fīn 1

CONFINE (v)
kən fīn′ 4

CONFISCATE +
kän′ fi skāt′ 2*
kän′ fə skāt′ 2
kən fis′ kāt 1
kən fis′ kət 1

CONFISCATORY
kən fis′ kə tôr′ ē 3*
kən fis′ kə tōr′ ē 2

CONFLAGRATION +
kän′ flə grā′ sħən 4

CONFLICT (n) +
kän′ flikt 3*
kän′ flikt′ 1

CONFLICT (v) +
kən flikt′ 4*
kän′ flikt′ 1

CONFORM
kən fôrm′ 4

CONFOUND +
kən found′ 4
kän found′ 3*

CONFRERE +
kän′ frer 4*
kōn′ frer 1
kän frer′ 1
kən frer′ 1

CONFRONT
kən frunt′ 4

CONFRONTATION +
kän′ frən tā′ sħən 3*
kän′ frun tā′ sħən 1
kän frən′ tā′ sħən 1

CONGEAL
kən jēl′ 4*
kən jē əl′ 1

CONGENIAL
kən jēn′ yəl 4

CONGENITAL
kən jen′ ə t′l 2*
kən jen′ ə təl 1
kən jen′ i t′l 1

CONGERIES + ○
kän jir′ ēz 2*
kän′ jə rēz′ 2
kən jir′ ēz 1
kän′ jə rēz 1

CONGLOMERATE (n) +
kən gläm′ ər it 3*
kən gläm′ ər ət 1
kən gläm′ rət 1

CONGLOMERATE (v) +
kən gläm′ ə rāt′ 4

CONGRATULATORY
kən grach′ ə lə tôr′ ē 3*
kən grach′ ə lə tōr′ ē 2
kən grach′ oo lə tôr′ ē 1
kən grach′ oo lə tōr′ ē 1
kən grach′ lə tôr′ ē 1
kən grach′ lə tōr′ ē 1

CONGRUENCE +
kən groo′ əns 3
kän′ groo əns 2*
käŋ′ groo wəns 1

CONICAL +
kän′ i kəl 3*
kän′ i k′l 1

CONIFER
kän′ ə fər 4*
kō′ nə fər 4

CONJECTURE
kən jek′ chər 4

CONJUGAL +
kän′ jə gəl 3*
kən joo′ gəl 2
kän′ joo gəl 1
kän′ ji gəl 1

CONJUNCTIVITIS
kən juŋk′ tə vīt′ is 3*
kən juŋk′ ti vīt′ əs 1

CONJURE +
kän′ jər 4*
kun′ jər 2
kən joor′ 1

CONJUROR +
kän′ jər ər 4*
kun′ jər ər 3
kən joor′ ər 1

CONNIVANCE
kə nī′ vəns 4*
kə nī′ vənts 1

CONNOISSEUR +
kän′ ə sur′ 4*
kän′ ə soor′ 1
kän′ ə soor′ 1
kän ə soor′ 1

CONNUBIAL
kə noo′ bē əl 4*
kə nyoo′ bē əl 3

PRONUNCIATION KEY

Symbol	Key words	Symbol	Key words	Symbol	Key words
a	asp, fat, parrot	†ə	a in ago	r	red, port, dear
ā	ape, date, play		e in agent	s	sell, castle, pass
†ä	ah, car, father		i in sanity	t	top, cattle, hat
e	elf, ten, berry		o in comply	v	vat, hovel, have
ē	even, meet, money		u in focus	w	will, always, swear
i	is, hit, mirror	ər	perhaps, murder	y	yet, onion, yard
ī	ice, bite, high	b	bed, fable, dub	z	zebra, dazzle, haze
ō	open, tone, go	d	dip, beadle, had	ch	chin, catcher, arch
ô	all, horn, law	f	fall, after, off	sh	she, cushion, dash
oo	ooze, tool, crew	g	get, haggle, dog	th	thin, nothing, truth
oo	look, pull, moor	h	he, ahead, hotel	th	then, father, lathe
yoo	use, cute, few	j	joy, agile, badge	zh	azure, leisure
yoo	united, cure, globule	k	kill, tackle, bake	ŋ	ring, anger, drink
oi	oil, point, toy	l	let, yellow, ball	″	see p. 15.
ou	out, crowd, plow	m	met, camel, trim	✓	see p. 15.
u	up, cut, color	n	not, flannel, ton	+	see p. 14.
ur	urn, fur, deter	p	put, apple, tap	′	see p. 15.
†See p. 14.		†See p. 16.		○	see p. 14.

CONSANGUINITY   +
kän′ saŋ gwin′ ə tē   2
kän′ san gwin′ ə tē   2
kän′ saŋ gwin′ i tē   1*

CONSCIENCE   +
kän′ shəns   3*
kän′ chəns   1
kän′ chənts   1

CONSCIENTIOUS   +
kän′ shē en′ shəs   3*
kän′ shē en′ chəs   1
kän′ sē en′ shəs   1
kän′ chē en′ chəs   1

CONSCIOUS   +
kän′ shəs   3*
kän′ chəs   1

CONSCRIPT (n,a)   +
kän′ skript   3*
kän′ skript′   1

CONSCRIPT (v)
kən skript′   4

CONSECUTIVE
kən sek′ yə tiv   4*
kən sek′ ət iv   1

CONSENSUAL
kən sen′ sho͞o əl   2*
kən sen′ sho͞o wəl   1
kən sench′ wəl   1
kən sench′ əl   1

CONSENSUS
kən sen′ səs   4*
kən sent′ səs   1

CONSEQUENCE   +
kän′ sə kwens′   3
kän′ sə kwens   2*
kän′ sə kwəns   2
kän′ sə kwents   1
kän′ si kwəns   1

CONSEQUENTLY   +
kän′ sə kwent′ lē   4*
kän′ sə kwənt lē   3

CONSERVATORY
kən sur′ və tôr′ ē   4*
kən sur′ və tōr′ ē   3

CONSERVE (v)
kən surv′   4

CONSERVE (n)   +
kän′ surv′   2*
kän′ sərv   2
kən surv′   1

CONSIDERABLE
kən sid′ ər ə bəl   3*
kən sid′ ər ə b'l   1
kən sid′ ər bəl   1
kən sid′ rə bəl   1

CONSISTORY
kən sis′ tər ē   4*
kən sis′ trē   1

CONSOLE (n)
kän′ sōl   3*
kän′ sōl′   1

CONSOLE (v)
kən sōl′   4

CONSOMMÉ   +
kän′ sə mä′   4*
kän′ sə mä′   1
känt sə mä′   1

CONSONANCE   +
kän′ sə nəns   4*
kän′ snəns   1
känt′ sə nənts   1

CONSONANT   +
kän′ sə nənt   4*
kän′ snənt   1
känt′ sə nənt   1

CONSORT (n)   +
kän′ sôrt   4

CONSORT (v)   +
kən sôrt′   4*
kän′ sôrt′   1

CONSORTIUM
kən sôr′ shē əm   4*
kən sôr′ shəm   1
kən sôrt′ ē əm   1

CONSPICUOUS
kən spik′ yo͞o əs   2*
kən spik′ yoo wəs   1
kən spik′ yə wəs   1

CONSPIRACY   ○
kən spir′ ə sē   4

CONSTABLE   +
kän′ stə bəl   3*
kun′ stə bəl   2
kän′ stə b'l   1
känt′ stə bəl   1

CONSTABULARY   ○
kən stab′ yə ler′ ē   4

CONSTANCY   +
kän′ stən sē   4*
känt′ stən sē   1

CONSTELLATION   +
kän stə lā′ shən   3*
kän′ stə lā′ shən   1
känt′ stə lā′ shən   1

CONSTITUENCY
kən stich′ o͞o ən sē   2*
kən stich′ oo wən sē   1
kən stich′ wən sē   1

CONSTITUTE   +
kän′ stə to͞ot′   3*
kän′ stə tyo͞ot′   3
kän′ sti to͞ot′   1
kän′ sti tyo͞ot′   1

CONSTITUTION   +
kän′ stə to͞o′ sh̶ən   3∗
kän′ stə tyo͞o′ sh̶ən   3
kän′ sti to͞o′ sh̶ən   1
kän′ sti tyo͞o′ sh̶ən   1

CONSTITUTIONAL   +
kän′ stə to͞o′ sh̶ən əl   2∗
kän′ stə tyo͞o′ sh̶ən əl   2
kän′ sti to͞o′ sh̶ə n′l   1
kän′ sti tyo͞o′ sh̶ə n′l   1
kän′ stə to͞o′ sh̶nəl   1
kän′ stə tyo͞o′ sh̶nəl   1

CONSTRUCT (n)   +
kän′ strukt   3∗
kän′ strukt′   1

CONSTRUCT (v)
kən strukt′   4

CONSUL   +
kän′ səl   3∗
kän′ s′l   1
känt′ səl   1

CONSULATE   +
kän′ sə lit   3∗
kän′ slət   1
känt′ slət   1

CONSUMMATE (adj)   +
kən sum′ it   3∗
kən sum′ ət   1
kän′ sə mit   1
kän′ sə mət   1

CONSUMMATE (v)   +
kän′ sə mat′   3∗
kän′ sə mat   1
känt′ sə mat′   1

CONTAGIOUS
kən ta′ jəs   4

CONTEMN
kən tem′   4

CONTEMPLATE   +
kän′ təm plat′   4

CONTEMPLATIVE   +
kən tem′ plə tiv   4∗
kän′ tem pla′ tiv   3

CONTEMPORANEITY
kən tem′ pər ə ne′ i te   2∗
kən tem′ pər ə ne′ ə te   2
kən tem′ prə ne′ ə te   1
kən tem′ pər ə na′ ə te   1
kən tem′ prə na′ ə te   1

CONTEMPORANEOUS
kən tem′ pə ra′ ne əs   4

CONTEMPORARY   ✓
kən tem′ pə rer′ e   4

CONTEMPTUOUS
kən temp′ ch̶o͞o əs   3∗
kən tem′ ch̶əs   1
kən temp′ ch̶ə wəs   1
kən temsh̶′ wəs   1
kən tempsh̶′ wəs   1

CONTENTION
kən ten′ sh̶ən   3∗
kən ten′ ch̶ən   1

CONTENTIOUS
kən ten′ sh̶əs   3∗
kən ten′ ch̶əs   1

CONTESTANT　+
kən tes′ tənt　4*
kän′ tes′ tənt　2

CONTIGUITY　+
kän′ tə gyōō′ ə tē　3*
kän′ tə gyōō′ i tē　1

CONTIGUOUS
kən tig′ yōō əs　2*
kən tig′ yoo wəs　1
kən tig′ yə wəs　1

CONTINENCE　+
känt′ ′n əns　3
känt′ ə nəns　1*

CONTINGENCY
kən tin′ jən sē　4

CONTINUITY　+
kän′ tə nōō′ ə tē　2
kän′ tə nyōō′ ə tē　2
kän′ ti nyōō′ i tē　1*
kän′ ti nōō′ i tē　1

CONTINUO
kən tin′ yōō ō′　1*
kən tin′ yōō ō　1
kən tin′ yoo wō′　1
kən tin′ ə wō′　1
kən tin′ yə wō′　1

CONTINUUM
kən tin′ yōō əm　2*
kən tin′ yoo wəm　1
kən tin′ yə wəm　1

CONTOUR　+
kän′ toor　4

CONTRABAND　+
kän′ trə band′　4

CONTRABASS　+
kän′ trə bās′　4

CONTRACT　+ (n)
kän′ trakt　2*
kän′ trakt′　2

CONTRACT　+ (v)
kən trakt′　4*
kän′ trakt′　2

CONTRACTOR　+
kən trak′ tər　3*
kän′ trak tər　3
kän′ trak′ tər　1

CONTRACTUAL　+
kən trak′ chōō əl　2*
kən trak′ choo wəl　1
kən trak′ chə wəl　1
kän trak′ chəl　1
kän trak′ chə wəl　1
kən trak′ chəl　1

CONTRARIETY　+
kän′ trə rī′ ə tē　3*
kän′ trə rī′ i tē　1

CONTRARY　+　○
kän′ trer ē　2
kän′ trer′ ē　2

CONTRARY ✓ +
(perverse)
kən trer′ ē　3
kän′ trer′ ē　1

CONTRAST　+ (n)
kän′ trast′　3*
kän′ trast　1

CONTRAST　+ (v)
kən trast′　4*
kän′ trast′　1

CONTRAVENE　+
kän′ trə vēn′　4

CONTRIBUTE
kən trib′ yōōt　3
kən trib′ yət　1*

CONTRITE　+
kən trīt′　4*
kän′ trīt′　3
kän′ trīt　1

CONTRITION
kən trish′ ən　4

CONTRIVANCE
kən trī′ vəns　4*
kən trī′ vənts　1

CONTROLLER
kən trōl′ ər　4

CONTROVERSIAL　+
kän′ trə vʉr′ shəl　4*
kän′ trə vʉr′ sē əl　1

CONTROVERSY　+
kän′ trə vʉr′ sē　4

CONTUMACIOUS
kän′ too mā′ shəs　3*
kän′ tyoo mā′ shəs　3
kän′ tə mā′ shəs　1
kän′ tyə mā′ shəs　1
kän′ chə mā′ shəs　1

CONTUMACY　+
kän′ too mə sē　3*
kän′ tyoo mə sē　3
kən tōō′ mə sē　2
kən tyōō′ mə sē　1
kän′ tə mə sē　1
kän′ tyə mə sē　1
kän′ chə mə sē　1

CONTUMELY　+
kän′ təm lē　3
kän′ too mə lē　2*
kän′ tyoo mə lē　2
kən tōō′ mə lē　2
kan tyōō′ mə lē　1
kän′ too mē′ lē　1
kän′ tyoo mē′ lē　1
kän′ tōō mə lē　1
kän′ tyōō mə lē　1

CONUNDRUM
kə nun′ drəm　4

CONVALESCE +
kän' və les' 4

CONVALESCENCE +
kän' və les' 'ns 2*
kän' və les' əns 2
kän' və les' 'nts 1

CONVERSANT +
kən vʉr' sənt 3
kän' vər sənt 2*
kən vʉr' s'nt 2
kän' vər s'nt 1

CONVERSE (v)
kən vʉrs' 4

CONVERSE (n) +
kän' vʉrs' 2*
kän' vʉrs 1
kän' vərs 1

CONVERSION
kən vʉr' zhən 4*
kən vʉr' shən 4

CONVERT (v)
kən vʉrt' 4

CONVERT (n) +
kän' vʉrt 2*
kän' vʉrt' 1
kän' vərt 1

CONVEX +
kän' veks 4
kän veks' 4*
kən' veks' 1
kän' veks' 1

CONVEY
kən vā' 4

CONVICT (n)
kän' vikt 4

CONVICT (v)
kən vikt' 4

CONVIVIAL
kən viv' ē əl 4*
kən viv' yəl 1

CONVOY (n) +
kän' voi 3*
kän' voi' 1

CONVOY (v) +
kən voi' 4*
kän' voi' 2
kän' voi 2

CONVULSE
kən vuls' 4

COOLANT
kōōl' ənt 4

COOPERATE +
kō äp' ə rāt' 4*
kō äp' rāt' 1

COOPERATIVE +
kō äp' ər ə tiv 3*
kō äp' ə rāt' iv 3
kō äp' rə tiv 2

COOPT +
kō äpt' 4

COPIOUS
kō' pē əs 4

COPULATE +
käp' yə lāt' 4

PRONUNCIATION KEY

Symbol	Key words	Symbol	Key words	Symbol	Key words
a	asp, fat, parrot	†ə	a in ago	r	red, port, dear
ā	ape, date, play		e in agent	s	sell, castle, pass
†ä	ah, car, father		i in sanity	t	top, cattle, hat
e	elf, ten, berry		o in comply	v	vat, hovel, have
ē	even, meet, money		u in focus	w	will, always, swear
i	is, hit, mirror	ər	perhaps, murder	y	yet, onion, yard
ī	ice, bite, high	b	bed, fable, dub	z	zebra, dazzle, haze
ō	open, tone, go	d	dip, beadle, had	ch	chin, catcher, arch
ô	all, horn, law	f	fall, after, off	sh	she, cushion, dash
ōo	ooze, tool, crew	g	get, haggle, dog	th	thin, nothing, truth
oo	look, pull, moor	h	he, ahead, hotel	th	then, father, lathe
yōo	use, cute, few	j	joy, agile, badge	zh	azure, leisure
yoo	united, cure, globule	k	kill, tackle, bake	ŋ	ring, anger, drink
oi	oil, point, toy	l	let, yellow, ball	''	see p. 15.
ou	out, crowd, plow	m	met, camel, trim	✓	see p. 15.
u	up, cut, color	n	not, flannel, ton	+	see p. 14.
ʉr	urn, fur, deter	p	put, apple, tap	'	see p. 15.
†See p. 14.		†See p. 16.		○	see p. 14.

COPULATIVE +
käp′ yə lə tiv   4*
· käp′ yə lāt′ iv   4

COQUETRY
kō ket′ rē   4
kōk′ ə trē   3*
kōk′ i trē   1

COQUETTE
kō ket′   4

CORAL +
kär′ əl   4*
kôr′ əl   4

CORDIAL
kôr′ jəl   4

CORDON
kôr′ d'n   3*
kôr′ dən   1

CORDOVAN
kôr′ də vən   4

CORDUROY
kôr′ də roi′   4*
kôr də roi′   2

CO-RESPONDENT +
kō′ ri spän′ dənt   4

CORMORANT
kôr′ mə rənt   3*
korm′ rənt   1
kôr′ mə rant′   1

CORNEA
kôr nē ə   4

CORNET
kôr net′   4*
kôr′ nit   2

CORNICE
kôr′ nis   3*
kôr′ nəs   1
kôr′ nish   1

CORNUCOPIA
kôr′ nə kō′ pē ə   4
kôr′ nyōo kō′ pē ə   1*
kôr′ nyə kō′ pē ə   1

COROLLARY ✓ +
kär′ ə ler′ ē   3*
kôr′ ə ler′ ē   3
kôr′ ə ler ē   1
kär′ ə ler ē   1

CORONA
kə rō′ nə   4

CORONARY +✓
kär′ ə ner′ ē   4*
kôr′ ə ner′ ē   4

CORONER +
kär′ ə nər   4*
kôr′ ə nər   4

CORONET +
kôr′ ə net′   3
kär′ ə net′   3
kär′ ə net′   2*
kôr′ ə net′   2
kôr′ ə nit   2
kär′ ə nit′   1
kär′ ə nit′   1

CORPORAL
kôr′ pə rəl   3*
kôr′ prəl   2

CORPORATE
kôr′ pər it   3*
kôr′ prit   1
kôr′ prət   1

CORPOREAL
kôr pôr′ ē əl   4*
kôr pōr′ ē əl   3

CORPS
kôr   4*
kōr   3

CORPSE
kôrps   4

CORPULENT
kôr′ pyə lənt   3*
kôr′ pyoo lənt   1

CORPUSCLE
kôr′ pəs əl   3*
kôr′ pus əl   2
kôr′ pəs 'l   1

CORPUS DELICTI
kôr′ pəs di lik′ tī   3*
kôr′ pəs di lik′ tī′   1
kôr′ pəs di lik′ tē′   1

CORRAL
kə ral′   4

CORRELATE +
kär′ ə lāt′   4*
kôr′ ə lāt′   4
kôr′ ə lət   1
kär′ ə lət   1

CORRELATIVE
kə rel′ ə tiv   4

CORRESPOND +
kär′ ə spänd′   3*
kôr′ ə spänd′   3
kôr′ i spänd′   1
kär′ i spänd′   1

CORRESPONDENT +
kär′ ə spän′ dənt   2*
kôr′ ə spän′ dənt   2

CORRIDOR +
kôr′ ə dər   2
kär′ ə dər   2*
kôr′ i dər   2
kär′ ə dôr′   2
kär′ i dôr   1
kôr′ i dôr   1

CORROBORATE +
kə räb′ ə rāt′   4

CORROSION
kə rō′ zhən   4

CORRUGATED   +
kôr′ ə gāt′ əd   4
kär′ ə gāt′ əd   3*
kär′ yə gāt′ id   1
kôr′ yo͞o gāt′ əd   1
kär′ yo͞o gāt′ əd   1
kôr′ yə gāt′ id   1

CORSAGE
kôr säzh′   4*
kôr säj′   2
kôr′ säzh   1
kôr′ säj   1

CORSAIR ✓
kôr′ ser   4

CORTEGE
kôr tezh′   4*
kôr tāzh′   3
kôr′ tezh′   1

CORTISONE
kôrt′ ə zōn′   2*
kôrt′ ə sōn′   2
kort′ i sōn′   1
kort′ i zōn′   1

CORUSCATE   +
kôr′ əs kāt′   4
kär′ əs kāt′   2*

CORVÉE
kôr vā′   4*
kôr′ vā′   1

COSMOGONY   +
käz mäg′ ə nē   4

COSMONAUT   +
käz′ mə nôt′   3*
käz′ mə nät   3
käz′ mə nôt   1

COSMOPOLITAN   +
käz′ mə päl′ ə t′n   2*
käz′ mə päl′ ə tən   1
käz′ mə päl′ i tən   1

COSMOS   +
käz′ məs   4*
käz′ mäs   2
käz′ mōs   2
käz′ mäs′   1
käz′ mōs′   1

COSSET   +
käs′ it   3*
käs′ ət   1

COTERIE
kōt′ ər ē   4

COTILLION
kō til′ yən   4
kə til′ yən   3*

COUGAR
ko͞o′ gər   4*
ko͞o′ gär   2

COUNCIL
koun′ səl   3*
koun′ s′l   1
kount′ səl   1

COUNSEL
koun′ səl   3*
koun′ s′l   1
kount′ səl   1

PRONUNCIATION KEY

Symbol	Key words	Symbol	Key words	Symbol	Key words
a	asp, fat, parrot	†ə	a in ago	r	red, port, dear
ā	ape, date, play		e in agent	s	sell, castle, pass
†ä	ah, car, father		i in sanity	t	top, cattle, hat
e	elf, ten, berry		o in comply	v	vat, hovel, have
ē	even, meet, money		u in focus	w	will, always, swear
i	is, hit, mirror	ər	perhaps, murder	y	yet, onion, yard
ī	ice, bite, high	b	bed, fable, dub	z	zebra, dazzle, haze
ō	open, tone, go	d	dip, beadle, had	ch	chin, catcher, arch
ô	all, horn, law	f	fall, after, off	sh	she, cushion, dash
o͞o	ooze, tool, crew	g	get, haggle, dog	th	thin, nothing, truth
oo	look, pull, moor	h	he, ahead, hotel	th	then, father, lathe
yo͞o	use, cute, few	j	joy, agile, badge	zh	azure, leisure
yoo	united, cure, globule	k	kill, tackle, bake	ŋ	ring, anger, drink
oi	oil, point, toy	l	let, yellow, ball	″	see p. 15.
ou	out, crowd, plow	m	met, camel, trim	✓	see p. 15.
u	up, cut, color	n	not, flannel, ton	+	see p. 14.
ʉr	urn, fur, deter	p	put, apple, tap	′	see p. 15.
†See p. 14.		†See p. 16.		◯	see p. 14.

COUNSELOR
koun′ sə lər 2*
koun′ s′l ər 1
koun′ slər 1
kount′ slər 1

COUNTERFEIT
koun′ tər fit 4

COUP
ko͞o 4

COUPE
ko͞op 4

COUPLET
kup′ lit 3*
kup′ lət 1

COUPON
ko͞o′ pän′ 2*
kyo͞o′ pän′ 2
ko͞o′ pän 2
kyo͞o′ pän 2

COURAGEOUS
kə rā′ jəs 4

COURIER
ko͞or′ ē ər 4*
kur′ ē ər 3

COURSE
kôrs 4*
kōrs 3

COURTEOUS
kur′ tē əs 4

COURTESAN
kôr′ tə zən 2*
kōr′ tə zən 2
kôr′ ti zən 1
kōr′ ti zən 1
kôr′ tə z′n 1

COURTESY
kur′ tə sē 3*
kur′ ti sē 1

COURTIER
kôr′ tē ər 4*
kōr′ tē ər 3
kôr′ tyər 2
kōr′ tyər 2
kôr′ chər 1
kōr′ chər 1

COUTURIER
ko͞o toor′ ē ā′ 3*
ko͞o toor′ ē ər 2
ko͞o to͞o ryā′ 1

COVE
kōv 4

COVEN
kuv′ ən 3*
kō′ vən 3

COVENANT
kuv′ ə nənt 4*
kuv′ nənt 1

COVERT
kō′ vərt 4*
kuv′ ərt 3

COVET
kuv′ it 4

COVETOUS
kuv′ ət əs 2*
kuv′ it əs 2

COVEY
kuv′ ē 4

COWARDICE
kou′ ərd is 3*
kou′ ərd əs 1

COWER
kou′ ər 3*
kour 1

COXSWAIN   +
käk′ swān′ 4
käk′ sən 3*
käk′ s′n 1

COYOTE
kī ōt′ ē 4*
kī′ ōt 3
kī′ ōt′ 1

COZEN
kuz′ ən 2*
kuz′ ′n 2

CRANIAL
krā nē əl 4

CRANIUM
krā′ nē əm 4

CRATER
krāt′ ər 4

CRAVAT
krə vat′ 4

CRAVEN
krā′ vən 4

CRAYON   +
krā′ ən 4
krā′ än′ 3*
krā′ än 1
kran 1

CREATIVE
krē′ āt′ iv 4

CREATURE
krē′ chər 4

CRÈCHE
kresh 4*
krāsh 3

CREDENCE
krēd′ ′ns 3*
krēd′ əns 2

CREDENTIAL
kri den′ shəl 4*
kri den′ chəl 2

CREDENZA
kri den′ zə 4

CREDO
krā′ dō 4*
krē′ dō 4

CREDULITY
kri dyōō′ lə tē 2*
kri dōō′ lə tē 2
krə dōō′ lə tē 1
krə dyōō′ lə tē 1
kri dōō′ li tē 1
kri dyōō′ li tē 1

CREDULOUS
krej′ oo ləs 3*
kred′ yōō ləs 1
krej′ ə ləs 1

CREMATE
kri māt′ 3*
krē′ māt 2
krē′ māt′ 2

CREMATORY
krē′ mə tôr′ ē 4*
krem′ ə tôr′ ē 3
krē′ mə tōr′ ē 2
krem′ ə tōr′ ē 2

CRENELATED
kren′ ′l āt′ id 2
kren′ ′l āt′ əd 1*
kren′ əl āt′ id 1

CREOLE
krē′ ōl 2*
krē′ ōl′ 2

CREOSOTE
krē′ ə sōt′ 4

CREPE
krāp 4*
krep 1

CREPES SUZETTE
krāp′ sōō zet′ 3
krāp′ soo zet′ 1

CREPUSCULAR
krə pus′ kyə lər 3*
kri pus′ kyoo lər 1

CRESCENT
kres′ ənt 2*
kres′ ′nt 2

CRETIN
krēt′ ′n 4*
krē′ tin 2

CRETONNE   +
kri tän′ 4
krē′ tän′ 2*
krē′ tän 2

CREVASSE
krə vas′ 2*
kri vas′ 2

CREVICE
krev′ is 3*
krev′ əs 1

CRESCENDO
krə shen′ dō 3*
krə sen′ dō 1
kri shen′ dō 1
kri sen′ dō 1
krə shen′ dō′ 1

CREWEL
krōō əl 4

CRIMSON
krim′ zən 3*
krim′ sən 1
krim′ z'n 1

CRINOLINE
krin′ 'l in 2
krin′ ə lin 1*
krin′ 'l ēn 1
krin′ 'l ən 1

CRISIS
krī′ sis 3*
krī′ səs 1

CRISES
krī′ sēz′ 2*
krī′ sēz 2

CRITERION ○
krī tir′ ē ən 4

CRITIQUE
kri tēk′ 4*
krə tēk′ 1

CROCHET
krō s·hā′ 4

CROCODILE +
kräk′ ə dīl′ 4

CROCUS
krō′ kəs 4

CRONY
krō′ nē 4

CROQUET
krō kā′ 4

CROQUETTE
krō ket′ 4

CROSIER
krō′ zhər 4

CROTCHET +
kräch′ it 3*
kräch′ ət 1

CROUP
krо̄о̄p 4

CROUPIER
krо̄о̄′ pē ā′ 4*
krо̄о̄′ pē ər 4

CROUTON +
krо̄о̄ tän′ 4
krо̄о̄′ tän′ 2*
krо̄о̄′ tän 2

CRUCIAL
krо̄о̄ s·həl 4

CRUCIBLE
krо̄о̄′ sə bəl 3*
krо̄о̄′ sə b'l 1

CRUCIFIX
krо̄о̄′ sə fiks′ 3*
krо̄о̄′ sə fiks 1

CRUCIFIXION
krо̄о̄′ sə fik′ s·hən 4

CRUCIFY
krо̄о̄′ sə fī′ 4

CRUET
krо̄о̄ it 4

CRUSTACEAN
krus tā′ s·hən 4

CRYPT
kript 4

CRYSTALLINE
kris′ tə lin 2*
kris′ t'lin 1
kris′ t'līn 1
kris′ tə lən 1
kris′ tə līn′ 1
kris′ tə lēn′ 1

CUBEB
kyо̄о̄′ beb′ 2*
kyо̄о̄′ beb 2

CUBIC
kyо̄о̄′ bik 4

CUBICLE
kyо̄о̄′ bi kəl 3*
kyо̄о̄′ bi k'l 1

CUBISM
kyо̄о̄′ biz′ əm 2*
kyо̄о̄′ biz əm 1
kyо̄о̄′ biz'm 1

CUBIT
kyо̄о̄′ bit 3*
kyо̄о̄′ bət 1

CUCKOLD
kuk′ əld 3*
kuk′ 'ld 1
kook′ əld 1

CUCKOO
kо̄о̄′ kо̄о̄ 4*
kook′ о̄о̄ 4

CUCUMBER
kyо̄о̄′ kum bər 2*
kyо̄о̄′ kum′ bər 1
kyо̄о̄′ kəm′ bər 1
kyо̄о̄′ kəm bər 1

CUDGEL
kuj′ əl 4

CUIRASS
kwi ras′ 4*
kyoo ras′ 1

CUISINE
kwi zēn′ 4

CUL-DE-SAC
kul′ di sak′ 2*
kool′ di sak′ 2
kul′ də sak′ 1
kul′ də sak 1
kool′ də sak′ 1
kool′ də sak 1
kul′ də sak′ 1
kool də sak′ 1

CULINARY ✓
kyo͞o′ lə ner′ ē   4*
kul′ ə ner′ ē   4

CULOTTE   +
ko͞o lät′   4*
kyo͞o lät′   4
ko͞o′ lät   1
kyo͞o′ lät   1
koo lät′   1
kyoo lät′   1
ko͞o′ lät′   1
kyo͞o′ lät′   1

CULPABLE
kul′ pə bəl   3*
kul′ pə b'l   1

CULPRIT
kul′ prit   4

CULVERT
kul′ vərt   4

CUM LAUDE
koom lou′ dē   3*
koom lou′ də   3
koom lô′ dē   3
koom lou′ dā   1

CUMMERBUND
kum′ ər bund′   4

CUMULATIVE
kyo͞om′ yə lāt′ iv   4
kyo͞om′ yə lə tiv   3*

CUMULUS
kyo͞om′ yə ləs   4

CUNEIFORM
kyo͞o′ nē ə fôrm′   4*
kyo͞o nē′ ə fôrm′   4
kyo͞o′ nə fôrm′   1

CUPIDITY
kyo͞o pid′ ə tē   3*
kyo͞o pid′ i tē   1

CUPOLA
kyo͞o′ pə lə   4*
kyo͞o′ pə lō′   1

CURAÇAO
koor′ ə sou′   4*
kyoor′ ə sō′   4
koor′ ə sō′   1
kyoor′ ə sō′   1
koor′ ə sou′   1
kyoor′ ə sou′   1
koor′ ə sō′   1

CURARE
kyo͞o rä′ rē   3*
koo rä′ rē   2

CURATE
kyoor′ it   3*
kyoor′ ət   1
kyoor′ āt′   1

CURATOR
kyoo rāt′ ər   4*
kyoor′ ə tər   3

CURÉ
kyoo′ rā   4

CURET (CURETTE)
kyoo ret′   4

PRONUNCIATION KEY

Symbol	Key words	Symbol	Key words	Symbol	Key words
a	asp, fat, parrot	†ə	a in ago	r	red, port, dear
ā	ape, date, play		e in agent	s	sell, castle, pass
†ä	ah, car, father		i in sanity	t	top, cattle, hat
e	elf, ten, berry		o in comply	v	vat, hovel, have
ē	even, meet, money		u in focus	w	will, always, swear
i	is, hit, mirror	ər	perhaps, murder	y	yet, onion, yard
ī	ice, bite, high	b	bed, fable, dub	z	zebra, dazzle, haze
ō	open, tone, go	d	dip, beadle, had	ch	chin, catcher, arch
ô	all, horn, law	f	fall, after, off	sh	she, cushion, dash
o͞o	ooze, tool, crew	g	get, haggle, dog	th	thin, nothing, truth
oo	look, pull, moor	h	he, ahead, hotel	th	then, father, lathe
yo͞o	use, cute, few	j	joy, agile, badge	zh	azure, leisure
yoo	united, cure, globule	k	kill, tackle, bake	ŋ	ring, anger, drink
oi	oil, point, toy	l	let, yellow, ball	″	see p. 15.
ou	out, crowd, plow	m	met, camel, trim	✓	see p. 15.
u	up, cut, color	n	not, flannel, ton	+	see p. 14.
ur	urn, fur, deter	p	put, apple, tap	′	see p. 15.
†See p. 14.		†See p. 16.		○	see p. 14.

CURETTAGE
kyoor' ə täzh'   3*
kyoo ret' ij   3
kyoor i täzh'   1

CURFEW
kɐr' fyo͞o   3*
kɐr' fyo͞o'   2

CURIA
kyo͞or' ē ə   4*
koor' ē ə   1

CURIO
kyoor' ē ō'   4

CURIOSITY   +
kyoor' ē äs' ə tē   3*
kyoor' ē äs' i tē   1

CURMUDGEON
kər muj' ən   4*
kər' muj' ən   1

CURSORY
kɐr' sər ē   3*
kɐrs' rē   1

CURTAIL
kər tāl   4

CURVACEOUS
kər vā' shəs   4

CURVATURE
kɐr' və chər   3*
kɐr' və choor   2
kɐr' və toor   1
kɐr' və tyoor   1

CUSTODIAN
kus tō' dē ən   2*
kus' tō' dē ən   1
kəs tō' dē ən   1

CUSTODY
kus' tə dē   4

CUSTOMER
kus' tə mər   4

CUTICLE
kyo͞ot' i kəl   3*
kyo͞ot' i k'l   1

CUTLASS
kut' ləs   3*
kut' las   1

CYANIDE
sī' ə nīd'   4*
sī' ə nid   2
sī ə nəd   1

CYBERNETICS
sī' bər net' iks   4

CYCLAMATE
sī' klə māt'   2*
sik' lə māt'   2

CYCLIC
sī' klik   4*
sik' lik   4

CYCLONE
sī' klōn'   2*
sī' klōn   2

CYCLONIC   +
sī klän' ik   4

CYGNET
sig' nit   2*
sig' nət   2

CYLINDER
sil' ən dər   3*
sil' in dər   1

CYLINDRICAL
sə lin' dri kəl   2*
si lin' dri kəl   1
sə lin' dri k'l   1

CYMBAL
sim' bəl   3*
sim' b'l   1

CYNIC
sin' ik   4

CYNICISM
sin' ə siz' əm   2*
sin' i siz' əm   1
sin' ə siz'm   1

CYNOSURE
sī' nə shoor'   4*
sin' ə shoor'   4

CYPRESS
sī' prəs   4

CYST
sist   4

CZAR
zär   4

CZARDAS
chär' däsh   4*
chär' dəsh   1
chär' dash'   1

CZARINA
zä rē' nə   4

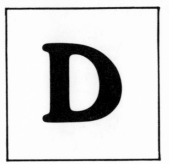

DACHA
dä′ chə 4

DACHSHUND
däks′ hoont′ 2*
daks′ hoond′ 1
däks′ hoond′ 1

DACRON
dā′ krän′ 2*
dak′ rän′ 2
dā′ krän 2
dak′ rän 2
dā′ krən 1
dak′ rən 1

DADA
dä′ dä 4*
dä′ də 1
dä′ dä′ 1

DADO
dā′ dō 4*
dā′ dō′ 1

DAGUERREOTYPE ✓
də ger′ ə tīp′ 4*
də ger′ ē ə tīp′ 1

DAHLIA
däl′ yə 4*
dal′ yə 4
dāl′ yə 1

DAIQUIRI
dīk′ ər ē 4*
dak′ ər ē 4

DAIS
dā′ is 3*
dī′ is 2
dās 2

DAMASK
dam′ əsk 4

DAMNABLE
dam′ nə bəl 3*
dam′ nə b′l 1

DAMSEL
dam′ zəl 3*
dam′ z′l 1

DAMSON
dam′ zən 3
dam′ s′n 1*
dam′ sən 1
dam′ z′n 1

DANDELION
dan′ d′lī′ ən 2
dan′ də lī′ ən 2*
dan′ dē lī′ ən 1

DATA
dāt′ ə 4*
dat′ ə 4
dät′ ə 4

DAUB
dôb 4*
däb 1

DAUNTED
dônt′ əd 4*
dänt′ əd 4

DAUPHIN
dô′ fin 3*
dô′ fən 1

DEAF
def 4

DEARTH
durth 4

DEBACLE
di bak′ əl   2*
di bäk′ əl   2
di bäk′ ′l   1
di bak′ ′l   1
dā bäk′ ′l   1
dā bäk′ əl   1
dā bak′ ′l   1
dā bak′ əl   1
deb′ i kəl   1

DEBAUCH
di bôch′   4*
di bäch′   1

DEBAUCHERY
di bôch′ ər ē   4*
di bôch′ rē   1
di bäch′ rē   1

DEBENTURE
di ben′ chər   4

DEBILITATE
di bil′ ə tāt′   3*
di bil′ i tāt′   1

DEBONAIR ✓ ○
deb′ ə ner′   4

DEBOUCH
di boosh′   4
di bouch′   2*

DEBRIS
də brē′   4*
dā′ brē′   3

DEBT
det   4

DEBTOR
det′ ər   4

DEBUT
dā byoo′   4
dā′ byoo   3*
di byoo′   3
deb′ yoo′   1
dā′ byoo′   1

DEBUTANTE
deb′ yoo tänt′   4*
deb′ yoo tänt′   2

DECADE
de kād′   3
dek′ ād   2*
dek′ əd   1

DECADENCE
dek′ ə dəns   4
di kād′ ′ns   3*
di kād′ əns   1
dek′ ə dənts   1

DECAL
di kal′   3
dē′ kal   2*
dek′ əl   2
dē kal′   1

DECALCOMANIA
di kal′ kə mā′ nē ə   3*
dē′ kal kə mā′ nē ə   1
di kal′ kə mān′ yə   1

DECANT
di kant′   4

DECATHLON   +
di kath′ län   3*
di kath′ lən   3
di kath′ län′   1

DECEASE
di sēs′   4

DECEDENT
di sēd′ ′nt   3*
di sē′ dənt   1

DECELERATE
dē sel′ ə rāt′   4

DECIBEL
des′ ə bel′   3*
des′ i bəl   1
des′ i bel′   1
des′ ə bəl   1
des′ ə b′l   1

DECIDUOUS
di sij′ oo əs   2*
di sid′ yoo əs   1
di sij′ oo wəs   1
di sij′ ə wəs   1

DECIMAL
des′ ə məl   3*
des′ məl   1
des′ ə m′l   1

DECIMALIZE
des′ ə mə līz′   3*
des′ mə līz′   1
des′ ə m′l īz′   1

DECIMATE
des′ ə māt′   3*
des′ i māt′   1

DECISIVE
di sī′ siv   4

DECLAMATION
dek lə mā′ shən   2*
dek′ lə mā′ shən   2

DECLAMATORY
di klam′ ə tôr′ ē   4*
di klam′ ə tōr′ ē   3

DECLARATIVE ✓
di klar′ ə tiv   3*
di kler′ ə tiv   3

DÉCLASSÉ
dā′ klä sā′   3
dā′ klə sā′   3
dā′ kla sā′   1*

DECLENSION
di klen′ shən   3*
di klen′ chən   1

DECLINATION
dek lə nā′ shən   2*
dek′ lə nā′ shən   2

DECOLLETAGE   +
dā käl′ ə täzh′   3
dek′ ə lə täzh′   2*
dā käl täzh′   1

DECOLLETÉ   +
dā käl′ ə tā′   2
dek′ ə lə tā′   1*
dā′ kôl tā′   1
dā käl tā′   1
dek′ lə tā′   1

DECOR
dā′ kôr′   3*
dā kôr′   3
dā′ kôr′   2
di kôr′   2
dā′ kôr   1
dek′ ôr′   1

DECORATIVE
dek′ ər ə tiv   4*
dek′ ə rāt′ iv   3
dek′ rə tiv   3

DECOROUS
di kôr′ əs   4
dek′ ər əs   3*
di kōr′ əs   2
dek′ rəs   1

DECORUM
di kôr′ əm   4*
di kōr′ əm   3

DECOUPAGE
dā′ kōō päzh′   2*
dā kōō päzh′   1
dā′ kōō′ päzh′   1

DECOY
di koi   4
dē′ koi   2*

DECREPIT
di krep′ it   3*
di krep′ ət   1

DE FACTO
dā fak′ tō   2*
dē fak′ tō   2
di fak′ tō   2
di fak′ tō′   1
dā fak′ tō′   1

DEFALCATE
di fal′ kāt′   2*
di fôl′ kāt′   2
def′ əl kāt′   2
di fal′ kāt   2
di fôl′ kāt   2

DEFAMATION
def′ ə mā′ shən   4*
dē′ fə mā′ shən   1

DEFAMATORY
di fam′ ə tôr′ ē   4*
di fam′ ə tōr′ ē   3

DEFAULT
di fôlt′   4

DEFECATE
def′ ə kāt′   3*
def′ i kāt′   1

DEFECT (n)
di fekt′   4*
dē′ fekt′   2
dē′ fekt   2

DEFECT (v)
di fekt′   4

PRONUNCIATION KEY

Symbol	Key words	Symbol	Key words	Symbol	Key words
a	asp, fat, parrot	†ə	a in ago	r	red, port, dear
ā	ape, date, play		e in agent	s	sell, castle, pass
†ä	ah, car, father		i in sanity	t	top, cattle, hat
e	elf, ten, berry		o in comply	v	vat, hovel, have
ē	even, meet, money		u in focus	w	will, always, swear
i	is, hit, mirror	ər	perhaps, murder	y	yet, onion, yard
ī	ice, bite, high	b	bed, fable, dub	z	zebra, dazzle, haze
ō	open, tone, go	d	dip, beadle, had	ch	chin, catcher, arch
ô	all, horn, law	f	fall, after, off	sh	she, cushion, dash
ōō	ooze, tool, crew	g	get, haggle, dog	th	thin, nothing, truth
oo	look, pull, moor	h	he, ahead, hotel	th	then, father, lathe
yōō	use, cute, few	j	joy, agile, badge	zh	azure, leisure
yoo	united, cure, globule	k	kill, tackle, bake	ŋ	ring, anger, drink
oi	oil, point, toy	l	let, yellow, ball	″	see p. 15.
ou	out, crowd, plow	m	met, camel, trim	✓	see p. 15.
u	up, cut, color	n	not, flannel, ton	+	see p. 14.
ʉr	urn, fur, deter	p	put, apple, tap	′	see p. 15.
†See p. 14.		†See p. 16.		○	see p. 14.

DEFERENCE
def′ ər əns 3*
def′ rəns 1
def′ rənts 1

DEFERENTIAL
def′ ə ren′ shəl 3*
def′ ə ren′ chəl 1

DEFIANCE
di fī′ əns 4*
di fī′ ənts 1

DEFICIENT
di fish′ ənt 4

DEFICIT
def′ ə sit 2*
def′ i ṣit 1
def′ ə sət 1

DEFINITE
def′ ə nit 3*
def′ ə nət 1
def′ nət 1

DEFINITIVE
di fin′ ə tiv 3*
di fin′ i tiv 1

DEFOLIANT
dē fō′ lē ənt 3*
di fō′ lē ənt 1

DEFOLIATE
dē fō′ lē āt′ 3*
di fō′ lē āt′ 1
dē′ fō′ lē āt′ 1

DEFRAUD
di frôd′ 4

DEFUNCT
di fuŋkt′ 4

DEGRADATION
deg′ rə dā′ shən 4

DEHUMIDIFY
dē′ hyo͞o mid′ ə fī′ 4*
dē′ yo͞o mid′ ə fī′ 1

DEICIDE
dē′ ə sīd′ 3*
dē′ i sīd 1
dā′ ə sīd′ 1

DEIFY
dē′ ə fī′ 4

DEIGN
dān 4

DEITY
dē′ ə tē 3*
dē′ i tē 1
dā′ ə tē 1

DELECTATION
dē′ lek tā′ shən 3*
di lek′ tā′ shən 2
dē lek′ tā′ shən 1
del′ ək tā′ shən 1

DELEGATE (n)
del′ ə gāt′ 3*
del′ ə git 3
del′ i gət 1
del′ i gāt′ 1

DELEGATE (v)
del′ ə gāt′ 4

DELETE
di lēt′ 4

DELETERIOUS ○
del′ ə tir′ ē əs 3*
del′ i tir′ ē əs 1

DELIBERATE (adj)
di lib′ ər it 3*
di lib′ rət 1

DELIBERATE (v)
di lib′ ər āt′ 4

DELICACY
del′ i kə sē 3*
del ə kə sē 1

DELICATESSEN
del′ i kə tes′ ′n 2*
del′ i kə tes′ ən 1
del′ ə kə tes′ ən 1

DELICIOUS
di lish′ əs 4

DELINEATE
di lin′ ē āt′ 4

DELINQUENCY
di liŋ′ kwən sē 4*
di lin′ kwən sē 1

DELIQUESCE
del′ ə kwes′ 3*
del′ i kwes′ 1

DELIRIUM ○
di lir′ ē əm 4

DELIRIUM TREMENS ○
di lir′ ē əm trē′ mənz 4*
di lir′ ē əm trem′ ənz 1

DELUGE
del′ yo͞oj 3*
del′ yooj 1

DELUXE
di looks′ 4*
di luks′ 4
di lo͞oks′ 2

DEMAGOGUE +
dem′ ə gäg′ 4*
dem′ ə gôg′ 3

DEMARCATE
dē′ mär kāt′ 3*
di mär′ kāt′ 2
di mär′ kāt 2
dē′ mär′ kāt′ 1

DEMEANOR
di mēn' ər   4

DEMENTIA PRAECOX   +
di men' shə prē' käks   2*
di men' shə prē' käks'   1
di men' shē ə prē' käks'   1

di men' shē ə prē' käks   1

di men' shə prā' käks   1
di men' chə prē' käks'   1

DEMIMONDE   +
dem' ē mänd'   2*
dem' ē mänd'   2
dem' ē mänd   1
dem' i mänd'   1

DEMISE
di mīz'   4

DEMITASSE
dem' i tas'   2*
dem' i täs'   2
dem' ē tas'   2
dem' ē täs'   2

DEMIURGE
dem' ē urj'   4

DEMOCRATIZE   +
di mäk' rə tīz'   4

DEMOGRAPHY   +
di mäg' rə fē   4

DEMOLITION
dem' ·ə lish' ən   4*
dē' mə lish' ən   3

DEMONIACAL
dē' mə nī' ə kəl   3*
dē' mə nī' ə k'l   1

DEMONOLOGY   +
dē' mə näl' ə jē   4

DEMONSTRABLE   +
di män' strə bəl   3*
di mänt' strə bəl   1
di män' strə b'l   1
dem' ən strə bəl   1
dem' ən strə b'l   1

DEMONSTRATE
dem' ən strāt'   4

DEMONSTRATIVE   +
di män' strə tiv   4*
di mänt strə tiv   1

DEMULCENT
di mul' sənt   3*
di mul' s'nt   1

DEMUR
di mur'   4

DEMURE
di myoor'   4

DEMURRAGE
di mur' ij   4

DENIER
(unit of weight for thread)
den' yər   4*
də nyā'   1

DENIGRATE
den' i grāt'   2*
den' ə grāt'   2

PRONUNCIATION KEY

Symbol	Key words	Symbol	Key words	Symbol	Key words
a	asp, fat, parrot	†ə	a in ago	r	red, port, dear
ā	ape, date, play		e in agent	s	sell, castle, pass
†ä	ah, car, father		i in sanity	t	top, cattle, hat
e	elf, ten, berry		o in comply	v	vat, hovel, have
ē	even, meet, money		u in focus	w	will, always, swear
i	is, hit, mirror	ər	perhaps, murder	y	yet, onion, yard
ī	ice, bite, high	b	bed, fable, dub	z	zebra, dazzle, haze
ō	open, tone, go	d	dip, beadle, had	ch	chin, catcher, arch
ô	all, horn, law	f	fall, after, off	sh	she, cushion, dash
ōō	ooze, tool, crew	g	get, haggle, dog	th	thin, nothing, truth
oo	look, pull, moor	h	he, ahead, hotel	th	then, father, lathe
yōō	use, cute, few	j	joy, agile, badge	zh	azure, leisure
yoo	united, cure, globule	k	kill, tackle, bake	ŋ	ring, anger, drink
oi	oil, point, toy	l	let, yellow, ball	''	see p. 15.
ou	out, crowd, plow	m	met, camel, trim	✓	see p. 15.
u	up, cut, color	n	not, flannel, ton	+	see p. 14.
ur	urn, fur, deter	p	put, apple, tap	'	see p. 15.
†See p. 14.		†See p. 16.		○	see p. 14.

DENIZEN
den' ə zən   3
den' i zən   1*

DENTIFRICE
den' tə fris   2*
den' tə fris'   1
den' tə frəs   1

DENTURE
den' chər   4

DENUNCIATION
di nun' sē ā' shən   4*
di nun' shē ā' shən   2
di nunt' sē ā' shən   1

DEO VOLENTE
dā' ō vō len' tē   2*
dē' ō vō len' tē   2
dā' ō vō len' tā   1
dā' ō və len' tē   1
dē' ō və len' tē   1

DEPILATORY
di pil' ə tôr ē   2*
di pil' ə tōr ē   2
di pil' ə tôr' ē   2
di pil' ə tōr' ē   1

DEPLETE
di plēt   4

DEPORTEE
dē' pôr tē'   3*
dē' pōr tē'   2
dē' pōr' tē'   1
di pōr tē'   1
dē' pôr' tē'   1
di pôr' tē'   1

DEPOSITION
dep' ə zish' ən   4*
dē' pə zish' ən   3

DEPOSITORY   +
di päz' ə tôr' ē   2*
di päz' ə tôr ē   1
di päz' ə tōr ē   1
di päz' i tôr ē   1
di päz' i tōr ē   1
di päz' ə tōr' ̣ē   1

DEPOT
dē' pō   4

DEPOT (military)
dep' ō   3

DEPRAVITY
di prav' ə tē   3*
di prav' i tē   1
di prāv' ə tē   1

DEPRECATE
dep' rə kāt'   2*
dep' ri kāt'   2

DEPRECATORY
dep' rə kə tôr ē   3*
dep' rə kə tōr ē   2
dep' ri kə tôr' ē   1
dep' ri kə tōr' ē   1

DEPRECIATE
di prē' shē āt'   4

DEPREDATION
dep' rə dā' shən   3*
dep' ri dā' shən   1

DEPRIVATION
dep' rə vā' shən   4*
dē' prī vā' shən   1

DEPUTY
dep' yə tē   4

DERACINATE
di ras' ə nāt'   3*
dē ras' 'n āt'   1

DERELICT
der' ə likt'   2*
der' ə likt   2

DERELICTION
der' ə lik' shən   4

DERISION
di rizh' ən   4

DERISIVE
di rī' siv   4

DERIVATION
der' ə vā' shən   4

DERIVATIVE
di riv' ə tiv   3
də riv' ə tiv   1*

DEROGATE
der' ə gāt'   4

DEROGATORY   +
di räg' ə tôr' ē   4*
di räg' ə tōr' ē   3

DERRIÈRE   ✓
der' ē er'   4

DERRINGER
der' in jər   3*
der' ən jər   1

DESCRY
di skrī'   4

DESECRATE
des' ə krāt'   3*
des' i krāt'   1

DESERT
(barren region, n)
dez' ərt   4

DESERTS
(deserved reward or
punishment, n)
di zurts'   4

DESERT (v)
di zurt'   4

DESICCATE
des′ i kāt′ 4

DESIDERATUM
di sid′ ə rāt′ əm 4*
di zid′ ə rāt′ əm 2
di sid′ ə rät′ əm 1
di zid′ ə rät′ əm 1

DESIGN
di zīn′ 4

DESIGNATE (v)
dez′ ig nāt′ 4

DESIROUS
di zīr′ əs 4

DESOLATE (adj)
des′ ə lit 3*
des′ ə lət 1
dez′ ə lət 1

DESPERADO
des′ pə rä′ dō 4*
des′ pə rā′ dō 4
des′ pə rä′ dō′ 1
des′ pə rā′ dō′ 1

DESPICABLE
des′ pik ə bəl 3*
di spik′ ə bəl 3
des′ pik ə b'l 1
di spik′ ə b'l 1

DESPISE
di spīz′ 4

DESPOND (n) +
di spänd′ 3
des′ pänd 1*

DESPOT +
des′ pət 3*
des′ pät 2
des′ pät′ 1

DESSERT
di zʉrt′ 4

DESTINE
des′ tin 3*
des′ tən 1

DESTITUTE
des′ tə to͞ot′ 3*
des′ tə tyo͞ot′ 3
des′ ti to͞ot′ 1
des′ ti tyo͞ot′ 1

DESTRUCT
di strukt′ 4*
dē′ strukt 1

DESUETUDE
des′ wi to͞od′ 3*
des′ wi tyo͞od′ 3
des′ wə to͞od′ 1
des′ wə tyo͞od′ 1
di so͞o′ ə to͞od′ 1
di so͞o′ ə tyo͞od′ 1

DESULTORY
des′ əl tôr′ ē 3*
des′ əl tōr′ ē 3
des′ 'l tôr′ ē 1
dez′ əl tôr′ ē 1
dez′ əl tōr′ ē 1

DETAIL (n)
di tāl′ 4*
dē′ tāl 3

PRONUNCIATION KEY

Symbol	Key words	Symbol	Key words	Symbol	Key words
a	asp, fat, parrot	†ə	a in ago	r	red, port, dear
ā	ape, date, play		e in agent	s	sell, castle, pass
†ä	ah, car, father		i in sanity	t	top, cattle, hat
e	elf, ten, berry		o in comply	v	vat, hovel, have
ē	even, meet, money		u in focus	w	will, always, swear
i	is, hit, mirror	ər	perhaps, murder	y	yet, onion, yard
ī	ice, bite, high	b	bed, fable, dub	z	zebra, dazzle, haze
ō	open, tone, go	d	dip, beadle, had	ch	chin, catcher, arch
ô	all, horn, law	f	fall, after, off	sh	she, cushion, dash
o͞o	ooze, tool, crew	g	get, haggle, dog	th	thin, nothing, truth
oo	look, pull, moor	h	he, ahead, hotel	th	then, father, lathe
yo͞o	use, cute, few	j	joy, agile, badge	zh	azure, leisure
yoo	united, cure, globule	k	kill, tackle, bake	ŋ	ring, anger, drink
oi	oil, point, toy	l	let, yellow, ball	ʺ	see p. 15.
ou	out, crowd, plow	m	met, camel, trim	✓	see p. 15.
u	up, cut, color	n	not, flannel, ton	+	see p. 14.
ʉr	urn, fur, deter	p	put, apple, tap	′	see p. 15.
†See p. 14.		†See p. 16.		○	see p. 14.

DETAIL (v)
di tāl′ 4*
dē′ tāl 1
dē′ tāl′ 1

DETAIN
di tān′ 4

DETECT
di tekt′ 4

DÉTENTE
dā tänt′ 3

DETERIORATE ○
di tir′ ē ə rāt′ 3*
di tir′ ē ə rāt 1

DETERRENT
di tur′ ənt 4*
di ter′ ənt 1

DETONATE
det′ 'n āt′ 4*
det′ ə nāt′ 1

DETOUR
di toor′ 4*
dē′ toor′ 2
dē′ toor 2

DETRIMENT
det′ rə mənt 4

DETRITUS
di trīt′ əs 4

DE TROP
də trō′ 4

DEUCE
do͞os 4*
dyo͞os 4

DEVASTATE
dev′ ə stāt′ 4

DEVIANT
dē′ vē ənt 4

DEVIATE (n, adj)
dē′ vē it 3*
dē′ vē ət 1
dē′ vē āt′ 1

DEVIATE (v)
dē′ vē āt′ 4

DEVICE
di vīs′ 4

DEVIOUS
dē′ və əs 4

DEVISE
di vīz′ 4

DEVOID
di void′ 4

DEVOTEE
dev′ ə tē′ 4
dev′ ə tā′ 3*
di vō′ tē′ 1

DEVOUT
di vout′ 4

DEW
dyo͞o 4*
do͞o 4

DEXTERITY
dek ster′ ə tē 3*
dek ster′ i tē 1

DEXTEROUS
dek′ strəs 4*
dek′ stər əs 2

DIABETES
dī′ ə bēt′ ēz 4*
dī′ ə bēt′ is 3
dī′ ə bēt′ əs 1

DIABETIC
dī′ ə bet′ ik 4

DIABOLIC +
dī′ ə bäl′ ik 4

DIABOLISM
dī ab′ ə liz′ əm 4

DIACRITICAL
dī′ ə krit′ i kəl 3*
dī′ ə krit′ i k'l 1

DIADEM
dī′ ə dem′ 4*
dī′ ə dəm 2

DIAGNOSE
dī′ əg nōz′ 4*
dī′ əg nōs′ 4
dī′ ig nōs′ 1
dī′ ig nōz′ 1
dī′ ig nōs 1
dī′ ig nōz 1

DIAGNOSIS
dī′ əg nō′ sis 4*
dī′ ig nō′ səs 1

DIAGNOSTICIAN +
dī′ əg näs tish′ ən 3*
dī′ ig näs tish′ ən 1
dī′ ig näs′ tish′ ən 1

DIAGONAL
dī ag′ ə n'l 3
dī ag′ ə nəl 1*
dī ag′ nəl 1

DIAL
dī′ əl 4*
dīl 3

DIALOGUE +
dī′ ə läg′ 4*
dī′ ə lôg′ 4

DIALYSIS
dī al′ ə sis 2*
dī al′ i sis 1
dī al′ ə səs 1

DIAMETER
dī am′ ət ər 3*
dī am′ it ər 1

DIONYSIAN
dī′ ə nis′ ē ən   4*
dī′ ə nish′ ən   4
dī′ ə nizh′ ən   2
dī′ ə nī′ sē ən   2
dī′ ə niz′ ē ən   1

DIORAMA
dī′ ə räm′ ə   4*
dī′ ə ram′ ə   4

DIPHTHERIA ○
dif thir′ ē ə   4*
dip thir′ ē ə   4

DIPHTHONG +
dif′ thôŋ′   2
dip′ thôŋ′   2
dif′ thôŋ   2
dip′ thôŋ   2
dif′ thäŋ′   1*
dip′ thäŋ′   1
dif′ thäŋ   1
dip′ thäŋ   1

DIPLOMACY
di plō′ mə sē   3*
də plō′ mə sē   1

DIPLOMAT
dip′ lə mat′   4

DIPLOMATE
dip′ lə māt′   4

DIPTYCH
dip′ tik   4*

DIRE
dīr   3*
dī′ ′r   1

DIRECT
dī rekt′   4
di rekt′   3*
də rekt′   1

DIRGE
dʉrj   4

DIRIGIBLE
dir′ ə jə bəl   3*
di rij′ ə bəl   2
dir′ i jə b'l   1

DIRNDL
dʉrn′ d'l   4

DISASTER
di zas′ tər   4*
di zäs′ tər   3
di sas′ tər   1

DISASTROUS
di zas′ trəs   4*
di zäs′ trəs   3
di sas′ trəs   1

DISCARD (n)
dis′ kärd′   4

DISCARD (v)
dis kärd′   4*
dis′ kärd′   1

DISCERN
di zʉrn′   4*
di sʉrn′   4

DISCHARGE (n)
dis chärj′   3
dis′ chärj′   2*
dis′ chärj   2
dish′ chärj′   1
dish′ chärj′   1

PRONUNCIATION KEY

Symbol	Key words	Symbol	Key words	Symbol	Key words
a	asp, fat, parrot	†ə	a in ago	r	red, port, dear
ā	ape, date, play		e in agent	s	sell, castle, pass
†ä	ah, car, father		i in sanity	t	top, cattle, hat
e	elf, ten, berry		o in comply	v	vat, hovel, have
ē	even, meet, money		u in focus	w	will, always, swear
i	is, hit, mirror	ər	perhaps, murder	y	yet, onion, yard
ī	ice, bite, high	b	bed, fable, dub	z	zebra, dazzle, haze
ō	open, tone, go	d	dip, beadle, had	ch	chin, catcher, arch
ô	all, horn, law	f	fall, after, off	sh	she, cushion, dash
o͞o	ooze, tool, crew	g	get, haggle, dog	th	thin, nothing, truth
oo	look, pull, moor	h	he, ahead, hotel	th	then, father, lathe
yo͞o	use, cute, few	j	joy, agile, badge	zh	azure, leisure
yoo	united, cure, globule	k	kill, tackle, bake	ŋ	ring, anger, drink
oi	oil, point, toy	l	let, yellow, ball	″	see p. 15.
ou	out, crowd, plow	m	met, camel, trim	∕	see p. 15.
u	up, cut, color	n	not, flannel, ton	+	see p. 14.
ʉr	urn, fur, deter	p	put, apple, tap	′	see p. 15.
†See p. 14.		†See p. 16.		○	see p. 14.

DISCHARGE (v)
dis chärj′ 4*
dish chärj′ 1
dis′ chärj′ 1
dish′ chärj′ 1

DISCIPLE
di sī′ pəl 3*
di sī′ p'l 1

DISCIPLINARY ✓
dis′ ə plə ner′ ē 3*
dis′ ə pli ner′ ē 1

DISCIPLINE
dis′ ə plin 3*
dis′ ə plən 1

DISCOGRAPHY +
dis käg′ rə fē 4

DISCOMFIT
dis kum′ fit 3*
dis kum′ fət 1

DISCOMFITURE
dis kum′ fi chər 2*
dis kum′ fi choor′ 1
dis kum′ fə choor′ 1
dis kump′ fə choor′ 1
dis kum′ fə chər 1
dis kum′ fə toor′ 1
dis kum′ fə tyoor′ 1

DISCONCERT
dis′ kən surt′ 4

DISCONSOLATE +
dis kän′ sə lit 3*
dis kän′ slət 1
dis känt′ slət 1

DISCONTENT
dis kən tent′ 4

DISCORD
dis′ kôrd 3
dis′ kôrd′ 2*

DISCORDANT
dis kôr′ d'nt 3*
dis kôr′ dənt 1

DISCOTHEQUE
dis′ kə tek′ 3*
dis kə tek′ 1
dis′ kō tek′ 1
dis′ kō tek′ 1
dis′ kə tek 1

DISCOUNT (n)
dis′ kount 3*
dis′ kount′ 1

DISCOUNT (v)
dis kount′ 4*
dis′ kount′ 2
dis′ kount 2

DISCOURSE (n)
dis′ kôrs 3*
dis′ kōrs 3
dis′ kôrs′ 2
dis′ kōrs′ 2

DISCOURSE (v)
dis kôrs′ 4*
dis kōrs′ 3
dis′ kôrs′ 1
dis′ kōrs′ 1

DISCREET
dis krēt′ 4

DISCREPANCY
dis krep′ ən sē 4

DISCRETE
dis krēt′ 4*
dis′ krēt′ 1

DISCRETION
dis kresh′ ən 4

DISCRIMINATE
dis krim′ ə nāt′ 4

DISCURSIVE
dis kur′ siv 4

DISCUS
dis′ kəs 4

DISCUSS
dis kus′ 4

DISEASE
di zēz′ 4

DISGRACE
dis grās′ 4

DISGUISE
dis gīz′ 4*
dis kīz′ 1

DISGUST
dis gust′ 4*
dis kust′ 1

DISHABILLE
dis′ ə bēl′ 4*
dis′ ə bē′ 3
dis′ ə bil′ 1

DISHEVELED
di shev′ əld 3*
di shev′ 'ld 1

DISINGENUOUS
dis′ in jen′ yoo əs 2*
dis′ in jen′ yoo wəs 1
dis′ 'n jen′ yə wəs 1

DISINTEGRATE
dis in′ tə grāt′ 4*

DISINTER
dis′ in tur′ 3*
dis′ 'n tur′ 1

DISMAL
diz′ məl 3*
diz′ m'l 1

DISPARAGE
dis par′ ij 4

DISPARATE
dis′ pər it   3*
dis par′ it   2
dis par′ ət   1
dis′ prət   1

DISPARITY
dis par′ ə tē   3*
dis par′ i tē   1

DISPOSSESS
dis′ pə zes′   4*
dis′ pə ses′   1

DISPUTANT
dis pyo͞ot′ ′nt   3
dis′ pyoot ənt   2
dis′ pyət ənt   1*
dis pyo͞ot′ ənt   1

DISPUTATIOUS
dis′ pyoo tā′ shəs   3*
dis′ pyə tā′ shəs   1

DISREPUTABLE
dis rep′ yə tə bəl   3*
dis rep′ yoo tə b′l   1

DISREPUTE
dis′ ri pyo͞ot′   4

DISSENT
di sent′   4

DISSIDENCE
dis′ ə dəns   3*
dis′ i d′ns   1
dis′ ə dənts   1

DISSIMULATE
di sim′ yə lāt′   4

DISSOLUTE
dis′ ə lo͞ot′   4*
dis′ ə lət   1

DISSOLVE   +
di zälv′   4*
di zôlv′   2

DISSONANT
dis′ ə nənt   4

DISSUADE
di swād′   4

DISTAFF
dis′ taf′   2*
dis′ taf   2
dis′ täf   2
dis′ täf′   1

DISTEMPER
dis tem′ pər   4

DISTICH
dis′ tik   4*
dis′ tik′   1

DISTILLATE
dis′ tə lāt′   3
dis′ t′ lit   2*
dis til′ it   2
dis′ t′ lāt′   1
dis′ tə lət   1

DISTILLATION
dis′ tə lā′ shən   4*

DISTINGUÉ
dis′ taŋ gā′   3*
di staŋ′ gā   3
dis taŋ gā′   1
dēs′ taŋ′ gā′   1

PRONUNCIATION KEY

Symbol	Key words	Symbol	Key words	Symbol	Key words
a	asp, fat, parrot	†ə	a in ago	r	red, port, dear
ā	ape, date, play		e in agent	s	sell, castle, pass
†ä	ah, car, father		i in sanity	t	top, cattle, hat
e	elf, ten, berry		o in comply	v	vat, hovel, have
ē	even, meet, money		u in focus	w	will, always, swear
i	is, hit, mirror	ər	perhaps, murder	y	yet, onion, yard
ī	ice, bite, high	b	bed, fable, dub	z	zebra, dazzle, haze
ō	open, tone, go	d	dip, beadle, had	ch	chin, catcher, arch
ô	all, horn, law	f	fall, after, off	sh	she, cushion, dash
o͞o	ooze, tool, crew	g	get, haggle, dog	th	thin, nothing, truth
oo	look, pull, moor	h	he, ahead, hotel	th	then, father, lathe
yo͞o	use, cute, few	j	joy, agile, badge	zh	azure, leisure
yoo	united, cure, globule	k	kill, tackle, bake	ŋ	ring, anger, drink
oi	oil, point, toy	l	let, yellow, ball	″	see p. 15.
ou	out, crowd, plow	m	met, camel, trim	✓	see p. 15.
u	up, cut, color	n	not, flannel, ton	+	see p. 14.
ʉr	urn, fur, deter	p	put, apple, tap	′	see p. 15.
†See p. 14.		†See p. 16.		○	see p. 14.

DISTRAUGHT
dis trôt′ 4

DISTRIBUTE
dis trib′ yoot 2*
dis trib′ yo͞ot 1
dis trib′ yət 1

DISTRIBUTION
dis′ trə byo͞o′ shən 4

DITHER
di*th* ər 4

DITHYRAMB
dit*h*′ i ram′ 2*
dit*h*′ i ramb′ 2
dit*h*′ ə ram′ 2
dit*h*′ ə ramb′ 2

DIURETIC
dī′ yoo ret′ ik 3*
dī ə ret′ ik 1
dī yə ret′ ik 1

DIURNAL
dī ʉr′ n′l 3*
dī ʉr′ nəl 1

DIVA
dē′ və 3*
dē′ vä 1

DIVAGATE
dī′ və gāt′ 4

DIVAN
di van′ 4
di vän′ 3
dī′ van′ 2*

DIVERGENT
də vʉr′ jənt 3*
dī vʉr′ jənt 2
di vʉr′ jənt 1

DIVERS
dī′ vərz 4

DIVERSE
di vʉrs′ 3*
dī′ vʉrs′ 3
dī′ vʉrs 2
də vʉrs′ 1

DIVERSITY
də vʉr′ sə tē 3*
dī vʉr′ sə tē 2
di vʉr′ si tē 1
dī vʉr′ si tē 1

DIVERT
dī vʉrt′ 4
di vʉrt′ 2*
də vʉrt′ 2

DIVEST
dī vest′ 4
di vest′ 2*
də vest′ 2

DIVINATION
div′ ə nā′ shən 4

DIVINITY
də vin′ ə tē 3
di vin′ i tē 1*

DIVISIBLE
di viz′ ə bəl 3*
də viz′ ə b′l 1
də viz′ ə bəl 1

DIVISIVE
də vī′ siv 2*
di vī′ siv 2
də vis′ iv 2
də viz′ iv 1

DIVORCÉE
di vôr sā′ 2
di vōr sā′ 2
di vôr sē′ 1*
di vôr′ sā′ 1
di vōr′ sā′ 1
di vōr sē′ 1
di vôr′ sē′ 1
di vōr′ sē′ 1
də vôr sā′ 1
də vôr sē′ 1
də vôr′ sā 1
də vôr′ sē 1
də vōr sē′ 1
də vōr′ sē′ 1

DIVOT
div′ ət 4

DIVULGE
di vulj′ 2*
də vulj′ 2
dī vulj′ 1

DO (music)
dō 4

DOCENT
dō′ s′nt 3*
dō′ sənt 2
dō sent′ 2

DOCILE   +
däs′ əl 3*
däs′ 'l 1
däs′ il′ 1

DOCTORATE   +
däk′ tər it 3*
däk′ trət 1

DOCTRINAIRE   + ✓
däk′ trə ner′ 4

DOCTRINAL   +
däk′ trə nəl 2*
däk′ trə n′l 2

DOCUMENTARY   +
däk′ yə men′ tə rē 4

DODO
dō' dō 4*
dō' dō' 1

DOFF +
däf 4*
dôf 4

DOG +
dôg 4*
däg 3

DOGE
dōj 4

DOGGED (adj) +
dôg' id 3
däg' id 2*
dôg' əd 1

DOGGEREL +
däg' ər əl 4*
dôg' ər əl 4
dôg' rəl 1
däg' rəl 1

DOGIE
dō' gē 4

DOGMA +
dôg' mə 4*
däg' mə 4

DOGMATIC +
dôg mat' ik 4*
däg mat' ik 4

DOGMATISM +
dôg' mə tiz' əm 4*
däg' mə tiz' əm 4

DOILY
doi' lē 4

DOLDRUMS +
dōl' drəmz 3*
däl' drəmz 3
dōl' drəmz' 1
dôl' drəmz' 1
däl' drəmz' 1
dôl' drəmz 1

DOLMAN +
dōl' mən 3*
däl' mən 3
dôl' mən 1

DOLMEN +
däl' mən 4
dōl' mən 3*
dōl' men 1
däl' men 1
dôl' mən 1

DOLOR +
dō' lər 4*
dä' lər 1

DOLOROUS +
dō' lər əs 4*
däl' ər əs 4

DOLPHIN +
däl' fin 2*
dôl' fin 2
däl' fən 2
dôl' fən 2

DOLT
dōlt 4

DOMAIN
dō mān' 4*
də mān' 2

PRONUNCIATION KEY

Symbol	Key words	Symbol	Key words	Symbol	Key words
a	asp, fat, parrot	†ə	a in ago	r	red, port, dear
ā	ape, date, play		e in agent	s	sell, castle, pass
†ä	ah, car, father		i in sanity	t	top, cattle, hat
e	elf, ten, berry		o in comply	v	vat, hovel, have
ē	even, meet, money		u in focus	w	will, always, swear
i	is, hit, mirror	ər	perhaps, murder	y	yet, onion, yard
ī	ice, bite, high	b	bed, fable, dub	z	zebra, dazzle, haze
ō	open, tone, go	d	dip, beadle, had	ch	chin, catcher, arch
ô	all, horn, law	f	fall, after, off	sh	she, cushion, dash
ōō	ooze, tool, crew	g	get, haggle, dog	th	thin, nothing, truth
oo	look, pull, moor	h	he, ahead, hotel	th	then, father, lathe
yōō	use, cute, few	j	joy, agile, badge	zh	azure, leisure
yoo	united, cure, globule	k	kill, tackle, bake	ŋ	ring, anger, drink
oi	oil, point, toy	l	let, yellow, ball	"	see p. 15.
ou	out, crowd, plow	m	met, camel, trim	✓	see p. 15.
u	up, cut, color	n	not, flannel, ton	+	see p. 14.
ʉr	urn, fur, deter	p	put, apple, tap	'	see p. 15.
†See p. 14.		†See p. 16.		○	see p. 14.

DOMICILE +
dō′ mə sīl 3*
däm′ ə sīl′ 3
däm′ ə səl 2
dō′ mə səl 2
dō′ mi səl 2
däm′ i sīl′ 1
däm′ i səl 1
dō′ mi sīl′ 1
däm′ ə sil 1

DOMINANT +
däm′ ə nənt 4

DOMINIE +
däm′ ə nē 3*
dō′ mə nē 3
däm′ ə nē′ 1
dō′ mə nē′ 1

DOMINO +
däm′ ə nō′ 3

DONATE
dō nāt′ 3
dō′ nāt 3*
dō′ nāt′ 2

DON JUAN +
dän wän′ 3*
dän jōō′ ən 3
dän′ wän′ 1
dän′ hwän′ 1

DONKEY +
duŋ′ kē 4*
däŋ′ kē 4
dôŋ′ kē 3

DONOR
dō′ nər 4*
dō′ nôr 1

DON QUIXOTE +
dän′ kē hō′ tē 3*
dän kwik′ sət 3
dän′ kwik′ sət 1
dän′ kē ōt′ ē 1

DOSAGE
dōs′ ij 4

DOSSIER +
däs′ ē ā′ 4
dôs′ yā 2*
dôs′ ē ā′ 2
däs′ ē ər 1
dôs′ ē ər 1
däs′ yā 1

DOTAGE
dōt′ ij 4

DOTARD
dōt′ ərd 4

DOTH
duth 3

DOUCHE
dōōsh 4

DOUGHTY
dout′ ē 4

DOUR
dŏor 4
dour 4
dou′ ər 2
dōōr 1*

DOUSE
dous 4

DOWAGER
dou′ ə jər 3*
dou′ i jər 1

DOWEL
dou′ əl 4*
doul 1

DOWRY
dou′ rē 4

DOYEN
doi′ ən 4*
doi en′ 2
doi′ en′ 1

DRACHMA
drak′ mə 4

DRACONIAN
drā kō′ nē ən 4*
drə kō′ nē ən 2

DRACONIC +
drā kän′ ik 4*
drə kän′ ik 1

DRAGOMAN
drag′ ə mən 4

DRAMA
drä′ mə 4*
dram′ ə 4

DRAMATIS PERSONAE
dram′ ə tis pər sō′ nē 3*
dräm′ ə tis pər sō′ nī′ 1
dräm′ ə tis pər sō′ nē 1
dram′ ə təs pər sō′ nē 1
dräm′ ə təs pər sō′ nē 1
dräm′ ə təs pər sō′ nī′ 1

DRAMATIST
dram′ ə tist 3
dräm′ ə tist 2*
dram′ ə təst 1
dräm′ ə təst 1

DRAUGHTS
drafts 4*
dräfts 3
drafs 1

DRIVEL
driv′ əl 3*
driv′ ′l 1

DROLL
drōl 4

DROMEDARY +✓
dräm′ ə der′ ē 3*
drum′ ə der′ ē 2
dräm′ i der′ ē 1
drum′ i der′ ē 1

DROSHKY   +
dräsh′ kē   4
drôsh′ kē   1*

DROSS   +
dräs   4*
drôs   4

DROUGHT
drout   4

DRUID
drōō′ id   3*
drōō′ əd   1

DUAL
dōō′ əl   4*
dyōō′ əl   4

DUBIETY
dōō bī′ ə tē   3*
dyōō bī′ ə tē   3
dōō bī′ i tē   1
dyōō bī′ i tē   1

DUBIOUS
dōō′ bē əs   4*
dyōō′ bē əs   4

DUCAL
dyōō′ kəl   3*
dōō′ kəl   3
dōō′ k'l   1
dyōō′ k'l   1

DUCAT
duk′ ət   4

DUCE
dōō′ chā   3*
dōō′ che   1
dōō′ chā′   1

DUCHESS
duch′ is   3*
duch′ əs   1

DUCHY
duch′ ē   4

DUCTILE
duk′ t'l   3*
duk′ til   2
duk′ tīl′   1

DUDE
dōōd   4*
dyōōd   3

DUDGEON
duj′ ən   4

DUE
dyōō   4*
dōō   4

DUEL
dyōō′ əl   4*
dōō′ əl   4

DUENNA
dōō en′ ə   4*
dyōō en′ ə   4

DUET
dōō et′   4*
dyōō et′   4

DUKE
dyōōk   4*
dōōk   4

DULCET
dul′ sit   3*
dul′ sət   1

DULCIMER
dul′ sə mər   4

PRONUNCIATION KEY

Symbol	Key words	Symbol	Key words	Symbol	Key words
a	asp, fat, parrot	†ə	a in ago	r	red, port, dear
ā	ape, date, play		e in agent	s	sell, castle, pass
†ä	ah, car, father		i in sanity	t	top, cattle, hat
e	elf, ten, berry		o in comply	v	vat, hovel, have
ē	even, meet, money		u in focus	w	will, always, swear
i	is, hit, mirror	ər	perhaps, murder	y	yet, onion, yard
ī	ice, bite, high	b	bed, fable, dub	z	zebra, dazzle, haze
ō	open, tone, go	d	dip, beadle, had	ch	chin, catcher, arch
ô	all, horn, law	f	fall, after, off	sh	she, cushion, dash
ōō	ooze, tool, crew	g	get, haggle, dog	th	thin, nothing, truth
oo	look, pull, moor	h	he, ahead, hotel	th	then, father, lathe
yōō	use, cute, few	j	joy, agile, badge	zh	azure, leisure
yoo	united, cure, globule	k	kill, tackle, bake	ŋ	ring, anger, drink
oi	oil, point, toy	l	let, yellow, ball	″	see p. 15.
ou	out, crowd, plow	m	met, camel, trim	✓	see p. 15.
u	up, cut, color	n	not, flannel, ton	+	see p. 14.
ʉr	urn, fur, deter	p	put, apple, tap	′	see p. 15.
†See p. 14.		†See p. 16.		○	see p. 14.

DULY
dyo͞o′ lē　4*
do͞o′ lē　4

DUNE
dyo͞on　4*
do͞on　4

DUNGEON
dun′ jən　4

DUO
do͞o′ ō　4*
dyo͞o′ ō　4
do͞o′ ō′　1
dyo͞o′ ō′　1

DUODENUM　+
do͞o äd′ 'n əm　4*
dyo͞o′ ə dē′ nəm　4
dyo͞o äd′ 'n əm　3
do͞o ə dē′ nəm　2
do͞o′ ə dē′ nəm　1

DUPE
dyo͞op　4*
do͞op　4

DUPLEX
do͞o′ pleks′　4*
dyo͞o′ pleks′　4

DUPLICATE (n, adj)
do͞o′ plə kit　2*
dyo͞o′ plə kit　2
do͞o′ pli kit　1
dyo͞o′ pli kit　1
do͞o′ pli kət　1
dyo͞o′ pli kət　1

DUPLICATE (v)
do͞o′ pli kāt′　2*
dyo͞o′ pli kāt′　2
do͞o′ plə kāt′　2
dyo͞o′ plə kāt′　2

DUPLICITY
do͞o plis′ ə tē　3*
dyo͞o plis′ ə tē　3
do͞o plis′ i tē　1
dyo͞o plis′ i tē　1

DURABLE
door′ ə bəl　4*
dyoor′ ə bəl　4

DURESS
doo res′　4*
dyoo res′　4
door′ is　3
dyoor′ is　3

DURUM
door′ əm　4*
dyoor′ əm　4
dur′ əm　1

DUTIFUL
dyo͞ot′ i fəl　3*
do͞ot′ i fəl　3
do͞ot′ ə fəl　1
dyo͞ot′ ə fəl　1

DUTY
dyo͞o′ tē　4*
do͞o′ tē　4

DYBBUK
dib′ ək　3

DYNAMIC
dī nam′ ik　4

DYNAMITE
dī′ nə mīt′　4

DYNAMO
dī′ nə mō′　4

DYNAST
dī′ nəst　4
dī′ nast′　2*
dī′ nast　2

DYNASTY
dī′ nəs tē　4

DYSENTERY　✓
dis′ 'n ter′ ē　2*
dis′ ən ter′ ē　2

DYSLEXIA
dis lek′ sē ə　3

DYSPEPSIA
dis pep′ sē ə　4*
dis pep′ shə　4

DYSTROPHY
dis′ trə fē　4

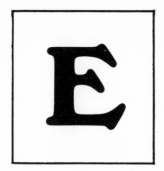

EASEL
ē′ zəl   3*
ē′ z′l   1

EAU DE COLOGNE
ō də kə lōn′   4

EBONY
eb′ ən ē   4

EBULLIENT
i bul′ yənt   3*
i bool yənt   2

ECCENTRIC
ik sen′ trik   4*
ek sen′ trik   3

ECCLESIASTIC
i klē′ zē as′ tik   4

ECDYSIAST
ek diz′ ē ast′   4*
ek diz′ ē əst   2

ECHELON   +
esh′ ə län   4

ÉCLAIR   ✓
ā kler′   4
ā′ kler   3*
i kler′   3

ÉCLAT
ā klä′   4*
i klä′   1

ECLECTIC
i klek′ tik   4*
e klek′ tik   1

ECLIPSE
i klips′   4*
ē klips′   1

ECLOGUE   +
ek′ läg′   3*
ek′ lôg′   2
ek′ lôg   1
ek′ läg   1

ECOLOGY   +
i käl′ ə jē   3*
ē käl′ ə jē   1
e käl′ ə jē   1

ECONOMICAL   +
ek′ ə näm′ i kəl   3*
ē′ kə näm′ i kəl   2
ē′ kə näm′ i k′l   1
ek′ kə näm′ i k′l   1

ECONOMICS   +
ek′ ə näm′ iks   4*
ē′ kə näm′ iks   4

ECONOMIST   +
i kän′ ə mist   3*
i kän′ ə məst   1

ECRU
ek′ rōō   4*
ā′ krōō   4

ECSTASY
ek′ stə sē   4

ECSTATIC
ek stat′ ik   4*
ik stat′ ik   2

ECUMENICAL
ek′ yoo men′ i kəl   2*
ek′ yoo men′ i k′l   1
ek′ yə men′ i kəl   1

ECZEMA
ig zē′ mə   4
ek′ sə mə   4
eg′ zə mə   4*
eg zē′ mə   1

EDELWEISS
ā′ d′l vīs′   3*
ā′ d′l wīs′   2
ā′ dəl vīs′   1

EDEMA
i dē′ mə   4

EDIBLE
ed′ ə bəl   3*
ed′ ə b'l   1

EDICT
ē dikt′   2*
ē dikt   2

EDIFICE
ed′ ə fis   3*
ed′ ə fəs   1

EDUCABLE
ej′ oo kə bəl   2
ej′ ə kə b'l   1*
ed′ yoo kə bəl   1
ej′ ə kə bəl   1

EDUCATION
ej′ ə kā′ shən   2*
ej′ oo kā′ shən   2
ed′ yoo kā′ shən   2

E'ER ✓
er   4*
ar   2

EFFACE
i fās′   4*
e fās′   2

EFFEMINATE
i fem′ ə nit   3*
ə fem′ ə nət   1

EFFERVESCENT
ef′ ər ves′ 'nt   2*
ef′ ər ves′ ənt   2

EFFETE
i fēt′   4*
e fēt′   2

EFFICACIOUS
ef′ ə kā′ shəs   4

EFFICACY
ef′ ə kə sē   2*
ef′ i kə sē   2

EFFIGY
ef′ ə jē   4

EFFLORESCENCE
ef′ lə res′ 'ns   2*
ef′ lô res′ əns   1
ef′ lə res′ əns   1
ef′ lô res′ 'ns   1

EFFLUENT
ef′ lōō ənt   3*
ef′ lōō wənt   1
ef′ lə wənt   1

EFFLUVIUM
i flōō′ vē əm   3*
e flōō′ vē əm   2

EFFRONTERY
i frun′ tər ē   4*
e frun′ tər ē   1

EFFULGENCE
i ful′ jəns   4*
e ful′ jəns   2
i fool′ jəns   1
e fool′ jəns   1

EFFUSIVE
i fyōō′ siv   4*
e fyōō′ siv   2
i fyōō′ ziv   1
e fyōō′ ziv   1

EGALITARIAN ✓
i gal′ ə ter′ ē ən   3*
i gal′ i ter′ ē ən   1
ē gal′ ə ter′ ē ən   1

EGO
ē′ gō   4*
eg′ ō   4

EGOCENTRIC
ē′ gō sen′ trik   4*
eg′ ō sen′ trik   4

EGOIST
ē′ gō ist   3*
eg′ ō ist   3
ē′ gə wəst   1
eg′ ə wəst   1

EGOTIST
ē′ gə tist   3*
eg′ ə tist   3
ē′ gə təst   1
eg′ ə təst   1

EGREGIOUS
i grē′ jəs   4*
i grē′ jē əs   3

EGRESS
ē′ gres   3*
e′ gres′   1

EGRET ✓
ē′ grit   3*
eg′ rit   3
ē′ grət   1
i gret′   1

EIDER
ī′ dər   4

EIGHTH
āt′ th   4*
āth   2

EITHER
ē′ thər   4*
ī′ thər   4

EJACULATE
i jak′ yə lāt′   4

EKE
ēk   4

ELABORATE (adj)
i lab′ ər it   3*
i lab′ rət   1

ELABORATE (v)
i lab′ ə rāt′   4

ÉLAN
ā län'   3*
ā lan'   1

ELAND
ē' land   2*
ē' lənd   2
ē' land'   1

ELECT
i lekt'   4

ELECTORAL
i lek' tər əl   4*
i lek' trəl   2

ELECTRICITY
i lek' tris' ə tē   3*
ē' lek tris' ə tē   2
i lek tris' i tē   1
i lek' tris' tē   1
ē' lek tris' i tē   1

ELECTROCUTE
i lek' trə kyo͞ot'   4

ELECTRODE
i lek' trōd'   2*
i lek' trōd   2

ELECTROLYSIS   +
i lek' träl' ə sis   2*
ē lek' träl' ə sis   1
i lek' träl' ə səs   1
i lek' träl' i sis   1

ELECTROLYTE
i lek' trə līt'   4

ELECTRON   +
i lek' trän'   2*
i lek' trän   2

ELECTRONIC   +
i lek' trän' ik   3*
ē' lek trän' ik   3
i lek trän' ik   1

ELEEMOSYNARY   +✓
el' ē ə mäs' ə ner' ē   3
el' ə mäs' ə ner' ē   2*
el' i mäs' ə ner' ē   2
el' ə mäz' ə ner' ē   1
el' i mäz' 'n er' ē   1

ELEGIAC
el' ə jī' ək   4*
i lē' jē ak'   4

ELEGY
el' ə jē   3*
el' i jē   1

ELEMENTARY   ✓
el' ə men' tər ē   4*
el' ə men' trē   4

ELEPHANTIASIS
el' ə fən tī' ə sis   3*
el' ə fən tī ə səs   1
el' ə fan' tī' ə səs   1

ELEPHANTINE
el' ə fan' tēn'   4
el' ə fan' tīn   3*
el' ə fan' tin'   2
el' ə fan' tin   1
el' ə fan' tīn'   1

ELICIT
i lis' it   3*
i lis' ət   1

ELIGIBLE
el' ə jə bəl   2
el' i jə b'l   1*
el' i jə bəl   1

PRONUNCIATION KEY

Symbol	Key words	Symbol	Key words	Symbol	Key words
a	asp, fat, parrot	†ə	a in ago	r	red, port, dear
ā	ape, date, play		e in agent	s	sell, castle, pass
†ä	ah, car, father		i in sanity	t	top, cattle, hat
e	elf, ten, berry		o in comply	v	vat, hovel, have
ē	even, meet, money		u in focus	w	will, always, swear
i	is, hit, mirror	ər	perhaps, murder	y	yet, onion, yard
ī	ice, bite, high	b	bed, fable, dub	z	zebra, dazzle, haze
ō	open, tone, go	d	dip, beadle, had	ch	chin, catcher, arch
ô	all, horn, law	f	fall, after, off	sh	she, cushion, dash
o͞o	ooze, tool, crew	g	get, haggle, dog	th	thin, nothing, truth
oo	look, pull, moor	h	he, ahead, hotel	th	then, father, lathe
yo͞o	use, cute, few	j	joy, agile, badge	zh	azure, leisure
yoo	united, cure, globule	k	kill, tackle, bake	ŋ	ring, anger, drink
oi	oil, point, toy	l	let, yellow, ball	''	see p. 15.
ou	out, crowd, plow	m	met, camel, trim	✓	see p. 15.
u	up, cut, color	n	not, flannel, ton	+	see p. 14.
ʉr	urn, fur, deter	p	put, apple, tap	'	see p. 15.
†See p. 14.		†See p. 16.		◯	see p. 14.

ELISION
i lizh′ ən 4

ELITE
ā lēt′ 4*
i lēt′ 4

ELIXIR
i lik′ sər 4

ELLIPSE
i lips′ 4*
ə lips 1
e lips 1

ELOCUTION
el ə kyōō′ shən 4

ELONGATE +
i lôŋ′ gāt′ 2
i lôŋ′ gāt 2*
i läŋ′ gāt′ 2
ē lôŋ gāt′ 1
ē′ läŋ gāt′ 1

ELOQUENT
el′ ə kwənt 4

ELUCIDATE
i lōō′ sə dāt′ 4
i lōō′ si dāt′ 1*
ə lōō′ sə dāt′ 1

ELUDE
i lōōd′ 3*
ē lōōd′ 1

ELUSIVE
i lōō′ siv 3*
ē lōō′ siv 1
ē lōō′ ziv 1

ELYSIUM
i liz′ ē əm 4*
i lizh′ ē əm 3
i lē′ zhē əm 1
i lē′ zē əm 1

EMACIATE
i mā′ shē āt′ 4*
i mā′ sē āt′ 1

EMANATE
em′ ə nāt′ 4

EMANCIPATE
i man′ sə pāt′ 4*
i mant′ sə pāt′ 1

EMASCULATE
i mas′ kyə lāt′ 4

EMBALM
im bäm′ 3
em bäm′ 2*

EMBARGO
im bär′ gō 3
em bär′ gō 2*

EMBARK
em bärk′ 2*
im bärk′ 2

EMBARRASS ✓
em bar′ əs 2*
im bar′ əs 2
em ber′ əs 1

EMBASSY
em′ bə sē 4

EMBELLISH
im bel′ ish 3
em bel′ ish 2*

EMBEZZLE
em bez′ əl 2*
im bez′ əl 2
im bez′ ′l 1

EMBLAZON
em blā′ zən 2*
im blā′ z′n 2
im blā′ zən 1

EMBLEM
em′ bləm 4

EMBLEMATIC
em′ blə mat′ ik 4

EMBODIMENT +
em bäd′ i mənt 2
em bäd′ ē mənt 1*
im bäd′ i mənt 1
im bäd′ ē mənt 1

EMBOLISM
em′ bə liz′ əm 3*
em′ bə liz′m 1

EMBOLUS
em′ bə ləs 4

EMBOSS +
im bôs′ 3
im bäs′ 3
em bôs′ 2*
em bäs′ 2

EMBOUCHURE
äm′ boo shoor′ 4*
am′ boo shoor′ 2

EMBRASURE
im brā′ zhər 3
em brā′ zhər 2*

EMBROCATE
em′ brō kāt′ 3
em′ brə kāt′ 2*

EMBROIDER
im broi′ dər 3
em broi′ dər 2*

EMBROIDERY
em broi′ də rē 3*
im broi′ də rē 3
im broid′ rē 1

EMBRYO
em′ brē ō′ 4

EMBRYONIC +
em′ brē än′ ik 4

EMEND
i mend′ 3
ē mend′ 1*

EMENDATION
ē′ men dā′ shən 3*
em′ ən dā′ shən 3
ē′ mən dā′ shən 1
i men′ dā′ shən 1

EMERALD
em′ rəld 4
em′ ər əld 3*

EMERITUS
i mer′ ə təs 3*
i mer′ i təs 1

EMERY
em′ ər ē 4*
em′ rē 4

EMETIC
i met′ ik 3*
ə met′ ik 1

EMIGRÉ
em′ ə grā′ 2
em′ i grā 1*
ā mə grā′ 1
em′ i grā′ 1

EMIR ○
i mir′ 2
ə mir′ 1*
e mir′ 1
ā mir′ 1

EMISSARY ✓
em′ ə ser′ ē 3*
em′ i ser′ ē 1

EMIT
i mit′ 3*
ē mit′ 1

EMOLLIENT +
i mäl′ yənt 4*
i mäl ē ənt 2

EMOLUMENT +
i mäl′ yə mənt 3*
i mäl′ yoo mənt 1

EMPATHY
em′ pə thē 4

EMPHYSEMA
em′ fə sē′ mə 3*
em′ fi sē′ mə 1
em′ fi zē′ mə 1
em′ fə zē′ mə 1

EMPIRE
em′ pīr′ 3*
em′ pī ər 2

EMPIRICAL ○
em pir′ i kəl 2*
im pir′ i kəl 2
em pir′ i k'l 1

EMPLOYEE
em ploi′ ē 3*
im ploi′ ē 2
im plô ē′ 1
em plô ē′ 1
im plô′ ē 1
em plô′ ē′ 1

PRONUNCIATION KEY

Symbol	Key words	Symbol	Key words	Symbol	Key words
a	asp, fat, parrot	†ə	a in ago	r	red, port, dear
ā	ape, date, play		e in agent	s	sell, castle, pass
†ä	ah, car, father		i in sanity	t	top, cattle, hat
e	elf, ten, berry		o in comply	v	vat, hovel, have
ē	even, meet, money		u in focus	w	will, always, swear
i	is, hit, mirror	ər	perhaps, murder	y	yet, onion, yard
ī	ice, bite, high	b	bed, fable, dub	z	zebra, dazzle, haze
ō	open, tone, go	d	dip, beadle, had	ch	chin, catcher, arch
ô	all, horn, law	f	fall, after, off	sh	she, cushion, dash
o͞o	ooze, tool, crew	g	get, haggle, dog	th	thin, nothing, truth
oo	look, pull, moor	h	he, ahead, hotel	th	then, father, lathe
yo͞o	use, cute, few	j	joy, agile, badge	zh	azure, leisure
yoo	united, cure, globule	k	kill, tackle, bake	ŋ	ring, anger, drink
oi	oil, point, toy	l	let, yellow, ball	″	see p. 15.
ou	out, crowd, plow	m	met, camel, trim	✓	see p. 15.
u	up, cut, color	n	not, flannel, ton	+	see p. 14.
ur	urn, fur, deter	p	put, apple, tap	′	see p. 15.
†See p. 14.		†See p. 16.		○	see p. 14.

EMPORIUM
em pôr′ ē əm 4*
em pōr′ ē əm 3
im pôr′ ē əm 2
im pōr′ ē əm 2

EMPYREAN ○
em′ pī rē′ ən 4*
em′ pə rē′ ən 2
em′ pir′ ē ən 2

EMU
ē′ myōō 4

EMULATE
em′ yə lāt′ 4

EMULSION
i mul′ shən 4

ENAMOR
in am′ ər 3*
en am′ ər 1

ENCEPHALITIS
en sef′ ə līt′ is 3*
en′ sef ə līt′ is 2
in sef′ ə līt′ əs 1

ENCHILADA
en′ chə lä′ də 4*
en′ chə la′ də 1

ENCLAVE
en′ klāv 4*
än′ klāv 2

ENCOMIUM
en kō′ mē əm 4

ENCOMPASS
in kum′ pəs 3
en kum′ pəs 2*

ENCORE
än′ kôr 2*
än′ kōr′ 2
än′ kôr′ 2
äŋ′ kôr 2
äŋ′ kōr 1
äŋ′ kôr′ 1
än kôr′ 1

ENCYCLICAL
en sik′ li kəl 3*
in sik′ li kəl 2
in sik′ li k'l 1
en sī′ kli kəl 1

ENCYCLOPEDIA
in sī′ klə pē′ dē ə 3
en sī′ klə pē′ dē ə 2*

ENDEAVOR
in dev′ ər 4

ENDEMIC
en dem′ ik 4

ENDIVE
än dēv 2*
en′ dīv 2
än′ dēv′ 1

ENDOCRINE
en′ də krēn′ 4
en′ də krīn′ 4
en′ də krin 3*
en′ də krən 1

ENDURANCE
in door′ əns 3
en door′ əns 2*
en dyoor′ əns 2
in dyoor′ əns 2

ENDURE
in door′ 3
en door′ 2
en dyoor′ 2*
in dyoor′ 2

ENEMA
en′ ə mə 4

ENERVATE
en′ ər vāt′ 4

ENFILADE
en′ fə lād′ 3
en′ fə lād′ 3
en′ fə läd′ 1*

ENGENDER
in jen′ dər 3
en jen′ dər 2*

ENGINE
en′ jən 4

ENHANCE
en hans′ 3*
en häns′ 3
in hans′ 2
in hants′ 1

ENIGMA
ə nig′ mə 2*
i nig′ mə 2

ENIGMATIC
en′ ig mat′ ik 4

EN MASSE
en mas′ 3
än mas′ 1*

ENMITY
en′ mə tē 3*
en′ mi tē 1

ENNUI
än′ wē 2*
än wē′ 1
an′ wē′ 1

ENORMOUS
i nôr′ məs 3*
e nôr′ məs 1

ENOUGH
i nuf′ 4

EN ROUTE
än root' 3*
en root' 1

ENSCONCE   +
in skäns' 3
en skäns' 2*
in skänts' 1

ENSEMBLE
än säm' bəl 3*
än säm' b'l 1

ENSIGN
(badge, flag, banner)
en' sīn' 2*
en' sīn 2

ENSIGN (naval officer)
en' sən 3
en' s'n 1*

ENSILAGE
en' sə lij 2*
en' s'l ij 1
en' slij 1

ENSUE
in soo' 3
en soo' 2*
in syoo' 1

ENTENTE
än tänt' 4

ENTERIC
en ter' ik 4

ENTERPRISE
en' tər prīz' 4*
en' tə prīz' 1

ENTIRE
in tīr' 4
en tīr' 3*
en tī' ər 2
in tī' ər 1

ENTIRETY
in tīr' te 2
in tī' rə te 2
en tī' 'r te 1*
en tī' rə te 1

ENTITY
en' tə te 3*
en' ti te 1

ENTOURAGE
an' too räzh' 4*
ant' ə räzh' 1

ENTR' ACTE
än trakt' 3*
än' trakt 1

ENTRAILS
en' trəlz 4
en' trālz 3*

ENTRANCE (n)
en' trəns 4*
en' trənts 1

ENTRANCE (v)
in trans' 3
en trans' 2*
en träns' 2
in träns' 2

ENTRÉE
än' trā 3*
än' trā' 1

PRONUNCIATION KEY

Symbol	Key words	Symbol	Key words	Symbol	Key words
a	asp, fat, parrot	†ə	a in ago	r	red, port, dear
ā	ape, date, play		e in agent	s	sell, castle, pass
†ä	ah, car, father		i in sanity	t	top, cattle, hat
e	elf, ten, berry		o in comply	v	vat, hovel, have
ē	even, meet, money		u in focus	w	will, always, swear
i	is, hit, mirror	ər	perhaps, murder	y	yet, onion, yard
ī	ice, bite, high	b	bed, fable, dub	z	zebra, dazzle, haze
ō	open, tone, go	d	dip, beadle, had	ch	chin, catcher, arch
ô	all, horn, law	f	fall, after, off	sh	she, cushion, dash
oo	ooze, tool, crew	g	get, haggle, dog	th	thin, nothing, truth
oo	look, pull, moor	h	he, ahead, hotel	th	then, father, lathe
yoo	use, cute, few	j	joy, agile, badge	zh	azure, leisure
yoo	united, cure, globule	k	kill, tackle, bake	ŋ	ring, anger, drink
oi	oil, point, toy	l	let, yellow, ball	''	see p. 15.
ou	out, crowd, plow	m	met, camel, trim	⎷	see p. 15.
u	up, cut, color	n	not, flannel, ton	+	see p. 14.
ur	urn, fur, deter	p	put, apple, tap	'	see p. 15.
†See p. 14.		†See p. 16.		◯	see p. 14.

ENTREPRENEUR
än′ trə prə nʉr′ 3*
än′ trə prə noor′ 2
än′ trə prə nyoor′ 1

ENUCLEATE
i nōō′ klē āt′ 3*
i nyōō′ klē āt′ 3
ē nōō′ klē āt′ 1

ENUMERATE
i nōō′ mə rāt′ 4*
i nyōō′ mə rāt′ 4

ENUNCIATE
i nun′ sē āt′ 3*
i nun′ shē āt′ 2
ē nun′ sē āt′ 1
ē nunt′ sē āt′ 1

ENURESIS
en′ yə rē′ sis 2*
en′ yoo rē′ sis 1
en′ yoo rē′ səs 1

ENURETIC
en′ yoo ret′ ik 3
en′ yə ret′ ik 1*

ENVELOP
in vel′ əp 3
en vel′ əp 2*

ENVELOPE
en′ və lōp′ 4*
än′ və lōp′ 4

ENVIRONMENT
in vī′ rən mənt 3
en vī′ rən mənt 2*
en vī′ ərn mənt 1
in vī′ ərn mənt 1
in vīrn′ mənt 1

ENVIRONS
in vī′ rənz 3
en′ vər ənz 3
en vī′ rənz 2*
in vī′ ərnz 2
en vī′ ərnz 1

ENVISAGE
en viz′ ij 3*
in viz′ ij 2

ENVOY
än′ voi 3*
en′ voi 3
en′ voi′ 1

ENZYME
en′ zīm′ 3*
en′ zīm 1

EON +
ē′ ən 4
ē′ än 2*

EPAULET
ep′ ə let′ 4*
ep′ ə let′ 3
ep′ ə lit 1
ep′ ə lət 1

ÉPÉE
ā pā′ 4*
e pā′ 1
ep′ ā 1

EPERGNE ✓
i pʉrn′ 4*
ā pern′ 3
ā pʉrn′ 1

EPHEDRINE
i fed′ rin 3*
i fed′ rən 1
ef′ ə drēn′ 1
ef′ i drin 1
ef′ i drēn′ 1

EPHEMERAL
i fem′ ər əl 4*
i fem′ rəl 1

EPICENE
ep′ ə sēn′ 3*
ep′ i sēn′ 1

EPICURE
ep′ i kyoor′ 3*
ep′ ə kyoor′ 1

EPICUREAN
ep′ i kyoo rē′ ən 3*
ep′ ə kyoo rē′ ən 1
ep′ ə kyoor′ ē ən 1
ep′ i kyoor′ ē ən 1

EPIDEMIOLOGY +
ep′ ə dē′ mē äl′ ə jē 3*
ep′ ə dem′ ē äl′ ə jē 3
ep′ i dē′ mē äl′ ə jē 1

EPIDERMIS
ep′ ə dʉr′ mis 3*
ep′ i dʉr′ mis 1

EPILEPSY
ep′ ə ləp′ sē 4

EPILEPTIC
ep′ ə lep′ tik 4

EPILOGUE +
ep′ ə läg′ 4*
ep′ ə lôg′ 4

EPIPHANY
i pif′ ə nē 4

EPISCOPAL
i pis′ kə pəl 4

EPISODE
ep′ ə sōd′ 3*
ep′ ə zōd′ 1
ep′ i sōd′ 1
ep′ i zōd′ 1

EPISODIC +
ep′ ə säd′ ik 3*
ep′ i säd′ ik 1
ep′ i zäd′ ik 1

EPISTLE
i pis′ əl 3*
i pis′ ′l 1

EPISTOLARY ✓
i pis' tə ler' ē   4

EPITAPH
ep' ə taf'   3*
ep' ə täf'   2
ep' i taf'   1
ep' i täf'   1

EPITHELIUM
ep' ə thē' lē əm   4

EPITHET
ep' ə thet'   4*
ep' ə thət   2

EPITOME
i pit' ə mē   4

EPOCH   +
ep' ək   4*
ep' äk'   1
ē' päk'   1

EPOCHAL   +
ep' ə kəl   3*
ep' äk' əl   1

EPONYMOUS   +
i pän' ə məs   3*
ə pän' ə məs   2

EPOXY   +
i päk' sē   2*
e päk' sē   1
ep' äk' sē   1

EQUABLE
ē' kwə bəl   3*
ek' wə bəl   3
ek' wə b'l   1
ē' kwə b'l   1

EQUANIMITY
ē' kwə nim' ə tē   3*
ek' wə nim' ə tē   3
ek' wə nim' i tē   1
ē' kwə nim' i tē   1

EQUATE
i kwāt'   4*
ē' kwāt'   1

EQUATION
i kwā' zhən   4*
i kwā' shən   3

EQUATOR
i kwāt' ər   4*
ē kwāt' ər   1

EQUATORIAL
ek' wə tôr' ē əl   4
ē' kwə tôr' ē əl   3*
ē' kwə tōr' ē əl   3
ek' wə tōr' ē əl   3

EQUERRY
ek' wər ē   4*
i kwer' ē   1

EQUESTRIAN
i kwes' trē ən   4

EQUESTRIENNE
i kwes' trē en'   4

EQUILIBRIUM
ē' kwə lib' rē əm   4*
ek' wə lib' rē əm   1

EQUINE
ē' kwīn'   2*
ē' kwīn   2
ek' wīn   1
ek' wīn'   1

PRONUNCIATION KEY

Symbol	Key words	Symbol	Key words	Symbol	Key words
a	asp, fat, parrot	†ə	a in ago	r	red, port, dear
ā	ape, date, play		e in agent	s	sell, castle, pass
†ä	ah, car, father		i in sanity	t	top, cattle, hat
e	elf, ten, berry		o in comply	v	vat, hovel, have
ē	even, meet, money		u in focus	w	will, always, swear
i	is, hit, mirror	ər	perhaps, murder	y	yet, onion, yard
ī	ice, bite, high	b	bed, fable, dub	z	zebra, dazzle, haze
ō	open, tone, go	d	dip, beadle, had	ch	chin, catcher, arch
ô	all, horn, law	f	fall, after, off	sh	she, cushion, dash
oo	ooze, tool, crew	g	get, haggle, dog	th	thin, nothing, truth
oo	look, pull, moor	h	he, ahead, hotel	th	then, father, lathe
yoo	use, cute, few	j	joy, agile, badge	zh	azure, leisure
yoo	united, cure, globule	k	kill, tackle, bake	ŋ	ring, anger, drink
oi	oil, point, toy	l	let, yellow, ball	''	see p. 15.
ou	out, crowd, plow	m	met, camel, trim	✓	see p. 15.
u	up, cut, color	n	not, flannel, ton	+	see p. 14.
ʉr	urn, fur, deter	p	put, apple, tap	'	see p. 15.
†See p. 14.		†See p. 16.		○	see p. 14.

EQUINOCTIAL   +
ē′ kwə näk′ shəl   4*
ek′ wə näk′ shəl   2

EQUINOX   +
ē′ kwə näks′   4*
ek′ wə näks′   3

EQUIPAGE
ek′ wə pij   4

EQUIPOISE
ē′ kwə poiz′   4
ek′ wə poiz′   4*

EQUITABLE
ek′ wət ə bəl   2
ek′ wit ə b'l   1*
ek′ wit ə bəl   1

EQUITY
ek′ wət ē   3
ek′ wit ē   1*

EQUIVOCAL
i kwiv′ ə kəl   3*
i kwiv′ ə k'l   1

EQUIVOCATE
i kwiv′ ə kāt′   4

ERA   ○
ir′ ə   4*
er′ ə   4

ERASURE
i rā′ shər   4*
i rā′ zhər   1

ERE   ✓
er   4*
ar   1

EREMITE
er′ ə mīt′   4

ERG
ʉrg   4

ERGO   ✓
ʉr′ gō   4*
er′ gō   3

ERGOT   +
ʉr′ gət   4*
ʉr′ gät   2

ERMINE
ʉr′ min   2*
ʉr′ mən   2

EROGENOUS   +
i räj′ ə nəs   4

EROTIC   +
i rät′ ik   4

EROTICA   +
i rät′ i kə   4

ERR   ✓
ʉr′   4*
er′   4

ERRANT   ✓
er′ ənt   4

ERRATIC
i rat′ ik   4

ERRATUM
e rät′ əm   2*
e rāt′ əm   2
e rat′ əm   2
i rät′ əm   1
i rāt′ əm   1

ERRONEOUS
e rō′ nē əs   3
ə rō′ nē əs   2*
i rō′ nē əs   2

ERROR   ✓
er′ ər   4

ERSATZ   ✓
er′ zäts   3*
er zäts′   2
ʉr′ zäts   1
er′ zäts′   1

ERUDITE   ✓
er′ yoo dīt′   3*
er′ oo dīt′   3
er′ ə dīt′   1
er′ yə dīt′   1

ERUDITION   ✓
er′ oo dish′ ən   3
er′ yoo dish′ ən   2*
er′ yoo dish′ ən   1
er′ ə dish′ ən   1
er′ yə dish′ ən   1

ESCADRILLE
es′ kə dril′   3
es′ kə dril′   1*
es′ kə drē′   1

ESCALATOR
es′ kə lāt′ ər   4

ESCAPADE
es′ kə pād′   4*
es′ kə pād′   1

ESCAROLE
es′ kə rōl′   4

ESCHATOLOGY   +
es′ kə täl′ ə jē   4

ESCHEW
es choo′   3*
is choo′   1

ESCORT (n)
es′ kôrt′   3*
es′ kôrt   1

ESCORT (v)
e skôrt′   3*
i skôrt′   2
e′ skôrt′   1

ESCRITOIRE
es' kri twär' 2*
es' krə twär' 1
es' krə twär' 1

ESCROW
es' krō 4*
es krō' 2
es' krō' 1
is krō' 1

ESCUTCHEON
e skuch' ən 2*
i skuch' ən 2

ESOPHAGUS +
i säf' ə gəs 4*
ē säf' ə gəs 1

ESOTERIC
es' ə ter' ik 4

ESPADRILLE
es' pə dril' 4

ESPALIER
es pal' yər 3
is pal' yā' 2*
is pal' yər 2
es pal' yā' 1

ESPERANTO
es' pə ran' tō 4
es' pə rän' tō 3*

ESPIONAGE
es' pē ə näzh' 4*
es' pē ə nij' 4
es' pē ə näzh' 1
es' pē ə näj' 1
is pē' ə nij 1

ESPLANADE
es' plə näd' 2*
es' plə nād' 2
es' plə nād' 2
es' plə näd' 2

ESPOUSE
i spouz' 3
e spouz' 2*
i spous' 1

ESPRESSO
es pres' ō 4*
es pres' ō' 1
is pres' ō 1

ESPRIT
es prē' 3*
is prē' 1

ESPRIT DE CORPS
es prē' də kôr' 3*
is prē' də kôr' 1
is prē' də kôr' 1

ESQUIRE
es' kwīr' 2*
es' kwī'r 1
es' kwīr 1
ə skwīr' 1
e skwī'r' 1

ESSAY (a composition, n)
es' ā 3*
es' a' 1

ESSAY (attempt, trial, n)
e sā' 4

PRONUNCIATION KEY

Symbol	Key words	Symbol	Key words	Symbol	Key words
a	asp, fat, parrot	†ə	a in ago	r	red, port, dear
ā	ape, date, play		e in agent	s	sell, castle, pass
†ä	ah, car, father		i in sanity	t	top, cattle, hat
e	elf, ten, berry		o in comply	v	vat, hovel, have
ē	even, meet, money		u in focus	w	will, always, swear
i	is, hit, mirror	ər	perhaps, murder	y	yet, onion, yard
ī	ice, bite, high	b	bed, fable, dub	z	zebra, dazzle, haze
ō	open, tone, go	d	dip, beadle, had	ch	chin, catcher, arch
ô	all, horn, law	f	fall, after, off	sh	she, cushion, dash
o͞o	ooze, tool, crew	g	get, haggle, dog	th	thin, nothing, truth
o͝o	look, pull, moor	h	he, ahead, hotel	th	then, father, lathe
yo͞o	use, cute, few	j	joy, agile, badge	zh	azure, leisure
yo͝o	united, cure, globule	k	kill, tackle, bake	ŋ	ring, anger, drink
oi	oil, point, toy	l	let, yellow, ball	ʻʻ	see p. 15.
ou	out, crowd, plow	m	met, camel, trim	✓	see p. 15.
u	up, cut, color	n	not, flannel, ton	+	see p. 14.
ur	urn, fur, deter	p	put, apple, tap	'	see p. 15.
†See p. 14.		†See p. 16.		○	see p. 14.

ESSAY (v)
e sā′   4*
es′ a′   1

ESSENCE
es′ əns   2*
es′ ′ns   2
es′ ′nts   1

ESSENTIAL
ə sen′ shəl   2*
i sen′ shəl   1
i sen′ chəl   1

ESTHETE
es′ thēt′   3*
es′ thēt   1

ESTHETICS
es thet′ iks   4*
is thet′ iks   1

ESTIMATE (n)
es′ tə mit   3*
es′ tə mət   1
es′ tə māt′   1

ESTIMATE (v)
es′ tə māt′   4

ESTROGEN
es′ trə jən   4

ESTUARY ✓
es′ choo er′ ē   2*
es′ choo wer′ ē   1
es′ chə wer′ ē   1

ESURIENT
i soor′ ē ənt   4

ET CETERA
et set′ ər ə   4*
et set′ rə   4

ETHER
ē′ thər   4

ETHEREAL ○
i thir′ ē əl   4

ETHOS   +
ē′ thäs′   3*
ē′ thäs   1
eth′ äs   1

ETIOLOGY   +
ēt ē äl′ ə jē   4

ETIQUETTE
et′ ə kit′   2*
et′ ə ket′   2
et′ i kət   2
et′ i ket′   2

ETUDE
ā′ tōōd′   2*
ā′ tyōōd′   2
ā′ tōōd   2
ā′ tyōōd   2
ā tōōd′   1
ā tyōōd′   1

ETYMOLOGY   +
et′ ə mäl′ ə jē   4

EUCALYPTUS
yōō′ kə lip′ təs   4

EUCHARIST
yōō′ kə rist   3*
yōō′ krəst   1
yōō′ kə rəst   1

EUCHRE
yōō′ kər   4

EUGENICS
yōō jen′ iks   4

EULOGY
yōō′ lə jē   4

EUNUCH
yōō′ nək   4*
yōō′ nik   1

EUPHEMISM
yōō′ fə miz′ əm   3*
yōō fə miz′m   1

EUPHEMISTIC
yōō fə mis′ tik   3*
yōō′ fə mis′ tik   1

EUPHONIOUS
yōō fō′ nē əs   3*
yoo fō′ nē əs   1

EUPHONY
yōō′ fə nē   4

EUPHORIA
yōō fôr′ ē ə   3*
yōō fōr′ ē ə   2
yoo fôr′ ē ə   1
yoo fōr′ ē ə   1

EUREKA
yoo rē′ kə   4

EURHYTHMICS
yoo rith′ miks   4

EUTHANASIA
yōō′ thə nā′ zhə   4*
yoo′ thə nā′ zhē ə   3
yōō′ thə nā′ shə   1
yoo′ thə nā′ zē ə   1

EVACUATE
i vak′ yoo āt′   1
i vak′ yoo wāt′   1
i vak′ yə wāt′   1
i vak′ yōō āt′   1*

EVANESCENT
ev′ ə nes′ ′nt   2*
ev′ ə nes′ ənt   2

EVANGELICAL
ē′ van jel′ i kəl   3*
ev′ ən jel′ i kəl   2
ē′ van jel′ i k'l   1
ev′ ən jel′ i k'l   1

EVANGELIST
i van′ jə list   3*
i van′ jə ləst   1

EVASIVE
i vā′ siv   4*
i vā′ ziv   1

EVENT
i vent′   4

EVERY
ev′ rē   4*
ev′ ə rē   1

EVIDENT
ev′ ə dənt   3*
ev′ ə dent′   2
ev′ i dənt   1

EVISCERATE
i vis′ ə rāt′   4

EVOCATIVE   +
i väk′ ə tiv   4
i vōk′ ə tiv   1

EVOLUTION
ev′ ə lōō′ shən   4*
ē′ və lōō′ shən   1

EWE
yōō   4*
yō   1

EWER
yōō′ ər   4*
yoor   1

EXACERBATE
ig zas′ ər bāt′   4*
ik sas′ ər bāt′   2
eg zas′ ər bāt′   1
ek sas′ ər bāt′   1

EXALT
ig zôlt′   3*
eg zôlt′   1

EXASPERATE
ig zas′ pə rāt′   4*
eg zas′ pə rāt′   1

EX CATHEDRA
eks kə thē′ drə   2*
eks′ kə thē′ drə   2
eks′ kath′ i drə   1
eks kath′ i drə   1

EXCELSIOR
ik sel′ sē ər   4
ek sel′ sē ər   2*
ek sel′ sē ôr′   1

EXCERPT (n)
ek′ surpt′   4*
eg′ zurpt′   1

EXCERPT (v)
ik surpt′   3
ek′ surpt′   2
ek surpt′   1*
eg zurpt′   1
eg′ surpt   1

EXCHEQUER
iks chek′ ər   4
eks′ chek ər   2
eks′ chek′ ər   2
eks chek′ ər   1*

EXCISE (n)
ek′ sīz   3
ek′ sīs   2*

EXCISE (v)
ik sīz′   3
ek sīz′   2*

PRONUNCIATION KEY

Symbol	Key words	Symbol	Key words	Symbol	Key words
a	asp, fat, parrot	†ə	a in ago	r	red, port, dear
ā	ape, date, play		e in agent	s	sell, castle, pass
†ä	ah, car, father		i in sanity	t	top, cattle, hat
e	elf, ten, berry		o in comply	v	vat, hovel, have
ē	even, meet, money		u in focus	w	will, always, swear
i	is, hit, mirror	ər	perhaps, murder	y	yet, onion, yard
ī	ice, bite, high	b	bed, fable, dub	z	zebra, dazzle, haze
ō	open, tone, go	d	dip, beadle, had	ch	chin, catcher, arch
ô	all, horn, law	f	fall, after, off	sh	she, cushion, dash
ōō	ooze, tool, crew	g	get, haggle, dog	th	thin, nothing, truth
oo	look, pull, moor	h	he, ahead, hotel	th	then, father, lathe
yōō	use, cute, few	j	joy, agile, badge	zh	azure, leisure
yoo	united, cure, globule	k	kill, tackle, bake	ŋ	ring, anger, drink
oi	oil, point, toy	l	let, yellow, ball	″	see p. 15.
ou	out, crowd, plow	m	met, camel, trim	✓	see p. 15.
u	up, cut, color	n	not, flannel, ton	+	see p. 14.
ur	urn, fur, deter	p	put, apple, tap	′	see p. 15.
†See p. 14.		†See p. 16.		○	see p. 14.

EXCITATION
ek′ si tā′ shən 2*
ek′ sī tā′ shən 2
ek′ si′ tā′ shən 1
ek′ sə tā′ shən 1

EXCLAMATORY
iks klam′ ə tôr′ ē 4
iks klam′ ə tōr′ ē 3
eks klam′ ə tôr′ ē 1*
eks klam′ ə tōr′ ē 1

EXCLUSIVE
iks klo͞o′ siv 4
eks klo͞o′ siv 1*
iks klo͞o′ ziv 1

EXCORIATE
ik skôr′ ē āt′ 3
ek skôr′ ē āt′ 2*
ik skōr′ ē āt′ 2
ek skōr′ ē āt′ 2

EXCREMENT
eks′ krə mənt 4

EXCRESCENCE
iks kres′ ′ns 2
eks kres′ əns 1*
iks kres′ əns 1
iks kres′ ′nts 1

EXCRETA
iks krēt′ ə 3
eks krēt′ ə 2*

EXCRETORY
eks′ krə tôr′ ē 3*
eks′ krə tōr′ ē 2
eks′ kri tôr′ ē 1
eks′ kri tōr′ ē 1
ik skrē′ tə rē 1

EXCRUCIATING
iks kro͞o′ shē āt′ ing 4
eks kro͞o′ shē āt′ ing 1*

EXCULPATE
eks′ kəl pāt′ 4*
ik skul′ pāt 3
ek skul′ pāt′ 1
ik′ skul pāt′ 1

EXCUSE (n)
ik skyo͞os′ 4
ek skyo͞os′ 1*

EXCUSE (v)
ik skyo͞oz′ 4
ek skyo͞oz′ 1*

EXECRABLE
ek′ si krə bəl 2*
ek′ sə krə bəl 1
ek′ si krə b′l 1

EXECRATE
ek′ sə krāt 1*
ek′ si krāt 1
ek′ si krāt′ 1
ek′ sə krāt′ 1

EXECUTE
ek′ sə kyo͞ot′ 2*
ek′ si kyo͞ot 1
ek′ si kyo͞ot′ 1

EXECUTIVE
ig zek′ yə tiv 4
eg zek′ yə tiv 1*
ig zek′ ə tiv 1

EXECUTOR
ig zek′ yə tər 3
eg zek′ yə tər 1*
ig zek′ ət ər 1

EXEGESIS
ek′ sə jē′ sis 2*
ek′ si jē′ sis 1
ek′ sə jē′ səs 1

EXEMPLAR
ig zem′ plər 4
ig zem′ plär′ 3
eg zem′ plär′ 1*
ig zem′ plär 1
eg zem′ plər 1

EXEMPLARY ✓
ig zem′ plə rē 4
eg zem′ plə rē 1*
eg′ zəm pler ē 1

EXEUNT
ek′ sē ənt 4
ek′ sē o͞ont′ 2*
ek′ sē o͞ont 1

EXHALATION
eks′ hə lā′ shən 4*
ek sə lā′ shən 2
eg′ zə lā′ shən 1

EXHAUST
ig zôst′ 4*
eg zôst′ 1

EXHIBIT
ig zib′ it 3
eg zib′ it 1*
ig zib′ ət 1

EXHILARATE
ig zil′ ə rāt′ 4
eg zil′ ə rāt′ 1*

EXHORT
ig zôrt′ 4
eg zôrt′ 1*

EXHUME
ig zyo͞om′ 3
eks hyo͞om′ 2*
iks hyo͞om′ 2
iks yo͞om′ 1
ig zo͞om′ 1

EXIGENCY
ek′ sə jən sē   3*
ek′ si jən sē   1
ek sij′ ən sē   1
ig zij′ ən sē   1

EXILE
eg′ zīl′   2*
ek′ sīl′   2
eg′ zīl   2

EXISTENTIAL
eg′ zis ten′ shəl   3*
ek′ sis ten′ shəl   3
eg′ zis ten′ chəl   1
ek′ sis ten′ chəl   1

EXIT
eg′ zit   3*
ek′ zit   3
eg′ zət   1
ek′ sət   1

EX LIBRIS
eks lē′ bris   3*
eks lī′ bris   3
eks lē′ brəs   1
eks lē′ brēs′   1

EXODUS
ek′ sə dəs   4*
eg′ zə dəs   1

EX OFFICIO
eks′ ə fish′ ē ō′   4

EXONERATE   +
ig zän′ ə rāt′   4
eg zän′ ə rāt′   1*

EXORBITANT
ig zôr′ bə tənt   3
eg zôr′ bə tənt   1*
ig zôr′ bi t′nt   1

EXORCISE
ek′ sôr sīz′   4*
ek′ sər sīz′   2

EXORCISM
ek′ sôr siz′ əm   2*
ek′ sôr siz′m   1
ek′ sôr′ siz′ əm   1
ek′ sər siz′ əm   1

EXORCIST
ek′ sôr sist   2
ek′ sôr sist′   2*

EXOTIC   +
ig zät′ ik   4
eg zät′ ik   1*

EXPATIATE
ik spā′ shē āt′   4
ek spā′ shē āt′   1*

EXPATRIATE (n, adj)
eks pā′ trē it   3*
eks pā′ trē āt′   3
eks pā′ trē ət   1

EXPATRIATE (v)
eks pā′ trē āt′   4

EXPECTORANT
ik spek′ tər ənt   3
ek spek′ tər ənt   1*
ik spek′ trənt   1

EXPECTORATE
ik spek′ te rāt′   4*
eg spek′ tə rāt′   1

EXPEDIENT
ik spē′ dē ənt   3
ek spē′ dē ənt   1*

PRONUNCIATION KEY

Symbol	Key words	Symbol	Key words	Symbol	Key words
a	asp, fat, parrot	†ə	a in ago	r	red, port, dear
ā	ape, date, play		e in agent	s	sell, castle, pass
†ä	ah, car, father		i in sanity	t	top, cattle, hat
e	elf, ten, berry		o in comply	v	vat, hovel, have
ē	even, meet, money		u in focus	w	will, always, swear
i	is, hit, mirror	ər	perhaps, murder	y	yet, onion, yard
ī	ice, bite, high	b	bed, fable, dub	z	zebra, dazzle, haze
ō	open, tone, go	d	dip, beadle, had	ch	chin, catcher, arch
ô	all, horn, law	f	fall, after, off	sh	she, cushion, dash
ōō	ooze, tool, crew	g	get, haggle, dog	th	thin, nothing, truth
oo	look, pull, moor	h	he, ahead, hotel	th	then, father, lathe
yōō	use, cute, few	j	joy, agile, badge	zh	azure, leisure
yoo	united, cure, globule	k	kill, tackle, bake	ŋ	ring, anger, drink
oi	oil, point, toy	l	let, yellow, ball	″	see p. 15.
ou	out, crowd, plow	m	met, camel, trim	✓	see p. 15.
u	up, cut, color	n	not, flannel, ton	+	see p. 14.
ur	urn, fur, deter	p	put, apple, tap	′	see p. 15.
†See p. 14.		†See p. 16.		○	see p. 14.

EXPEDITE
ek′ spə dīt′   3*
ek′ spi dīt′   1

EXPEDITIOUS
ek′ spə dish′ əs   3*
ek′ spi dish′ əs   1

EXPERIENTIAL ○
ik spir′ ē en′ shəl   3
ek spir′ ē en′ shəl   1*
ik spir′ ē en′ chəl   1

EXPERIMENT (n) ○
ik sper′ ə mənt   3
ik spir′ ə mənt   2
ik sper′ ə ment   2
ek sper′ ə mənt   1*
ek sper′ ə ment   1

EXPERIMENT (v) ○
ik sper′ ə ment′   3
ik spir′ ə ment′   3
ik sper′ ə mənt   3
ek sper′ ə ment′   1*
ik spir′ ə mənt   1
ek sper′ ə mənt   1

EXPERIMENTAL ○
ik sper′ ə ment″l   3
ik spir′ ə ment″l   2
ek sper′ ə ment″l   1*

EXPERT (n)
ek′ spʉrt′   2*
ek′ spʉrt   1
ek′ spərt   1

EXPERT (adj)
ik spʉrt′   4*
ek′ spʉrt   2
ek′ spʉrt′   1

EXPERTISE
ek′ spər tēz′   3*
ek′ spʉr tēz′   1
ek′ spər′ tēz′   1
ek′ spər tēs′   1

EXPIATE
ek′ spē āt′   4

EXPLANATORY
ik splan′ ə tôr ē   3
ik splan′ ə tōr′ ē   2
ek splan′ ə tôr ē   1*
ek splan′ ə tōr ē   1

EXPLETIVE
eks′ plə tiv   3*
eks′ pli tiv   1

EXPLICABLE
eks′ pli kə b′l   2*
eks′ pli kə bəl   1
iks plik′ ə b′l   1
eks′ plik′ ə bəl   1
iks plik′ ə bəl   1

EXPLICIT
ik splis′ it   3
ek splis′ it   1*
ik splis′ ət   1

EXPLOIT (n)
eks′ ploit   2*
eks′ ploit   2
iks ploit′   2

EXPLOIT (v)
ik sploit′   4*
ek sploit′   1
ek′ sploit′   1

EXPLORATORY
ik splôr′ ə tôr′ ē   3
ik splōr′ ə tôr′ ē   2
ik splōr′ ə tōr ē   2
ek splôr′ ə tôr′ ē   1*
ek splōr′ ə tōr′ ē   1

EXPLOSIVE
ik splō′ siv   4
ek splō′ siv   1*
ik splō′ ziv   1

EXPONENT
ik spō′ nənt   4
ek spō′ nənt   1*

EXPORT (n)
eks′ pôrt   4*
eks′ pōrt   3

EXPORT (v)
ik spôrt′   3
ek spôrt′   2*
ik spōrt′   2
ek spōrt′   2
ek′ spôrt   2
ek′ spōrt   2

EXPOSÉ
eks′ pō zā′   4*
eks′ pə zā′   1

EXPOSITORY +
ik späz′ ə tôr′ ē   2
ek späz′ ə tôr′ ē   1*
ik späz′ ə tōr′ ē   1
ik späz′ i tōr′ ē   1
ik späz′ i tôr′ ē   1
ek späz′ ə tōr′ ē   1

EXPOSTULATE +
ik späs′ chə lāt′   3
ek späs′ choo lāt′   1*
ik späs′ choo lāt′   1

EXPROPRIATE
eks prō′ prē āt′   4

EXPUNGE
ik spunj′   4
ek spunj′   1*

EXPURGATE
eks′ pər gāt′   4*
iks′ pər gāt′   1
eks′ pʉr gāt   1

EXQUISITE
eks′ kwi zit   3*
iks kwiz′ it   2
eks′ kwi zət   1
eks′ kwi′ zət   1

EXTANT
ek′ stənt   4*
ik′ stənt   3
ek stant′   2
ik stant′   1

EXTEMPORANEOUS
ik stem′ pə rā′ nē əs   3
ek stem′ pə rā′ nē əs   2*

EXTEMPORE
ik stem′ pə rē   4
ek stem′ pə rē   1*

EXTENUATING
ik sten′ yo͞o āt′ iŋ   2
ek sten′ yo͞o āt′ iŋ   1*
ik sten′ yoo wāt′ iŋ   1
ik sten′ yə wāt′ iŋ   1

EXTINCT
ik stiŋkt′   3
ek stiŋkt′   1*
ek′ stiŋkt′   1

EXTINGUISH
ik stiŋ′ gwish   4
ek stiŋ′ gwish   1*

EXTIRPATE
ek′ stər pāt′   4*
ik stʉr′ pāt′   2
ik′ stər pāt′   1
ek stʉr′ pāt′   1

EXTOL   +
ik sto͞ol′   4
ek sto͞ol′   1*
ik stäl′   1

EXTRACT (n)
eks′ trakt   3*
eks′ trakt′   1

EXTRACT (v)
ik strakt′   4
ek strakt′   1*

EXTRANEOUS
ik strā′ nē əs   3
ek strā′ nē əs   2*

EXTRAORDINARY ✓
ik strôr′ d'n er′ ē   3*
ek′ strə or′ d'n er′ ē   2
ek strôr′ dən er ē   1
ik strôr′ dən er ē   1
ek′ strə ôr′ dən er ē   1

EXTRAPOLATE
ik strap′ ə lāt′   4
ek strap′ ə lāt′   1*

EXTRAVAGANZA
ik strav′ ə gan′ zə   4
ek strav′ ə gan′ zə   1*

EXTREMIST
ik strēm′ ist   3
ek strēm′ ist   1*
ik strēm′ əst   1

EXTREMITY
ik strem′ ə tē   3
ek strem′ ə tē   1*
ik strem′ i tē   1

EXTRICATE
eks′ trə kāt′   3*
eks′ tri kāt′   1

EXTRINSIC
ek strin′ sik   3*
ek strin′ zik   2
ik strin′ sik   2
ik strin′ zik   1

PRONUNCIATION KEY

Symbol	Key words	Symbol	Key words	Symbol	Key words
a	asp, fat, parrot	†ə	a in ago	r	red, port, dear
ā	ape, date, play		e in agent	s	sell, castle, pass
†ä	ah, car, father		i in sanity	t	top, cattle, hat
e	elf, ten, berry		o in comply	v	vat, hovel, have
ē	even, meet, money		u in focus	w	will, always, swear
i	is, hit, mirror	ər	perhaps, murder	y	yet, onion, yard
ī	ice, bite, high	b	bed, fable, dub	z	zebra, dazzle, haze
ō	open, tone, go	d	dip, beadle, had	ch	chin, catcher, arch
ô	all, horn, law	f	fall, after, off	sh	she, cushion, dash
o͞o	ooze, tool, crew	g	get, haggle, dog	th	thin, nothing, truth
oo	look, pull, moor	h	he, ahead, hotel	th	then, father, lathe
yo͞o	use, cute, few	j	joy, agile, badge	zh	azure, leisure
yoo	united, cure, globule	k	kill, tackle, bake	ŋ	ring, anger, drink
oi	oil, point, toy	l	let, yellow, ball	′′	see p. 15.
ou	out, crowd, plow	m	met, camel, trim	✓	see p. 15.
u	up, cut, color	n	not, flannel, ton	+	see p. 14.
ʉr	urn, fur, deter	p	put, apple, tap	′	see p. 15.
†See p. 14.		†See p. 16.		○	see p. 14.

EXUBERANT
ig zo͞o′ bər ənt   4
eg zo͞o′ bər ənt   1*
ig zo͞o′ brənt   1

EXUDATE
eks′ yə dāt′   1*
eks′ yo͞o dāt′   1
eks′ yoo dāt′   1
ek′ soo dāt′   1
ek′ sə dāt′   1
ek′ shoo dāt′   1

EXUDE
ig zo͞od′   4
ik so͞od′   2
eg zo͞od′   1*
ek so͞od′   1

EXULT
ig zult′   4
eg zult′   1*

EYRIE (AERIE) ○ ✓
er′ ē   3*
ir′ ē   3

FAÇADE
fə säd′ 4*
fa säd′ 1

FACET
fas′ it 3*
fas′ ət 1

FACETIOUS
fə sē′ shəs 4

FACIAL
fā′ shəl 4

FACILE
fas′ əl 2*
fas′ il 2
fas′ 'l 1

FACILITATE
fə sil′ ə tāt′ 3*
fə sil′ i tāt′ 1

FACSIMILE
fak sim′ ə lē 4

FACTITIOUS
fak tish′ əs 4

FACTOTUM
fak tōt′ əm 4

FACTUAL
fak′ choo əl 2*
fak′ choo wəl 1
fak′ chəl 1

FAHRENHEIT ✓
far′ ən hīt′ 3*
fer′ ən hīt′ 1
fär′ ən hīt′ 1

FAIENCE
fī äns′ 4*
fā äns′ 4
fī änts′ 1
fā änts′ 1

FAILLE
fīl 4*
fāl 3

FAKIR ○
fə kir′ 4*
fā′ kər 2

FALCON
fal′ kən 4*
fôl′ kən 4
fô′ kən 4

FALLACIOUS
fə lā′ shəs 4

FALLACY
fal′ ə sē 4

FALSETTO
fôl set′ ō 4*
fôl set′ ō′ 1

FALSIFY
fôl′ sə fī′ 4

FALTER
fôl′ tər 4

FAMILIAL
fə mil′ yəl 4*
fə mil′ ē əl 1

FAMILIARITY
fə mil′ yar′ ə tē 3*
fə mil′ ē ar′ ə tē 3
fə mil′ ē ar′ i tē 1

FAMILIARIZE
fə mil′ yə rīz′ 4

FAMINE
fam′ in 2*
fam′ ən 2

FANATIC
fə nat′ ik 4

FANATICISM
fə nat′ ə siz′ əm   2*
fə nat′ i siz′ əm   1
fə nat′ i siz′ ′m   1

FANFARE ✓
fan′ fer′   3*
fan′ fer   1

FANTASIA
fan tā′ zhə   4*
fan tā′ zhē ə   3
fan′ tə zē′ ə   3
fan tā′ zē ə   2

FANTASY
fan′ tə sē   4*
fan′ tə zē   4

FARCE
färs   4

FARCICAL
fär′ si kəl   3
fär′ si k′l   1*

FARINACEOUS
far′ ə nā′ shəs   4

FARO ✓
fer′ ō   2*
fär′ ō   2
far′ ō   1

FARRAGO
fə rä′ gō   4*
fə rā′ gō   4

FARTHING
fär′ thiŋ   4

FARTHINGALE
fär′ thiŋ gāl′   4*
fär′ thən gāl′   1

FASCES
fas′ ēz′   2*
fas′ ēz   2

FASCIA
fash′ ē ə   4
fash′ ə   2*
fāsh′ ə   1
fāsh′ ē ə   1

FASCIST
fash′ ist   3*
fash′ əst   1
fas′ əst   1

FASCISM
fash′ iz əm   2*
fash′ iz′m   1
fash′ iz′ əm   1
fas′ iz′ əm   1

FASTIDIOUS
fa stid′ ē əs   4*
fə stid′ ē əs   2

FATHOM
fath əm   4

FATIGUE
fə tēg′   4

FATUOUS
fach′ ōō əs   2*
fach′ oo wəs   1
fach′ wəs   1

FAUCET
fô′ sit   3
fô′ sət   1*
fäs′ ət   1

FAULT
fôlt   4

FAUN
fôn   4

FAUNA
fô′ nə   4

FAUX PAS
fō pä′   4

FEASIBLE
fē′ zə bəl   3
fē′ zə b′l   1*

FEALTY
fē′ əl tē   3*
fēl′ tē   1

FEBRIFUGE
feb′ rə fyōōj′   4

FEBRILE
feb′ rəl   4*
fē′ brəl   3
fē′ brīl   1

FEBRUARY ✓
feb′ rōō er′ ē   2*
feb′ yōō er′ ē   2
feb′ rə wer′ ē   2
feb′ yoo wer′ ē   1
feb′ ə wer′ ē   1

FECAL
fē′ kəl   4

FECES
fē′ sēz   4*
fē′ sēz′   1

FECUND
fek′ ənd   4*
fē′ kənd   3
fē′ kund   1
fek′ und   1

FECUNDITY
fi kun′ də tē   3*
fi kun′ di tē   1

FEDAYEEN
fed′ ä yēn′   1*
fə dä′ yēn   1
fid′ a ēn′   1
fid′ a yēn′   1
fid′ ä ēn′   1
fid′ ä yēn′   1

FEDORA
fi dôr′ ə   4*
fi dōr′ ə   3

FEIGN
fān   4

FEINT
fānt   4

FEISTY
fī′ stē   4

FELICITOUS
fə lis′ ə təs   3*
fə lis′ i təs   1

FELICITY
fə lis′ ə tē   3*
fə lis′ i tē   1

FELINE
fē′ līn′   3*
fē′ lin   1

FELLAH
fel′ ə   4*
fə lä′   2

FELLATIO
fə lā′ shē ō′   4*
fe lā′ shē ō′   3
fə lät′ ē ō′   2
fə lat′ ē ō′   1

FELON
fel′ ən   4

FELONIOUS
fə lō′ nē əs   4

FELONY
fel′ ə nē   4

FEMUR
fē′ mər   4

FENESTRATION
fen′ ə strā′ shən   3*
fen′ i strā′ shən   1

FERAL ◯ ✓
fir′ əl   4*
fer′ əl   3

FERMENT (n)
fur′ ment′   2*
fur′ ment   2
fər ment′   1

FERMENT (v)
fər ment′   4

FEROCIOUS
fə rō′ shəs   4

FEROCITY +
fə räs′ ə tē   3*
fə räs′ i tē   1

FERRULE (FERULE)
fer′ əl   4*
fer′ ōōl′   2
fer′ ool   1
fer′ ōōl   1

FERTILE
fur′ t′l   4

FETAL
fēt′ ′l   2*
fēt′ əl   2

PRONUNCIATION KEY

Symbol	Key words	Symbol	Key words	Symbol	Key words
a	asp, fat, parrot	†ə	a in ago	r	red, port, dear
ā	ape, date, play		e in agent	s	sell, castle, pass
†ä	ah, car, father		i in sanity	t	top, cattle, hat
e	elf, ten, berry		o in comply	v	vat, hovel, have
ē	even, meet, money		u in focus	w	will, always, swear
i	is, hit, mirror	ər	perhaps, murder	y	yet, onion, yard
ī	ice, bite, high	b	bed, fable, dub	z	zebra, dazzle, haze
ō	open, tone, go	d	dip, beadle, had	ch	chin, catcher, arch
ô	all, horn, law	f	fall, after, off	sh	she, cushion, dash
ōō	ooze, tool, crew	g	get, haggle, dog	th	thin, nothing, truth
oo	look, pull, moor	h	he, ahead, hotel	th	then, father, lathe
yōō	use, cute, few	j	joy, agile, badge	zh	azure, leisure
yoo	united, cure, globule	k	kill, tackle, bake	ŋ	ring, anger, drink
oi	oil, point, toy	l	let, yellow, ball	′′	see p. 15.
ou	out, crowd, plow	m	met, camel, trim	✓	see p. 15.
u	up, cut, color	n	not, flannel, ton	+	see p. 14.
ur	urn, fur, deter	p	put, apple, tap	′	see p. 15.
†See p. 14.		†See p. 16.		◯	see p. 14.

FETE (FÊTE)
fāt 4*
fet 2

FETID
fet′ id 3*
fē′ tid 2
fet′ əd 1

FETISH
fet′ ish 4*
fēt′ ish 4

FETISHISM
fet′ ish iz əm 3*
fēt′ ish iz əm 3
fet′ ish iz ′m 1
fēt′ ish iz ′m 1

FETUS
fē′ təs 4

FEUD
fyo͞od 4

FEY
fā 4

FIANCÉ (FIANCÉE)
fē′ än sā′ 4*
fē än′ sā′ 3

FIASCO
fē as′ kō 3*
fē äs′ kō 1
fē äs′ kō′ 1

FIAT
fī′ ət 4
fī′ at′ 2*
fē′ ät 2
fī′ at 2
fē′ ət 1
fē′ at′ 1

FIBRILLATION
fib′ rə lā′ shən 4*
fī′ brə lā shən 3

FIBRIN
fī′ brin 3*
fī′ brən 1

FIBROID
fī′ broid 3*
fī′ broid′ 1

FIBROSIS
fī brō′ sis 3*
fī brō′ səs 1

FICHU
fish′ o͞o 4*
fish′ o͞o′ 1
fesh′ o͞o 1

FICTITIOUS
fik tish′ əs 4

FIDELITY
fi del′ ə tē 3*
fī del′ ə tē 3
fi del′ i tē 1
fī del′ i tē 1

FIDUCIARY ✓
fi do͞o′ shē er′ ē 3*
fi dyo͞o′ shē er′ ē 2
fī do͞o′ shē er′ ē 1
fī dyo͞o′ shē er′ ē 1
fi do͞o′ shə rē 1
fə do͞o′ shē er′ ē 1
fə do͞o′ shə rē 1
fə dyo͞o′ shə rē 1

FIEF
fēf 4

FIEND
fēnd 4

FIERY
fī′ ər ē 4*
fī′ rē 2

FIESTA
fē es′ tə 4

FIFTH
fifth 4*
fiftth 1

FIGURATIVE
fig′ yər ə tiv 4*
fig′ ər ə tiv 1

FIGURINE
fig′ yə rēn′ 4*
fig′ ə rēn′ 1

FILET
fi lā′ 4*
fil′ ā 3

FILIAL
fil′ ē əl 4*
fil′ yəl 2

FILIBUSTER
fil′ ə bus′ tər 4

FILIGREE
fil′ ə grē′ 4

FILLIP
fil′ əp 4

FINAGLE
fi nā′ gəl 3*
fi nā′ g′l 1

FINALE
fi nä′ lē 3
fi nal′ ē 2*
fə nal′ ē 2
fə nä′ lē 1

FINALIST
fī′ n′l ist 2*
fī′ n′l əst 1
fī′ nəl ist 1

FINALITY
fī nal′ ə tē 3
fə nal′ ə tē 2
fi nal′ ə tē 1*
fī nal′ i tē 1

FINANCE
fī′ nans′ 3
fə nans′ 2*
fi nans′ 2
fī′ nans 2
fī nans′ 1
fī′ nants′ 1

FINANCIAL
fi nan′ shəl 2*
fī nan′ shəl 3
fə nan′ chəl 1
fī nan′ chəl 1
fə nan′ shəl 1

FINANCIER ○
fin′ ən sir′ 4*
fī′ nan′ sir′ 2
fə nan′ sir′ 1
fī nən sir′ 1

FINERY
fīn′ ər ē 4*
fīn′ rē 1

FINESSE
fi nes′ 3*
fə nes′ 1

FINIAL
fin′ ē əl 4*
fī′ nē əl 1

FINIS
fin′ is 3*
fī′ nis 3
fin′ əs 1
fī nəs 1
fē′ nē′ 1

FINITE
fī′ nīt′ 2*
fī′ nīt 2

FISSURE
fish′ ər 4

FISTULA
fis′ choo lə 3
fis′ chə lə 1*
fish′ chə lə 1

FIXATIVE
fik′ sə tiv 4

FJORD (FIORD)
fyôrd 3*
fyōrd 2
fē ôrd′ 1

FLACCID
flak′ sid 3*
flak′ səd 1
flas′ id 1
flas′ əd 1

FLACON   +
flak′ ən 3*
flak′ ′n 1
flak′ än′ 1

FLAGELLANT
flə jel′ ənt 4*
flaj′ ə lənt 4

FLAGELLATE (n)
flaj′ ə lāt′ 4
flə jel′ ət 1*
flaj′ ə lət 1

FLAGELLATE (v)
flaj′ ə lāt′ 4

PRONUNCIATION KEY

Symbol	Key words	Symbol	Key words	Symbol	Key words
a	asp, fat, parrot	†ə	a in ago	r	red, port, dear
ā	ape, date, play		e in agent	s	sell, castle, pass
†ä	ah, car, father		i in sanity	t	top, cattle, hat
e	elf, ten, berry		o in comply	v	vat, hovel, have
ē	even, meet, money		u in focus	w	will, always, swear
i	is, hit, mirror	ər	perhaps, murder	y	yet, onion, yard
ī	ice, bite, high	b	bed, fable, dub	z	zebra, dazzle, haze
ō	open, tone, go	d	dip, beadle, had	ch	chin, catcher, arch
ô	all, horn, law	f	fall, after, off	sh	she, cushion, dash
oo	ooze, tool, crew	g	get, haggle, dog	th	thin, nothing, truth
oo	look, pull, moor	h	he, ahead, hotel	th	then, father, lathe
yoo	use, cute, few	j	joy, agile, badge	zh	azure, leisure
yoo	united, cure, globule	k	kill, tackle, bake	ŋ	ring, anger, drink
oi	oil, point, toy	l	let, yellow, ball	″	see p. 15.
ou	out, crowd, plow	m	met, camel, trim	✓	see p. 15.
u	up, cut, color	n	not, flannel, ton	+	see p. 14.
ʉr	urn, fur, deter	p	put, apple, tap	′	see p. 15.
†See p. 14.		†See p. 16.		○	see p. 14.

FLAGEOLET
flaj′ ə let′ 4*
flaj′ ə lā′ 3

FLAGON
flag′ ən 4

FLAGRANT
flā′ grənt 4

FLAMBÉ
fläm bā′ 3

FLAMBEAU
flam′ bō′ 3*
flam′ bō 1

FLAMBOYANT
flam boi′ ənt 4

FLAMENCO
flə meŋ′ kō 4*
flə meŋ′ kō′ 1

FLAMINGO
flə miŋ′ gō 4*
flə miŋ′ gō′ 1

FLAN
flan 4*
flän 2

FLANGE
flanj 4

FLATULENCE
flach′ ə ləns 3*
flach′ oo ləns 1
flach′ yoo ləns 1
flach′ ə lənts 1

FLATUS
flā′ təs 4

FLAUNT
flônt 4*
flänt 1

FLAUTIST
flô′ tist 3*
flou′ tist 3
flô′ təst 1
flou′ təst 1

FLORAL
flôr′ əl 4*
flōr′ əl 3

FLORID +
flär′ id 3*
flôr′ id 3
flôr′ əd 1
flär′ əd 1

FLORIST +
flär′ ist 3*
flôr′ ist 3
flōr′ ist 2
flōr′ əst 1
flôr′ əst 1

FLOTILLA
flō til′ ə 4

FLOTSAM +
flät′ səm 4

FLOURISH
flʉr′ ish 4*
flur′ ish 1

FLOUT
flout 4

FLUCTUATE
fluk′ choo āt′ 2*
fluk′ choo wāt′ 1
fluk′ chə wāt′ 1

FLUENT
floo′ ənt 4

FLUORESCENT
flô res′ ənt 2
floo ər es′ ənt 2*
floo res′ ənt 2
floo res′ ′nt 2
flō res′ ənt 1

FLUORIDATE
floor′ ə dāt′ 3*
flôr′ ə dāt′ 2
floo′ ər ə dāt′ 1
flōr′ ə dāt′ 1

FLUORIDE
floo′ ə rīd′ 3*
flôr′ īd 2
floor′ īd′ 2
floor′ īd 2
flōr′ īd 1

FLUOROSCOPE
floor′ ə skōp′ 4*
floo′ ər ə skōp′ 3
flôr′ ə skōp′ 2
flōr′ ə skōp′ 1

FLUTIST
floot′ ist 3*
floot′ əst 1

FOCAL
fō′ kəl 3
fō′ k'l 1*

FOCUS
fō′ kəs 4

FOCI
fō′ sī′ 2*
fō′ sī 2

FOGY
fō′ gē 4

FOLIAGE
fō′ lē ij 4*
fō′ lij 1
fō′ lyij 1

FOLIO
fō′ lē ō′ 4

FOLK
fōk 4

FOLLICLE   +
fäl′ i kəl   3
fäl′ i k'l   1*

FOMENT
fō ment′   4

FONDANT   +
fän′ dənt   4

FONDUE   +
fän dōō′   4*
fän′ dōō   2
fän′ dōō′   1
fän′ dyōō′   1
fän dyōō′   1

FORAGE   +
fär′ ij   4*
fôr′ ij   4

FORAY   +
fôr′ ā   2*
fôr′ ā′   2
fōr′ ā′   1
fär′ ā   1

FORBADE
fər bad′   4*
fər bād′   3
fôr bad′   2
fôr bād′   1

FORBEAR (n) ✓
fôr′ ber′   4*
fōr′ ber′   2
fôr′ bar′   1
fōr′ bar′   1

FORBEAR (v) ✓
fôr ber′   4*
fər ber′   1
fôr bar′   1
fər bar′   1

FORCEPS
fôr′ seps   2*
fôr′ səps   2

FORECASTLE
fōk′ səl   3*
fōr′ kas′ əl   3
fôr′ kas′ əl   2
fōr′ käs′ əl   2
fôr′ käs′ əl   1
fōk′ s'l   1
fôr′ kas′ 'l   1

FOREHEAD   +
fôr′ hed′   4
fôr′ id   3
fär′ id   2*
fär′ hed′   2
fōr′ hed′   1
fôr′ əd   1
fär′ əd   1

FOREIGN   +
fär′ in   3*
fôr′ in   3
fôr′ ən   1
fär′ ən   1

FORENSIC
fə ren′ sik   4*
fə rent′ sik   1
fə ren′ zik   1

PRONUNCIATION KEY

Symbol	Key words	Symbol	Key words	Symbol	Key words
a	asp, fat, parrot	†ə	a in ago	r	red, port, dear
ā	ape, date, play		e in agent	s	sell, castle, pass
†ä	ah, car, father		i in sanity	t	top, cattle, hat
e	elf, ten, berry		o in comply	v	vat, hovel, have
ē	even, meet, money		u in focus	w	will, always, swear
i	is, hit, mirror	ər	perhaps, murder	y	yet, onion, yard
ī	ice, bite, high	b	bed, fable, dub	z	zebra, dazzle, haze
ō	open, tone, go	d	dip, beadle, had	ch	chin, catcher, arch
ô	all, horn, law	f	fall, after, off	sh	she, cushion, dash
ōō	ooze, tool, crew	g	get, haggle, dog	th	thin, nothing, truth
oo	look, pull, moor	h	he, ahead, hotel	th	then, father, lathe
yōō	use, cute, few	j	joy, agile, badge	zh	azure, leisure
yoo	united, cure, globule	k	kill, tackle, bake	ŋ	ring, anger, drink
oi	oil, point, toy	l	let, yellow, ball	″	see p. 15.
ou	out, crowd, plow	m	met, camel, trim	✓	see p. 15.
u	up, cut, color	n	not, flannel, ton	+	see p. 14.
ur	urn, fur, deter	p	put, apple, tap	′	see p. 15.
†See p. 14.		†See p. 16.		○	see p. 14.

FORFEIT
fôr′ fit 3*
fôr′ fət 1

FORFEITURE
fôr′ fə chər 2*
fôr′ fi chər 1
fôr′ fi choor′ 1
fôr′ fə choor′ 1
fôr′ fə toor′ 1
fôr′ fə tyoor′ 1

FORMALDEHYDE
fôr mal′ də hīd′ 4*
fər mal′ də hīd′ 1

FORMICA
fôr mī′ kə 4*
fər mī′ kə 1

FORMIDABLE
fôr′ mə də bəl 2*
fôr′ mə də b'l 1
fôr′ mi də b'l 1
fôr mid′ ə bəl 1

FORSYTHIA
fər sith′ ē ə 4*
fôr sith′ ē ə 3
fôr sī′ thē ə 1

FORTE (n)
fôrt 4*
fōrt 3
fôr′ tā 2

FORTE (music)
fôr′ tā 3*
fôr′ tē 1
fôr′ tā′ 1

FORTHWITH
fôrth′ with′ 3*
fôrth′ with′ 3
fōrth′ with′ 3
fōrth′ with′ 3
fôrth with′ 2
fôrth with′ 2
fōrth with′ 1
fōrth with′ 1

FORTISSIMO
fôr tis′ ə mō 2*
fôr tis′ ə mō′ 2

FORTITUDE
fôr′ tə tood′ 3*
fôr′ tə tyood′ 3
fôr′ ti tood′ 1
fôr′ ti tyood′ 1

FORTNIGHT
fôrt′ nīt′ 4*
fôrt′ nit 2
fôrt′ nīt 1

FORTUITOUS
fôr tyoo′ ə təs 3*
fôr too′ ə təs 3
fôr too′ i təs 1
fôr tyoo′ i təs 1

FORTUNE
fôr′ chən 4

FORUM
fôr′ əm 4*
fōr′ əm 3

FOSTER +
fôs′ tər 4*
fäs′ tər 4

FOULARD
foo lärd′ 4*
fə lärd′ 1

FOUR
fôr 4*
fōr 3

FOYER
foi′ ər 4*
foi′ ā 2
foi yā′ 2
foi′ ā′ 1
fwä′ yā′ 1
foir 1

FRACAS
frā′ kəs 3*
frak′ əs 1

FRACTIOUS
frak′ shəs 4

FRAGILE
fraj′ əl 3*
fraj′ īl′ 2
fraj′ 'l 1

FRAGMENT (n)
frag′ mənt 4

FRAGMENT (v)
frag′ mənt 3
frag ment′ 1*
frag′ ment′ 1

FRAGMENTARY ✓
frag′ mən ter′ ē 4

FRAGRANT
frā′ grənt 4

FRAILTY
frāl′ tē 3*
frā əl′ tē 1

FRANCHISE
fran′ chīz 2*
fran′ chīz′ 2

FRANGIBLE
fran′ jə bəl 3
fran′ jə b'l 1*

FRANGIPANI +
fran′ jə pan′ ē 3*
fran′ jə pän′ ē 3
fran′ jə pan′ ē 1
fran′ jə pän′ ē 1

FRANKFURTER
fraŋk′ fər tər 3*
fraŋk′ fət ər 1

FRANKINCENSE
fraŋ′ kin sens′   2*
fraŋ′ kən sens′   2

FRATERNAL
frə tʉr′ n'l   3*
frə tʉr′ nəl   1

FRATERNIZE
frat′ ər nīz′   4

FRAU
frou   4

FRAUD
frôd   4

FRAUDULENT
frô′ jə lənt   4

FRAUGHT
frôt   4

FRÄULEIN
froi′ līn   2*
froi′ līn′   2
frou′ līn   2

FRENETIC
frə net′ ik   3*
fri net′ ik   1

FREQUENCY
frē′ kwən sē   4

FREQUENT (adj)
frē′ kwənt   4

FREQUENT (v)
frē kwent′   3*
frē′ kwənt   3
fri kwent′   1

FREUDIAN
froi′ dē ən   4

FRIABLE
frī′ ə bəl   3
frī′ ə b'l   1*

FRIAR
frī′ ər   4*
frīr   1

FRICASSEE
frik′ ə sē′   4*
frik′ ə sē′   2

FRIEZE
frēz   4

FRIGATE
frig′ it   3*
frig′ ət   1

FRIGID
frij′ id   3*
frij′ əd   1

FRIJOLE
frē hō′ lē   3*
frē hōl′   1

FRIVOLITY   +
fri väl′ ə tē   3*
fri väl′ i tē   1

FRIVOLOUS
friv′ ə ləs   4
friv′ ləs   1

FRONTAL
frunt′ 'l   4

PRONUNCIATION KEY

Symbol	Key words	Symbol	Key words	Symbol	Key words
a	asp, fat, parrot	†ə a in ago		r	red, port, dear
ā	ape, date, play	e in agent		s	sell, castle, pass
†ä	ah, car, father	i in sanity		t	top, cattle, hat
e	elf, ten, berry	o in comply		v	vat, hovel, have
ē	even, meet, money	u in focus		w	will, always, swear
i	is, hit, mirror	ər	perhaps, murder	y	yet, onion, yard
ī	ice, bite, high	b	bed, fable, dub	z	zebra, dazzle, haze
ō	open, tone, go	d	dip, beadle, had	ch	chin, catcher, arch
ô	all, horn, law	f	fall, after, off	sh	she, cushion, dash
o͞o	ooze, tool, crew	g	get, haggle, dog	th	thin, nothing, truth
o͝o	look, pull, moor	h	he, ahead, hotel	t̸h	then, father, lathe
yo͞o	use, cute, few	j	joy, agile, badge	zh	azure, leisure
yo͝o	united, cure, globule	k	kill, tackle, bake	ŋ	ring, anger, drink
oi	oil, point, toy	l	let, yellow, ball	″	see p. 15.
ou	out, crowd, plow	m	met, camel, trim	✓	see p. 15.
u	up, cut, color	n	not, flannel, ton	+	see p. 14.
ʉr	urn, fur, deter	p	put, apple, tap	′	see p. 15.
†See p. 14.		†See p. 16.		○	see p. 14.

FRONTIER   +   ○
frun tir'   4*
frən tir'   1
frun' tir   1
frän tir'   1
frän' tir   1

FRONTISPIECE   +
frun' tis pēs'   3*
frun' təs pēs'   1
frän' tis pēs'   1

FROTH (n)   +
frôth   4*
fräth   3

FROTH (v)   +
frôth   3
frôth   2*
fräth   2
fräth   1

FROUFROU
froo' froo   4*
froo' froo'   1

FRUGAL
froo' gəl   3
froo' g'l   1*

FRUITION
froo ish' ən   4

FUCHSIA
fyoo' shə   4

FUGITIVE
fyoo' jə tiv   3*
fyoo' ji tiv   1

FUGUE
fyoog

FÜHRER   ○
  (FUEHRER)
fyoor' ər   4
fir' ər   1*

FULCRUM
fool' krəm   4*
ful' krəm   4

FULMINATE
fool' mə nāt'   3*
ful' mə nāt'   3

FULSOME
fool' səm   4*
ful' səm   2

FUMIGATE
fyoo' mə gāt'   3*
fyoo' mi gāt'   1

FUNEREAL   ○
fyoo nir' ē əl   4

FUNGI
fun' jī   2*
fun' jī'   2
fuŋ' gī'   1
fuŋ' gī   1

FUNGICIDE
fun' jə sīd'   3*
fuŋ' gə sīd'   3
fun' ji sīd'   1

FUNGUS
fuŋ' gəs   4

FUNICULAR
fyoo nik' yə lər   2*
fə nik' yə lər   2
fyoo nik' yoo lər   1
fyoo nik' yə lər   1

FURLOUGH
fur' lō   4*
fur' lō'   1

FUROR
fyoor' ôr   3*
fyoor' ōr   2
fyoor' ôr'   1
fyoor' ōr'   1

FURUNCLE
fyoor' uŋ' kəl   2*
fyoor' uŋ kəl   1
fyoor' uŋ k'l   1

FUSELAGE
fyoo' sə läzh'   4*
fyoo' zə läzh'   4
fyoo' sə lij   2
fyoo' zə lij   1
fyoo' sə läj'   1
fyoo' zə läj'   1

FUSILLADE
fyoo' sə läd'   4*
fyoo' sə lād'   4
fyoo' zə lād'   3
fyoo' zə läd'   3
fyoo sə läd'   1
fyoo sə lād'   1
fyoo zə läd'   1
fyoo zə lād'   1

FUSION
fyoo' zhən   4

FUSTIAN
fus' chən   4

FUTILE
fyoot' 'l   4*
fyoo' tīl'   2
fyoo' til   1

FUTURITY
fyoo choor' ə tē   3*
fyoo toor' ə tē   3
fyoo tyoor' ə tē   3
fyoo toor' i tē   1
fyoo tyoor' i tē   1

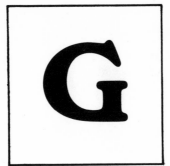

GAFFE
gaf   4

GAIETY
gā′ ə tē   3*
gā′ i tē   1

GALA
gā′ lə   4*
gal′ ə   4
gä′ lə   3

GALAXY
gal′ ək sē   4

GALL
gôl   4

GALLANT (n)
gə länt′   4*
gə lant′   4
gal′ ənt   4

GALLANT (adj)
gal′ ənt   4*
gə lant′   4
gə länt′   4

GALLEON
gal′ ē ən   4*
gal′ yən   1

GALLICISM
gal′ i siz′ əm   2*
gal′ ə siz′m   1
gal′ ə siz′ əm   1

GALLIMAUFRY
gal′ ə mô′ frē   4

GALLINACEOUS
gal′ ə nā′ shəs   4

GALORE
gə lôr′   4*
gə lōr′   3

GALOSH   +
gə läsh   4

GALVANIC
gal van′ ik   4

GALVANIZE
gal′ və nīz′   4

GAMBOL
gam′ bəl   3
gam′ b'l   1*

GAMETE
gə mēt′   4
gam′ ēt   3*

GAMIN
gam′ in   2*
gam′ ən   2

GAMUT
gam′ ət   4

GAMY
gā′ mē   4

GANEF   +
gä′ nəf   4

GANGLION
gaŋ′ glē ən   4

GANGRENE
gaŋ grēn′   4
gaŋ′ grēn   2*
gan′ grēn′   1
gan grēn′   1

GANGRENOUS
gaŋ′ grə nəs   4

GANTLET
gônt′ lit   3*
gant′ lit   3
gônt′ lət   1
gant′ lət   1

GAOL
jāl   4

GARAGE
gə räzh′   4*
gə räj′   4

GARDENIA
gär dēn′ yə   4*
gär dē′ nē ə   3

GARGANTUAN
gär gan′ chōō ən   2*
gär gan′ choo wən   1
gär ganch′ wən   1

GARGOYLE
gär′ goil′   2*
gär′ goil   2

GARISH ✓
gar′ ish   3*
ger′ ish   2

GARNET
gär′ nit   3*
gär′ nət   1

GARNISHEE
gär′ ni shē′   2*
gär′ nə shē′   2

GARNITURE
gär′ ni chər   4*
gär′ nə choor′   1

GARROTTE   +
gə rät′   4*
gə rōt′   4

GARRULITY
gə rōō′ lə tē   3*
gə rōō′ li tē   1
ga rōō′ lə tē   1

GARRULOUS
gar′ ə ləs   4*
gar′ yə ləs   3
gar′ yoo ləs   1

GASCONADE
gas kə nād′   3*
gas′ kə nād′   1

GASEOUS
gash′ əs   4*
gas′ ē əs   4
gas′ yəs   2

GASOLINE
gas′ ə lēn′   4*
gas′ ə lēn′   4

GASTRONOMIC   +
gas′ trə näm′ ik   4

GASTRONOMY   +
gas trän′ ə mē   2*
gə strän′ ə mē   2

GAUCHE
gōsh   4

GAUCHERIE
gō′ shə rē′   4*
gōsh′ rē   1

GAUCHO
gou′ chō   4

GAUDY
gôd′ ē   4*
gäd′ ē   1

GAUGE
gāj   4

GAUNT
gônt   4*
gänt   1

GAUNTLET
gônt′ lit   3*
gänt′ lit   3
gônt′ lət   1
gänt′ lət   1

GAUZE
gôz   4

GAVOTTE   +
gə vät′   4

GAZEBO
gə zē′ bō   4*
gə zā′ bō   4

GAZELLE
gə zel′   4

GAZETEER   ○
gaz′ ə tir′   3*
gaz′ i tir′   1

GAZETTE
gə zet′   4

GEISHA
gā′ shə   4*
gē′ shə   3

GEL
jel   4

GELATIN
jel′ ət ′n   3*
jel′ ət in   1
jel′ ət ən   1

GELATINOUS
je lat′ ′n əs   4*
je lat′ nəs   1

GELDING
gel′ diŋ   4

GELID
jel′ id   3*
jel′ əd   1

GEMINI
jem′ ə nī′   4*
jem′ ə nē′   3
gem′ ə nē′   1
jim′ ə nī′   1

GENDARME
zhän′ därm′   2*
zhän′ därm   2
jän′ därm′   1

GENE
jēn 4

GENEALOGY +
jē' nē äl' ə jē 3*
jē' nē al' ə jē 3
jen' ē äl' ə jē 2
jen' ē al' ə jē 2

GENERIC
ji ner' ik 4

GENESIS
jen' ə sis 2*
jen' i sis 1
jen' ə səs 1

GENETIC
jə net' ik 4

GENIAL
jēn' yəl 3*
jē' nē əl 2
jē' nyəl 1

GENIE
jē' nē 4*
jen' ē 1

GENITAL
jen' i t'l 2*
jen' ə t'l 1
jen' ə təl 1

GENITALIA
jen' ə tāl' yə 3*
jen' ə tā' lē ə 2
jen' i tā' lē ə 1
jen' i tāl' yə 1

GENOCIDE
jen' ə sīd' 4

GENRE
zhän' rə 4

GENTEEL
jen tēl' 4*
jen tē' əl 1

GENTIAN
jen' shən 3*
jen' chən 1

GENTILE
jen' tīl 3*
jen' tīl' 1

GENUFLECT
jen' yə flekt' 3*
jen' yoo flekt' 1

GENUINE
jen' yoo in 2*
jen' yoo wən 1
jen' yə wən 1

GENUS
jē' nəs 4

GEODESIC
jē' ə des' ik 4*
jē' ə dē' sik 3
jē' ə dez' ik 1
jē' ə dē' zik 1

GEOMETRIC
jē' ə met' rik 4

GEORGETTE
jôr jet' 4

GERANIUM
jə rā' nē əm 2*
ji rā' nē əm 2
jə rān' yəm 2

PRONUNCIATION KEY

Symbol	Key words	Symbol	Key words	Symbol	Key words
a	asp, fat, parrot	†ə	a in ago	r	red, port, dear
ā	ape, date, play		e in agent	s	sell, castle, pass
†ä	ah, car, father		i in sanity	t	top, cattle, hat
e	elf, ten, berry		o in comply	v	vat, hovel, have
ē	even, meet, money		u in focus	w	will, always, swear
i	is, hit, mirror	ər	perhaps, murder	y	yet, onion, yard
ī	ice, bite, high	b	bed, fable, dub	z	zebra, dazzle, haze
ō	open, tone, go	d	dip, beadle, had	ch	chin, catcher, arch
ô	all, horn, law	f	fall, after, off	sh	she, cushion, dash
oo	ooze, tool, crew	g	get, haggle, dog	th	thin, nothing, truth
oo	look, pull, moor	h	he, ahead, hotel	th	then, father, lathe
yoo	use, cute, few	j	joy, agile, badge	zh	azure, leisure
yoo	united, cure, globule	k	kill, tackle, bake	ŋ	ring, anger, drink
oi	oil, point, toy	l	let, yellow, ball	''	see p. 15.
ou	out, crowd, plow	m	met, camel, trim	✓	see p. 15.
u	up, cut, color	n	not, flannel, ton	+	see p. 14.
ʉr	urn, fur, deter	p	put, apple, tap	'	see p. 15.
†See p. 14.		†See p. 16.		○	see p. 14.

GERBIL
jʉr' bəl   2*
jʉr' bil   1
jʉr' b'l   1

GERIATRICS   ○
jer' ē at' riks   4
jir' ē at' riks   1*

GERMANE
jər mān'   4

GERMICIDE
jʉr' mə sīd'   2*
jʉr' mi sīd'   2

GERMINAL
jʉr' mə n'l   3*
jʉrm' nəl   1
jʉr' mə nəl   1

GERONTOLOGY   +
jer' ən täl' ə jē   4

GERRYMANDER
jer' ē man' dər   2*
ger' ē man' dər   2
jer' i man' dər   2
ger' i man' dər   2
jer' ē man' dər   1
ger' ē man' dər   1

GERUND
jer' ənd   4

GERUNDIVE
je run' div   4

GESSO
jes' ō   4

GEST
jest   4

GESTAPO
gə stä' pō   4*
gə stä' pō   1

GESTALT
gə sḥtält'   4*
gə sḥtôlt'   2
gə stält'   2
gə stôlt'   2

GESTATE
jes' tāt'   2*
jes' tāt   2

GESTICULATE
jə stik' yə lāt'   4

GESTURE
jes' chər   4*
jesḥ' chər   2

GESUNDHEIT
gə zoont' hīt'   2*
gə zoont' hīt   2

GETHSEMANE
getḥ sem' ə nē   4

GEW-GAW
gyoo' gô   3*
goo' gô   3

GEYSER
gī' zər   4*
gī' sər   2

GHAT
gôt   4
gät   3*

GHEE
gē   4

GHERKIN
gʉr' kin   4

GHETTO
get' ō   4

GHILLIE (GILLIE)
gil' ē   4

GHOUL
gool   4

GIBBER
jib' ər   4*
gib' ər   3

GIBBERISH
jib' ər isḥ   4*
gib' ər isḥ   4
jib' risḥ   1
gib' risḥ   1

GIBBET
jib' it   3*
jib' ət   1

GIBBON
gib' ən   4

GIBBOUS
gib' əs   4*
jib' əs   1

GIBE
jīb   4

GIBLETS
jib' lits   3*
jib' ləts   1

GIG
gig   4

GIGANTESQUE
jī' gan tesk'   4*
jī' gən tesk'   1

GIGANTIC
jī gan' tik   4*
jə gan' tik   1

GIGOLO
zhig' ə lō'   3*
jig' ə lō'   3
jig' ə lō   1

GILL (of a fisḥ)
gil   4

GILL (liquid measure)
jil   4

GIMCRACK
jim′ krak′   4

GIMLET
gim′ lit   4*
gim′ lət   1

GINGER
jin′ jər   4

GINGHAM
giŋ′ əm   4

GINGIVITIS
jin′ jə vīt′ is   2*
jin′ jə vīt′ əs   2

GINGKO
giŋ′ kō   3*
jiŋk′ gō   1

GIRANDOLE
jir′ ən dōl′   4

GIST
jist   4

GLABROUS
glā′ brəs   4

GLACÉ
gla sā′   4

GLACIAL
glā′ shəl   4

GLACIER
glā′ shər   4*
glā′ zhər   1

GLADIATOR
glad′ ē at′ ər   4

GLADIOLA
glad′ ē ō′ lə   4

GLADIOLUS
glad′ ē ō′ ləs   4

GLAMOR
glam′ ər   4

GLAUCOMA
glou kō′ mə   4*
glô kō′ mə   4

GLAZIER
glā′ zhər   4*
glā′ zē ər   1

GLISSADE
gli sād′   4*
gli säd′   4

GLOBAL
glō′ bəl   3*
glō′ b'l   1

GLOBULAR   +
gläb′ yə lər   4

GLOBULE   +
glab′ yo͞ol   4

GLOBULIN   +
gläb′ yə lən   3*
gläb′ yə lin   1

GLOCKENSPIEL   +
gläk′ ən shpēl′   4*
gläk′ ən spēl′   4

GLORY
glôr′ ē   4*
glōr′ ē   3

PRONUNCIATION KEY

Symbol	Key words	Symbol	Key words	Symbol	Key words
a	asp, fat, parrot	†ə	a in ago	r	red, port, dear
ā	ape, date, play		e in agent	s	sell, castle, pass
†ä	ah, car, father		i in sanity	t	top, cattle, hat
e	elf, ten, berry		o in comply	v	vat, hovel, have
ē	even, meet, money		u in focus	w	will, always, swear
i	is, hit, mirror	ər	perhaps, murder	y	yet, onion, yard
ī	ice, bite, high	b	bed, fable, dub	z	zebra, dazzle, haze
ō	open, tone, go	d	dip, beadle, had	ch	chin, catcher, arch
ô	all, horn, law	f	fall, after, off	sh	she, cushion, dash
o͞o	ooze, tool, crew	g	get, haggle, dog	th	thin, nothing, truth
oo	look, pull, moor	h	he, ahead, hotel	th	then, father, lathe
yo͞o	use, cute, few	j	joy, agile, badge	zh	azure, leisure
yoo	united, cure, globule	k	kill, tackle, bake	ŋ	ring, anger, drink
oi	oil, point, toy	l	let, yellow, ball	″	see p. 15.
ou	out, crowd, plow	m	met, camel, trim	✓	see p. 15.
u	up, cut, color	n	not, flannel, ton	+	see p. 14.
ur	urn, fur, deter	p	put, apple, tap	′	see p. 15.
†See p. 14.		†See p. 16.		○	see p. 14.

GLOSSARY   +
gläs′ ə rē   4*
glôs′ ə rē   2
gläs′ rē   1

GLOWER
glou′ ər   4*
glour   1

GLUCOSE
glo͞o′ kōs′   2*
glo͞o′ kōs   2
glo͞o′ kōz′   1

GLUTEN
glo͞ot′ ′n   4

GLUTINOUS
glo͞ot′ ′n əs   4*
glo͞ot′ nəs   1

GLUTTON
glut′ ′n   4

GLYCERINE
glis′ ər in   3*
glis′ rin   1
glis′ rən   1

GNEISS
nīs   4

GNOME
nōm   4

GNOMIC   +
nō′ mik   4*
näm′ ik   1

GNU
no͞o   4*
nyo͞o   4

GOATEE
gō tē′   4

GOBBLEDYGOOK   +
(GOBBLEDEGOOK)
gäb′ əl dē go͝ok′   2*
gäb′ ′l dē go͝ok′   1
gäb′ əl dē go͝ok′   1
gäb′ əl dē go͞ok′   1

GOLEM
gō′ ləm   4*
gō′ lem   2
goi′ ləm   1
gä′ ləm   1

GONAD   +
gō′ nad′   2*
gō′ nad   2
gän′ ad   1

GONDOLA   +
gän′ də lə   2*
gän dō′ lə   2
gän′ d′l ə   2

GONDOLIER   ○
gän′ də lir′   2*
gän′ d′ lir′   2

GONFALON   +
gän′ fə lən   3
gän′ fə län′   2*

GONORRHEA   +
gän′ ə rē′ ə   4

GOOGOL   +
go͞o′ gôl′   1*
go͞o′ gäl′   1
go͞o′ gäl   1
go͞o′ gəl   1
go͞o′ gôl   1

GOOK
gook   4*
go͞ok   4

GOOSEBERRY
go͞os′ ber′ ē   4*
go͞os′ bə rē   4
go͞oz′ ber′ ē   4
go͞oz′ bə rē   4

GOPHER
gō′ fər   4

GORGE
gôrj   4

GORGON
gôr′ gən   4

GORMAND
(see GOURMAND)

GOSLING   +
gäz′ liŋ   3*
gôz′ liŋ   1

GOSSAMER   +
gäs′ ə mər   4

GOUACHE
gwäsh′   4
go͞o äsh′   2*

GOUGE
gouj   4

GOULASH
go͞o′ läsh   3
go͞o′ lash   3
go͞o′ läsh′   1*
go͞o′ lash′   1

GOURD
goord   4*
gôrd   4
gōrd   3

GOURMAND
goor′ mənd   4
goor mänd′   1*
goor′ mänd   1

GOURMET
goor mā′   3*
goor′ mā   2
goor′ mā′   1

GOUT
gout   4

GOVERNANCE
guv′ ər nəns   4

GOVERNMENT
guv′ ərn mənt   4*
guv′ ər mənt   3
guv′ ′m ənt   1

GRADIENT
grā′ dē ənt   4*
grā′ dyənt   1

GRADUATE (n)
graj′ o͞o it   2*
graj′ o͞o āt′   1
graj′ oo wit   1
graj′ oo wāt′   1
graj′ wət   1
graj′ ə wāt′   1

GRADUATE (v)
graj′ o͞o āt′   2*
graj′ oo wāt′   1
graj′ ə wāt′   1

GRAFFITI
grə fēt′ ē   4

GRAHAM
grā′ əm   3*
gram′   1

GRAMERCY
grə mur′ sē   4*
gram′ ər sē   2

GRANARY
gran′ ə rē   4*
grān′ ə rē   4
grān′ rē   1

GRANDEE
gran dē′   4

GRANDEUR
gran′ jər   4*
gran′ joor   3
gran′ door   1
gran′ dər   1

GRANDILOQUENCE
gran dil′ ə kwəns   4*
gran dil′ ə kwənts   1

GRANDIOSE
gran′ dē ōs′   4*
gran′ dē ōs′   2

GRANITE
gran′ it   3*
gran′ ət   1

GRANULE
gran′ yo͞ol   4

GRATIS
grat′ is   2*
grāt′ is   2
grat′ əs   1
grāt′ əs   1

GRATITUDE
grat′ ə tyo͞od′   3
grat′ ə to͞od′   2*
grat′ i to͞od′   1
grat′ i tyo͞od′   1

GRATUITOUS
gra to͞o′ ə təs   2
gra tyo͞o′ ə təs   2
grə to͞o′ i təs   1*
grə tyo͞o′ i təs   1
grə to͞o′ ə təs   1
grə tyo͞o′ ə təs   1

GRATUITY
grə tōō′ i tē 1*
gra tōō′ ə tē 1
gra tyōō′ ə tē 1
grə tyōō′ i tē 1
grə tōō′ ə tē 1
grə tyōō′ ə tē 1

GRAVAMEN
grə vā′ mən 4

GRAVID
grav′ id 3*
grav′ əd 1

GRAVURE
grə vyoor′ 2*
grə vyōōr′ 2
grā vyoor′ 1
grā′ vyər 1
grā′ vyoor 1

GREASE (n)
grēs 4

GREASE (v)
grēs 4*
grēz 3

GREASY
grē′ sē 4*
grē′ zē 4

GREGARIOUS ✓
gri ger′ ē əs 4*
grə ger′ ē əs 1

GREMLIN
grem′ lən 3*
grem′ lin 1

GRENADE
grə nād′ 3*
gri nād′ 1

GRENADIER ○
gren′ ə dir′ 4

GRENADINE
gren′ ə dēn′ 4*
gren′ ə dēn′ 4

GRIDIRON
grid′ ī′ ərn 4*
grid′ īrn 1

GRIEVOUS
grē′ vəs 4

GRIMACE
gri mās′ 4*
grim′ əs 3
grim′ is 1

GRIMY
grī′ mē 4

GRINGO
griŋ′ gō 4

GRIPE
grīp 4

GRIPPE
grip 4

GRISAILLE
gri zāl′ 4*
gri zī′ 3

GRISLY
griz′ lē 4

GRISTLY
gris′ lē 4

GROSCHEN
grō′ shən 4*
grô′ shən 1

GROSGRAIN
grō′ grān′ 4

GROTESQUE
grō tesk′ 4

GROUSE
grous 4

GROUT
grout 4

GROVEL +
gruv′ əl 3*
gräv′ əl 3
gruv′ ′l 1
gräv′ ′l 1

GRUEL
grōō′ əl 4*
grōōl 1

GUANO
gwä′ nō 4

GUARANTEE
gar′ ən tē′ 4*
gär′ ən tē′ 2

GUARANTY
gar′ ən tē 3*
gär′ ən tē 2
gar′ ən tē′ 1

GUAVA
gwä′ və 4

GUBERNATORIAL
gōō′ bər nə tôr′ ē əl 3*
gōō′ bər nə tōr′ ē əl 3
gyōō′ bər nə tôr′ ē əl 3
gyōō′ bər nə tōr′ ē əl 3
gōō′ bə nə tôr′ ē əl 1
gyōō′ bə nə tōr′ ē əl 1
gōō′ bə nə tôr′ ē əl 1
gyōō′ bə nə tôr′ ē əl 1

GUERDON
gur′ d′n 4

GUERILLA
gə ril′ ə 4*
ge ril′ ə 1

GUFFAW
gə fô′ 4

GUIDON +
gīd' 'n 4*
gī' dän' 2

GUILD
gild 4

GUILE
gīl 4

GUILLOTINE
gil' ə tēn' 4*
gē' ə tēn' 4
gē' ə tēn' 1

GUIMPE
gamp 4*
gimp 4

GUINEA
gin' ē 4

GUISE
gīz 4

GUITAR
gi tär' 4*
gə tär' 1

GULDEN
gool' dən 3*
gool' d'n 1
gool' dən 1

GULLET
gul' it 2*
gul' ət 2

GUNWALE
gun' 'l 3*
gun' əl 1

GURU
goo roo' 3
goo' roo' 2
goo' roo 1*
gə roo' 1

GUSTATORY
gus' tə tôr' ē 4*
gus' tə tōr' ē 3

GUTTA PERCHA
gut' ə pur' chə 4

GUTTURAL
gut' ər əl 4*
gut' rəl 1

GYNECOLOGY +
gī' nə käl' ə jē 4*
jī' nə käl' ə jē 4
ji nə käl' ə jē 2
ji' nə käl' ə jē 2

GYP
jip 4

GYPSUM
jip' səm 4

GYRATE
jī' rāt' 2*
jī' rāt 2
jī rāt' 1

GYROSCOPE
jī' rə skōp' 4

GYVE
jīv 4*
gīv 1

PRONUNCIATION KEY

Symbol	Key words	Symbol	Key words	Symbol	Key words
a	asp, fat, parrot	†ə	a in ago	r	red, port, dear
ā	ape, date, play		e in agent	s	sell, castle, pass
†ä	ah, car, father		i in sanity	t	top, cattle, hat
e	elf, ten, berry		o in comply	v	vat, hovel, have
ē	even, meet, money		u in focus	w	will, always, swear
i	is, hit, mirror	ər	perhaps, murder	y	yet, onion, yard
ī	ice, bite, high	b	bed, fable, dub	z	zebra, dazzle, haze
ō	open, tone, go	d	dip, beadle, had	ch	chin, catcher, arch
ô	all, horn, law	f	fall, after, off	sh	she, cushion, dash
oo	ooze, tool, crew	g	get, haggle, dog	th	thin, nothing, truth
oo	look, pull, moor	h	he, ahead, hotel	th	then, father, lathe
yoo	use, cute, few	j	joy, agile, badge	zh	azure, leisure
yoo	united, cure, globule	k	kill, tackle, bake	ŋ	ring, anger, drink
oi	oil, point, toy	l	let, yellow, ball	"	see p. 15.
ou	out, crowd, plow	m	met, camel, trim	✓	see p. 15.
u	up, cut, color	n	not, flannel, ton	+	see p. 14.
ur	urn, fur, deter	p	put, apple, tap	'	see p. 15.
†See p. 14.		†See p. 16.		○	see p. 14.

H

HABEAS CORPUS
hā′ bē əs kôr′ pəs 3
hā′ bē əs kôr′ pəs 1*

HABILIMENT
hə bil′ ə mənt 4

HABITABLE
hab′ ə tə bəl 2*
hab′ i tə bəl 1
hab′ i tə b′l 1

HABITAT
hab′ ə tat′ 3*
hab′ i tat′ 1

HABITUAL
hə bich′ o͞o əl 2*
hə bich′ oo wəl 1
hə bich′ əl 1
ha bich′ əl 1
hə bich′ wəl 1
hə bich′ ə wəl 1

HABITUÉ
hə bich′ o͞o ā′ 2
hə bich′ o͞o ā′ 2*
hə bich′ oo wā′ 1
hə bich′ ə wā′ 1
ha bich′ ə wā′ 1

HACIENDA
hä′ sē en′ də 4*
ä′ sē en′ də 1

HADES
hā′ dēz 4

HADJ (HAJJ)
haj 4

HAGGIS
hag′ is 3*
hag′ əs 1

HAGIOLOGY +
hā′ jē äl′ ə jē 4*
hag′ ē äl′ ə jē 4

HAIKU
hī′ ko͞o 4*
hī′ ko͞o′ 1

HALBERD
hal′ bərd 4*
hôl′ bərd 2
häl′ bərd 1

HALCYON
hal′ sē ən 4

HALFPENNY
hāp′ nē 3
hā′ pə nē 2*
haf′ pen′ ē 1

HALLELUJAH
hal′ ə lo͞o′ yə 4

HALLUCINATION
hə lo͞o′ sə nā′ shən 3*
hə lo͞o′ s′n ā′ shən 1

HALLUCINOGEN
hə lo͞o′ sə nə jən 2*
hə lo͞o′ s′n ə jən 1
hal′ yə sin′ ə jən 1

HALO
hā′ lō 4*
hā′ lō′ 1

HALVAH
häl vä′ 3*
häl′ vä 3
häl′ vä′ 1
häl′ və 1

HALYARD
hal′ yərd 4

HANDKERCHIEF
haŋ′ kər chif 4*
haŋ′ kər chēf′ 3
haŋ′ kər chəf 1
haŋ′ kər chif′ 1

HANDSOME
han′ səm 4*
hant′ səm 1

HANGAR
haŋ′ ər 4

HANGER
haŋ′ ər 4

HAPHAZARD
hap haz′ ərd 4*
hap′ haz′ ərd 1

HARA KIRI ○ ✓
här′ ə kir ē 3*
här′ ē kir′ ē 2
har′ i kir′ ē 1
har′ i kar′ ē 1
har′ ē kir′ ē 1
här′ ē kär′ ē 1
her′ ē ker′ ē 1

HARANGUE
hə raŋ′ 4

HARASS
har′ əs 4*
hə ras′ 4

HARBINGER
här′ bən jər 2*
här′ bin jər 2

HAREM ✓
her′ əm 4*
har′ əm 4

HARLEQUIN
här′ lə kwən 2
här′ lə kin 2
här′ lə kwin 1*
här′ lə kən 1
här′ li kən 1
här′ li kwən 1

HARLEQUINADE
här′ lə kwi nād′ 2*
här′ lə kwə näd′ 1
här′ lə ki nād′ 1
här′ li kə nād′ 1
här′ li kwə nād′ 1

HARLOT
här′ lət 4

HARPSICHORD
härp′ si kôrd′ 4*
härp′ si kōrd′ 1

HARQUEBUS
här′ kə bəs 3
här′ kwi bəs 2*
här′ kwə bus′ 1
här′ kwi bəs′ 1

HARRIDAN
har′ i d'n 2*
har′ ə d'n 1
har′ ə dən 1

HARTEBEEST
härt′ bēst′ 4*
här′ tə bēst′ 3

HASHISH
hash′ ish 3
hash′ ēsh′ 2*
hash′ ish′ 2
hash′ ēsh 2

HAUBERK
hô′ bᵘrk 4*
hô′ bᵘrk′ 1

HAUGHTY
hôt′ ē 4*
hät′ ē 1

HAUNCH
hônch 4*
hänch 4

HAUNT
hônt 4*
hänt 4

HAUTBOY
ō′ boi′ 3*
hō′ boi′ 3
hō′ boi 1
ō′ boi 1

HAUTEUR
hō tᵘr′ 4*
hô tᵘr′ 1
ō tᵘr′ 1

HAVOC
hav′ ək 4*
hav′ ik 1

HAWSE
hôz 4*
hôs 1

HEARKEN
här′ kən 4

HEARSE
hᵘrs 4

HEARTH
härth 4

HEATH
hēth 4

HEATHEN
hē′ thən 4

HEATHER
heth′ ər 4

HEBRAIC
hi brā′ ik 1

HEDONISM
hēd' 'n iz' əm   3
hēd' 'n iz' 'm   1*

HEGEMONY
hi jem' ə nē   3*
hej' ə mō' nē   3
hi gem' ə nē   1

HEGIRA (HEJIRA)
hi jī' rə   4*
hej' ər ə   4
hej' rə   1

HEIFER
hef' ər   4

HEIGH-HO
hī' hō'   4*
hā' hō'   4

HEIGHT
hīt   4*

HEINOUS
hā' nəs   4

HEIR ✓
er   4*
ar   1

HEIRESS ✓
er' is   3*
er' əs   1
ar' əs   1

HEJIRA (see HEGIRA)

HELICAL
hel' i kəl   4*
hē' lə kəl   1
hē' li kəl   1

HELICOPTER   +
hel' ə käp' tər   3*
hē' lə käp' tər   3
hel' i käp tər   1

HELIOCENTRIC
hē lē ō sen' trik   3*
hē' lē ō sen' trik   1

HELIOTROPE
hē' lē ə trōp'   3*
hēl' yə trōp'   3

HELIPORT
hel' ə pôrt'   4*
hel' ə pōrt'   3
hē' lə pôrt'   2
hē' lə pōrt'   2

HELIUM
hē' lē əm   4

HELIX
hē' liks   4

HELOT
hel' ət   4*
hēl' ət   3

HEMATOLOGY   +
hē' mə täl' ə jē   4*
hem' ə täl' ə jē   2

HEMISPHERIC   ○
hem' ə sfer' ik   2*
hem i sfir' ik   1
hem i sfer' ik   1
hem' ə sfir' ik   1

PRONUNCIATION KEY

Symbol	Key words	Symbol	Key words	Symbol	Key words
a	asp, fat, parrot	†ə	a in ago	r	red, port, dear
ā	ape, date, play		e in agent	s	sell, castle, pass
†ä	ah, car, father		i in sanity	t	top, cattle, hat
e	elf, ten, berry		o in comply	v	vat, hovel, have
ē	even, meet, money		u in focus	w	will, always, swear
i	is, hit, mirror	ər	perhaps, murder	y	yet, onion, yard
ī	ice, bite, high	b	bed, fable, dub	z	zebra, dazzle, haze
ō	open, tone, go	d	dip, beadle, had	ch	chin, catcher, arch
ô	all, horn, law	f	fall, after, off	sh	she, cushion, dash
o͞o	ooze, tool, crew	g	get, haggle, dog	th	thin, nothing, truth
oo	look, pull, moor	h	he, ahead, hotel	th	then, father, lathe
yo͞o	use, cute, few	j	joy, agile, badge	zh	azure, leisure
yoo	united, cure, globule	k	kill, tackle, bake	ŋ	ring, anger, drink
oi	oil, point, toy	l	let, yellow, ball	''	see p. 15.
ou	out, crowd, plow	m	met, camel, trim	✓	see p. 15.
u	up, cut, color	n	not, flannel, ton	+	see p. 14.
ur	urn, fur, deter	p	put, apple, tap	'	see p. 15.
†See p. 14.		†See p. 16.		○	see p. 14.

HEMOGLOBIN
hē′ mə glō′ bin 2*
hē′ mə glō′ bən 2
hem′ ə glō′ bin 2
hem′ ə glō′ bən 1
hē′ mə glō′ bin 1
hem′ ə glō′ bin 1

HEMOPHILIA
hē mə fil′ ē ə 3*
hē′ mə fēl′ yə 3
hem ə fil′ ē ə 2
hem′ ə fēl′ yə 1
hem′ ə fil′ yə 1

HEMORRHAGE
hem′ ər ij 4*
hem′ rij 3

HEMORRHOID
hem′ ə roid′ 4*
hem′ roid 2
hem′ roid′ 1

HEPATITIS
hep′ ə tī′ tis 3*
hep′ ə tī′ təs 1

HERALD
her′ əld 4

HERALDIC
hə ral′ dik 4*
he ral′ dik 1

HERB
ʉrb 4*
hʉrb 4

HERBACEOUS
hʉr bā′ s̸həs 4*
ʉr bā′ s̸həs 3

HERBICIDE
hʉr′ bi sīd′ 3*
ʉr′ bi sīd′ 2
hʉr′ bə sīd′ 1
ʉr′ bə sīd′ 1

HERBIVOROUS
hər biv′ ər əs 4*
ər biv′ ər əs 1

HERCULEAN
hʉr′ kyōō′ lē ən 4*
hʉr′ kyə lē′ ən 4

HEREDITARY ✓
hə red′ ə ter′ ē 3*
hə red′ i ter′ ē 1

HEREDITY
hə red′ ə tē 3*
hə red′ i tē 1

HERESY
her′ ə sē 3*
her′ i sē 1

HERETIC
her′ ə tik 2*
her′ i tik 1
her′ ə tik′ 1

HERETICAL
hə ret′ i kəl 3*
hə ret′ i k′l 1

HERMAPHRODITE
hər maf′ rə dīt′ 4*
hər maf′ rə dit′ 1

HERMETIC
hər met′ ik 4

HERNIA
hʉr′ nē ə 4

HEROIC
hi rō′ ik 4

HEROIN
her′ ō in 1*
her′ ō ən 1
her′ ə win 1
her′ ə wən 1

HEROINE
her′ ō in 2*
her′ ə win 1
her′ ə wən 1

HEROISM
her′ ō iz′ əm 2*
her′ ō wiz′m 1
her′ ə wiz′ əm 1

HERON
her′ ən 4

HERPES
hʉr′ pēz 3*
hʉr′ pēz′ 2

HERPETOLOGIST +
hʉr′ pə täl′ ə jist 2*
hʉr′ pi täl′ ə jist 1
hʉr′ pə täl′ ə jəst 1

HESITANCY
hez′ ə tən sē 3*
hez′ i tən sē 1

HETAERA ○
hi tir′ ə 4

HETERODOX +
het′ ər ə däks′ 4*
he′ trə däks′ 1

HETEROGENEITY
het′ ə rō jə nē′ ə tē 2*
het′ ə rō jə nē′ i tē 1
het′ ə rə jə nē′ ə tē 1
he′ trō jə nē′ ə tē 1

HETEROGENEOUS
het′ ər ə jē′ nē əs 4*
het′ ər ə jēn′ yəs 3
het′ rə jēn′ yəs 2

HETEROSEXUAL
het′ ə rō sek′ s̸hōō əl 1*
het′ ər ə sek′ s̸hōō əl 1
het′ ər ə sek′ s̸hōō wəl 1
het′ ə rō seks̸h′ wəl 1

HEURISTIC
hyo͞o ris' tik   4

HIATUS
hī āt' əs   4

HIBACHI
hi bä' chē   3*
hē bä' chē   1

HIBERNATE
hī' bər nāt'   4

HIBISCUS
hī bis' kəs   4*
hi bis' kəs   2
hə bis' kəs   1

HICCOUGH
hik' əp   3*
hik' up   2
hik' əp'   1

HIDALGO
hi dal' gō   4

HIDEOUS
hid' ē əs   4

HIERARCHY
hī' ə rär' kē   4*
hī' rär' kē   2
hī' rär kē   1

HIERATIC
hī' ə rat' ik   4*
hī rat' ik   2
hī' rat' ik   1

HIEROGLYPHIC
hī' rə glif' ik   4*
hī' ər ə glif' ik   4

HILARIOUS ✓
hi ler' ē əs   4*
hī ler' ē əs   4
hi lar' ē əs   3
hī lar' ē əs   3

HILARITY
hi lar' ə tē   3*
hī lar' ə tē   3
hi ler' ə tē   2
hī ler' ə tē   2
hi lar' i tē   1
hī ler' i tē   1
hi ler' i tē   1
hī lar' i tē   1

HIRSUTE
hʉr so͞ot'   3*
hʉr' so͞ot   3
hʉr' so͞ot'   2
hir' so͞ot   2

HISTAMINE
his' tə mēn'   4*
his' tə min   2
his' tə mən   2

HISTORICAL   +
his tär' i kəl   3*
his tôr' i kəl   3
his tôr' i k'l   1
his tär' i k'l   1

HISTORY
his' tə rē   4*
his' trē   3

HISTRIONIC   +
his' trē än' ik   4

HOARD
hôrd   4*
hōrd   3

HOAX
hōks 4

HOI POLLOI
hoi' pə loi' 3*
hoi' pə loi' 1

HOKUM
hō' kəm 4

HOLLANDAISE   +
häl' ən dāz' 3*
häl' ən dāz' 2

HOLOCAUST   +
häl' ə käst' 2
häl' ə kôst' 1*
häl' ə kôst 1
hō' lə käst' 1
hō' lə kôst' 1

HOMAGE   +
häm' ij 4*
äm' ij 4

HOMBRE   +
äm' brē 4
äm' brä 3*
um' brē 1
um' brä' 1

HOMBURG   +
häm' bʉrg 3*
häm' bʉrg' 1

HOMEOPATHY   +
hō' mē äp' ə thē 4*
häm' ē äp' ə thē 3

HOMERIC
hō mer' ik 4

HOMICIDAL   +
häm ə sīd' 'l 3*
hō' mə sīd' 'l 2
hō mə sīd' 'l 1
häm' i sīd' 'l 1

HOMICIDE   +
häm' ə sīd' 3*
hō' mə sīd' 3
häm' i sīd' 1

HOMILETIC   +
häm' ə let' ik 4

HOMILY   +
häm' ə lē 4

HOMINY   +
häm' ə nē 4

HOMOGENEITY   +
hō' mə jə nē' i tē 2*
häm' ə jə nē' i tē 2
hō' mō ji nē' ə tē 1
häm' ō ji nē' ə tē 1

HOMOGENEOUS   +
hō' mə jē' nē əs 4
hō' mə jēn' yəs 3*
häm' ə jē' nē əs 3
häm' ə jēn' yəs 2

HOMOGENIZE   +
hə mäj' ə nīz' 4*
hō mäj' ə nīz' 3

HOMONYM   +
häm' ə nim' 3*
hō' mə nim' 3
häm' ə nim 1

HOMO SAPIENS
hō' mō sā' pē ənz 4*
hō' mō sap' ē ənz 2
hō' mō sap' ē enz 1
hō' mō sā' pē enz 1

HONORARIUM   +   ✓
än' ə rer' ē əm 4

HOOF
hoof 4*
ho͞of 4

HOOKAH
hook' ə 4
ho͞ok' ə 1

HOOLIGAN
ho͞o li gən 3*
ho͞o lə gən 1

HOOTENANNY
ho͞ot' 'n an' ē 4

HORDE
hôrd 4*
hōrd 3

HORIZON
hə rī' z'n 2*
hə rī' zən 2

HORIZONTAL   +
här' ə zän' t'l 3*
hôr' ə zän' t'l 3
hôr' i zän' t'l 1
här' i zän' t'l 1

HORMONE
hôr' mōn' 2*
hôr' mōn 2

HOROSCOPE   +
här' ə skōp' 4*
hôr' ə skōp' 4

HORRENDOUS   +
hô ren' dəs 4*
hä ren' dəs 2
hə ren' dəs 2
hō ren' dəs 1

HORS D'OEUVRE
ôr dʉrv' 3*
ôr' dʉrv 1
ôr' duv' 1

HORTATORY
hôr' tə tôr' ē 4*
hôr' tə tōr' ē 3

HOSANNA
hō zan' ə 4*
hō zän' ə 1

HOSIERY
hō' zhər ē 3*
hōzh' rē 1

HOSPICE +
häs' pis 3*
häs' pəs 1

HOSPITABLE +
häs pit' ə bəl 3
häs' pi tə bəl 2*
häs' pi tə b'l 1
häs' pə tə bəl 1
häs pit' ə b'l 1

HOSTAGE +
häs' tij 4

HOSTEL +
häs' t'l 3*
häs' təl 1

HOSTELRY +
häs' t'l rē 3*
häs' təl rē 1

HOSTILE +
häs' t'l 3*
häs' təl 1
häs' tīl' 1

HOURI
hoor' ē 3
ho͞or' ē 3
hou' rē 1*

HOUSE (v)
houz 4

HOUSING
hou' ziŋ 4

HOVEL +
huv' əl 3*
häv' əl 3
huv' 'l 1
häv' 'l 1

HOVER +
huv' ər 4*
häv' ər 4

HOWBEIT
hou bē' it 3*
hou bē' ət 1

HOWDAH
hou' də 4

HOWITZER
hou' it sər 3*
hou' ət sər 1

HOYDEN
hoid' 'n 4

HUARACHE
wə rä' che 3*
hə rä' che 2
wə rä' chä 1
hoo rä' che 1
hoo rä' chä 1

HUBRIS
hyoo' bris 3*
hyoo' brəs 1
hoo' bris 1

HUE
hyoo 4

HUGE
hyooj 4*
yooj 3

PRONUNCIATION KEY

Symbol	Key words	Symbol	Key words	Symbol	Key words
a	asp, fat, parrot	†ə	a in ago	r	red, port, dear
ā	ape, date, play		e in agent	s	sell, castle, pass
†ä	ah, car, father		i in sanity	t	top, cattle, hat
e	elf, ten, berry		o in comply	v	vat, hovel, have
ē	even, meet, money		u in focus	w	will, always, swear
i	is, hit, mirror	ər	perhaps, murder	y	yet, onion, yard
ī	ice, bite, high	b	bed, fable, dub	z	zebra, dazzle, haze
ō	open, tone, go	d	dip, beadle, had	ch	chin, catcher, arch
ô	all, horn, law	f	fall, after, off	sh	she, cushion, dash
oo	ooze, tool, crew	g	get, haggle, dog	th	thin, nothing, truth
oo	look, pull, moor	h	he, ahead, hotel	th	then, father, lathe
yoo	use, cute, few	j	joy, agile, badge	zh	azure, leisure
yoo	united, cure, globule	k	kill, tackle, bake	ŋ	ring, anger, drink
oi	oil, point, toy	l	let, yellow, ball	''	see p. 15.
ou	out, crowd, plow	m	met, camel, trim	✓	see p. 15.
u	up, cut, color	n	not, flannel, ton	+	see p. 14.
ur	urn, fur, deter	p	put, apple, tap	'	see p. 15.
†See p. 14.		†See p. 16.		○	see p. 14.

HUMAN
hyo͞o′ mən   4*
yo͞o′ mən   3

HUMANE
hyo͞o mān′   4*
yo͞o mān′   3

HUMBLE
hum′ bəl   3*
um′ bəl   2
um′ b'l   2
hum′ b'l   1

HUMID
hyo͞o′ mid   3*
yo͞o′ mid   2
hyo͞o′ məd   1
yo͞o′ məd   1

HUMIDITY
hyo͞o mid′ ə tē   3*
hyo͞o mid′ i tē   1
yo͞o mid′ ə tē   1
yo͞o mid′ i tē   1

HUMILIATE
hyo͞o mil′ ē āt′   4*
yo͞o mil′ ē āt′   3
hyo͞o mil′ ē āt′   1

HUMILITY
hyo͞o mil′ ə tē   3*
hyo͞o mil′ i tē   1
yo͞o mil′ ə tē   1
yo͞o mil′ i tē   1

HUMOR
hyo͞o′ mər   4*
yo͞o′ mər   3

HUMUS
hyo͞o′ məs   4*
yo͞o′ məs   3

HUNDRED
hun′ drid   3*
hun′ dərd   2
hun′ drəd   1

HUNDREDTH
hun′ dridth   3*
hun′ dritth   1
hun′ drədth   1
hun′ drətth   1

HURLY BURLY
hur′ lē bur′ lē   2*
hur′ lē bur′ lē   2
hur′ lē bur′ lē   1

HURRAH
hə rä′   2*
hoo rä′   2
hoo rô′   2
hə rô′   2

HUSSAR
hə zär′   3*
hoo zär′   3
hə sär′   1

HUSSY
huz′ ē   4*
hus′ ē   4

HYACINTH
hī′ ə sinth   3*
hī′ ə sinth′   2
hī′ ə sintth′   1
hī′ ə sənth   1
hī′ ə səntth   1

HYBRID
hī brid   3*
hī brəd   1

HYDRA
hī′ drə   4

HYDRANGEA
hī drān′ jə   4*
hī drān′ jē ə   3
hī dran′ jə   2
hī dran′ jē ə   2

HYDRAULIC
hī drô′ lik   4*
hī drä′ lik   2

HYDROGENATE   +
hī dräj′ ə nāt′   4*
hī′ drə jə nāt′   4

HYDROLYSIS   +
hī dräl′ ə sis   2*
hī dräl′ i sis   1
hī dräl′ ə səs   1
hī′ drə lī′ səs   1

HYDROMETER   +
hī dräm′ ə tər   3*
hī dräm′ i tər   1

HYDROPHOBIA
hī drə fō′ bē ə   4

HYENA
hī ē′ nə   4

HYGIENE
hī′ jēn′   2
hī′ jēn   2
hī jēn′   1*
hī′ jē ən′   1

HYGIENIC
hī′ jē en′ ik   4*
hī′ jē′ nik   2
hī′ jen′ ik   2

HYMENEAL
hī′ mə nē′ əl   4

HYMN
him   4

HYMNAL
him′ nəl   3*
him′ n'l   1

HYPERBOLE
hī pur′ bə lē   4*
hī pur′ bə lē′   1

HYPERTROPHY
hī pur′ trə fē   4

HYPNOSIS
hip nō' sis   3*
hip nō' səs   1

HYPNOTIC   +
hip nät' ik   4

HYPNOTISM
hip' nə tiz' əm   3*
hip' nə tiz'm   1

HYPOCHONDRIA   +
hī' pə kän' drē ə   4

HYPOCHONDRIAC
hī' pə kän' drē ak'   4

HYPOCHONDRIACAL   +
hī' pə kən drī' ə kəl   2*
hī' pō kän drī' ə kəl   1
hī' pə kən drī' ə k'l   1

HYPOCRISY   +
hi päk' rə sē   4*
hī päk' rə sē   1

HYPOCRITE
hip' ə krit'   2*
hip' ə krit   2

HYPODERMIC
hī' pə dʉr' mik   3*
hī pə dʉr' mik   1

HYPOTHESIS   +
hī päth' ə sis   2*
hī päth' i sis   1
hī päth' ə səs   1
hi päth' i sis   1
hi päth' ə sis   1

HYPOTHETICAL
hī pə thet' i kəl   2*
hī' pə thet' i kəl   1
hī' pə thet' i k'l   1

HYSSOP
his' əp   4

HYSTERECTOMY
his' tə rek' tə mē   4

HYSTERIA   ○
his tir' ē ə   3*
his ter' ē ə   4

HYSTERICS
his ter' iks   4

PRONUNCIATION KEY

Symbol	Key words	Symbol	Key words	Symbol	Key words
a	asp, fat, parrot	†ə	a in ago	r	red, port, dear
ā	ape, date, play		e in agent	s	sell, castle, pass
†ä	ah, car, father		i in sanity	t	top, cattle, hat
e	elf, ten, berry		o in comply	v	vat, hovel, have
ē	even, meet, money		u in focus	w	will, always, swear
i	is, hit, mirror	ər	perhaps, murder	y	yet, onion, yard
ī	ice, bite, high	b	bed, fable, dub	z	zebra, dazzle, haze
ō	open, tone, go	d	dip, beadle, had	ch	chin, catcher, arch
ô	all, horn, law	f	fall, after, off	sh	she, cushion, dash
ōō	ooze, tool, crew	g	get, haggle, dog	th	thin, nothing, truth
oo	look, pull, moor	h	he, ahead, hotel	th	then, father, lathe
yōō	use, cute, few	j	joy, agile, badge	zh	azure, leisure
yoo	united, cure, globule	k	kill, tackle, bake	ŋ	ring, anger, drink
oi	oil, point, toy	l	let, yellow, ball	"	see p. 15.
ou	out, crowd, plow	m	met, camel, trim	✓	see p. 15.
u	up, cut, color	n	not, flannel, ton	+	see p. 14.
ʉr	urn, fur, deter	p	put, apple, tap	'	see p. 15.
†See p. 14.		†See p. 16.		○	see p. 14.

IBEX
ī′ beks′ 4

IBIS
ī′ bis 3*
ī′ bəs 1

ICHOR
ī′ kər 3
ī′ kôr′ 2*
ī′ kôr 2

ICHTHYOLOGY +
ik′ thē äl′ ə jē 4

ICON +
ī′ kän 3*
ī′ kän′ 1

ICONOCLAST +
ī kän′ ə klast′ 4

IDEA
ī dē′ ə 4*
īd′ ē ə 1

IDEALISM
ī dē′ ə liz′ əm 3*
ī dē′ ə liz′m 1
ī dē′ liz′ əm 1

IDÉE FIXE
ē dā fēks′ 3

IDENTIFY
ī den′ tə fī′ 4*
i den′ tə fī 2
ə den′ tə fī′ 1

IDEOLOGY +
ī′ dē äl′ ə jē 2*
id′ ē äl′ ə jē 2
ī dē äl′ ə jē 1

IDES
īdz 4

IDIOM
id′ ē əm 4

IDIOSYNCRASY
id′ ē ə sin′ krə sē 3*
id′ ē ə sin′ krə sē 2
id′ ē ō sin′ krə sē 1

IDOLATROUS +
ī däl′ ə trəs 4

IDOLATRY +
ī däl′ ə trē 4

IDYLL
īd′ ′l 4

IDYLLIC
ī dil′ ik 4

IGLOO
ig′ loo 4

IGNEOUS
ig′ nē əs 4

IGNOBLE
ig nō′ bəl 3*
ig nō′ b′l 1

IGNOMINIOUS
ig′ nə min′ ē əs 3*
ig′ nō min′ ē əs 1

IGNOMINY +
ig′ nə min′ ē 4*
ig näm′ ə nē 1

IGNORAMUS
ig′ nə rā′ məs 3*
ig′ nə ram′ əs 2

IGUANA
i gwä′ nə 4

ILEITIS
il′ ē ī′ tis 4

ILLICIT
i lis′ it   3*
i lis′ ət   1

ILLITERATE
i lit′ ər it   3*
i lit′ ər ət   1
i lit′ rət   1

ILLUMINATE
i lo͞o′ mə nāt′   4

ILLUSION
i lo͞o′ zhən   4

ILLUSORY
i lo͞o′ sər ē   4*
i lo͞o′ zər ē   3
i lo͞os′ rē   1

ILLUSTRATE
il′ ə strāt′   4*
i lus′ trāt   2
i lus′ trāt′   2

ILLUSTRATION
il′ ə strā′ shən   4

ILLUSTRATIVE
i lus′ trə tiv   4*
il′ ə strā′ tiv   3

ILLUSTRIOUS
i lus′ trē əs   4

IMAGERY
im′ ij rē   4*
im′ ij ə rē   2

IMAGISM
im′ ə jiz′ əm   2*
im′ ə jiz ′m   1
im′ i jiz′ əm   1

IMAGO
i mā′ gō   4*
i mä′ gō   1

IMBECILE
im′ bə səl   2*
im′ bə sil   1
im′ bi sil   1
im′ bi səl   1
im′ bə s′l   1

IMBROGLIO
im brōl′ yō   4

IMBUE
im byo͞o′   4

IMMACULATE
i mak′ yə lit   3*
i mak′ yə lət   1

IMMANENT
im′ ə nənt   4

IMMATURE
im′ ə cho͝or′   4*
im′ ə to͝or′   4
im′ ə tyo͝or′   3

IMMERSE
i mʉrs′   4

IMMERSION
i mʉr′ zhən   4*
i mʉr′ shən   4

IMMOBILE
i mō′ bəl   2*
i mō′ bēl   2
i mō′ bēl′   2
i mō′ bīl′   2
i mō′ b′l   1
i mō′ bil   1

IMMOLATE
im′ ə lāt′   4

IMMORAL   +
i mär′ əl   4*
i môr′ əl   4

IMMORTAL
i môr′ t′l   4

IMMUNE
i myo͞on′   4

IMMUNITY
i myo͞on′ ə tē   3*
i myo͞on′ i tē   1

IMMUNIZE
im′ yə nīz′   4*
i myo͞o′ nīz   1

IMMUNOLOGY   +
im′ yə näl′ ə jē   3*
im′ yoo näl′ ə jē   1

IMMURE
i myo͞or′   2*
i myoor′   2

IMPASSE
im pas′   3
im′ pas   2*
im′ pas′   1

IMPECCABLE
im pek′ ə bəl   4*
im pek′ ə b′l   1

IMPECUNIOUS
im′ pi kyo͞o′ nē əs   3*
im′ pə kyo͞o′ nē əs   1
im′ pi kyo͞o′ nyəs   1

IMPEDIMENT
im ped′ ə mənt   4

IMPEDIMENTA
im ped′ ə men′ tə   4*

IMPENETRABLE
im pen′ ə trə bəl   3*
im pen′ i trə bəl   1
im pen′ i trə b′l   1

IMPERATIVE
im per′ ə tiv   4

IMPERIAL   ○
im pir′ ē əl   4

IMPERIOUS ○
im pir′ ē əs 4

IMPERTURBABLE
im′ pər tur′ bə bəl 3*
im′ pər tur′ bə b'l 1

IMPERVIOUS
im pur′ vē əs 4

IMPETIGO
im′ pə tī′ gō 3*
im′ pə tē′ gō 2
im′ pi tī′ gō 1

IMPETUOUS
im pech′ oo əs 2*
im pech′ oo wəs 1
im pech′ wəs 1

IMPETUOSITY +
im pech′ oo äs′ ə tē 1*
im pech′ oo wäs′ ə tē 1
im pech′ ə wäs′ ə tē 1
im pech′ oo äs′ i tē 1

IMPETUS
im′ pə təs 3*
im′ pi təs 1

IMPINGE
im pinj′ 4

IMPIOUS
im′ pē əs 4*
im pī′ əs 2

IMPLACABLE
im plā′ kə bəl 3*
im plak′ ə bəl 3
im plak′ ə b'l 1
im plā′ kə b'l 1

IMPLICIT
im plis′ it 3*
im plis′ ət 1

IMPOLITIC +
im päl′ i tik 2*
im päl′ ə tik 1
im päl′ ə tik′ 1

IMPORT (n)
im′ pōrt′ 3
im′ pôrt′ 2*

IMPORT (v)
im pôrt′ 4*
im pōrt′ 3
im′ pôrt 1

IMPORTUNATE
im pôr′ chə nit 2*
im pôr′ choo nit 1
im porch′ nət 1

IMPORTUNE
im′ pôr′ chən 4
im′ pôr tyoon′ 3*
im′ pôr toon′ 3
im′ pər toon′ 1

IMPOSTOR +
im päs′ tər 4

IMPOSTURE +
im päs′ chər 4

IMPOTENCE
im′ pə təns 3*
im′ pə t'ns 1
im′ pə tənts 1

PRONUNCIATION KEY

Symbol	Key words	Symbol	Key words	Symbol	Key words
a	asp, fat, parrot	†ə	a in ago	r	red, port, dear
ā	ape, date, play		e in agent	s	sell, castle, pass
†ä	ah, car, father		i in sanity	t	top, cattle, hat
e	elf, ten, berry		o in comply	v	vat, hovel, have
ē	even, meet, money		u in focus	w	will, always, swear
i	is, hit, mirror	ər	perhaps, murder	y	yet, onion, yard
ī	ice, bite, high	b	bed, fable, dub	z	zebra, dazzle, haze
ō	open, tone, go	d	dip, beadle, had	ch	chin, catcher, arch
ô	all, horn, law	f	fall, after, off	sh	she, cushion, dash
oo	ooze, tool, crew	g	get, haggle, dog	th	thin, nothing, truth
oo	look, pull, moor	h	he, ahead, hotel	th	then, father, lathe
yoo	use, cute, few	j	joy, agile, badge	zh	azure, leisure
yoo	united, cure, globule	k	kill, tackle, bake	ŋ	ring, anger, drink
oi	oil, point, toy	l	let, yellow, ball	″	see p. 15.
ou	out, crowd, plow	m	met, camel, trim	╱	see p. 15.
u	up, cut, color	n	not, flannel, ton	+	see p. 14.
ur	urn, fur, deter	p	put, apple, tap	′	see p. 15.
†See p. 14.		†See p. 16.		○	see p. 14.

IMPOTENT
im′ pə tənt 3*
im′ pə t′nt 1

IMPRECATION
im′ prə kā′ shən 3*
im′ pri kā′ shən 1

IMPREGNATE
im preg′ nāt′ 3
im′ preg nāt′ 2*

IMPRESARIO ✓
im′ prə sär′ ē ō′ 2*
im′ prə ser′ ē ō′ 2
im′ prə sär′ ē ō 1
im′ prə ser′ ē ō 1
im′ pri sär′ ē ō′ 1
im′ pri ser′ ē ō′ 1

IMPRESS (n)
im′ pres′ 2*
im′ pres 2
im pres′ 1

IMPRESS (v)
im press′ 4

IMPRIMATUR
im′ pri māt′ ər 2*
im′ pri mät′ ər 2
im′ prə mät′ ər 1
im′ prə māt′ ər 1
im prə mä′ toor′ 1
im prim′ ə toor′ 1

IMPRINT (n)
im′ print′ 2*
im′ print 2

IMPRINT (v)
im print′ 4

IMPROMPTU +
im prämp′ tōō 3*
im prämp′ tyōō 3
im präm′ tōō 1

IMPROPRIETY
im′ prə prī′ ə tē 2*
im′ prə prī′ i tē 1
im′ pə prī′ ə tē 1

IMPROVIDENT +
im präv′ ə dənt 3*
im präv′ i dənt 1

IMPROVISATION +
im präv′ ə zā′ shən 3*
im′ prə vi zā′ shən 2
im präv′ i zā′ shən 1
im prə və zā′ shən 1

IMPROVISE
im′ prə vīz′ 4*
im′ prə vīz′ 1

IMPUDENT
im′ pyə dənt 3*
im′ pyōō dənt 1

IMPUGN
im pyōōn′ 4

IMPUNITY
im pyōō′ nə tē 3*
im pyōō′ ni tē 1

IMPUTE
im pyōōt′ 4

IN ABSENTIA
in ab sen′ shē ə 3*
in ab sen′ shə 2
in ab sen′ tē ə 1
in əb sen′ shə 1
in′ ab sen′ chə 1

INADVERTENT
in′ əd vʉr′ t′nt 2*
in′ əd vʉr′ tənt 2

INALIENABLE
in āl′ yən ə bəl 3*
in āl′ yən ə b′l 1

INAMORATA
in am′ ə rät′ ə 4*
in′ am ə rät′ ə 2
in am ə rät′ ə 1

INANIMATE
in an′ ə mit 3*
in an′ ə mət 1

INANITION
in′ ə nish′ ən 4

INAUGURAL
in ô′ gyə rəl 4*
in ô′ gə rəl 3
in ô′ grəl 1

INAUGURATE
in ô′ gyə rāt′ 4*
in ô′ gə rāt′ 2

INCALCULABLE
in kal′ kyə lə bəl 3*
in kal′ kyə lə b′l 1

INCANDESCENT
in′ kən des′ ənt 2*
in′ kən des′ ′nt 2

INCARCERATE
in kär′ sə rāt′ 4

INCARNADINE ✓
in kär′ nə dīn′ 4*
in kär′ nə dēn′ 4
in kär′ nə din 2
in kär′ nə din′ 1

INCARNATE (adj)
in kär′ nit 3*
in kär′ nāt 2
in kär′ nət 1

INCARNATE (v)
in kär′ nāt 4*
in′ kär′ nāt′ 1

INCENDIARY ✓
in sen′ dē er′ ē 4

INCENSE (n)
in′ sens 2*
in′ sens′ 2
in′ sents 1

INCENSE (v)
in sens′ 4*
in sents′ 1

INCEST
in′ sest′ 2*
in′ sest 2

INCESTUOUS
in ses′ c𝘩o͞o əs 2*
in ses′ c𝘩oo wəs 1
in ses′ c𝘩ə wəs 1

INCHOATE
in kō′ it 3*
in kō′ ət 1
in′ kə wāt′ 1

INCINERATE
in sin′ ə rāt′ 4

INCIPIENT
in sip′ ē ənt 4

INCISE
in sīz′ 4*
in sīs′ 1

INCISION
in sizh′ ən 4

INCISOR
in sī′ zər 4

INCLEMENT
in klem′ ənt 4

INCLINE (n)
in′ klīn 3*
in klīn′ 2
in′ klīn′ 1

INCLINE (v)
in klīn′ 4

INCOGNITO +
in′ käg net′ ō 3
in käg′ nə tō′ 2*
in′ käg net′ ō′ 2
in käg′ ni tō′ 2

INCOHERENT ○
in′ kō hir′ ənt 4

INCOMMUNICADO
in′ kə myo͞o nə kä′ dō 3*
in′ kə myo͞o′ ni kä′ dō 1

INCOMPARABLE +
in käm′ pər ə bəl 2*
in käm′ pər ə b'l 1
in käm′ prə bəl 1

INCOMPATIBLE
in′ kəm pat′ ə bəl 3*
in′ kəm pat′ ə b'l 1

INCONGRUITY +
in′ kən gro͞o′ ə tē 2*
in′ käŋ gro͞o′ ə tē 1
in′ käŋ gro͞o′ i tē 1

INCONGRUOUS +
in käŋ′ gro͞o əs 2*
in kän′ gro͞o wəs 1
in käŋ′ grə wəs 1

INCONSEQUENTIAL +
in kän′ sə kwen′ shəl 2*
in′ kän sə kwen′ shəl 2
in kän sə kwen′ c𝘩əl 1

INCONTINENT   +
in känt′ ′n ənt   3*
in känt′ ən ənt   1

INCONTROVERTIBLE   +
in′ kän trə vɐr′ tə bəl   3*
in kän trə vɐr′ tə bəl   2
in′ kän trə vɐr′ tə b′l   1
in kän trə vɐr′ tə b′l   1

INCORPOREAL
in′ kôr pôr′ ē əl   4*
in′ kôr pōr′ ē əl   3

INCORRIGIBLE   +
in kär′ ə jə bəl   2*
in kôr′ ə jə bəl   2
in kôr′ i jə bəl   1
in kär′ i jə bəl   1
in kôr′ i jə b′l   1
in kär′ i jə b′l   1

INCREASE (n)
in′ krēs′   2*
in′ krēs   2
in krēs′   1

INCREASE (v)
in krēs′   4*
in′ krēs   1

INCREDULITY
in′ krə dyo͞o′ lə tē   2*
in′ krə do͞o′ lə tē   2
in′ kri do͞o′ li tē   1
in′ kri dyo͞o′ li tē   1
in kri do͞o′ lə tē   1
in kri dyo͞o′ lə tē   1

INCREMENT
in′ krə mənt   4*
iŋ′ krə mənt   3

INCUBATE
in′ kyə bāt′   4*
iŋ′ kyə bāt′   4

INCUBUS
in′ kyə bəs   4*
iŋ′ kyə bəs   4

INCULCATE
in′ kul kāt′   2*
in kul′ kāt′   2
in kul′ kāt   2
in′ kəl′ kāt′   1

INCUMBENT
in kum′ bənt   4

INCUNABULA
in′ kyo͞o nab′ yə lə   3*
in′ kyə nab′ yə lə   1

INDEFATIGABLE
in′ di fat′ ə gə bəl   2*
in′ di fat′ i gə b′l   1
in′ di fat′ i gə bəl   1

INDEMNITY
in dem′ nə tē   3*
in dem′ ni tē   1

INDENTURE
in den′ chər   4

INDETERMINATE
in′ di tɐr′ mə nit   2*
in′ di tɐr′ mi nit   1
in′ di tɐrm′ nət   1

INDICATIVE
in dik′ ə tiv   4

INDICES
in′ də sēz′   3*
in′ di sēz′   1

INDICIA
in dish′ ē ə   4*
in dish′ ə   3

INDICT
in dīt′   4

INDIGENOUS
in dij′ ə nəs   4

INDIGENT
in′ di jənt   3*
in′ də jənt   1

INDIGESTION
in′ dī jes′ chən   4
in′ di jes′ chən   3*
in′ dī jesh′ chən   3
in′ di jesh′ chən   2

INDIGO
in′ di go′   3*
in′ də go′   1

INDISCREET
in′ dis krēt′   4

INDISCRETION
in′ dis kresh′ ən   4

INDISCRIMINATE
in′ dis krim′ ə nit   3*
in′ dis krim′ nət   1
in′ dis krim′ ə nət   1

INDISPUTABLE
in dis′ pyət ə bəl   2*
in′ dis pyo͞ot′ ə bəl   2
in dis pyo͞ot′ ə bəl   1
in′ dis pyo͞ot′ ə b′l   1
in dis′ pyo͞o tə b′l   1

INDISSOLUBLE   +
in′ di säl′ yə bəl   3*
in′ di säl′ yoo b′l   1

INDITE
in dīt′   4

INDOMITABLE   +
in däm′ ət ə bəl   2*
in däm′ it ə bəl   1
in däm′ it ə b′l   1

INDOLENT
in′ də lənt   4

INDUBITABLE
in do͞o′ bi tə bəl   2*
in dyo͞o′ bi tə bəl   2
in do͞o′ bi tə b′l   1
in dyo͞o′ bi tə b′l   1
in do͞o′ bə tə bəl   1
in dyo͞o′ bə tə bəl   1

INDUCE
in dyo͞os′ 4*
in do͞os′ 3

INDURATE
in′ dyo͞o rāt′ 3*
in′ do͞o rāt′ 3
in′ də rāt′ 1

INEBRIATED
in ē′ brē āt′ id 3*
in ē′ brē āt′ əd 1

INEBRIETY
in i brī′ ə tē 2*
in i brī′ i tē 1
in ē brī′ ə tē 1

INEDUCABLE
in ej′ o͞o kə bəl 2
in ej′ ə kə bəl 1*
in ej′ ə kə b′l 1
in ed′ yo͞o kə bəl 1

INEFFABLE
in ef′ ə bəl 3*
in ef′ ə b′l 1

INELUCTABLE
in′ i luk′ tə bəl 3*
in′ i luk′ tə b′l 1

INEPTITUDE
in ep′ tə to͞od′ 3
in ep′ tə tyo͞od′ 3*
in ep′ ti tyo͞od′ 1
in ep′ ti to͞od′ 1

INEQUITABLE
in ek′ wət ə bəl 2*
in ek′ wit ə bəl 1
in ek′ wit ə b′l 1

INERADICABLE
in′ i rad′ i kə bəl 2*
in′ i rad′ ə kə bəl 1
in′ i rad′ ə kə b′l 1

INERTIA
in ʉr′ shə 4*
in ʉr′ shē ə 1

INESTIMABLE
in es′ tə mə bəl 3*
in es′ tə mə b′l 1

INEVITABLE
in ev′ ə tə bəl 2*
in ev′ ə tə b′l 1
in ev′ i tə bəl 1

INEXHAUSTIBLE
in′ ig zôs′ tə bəl 3*
in′ ig zôs′ tə b′l 1

INEXORABLE
in ek′ sər ə bəl 2*
in ek′ sər ə b′l 1
in eks′ rə bəl 1
in egz′ ə rə bəl 1

INEXPLICABLE
in′ iks plik′ ə bəl 3
in eks′ pli kə bəl 2*
in eks′ plə kə bəl 1
in eks′ pli kə b′l 1
in′ iks plik′ ə b′l 1

IN EXTREMIS
in ik strē′ mis 3*
in ek strē′ mis 1
in′ ik strā′ məs 1

PRONUNCIATION KEY

Symbol	Key words	Symbol	Key words	Symbol	Key words
a	asp, fat, parrot	†ə a in ago		r	red, port, dear
ā	ape, date, play		e in agent	s	sell, castle, pass
†ä	ah, car, father		i in sanity	t	top, cattle, hat
e	elf, ten, berry		o in comply	v	vat, hovel, have
ē	even, meet, money		u in focus	w	will, always, swear
i	is, hit, mirror	ər	perhaps, murder	y	yet, onion, yard
ī	ice, bite, high	b	bed, fable, dub	z	zebra, dazzle, haze
ō	open, tone, go	d	dip, beadle, had	ch	chin, catcher, arch
ô	all, horn, law	f	fall, after, off	sh	she, cushion, dash
o͞o	ooze, tool, crew	g	get, haggle, dog	th	thin, nothing, truth
o͝o	look, pull, moor	h	he, ahead, hotel	th	then, father, lathe
yo͞o	use, cute, few	j	joy, agile, badge	zh	azure, leisure
yo͝o	united, cure, globule	k	kill, tackle, bake	ŋ	ring, anger, drink
oi	oil, point, toy	l	let, yellow, ball	″	see p. 15.
ou	out, crowd, plow	m	met, camel, trim	╱	see p. 15.
u	up, cut, color	n	not, flannel, ton	+	see p. 14.
ʉr	urn, fur, deter	p	put, apple, tap	′	see p. 15.
†See p. 14.		†See p. 16.		○	see p. 14.

INEXTRICABLE
in eks′ tri kə bəl   2*
in eks′ tri kə b'l   1
in eks′ trə kə bəl   1
in′ ik strik′ ə bəl   1
in′ ik strik′ ə b'l   1

INFAMOUS
in′ fə məs   4

INFAMY
in′ fə mē   4

INFANTILE
in′ fən tīl′   4*
in′ fən til   4
in′ fən t'l   1

INFATUATION
in fach′ o͞o ā′ shən   2*
in fach′ oo wā′ shən   1
in fach′ ə wā′ shən   1

INFECTIOUS
in fek′ shəs   4

INFER
in fu̇r′   4

INFERENCE ✓
in′ fər əns   3*
in′ frəns   2

INFERNO
in fu̇r′ nō   4

INFIDEL
in′ fə d'l   2*
in′ fə del′   2
in′ fi d'l   1
in′ fə dəl   1

INFIDELITY
in′ fə del′ ə tē   3*
in′ fi del′ i tē   1
in′ fĭ del′ ə tē   1

INFILTRATE
in′ fil trāt′   3*
in fil′ trāt′   2
in fil′ trāt   2
in′ fil trāt   1

INFINITE
in′ fə nit   3*
in′ fə nət   1

INFINITESIMAL
in′ fin′ ə tes′ ə məl   2
in fin′ ə tes′ ə məl   2
in fin′ ə tez′ ə məl   1*
in′ fin i tes′ ə məl   1
in′ fən ə tes′ ə məl   1

INFINITUDE
in fin′ ə tyo͞od′   3*
in fin′ ə to͞od′   3
in fin′ i to͞od′   1
in fin′ i tyo͞od′   1

INFLAMMABLE
in flam′ ə bəl   3*
in flam′ ə b'l   1

INFLUENCE
in′ flo͞o əns   3*
in′ floo wəns   1
in flo͞o′ əns   1
in′ flo͞o ənts   1

INFLUENTIAL
in′ flo͞o en′ shəl   2*
in′ floo wen′ shəl   1
in′ flo͞o en′ chəl   1

INFLUENZA
in′ flo͞o en′ zə   3*
in′ floo wen′ zə   1

INGENIOUS
in jēn′ yəs   4

INGÉNUE
an′ zhə no͞o′   2*
an′ zhə nyo͞o′   2
an′ zhə no͞o′   1
an′ jə no͞o′   2
än′ jə no͞o′   1

INGENUITY
in′ jə no͞o′ ə tē   3*
in′ jə nyo͞o′ ə tē   3
in′ jə no͞o′ i tē   1
in′ jə nyo͞o′ i tē   1

INGENUOUS
in jen′ yo͞o əs   2*
in jen′ yoo wəs   1
in jen′ yə wəs   1

INGEST
in jest′   4

INGOT
iŋ′ gət   4

INGRATE
in′ grāt′   2*
in′ grāt   2

INGRATIATE
in grā′ shē āt′   4

INGREDIENT
in grē′ dē ənt   4

INHALANT
in hā′ lənt   4

INHALATOR
in′ hə lāt′ ər   4

INHERENT ○ ✓
in hir′ ənt   4*
in her′ ənt   4

INHIBIT
in hib′ it   3*
in hib′ ət   1

INHIBITION
in′ hi bish′ ən   3
in′ i bish′ ən   2
in′ ə bish′ ən   2

INHUMAN
in hyo͞o′ mən   4*
in yo͞o′ mən   3

INHUMANE
in′ hyo͞o mān′   4*
in′ yo͞o mān′   2
in′ yoo mān′   1

INIMICAL
in im′ i kəl   3*
in im′ i k′l   1

INIMITABLE
in im′ i tə bəl   2*
in im′ ə tə bəl   1
in im′ ə tə b′l   1

INIQUITOUS
in ik′ wə təs   3*
in ik′ wi təs   1

INIQUITY
in ik′ wə te̅   3*
in ik′ wi te̅   1

INITIATE (v)
i nish′ e̅ āt′   4

INITIATE (adj, n)
i nish′ e̅ it   3*
i nish′ e̅ āt′   2
i nish′ e̅ ət   1
i nish′ ət   1

INITIATIVE
i nish′ ə tiv   4
i nish′ e̅ ə tiv   3*
i nish′ e̅ ā tiv   1

INJURIOUS
in joor′ e əs   4

IN LOCO PARENTIS
in lo̅′ ko̅ pə ren′ tis   3*
in lo̅′ ko̅ pə ren′ tis   1

IN MEMORIAM
in mə môr′ e̅ əm   4*
in mə mo̅r′ e̅ əm   3

INNATE
i nāt′   4*
in′ āt   2
in′ āt′   2

INNOCUOUS   +
i näk′ yo͞o əs   2*
i näk′ yoo wəs   1
i näk′ yə wəs   1

INNUENDO
in yo͞o en′ do̅   1*
in yo͞o′ en′ do̅   1
in′ yoo wen′ do̅   1
in′ yə wen′ do̅   1

INOCULATE   +
i näk′ yə lāt′   3*
i näk′ yoo lāt′   1

INOPERABLE   +
in äp′ ər ə bəl   3*
in äp′ ər ə b′l   1
in äp′ rə bəl   1

PRONUNCIATION KEY

Symbol	Key words	Symbol	Key words	Symbol	Key words
a	asp, fat, parrot	†ə	a in ago	r	red, port, dear
ā	ape, date, play		e in agent	s	sell, castle, pass
†ä	ah, car, father		i in sanity	t	top, cattle, hat
e	elf, ten, berry		o in comply	v	vat, hovel, have
e̅	even, meet, money		u in focus	w	will, always, swear
i	is, hit, mirror	ər	perhaps, murder	y	yet, onion, yard
ī	ice, bite, high	b	bed, fable, dub	z	zebra, dazzle, haze
o̅	open, tone, go	d	dip, beadle, had	ch	chin, catcher, arch
ô	all, horn, law	f	fall, after, off	sh	she, cushion, dash
o͞o	ooze, tool, crew	g	get, haggle, dog	th	thin, nothing, truth
oo	look, pull, moor	h	he, ahead, hotel	th	then, father, lathe
yo͞o	use, cute, few	j	joy, agile, badge	zh	azure, leisure
yoo	united, cure, globule	k	kill, tackle, bake	ŋ	ring, anger, drink
oi	oil, point, toy	l	let, yellow, ball	″	see p. 15.
ou	out, crowd, plow	m	met, camel, trim	✓	see p. 15.
u	up, cut, color	n	not, flannel, ton	+	see p. 14.
ur	urn, fur, deter	p	put, apple, tap	′	see p. 15.
†See p. 14.		†See p. 16.		○	see p. 14.

INOPERATIVE +
in äp′ ər ə tiv 4*
in äp′ ə rāt′ iv 2
in äp′ rə tiv 1
in äp′ rāt′ iv 1

INQUEST
in′ kwest′ 2*
in′ kwest 2

INQUIRE
in kwīr′ 3*
in kwī′ ər 1

INQUIRY
in′ kwə rē 4
in′ kwī′ rē 2
in kwīr′ ē 2*
in′ kwīr′ ē 2
in kwi ər ē 2
iŋ′ kwə rē 1

INSANE
in sān′ 4*
in′ sān′ 1

INSATIABLE ✓
in sā′ sһə bəl 3*
in sā′ sһē ə bəl 2
in sā′ sһə b'l 1

INSCRIBE
in skrīb′ 4

INSCRUTABLE
in skrōōt′ ə bəl 3*
in skrōōt′ ə b'l 1

INSECTICIDE
in sek′ tə sīd′ 3*
in sek′ ti sīd′ 1

INSENSATE
in sen′ sit 3*
in sen′ sāt′ 2
in sen′ sāt 2
in sen′ sət 1

INSEPARABLE
in sep′ ər ə bəl 3*
in sep′ rə bəl 2
in sep′ ər ə b'l 1

INSERT (n)
in′ sᵤrt′ 2*
in′ sᵤrt 1
in′ sərt 1

INSERT (v)
in sᵤrt′ 4

INSIDIOUS
in sid′ ē əs 4

INSIGHT
in′ sīt′ 4

INSIGNIA
in sig′ nē ə 4

INSINUATE
in sin′ yōō āt′ 2*
in sin′ yoo wāt′ 1
in sin′ yə wāt′ 1

INSIPID
in sip′ id 3*
in sip′ əd 1

INSOLENT
in′ sə lənt 4
in′ slənt 1

INSOLUBLE +
in säl′ yə bəl 3*
in säl′ yoo b'l 1

INSOMNIA +
in säm′ nē ə 4

INSOUCIANCE
in sōō′ sē əns 4*
in sōō′ sē ənts 1

INSTANTANEOUS
in′ stən tā′ nē əs 4*
in′ stən tān′ yəs 2

INSTINCT (n)
in′ stiŋkt′ 2*
in′ stiŋkt 2

INSTITUTE
in′ stə tōōt′ 3*
in′ stə tyōōt′ 3
in′ sti tōōt′ 1
in′ sti tyōōt′ 1

INSTITUTION
in′ stə tōō′ sһən 3*
in′ stə tyōō′ sһən 3
in′ sti tōō′ sһən 1
in′ sti tyōō′ sһən 1

INSULAR
in′ sə lər 4
in′ syə lər 2*
in′ syoo lər 1
in′ sһə lər 1

INSULATE
in′ sə lāt′ 4
in′ syə lāt′ 1*
in′ syoo lāt′ 1

INSULIN
in′ sə lin 2*
in′ sə lən 2
in′ syə lin 1
in′ syə lən 1
in′ syoo lin 1
in′ slən 1

INSULT (n)
in′ sult 2
in′ sult′ 1*
in′ səlt 1

INSULT (v)
in sult′ 4

INSUPERABLE
in sōō′ pər ə bəl 3*
in sōō′ pər ə b'l 1
in sōō′ prə bəl 1

INSURGENT
in sᵤr′ jənt 4

INSURRECTION
in′ sə rek′ shən   4

INTACT
in takt′   4

INTAGLIO
in tal′ yō   3*
in täl′ yō   3
in tag′ lē ō′   1
in täg′ lē ō′   1

INTEGER
in′ tə jər   2*
in′ ti jər   2

INTEGRAL
in′ tə grəl   3*
in teg′ rəl   2
in′ ti grəl   1
in tēg′ rəl   1

INTEGRITY
in teg′ rə tē   3*
in teg′ ri tē   1

INTEGUMENT
in teg′ yoo mənt   2*
in teg′ yə mənt   2

INTELLIGENTSIA
in tel′ ə gent′ sē ə   3*
in tel′ ə jent′ sē ə   3
in tel′ i jent′ sē ə   1
in tel′ i gent′ sē ə   1
in tel′ ə jen′ sē ə   1
in tel′ ə gen′ sē ə   1

INTENT
in tent′   4

INTER
in tur′   4

INTERCOM   +
in′ tər käm′   4

INTERDICT (n)
in′ tər dikt′   3

INTERDICT (v)
in′ tər dikt′   3*
in tər dikt′   1

INTERDICTION
in′ tər dik′ shən   4

INTEREST
in′ trist   3*
in′ tər ist   3
in′ tər əst   1
in′ trəst   1
in′ tər est′   1
in tərst   1

INTERIM
in′ tər im   3*
in′ tər əm   1

INTERLOCUTOR   +
in′ tər läk′ yə tər   4*
in′ tər läk′ ə tər   1

INTERMEDIARY   ✓
in′ tər mē′ dē er′ ē   4

INTERMEDIATE
in′ tər mē′ dē it   3*
in′ tər mē′ dē ət   1

INTERMENT
in tur′ mənt   4

INTERMEZZO
in′ tər met′ sō   4*
in′ tər med′ zō   4

PRONUNCIATION KEY					
Symbol	*Key words*	*Symbol*	*Key words*	*Symbol*	*Key words*
a	asp, fat, parrot	†ə	a in ago	r	red, port, dear
ā	ape, date, play		e in agent	s	sell, castle, pass
†ä	ah, car, father		i in sanity	t	top, cattle, hat
e	elf, ten, berry		o in comply	v	vat, hovel, have
ē	even, meet, money		u in focus	w	will, always, swear
i	is, hit, mirror	ər	perhaps, murder	y	yet, onion, yard
ī	ice, bite, high	b	bed, fable, dub	z	zebra, dazzle, haze
ō	open, tone, go	d	dip, beadle, had	ch	chin, catcher, arch
ô	all, horn, law	f	fall, after, off	sh	she, cushion, dash
o͞o	ooze, tool, crew	g	get, haggle, dog	th	thin, nothing, truth
oo	look, pull, moor	h	he, ahead, hotel	th	then, father, lathe
yo͞o	use, cute, few	j	joy, agile, badge	zh	azure, leisure
yoo	united, cure, globule	k	kill, tackle, bake	ŋ	ring, anger, drink
oi	oil, point, toy	l	let, yellow, ball	″	see p. 15.
ou	out, crowd, plow	m	met, camel, trim	✓	see p. 15.
u	up, cut, color	n	not, flannel, ton	+	see p. 14.
ur	urn, fur, deter	p	put, apple, tap	′	see p. 15.
†See p. 14.		†See p. 16.		○	see p. 14.

INTERMINABLE
in tʉr′ mə nə bəl   2*
in tʉr′ mi nə b′l   1
in tʉrm′ nə bəl   1

INTERN(E) (n)
in′ tʉrn′   1*
in′ tʉrn   1
in′ tərn   1
in′ tərn′   1

INTERN (v)
in tʉrn′   4*
in′ tərn′   1

INTERNECINE
in′ tər nē′ sīn   3*
in′ tər nes′ ēn   3
in′ tər nē′ sin   2
in′ tər nes′ ′n   2
in′ tər nes′ ən   2
in tʉr′ nə sēn′   1
in tʉr′ nə sən   1

INTERPOLATE
in tʉr′ pə lāt′   4

INTERPRET
in tʉr′ prit   3*
in tʉr′ prət   1
in tʉr′ pət   1

INTERPRETATIVE
in tʉr′ prə tāt′ iv   3*
in tʉr′ pri tāt′ iv   1

INTERREGNUM
in′ tər reg′ nəm   3*
in′ tə reg′ nəm   1

INTERROGATE
in ter′ ə gāt′   4

INTERROGATIVE   +
in′ tə räg′ ə tiv   4

INTERROGATORY   +
in′ tə räg′ ə tôr′ ē   3*
in′ tə räg′ ə tōr′ ē   3

INTERSTICES
in tʉr′ sti siz   3
in tʉr′ sti sēz′   2*
in tʉr′ stə sēz′   2
in tʉr′ stə səz   1

INTERSTITIAL
in′ tər stishʹ əl   4

INTESTATE
in tes′ tit   3
in tes′ tāt′   2*
in tes′ tāt   2
in tes′ tət   1

INTESTINE
in tes′ tən   2*
in tes′ tin   2

INTIMATE (adj, n)
in′ tə mit   3*
in′ tə mət   1

INTIMATE (v)
in′ tə māt′   4

INTRANSIGENT
in tran′ sə jənt   3*
in tran′ si jənt   1
in trant′ sə jənt   1

INTRAVENOUS
in′ trə vē′ nəs   4

INTREPID
in trep′ id   3*
in trep′ əd   1

INTRICACY
in′ tri kə sē   3*
in′ trə kə sē   1

INTRIGUE (n)
in trēg′   4
in′ trēg′   2*
in′ trēg   2

INTRIGUE (v)
in trēg′   4

INTRINSIC
in trin′ sik   4*
in trin′ zik   3

INTRODUCE
in′ trə do͞os′   4*
in′ trə dyo͞os′   4

INTROIT
in trō′ it   2*
in′ trō it   2
in′ troit   2
in troit′   1
in tro′ ət   1

INTRUSION
in tro͞o′ zhən   4

INTUITION
in′ to͞o ishʹ ən   3*
in′ tyo͞o ishʹ ən   3
in′ too wishʹ ən   1
in′ tyoo wishʹ ən   1

INTUITIVE
in tyo͞o′ i tiv   2*
in to͞o′ i tiv   2
in to͞o′ ə tiv   2
in tyo͞o′ ə tiv   2

INUNDATE
in′ ən dāt′   3*
in′ un dāt′   2
in un′ dāt   1

INURE
in yoor′   4*
in oor′   2

INVALID (n)
in′ və lid   3*
in′ və ləd   1

INVALID (adj)
in val′ id   3*
in val′ əd   1

INVARIABLE ✓
in ver′ ē ə bəl   3*
in ver′ ē ə b′l   1

INVEIGH
in vā' 4

INVEIGLE
in vē' gəl 3*
in vā' gəl 3
in vē' g'l 1
in vā' g'l 1

INVENTORY
in' vən tôr' ē 4*
in' vən tōr' ē 3

INVERTEBRATE
in vʉr' tə brāt' 4
in vʉr' tə brit 3*
in vʉr' tə brət 1

INVESTITURE
in ves' tə chər 2*
in ves' tə choor 2
in ves' ti chər 1
in ves' tə toor 1
in ves' tə tyoor 1

INVETERATE
in vet' ər it 3*
in vet' ər ət 1
in ve' trət 1

INVIDIOUS
in vid' ē əs 4

INVIOLABLE
in vī' ə lə bəl 3*
in vī' ə lə b'l 1

INVIOLATE
in vī' ə lit 3*
in vī' ə lāt 2
in vī' ə lət 1

IN VITRO
in vē' trō 4

IN VIVO
in vē' vō 4

INVOICE
in' vois' 2*
in' vois 2

IODINE
ī' ə dīn' 3
ī' ə din 3
ī' ə dēn' 2*

ION   +
ī' ən 4
ī' än 3*

IONOSPHERE   + ○
ī än' ə sfir' 4

IOTA
ī ōt' ə 4*
ē ōt' ə 1

IPSO FACTO
ip' sō fak' tō 3*
ip' sō fak' tō 1

IRASCIBLE
ī ras' ə bəl 3*
i ras' ə bəl 3
ī ras' ə b'l 1
i ras' ə b'l 1

IRATE
ī rāt' 4*
ī' rāt 3

IRIDESCENT ○
ir ə des' 'nt 2*
ir ə des' ənt 1
ir i des' ənt 1

PRONUNCIATION KEY

Symbol	Key words	Symbol	Key words	Symbol	Key words
a	asp, fat, parrot	†ə	a in ago	r	red, port, dear
ā	ape, date, play		e in agent	s	sell, castle, pass
†ä	ah, car, father		i in sanity	t	top, cattle, hat
e	elf, ten, berry		o in comply	v	vat, hovel, have
ē	even, meet, money		u in focus	w	will, always, swear
i	is, hit, mirror	ər	perhaps, murder	y	yet, onion, yard
ī	ice, bite, high	b	bed, fable, dub	z	zebra, dazzle, haze
ō	open, tone, go	d	dip, beadle, had	ch	chin, catcher, arch
ô	all, horn, law	f	fall, after, off	sh	she, cushion, dash
o͞o	ooze, tool, crew	g	get, haggle, dog	th	thin, nothing, truth
oo	look, pull, moor	h	he, ahead, hotel	th	then, father, lathe
yo͞o	use, cute, few	j	joy, agile, badge	zh	azure, leisure
yoo	united, cure, globule	k	kill, tackle, bake	ŋ	ring, anger, drink
oi	oil, point, toy	l	let, yellow, ball	''	see p. 15.
ou	out, crowd, plow	m	met, camel, trim	✓	see p. 15.
u	up, cut, color	n	not, flannel, ton	+	see p. 14.
ʉr	urn, fur, deter	p	put, apple, tap	'	see p. 15.
†See p. 14.		†See p. 16.		○	see p. 14.

IRIS
ī′ ris 3*
ī′ rəs 1

IRON
ī′ ərn 4*
īrn 1

IRONIC +
ī rän′ ik 4

IRONY
ī′ rən ē 4*
ī′ ər nē 2

IRRADIATE
i rā′ dē āt′ 4

IRRATIONAL
i rash′ ə nəl 2*
i rash′ ə n'l 2
i rash′ nəl 1

IRRECONCILABLE
i rek′ ən sīl′ ə bəl 4*
i rek′ ən sīl′ ə bəl 4
i rek′ ən sīl′ ə b'l 1

IRREFRAGABLE
i ref′ rə gə bəl 3*
ir′ i frag′ ə bəl 1
i ref′ rə gə b'l 1

IRREFUTABLE
i ref′ yə tə bəl 3*
ir′ i fyōō′ tə bəl 2
i ref′ yoo tə b'l 1
ir′ i fyōō′ tə b'l 1

IRRELEVANT
i rel′ ə vənt 4

IRRELIGIOUS
ir′ i lij′ əs 4

IRREMEDIABLE
ir′ i mē′ dē ə bəl 4

IRREPARABLE
i rep′ ər ə bəl 3*
i rep′ ər ə b'l 1
i rep′ rə bəl 1

IRREPRESSIBLE
ir′ i pres′ ə bəl 4*
ir′ i pres′ ə b'l 1

IRREPROACHABLE
ir′ i prō′ chə bəl 3*
ir′ i prō′ chə b'l 1

IRRESISTIBLE
ir′ i zis′ tə bəl 3*
ir′ i zis′ tə b'l 1

IRRESOLUTE
i rez′ ə lōōt′ 4*
i rez′ ə lət 1

IRRESPECTIVE
ir′ i spek′ tiv 4

IRRESPONSIBLE +
ir′ i spän′ sə bəl 3*
ir′ i spän′ sə b'l 1

IRRETRIEVABLE
ir′ i trē′ və bəl 3*
ir′ i trē′ və b'l 1

IRREVERENT
i rev′ ər ənt 4*
i rev′ rənt 1
i rev′ ərnt 1

IRREVOCABLE
i rev′ ə kə bəl 3*
i rev′ ə kə b'l 1

IRRITABLE
ir′ ə tə bəl 2*
ir′ i tə bəl 1
ir′ i tə b'l 1

ISLET
ī′ lit 3*
ī′ lət 1

ISOBAR
ī′ sə bär′ 4

ISOLATE
ī′ sə lāt′ 4*
is′ ə lāt′ 4

ISOMER
ī′ sə mər 4

ISOMETRIC
ī sə met′ rik 2*
ī′ sə met′ rik 2

ISOTOPE
ī′ sə tōp′ 4

ISSUE
ish′ ōō 4*
ish ə 1

ISTHMUS
is′ məs 4

ITALICS
i tal′ iks 4*
ī tal′ iks 4
ə tal′ iks 1

ITALICIZE
i tal′ i sīz′ 3*
ī tal′ i sīz′ 1
ə tal′ ə siz′ 1
i tal′ ə sīz′ 1

ITERATE
it′ ə rāt′ 4

ITINERANT
ī tin′ ə rənt 4*
i tin′ ə rənt 3

ITINERARY ✓
ī tin′ ə rer′ ē 4*
i tin′ ə rer′ ē 3
ə tin′ ə rer′ ē 1

IVORY
ī′ və rē 4
īv′ rē 3*

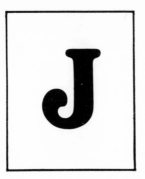

JABOT
zha bō′ 4*
ja bō′ 2
jab′ ō′ 1

JAGUAR
jag′ wär′ 2*
jag′ wär 2
jag′ yo͞o är′ 1
jag′ yoo wär′ 1
jag′ yə wär′ 1

JAI-ALAI
hī′ lī′ 4*
hī′ ə lī′ 3
hī′ ə lī′ 2

JALOPY +
jə läp′ ē 4

JALOUSIE
jal′ ə sē 2*
jal′ o͞o sē 1
jal′ ə sē′ 1

JAMB
jam 4

JAMBOREE
jam′ bə rē′ 4

JANISSARY ✓
jan′ ə ser′ ē 2*
jan′ ə zer′ ē 2
jan′ i ser′ ē 1

JARGON +
jär′ gən 4*
jär′ gän 1
jär′ gän′ 1

JASMINE
jaz′ min 2*
jaz′ mən 2
jas′ min 1

JAUNDICE
jôn′ dis 3*
jän′ dis 3
jôn′ dəs 1
jän′ dəs 1

JAUNT
jônt 4*
jänt 4

JAVELIN
jav′ ə lin 2*
jav′ lən 2
jav′ ə lən 2
jav′ lin 2

JEHOVAH
ji hō′ və 4

JEHU
jē′ hyo͞o 3*
je′ ho͞o 2
jē′ o͞o 1

JEJUNE
ji jo͞on′ 3*
jə jo͞on′ 1

JEOPARDIZE
jep′ ər dīz′ 4

JEOPARDY
jep′ ər dē 4

JEREMIAD
jer′ ə mī′ əd 3*
jer′ ə mī′ ad 3

JERKIN
jur′ kin 2*
jur′ kən 2

JEROBOAM
jer′ ə bō′ əm 4

JETSAM
jet′ səm 4

JETTISON
jet′ i sən 2*
jet′ i zən 2
jet′ ə s′n 1
jet′ ə z′n 1
jet′ ə sən 1
jet′ ə zən 1

JEWEL
jo͞o əl 4

JEWELRY
jo͞o′ əl rē 4

JINRIKISHA
jin rik′ shô 3*
jin rik′ shä 2
jin rik′ shô′ 1

JITNEY
jit′ nē 4

JOCOSE
jō kōs′ 4*
jə kōs′ 1

JOCULAR +
jäk′ yə lər 4

JOCUND +
jäk′ ənd 4*
jō′ kənd 4

JODHPUR +
jäd′ pər 4*
jōd′ pər 1

JONQUIL +
jän′ kwil 2*
jäŋ′ kwil 2
jäŋ′ kwəl 2
jän′ kwəl 2

JOUST
joust 4*
just 4
jo͞ost 4

JOVIAL
jō′ vē əl 4*
jō′ vyəl 2

JOWL
joul 4*
jōl 2

JUBILEE
jo͞o′ bə lē′ 4*
jo͞o′ bə lē′ 2
jo͞o bə lē′ 1
jo͞o′ bə lē 1

JUDAIC
jo͞o dā′ ik 4

JUDAISM
jo͞o′ dē iz′ əm 3*
jo͞o′ dā iz′ əm 1
jo͞o′ də iz′ ′m 1

JUDICIAL
jo͞o dish′ əl 4

JUDICIARY ✓
jo͞o dish′ ē er′ ē 4*
jo͞o dish′ ər ē 3

JUDO
jo͞o′ dō 4

JUGGERNAUT
jug′ ər nôt′ 4*
jug′ ər nät′ 1

JUGULAR
jug′ yə lər 3
jo͞og′ yə lər 2*
jug′ yoo lər 1

JUJUBE
jo͞o′ jo͞ob′ 2*
jo͞o′ jo͞ob 2
jo͞o′ jo͞o bē′ 1

JUJITSU
jo͞o jit′ so͞o 4

JULEP
jo͞o′ ləp 2*
jo͞o′ lip 2

JULIENNE
jo͞o′ lē en′ 4

JUNCTURE
juŋk′ chər 4*
juŋ′ chər 1

JUNIPER
jo͞o′ nə pər 4

JUNTA
ho͞on′ tə 4*
jun′ tə 4
ho͞on′ tə 2
hun′ tə 2

JURISPRUDENCE
jo͞or′ is pro͞o′ d′ns 2
jo͞or′ əs pro͞o′ d′ns 1*
jo͞or′ əs pro͞o′ dəns 1

JUTE
jo͞ot 4

JUVENILE
jo͞o′ və nīl′ 4
jo͞o′ və n′l 2
jo͞o′ və nil 1*

JUVENILIA
jo͞o′ və nil′ ē ə 4*
jo͞o′ və nil′ yə 2

JUXTAPOSITION
juk′ stə pə zish′ ən 4

KALEIDOSCOPE
kə lī′ də skōp′ 4

KALEIDOSCOPIC +
kə lī′ də skäp′ ik 4

KAMIKAZE
kä′ mi kä′ zē 2*
kä′ mə kä′ zē 1
kä mi kä′ zē 1

KANGAROO
kaŋ′ gə rōō′ 4

KAPOK +
kā′ päk′ 2*
kā′ päk 2
kap′ ək 1

KAPUT
kə pood′ 3*
kä pood′ 3
kə pōōt′ 2

KARAKUL (CARACUL)
kar′ ə kəl 4

KARAT
kar′ ət 4

KARATE
kə rät′ ē 3*
kä rät′ ā 1

KARMA
kär′ mə 4*
kʉr′ mə 3

KATYDID
kāt′ ē did′ 3*
kāt′ ē did 1

KAYAK
kī′ ak′ 3*
kī′ ak 1

KEBAB
kə bäb′ 4*
kā′ bäb 2

KEPI
kā′ pē 4*
kep′ ē 4

KERCHIEF
kʉr′ chif 3*
kʉr′ chəf 1
kʉr′ chēf′ 1

KEROSENE ✓
ker′ ə sēn′ 4*
ker′ ə sēn′ 4
kar′ ə sēn′ 2
kar ə sēn′ 2

KETCHUP
kech′ əp 4*
kach′ əp 3

KHAKI
kak′ ē 4*
käk′ ē 3

KHAN
kän 4*
kan 4

KHEDIVE
kə dēv′ 4

KIBBUTZ
ki boots′ 4*
ki bōōts′ 3

KIBITZ
kib′ its 3*
kib′ əts 1
kə bits′ 1

KIBITZER
kib' its ər 3*
kib' əts ər 1
kə bit' sər 1

KIBOSH +
ki bäsh' 4*
kī' bäsh' 2
kī' bäsh 3

KILN
kil 4*
kiln 4

KILO
kē' lō 4*
kil' ō 3
kē' lō' 1

KILOMETER +
ki läm' ə tər 3*
kil' ə mēt' ər 3

KIMONO
kə mō' nə 4*
kə mō' nō 4
kə mō' nō' 1

KINDERGARTEN
kin' dər gärt' 'n 3*
kin' dər gärd' 'n 2
kin' də gärt' 'n 1

KINESCOPE
kin' ə skōp' 3*
kin' i skōp' 1
kī' nə skop' 1

KINESTHESIA
kin' əs thē' zhə 2*
kin' is thē' zhə 2
kin' əs thē' zhē ə 1
kin' is thē' zhē ə 1
kī' nəs thē' zhə 1
kī' nəs thē' zhē ə 1

KINETIC
ki net' ik 3*
kī net' ik 2
kə net' ik 1

KINKAJOU
kiŋ' kə jōō' 4

KIOSK +
kē äsk' 4
kē' äsk' 2*
kī' äsk' 1

KIRSCH ○
kirsh 4

KISMET
kiz' mit 2*
kis' mit 2
kiz' met 2
kis' met 1
kiz' met' 1

KIWI
kē' wē 4*
kē' wē' 1

KLIEG
klēg 4

KNACKWURST
näk' wurst' 3
näk' woorst' 2*

KNAPSACK
nap' sak' 4

KNISH
knish 2*
kə nish' 2

KNOLL
nōl 4

KNOUT
nout 3*
nōōt 1

KOALA
kō ä' lə 4*
kə wäl' ə 1

KOHLRABI
kōl rä' bē 4*
kōl' rä' bē 3
kōl ra' bē 1

KOPECK
kō' pek' 2*
kō' pek 2

KORAN
kô ran' 3*
kô rän' 3
kō ran' 2
kō rän' 2
kə ran' 2
kə rän' 2
kō' ran 1
kō' rän 1

KOSHER
kō' shər 4

KOWTOW
kou' tou' 3
kou' tou' 2*
kō' tou' 2
kō' tou' 2
kou tou' 1

KRAAL
kräl 4*
krôl 2

KRIS
krēs 4

KUDOS
kyōō' däs 4
kyōō dōs 3
kōō' däs 3
kōō' dōs 2*
kōō' dōz 1
kyōō' dōz 1

KU KLUX KLAN
kyōō' kluks' klan'   3*
kōō' kluks' klan'   3
kōō' kluks' klan'   1
kyōō' kluks' klan'   1
klōō' kluks' klan'   1

KULAK
kōō' läk   3*
koo lak'   2
koo läk'   2
kyōō lak'   1
kyōō' läk'   1

KULTUR
kool toor'   4

KUMQUAT
kum' kwät'   2*
kum' kwät   2
kum' kwôt   1

PRONUNCIATION KEY

Symbol	Key words	Symbol	Key words	Symbol	Key words
a	asp, fat, parrot	†ə	a in ago	r	red, port, dear
ā	ape, date, play		e in agent	s	sell, castle, pass
†ä	ah, car, father		i in sanity	t	top, cattle, hat
e	elf, ten, berry		o in comply	v	vat, hovel, have
ē	even, meet, money		u in focus	w	will, always, swear
i	is, hit, mirror	ər	perhaps, murder	y	yet, onion, yard
ī	ice, bite, high	b	bed, fable, dub	z	zebra, dazzle, haze
ō	open, tone, go	d	dip, beadle, had	ch	chin, catcher, arch
ô	all, horn, law	f	fall, after, off	sh	she, cushion, dash
ōō	ooze, tool, crew	g	get, haggle, dog	th	thin, nothing, truth
oo	look, pull, moor	h	he, ahead, hotel	th	then, father, lathe
yōō	use, cute, few	j	joy, agile, badge	zh	azure, leisure
yoo	united, cure, globule	k	kill, tackle, bake	ŋ	ring, anger, drink
oi	oil, point, toy	l	let, yellow, ball	''	see p. 15.
ou	out, crowd, plow	m	met, camel, trim	✓	see p. 15.
u	up, cut, color	n	not, flannel, ton	+	see p. 14.
ur	urn, fur, deter	p	put, apple, tap	'	see p. 15.
†See p. 14.		†See p. 16.		○	see p. 14.

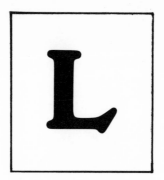

LABIAL
lā′ bē əl 4

LABILE
lā′ bīl 2*
lā′ bil 1
lā′ b'l 1
lā′ bīl′ 1
lā′ bəl 1

LABORATORY
lab′ rə tôr′ ē 4*
lab′ rə tōr′ ē 3
lab′ ər ə tôr′ ē 1
lab′ ər ə tōr′ ē 1

LABORIOUS
lə bôr′ ē əs 3*
lə bōr′ ē əs 3

LABURNUM
lə bur′ nəm 4

LABYRINTH
lab′ ə rinth′ 3*
lab′ ə rinth 1
lab′ ə rintth′ 1
lab′ ə rənth 1
lab′ ə rəntth 1

LABYRINTHINE
lab′ ə rin′ thin′ 3*
lab′ ə rin′ thēn′ 3
lab′ ə rin′ thin 1
lab′ ə rin′ thēn 1
lab′ ə rin′ thən 1
lab′ ə rint′ thən 1

LACERATE
las′ ə rāt′ 4*
las′ ə rət 1

LACHRYMAL
lak′ rə məl 4

LACHRYMOSE
lak′ rə mōs′ 4

LACKADAISICAL
lak ə dā′ zi kəl 2*
lak′ ə dā′ zi k'l 1
lak′ ə dā′ zi kəl 1

LACONIC +
lə kän′ ik 4

LACQUER
lak′ ər 4

LACROSSE +
lə krôs′ 4*
lə kräs′ 3

LACTOSE
lak′ tōs′ 2*
lak′ tōs 2
lak′ tōz′ 1

LACUNA
lə kyoo′ nə 4*
lə koo′ nə 1

LADLE
lād′ 'l 4

LAGER
lä′ gər 4*
lô′ gər 1

LAGNIAPPE
lan yap′ 4*
lan′ yap 3
lan′ yap′ 1

LAIRD ✓
lerd 4
lard 1

LAITY
lā′ ət ē 3*
lā′ it ē 1

LAMA
lä′ mə 4

LAMBASTE
lam bāst′ 4*
lam bast′ 3

LAMBREQUIN
lam′ brə kin 3*
lam′ bər kin 3
lam′ bər kən 1
lam′ bri kən 1

LAMÉ
la mā′ 4*
lä mā′ 1

LAMENT
lə ment′ 4

LAMENTABLE
lam′ ən tə bəl 3*
lə men′ tə bəl 2
lam′ ən tə b′l 1
lə men′ tə b′l 1

LAMPOON
lam po͞on′ 4

LAMPREY
lam′ prē 4*
lam′ prā 1

LANCET
lan′ sit 3*
län′ sit 3
lan′ sət 1
lant′ sət 1

LANDAU
lan′ dô 4
lan′ dou′ 2*
lan′ dou 2

LANGUID
laŋ′ gwid 3*
laŋ′ gwəd 1

LANGUISH
laŋ′ gwish 4

LANGUOR
laŋ′ gər 4*
laŋ′ ər 1

LANUGO
lə no͞o′ gō 4*
lə nyo͞o′ gō 4

LANYARD
lan′ yərd 4

LAPEL
lə pel′ 4

LAPIDARY ✓
lap′ ə der′ ē 3*
lap′ i der′ ē 1

LAPIN
lap′ ən 2*
lap′ in 2

LARCENY
lär′ sə nē 3*
lärs′ nē 1
lärs′ ′n ē 1

LARGESS
lär jes′ 4*
lär′ jis 3
lär′ jes′ 2
lär zhes′ 1

LARIAT ✓
lar′ ē ət 3*
lar′ ē it 1
ler′ ē ət 1

LARYNGEAL
lə rin′ jē əl 4*
lə rin′ jəl 4
lar′ ən jē′ əl 3

LARYNGITIS
lar′ ən jī′ tis 3*
lar′ ən jī′ təs 1

LARYNX
lar′ iŋks 4*
lar′ iŋs 1

LASAGNA
lə zän′ yə 4*
lä zän′ yə 1

LASCIVIOUS
lə siv′ ē əs 4

LASER
lā′ zər 4

LASSO
las′ ō 4*
la so͞o′ 3
la′ so͞o 1

LATENT
lāt′ ′nt 3*
lāt′ ənt 1

LATERAL
lat′ ər əl 4*
lat′ rəl 1

LATEX
lā′ teks′ 2*
lā′ teks 2

LATH
latħ 4*
lätħ 3
latħ 1

LATHE
lātħ 4

LATHER
latħ′ ər 4

LATITUDE
lat′ ə to͞od′ 3*
lat′ ə tyo͞od′ 3
lat′ i to͞od′ 1
lat′ i tyo͞od′ 1

LATRINE
lə trēn′ 4

LATTICE
lat′ is 3*
lat′ əs 1

LAUD
lôd 4

LAUNCH
lônch 4*
länch 4

LAUNDER
lôn' dər 4*
län' dər 4

LAUREATE
lôr' ē it 3*
lôr' ē ət 1
lär' ē ət 1

LAUREL
lôr' əl 4*
lär' əl 4

LAVA
lä' və 3*
lav' ə 3

LAVABO
lə vä' bō 4*
lə vā' bō 3

LAVAGE
lə väzh' 3*
lav' ij 3

LAVALIERE ○
lav' ə lir' 3
lä və lir' 2*
läv lir' 2

LAVATORY
lav' ə tôr' ē 4*
lav' ə tōr' ē 2

LAYETTE
lā et' 4

LEARNED (adj)
lʉr' nid 3*
lʉr' nəd 1

LEAVEN
lev' ən 3*
lev' 'n 1

LEBENSRAUM
lā' bəns roum' 4*
lā' bənz roum' 2
lā' bənts roum' 1

LECHER
lech' ər 4

LECHEROUS
lech' ər əs 4*
lech' rəs 1

LECITHIN
les' ə thin 2*
les' ə thən 2

LECTERN
lek' tərn 4

LEEWARD
lo͞o' ərd 4*
lē' wərd 4

LEGATE
leg' it 3*
leg' ət 1

LEGATEE
leg' ə tē' 4

LEGATO
lə gät' ō 2*
li gät' ō 2

PRONUNCIATION KEY

Symbol	Key words	Symbol	Key words	Symbol	Key words
a	asp, fat, parrot	†ə	a in ago	r	red, port, dear
ā	ape, date, play		e in agent	s	sell, castle, pass
†ä	ah, car, father		i in sanity	t	top, cattle, hat
e	elf, ten, berry		o in comply	v	vat, hovel, have
ē	even, meet, money		u in focus	w	will, always, swear
i	is, hit, mirror	ər	perhaps, murder	y	yet, onion, yard
ī	ice, bite, high	b	bed, fable, dub	z	zebra, dazzle, haze
ō	open, tone, go	d	dip, beadle, had	ch	chin, catcher, arch
ô	all, horn, law	f	fall, after, off	sh	she, cushion, dash
o͞o	ooze, tool, crew	g	get, haggle, dog	th	thin, nothing, truth
o͝o	look, pull, moor	h	he, ahead, hotel	th	then, father, lathe
yo͞o	use, cute, few	j	joy, agile, badge	zh	azure, leisure
yo͝o	united, cure, globule	k	kill, tackle, bake	ŋ	ring, anger, drink
oi	oil, point, toy	l	let, yellow, ball	''	see p. 15.
ou	out, crowd, plow	m	met, camel, trim	✓	see p. 15.
u	up, cut, color	n	not, flannel, ton	+	see p. 14.
ʉr	urn, fur, deter	p	put, apple, tap	'	see p. 15.
†See p. 14.		†See p. 16.		○	see p. 14.

LEGEND
lej' ənd 4

LEGENDARY ✓
lej' ən der' ē 4

LEGERDEMAIN
lej' ər də mān' 3*
lej' ər di mān' 1

LEGION
lē' jən 4

LEGIONNAIRE ✓
lē' jə ner' 2*
lē jə ner' 2
lē' jē nar' 1

LEGISLATIVE
lej' is lā' tiv 3*
lej' əs lā' tiv 1

LEGISLATURE
lej' is lā' chər 3*
lej' əs lā' chər 1

LEGITIMATE
lə jit' ə mit 2*
li jit' ə mət 2

LEGUME
leg' yōōm' 3*
li gyōōm' 3
lə gyōōm' 1

LEGUMINOUS
li gyōō' mə nəs 3
lə gyōō' mə nəs 2*

LEI
lā 4*
lā' ē 3
lā' ē' 1

LEISURE
lē' zhər 4*
lezh' ər 4
lāzh' ər 1

LEIT MOTIF
līt' mō tēf' 4

LEMUR
lē' mər 4

LENGTH
leŋkth 4*
leŋth 4

LENIENCY
lēn' yən sē 4*
lē' nē ən sē 4

LENIENT
lēn' yənt 4*
lē' nē ənt 3
lē' ni ənt 1

LENS
lenz 4

LEO
lē' ō 4

LEONINE
lē' ə nīn' 4

LEOPARD
lep' ərd 4

LEOTARD
lē' ə tärd' 4

LEPER
lep' ər 4

LEPRECHAUN
lep' rə kôn' 4*
lep' rə kän' 4

LEPROSY
lep' rə sē 4

LEPROUS
lep' rəs

LESBIAN
lez' bē ən 4

LESE MAJESTY
lēz' maj' is tē 3*
lēz' maj' əs tē 1

LESION
lē' zhən 4

LESSEE
le sē' 4

LESSOR
les' ôr' 4*
les ôr' 4

LETHAL
lē' thəl 4

LETHARGIC
lə thär' jik 4

LETHARGY
leth' ər jē 4

LEUKEMIA
lōō kē' mē ə 4

LEVEE
lev' ē 4

LEVEE (reception)
lev' ē 4*
lə vē' 3
lə vā' 2
le vē' 1

LEVER
lē' vər 4*
lev' ər 4

LEVERAGE
lē' vər ij 4*
lev' ər rij 4
lev' rij 1
lēv' rij 1

LEVI
lē' vī' 2*
lē' vī 2

LEVIATHAN
lə vī′ ə thən   2*
li vī′ ə thən   2

LEVITY
lev′ ə tē   3*
lev′ i tē   1

LEVY
lev′ ē   4

LEWD
lo͞od   4

LEXICOGRAPHER   +
lek′ sə käg′ rə fər   3*
lek′ si käg′ rə fər   1

LEXICON   +
lek′ si kän′   2*
lek′ sə kän′   2
lek′ si kən   2
lek′ sə kən   1

LIABILITY
lī′ ə bil′ ə tē   3*
lī′ ə bil′ i tē   1

LIABLE
lī′ ə bəl   3*
lī′ ə b'l   1
lī′ b'l   1

LIAISON   +
lē′ ə zän′   4*
lē ā′ zän′   3
lē′ ā zän′   1
lē ā zôn′   1
lē′ ə zən   1
lē ā′ zən   1
lē′ ə zōn   1
lā′ ə zän′   1

LIBATION
lī bā′ shən   4

LIBEL
lī′ bəl   3*
lī′ b'l   1

LIBELOUS
lī′ bə ləs   3*
lī′ b'l əs   1
lī′ bləs   1

LIBERTARIAN   ✓
lib′ ər ter′ ē ən   4

LIBERTINE
lib′ ər tēn′   4*
lib′ ər tin   2

LIBIDINOUS
li bid′ 'n əs   3
lə bid′ 'n əs   2*

LIBIDO
li bē′ dō   3*
li bī′ dō   3
lə bē′ dō   1
lib′ ə dō′   1

LIBRARY   ✓
lī′ brer′ ē   4*
lī′ brə rē   2
lī′ brē   1

LIBRA
lē′ brə   4*
lī′ brə   4

LIBRETTO
li bret′ ō   3*
lə bret′ ō   1
lə bret′ ō′   1

PRONUNCIATION KEY

Symbol	Key words	Symbol	Key words	Symbol	Key words
a	asp, fat, parrot	†ə	a in ago	r	red, port, dear
ā	ape, date, play		e in agent	s	sell, castle, pass
†ä	ah, car, father		i in sanity	t	top, cattle, hat
e	elf, ten, berry		o in comply	v	vat, hovel, have
ē	even, meet, money		u in focus	w	will, always, swear
i	is, hit, mirror	ər	perhaps, murder	y	yet, onion, yard
ī	ice, bite, high	b	bed, fable, dub	z	zebra, dazzle, haze
ō	open, tone, go	d	dip, beadle, had	ch	chin, catcher, arch
ô	all, horn, law	f	fall, after, off	sh	she, cushion, dash
o͞o	ooze, tool, crew	g	get, haggle, dog	th	thin, nothing, truth
oo	look, pull, moor	h	he, ahead, hotel	th	then, father, lathe
yo͞o	use, cute, few	j	joy, agile, badge	zh	azure, leisure
yoo	united, cure, globule	k	kill, tackle, bake	ŋ	ring, anger, drink
oi	oil, point, toy	l	let, yellow, ball	″	see p. 15.
ou	out, crowd, plow	m	met, camel, trim	✓	see p. 15.
u	up, cut, color	n	not, flannel, ton	+	see p. 14.
ur	urn, fur, deter	p	put, apple, tap	′	see p. 15.
†See p. 14.		†See p. 16.		○	see p. 14.

LICENTIATE
lī sen' shē it   3*
lī sen' shē āt'   3
lī sen' chē ət   1

LICENTIOUS
lī sen' shəs   3*
lī sen' chəs   1

LICHEE
lē' chē   3*
lē' chē'   2
lī' chē   1
lī' chē'   1

LICHEN
lī' kən   4

LICIT
lis' it   3*
lis' ət   1

LICORICE
lik' ər is   3*
lik' ər ish   3
lik' rish   3
lik rəs   1
lik ə rəs   1

LIED (song)
lēd   3*
lēt   1

LIEF
lēf   4*
lēv   1

LIEGE
lēj   4

LIEN
lēn   4*
lē' ən   4

LIEU
loo͞   4

LIEUTENANT
loo͞ ten' ənt   4

LIGAMENT
lig' ə mənt   4

LIGATE
lī' gāt'   2*
lī' gāt   2
lī gāt'   1

LIGATURE
lig' ə choor'   3*
lig' ə chər   2

LIGHTNING
līt' ning   4

LIGNEOUS
lig' nē əs   4

LILAC
lī' lək   4
lī' lak   3*
lī' läk'   2
lī' läk   2

LILLIPUTIAN
lil' ə pyoo͞' shən   3*
lil' i pyoo͞' shən   1

LIMN
lim   4

LIMOUSINE
lim' ə zēn'   4*
lim' ə zēn'   4

LINAGE
lī' nij   4

LINEAGE
lin' ē ij   4

LINEAL
lin' ē əl   4

LINEAMENT
lin' ē ə mənt   4

LINEAR
lin' ē ər   4

LINGERIE
län' zhə rā'   4
län' zhə rē'   2
lan' zhə rē'   1*
lan' jə rē'   1
lan zhə rā'   1
lan zhə rē'   1

LINGUA FRANCA
liŋ' gwə fraŋ' kə   4*
liŋ' gwə fraŋ' kə   1

LINGUINE
liŋ gwē' nē   4

LINGUIST
liŋ' gwist   3*
liŋ' gwəst   1

LINGUISTIC
liŋ gwis' tik   4

LINOLEUM
li nō' lē əm   3*
lə nō' lē əm   1
lə nōl' yəm   1

LINOTYPE
lī' nə tīp'   4

LIPID
lip' id   3*
lī' pid   3
lip' əd   1

LIQUEUR
li kur'   3*
li kyoor'   3
li koor'   1

LIRA ○
lir' ə   4

LISLE
līl   4

LISSOME
lis' əm   4

LITANY
lit' 'n ē 4*
lit' nē 1

LITER
lēt' ər 4

LITERACY
lit' ər ə sē 4*
lī' trə sē 1

LITERAL
lit' ər əl 4*
li' trəl 1

LITERARY ✓
lit' ə rer' ē 4

LITERATI
lit' ə rät' ē 4*
lit' ə rā' tī 3

LITERATURE
lit' ər ə choor' 3*
lit' rə choor' 3
lit' ər ə chər 2
lit' rə chər 1

LITHE
līth 4*
lī th 1

LITHOGRAPH
lith' ə graf' 4*
lith' ə gräf' 3

LITHOGRAPHY +
li thäg' rə fē 4

LITIGANT
lit' i gənt 2*
lit' ə gənt 2

LITIGIOUS
li tij' əs 4*
lə tij' əs 1

LITTÉRATEUR
lit' ər ə tur' 4*
li' trə tur' 1

LITTORAL
lit' ər əl 4*
lit' ər al' 1
lit' ər äl' 1

LITURGICAL
li tur' ji kəl 3*
li tur' jə k'l 1
lə tur' ji kəl 1

LITURGY
lit' ər jē 4

LIVELONG +
liv' lôn' 3*
liv' län' 2

LIVERWURST
liv' ər wurst' 4
liv' ər woorst' 2*
liv' ə woorst' 1
liv' ər woost' 1
liv' ər woosht' 1

LIVERY
liv' ər ē 4*
liv' rē 2

LIVID
liv' id 3*
liv' əd 1

LLAMA
lä' mə 4

PRONUNCIATION KEY

Symbol	Key words	Symbol	Key words	Symbol	Key words
a	asp, fat, parrot	†ə	a in ago	r	red, port, dear
ā	ape, date, play		e in agent	s	sell, castle, pass
†ä	ah, car, father		i in sanity	t	top, cattle, hat
e	elf, ten, berry		o in comply	v	vat, hovel, have
ē	even, meet, money		u in focus	w	will, always, swear
i	is, hit, mirror	ər	perhaps, murder	y	yet, onion, yard
ī	ice, bite, high	b	bed, fable, dub	z	zebra, dazzle, haze
ō	open, tone, go	d	dip, beadle, had	ch	chin, catcher, arch
ô	all, horn, law	f	fall, after, off	sh	she, cushion, dash
o͞o	ooze, tool, crew	g	get, haggle, dog	th	thin, nothing, truth
oo	look, pull, moor	h	he, ahead, hotel	th	then, father, lathe
yo͞o	use, cute, few	j	joy, agile, badge	zh	azure, leisure
yoo	united, cure, globule	k	kill, tackle, bake	ŋ	ring, anger, drink
oi	oil, point, toy	l	let, yellow, ball	''	see p. 15.
ou	out, crowd, plow	m	met, camel, trim	✓	see p. 15.
u	up, cut, color	n	not, flannel, ton	+	see p. 14.
ur	urn, fur, deter	p	put, apple, tap	'	see p. 15.
†See p. 14.		†See p. 16.		○	see p. 14.

LOATH
lōth   4*
lō*th*   3

LOATHE
lō*th*   4

LOBOTOMY   +
lō bät′ ə mē   4*
lə bät′ ə mē   2

LOCALE
lō kal′   4*
lō käl′   2

LOCO
lō′ kō   4*
lō′ kō′   1

LOCUS
lō′ kəs   4

LOCUST
lō′ kəst   4

LOCUTION
lō kyōō′ shən   4

LOGE
lōzh   4

LOGGIA   +
lô′ jē ə   3*
lä′ jē ə   2
lä′ jə   2
lô′ jə   1
lô′ jä   1

LOGISTICS
lō jis′ tiks   4

LOGO   +
läg′ ō   3*
lôg′ ō   3
lō′ gō′   1

LOLL   +
läl   4

LONGEVITY   +
län jev′ ə tē   3
lôn jev′ ə tē   2*
län jev′ i tē   1

LONGITUDE   +
län′ jə tōōd′   3*
län′ jə tyōōd′   3
län′ ji tōōd′   1
län′ ji tyōōd′   1

LONG-LIVED   +
lôŋ′ līvd′   4*
lôŋ′ livd′   4
läŋ′ līvd′   2
läŋ′ livd′   2

LOOSE
lōōs   4

LOQUACIOUS
lō kwā′ shəs   4

LOQUACITY
lō kwas′ ə tē   3*
lō kwas′ i tē   1

LORELEI
lôr′ ə lī′   4*
lōr′ ə lī′   1

LORGNETTE
lôrn yet′   4

LORRY   +
lôr′ ē   4*
lär′ ē   2
lōr′ ē   2

LOTHARIO   ✓
lō ther′ ē ō′   2*
lō ther′ ē ō   2
lō thar′ ē ō′   1
lō thär′ ē ō′   1

LOTUS
lō′ təs   4

LOUNGE
lounj   4

LOUPE
lōōp   4

LOUVER
lōō vər   4

LOWER (to be angry, sullen)
lou′ ər   3*
lour   3

LOZENGE   +
läz′ inj   2*
läz′ 'nj   2

LUAU
lōō ou′   3
lōō′ ou   2*

LUBRICANT
lōō′ bri kənt   2*
loo′ brə kənt   2

LUBRICATE
lōō′ brə kāt′   3*
lōō′ bri kāt′   1

LUBRICITY
lōō bris′ ə tē   3*
lōō bris′ i tē   1

LUCID
lōō′ sid   3*
lōō′ səd   1

LUCITE
lōō′ sīt   3*
lōō′ sīt′   1

LUCRATIVE
lōō′ krə tiv   4

LUCRE
lōō′ kər   4

LUCUBRATION
lōō′ kyoo brā′ shən   3*
lōō′ kə brā′ shən   1
lōō′ kyə brā′ shən   1

LUCULLAN
lo͞o kul' ən 4

LUDICROUS
lo͞o' də krəs 2*
lo͞o' di krəs 2

LUGUBRIOUS
loo go͞o' brē əs 4*
loo gyo͞o' brē əs 4

LUMBAGO
lum bā' gō 3*
ləm' bā' gō 1
ləm' bā' gō' 1

LUMBAR
lum' bər 4*
lum' bär' 2
lum' bär 2

LUMINARY ✓
lo͞o' mə ner' ē 4

LUMINOUS
lo͞o' mə nəs 4

LUNACY
lo͞o' nə sē 4

LUNAR
lo͞o' nər 4*
lo͞o' när' 1

LUNATIC
lo͞o' nə tik 3*
lo͞o' nə tik' 1

LUNETTE
lo͞o net' 4

LUPIN (n)
lo͞o' pən 4

LUPINE (adj)
lo͞o' pīn 3*
lo͞o' pīn' 1

LUPUS
lo͞o' pəs 4

LURE
loor 4

LURID
loor' id 3*
loor' əd 1

LUSCIOUS
lush' əs 4

LUTE
lo͞ot 4

LUXURIANT
luk shoor' ē ənt 4*
lug zhoor' ē ənt 4
lug' zhoor' ē ənt 1
luk' shoor' ē ənt 1

LUXURIOUS
luk shoor' ē əs 4*
lug zhoor' ē əs 4
lug' zhoor' ē əs 1
luk' shoor' ē əs 1

LUXURY
luk' shə rē 3*
lug' shə rē 3
luksh' rē 1
lugsh' rē 1

LYCÉE
lē sā' 3

PRONUNCIATION KEY

Symbol	Key words	Symbol	Key words	Symbol	Key words
a	asp, fat, parrot	†ə	a in ago	r	red, port, dear
ā	ape, date, play		e in agent	s	sell, castle, pass
†ä	ah, car, father		i in sanity	t	top, cattle, hat
e	elf, ten, berry		o in comply	v	vat, hovel, have
ē	even, meet, money		u in focus	w	will, always, swear
i	is, hit, mirror	ər	perhaps, murder	y	yet, onion, yard
ī	ice, bite, high	b	bed, fable, dub	z	zebra, dazzle, haze
ō	open, tone, go	d	dip, beadle, had	ch	chin, catcher, arch
ô	all, horn, law	f	fall, after, off	sh	she, cushion, dash
o͞o	ooze, tool, crew	g	get, haggle, dog	th	thin, nothing, truth
oo	look, pull, moor	h	he, ahead, hotel	th	then, father, lathe
yo͞o	use, cute, few	j	joy, agile, badge	zh	azure, leisure
yoo	united, cure, globule	k	kill, tackle, bake	ŋ	ring, anger, drink
oi	oil, point, toy	l	let, yellow, ball	″	see p. 15.
ou	out, crowd, plow	m	met, camel, trim	✓	see p. 15.
u	up, cut, color	n	not, flannel, ton	+	see p. 14.
ʉr	urn, fur, deter	p	put, apple, tap	'	see p. 15.
†See p. 14.		†See p. 16.		○	see p. 14.

LYCEUM
lī sē′ əm 4
lī′ sē əm 2*

LYONNAISE
lī ə nāz′ 3*
lī′ ə nāz′ 1

LYRE
līr 4

LYRIC ○
lir′ ik 4

LYRICISM ○
lir′ ə siz′ əm 2*
lir′ i siz′ əm 1
lir′ ə siz'm 1

MACABRE
mə käb′ rə 4*
mə käb′ ər 4
mə käb′ 3

MACADAM
mə kad′ əm 4

MACADAMIA
mak′ ə dā′ mē ə 4

MACAQUE
mə käk′ 4
mə kak′ 2*

MACARONI
mak′ ə rō′ nē 4

MACARONIC   +
mak′ ə rän′ ik 4

MACAW
mə kô′ 4

MACEDOINE
mas′ ə dwän′ 2*
mas′ i dwän′ 2

MACERATE
mas′ ə rāt′ 4

MACH
mäk 4

MACHETE
mə s̸het′ ē 4*
mə c̸het′ ē 4
mə s̸het′ 1

MACHIAVELLIAN
mak′ ē ə vel′ ē ən 4*
mak′ ē ə vel′ yən 2

MACHINATION
mak′ ə nā′ s̸hən 3*
mas̸h′ ə nā′ s̸hən 3
mak′ i nā′ s̸hən 1
mas̸h′ i nā′ s̸hən 1

MACHISMO
ma c̸hēz′ mō 2*
mä c̸hēz′ mō 1
mä c̸hiz′ mō 1

MACKEREL
mak′ rəl 4*
mak′ ər əl 3

MACRAMÉ
mak′ rə mā′ 2*
mak′ rə mā′ 2

MACROBIOTIC   +
mak′ rō bī ät′ ik 3*
mak′ rō bē ät′ ik 1

MACROCOSM   +
mak′ rə käz′ əm 2*
mak′ rō käz′ əm 1
mak′ rə käz′ ′m 1

MACRON   +
mā′ krən 3
mā′ krän 2*
mak′ rän 1
mak′ rän′ 1
mak′ rən 1

MADAME
mad′ əm 3*
mə dam′ 3
ma dam′ 2
mə däm′ 1

MADEMOISELLE
mad′ ə mə zel′ 3*
mam zel′ 2
mad′ mwä zel′ 1
mad′ mə zel′ 1

MADONNA   +
mə dän′ ə 4

MADRAS
mad' rəs   4*
mə dras'   3
mə dräs'   3
mäd' rəs   1

MADRIGAL
mad' ri gəl   3*
mad' rə gəl   1

MADRILÈNE
mad' rə len'   2*
mad' ri len'   1
mad' rə län'   1
mad' rə len'   1

MAELSTROM   +
māl' strəm   4

MAESTRO
mīs' trō   4*
mä es' trō   1

MAFIA
mä' fē ə   4*
ma' fē ə   1

MAGENTA
mə jen' tə   4

MAGI
mā' jī   3*
mā' jī'   1

MAGISTERIAL   ○
maj' is tir' ē əl   4

MAGISTRACY
maj' is trə sē   3*
maj' əs trə sē   1

MAGNA CHARTA
mag' nə kär' tə   3*
mag' nə kär' tə   1

MAGNANIMOUS
mag nan' ə məs   4

MAGNATE
mag' nāt'   2*
mag' nāt   2
mag' nit   1
mag' nət   1

MAGNESIA
mag nē' zhə   4*
mag nē' shə   4

MAGNANIMITY
mag' nə nim' ə tē   2*
mag' nə nim' i tē   2*

MAGNET
mag' nit   3*
mag' nət   1

MAGNETO
mag nēt' ō   4

MAGNIFICO
mag nif' i kō'   2*
mag nif' ə kō'   2

MAGNILOQUENT
mag nil' ə kwənt   4

MAGNOLIA
mag nōl' yə   4*
mag nō' lē ə   2

MAHARAJA (H)
mä' hə rä' jə   3*
mä' hə rä' zhä   2
mä' hə rä' jä   1

MAHARANEE
mä' hə rä' nē   4

MAHATMA
mə hat' mə   3
mə hät' mə   3*
mä hät' mä   1

MAH JONG   +
mä' zhäng'   4*
mä' zhông'   3
mä' jäng'   3
mä' jông'   2

MAHOGANY   +
mə häg' ə nē   4*
mə hôg' ə nē   1

MAHOUT
mə hout'   4

MAINSAIL
mān' səl   3*
mān' sāl'   3
mān' s'l   1

MAINTAIN
mān tān'   4*
mən tān'   1

MAINTENANCE
mān' t'n əns   3*
mān' tən əns   1
mānt' nəns   1

MAJOLICA   +
mə jäl' i kə   3*
mə yäl' i kə   2
mə jäl' ə kə   1
mə yäl' ə kə   1

MAJOR DOMO
mā' jər dō' mō   4

MAJORITY   +
mə jär' ə tē   2*
mə jôr' ə tē   2
mə jôr' i tē   1
mə jär' i tē   1

MALADY
mal' ə dē   4

MALACHITE
mal' ə kīt'   4

MALAISE
mal āz'   3*
mə lāz'   1
mal ez'   1

MALADROIT
mal' ə droit'   4

MALAGA
mal′ ə gə   4

MALAMUTE
mal′ ə myoot′   4*
mäl′ ə myoot′   1

MALFEASANCE
mal fē′ z′ns   3*
mal fē′ zəns   1

MALODOROUS
mal′ ō′ dər əs   4

MALAPROPISM   +
mal′ ə präp iz′ əm   3*
mal′ ə präp iz′m   1

MALAPROPOS
mal′ ap rə pō′   4

MALARIA   ✓
mə ler′ ē ə   4

MALEDICTION
mal′ ə dik′ sлən   3*
mal′ i dik′ sлən   1

MALEFACTOR
mal′ ə fak′ tər   4

MALEFICENT
mə lef′ ə sənt   2*
mə lef′ i sənt   1
mə lef′ ə s′nt   1

MALEVOLENT
mə lev′ ə lənt   4

MALICE
mal′ is   3*
mal′ əs   1

MALICIOUS
mə lisл′ əs   4

MALIGN
mə līn′   4

MALIGNANT
mə lig′ nənt   4

MALINGER
mə liŋ′ gər   4

MALL
môl   4*
mall   3

MALLARD
mal′ ərd   4

MALLEABLE
mal′ ē ə bəl   3*
mal′ ē ə b′l   1
mal′ yə bəl   1

MALMSEY
mäm′ zē   4*
mälm′ zē   1

MALOCCLUSION
mal′ ə kloo′ zhən   4

MAMBO
mäm′ bō   4

MAMMALIAN
mə mā′ lē ən   3*
ma mā′ lē ən   3
mə māl′ yən   1

MAMMARY
mam′ ər ē   4

MAMMOTH
mam′ əth 4

MANACLE
man′ ə kəl 2
man′ ə k′l 1*
man′ i kəl 1

MANDALA
mun′ də lə 4

MAÑANA
mä nyä′ nä 3*
mə nyä′ nə 1

MANDAMUS
man dā′ məs 4

MANDARIN
man′ də rin 3*
man′ drən 1

MANDATORY
man′ də tôr′ ē 4*
man′ də tōr′ ē 3

MANÈGE
ma nezh′ 4*
ma näzh′ 3

MANDOLIN
man′ də lin′ 3
man′ də lin′ 1*
man′ d′l in′ 1

MANDRAGORA
man drag′ ə rə 4

MANEUVER
mə noo′ vər 4*
mə nyoo′ vər 3

MANGE
mānj 4

MANGER
mān′ jər 4

MANGY
mān′ jē 4

MANIA
mā′ nē ə 4*
mān′ yə 3

MANIACAL
mə nī′ ə kəl 3*
mə nī′ ə k′l 1

MANICOTTI   +
man′ i kät′ ē 2*
man′ ə kät′ ē 2

MANIFESTO
man′ ə fes′ tō 4

MANNA
man′ ə 4

MANNIKIN
man′ ə kin 2*
man′ i kin 1
man′ i kən 1

MANSARD
man′ särd 3*
man′ särd′ 1

MANTILLA
man til′ ə 4
man tē′ ə 3
man tē′ yə 2*

MANURE
mə noor′ 2*
mə nyoor′ 2
mə noor′ 2
mə nyoor′ 1

MARACA
mə rä′ kə 4*
mə ra′ kə 2

MARASCHINO
mar′ ə skē′ nō 4*
mar′ ə shē′ nō 4

MARATHON   +
mar′ ə thän′ 4*
mar′ ə thən 1

MARAUDER
mə rôd′ ər 4

MARCASITE
mär′ kə sīt′ 4
mär′ kə zīt′ 2*

MARCEL
mär sel′ 4

MARCHIONESS
mär′ shə nes′ 3*
mär′ shən is 2

MARDI GRAS
mär′ dē grä′ 1*
mär′ dē grä′ 1
mär′ dē grä′ 1
mär′ di grä′ 1

MARGARINE
mär′ jə rin 2*
mär′ jə rēn′ 1
märj′ rin 1
märj′ rən 1

MARIJUANA
mar′ ə wä′ nə 4*
mar′ ə hwä′ nə 2
mär′ ə wä′ nə 1

MARIMBA
mə rim′ bə 4

MARINA
mə rē′ nə 4

MARINATE
mar′ ə nāt′ 4

MARINADE
mar′ ə nād′ 4*
mar′ ə nād′ 1

MARINER
mar′ ə nər 4

MARIONETTE ✓
mar′ ē ə net′ 4*
mer′ ē ə net′ 1

MARITAL
mar′ ə t′l   2*
mar′ i t′l   1
mar′ ə təl   1

MARITIME
mar′ ə tīm′   3*
mar′ i tīm′   1

MARJORAM
mär′ jər əm   3*
marj′ rəm   1

MARMALADE
mär′ mə lād′   4*
mär′ mə lād′   1

MARMOREAL
mär môr′ ē əl   4*
mär mōr′ ē əl   3

MARMOSET
mär′ mə zet′   4
mär′ mə set′   3*

MAROON
mə rōōn′   4

MARQUEE
mär kē′   4

MARQUESS
mär′ kwis   4

MARQUETRY
mär′ kə trē   3*
mär′ ki trē   1

MARQUIS
mär′ kwis   3*
mär kē′   2
mär′ kwəs   1

MARQUISE
mär kēz′   4

MARQUISETTE
mär′ ki zet′   3*
mär′ kwi zet′   3
mär′ kə zet′   1

MARSHMALLOW
märsh′ mal′ ō   4*
märsh′ mel′ ō   4
märsh′ mel′ ə   1

MARSUPIAL
mär sōō′ pē əl   4

MARTIAL
mär′ shəl   4

MARTYR
mär′ tər   4

MARZIPAN
mär′ zə pan′   3*
märt′ sə pän′   2
mär′ zi pan′   1

MASCARA
mas kar′ ə   2*
məs kar′ ə   2

MASCOT
mas′ kət   4
mas′ kät   3*

MASCULINE
mas′ kyə lin   3*
mas′ kyə lən   1

PRONUNCIATION KEY

Symbol	Key words	Symbol	Key words	Symbol	Key words
a	asp, fat, parrot	†ə	a in ago	r	red, port, dear
ā	ape, date, play		e in agent	s	sell, castle, pass
†ä	ah, car, father		i in sanity	t	top, cattle, hat
e	elf, ten, berry		o in comply	v	vat, hovel, have
ē	even, meet, money		u in focus	w	will, always, swear
i	is, hit, mirror	ər	perhaps, murder	y	yet, onion, yard
ī	ice, bite, high	b	bed, fable, dub	z	zebra, dazzle, haze
ō	open, tone, go	d	dip, beadle, had	ch	chin, catcher, arch
ô	all, horn, law	f	fall, after, off	sh	she, cushion, dash
ōō	ooze, tool, crew	g	get, haggle, dog	th	thin, nothing, truth
oo	look, pull, moor	h	he, ahead, hotel	th	then, father, lathe
yōō	use, cute, few	j	joy, agile, badge	zh	azure, leisure
yoo	united, cure, globule	k	kill, tackle, bake	ŋ	ring, anger, drink
oi	oil, point, toy	l	let, yellow, ball	″	see p. 15.
ou	out, crowd, plow	m	met, camel, trim	╱	see p. 15.
u	up, cut, color	n	not, flannel, ton	+	see p. 14.
ur	urn, fur, deter	p	put, apple, tap	′	see p. 15.
†See p. 14.		†See p. 16.		○	see p. 14.

MASOCHISM
mas′ ə kiz′ əm   3*
mas′ ə kiz′ ′m   1
maz′ ə kiz′ əm   1

MASQUE
mask   4*
mäsk   3

MASQUERADE
mas′ kə rād′   4

MASSACRE
mas′ ə kər   3*
mas′ i kər   1

MASSAGE
mə säzh′   4*
mə säj′   2

MASSEUR
ma sᵾr′   4*
mə sᵾr′   2

MASSEUSE
mə sōōz′   3*
mə sōōs′   1
mə sooz′   1
ma sōōz′   1
ma suz′   1

MASTIFF
mas′ tif   3*
mas′ təf   1
mäs′ tif   1

MASTODON   +
mas′ tə dän′   4*
mas′ tə dən   1

MATADOR
mat′ ə dôr′   4

MATER
māt′ ər   4*
mät′ ər   1

MATERIA MEDICA   ○
mə tir′ ē ə med′ i kə   4

MATÉRIEL   ○
(MATERIEL)
mə tir′ ē el′   4

MATIN
mat′ ′n   3*
mat′ in   2

MATINÉE
mat′n ā′   2*
mat′ ′n ā′   1
mat′ ə nā′   1

MATRIARCH
mā′ trē ärk′   4

MATRICIDE
mat′ rə sīd′   2*
mā′ trə sīd′   2
mat′ ri sīd′   1
mā′ tri sīd′   1

MATRICULATE
mə trik′ yə lāt′   3*
mə trik′ yoo lāt′   1

MATRIX
mā′ triks   4*
ma′ triks   1

MATRONLY
mā′ trən lē   4

MATRONYMIC
mat′ rə nim′ ik   4

MATURE
mə toor′   4
mə choor′   4
mə tyoor′   3*

MATUTINAL
mə tōōt′ ′n əl   2*
mə tyōōt′ ′n əl   2
mach′ oo tīn′ əl   1
mach′ oo tīn′ ′l   1
mə tōōt′ nəl   1
mə tyōōt′ nəl   1

MATZOH
mät′ sə   4*
mät′ sō   2
mät′ sô   1
mät′ sōth′   1

MAUDLIN
môd′ lin   3*
môd′ lən   1

MAUNDER
môn′ dər   4*
män′ dər   2

MAUSOLEUM
mô′ sə lē′ əm   4*
mô′ zə lē′ əm   4

MAUVE
mōv   4*
môv   2

MAVERICK
mav′ ər ik   4*
mav′ rik   4

MAVOURNEEN
mə voor′ nēn′   2*
mə vôr′ nēn   2
mə voor′ nēn   2
mə vōr′ nēn   1

MAYHEM
mā′ əm   4*
mā′ hem′   2
mā′ hem   2

MAYONNAISE
mā′ ə nāz′   4*
mā′ ə nāz′   3

MAYORALTY   ✓
mā′ ər əl tē   4*
mer′ əl tē   4

MAZEL TOV
mä zəl tôf′   1*
mä′ z′l tōv′   1
mä′ zəl tôv′   1

MAZURKA
mə zʉr′ kə   4*
mə zoor′ kə   4

MEA CULPA
mē′ ə kul′ pə   3
mä′ ä kool pä   2*
mä′ ə kul′ pə   1

MEANDER
mē an′ dər   4

MEDALLION
mə dal′ yən   4

MEDIA
mē′ dē ə   4

MEDIAL
mē′ dē əl   4

MEDIATE
mē′ dē āt′   4

MEDICAMENT
mə dik′ ə mənt   2*
mi dik′ ə mənt   2
med′ i kə mənt   2
med′ ə kə mənt   2

MEDICINAL
mə dis′ ə nəl   2*
mə dis′ ′n′l   1
mə dis′ nəl   1

MEDIEVAL
med′ ē ē′ vəl   3*
mē′ dē ē′ vəl   2
mid′ ē ē′ vəl   2
me′ dē ē′ v′l   1
med′ ē′ vəl   1
mē dē′ vəl   1

MEDIOCRE
mē′ dē ō ′ kər   3*
mē′ dē ō′ kər   2

MEDIOCRITY   +
mē dē äk′ rə tē   2*
mē′ dē äk′ rə tē   1
mē′ dē äk′ ri tē   1

MEDLEY
med′ lē   4

MEERSCHAUM   ○
mir′ shəm   3*
mir′ shôm   3
mir′ shoum   1

MEGALOMANIA
meg′ ə lō mā′ nē ə   4*
meg′ ə lō mān′ yə   2

MEGALOPOLIS   +
meg′ ə läp ə lis   2*
meg′ ə läp ə ləs   2

MEGATON
meg′ ə tun′   4

MEGILLAH
me gil′ ə   4

MEISTERSINGER
mīs′ tər siŋ′ ər   4
mīs′ tər ziŋ′ ər   3*

MELANCHOLIC   +
mel′ ən käl′ ik   4

PRONUNCIATION KEY

Symbol	Key words	Symbol	Key words	Symbol	Key words
a	asp, fat, parrot	†ə	a in ago	r	red, port, dear
ā	ape, date, play		e in agent	s	sell, castle, pass
†ä	ah, car, father		i in sanity	t	top, cattle, hat
e	elf, ten, berry		o in comply	v	vat, hovel, have
ē	even, meet, money		u in focus	w	will, always, swear
i	is, hit, mirror	ər	perhaps, murder	y	yet, onion, yard
ī	ice, bite, high	b	bed, fable, dub	z	zebra, dazzle, haze
ō	open, tone, go	d	dip, beadle, had	ch	chin, catcher, arch
ô	all, horn, law	f	fall, after, off	sh	she, cushion, dash
ōo	ooze, tool, crew	g	get, haggle, dog	th	thin, nothing, truth
oo	look, pull, moor	h	he, ahead, hotel	th	then, father, lathe
yōo	use, cute, few	j	joy, agile, badge	zh	azure, leisure
yoo	united, cure, globule	k	kill, tackle, bake	ŋ	ring, anger, drink
oi	oil, point, toy	l	let, yellow, ball	′′	see p. 15.
ou	out, crowd, plow	m	met, camel, trim	✓	see p. 15.
u	up, cut, color	n	not, flannel, ton	+	see p. 14.
ʉr	urn, fur, deter	p	put, apple, tap	′	see p. 15.
†See p. 14.		†See p. 16.		○	see p. 14.

MELANCHOLY +
mel' ən käl' ē 4

MÉLANGE
mā länj' 2
mā länzh' 1*

MELÉE (MELEE)
mā lā' 4*
mā' lā 3
mel' ā 1

MELLIFLUOUS
mə lif' lōō əs 2*
mə lif' loo wəs 1
me lif' lə wəs 1
mə lif' lə wəs 1

MELODEON
mə lō' dē ən 4

MELODIC +
mə läd' ik 4

MELODIOUS
mə lō' dē əs 4

MELODRAMA
mel' ə dram' ə 4
mel' ə drä' mə 4*

MEMENTO
mə men' tō 3*
mi men' tō 2

MEMOIR
mem' wär 3*
mem' wôr 2
mem' wär' 1

MEMORABILIA
mem' ər ə bil' ē ə 4*
mem' ər ə bil' yə 4
mem' ər ə bēl' yə 1

MEMORABLE
mem' ər ə bəl 2*
mem' ər ə b'l 1
mem' rə bəl 1

MEMSAHIB
mem' sä' ib 4*
mem' sä' hib 2
mem' sä' ēb 1
mem säb' 1
mem' säb 1

MENACE
men' is 3*
men' əs 1

MÉNAGE
mā näzh' 4*
mə näzh' 1

MENAGERIE
mə naj' ər ē 4*
mə nazh' ər ē 4
mə naj' rē 1

MENDACIOUS
men dā' shəs 4

MENDACITY
men das' ə tē 3*
men das' i tē 1

MENDICANT
men' di kənt 4*
men' də kənt 1

MENHADEN
men hād'n' 4*
mən hād' 'n 1

MENHIR ○
men' hir 4

MENIAL
mē' nē əl 4*
mēn' yəl 3

MENINGITIS
men' in jīt' is 3*
men' in jīt' əs 1

MENORAH
mə nô' rə 4*
mə nō' rə 4

MENSHEVIK
men' shə vik 3*
men' chə vik' 1
men' chə vēk' 1

MENSTRUATE
men' strōō āt' 2*
men' stroo' wāt' 1
men' strə wāt' 1
men' strāt 1

MENTHOL +
men' thôl' 2*
men' thōl 2
men' thôl 2
men' thäl 2

MENU
men' yōō 4*
mān' yōō 3

MEPHITIC
mə fit' ik 4

MERCANTILE
mʉr' kən tēl' 4*
mʉr' kən tīl' 4
mʉr' kən til 3

MERCENARY ✓
mʉr' sə ner' ē 3*
mʉr' s'n er' ē 1

MERCHANDISE
mʉr' chən dīz' 4*
mʉr' chən dīs' 4

MERCURIAL
mər kyoor' ē əl 4

MERETRICIOUS
mer' ə trīsh' əs 3*
mer' i trīsh' əs 1

MERIDIAN
mə rid' ē ən 4

MERINGUE
mə raŋ' 4

MESA
mā′ sə   4

MESCALINE
mes′ kə lēn′   3*
mes′ kə lin   2
mes′ kə lən   1

MESMERIZE
mez′ mə rīz′   4*
mes′ mə rīz′   2

MESQUITE
məs kēt′   4*
mes kēt′   3
mes′ kēt   1

MESSIAH
mə sī′ ə   3*
mi sī′ ə   1

MESSIANIC
mes′ ē an′ ik   4

MESTIZO
mes tē′ zō   *
mis tē′ zō   2

METABOLISM
mə tab′ ə liz′ əm   3*
mə tab′ ə liz′ ′m   1

METALLIC
mə tal′ ik   4

METALLURGY
met′ ′l ʉr′ jē   4

METAMORPHOSIS
met′ ə môr′ fə sis   3*
met′ ə môr fō′ sis   1
met′ ə môr′ fə səs   1

METAPHOR
met′ ə fər   4*
met′ ə fôr′   4

METAPHORICAL   +
met′ ə fôr′ ik əl   4
met′ ə fōr′ ik əl   2
met′ ə fär′ ik əl   1*

METAPHYSICAL
met′ ə fiz′ i kəl   3
met′ ə fiz′ i k′l   1*

METASTASIS
mə tas′ tə sis   3*
mə tas′ tə səs   1

METE
mēt   4

METEOR
mē′ tē ər   4
mē′ tē ôr′   2*

METEORIC   +
mē′ tē är′ ik   4*
mē′ tē ôr′ ik   4

METEORITE
mē′ tē ə rīt′   4

METEOROLOGY   +
mē′ tē ə räl′ ə jē   4

METER
mē′ tər   4

METHADONE
meth′ ə dōn′   4

METHANE
meth′ ān′   2*
meth′ ān   2

METICULOUS
mə tik′ yə ləs   3*
mə tik′ yo͞o ləs   1

MÉTIER
mā tyā′   3*
mā tyā   1
me′ tyā′   1
me tyā′   1

METONYMY   +
mə tän′ ə mē   3*
mi tän′ ə mē   1

METRIC
met′ rik   4

METRONOME
met′ rə nōm′   4

METROPOLIS   +
mə träp′ ə lis   2*
mə träp′ ′l is   1
mə träp′ ləs   1

METROPOLITAN   +
met′ rə päl′ it ′n   2*
met′ rə päl′ ət ′n   1
met′ rə päl′ ət ən   1

MEZZANINE
mez′ ə nēn′   3*
mez′ ə nēn′   3
mez′ ′n ēn′   1

MEZZOTINT
met′ sō tint′   3*
med′ zō tint′   3
mez′ ō tint′   3

MIASMA
mī az′ mə   4*
mē az′ mə   4

MICA
mī′ kə   4

MICROBE
mī′ krōb′   2*
mī′ krōb   2

MICROCEPHALIC
mī′ krō sə fal′ ik   3*
mī krə si fal′ ik   1

MICROMETER   +
mī kräm′ ə tər   3*
mī kräm′ i tər   1

MICROCOSM   +
mī′ krə käz′ əm   3*
mī′ krə käz′ ′m   1

MICROFICHE
mī′ krə fēsh′   2*
mī′ krō fēsh′   1

MICRON   +
mī′ krän   3*
mī′ krän′   1

MICROSCOPIC   +
mī′ krə skäp′ ik   4

MICROSCOPY   +
mī kräs′ kə pē   4

MIDGET
mij′ it   3*
mij′ ət   1

MIDST
midst   4*
mitst   3

MIEN
mēn   4

MIGNONETTE
min′ yə net′   4

MIGRAINE
mī′ grān′   2*
mī′ grān   2

MIGRANT
mī′ grənt   4

MIGRATE
mī′ grāt′   2*
mī′ grāt   2
mī grāt′   1

MIGRATORY
mī′ grə tôr′ ē   4*
mī′ grə tōr′ ē   3

MIKADO
mi kä′ dō   4

MILADY
mi lā′ dē   4

MILDEW
mil′ do͞o   4*
mil′ dyo͞o′   4

MILEAGE
mīl′ ij   4

MILITIA
mə lish′ ə   3*
mi lish′ ə   1

MILENNIUM
mə len′ ē əm   2*
mi len′ ē əm   2

MIME
mīm   3*
mēm   2

MIMESIS
mi mē′ sis   3*
mī mē′ sis   3
mə mē′ səs   1

MIMETIC
mi met′ ik   3*
mī met′ ik   3
mə met′ ik   1

MIMIC
mim′ ik   4

MIMICRY
mim′ ik rē   4

MIMOSA
mi mō′ sə   3*
mi mō′ zə   2
mə mō′ sə   1
mī mō′ sə   1
mī mō′ zə   1

MINARET
min′ ə ret′   4*
min′ ə ret′   3

MINATORY
min′ ə tôr′ ē   4*
min′ ə tōr′ ē   3

MINERAL
min′ ər əl   4*
min′ rəl   3

MINERALOGY   +
min′ ə ral′ ə jē   4*
min′ ə räl′ ə jē   4

MINESTRONE
min′ ə strō′ nē   3*
min′ i strō′ nē   1

MINIATURE
min′ ē ə choor′   3*
min′ ē ə chər   2
min′ ə chər   1
min′ yə toor′   1
min′ yə chər   1

MINIATURIZE
min′ ē ə chə rīz′   4*
min′ ə chə rīz′   2
min′ i ə chə rīz′   1

MINION
min′ yən   4

MINISCULE
min′ ə skyōōl′   4*
mi nus′ kyōōl   3

MINISTERIAL   ○
min′ is tir′ ē əl   4

MINNESINGER
min′ i siŋ′ ər   4*
min′ ə ziŋ′ ər   2

MINORITY   +
mī nôr′ ə tē   4
mə nôr′ ə tē   3
mī när′ ə tē   3
mə när′ ə tē   2*
mi nôr′ i tē   1
mi när′ i tē   1

MINUET
min′ yōō et′   2*
min′ yoo wet′   1
min′ yə wet′   1

MINUTE (n)
min′ it   3*
min′ ət   1

MINUTE (adj)
mī nyōōt′   4*
mī nōōt′   4
mi nōōt′   3
mi nyōōt′   3

PRONUNCIATION KEY

Symbol	Key words	Symbol	Key words	Symbol	Key words
a	asp, fat, parrot	†ə	a in ago	r	red, port, dear
ā	ape, date, play		e in agent	s	sell, castle, pass
†ä	ah, car, father		i in sanity	t	top, cattle, hat
e	elf, ten, berry		o in comply	v	vat, hovel, have
ē	even, meet, money		u in focus	w	will, always, swear
i	is, hit, mirror	ər	perhaps, murder	y	yet, onion, yard
ī	ice, bite, high	b	bed, fable, dub	z	zebra, dazzle, haze
ō	open, tone, go	d	dip, beadle, had	ch	chin, catcher, arch
ô	all, horn, law	f	fall, after, off	sh	she, cushion, dash
ōō	ooze, tool, crew	g	get, haggle, dog	th	thin, nothing, truth
oo	look, pull, moor	h	he, ahead, hotel	th	then, father, lathe
yōō	use, cute, few	j	joy, agile, badge	zh	azure, leisure
yoo	united, cure, globule	k	kill, tackle, bake	ŋ	ring, anger, drink
oi	oil, point, toy	l	let, yellow, ball	″	see p. 15.
ou	out, crowd, plow	m	met, camel, trim	✓	see p. 15.
u	up, cut, color	n	not, flannel, ton	+	see p. 14.
ur	urn, fur, deter	p	put, apple, tap	′	see p. 15.
†See p. 14.		†See p. 16.		○	see p. 14.

MINUTIA
mi nōō′ shē ə   3*
mi nyōō′ shē ə   3
mi nōō′ shə   3
mi nyōō′ shə   3
mə nōō′ shə   1
mə nyōō′ shə   1

MIRACULOUS
mə rak′ yə ləs   3*
mi rak′ yoo ləs   1

MIRAGE
mi räzh′   3*
mə räzh′   1

MISALLIANCE
mis′ ə lī′ əns   4*
mis′ ə lī′ ənts   1

MISANTHROPE
mis′ ən thrōp′   3*
miz′ ən thrōp′   3
miz′ ′n thrōp′   1

MISANTHROPY
mis an′ thrə pē   4*
miz an′ thrə pē   2
mis ant′ thrə pē   1

MISCEGENATION
mis′ i jə nā′ shən   4
mi sej′ ə nā′ shən   2*
mi sej′ ə nā′ shən   2

MISCELLANEOUS
mis ə lā′ nē əs   4*
mis ə lān′ yəs   1

MISCELLANY
mis′ ə lā′ nē   4

MISCHIEF
mis′ chif   3*
mis chəf   1

MISCHIEVOUS
mis′ chə vəs   4

MISCIBLE
mis′ ə bəl   3*
mis′ ə b′l   1

MISCONSTRUE
mis′ kən strōō′   4

MISCREANT
mis′ krē ənt   4

MISDEMEANOR
mis′ di mē′ nər   4

MISERABLE
miz′ rə bəl   3*
miz′ ər ə bəl   3
miz′ ər ə b′l   1
miz′ ər bəl   1

MISERLY
mī′ zər lē   4

MISFEASANCE
mis fē′ z′ns   2*
mis fē′ zəns   2

MISHAP
mis hap′   3
mis′ hap′   2*
mis′ hap   2

MISHMASH   +
mish′ mäsh   4*
mish′ mash′   4

MISLED
mis led′   4

MISNOMER
mis nō′ mər   4

MISOGYNIST   +
mi säj′ ə nist   3*
mi säj′ ə nəst   1

MISOGYNY   +
mi säj′ ə nē   4*
mə säj′ ə nē   1

MISPRISION
mis prizh′ ən   4

MISSAL
mis′ əl   3*
mis′ ′l   1

MISSILE
mis′ əl   3*
mis′ ′l   1

MISTLETOE
mis′ əl tō′   3*
mis′ ′l tō   1

MISTRAL
mis′ trəl   4
mis träl′   1*

MITER
mīt′ ər   4

MITIGATE
mit′ ə gāt′   4

MITZVAH
mits′ və   4*
mits′ vä   2

MNEMONIC   +
ni män′ ik   3*
nē män′ ik   2

MOBILE (adj)
mō′ bəl   3*
mō′ bēl′   3
mō′ bīl′   2
mō′ b′l   1
mō′ bil   1

MOBILE (n)
mō′ bēl′   2*
mō′ bēl   2

MOBILIZE
mō′ bə līz′   4

MOBOCRACY   +
mäb äk′ rə sē   4

MOCCASIN   +
mäk′ ə sin   2
mäk′ ə sən   1*
mäk′ ə s'n   1
mäk′ ə zən   1

MOCHA
mō′ kə   4

MODAL
mōd′ 'l   4

MODALITY
mō dal′ ə tē   3*
mō dal′ i tē   1

MODERATOR   +
mäd′ ə rāt′ ər   4

MODERN   +
mäd′ ərn   4

MODICUM   +
mäd′ i kəm   3*
mäd′ ə kəm   1
mōd′ i kəm   1

MODISH
mōd′ ish   4

MODISTE
mō dēst′   4

MODULAR   +
mäj′ ə lər   3*
mäd′ yə lər   1
mäj′ oo lər   1
mäd′ yoo lər   1

MODULATE   +
mäj′ ə lāt′   3*
mäd′ yə lāt′   2
mäj′ oo lāt′   1

MODULE   +
mäj′ ool   4
mäd′ yool   2*

MODUS VIVENDI
mō′ dəs vi ven′ dī   3
mō′ dəs vi ven′ dē   2*
mō′ dəs vi ven′ dē   1
mō′ dəs vi ven′ dī   1

MOGUL
mō gul′   4
mō′ gəl   3*
mō′ gul   2

MOHAIR   ✓
mô′ her′   2*
mō′ her   1
mō′ har′   1

MOIETY
moi′ ə tē   3*
moi′ i tē   1

MOIRÉ
mwä rā′   4
mô rā′   2*
môr′ ā   2

MOLECULAR
mə lek′ yə lər   4*
mō lek′ yə lər   1

MOLECULE   +
mäl′ ə kyool′   3*
mäl′ i kyool′   1

MOLEST
mə lest′   4*
mō lest′   1

MOLESTATION   +
mäl′ əs tā′ shən   3*
mō′ les tā′ shən   2
mə les tā′ shən   1
mō′ les′ tā′ shən   1

MOLLUSC   +
mäl′ əsk   4

MOMENTOUS
mō men′ təs   4*
mə men′ təs   1

MOMENTUM
mō men′ təm   4*
mə men′ təm   1

MONAD   +
mō′ nad′   2*
mō′ nad   2
män′ ad   2

MONARCH   +
män′ ərk   4*
män′ ärk   2

MONARCHY   +
män′ ər kē   4*
män′ är kē   2

MONASTIC
mə nas′ tik   4

MONAURAL   +
män ôr′ əl   3
mōn ôr′ əl   1*

MONETARY   +✓
män′ ə ter′ ē   3*
mun′ ə ter′ ē   3
män′ i ter′ ē   1
mun′ i ter′ ē   1

MONGER   +
mäŋ′ gər   4*
muŋ′ gər   4

MONGOLISM
mäŋ′ gə liz′ əm   3*
mäŋ′ gə liz′ ′m   1
män′ gə liz′ əm   1

MONGOLOID   +
mäŋ′ gə loid′   3*
män′ gə loid′   2

MONGOOSE   +
mäŋ′ gōōs′   3*
män′ gōōs′   3

MONGREL   +
mäŋ′ grəl   4*
muŋ′ grəl   4

MONOCLE   +
män′ ə kəl   2*
män′ ə k′l   1
män′ i kəl   1

MONOGAMIST   +
mə näg′ ə mist   3*
mə näg ə məst   1

MONOGAMOUS   +
mə näg′ ə məs   4

MONOGAMY   +
mə näg′ ə mē   4

MONOLITH   +
män′ ə litℏ′   2*
män′ ə litℏ   1
män′ ′litℏ′   1

MONOLOGUE   +
män′ ə lôg′   4
män′ ə läg′   3*

MONOLOGIST   +
mə näl′ ə jist   3*
män′ ə lôg′ ist   2
män′ ə läg′ ist   2
mə näl′ ə jəst   1

MONONUCLEOSIS   +
män′ ə nōō′ klē ō′ sis   2*
män′ ə nyōō′ klē ō′ sis   2
män′ ō nōō′ klē ō′ sis   1
män′ ō nōō′ klē ō′ səs   1
män′ ō nyōō′ klē ō′ səs   1

MONOPOLY   +
mə näp′ ə lē   4
mə näp′ lē   1

MONOTONE   +
män′ ə tōn′   4

MONOTONOUS   +
mə nät′ ′n əs   4

MONOTONY   +
mə nät′ ′n ē   4*
mə nät′ nē   1

MONSIGNOR   +
män sēn′ yər   4*
mən sēn′ yər   1

MONSOON   +
män sōōn′   4

MONSTROSITY   +
män sträs′ ə tē   3*
män sträs′ i tē   1

MONSTROUS   +
män′ strəs   4*
mänt′ strəs   1

MONTAGE   +
män täƶ′   4*
mōn täƶ′   1

MOOT
mōōt   4

MORAINE
mə rān′   4
mô rān′   1

MORAL   +
mär′ əl   4*
môr′ əl   4

MORALE
mə ral′ 4*
mô ral′ 1

MORALITY
mə ral′ ə tē 3*
mô ral′ ə tē 3
mə ral′ i tē 1
mô ral′ i tē 1

MORASS
mə ras′ 4*
mô ras′ 3

MORATORIUM +
môr′ ə tôr′ ē əm 4*
môr′ ə tōr′ ē əm 3
mär ə tôr′ ē əm 2
mär ə tōr′ ē əm 2

MORDANT
môr′ d'nt 3*
môr′ dənt 1

MORE
môr 4*
mōr 3

MORES
môr′ āz 3*
môr′ ēz 3
mōr′ ēz 3
mōr′ āz 2
môr′ āz′ 1
mōr′ āz′ 1

MORGANATIC
môr′ gə nat′ ik 4

MORGUE
môrg 4

MORIBUND +
môr′ ə bund′ 4*
mär′ ə bund′ 3
môr′ ə bənd 1

MORON +
môr′ än′ 4*
mōr′ än′ 3

MOROSE
mə rōs′ 4*
mô rōs′ 3

MORPHINE
môr′ fēn′ 2*
môr′ fēn 2

MORTAR
môr′ tər 4

MORTGAGE
môr′ gij 4

MORTICIAN
môr tish′ ən 4

MORTIFY
môr′ tə fī′ 4

MORTISE
môr′ tis 3*
môr′ təs 1

MORTMAIN
môrt′ main 4

MORTUARY ✓
môr′ cho͞o er′ ē 2*
môr′ choo wer′ ē 1
môr′ chə wer′ ē 1

PRONUNCIATION KEY

Symbol	Key words	Symbol	Key words	Symbol	Key words
a	asp, fat, parrot	†ə	a in ago	r	red, port, dear
ā	ape, date, play		e in agent	s	sell, castle, pass
†ä	ah, car, father		i in sanity	t	top, cattle, hat
e	elf, ten, berry		o in comply	v	vat, hovel, have
ē	even, meet, money		u in focus	w	will, always, swear
i	is, hit, mirror	ər	perhaps, murder	y	yet, onion, yard
ī	ice, bite, high	b	bed, fable, dub	z	zebra, dazzle, haze
ō	open, tone, go	d	dip, beadle, had	ch	chin, catcher, arch
ô	all, horn, law	f	fall, after, off	sh	she, cushion, dash
o͞o	ooze, tool, crew	g	get, haggle, dog	th	thin, nothing, truth
oo	look, pull, moor	h	he, ahead, hotel	th	then, father, lathe
yo͞o	use, cute, few	j	joy, agile, badge	zh	azure, leisure
yoo	united, cure, globule	k	kill, tackle, bake	ŋ	ring, anger, drink
oi	oil, point, toy	l	let, yellow, ball	″	see p. 15.
ou	out, crowd, plow	m	met, camel, trim	✓	see p. 15.
u	up, cut, color	n	not, flannel, ton	+	see p. 14.
ur	urn, fur, deter	p	put, apple, tap	′	see p. 15.
†See p. 14.		†See p. 16.		○	see p. 14.

MOSAIC
mō zā′ ik 4

MOSLEM   +
mäz′ ləm 4*
mäs′ ləm 4
muz′ ləm 1

MOSQUE   +
mäsk 4*
môsk 1

MOT
mō 4

MOTET
mō tet′ 4

MOTH   +
môth 4*
mäth 2

MOTHS   +
môthz 4*
môths 4
mäthz 2
mäths 2

MOTIF
mō tēf′ 4

MOTIVE
mō′ tiv 4

MOTILE
mōt′ ′l 4*
mō′ tīl′ 2
mō′ til 1

MOTLEY   +
mät′ lē 4

MOUE
mōō 4

MOUJIK
mōō zhik′ 3*
mōō zhēk′ 3
mōō′ zhik 2

MOULAGE
mōō läzh′ 4

MOULD
mōld 4

MOULT
mōlt 4

MOUNTEBANK
moun′ tə baŋk′ 3*
moun′ ti baŋk′ 1

MOUSSE
mōōs 4

MOUTH (n)
mouth 4

MOUTH (v)
mouth 4

MOUTON   +
mōō′ tän 2
mōō′ tän′ 2*
mōō tän′ 1

MOW
mō 4

MOZZARELLA   +
mät′ sə rel′ ə 4*
mōt′ sə rel′ ə 1
môt′ sə rel′ ə 1

MUCILAGE
myōō′ sə lij 4*
myōō′ slij 1

MUCILAGINOUS
myōō′ sə laj′ ə nəs 3*
myōō′ si laj′ ə nəs 1

MUCOUS
myōō′ kəs 4

MUENSTER
mōōn′ stər 4
mun′ stər 4
min′ stər 2*

MUEZZIN
myōō ez′ in 3
mōō ez′ in 2*
mōō ez′ ′n 1
mwez′ ′n 1

MUFTI (moslem judge)
muf′ tē 4*
mōof′ tē 2

MUFTI (civilian dress)
muf′ tē 4

MUKLUK
muk′ luk′ 3*
muk′ luk 1

MULATTO
mə lat′ ō 3
moo lat′ ō 2
myōō lat′ ō 2
moo lät′ ō 1*
myōō lät′ ō 1

MULCT
mulkt 4

MULETEER ○
myoo′ lə tir′ 4

MULLAH
mul′ ə 3*
mool′ ə 3

MULLEIN
mul′ ən 4

MULLIGATAWNY
mul′ i gə tô′ nē 3*
mul′ ə gə tô′ nē 1
mul′ i gə tä′ nē 1

MULLION
mul′ yən 4

MULTIFARIOUS ✓
mul′ tə fer′ ē əs 4*
mul′ tə far′ ē əs 2

MULTITUDE
mul' tə to͞od'   3*
mul' tə tyo͞od'   3
mul' ti to͞od'   1
mul' ti tyo͞od'   1

MUNDANE
mun' dān'   4*
mun' dān'   2
mun' dān   2

MUNICIPAL
myo͞o nis' ə pəl   2*
myo͞o nis' ə p'l   1
myo͞o nis' pəl   1

MUNIFICENT
myo͞o nif' ə sənt   2*
myo͞o nif' i sənt   1
myo͞o nif' ə s'nt   1

MURAL
myo͞or' əl   4

MURRAIN
mur' in   3*
mur' ən   1

MUSCATEL
mus' kə tel'   3*
mus' kə tel'   1

MUSE
myo͞oz   4

MUSETTE
myo͞o zet'   2*
myo͞o zet'   2

MUSEUM
myo͞o zē' əm   3*
myo͞o zē' əm   1

MUSICALE
myo͞o' zi kal'   3*
myo͞o zə kal'   1

MUSKELLUNGE
mus' kə lunj'   3*
mus' kə länj'   1

MUSKETEER ○
mus' kə tir'   2*
mus' ki tir'   2

MUSKMELON
musk' mel' ən   4

MUSLIM
mo͞oz' ləm   3*
muz' ləm   3
mo͞os' ləm   2
muz' lim   1

MUSTACHE
mə stash'   3*
mus' tash'   2
mus' tash   1

MUSTACHIO
məs tä' shē o   4
məs tä' shō   3
məs ta' shō   3
məs ta' shē ō'   2*

MUSTANG
mus' tang'   2*
mus' tang   2

MUTANT
myo͞ot' 'nt   3*
myo͞ot' ənt   1

MUTATION
myo͞o tā' shən   4

PRONUNCIATION KEY

Symbol	Key words	Symbol	Key words	Symbol	Key words
a	asp, fat, parrot	†ə a in ago		r	red, port, dear
ā	ape, date, play	e in agent		s	sell, castle, pass
†ä	ah, car, father	i in sanity		t	top, cattle, hat
e	elf, ten, berry	o in comply		v	vat, hovel, have
ē	even, meet, money	u in focus		w	will, always, swear
i	is, hit, mirror	ər	perhaps, murder	y	yet, onion, yard
ī	ice, bite, high	b	bed, fable, dub	z	zebra, dazzle, haze
ō	open, tone, go	d	dip, beadle, had	ch	chin, catcher, arch
ô	all, horn, law	f	fall, after, off	sh	she, cushion, dash
o͞o	ooze, tool, crew	g	get, haggle, dog	th	thin, nothing, truth
o͜o	look, pull, moor	h	he, ahead, hotel	th	then, father, lathe
yo͞o	use, cute, few	j	joy, agile, badge	zh	azure, leisure
yo͜o	united, cure, globule	k	kill, tackle, bake	ŋ	ring, anger, drink
oi	oil, point, toy	l	let, yellow, ball	''	see p. 15.
ou	out, crowd, plow	m	met, camel, trim	✓	see p. 15.
u	up, cut, color	n	not, flannel, ton	+	see p. 14.
ur	urn, fur, deter	p	put, apple, tap	'	see p. 15.
†See p. 14.		†See p. 16.		○	see p. 14.

MUTE
myo͞ot 4

MUTILATE
myo͞ot′ 'l āt′ 4

MUTINEER ○
myo͞ot′ 'n ir′ 4

MUTINOUS
myo͞ot′ 'n əs 4*
myo͞ot′ nəs 1

MUTINY
myo͞ot′ 'n ē 4*
myo͞ot′ nē 1

MUTUAL
myo͞o′ choo əl 2*
myo͞o′ choo wəl 1
myo͞och′ wəl 1

MYNA
mī′ nə 4

MYOPIA
mī ō′ pē ə 4

MYOPIC +
mī äp′ ik 4*
mī ō′ pik 2

MYRIAD ○
mir′ ē əd 4

MYRMIDON +
mur′ mə dän′ 2*
mur′ mə dän 2
mur′ mə dən 2
mur′ mi d'n 1

MYRRH
mur 4

MYSTIQUE
mi stēk′ 4

NABOB +
nā′ bäb 3*
nā′ bäb′ 1

NACRE
nā′ kər 4

NACREOUS
nā′ krē əs 4*
nā′ krəs 1
nā′ kə rəs 1

NADIR ○
nā′ dər 4
nā′ dir 4*

NAIAD
nī′ əd 4*
nā′ əd 4
nā′ ad′ 2
nā′ ad 2
nī′ ad′ 2
nī′ ad 2

NAIF
nä ēf′ 4

NAIVE
nä ēv′ 4

NAIVETE
nä′ ēv tā′ 2
nä ēv tā′ 2*
nä ēv′ tā′ 1
nä ē və tā′ 1
nä ē′ və tā 1

NAPALM
nā′ päm 4*
nā′ pälm 1

NAPERY
nā′ pə rē 4*
nā′ prē 1

NAPHTHA
naf′ thə 4*
nap′ thə 4

NARCISSISM
när′ sə siz′ əm 2*
när′ si siz′ əm 1
när′ sə siz′m 1

NARCISSUS
när sis′ əs 4

NARGHILE
när′ gə lē′ 2*
när′ gə lā′ 2
när′ gə lē 1
när′ gə le 1*

NARWHAL
när′ wəl 4*
när′ hwəl 1
när′ hwäl 1
när′ wäl 1

NASAL
nā′ zəl 3
nā′ z'l 1*

NASCENT
nā′ s'nt 2*
nā′ sənt 2
nas′ ənt 2
nas′ 'nt 2

NASTURTIUM
nə stʉr′ shəm 4*
na stʉr′ shəm 4

NATAL
nāt′ 'l 4

NATATORIUM
nāt′ ə tôr′ ē əm 4
nat ə tôr′ ē əm 3*
nat ə tōr′ ē əm 3
nāt′ ə tōr′ ē əm 2

NATIVITY
nə tiv′ ə tē   3*
nā tiv′ ə tē   3
nə tiv′ i tē   1
nā tiv′ i tē   1

NATURE
nā′ chər   4

NATUROPATH
nā′ chər ə pat*h*′   3
nə toor′ ə pat*h*′   1*
nə tyoor′ ə pat*h*′   1

NAUGHT
nôt   4*
nät   1

NAUSEA
nô′ shə   4*
nô′ zē ə   4
nô′ zhə   4
nô′ sē ə   4

NAUSEATE
nô′ zē āt′   4*
nô′ zhē āt′   4
nô′ sē āt′   4
nô′ shē āt′   4

NAUSEOUS
nô′ shəs   4*
nô′ zē əs   4
nô′ sē əs   1

NAUTICAL
nôt′ i kəl   3*
nôt′ i k′l   1
nät′ i kəl   1

NAUTILUS
nôt′ ′l əs   4*
nôt′ əl əs   1

NAVEL
nā′ vəl   3
nā′ v′l   1*

NAVIGABLE
nav′ ə gə bəl   2*
nav′ i gə bəl   1
nav′ i gə b′l   1

NAZI
nät′ sē   4*
nat′ sē   4

NEANDERTHAL
nē an′ dər t*h*ôl′   4*
nē an′ dər tôl′   3
nā än′ dər täl′   3
nē an′ dər täl   2

NEBULA
neb′ yə lə   4

NEBULOUS
neb′ yə ləs   4

NECESSARILY ✓
nes′ ə ser′ ə lē   3*
nes′ i ser′ ə lē   1
nes′ i ser′ ə lē   1
nes′ ə ser′ ə lē   1

NECESSARY ✓
nes′ ə ser′ ē   3*
nes′ i ser′ ē   1

NECESSITY
nə ses′ ə tē   2*
ni ses′ ə tē   2
nə ses′ i tē   1
ni ses′ tē   1

NECROMANCY
nek′ rə man′ sē   4

NECROPHILIA
nek′ rə fil′ ē ə   3*
nek′ rə fēl′ yə   1

NECTAR
nek′ tər   4

NECTARINE
nek′ tə rēn′   4*
nek′ tə rēn′   2

NÉE
nā   4*
nē   1

NE'ER ✓
ner   4

NEFARIOUS ✓
ni fer′ ē əs   4*
ni far′ ē əs   1

NEGATE
ni gāt′   3*
neg′ āt   1
nē′ gāt   1

NEGLIGÉE
neg′ li zhā′   2*
neg′ lə zhā′   2
neg′ li zhā′   1
neg′ lə zhā′   1

NEGLIGIBLE
neg′ li jə bəl   3*
neg′ li jə b′l   1

NEGOTIABLE
ni gō′ shē ə bəl   3*
ni gō′ shə bəl   3
ni gō′ shə b′l   1
ni gō′ shē ə b′l   1

NEGOTIATE
ni gō′ shē āt′   4

NEGUS
nē′ gəs   4*
ni gōōs′   1

NEIGH
nā   4

NEITHER
nē′ *th*ər   4*
nī′ *th*ər   4

NEMESIS
nem′ ə sis   2*
nem′ i sis   1
nem′ ə səs   1

NEOLITHIC
nē ə lith′ ik   4

NEOLOGISM   +
nē äl′ ə jiz′ əm   2*
nē äl′ ə jiz əm   1
nē äl′ ə jiz′m   1

NEON   +
nē′ än   4

NEOPHYTE
nē′ ə fīt′   4

NEPENTHE
ni pen′ the   3*
nə pen′ the   1
nə pent′ the   1

NEPOTISM
nep′ ə tiz′ əm   3*
nep′ ə tiz′m   1

NESTLE
nes′ əl   3
nes′ ′l   1*

NESTLING
nest′ liŋ   4
nes′ liŋ   2*

NETHER
neth′ ər   4

NETSUKE
net′ soo kā′   2
net′ skē   2
net′ soo kē′   1*
net′ skā   1

NEURALGIA
noo ral′ jə   4*
nyoo ral′ ja   3
nyoo ral′ jə   1

NEURASTHENIA
noor′ əs the′ nē ə   4*
nyoor′ əs the′ nē ə   4

NEURON   +
nyoor′ än   3*
noor′ än   3
noor′ än′   1
nyoor′än′   1
noor′ än   1
nyoor′ än   1

NEUROSES
nyoo rō′ sez′   3*
noo rō′ sez′   3
noo rō′ sez   1
nyoo rō′ sez   1

NEUROSIS
nyoo rō′ sis   3*
noo rō′ sis   3
noo rō′ səs   1
nyoo rō′ səs   1

NEUROTIC   +
nyoo rät′ ik   4*
noo rät′ ik   4

NEUTER
nyoot′ ər   4*
noot′ ər   4

NEUTRAL
nyoo′ trəl   4*
noo′ trəl   4

NEUTRON   +
noo′ trän   3
nyoo′ trän   2*
noo′ trän′   1
nyoo′ trän′   1

PRONUNCIATION KEY

Symbol	Key words	Symbol	Key words	Symbol	Key words
a	asp, fat, parrot	†ə	a in ago	r	red, port, dear
ā	ape, date, play		e in agent	s	sell, castle, pass
†ä	ah, car, father		i in sanity	t	top, cattle, hat
e	elf, ten, berry		o in comply	v	vat, hovel, have
ē	even, meet, money		u in focus	w	will, always, swear
i	is, hit, mirror	ər	perhaps, murder	y	yet, onion, yard
ī	ice, bite, high	b	bed, fable, dub	z	zebra, dazzle, haze
ō	open, tone, go	d	dip, beadle, had	ch	chin, catcher, arch
ô	all, horn, law	f	fall, after, off	sh	she, cushion, dash
oo	ooze, tool, crew	g	get, haggle, dog	th	thin, nothing, truth
oo	look, pull, moor	h	he, ahead, hotel	th	then, father, lathe
yoo	use, cute, few	j	joy, agile, badge	zh	azure, leisure
yoo	united, cure, globule	k	kill, tackle, bake	ŋ	ring, anger, drink
oi	oil, point, toy	l	let, yellow, ball	″	see p. 15.
ou	out, crowd, plow	m	met, camel, trim	✓	see p. 15.
u	up, cut, color	n	not, flannel, ton	+	see p. 14.
ur	urn, fur, deter	p	put, apple, tap	′	see p. 15.
†See p. 14.		†See p. 16.		○	see p. 14.

NEW
nyo͞o 4*
no͞o 4

NEWSPAPER
nyo͞oz' pā' pər 4*
no͞oz' pā' pər 4

NEWT
nyo͞ot 4*
no͞ot 4

NEXUS
nek' səs 4

NIACIN
nī' ə sin 3*
nī' ə sən 1

NICETY
nī' sə tē 3*
nī' si tē 1
nī' stē 1

NICHE
nich 4

NICKELODEON
nik ə lō' dē ən 4

NICOTINE
nik' ə tēn' 4*
nik' ə tin 2
nik' ə tēn 1

NIGH
nī 4

NIHILISM
nī' ə liz' əm 3*
ni' hi liz' əm 2
nē' ə liz' əm 2
nī' ə liz'm 1
nē' ə liz'm 1

NIMIETY
ni mī' ə tē 3*
ni mī' i tē 1

NIRVANA ○
nir vä' nə 4*
nər vä' nə 4
nir va' nə 2
nər va' nə 1

NISEI
nē' sā' 2*
nē sā' 2
nē' sā' 2
nē' sā 1

NITROGLYCERINE
nī' trō glis' ər in 2*
nī' trə glis' ər in 2
nī' trō glis' rən 1

NOBLESSE OBLIGE
nō bles' ō blēzh' 3*
nō' bles' ə blēzh' 1

NOCTURNAL +
näk tur' n'l 3*
näk tur' nəl 1

NOCTURNE +
näk' turn 3*
näk' turn' 1

NODULE +
näj' o͞ol 4*
näj' o͞o əl 1

NOLO CONTENDERE
nō' lō kən ten' də rē 4

NOMAD +
nō' mad' 2*
nō' mad 2
näm' ad 2

NOMADIC
nō mad' ik 4

NOM DE GUERRE + ✓
näm' də ger' 2*
näm də ger' 1
näm di ger' 1

NOM DE PLUME +
näm' də plo͞om' 3*
näm di plo͞om' 1

NOMENCLATURE
nō' mən klā' chər 4*
nō men' klə chər 4
nō men' klə choor 1
nō men' klə toor 1
nō men' klə tyoor 1

NOMINAL +
näm' ə n'l 2*
näm' ə nəl 1
näm' i n'l 1
näm' nəl 1

NOMINATIVE +
näm' ə nə tiv 3*
näm' ə nā' tiv 2
näm' nə tiv 2

NONAGE +
nän' ij 4*
nō' nij 4

NONAGENARIAN +✓
nän' ə jə ner' ē ən 3*
nō' nə jə ner' ē ən 3
nän' ə ji ner' ē ən 1
nō' nə ji ner' ē ən 1

NONCE +
näns 4*
nänts 1

NONCHALANCE +
nän' shə ləns 2*
nän' shə läns' 2
nän shə läns' 2
nän' shə länts' 1
nän chə läns' 1

NONCHALANT +
nän' shə lənt 2*
nän' shə länt' 2
nän shə länt' 2

NONCOMBATANT   +
nän′ kəm bat′ ənt   3
nän′ käm′ bə tənt   2*
nän käm′ bə tənt   1
nän′ käm′ bə t′nt   1
nän′ kəm bat′ ′nt   1

NONCOMMITAL   +
nän′ kə mit′ ′l   3*
nän kə mit′l   1

NONDESCRIPT   +
nän di skript′   4*
nän′ di skript′   1

NONENTITY   +
nän en′ tə tē   3*
nän en′ ti tē   1

NONPAREIL   +
nän′ pə rel′   4

NON SEQUITUR   +
nän sek′ wi toor′   1*
nän′ sek′ wi tər   1
nän sek′ wi tər   1
nän sek′ wə tər   1
nōn sek′ wə tər   1

NOOSE
nōōs   4

NOSTALGIA   +
näs tal′ jə   4
nəs tal′ jə   3*
nôs tal′ jə   2
näs tal′ jē ə   2
nəs tal′ jē ə   2
nôs tal′ jē ə   1
nəs täl′ jə   1
nōs tal′ jə   1

NOSTRUM   +
näs′ trəm   4

NOTARY
nōt′ ər ē   4

NOTORIETY
nōt′ ə rī′ ə tē   3*
nōt′ ə rī′ i tē   1

NOTORIOUS
nō tôr′ ē əs   4*
nō tōr′ ē əs   3
nə tôr′ ē əs   1
nə tōr′ ē əs   1

NOUGAT
nōō′ gət   4*
nōō′ gä   1

NOUVEAU RICHE
nōō vō rēsh′   2*
nōō′ vō resh′   1
nōō′ vō′ rēsh′   1

NOVELLA
nō vel′ ə   4

NOVENA
nō vē′ nə   4*
nə vē′ nə   1

NOVICE   +
näv′ is   3*
näv′ əs   1

NOVITIATE
nō vish′ ē it   3*
nō vish′ ē āt′   2
nō vish′ it   1
nō vish′ ət   1
nə vish′ ət   1

NOXIOUS   +
näk′ shəs   4

PRONUNCIATION KEY

Symbol	Key words	Symbol	Key words	Symbol	Key words
a	asp, fat, parrot	†ə	a in ago	r	red, port, dear
ā	ape, date, play		e in agent	s	sell, castle, pass
†ä	ah, car, father		i in sanity	t	top, cattle, hat
e	elf, ten, berry		o in comply	v	vat, hovel, have
ē	even, meet, money		u in focus	w	will, always, swear
i	is, hit, mirror	ər	perhaps, murder	y	yet, onion, yard
ī	ice, bite, high	b	bed, fable, dub	z	zebra, dazzle, haze
ō	open, tone, go	d	dip, beadle, had	ch	chin, catcher, arch
ô	all, horn, law	f	fall, after, off	sh	she, cushion, dash
ōō	ooze, tool, crew	g	get, haggle, dog	th	thin, nothing, truth
oo	look, pull, moor	h	he, ahead, hotel	th	then, father, lathe
yōō	use, cute, few	j	joy, agile, badge	zh	azure, leisure
yoo	united, cure, globule	k	kill, tackle, bake	ŋ	ring, anger, drink
oi	oil, point, toy	l	let, yellow, ball	″	see p. 15.
ou	out, crowd, plow	m	met, camel, trim	╰	see p. 15.
u	up, cut, color	n	not, flannel, ton	+	see p. 14.
ur	urn, fur, deter	p	put, apple, tap	′	see p. 15.
†See p. 14.		†See p. 16.		○	see p. 14.

NTH (degree)
entth   4*
enttth   1

NUANCE
nyo͞o′ äns   3*
no͞o äns′   3
no͞o′ äns   3
nyo͞o äns′   2
no͞o′ äns′   1
nyo͞o′ äns′   1
no͞o′ änts   1
nyo͞o′ änts   1

NUBILE
nyo͞o′ bīl′   2*
no͞o′ bīl′   2
nyo͞o′ bil   2
nyo͞o′ b'l   2
no͞o′ bil   1
no͞o′ b'l   1
no͞o′ bəl   1
nyo͞o′ bəl   1

NUCLEAR
no͞o′ klē ər   4*
nyo͞o′ klē ər   4

NUCLEUS
no͞o′ klē əs   4*
nyo͞o′ klē əs   4

NUCLEI
no͞o′ klē ī′   4*
nyo͞o′ klē ī′   4

NUDE
nyo͞od   4*
no͞od   4

NUDITY
no͞o′ də tē   3
nyo͞o′ də tē   2*
no͞o′ di tē   1
nyo͞o′ di tē   1

NUGATORY
no͞o′ gə tôr′ ē   4*
nyo͞o′ gə tôr′ ē   4
no͞o′ gə tōr′ ē   3
nyo͞o′ gə tōr′ ē   3

NUISANCE
no͞o′ s'ns   2*
no͞o′ səns   2
nyo͞o′ səns   2
nyo͞o′ s'ns   2
no͞o′ s'nts   1
nyo͞o′ s'nts   1

NUMERAL
no͞o′ mər əl   3*
nyo͞o′ mər əl   3
no͞om′ rəl   1

NUMERICAL
nyo͞o mer′ i kəl   3*
no͞o mer′ i kəl   3
noo mer′ i k'l   1
nyoo mer′ i k'l   1

NUMEROUS
nyo͞o′ mər əs   4*
no͞o′ mər əs   4
no͞om′ rəs   1

NUMISMATICS
no͞o′ miz mat′ iks   3*
no͞o′ mis mat′ iks   3
nyo͞o′ miz mat′ iks   3
nyo͞o′ mis mat′ iks   3
no͞o′ məz mat′ iks   1
nyo͞o′ məz mat′ iks   1
no͞o′ məs mat′ iks   1
nyo͞o′ məs mat′ iks   1

NUMISMATIST
no͞o miz′ mə tist   3*
no͞o mis′ mə tist   3
nyo͞o miz′ mə tist   3
nyo͞o mis′ mə tist   3
no͞o miz′ mə təst   1
nyo͞o miz′ mə təst   1

NUNCIO
nun′ sē ō′   3*
noon′ sē ō′   2
nun′ she ō   1
nun′ she ō′   1
nunt′ sē ō′   1
noont′ sē ō′   1

NUPTIAL
nup′ shəl   4
nup′ chəl   3*

NURTURE
nʉr′ chər   4

NUTRIA
no͞o′ trē ə   4*
nyo͞o′ trē ə   4

NUTRIENT
no͞o′ trē ənt   4*
nyo͞o′ trē ənt   4

NUTRIMENT
no͞o′ trə mənt   4*
nyo͞o′ trə mənt   4

NUTRITION
no͞o trish′ ən   4*
nyo͞o trish′ ən   4

NYMPH
nimf   4*
nimpf   1

NYMPHOMANIA
nim′ fə mā′ nē ə   4*
nim′ fə mān′ yə   3
nimp′ fə mā′ nē ə   1
nimp′ fə mān′ yə   1

NYSTAGMUS
nis tag′ məs   4

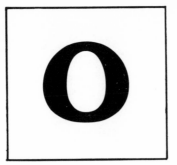

OAF
ōf   4

OASES
ō ā′ sēz′   2*
ō ā′ sēz   2

OASIS
ō ā′ sis   3*
ō′ ə sis   2
ō ā′ səs   1

OATH
ōth   4

OATHS
ōthz   4*
ōths   4

OBBLIGATO   +
äb′ lə gät′ ō   4*
äb′ lə gät′ ō′   1

OBDURATE   +
äb′ door ət   2*
äb′ dyoor ət   2
äb′ door it   2
äb′ dyoor it   2
äb′ dər ət   1
äb′ dyər ət   1
äb door′ ət   1
äb dyoor′ ət   1

OBEISANCE
ō bē′ səns   3
ō bā′ səns   2*
ō bā′ s'ns   2
ō bē′ s'ns   1
ō bā′ s'nts   1
ə bā′ səns   1
ə bā′ s'nts   1

OBELISK   +
äb′ ə lisk   4*
äb′ ə ləsk   1
ō′ bə lisk   1

OBESE
ō bēs′   4

OBESITY
ō bē′ sə tē   3*
ō bē′ si tē   1

OBFUSCATE   +
äb′ fəs kāt′   4*
äb fus′ kāt   3
äb fus′ kāt′   1
əb fus′ kāt′   1

OBIT   +
ō′ bit   3*
ō bit′   2
äb′ it   2
ō′ bət   1

OBITER DICTUM   +
ō′ bi tər dik′ təm   2*
äb′ i tər dik′ təm   2
ō′ bə tər dik′ təm   1

OBITUARY   ✓
ō bich′ ōo er′ ē   2*
ō bich′ oo wer′ ē   1
ə bich′ oo wer′ ē   1
ə bich′ ə wer′ ē   1
ō bich′ ə wer′ ē   1
ə bich′ ə rē   1
ō bich′ ə rē   1

OBJECT   + (v)
əb jekt′   4*
äb jekt′   1

OBJECT   + (n)
äb′ jikt   4*
äb′ jekt   2

OBJET D'ART   +
ôb zhe där′   1
ôb′ zhā′ där′   1*
äb′ zhā där′   1
ub′ zhā där′   1

OBJURGATORY   +
äb jur′ gə tôr′ ē   3*
əb jur′ gə tôr′ ē   1
əb jur′ gə tōr′ ē   1

OBLATE   +
äb′ lāt   3*
äb lāt′   2
äb′ lāt′   1
əb lāt′   1
ōb lāt′   1

OBLIGATORY   +
ə blig′ ə tôr′ ē   4*
ə blig′ ə tōr′ ē   3
äb′ li gə tôr′ ē   2
äb′ li gə tōr′ ē   2
ä blig′ ə tôr′ ē   1
ä blig′ ə tōr′ ē   1
äb′ lə gə tôr′ ē   1
äb′ lə gə tōr′ ē   1

OBLIQUE
ə blēk   4
ō blēk   3*

OBLITERATE
ə blit′ ə rāt′   4*
ō blit′ ə rāt′   2

OBLIVION   +
ə bliv′ ē ən   4*
ō bliv′ ē ən   2
ä bliv′ ē ən   1

OBLIVIOUS
ə bliv′ ē əs   4

OBLOQUY   +
äb′ lə kwē   4

OBNOXIOUS   +
əb näk′ shəs   4*
äb näk′ shəs   3

OBOE
ō′ bō   4*
ō′ bō′   1

OBSCENE   +
əb sēn′   4*
äb sēn′   3

OBSCENITY   +
əb sen′ ə tē   3*
äb sen′ ə tē   2
əb sen′ i tē   1
äb sen′ i tē   1

OBSEQUIES   +
äb′ sə kwēz   4

OBSEQUIOUS   +
əb sē′ kwē əs   4*
äb sē′ kwē əs   3

OBSESS   +
äb ses′   4*
əb ses′   3

OBSOLESCENT   +
äb sə les′ ′nt   2*
äb′ sə les′ ənt   2

OBSOLETE
äb′ sə lēt′   4*
äb′ sə lēt′   4

OBSTETRICIAN   +
äb′ stə trish′ ən   3*
äb′ sti trish′ ən   1

OBSTINACY   +
äb′ stə nə sē   4

OBSTINATE   +
äb′ stə nit   3*
äb′ stə nət   1

OBSTREPEROUS   +
əb strep′ ər əs   4*
äb strep′ ər əs   3
əb strep′ rəs   1
äb strep′ rəs   1

OBTUSE   +
əb tōōs′   4
əb tyōōs′   4
äb tōōs′   3*
äb tyoos′   3
äb′ tōōs   1
äb′ tyōōs   1

OBVIATE   +
äb′ vē āt′   4

OCARINA   +
äk′ ə rē′ nə   4

OCCASION
ə kā′ zhən   4

OCCIPITAL   +
äk sip′ ə t′l   2*
äk sip′ i t′l   1
äk sip′ ə təl   1

OCCULT   +
ə kult′   4*
ä kult′   2
ä′ kult   2
ä′ kult′   1

OCCULTISM   +
ə kul′ tiz′ əm   2*
äk′ əl tiz ′m   2
ä kul′ tiz′ əm   1
äk′ ul tiz′ əm   1
ə kul′ tiz əm   1
ə kul′ tiz ′m   1

OCEANIC
ō′ shē an′ ik   4

OCEANOGRAPHY   +
ō′ shə näg′ rə fē   4*
ō′ shē ə näg′ rə fē   2

OCELOT   +
äs′ ə lät′   4*
ō′ sə lät′   4

OCHER
ō′ kər   4

OCTAGONAL   +
äk tag′ ə n′l   3*
äk tag′ ə nəl   1

OCTAVE   +
äk′ tiv   4*
äk′ tāv   3
äk′ tāv′   1
äk′ təv   1

OCTAVO   +
äk tā′ vō   4*
äk tä′ vō   3

OCTOGENARIAN   ✓   +
äk tə jə ner′ ē ən   2*
äk′ tə ji ner′ ē ən   1
äk′ tə jə ner′ ē ən   1

OCTOPUS   +
äk′ tə pəs   4*
äk′ tə poos′   1

OCTOROON   +
äk tə rōon′   2*
äk′ tə rōon′   2

OCULAR   +
äk′ yə lər   4

ODALISQUE
ōd′ ′l isk   3*
ōd′ əl isk′   1

ODIOUS
ō′ dē əs   4

ODIUM
ō′ dē əm   4

ODOMETER   +
ō däm′ ət ər   1

ODORIFEROUS
ō′ də rif′ ər əs   4

ODOROUS
ō′ dər əs   4

ODYSSEY   +
äd′ ə sē   3*
äd′ i sē   1

OEDIPAL
ed′ ə pəl   4*
ē′ də pəl   4

OEDIPUS
ed′ ə pəs   4*
ē′ də pəs   4

OFFAL   +
ô′ fəl   3*
äf′ əl   3
ô′ f′l   1
äf′ ′l   1

OFFERTORY   +
äf′ ər tôr′ ē   4*
ôf′ ər tôr′ ē   4
äf′ ər tōr′ ē   3
ôf′ ər tōr′ ē   3
ôf′ ə tōr′ ē   1

OFFICIAL
ə fish′ əl   4

OFFICIATE
ə fish′ ē āt′   4

OFFICIOUS
ə fish′ əs   4

OFTEN   +
ôf′ ən   2
äf′ ən   2
ôf′ ′n   1*
ôf′ t′n   1

OGIVE
ō′ jīv′   3*
ō jīv′   2
ō′ jīv   1

OGLE   +
ō′ gəl   2
ō′ g′l   1*
ô′ gəl   1
ä′ g′l   1
ä′ gəl   1

OGRE
ō′ gər   4

OHM
ōm   4

OKAPI
ō kä′ pē   4

OKRA
ō′ krə   4

OLEAGINOUS
ō′ lē aj′ ə nəs   3*
ō′ lē aj′ i nəs   1

OLEANDER
ō′ lē an′ dər   4
ō′ lē an′ dər   3*

OLEOMARGARINE
ō′ lē ō mär′ jə rin   3*
ō′ lē ō mär′ jə rēn′   3
ō′ lē ō mär′ gə rin   1
ō′ lē ō mär′ gə rēn′   1
ō′ lē ō märj′ rən   1
ō′ lē ō mär′ jə rən   1
ō′ lē ō mär′ jə rēn   1

OLFACTORY   +
äl fak′ tər ē   4
ōl fak′ tər ē   3*
äl fak′ trē   3
ōl fak′ trē   3

OLIGARCH   +
äl′ ə gärk′   4

OLIGARCHY   +
äl′ ə gär′ kē   4

OLIO
ō′ lē ō′   4

OLYMPIAN
ō lim′ pē ən   4*
ə lim′ pē ən   1

OMBUDSMAN   +
äm′ budz mən   3
äm′ boodz man′   1*

OMEGA
ō meg′ ə   4
ō mē′ gə   4
ō mā′ gə   3*
ō′ meg ə   1

OMELET   +
äm′ lit   3*
äm′ ə lit   2
äm′ ə let   1
äm′ lət   1
äm′ ə lət   1

OMEN
ō′ mən   4

OMINOUS   +
äm′ ə nəs   4

OMNIBUS   +
äm′ ni bus′   4*
äm′ nə bəs   2
äm′ ni bəs   1

OMNIPOTENT   +
äm nip′ ə tənt   3*
äm nip′ ə t′nt   1

OMNIPRESENT   +
äm′ ni prez′ ′nt   2
äm′ ni prez′ ənt   1*
äm′ nə prez′ ənt   1

OMNISCIENT   +
äm nish′ ənt   4

OMNIVEROUS   +
äm niv′ ər əs   4*
äm niv′ rəs   1

ONEROUS   +
ō′ nər əs   4*
än′ ər əs   4

ONOMATOPOEIA   +
än′ ə mät′ ə pē′ ə   2*
än′ ə mat′ ə pē′ ə   2
än ə mat′ ə pē′ ə   2

ONTOGENY   +
än täj′ ə nē   4

ONTOLOGY   +
än täl′ ə jē   4

ONUS
ō′ nəs   4

ONYX   +
än′ iks   4*
ō′ niks   2

OPACITY
ō pas′ ə tē   3*
ō pas′ i tē   1

OPAL
ō′ pəl   3*
ō′ p′l   1

OPALESCENT
ō′ pə les′ ′nt   2*
ō′ pə les′ ənt   2

OPAQUE
ō pāk′   4

OPERABLE   +
äp′ ər ə bəl   3*
äp′ ər ə b′l   1
äp′ rə bəl   1

OPERATIC   +
äp ə rat′ ik   2*
äp′ ə rat′ ik   2

OPERATIVE   +
äp′ ər ə tiv   4*
äp′ ə rā′ tiv   4
äp′ rə tiv   3

OPHTHALMIC   +
äf t*h*al′ mik   4*
äp t*h*al′ mik   3

OPHTHALMOLOGIST   +
äf′ thə mäl′ ə jist   4*
äp′ thə mäl′ ə jist   4
äf′ thal mäl′ ə jist   3
äp′ thal mäl′ ə jist   3
äf′ thal mäl′ ə jəst   1
äp′ thal mäl′ ə jəst   1
äf′ thəl mäl′ ə jist   1

ORATOR   +
är′ ə tər   4*
ôr′ ə tər   4

OPIATE
ō′ pē āt′   4
ō′ pē it   3*
ō′ pē ət   1

OPIUM
ō′ pē əm   4

OPOSSUM   +
ə päs′ əm   4*
päs′ əm   3

OPPORTUNE   +
äp′ ər tōōn′   4*
äp′ ər tyōōn′   4

OPPROBRIOUS
ə prō′ brē əs   4

OPPROBRIUM
ə prō′ brē əm   4

OPTICIAN   +
äp tis*h*′ ən   4

OPTIMUM   +
äp′ tə məm   4

OPTOMETRIST   +
äp täm′ ə trist   2*
äp täm′ i trist   1
äp täm′ ə trəst   1

OPTOMETRY   +
äp täm′ ə trē   3*
äp täm′ i trē   1

OPULENT   +
äp′ yə lənt   4

OPUS
ō′ pəs   4

ORACLE   +
ôr′ ə kəl   3
är′ ə k'l   2*
är′ ə kəl   2
ôr′ ə k'l   1

ORACULAR
ô rak′ yə lər   3*
ō rak′ yə lər   1
ə rak′ yə lər   1
ô rak′ yoo lər   1

ORAL   +
ôr′ əl   4*
ōr′ əl   3
är′ əl   1

ORANGE   +
är′ inj   4*
ôr′ inj   4
ôr′ ənj   1
är′ ənj   1

PRONUNCIATION KEY

Symbol	Key words	Symbol	Key words	Symbol	Key words
a	asp, fat, parrot	†ə	a in ago	r	red, port, dear
ā	ape, date, play		e in agent	s	sell, castle, pass
†ä	ah, car, father		i in sanity	t	top, cattle, hat
e	elf, ten, berry		o in comply	v	vat, hovel, have
ē	even, meet, money		u in focus	w	will, always, swear
i	is, hit, mirror	ər	perhaps, murder	y	yet, onion, yard
ī	ice, bite, high	b	bed, fable, dub	z	zebra, dazzle, haze
ō	open, tone, go	d	dip, beadle, had	ch	chin, catcher, arch
ô	all, horn, law	f	fall, after, off	sh	she, cushion, dash
ōō	ooze, tool, crew	g	get, haggle, dog	th	thin, nothing, truth
oo	look, pull, moor	h	he, ahead, hotel	*th*	then, father, lathe
yōō	use, cute, few	j	joy, agile, badge	zh	azure, leisure
yoo	united, cure, globule	k	kill, tackle, bake	ŋ	ring, anger, drink
oi	oil, point, toy	l	let, yellow, ball	″	see p. 15.
ou	out, crowd, plow	m	met, camel, trim	✓	see p. 15.
u	up, cut, color	n	not, flannel, ton	+	see p. 14.
ur	urn, fur, deter	p	put, apple, tap	′	see p. 15.
†See p. 14.		†See p. 16.		○	see p. 14.

ORANG-OUTAN
ə raŋ′ ə tan′ 2*
ô raŋ′ oo tan′ 2
ō raŋ′ ə tan′ 1
ō raŋ′ oo tan′ 1
ə raŋ′ oo tan′ 1

ORATORIO +
är′ ə tôr′ ē ō′ 4
ôr′ ə tôr′ ē ō′ 3*
ôr′ ə tōr′ ē ō′ 3
är′ ə tōr′ ē ō′ 3

ORATORY +
är′ ə tôr′ ē 4
ôr′ ə tôr′ ē 4*
ôr′ ə tōr′ ē 3
är′ ə tōr′ ē 3

ORCHESTRA
ôr′ kis trə 3*
ôr′ kes′ trə 3
ôr′ kəs trə 1

ORCHESTRAL
ôr kes′ trəl 4

ORCHID
ôr′ kid 3*
ôr′ kəd 1

ORDAIN
ôr dān′ 4

ORDEAL
ôr dēl′ 4*
ôr dē′ əl 3
ôr′ dēl 3
ôr′ dē əl 1

ORDINANCE
ôr′ d'n əns 4*
ôrd′ nəns 1
ôrd′ nənts 1

ORDINARILY ✓
ôr′ d'n er′ ə lē 4*
ôr′ d'n er′ ə lē 2

ORDINARY ✓
ôr′ d'n er′ ē 4

ORDNANCE
ôrd′ nəns 4*
ôrd′ nənts 1

ORDURE
ôr jər 4
ôr dyoor 3*

OREGANO
ə reg′ ə nō′ 4*
ô reg′ ə nō′ 4

ORGANDY
ôr′ gən dē 4

ORGANZA
ôr gan′ zə 4

ORGASM
ôr′ gaz əm 2
ôr′ gaz'm 1*
ôr′ gaz′ əm 1

ORGIASTIC
ôr′ jē as′ tik 4

ORGY
ôr′ jē 4

ORIGAMI
ôr′ ə gä′ mē 3*
ôr′ i gä′ mē 1

ORIEL
ôr′ ē əl 4*
ōr′ ē əl 3

ORIENT (n)
ôr′ ē ənt 4*
ôr′ ē ent′ 4
ōr′ ē ənt 3
ōr′ ē ent′ 3

ORIENT (v)
ôr′ ē ent′ 4*
ōr′ ē ent′ 3

ORIFICE +
ôr′ ə fis 3*
är′ ə fis 3
ôr′ ə fəs 1
är′ ə fəs 1

ORIFLAMME +
ôr′ ə flam′ 4*
är′ ə flam′ 4

ORIGIN +
ôr′ ə jin 2
är′ ə jin 1*
ôr′ i jin 1
ôr′ ə jən 1
är′ i jin 1
är′ ə jən 1

ORIOLE
ôr′ ē ōl′ 4*
ōr′ ē ōl′ 3
ôr′ ē əl 1
ōr′ ē əl 1

ORISON +
ôr′ ə sən 2*
ôr′ ə zən 2
är′ ə sən 2
är′ ə zən 2
ôr′ i zən 1
är′ i zən 1
ôr′ i z'n 1
är′ i z'n 1
är′ i s'n 1

ORMOLU
ôr′ mə lōō′ 4

ORNATE
ôr nāt′ 4

ORNITHOLOGY +
ôr′ nə thäl′ ə jē 4

OROTUND +
ôr′ ə tund′ 3*
ōr′ ə tund′ 3
är′ ə tund′ 1

ORTHODONTIA   +
ôr′ thə dän′ shə   3*
ôr′ thə dän′ shē ə   2
ôr′ thə dän′ chə   1
ôr′ thə dän′ chē ə   1

ORTHODOX   +
ôr′ thə däks′   4

ORTHOEPY
ôr thō′ ə pē   4*
ôr′ thō ep′ ē   2
ôr′ thō ə pē   1
ôr′ thə wep′ ē   1

ORTHOGRAPHY   +
ôr thäg′ rə fē   4

ORTHOPEDIST
ôr′ thə pē′ dist   3*
ôr′ thə pē′ dəst   1

OSCILLATE   +
äs ə lāt′   4

OSCILLOGRAPH   +
ä sil′ ə graf′   3
ä sil′ ə gräf′   2
ə sil′ ə graf′   1*
ə sil′ ə gräf′   1

OSCULATE   +
äs kyə lāt′   4

OSMOSIS   +
äs mō′ sis   3*
äz mō′ sis   3
äs mō′ səs   1
äz mō′ səs   1

OSPREY   +
äs′ prē   4*
äs′ prā   2

OSTENTATIOUS   +
äs tən tā′ shəs   2*
äs′ ten tā′ shəs   2
äs′ tən tā′ shəs   1

OSTEOPATH   +
äs′ tē ə path′   4

OSTRACISM   +
äs′ trə siz′ əm   3*
äs′ trə siz′m   1

OSTRACIZE   +
äs′ trə sīz′   4

OSTRICH   +
äs′ trich   4*
ôs′ trich   3
äs′ trij   1
ôs′ trij   1

OTIOSE
ō′ shē ōs′   4*
ō′ tē ōs′   3

OTOLOGIST   +
ō täl′ ə jist   3

OTTOMAN   +
ät′ ə mən   4

OUIJA
wē′ jē   4*
wē′ jə   4

OUTRÉ
ōō trā′   4

PRONUNCIATION KEY

Symbol	Key words	Symbol	Key words	Symbol	Key words
a	asp, fat, parrot	†ə	a in ago	r	red, port, dear
ā	ape, date, play		e in agent	s	sell, castle, pass
†ä	ah, car, father		i in sanity	t	top, cattle, hat
e	elf, ten, berry		o in comply	v	vat, hovel, have
ē	even, meet, money		u in focus	w	will, always, swear
i	is, hit, mirror	ər	perhaps, murder	y	yet, onion, yard
ī	ice, bite, high	b	bed, fable, dub	z	zebra, dazzle, haze
ō	open, tone, go	d	dip, beadle, had	ch	chin, catcher, arch
ô	all, horn, law	f	fall, after, off	sh	she, cushion, dash
ōō	ooze, tool, crew	g	get, haggle, dog	th	thin, nothing, truth
oo	look, pull, moor	h	he, ahead, hotel	th	then, father, lathe
yōō	use, cute, few	j	joy, agile, badge	zh	azure, leisure
yoo	united, cure, globule	k	kill, tackle, bake	ŋ	ring, anger, drink
oi	oil, point, toy	l	let, yellow, ball	″	see p. 15.
ou	out, crowd, plow	m	met, camel, trim	✓	see p. 15.
u	up, cut, color	n	not, flannel, ton	+	see p. 14.
ur	urn, fur, deter	p	put, apple, tap	′	see p. 15.
†See p. 14.		†See p. 16.		○	see p. 14.

OVERDUE
ō′ vər dōō′   4*
ō′ vər dyōō′   4

OVERT
ō vʉrt′   4*
ō′ vʉrt   3
ō′ vʉrt′   1

OVERTURE
ō′ vər choor′   3*
ō′ vər chər   3
ō′ və chər   2
ō′ vər toor   1
ō′ vər tyoor   1

OVINE
ō′ vīn′   2*
ō′ vīn   2
ō′ vin   1

OVIPAROUS
ō vip′ ər əs   4*
ō vip′ rəs   1

OVULATE   +
ō′ vyə lāt′   3*
äv′ yə lāt′   3

OVUM
ō′ vəm   4

OXFORD   +
äks′ fərd   4

OYEZ
ō′ yez′   2*
ō′ yes′   2
ō′ yā′   2
ō′ yes′   1
ō′ yez′   1
ō′ yā   1
ō′ yes   1
ō′ yez   1

OZONE
ō′ zōn′   2*
ō′ zōn   2
ō zōn′   1

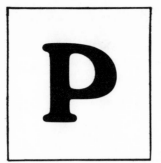

PABULUM
pab′ yə ləm ₃*
pab′ yoo ləm ₁

PACHYDERM
pak′ i dʉrm ₄

PACIFISM
pas′ ə fiz′ əm ₃*
pas′ ə fiz′m ₁

PACIFY
pas′ ə fī′ ₄

PADRE
pä′ drā ₄*
pä′ drē ₄

PADRONE
pə drō′ nē ₄*
pə drō′ nā ₂

PAEAN
pē′ ən ₄

PAGAN
pā′ gən ₄

PAGEANT
paj′ ənt ₄

PAGODA
pə gō′ də ₄

PAISANO
pī zä′ nō ₃*
pī sä′ nō ₁

PAISLEY
pāz′ lē ₄

PAJAMAS
pə jä′ məz ₄*
pə jam′ əz ₄

PALADIN
pal′ ə din ₃*
pal′ ə dən ₁

PALANQUIN
pal′ ən kēn′ ₄*
pal′ ən kin′ ₁
pal′ ən kwin′ ₁
pə laŋ′ kwən ₁
pə lan′ kwən ₁

PALATABLE
pal′ ət ə bəl ₂*
pal′ it ə bəl ₁
pal′ it ə b′l ₁

PALATE
pal′ it ₃*
pal′ ət ₁

PALATIAL
pə lā′ sħəl ₄

PALAVER
pə lav′ ər ₄*
pə läv′ ər ₃

PALEOLITHIC
pā′ lē ə litħ′ ik ₄*
pal′ ē ə litħ′ ik ₃

PALEONTOLOGY   +
pā′ lē än täl′ ə jē ₄*
pal′ ē än täl′ ə jē ₃

PALETTE
pal′ it ₃*
pal′ ət ₁

PALFREY
pôl′ frē ₄

PALINDROME
pal′ in drōm′ ₃*
pal′ ən drōm′ ₁

PALISADE
pal′ ə sād′   3*
pal′ i sād′   1
pal′ ə sād′   1

PALLADIAN
pə lā′ dē ən   3*
pə läd′ ē ən   1

PALLADIUM
pə lā′ də əm   4

PALLET
pal′ it   3*
pal′ ət   1

PALLIATE
pal′ ē āt′   4

PALLIATIVE
pal′ ē āt′ iv   4
pal′ ē ə tiv   3*
pal′ yə tiv   1

PALLID
pal′ id   3*
pal′ əd   1

PALLOR
pal′ ər   4

PALM
päm   4*
pälm   2

PALMETTO
pal met′ ō   4*
päl met′ ō′   1
pä met′ ō   1

PALMISTRY
päm′ is trē   3*
päm′ əs trē   1
päl′ mis trē   1
päl′ məs trē   1

PALOMINO
pal′ ə mē′ nō   4*
pal′ ə mē′ nō′   1
pal′ ə mē′ nə   1

PALPABLE
pal′ pə bəl   3
pal′ pə b'l   1*

PALSY
pôl′ zē   4

PALTRY
pôl′ trē   4

PAMPAS
pam′ pəz   4
pam′ pəs   1*

PAMPHLET
pam′ flit   3*
pam′ flət   1
pamp′ flət   1
pam′ plət   1

PANACEA
pan′ ə sē′ ə   4

PANACHE
pə nash′   4*
pə näsh′   4

PANATELA
pan′ ə tel′ ə   4

PANCREAS
pan′ krē əs   4*
paŋ′ krē əs   4

PANDEMONIUM
pan′ də mō′ nē əm   4

PANEGYRIC ○
pan′ ə jīr′ ik   3
pan′ i jir′ ik   2
pan′ ə jir′ ik   1*
pan′ i jī′ rik   1

PANJANDRUM
pan jan′ drəm   4

PANOPLY
pan′ ə plē   4

PANORAMA
pan′ ə räm′ ə   4*
pan′ ə ram′ ə   4

PANSY
pan′ zē   4

PANTHEISM
pan′ thē iz′ əm   3*
pan′ thē iz'm   1
pant′ thē iz əm   1

PANTHEON +
pan′ thē än′   4*
pan′ thē ən   4
pan thē ən   1
pant′ thē ən   1

PANTOMIME
pan′ tə mīm′   4

PANZER
pan′ zər   4*
pän′ sər   1
pänt′ sər   1

PAPACY
pā′ pə sē   4

PAPAL
pā′ pəl   4

PAPAYA
pə pä′ yə   3
pə pī′ ə   1*

PAPIER MACHÉ
pā′ pər mə shā′   4*
pā′ pər ma′ shā′   1

PAPIST
pā′ pist   3*
pā pəst   1

PAPOOSE
pə p\overline{oo}s′   4*
pa p\overline{oo}s′   4

PAPRIKA
pa prē′ kə   4
pə prē′ kə   4
pap′ ri kə   2*
pap′ rə kə   1

PAPYRUS
pə pī′ rəs   4

PARABLE
par′ ə bəl   3*
par′ ə b'l   1

PARABOLA
pə rab′ ə lə   4

PARACHUTE
par′ ə sho͞ot′   4

PARACLETE
par′ ə klēt′   4

PARADIGM
par′ ə dīm′   4*
par′ ə dim   2
par′ ə dim′   2

PARADISE
par′ ə dīs′   4*
par′ ə dīz′   3

PARADISIACAL
par′ ə di sī′ ə kəl   2*
par′ ə di zī′ ə kəl   2
par′ ə di sī′ ə k'l   1
par′ ə dī sā′ ə kəl   1
par′ ə dī zā′ ə kəl   1

PARADOX   +
par′ ə däks′   4

PARAFFIN
par′ ə fin   3*
par′ ə fən   1

PARAGON   +
par′ ə gən   4
par′ ə gän′   2*
par′ ə gän   2

PARALLEL
par′ ə lel′   4*
par′ ə ləl   2

PARALYSIS
pə ral′ ə sis   2*
pə ral′ i sis   1
pə ral′ ə səs   1

PARALYTIC
par′ ə lit′ ik   4

PARALYZE
par′ ə līz′   4

PARAMECIUM
par′ ə mē′ sē′ əm   4*
par′ ə mē′ shē əm   4
par′ ə mē′ shəm   1

PARAMETER
pə ram′ ə tər   3*
pə ram′ i tər   1

PARAMOUNT
par′ ə mount′   4

PARAMOUR
par′ ə mo͝or′   4

PARANOIA
par′ ə noi′ ə   4

PRONUNCIATION KEY

Symbol	Key words	Symbol	Key words	Symbol	Key words
a	asp, fat, parrot	†ə	a in ago	r	red, port, dear
ā	ape, date, play		e in agent	s	sell, castle, pass
†ä	ah, car, father		i in sanity	t	top, cattle, hat
e	elf, ten, berry		o in comply	v	vat, hovel, have
ē	even, meet, money		u in focus	w	will, always, swear
i	is, hit, mirror	ər	perhaps, murder	y	yet, onion, yard
ī	ice, bite, high	b	bed, fable, dub	z	zebra, dazzle, haze
ō	open, tone, go	d	dip, beadle, had	ch	chin, catcher, arch
ô	all, horn, law	f	fall, after, off	sh	she, cushion, dash
o͞o	ooze, tool, crew	g	get, haggle, dog	th	thin, nothing, truth
o͝o	look, pull, moor	h	he, ahead, hotel	th	then, father, lathe
yo͞o	use, cute, few	j	joy, agile, badge	zh	azure, leisure
yo͝o	united, cure, globule	k	kill, tackle, bake	ŋ	ring, anger, drink
oi	oil, point, toy	l	let, yellow, ball	″	see p. 15.
ou	out, crowd, plow	m	met, camel, trim	✓	see p. 15.
u	up, cut, color	n	not, flannel, ton	+	see p. 14.
ur	urn, fur, deter	p	put, apple, tap	′	see p. 15.
†See p. 14.		†See p. 16.		○	see p. 14.

PARANOIAC
par′ ə noi′ ak′ 2*
par′ ə noi′ ək 2
par′ ə noi′ ak 1
par′ ə noi′ ik 1

PARAPET
par′ ə pet′ 4*
par′ ə pit 3
par′ ə pət 1

PARAPHERNALIA
par′ ə fər nāl′ yə 4*
par′ ə fə nāl′ yə 4
par′ ə fər nā′ lē ə 1
par′ ə fə nā′ lē ə 1

PARAPHRASE
par′ ə frāz′ 4

PARAPLEGIA
par′ ə plē′ jə 4*
par′ ə plē′ jē ə 4

PARASITE
par′ ə sīt′ 4

PARASITIC
par′ ə sit′ ik 4

PARASOL +
par′ ə sôl′ 4*
par′ ə säl′ 4

PARCHEESI
pär chē′ zē 4*
pər chē′ zē 1

PAREGORIC +
par′ ə gär′ ik 4*
par′ ə gôr′ ik 4
par′ ə gōr′ ik 1

PARENT ✓
per′ ənt 4*
par′ ənt 3

PARENTAL
pə rent′ ′l 4

PARENTHESIS
pə ren′ thə sis 2*
pə ren′ thi sis 1
pə ren′ thə səs 1
pə rent′ thə səs 1

PARENTHETICAL
par′ ən thet′ i kəl 4

PARESIS
pə rē′ sis 3*
par′ ə sis 2
pə rē′ səs 1
par′ i sis 1

PARFAIT
pär fā′ 4

PARIAH
pə rī′ ə 4*
par′ ē ə 1
pär′ ē ə 1

PARIETAL
pə rī′ ə t′l 2*
pə rī′ ə təl 1
pə rī′ i t′l 1

PARI MUTUEL
par′ i myo͞o′ cho͞o əl 2*
par′ ə myo͞o′ choo wəl 1
par′ i myo͞och′ wəl 1
par′ i myo͞o′ chəl 1

PARITY
par′ ə tē 3*
par′ i tē 1

PARLANCE
pär′ ləns 4*
pär′ lənts 1

PARLAY
pär′ lē 4
pär′ lā 3*
pär lā′ 2

PARLEY
pär′ lē 4

PARLIAMENT
pär′ lə mənt 4*
pärl′ yə mənt 1

PARLIAMENTARIAN ✓
pär′ lə men ter′ ē ən 3*
pär′ lə mən ter′ ē ən 2
pär lə men′ ter′ ē ən 1
pärl yə men′ ter′ ē ən 1

PARLIAMENTARY
pär′ lə men′ tə rē 4*
pär′ lə men′ trē 4
pärl yə men′ tə rē 1
pärl yə men′ trē 1

PARLOUS
pär′ ləs 4

PARMESAN
pär′ mə zən′ 3*
pär′ mə zän′ 3
pär′ mə zan′ 3
par′ mi zän′ 1
par′ mi zan′ 1
par′ mi zən′ 1
pär′ mi zän′ 1
pär′ mi zan′ 1
par′ i myo͞o′ chəl 1

PAROCHIAL
pə rō′ kē əl 4

PARODY
par′ ə dē 4

PAROLE
pə rōl′ 4

PAROLEE
pə rō′ lē′ 3*
pə rō lē′ 1
pə rō′ lē′ 1
par′ ə lē′ 1

PAROXYSM
par′ ək siz′ əm 3*
par′ ək siz′m 1

PARQUET
pär kā′ 4*
pär ket′ 1

PARQUETRY •
pär′ kə trē 2*
pär′ ki trē 2

PARRICIDE
par′ ə sīd′ 3
par′ i sīd′ 1*

PARSIMONIOUS
pär′ sə mō′ nē əs 4

PARSIMONY
pär′ sə mō′ nē 4

PARTERRE ✓
pär ter′ 4

PARTHENOGENESIS
pär′ thə nō jen′ ə sis 2*
pär′ thə nō jen′ i sis 1
pär′ thə nō jen′ ə səs 1

PARTIALITY
pär′ shē al′ ə tē 3*
pär′ shal′ ə tē 2
pär′ shal′ i tē 1
pär′ shē al′ i tē 1

PARTICIPANT
pär tis′ ə pənt 4*
pər tis′ ə pənt 2
pər tis′ pənt 1

PARTICIPIAL
pär′ tə sip′ ē əl 3*
pär′ ti sip′ ē əl 1

PARTICULAR
pər tik′ yə lər 4*
pə tik′ yə lər 1

PARTISAN
pärt′ ə zən 2*
pärt′ ə sən 1
pärt′ ə s'n 1
pärt′ ə z'n 1
pärt′ i zən 1

PARVENU
pär′ və nyōō′ 4*
pär′ və nōō′ 4

PASCHAL
pas′ kəl 3*
pas′ k'l 1

PASHA
pä′ shə 4*
pash′ ə 4
pə shä′ 3
pə shô 1

PASQUINADE
pas′ kwə nād′ 4

PASSACAGLIA
päs′ ə käl′ yə 4*
pas′ ə kal′ yə 2
pas′ ə käl′ yə 2

PASSÉ
pa sā′ 4*
pas′ ā 2

PASSIM
pas′ im 3*
pas′ əm 1
päs′ im 1
päs′ əm 1

PRONUNCIATION KEY

Symbol	Key words	Symbol	Key words	Symbol	Key words
a	asp, fat, parrot	†ə	a in ago	r	red, port, dear
ā	ape, date, play		e in agent	s	sell, castle, pass
†ä	ah, car, father		i in sanity	t	top, cattle, hat
e	elf, ten, berry		o in comply	v	vat, hovel, have
ē	even, meet, money		u in focus	w	will, always, swear
i	is, hit, mirror	ər	perhaps, murder	y	yet, onion, yard
ī	ice, bite, high	b	bed, fable, dub	z	zebra, dazzle, haze
ō	open, tone, go	d	dip, beadle, had	ch	chin, catcher, arch
ô	all, horn, law	f	fall, after, off	sh	she, cushion, dash
ōō	ooze, tool, crew	g	get, haggle, dog	th	thin, nothing, truth
oo	look, pull, moor	h	he, ahead, hotel	th	then, father, lathe
yōō	use, cute, few	j	joy, agile, badge	zh	azure, leisure
yoo	united, cure, globule	k	kill, tackle, bake	ŋ	ring, anger, drink
oi	oil, point, toy	l	let, yellow, ball	″	see p. 15.
ou	out, crowd, plow	m	met, camel, trim	✓	see p. 15.
u	up, cut, color	n	not, flannel, ton	+	see p. 14.
ur	urn, fur, deter	p	put, apple, tap	′	see p. 15.
†See p. 14.		†See p. 16.		○	see p. 14.

PASTA
päs′ tə 4

PASTEL
pa stel′ 3*
pas′ təl 2

PASTEURIZE
pas′ chə rīz′ 4*
pas′ tə rīz′ 4

PASTICHE
pas tēsh′ 4*
päs tēsh′ 4

PASTILLE
pas tēl′ 4

PASTOR
pas′ tər 4*
päs′ tər 2

PASTORAL
pas′ tər əl 4*
päs′ tər əl 3
pas′ trəl 1

PASTORALE
pas′ tə ral′ 4*
pas′ tə räl′ 4
pas′ tə rä′ lē 3
päs′ tə ral′ 1
päs′ tə räl′ 1

PASTRAMI
pə strä′ mē 4

PASTURE
pas′ chər 4*
päs′ chər 3

PATCHOULI
pə choo′ lē 4*
pach′ oo lē 3
pach′ ə lē 1

PÂTÉ
pä tā′ 4

PATEN
pat′ ′n 4

PATENT (n)
pat′ ′nt 3*
pat′ ənt 1

PATENT (adj)
pāt′ ′nt 3*
pāt′ ənt 1

PATER
pāt′ ər 4

PATER FAMILIAS
pät′ ər fə mil′ ē əs 4*
pāt′ ər fə mil′ ē əs 4
pat′ ər fə mil′ ē əs 1

PATHOS +
pā′ thäs 3*
pā′ thôs 3
pā′ thäs′ 1

PATINA
pat′ ə nə 2*
pat′ ′n ə 2
pə tē′ nə 1

PATIO
pät′ ē ō′ 4
pat′ ē ō′ 3*

PATISSERIE
pə tis′ ə rē 2*
pä tēs rē′ 1

PATOIS
pat′ wä 2*
pat′ wä′ 2
pät′ wä′ 1

PATRIARCH
pā′ trē ärk′ 4

PATRICIAN
pə trish′ ən 4

PATRIMONY
pat′ rə mō′ nē 4

PATRIOT +
pā′ trē ət 4*
pā′ trē ät′ 4

PATRIOTISM
pā′ trē ə tiz′ əm 3*
pā′ trē ə tiz′m 1

PATRON
pā′ trən 4

PATRONAGE
pā′ trən ij 4*
pa′ trən ij 4

PATRONIZE
pā′ trə nīz′ 4*
pat′ rə nīz′ 4

PATRONYMIC
pa′ trə nim′ ik 4

PAUCITY
pô′ sə tē 3*
pô′ si tē 1

PAUNCH
pônch 4*
pänch 3

PAUPER
pô′ pər 4

PAVANE
pə van′ 4*
pə vän′ 4

PAVILION
pə vil′ yən 4

PAWN
pôn 4*
pän 1

PEAKED (sickly, pale)
pē′ kid 3*
pē′ kəd 1
pik′ əd 1

PECAN
pi kän′ 4
pi kan′ 4
pē′ kan 2*
pē′ kən 1
pē′ kän 1

PECCADILLO
pek′ ə dil′ ō 4
pek′ ə dil′ ō′ 1

PECCARY
pek′ ə rē 4

PECTORAL
pek′ tər əl 4*
pek′ trəl 1

PECUNIARY ✓
pi kyōō′ nē er′ ē 4

PEDAGOG (UE)
ped′ ə gäg′ 4*
ped′ ə gôg′ 3

PEDAGOGY +
ped′ ə gō′ jē 4*
ped′ ə gäj′ ē 4

PEDAL (adj)
pēd′ ′l 3*
ped′ ′l 3

PEDAL (n)
ped′ ′l 4

PEDANT
ped′ ′nt 3*
ped′ ənt 1

PEDANTRY
ped′ ′n trē 4

PEDERAST
ped′ ə rast′ 4*
pē′ də rast′ 2

PEDERASTY
ped′ ə ras′ tē 4*
pē′ də ras′ tē 2

PEDESTRIAN
pə des′ trē ən 4

PEDIATRICIAN
pē′ dē ə trish′ ən 4*
ped ē ə trish′ ən 1

PEDIATRICS
pē′ dē at′ riks 4*
ped′ ē at′ riks 1

PEDICULOSIS
pə dik′ yə lō′ sis 2*
pi dik′ yə lō′ sis 1
pi dik′ yə lō′ səs 1

PEDOMETER +
pi däm′ ə tər 3*
pi däm′ i tər 1

PEERAGE ○
pir′ ij 4

PEIGNOIR
pen wär′ 4*
pān wär′ 4
pān′ wär 3
pen′ wär 3

PEJORATIVE +
pi jär′ ə tiv 3*
pi jôr′ ə tiv 3
pē′ jə rāt′ iv 3
pej′ ə rāt′ iv 3

PRONUNCIATION KEY

Symbol	Key words	Symbol	Key words	Symbol	Key words
a	asp, fat, parrot	†ə	a in ago	r	red, port, dear
ā	ape, date, play		e in agent	s	sell, castle, pass
†ä	ah, car, father		i in sanity	t	top, cattle, hat
e	elf, ten, berry		o in comply	v	vat, hovel, have
ē	even, meet, money		u in focus	w	will, always, swear
i	is, hit, mirror	ər	perhaps, murder	y	yet, onion, yard
ī	ice, bite, high	b	bed, fable, dub	z	zebra, dazzle, haze
ō	open, tone, go	d	dip, beadle, had	ch	chin, catcher, arch
ô	all, horn, law	f	fall, after, off	sh	she, cushion, dash
ōō	ooze, tool, crew	g	get, haggle, dog	th	thin, nothing, truth
oo	look, pull, moor	h	he, ahead, hotel	th	then, father, lathe
yōō	use, cute, few	j	joy, agile, badge	zh	azure, leisure
yoo	united, cure, globule	k	kill, tackle, bake	ŋ	ring, anger, drink
oi	oil, point, toy	l	let, yellow, ball	″	see p. 15.
ou	out, crowd, plow	m	met, camel, trim	✓	see p. 15.
u	up, cut, color	n	not, flannel, ton	+	see p. 14.
ur	urn, fur, deter	p	put, apple, tap	′	see p. 15.
†See p. 14.		†See p. 16.		○	see p. 14.

PEKOE
pē′ kō 4*
pek′ ō 1

PELISSE
pə lēs′ 4*
pe lēs′ 1

PELLAGRA
pə lag′ rə 4*
pə lāg′ rə 4
pə läg′ rə 3

PELLUCID
pə lo͞o′ sid 3*
pə lo͞o′ səd 1

PENAL
pē′ n'l 2*
pē′ nəl 1
pe′ n'l 1

PENALIZE
pē′ n'l īz′ 3*
pen′ 'l īz′ 2
pen′ əl īz 2
pē′ nəl īz 1

PENALTY
pen′ 'l tē 3*
pen′ əl tē 1

PENANCE
pen′ əns 4*
pen′ ənts 1

PENATES
pə nāt′ ēz 2*
pi nāt′ ēz 2
pə nät′ ēz 2

PENCHANT
pen′ chənt 4

PENDULUM
pen′ dyə ləm 3*
pen′ joo ləm 2
pen′ də ləm 2
pen′ jə ləm 2
pen′ d'l əm 2
pen′ dyoo ləm 1

PENETRABLE
pen′ ə trə bəl 2*
pen′ i trə bəl 1
pen′ i trə b'l 1

PENGUIN
peŋ′ gwin 3*
pen′ gwin 3
pen′ gwən 1
peŋ′ gwən 1

PENICILLIN
pen′ ə sil′ in 2*
pen′ i sil′ in 1
pen′ ə sil′ ən 1

PENINSULA
pə nin′ sə lə 4
pə nin′ syə lə 3*
pə nin′ syoo lə 1
pə nint′ sə lə 1
pə nin′ chə lə 1
pə nin′ shə lə 1
pə nins′ lə 1
pə nints′ lə 1

PENIS
pē′ nis 3*
pē′ nəs 1

PENITENT
pen′ ə tənt 3*
pen′ i tənt 1

PENITENTIARY
pen′ ə ten′ shə rē 2*
pen′ ə tench′ ə rē′ 1
pen′ i ten′ shə rē 1
pen′ ə tench′ rē′ 1
pen′ tench′ rē′ 1
pen′ tench′ ə rē′ 1

PENOLOGY +
pē näl′ ə jē 4

PENSION
pen′ shən 3*
pen′ chən 1

PENTATEUCH
pen′ tə tyo͞ok′ 4*
pen′ tə to͞ok′ 4

PENTECOST +
pen′ ti käst′ 3*
pen′ ti kôst′ 3
pen′ tə kôst′ 1
pen′ tə käst′ 1

PENUCHE
pə no͞o′ chē 4

PENULTIMATE
pi nul′ tə mit 3*
pi nult′ mət 1

PENUMBRA
pi num′ brə 3*
pə num′ brə 1

PENURIOUS
pə nyoor′ ē əs 4*
pə noor′ ē əs 4

PENURY
pen′ yə rē 4

PEON +
pē′ ən 4*
pē′ än 3
pē′ än′ 1

PEONAGE
pē′ ə nij 4

PEONY
pē′ ə nē 4

PERADVENTURE
pʉr′ əd ven′ chər   4*
per′ əd ven′ chər   3
pʉr′ əd ven′ chər   1
per′ əd ven′ chər   1

PERAMBULATOR
pər am′ byə lāt′ ər   3*
pər am′ byōō lāt′ ər   1

PER ANNUM
pər an′ əm   4
pʉr′ an′ əm   1

PERCALE
pər kāl′   4*
pər kal′   2
pʉr′ kāl   1

PER CAPITA
pər kap′ ə tə   3*
pər kap′ i tə   1

PERCENTILE
pər sen′ tīl   4*
pər sen′ til   1
pər sen′ t′l   1

PERCHERON   +
pʉr′ shə rän′   4*
pʉr′ chə rän′   4

PERCOLATOR
pʉr′ kə lāt′ ər   4

PER DIEM
pər dē′ əm   4*
pər dī′ əm   4
pʉr dē′ əm   1
pʉr dī′ əm   1

PEREGRINATE
per′ ə grə nāt′   3*
per′ ə gri nāt′   1

PEREMPTORY
pə remp′ tər ē   4*
per′ əmp tōr′ ē   1
per′ əmp tôr′ ē   1
pə remp′ trē   1

PERENNIAL
pə ren′ ē əl   4

PERFECT (adj)
pʉr′ fikt   4

PERFECT (v)
pər fekt′   4*
pʉr′ fikt   3

PERFECTO
pər fek′ tō   4*
pər fek′ tō′   1

PERFIDIOUS
pər fid′ ē əs   4*
pʉr′ fid′ ē əs   1

PERFIDY
pʉr′ fə dē   3*
pʉr′ fi dē   1

PERFORATE
pʉr′ fə rāt′   4

PERFORCE
pər fôrs′   4*
pər fōrs′   3

PERFUME (n)
pʉr′ fyōōm′   4*
pər fyōōm′   4

PRONUNCIATION KEY

Symbol	Key words	Symbol	Key words	Symbol	Key words
a	asp, fat, parrot	†ə	a in ago	r	red, port, dear
ā	ape, date, play		e in agent	s	sell, castle, pass
†ä	ah, car, father		i in sanity	t	top, cattle, hat
e	elf, ten, berry		o in comply	v	vat, hovel, have
ē	even, meet, money		u in focus	w	will, always, swear
i	is, hit, mirror	ər	perhaps, murder	y	yet, onion, yard
ī	ice, bite, high	b	bed, fable, dub	z	zebra, dazzle, haze
ō	open, tone, go	d	dip, beadle, had	ch	chin, catcher, arch
ô	all, horn, law	f	fall, after, off	sh	she, cushion, dash
ōō	ooze, tool, crew	g	get, haggle, dog	th	thin, nothing, truth
oo	look, pull, moor	h	he, ahead, hotel	th	then, father, lathe
yōō	use, cute, few	j	joy, agile, badge	zh	azure, leisure
yoo	united, cure, globule	k	kill, tackle, bake	ŋ	ring, anger, drink
oi	oil, point, toy	l	let, yellow, ball	″	see p. 15.
ou	out, crowd, plow	m	met, camel, trim	✓	see p. 15.
u	up, cut, color	n	not, flannel, ton	+	see p. 14.
ʉr	urn, fur, deter	p	put, apple, tap	′	see p. 15.
†See p. 14.		†See p. 16.		○	see p. 14.

PERFUME (v)
pər fyōōm′   4*
pʉr fyōōm   1

PERFUNCTORY
pər fuŋk′ tər ē   3*
pər fuŋ′ trē   1

PERGOLA
pʉr′ gə lə   4*
pər gō′ lə   1

PERIGEE
per′ ə jē   2
per′ ə jē′   2*
per′ i jē′   1

PERIHELION
per′ ə hēl′ yən   4*
per′ ə hē′ lē ən   3

PERIMETER
pə rim′ ə tər   3*
pə rim′ i tər   1

PERIODONTIA   +
per′ ē ə dän′ sʰə   2*
per′ ē ə dän′ sʰē ə   2
per′ ē ō dän′ sʰə   1

PERIPATETIC
per′ ə pə tet′ ik   3*
per′ i pə tet′ ik   1

PERIPHERAL
pə rif′ ər əl   4*
pə rif′ rəl   1

PERIPHERY
pə rif′ ər ē   4*
pə rif′ rē   1

PERISTALSIS
per′ ə stôl′ sis   2*
per′ ə stal′ sis   2
per′ i stôl′ sis   1
per′ i stal′ sis   1
per′ ə stôl′ səs   1
per′ ə stal′ səs   1

PERITONITIS
per′ it ′n īt′ əs   2*
per′ ət ′n īt′ əs   1
per′ ət ən īt′ is   1

PERJURE
pʉr′ jər   4

PERJURY
pʉr′ jə rē   4*
pʉrj′ rē   1

PERMEATE
pʉr′ mē āt′   4

PERMIT (n)
pʉr′ mit   4*
pər mit′   4

PERMIT (v)
pər mit′   4

PERMUTATION
pʉr′ myoo tā′ sʰən   3*
pʉr′ myə tā′ sʰən   1

PERNICIOUS
pər nisʰ′ əs   4

PEROXIDE   +
pə räk′ sīd′   3*
pə räk′ sīd   1

PERPENDICULAR
pʉr pən dik′ yə lər   4

PERPETRATE
pʉr′ pə trāt′   3*
pʉr′ pi trāt′   1

PERPETUAL
pər pecʰ′ ōō əl   2*
pər pecʰ′ oo wəl   1
pər pecʰ′ ə wəl   1
pər pecʰ′ wəl   1
pər pecʰ′ əl   1

PERPETUITY
pʉr′ pə tyōō′ ə tē   3*
pʉr′ pə tōō′ ə tē   3
pʉr′ pi tōō′ i tē   1
pʉr′ pi tyōō′ i tē   1

PERPLEX
pər pleks′   4

PERQUISITE
pʉr′ kwə zit   2*
pʉr′ kwi zit   1
pʉr′ kwə zət   1

PER SE
pər sā′   2*
pʉr sā′   1
pʉr sē′   1
pər sē′   1
pʉr′ sā′   1
pʉr′ sē′   1
per sā′   1
per sē′   1

PERSIFLAGE
pʉr′ sə fläzʰ′   3*
pʉr′ si fläzʰ′   1
per′ si fläzʰ′   1

PERSIMMON
pər sim′ ən   4

PERSONA
pər sō′ nə   4*
pər sō′ nä   2

PERSONA NON GRATA   +
pər sō′ nə nän grä′ tə   4*
pər sō′ nə nän grat′ ə   3
pər sō′ nə nän grāt′ ə   2

PERSONAE
pər sō′ nē   3*
pər sō′ nē′   1
pər sō′ nī′   1

PERSONNEL
pʉr′ sə nel′   4

PERSPICACIOUS
pʉr′ spə kā′ shəs   3*
pʉr′ spi kā′ shəs   1

PERSPICACITY
pʉr′ spə kas′ ə tē   2*
pʉr′ spi kas′ ə tē   1
pʉr′ spə kas′ i tē   1

PERSPICUITY
pʉr′ spi kyo͞o′ ə tē   2*
pʉr′ spə kyo͞o′ i tē   1
pʉr′ spə kyo͞o′ ə tē   1

PERSPIRATION
pʉr′ spə rā′ shən   4*
pʉr′ sprā′ shən   1

PERSPIRE
pər spīr′   3
pər spī′ ər   2*

PERSUASION
pər swā′ zhən   4

PERSUASIVE
pər swā′ siv   4*
pər swā′ ziv   2

PERTINACIOUS
pʉr′ tə nā′ shəs   2*
pʉr′ t'n ā′ shəs   2

PERTINACITY
pʉr′ tə nas′ ə tē   3*
pʉr′ tə nas′ i tē   1

PERTURB
pər tʉrb′   4

PERTURBATION
pʉr′ tər bā′ shən   4

PERUKE
pə ro͞ok′   4

PERUSAL
pə ro͞o′ zəl   3*
pə ro͞o′ z'l   1

PERUSE
pə ro͞oz′

PERVERSE
pər vʉrs′   4*
pʉr′ vʉrs   1

PERVERT (n)
pʉr′ vʉrt′   3*
pʉr′ vərt   1

PERVERT (v)
pər vʉrt′   4

PESETA
pə sā′ tə   4

PESO
pā′ sō   3*
pe′ sō   2

PESSARY
pes′ ə rē   4*
pes′ rē   1

PESTIFEROUS
pes tif′ ər əs   4*
pes tif′ rəs   1

PESTILENCE
pes′ t'l əns   2*
pes′ təl əns   2

PRONUNCIATION KEY

Symbol	Key words	Symbol	Key words	Symbol	Key words
a	asp, fat, parrot	†ə	a in ago	r	red, port, dear
ā	ape, date, play		e in agent	s	sell, castle, pass
†ä	ah, car, father		i in sanity	t	top, cattle, hat
e	elf, ten, berry		o in comply	v	vat, hovel, have
ē	even, meet, money		u in focus	w	will, always, swear
i	is, hit, mirror	ər	perhaps, murder	y	yet, onion, yard
ī	ice, bite, high	b	bed, fable, dub	z	zebra, dazzle, haze
ō	open, tone, go	d	dip, beadle, had	ch	chin, catcher, arch
ô	all, horn, law	f	fall, after, off	sh	she, cushion, dash
o͞o	ooze, tool, crew	g	get, haggle, dog	th	thin, nothing, truth
oo	look, pull, moor	h	he, ahead, hotel	th	then, father, lathe
yo͞o	use, cute, few	j	joy, agile, badge	zh	azure, leisure
yoo	united, cure, globule	k	kill, tackle, bake	ŋ	ring, anger, drink
σi	oil, point, toy	l	let, yellow, ball	″	see p. 15.
σu	out, crowd, plow	m	met, camel, trim	✓	see p. 15.
u	up, cut, color	n	not, flannel, ton	+	see p. 14.
ʉr	urn, fur, deter	p	put, apple, tap	'	see p. 15.
†See p. 14.		†See p. 16.		○	see p. 14.

PESTLE
pes′ əl   3*
pes′ t′l   2
pes′ ′l   1

PETARD
pi tärd′   3*
pə tärd′   1
pə tär′   1

PETIT
pet′ ē   4*
pet′ ət   1

PETITE
pə tēt′   4

PETIT FOUR
pet′ ē fôr′   3*
pet′ ē fōr′   2
pet ē fôr′   1
pet ē fōr′   1
pə tē foor′   1

PETITION
pə tish′ ən   4

PETIT MAL
pə tē′ mal′   4*
pə tē′ mäl′   2

PETIT POINT
pet′ ē point′   4*

PETREL
pet′ rəl   4*
pē′ trəl   1

PETROL
pet′ rəl   4*
pe träl′   1

PETROLATUM
pet′ rə lā′ təm   4*
pet′ rə lä′ təm   3

PETROLEUM
pə trō′ lē əm   4*
pə trōl′ yəm   1

PETTIFOGGER   +
pet′ ē fäg′ ər   4*
pet′ ē fôg′ ər   4

PETULANT
pech′ ə lənt   2*
pech′ oo lənt   2

PETUNIA
pə tōōn′ yə   4*
pə tyōōn′ yə   4
pə tōō′ nē ə   2
pə tyōō′ nē ə   1

PEW
pyōō   4

PEWTER
pyōō′ tər   4

PEYOTE
pā ōt′ ē   4*
pē ōt′ ē   1

PFENNIG
fen′ ig   4*
fen′ ik   1

PHAETON
fā′ ət ′n   2*
fā′ it ′n   1
fā′ ət ən   1

PHAGOCYTE
fag′ ə sīt′   4

PHALANGE
fə lanj′   4*
fā′ lanj′   2
fal′ ənj   2
fā lanj′   1
fāl′ ənj   1

PHALANX
fā′ laŋks′   2*
fā′ laŋks   2
fal′ aŋks   1

PHALLIC
fal′ ik   4

PHALLUS
fal′ əs   4

PHANTASM
fan′ taz′ əm   2*
fan′ taz əm   1
fan′ taz′m   1

PHANTASMAGORIA
fan taz′ mə gôr′ ē ə   4*
fan taz′ mə gōr′ ē ə   3

PHARAOH   ✓
fer′ ō   4*
far′ ō   2
fãr′ ō   1

PHARISEE
far′ ə sē   3*
far′ i sē′   1

PHARMACEUTICAL
fär mə sōōt′ i kəl   3*
fär mə sōōt′ i k′l   1
fär mə syōōt′ i k′l   1

PHARMACOPOEIA
fär′ mə kə pē′ ə   4*
fär′ mə kə pē′ yə   2

PHARYNGITIS
far′ in jīt′ is   3*
far′ ən jīt′ əs   1

PHARYNX
far′ iŋks   4*
far′ iŋs   1

PHENOBARBITAL
fē′ nō bär′ bə tôl′   3*
fē′ nō bär′ bi tal′   2
fē′ nō bär′ bi tôl′   1
fē′ nə bär′ bi tal′   1
fē′ nə bär′ bi tôl′   1
fē′ nə bär′ bə tôl′   1

PHENOL   +
fē′ nōl′   3
fē′ nôl   2*
fē′ näl   2
fē′ nōl   1
fi nōl′   1

PHENOMENON   +
fi näm′ ə nän′   4

PHIAL
fī′ əl   4*
fīl′   1

PHILANTHROPIC   +
fil′ ən thräp′ ik   4

PHILANTHROPY
fi lan′ thrə pē   3*
fə lan′ thrə pē   1
fə lant′ thrə pē   1

PHILATELIC
fil′ ə tel′ ik   4

PHILATELIST
fi lat′ ′l ist   3*
fə lat′ ′l əst   1

PHILATELY
fi lat′ ′l ē   4

PHILIPPIC
fi lip′ ik   4

PHILISTINE
fil′ is tēn′   3*
fi lis′ tin   3
fi lis′ tēn   2
fil′ is tīn′   1
fil′ əs tēn′   1
fə lis′ tən   1

PHILODENDRON   \
fil′ ə den′ drən   4

PHILOLOGY   +
fi läl′ ə jē   3*
fə läl′ ə jē   1

PHLEBITIS
fli bīt′ is   3*
fli bit′ əs   1

PHLEGM
flem   4

PHLEGMATIC
fleg mat′ ik   4

PHLOX   +
fläks   4

PHOBIA
fō′ bē ə   4

PHOENIX
fē′ niks   4

PHONETIC
fə net′ ik   4*
fō net′ ik   1

PHONICS   +
fän′ iks   4

PHOSPHORESCENCE   +
fäs′ fə res′ ′ns   2*
fäs′ fə res′ əns   2
fäs′ fə res′ ′nts   1

PHOTOGENIC
fōt′ ə jen′ ik   4*
fōt′ ə jēn′ ik   1

PRONUNCIATION KEY

Symbol	Key words	Symbol	Key words	Symbol	Key words
a	asp, fat, parrot	†ə	a in ago	r	red, port, dear
ā	ape, date, play		e in agent	s	sell, castle, pass
†ä	ah, car, father		i in sanity	t	top, cattle, hat
e	elf, ten, berry		o in comply	v	vat, hovel, have
ē	even, meet, money		u in focus	w	will, always, swear
i	is, hit, mirror	ər	perhaps, murder	y	yet, onion, yard
ī	ice, bite, high	b	bed, fable, dub	z	zebra, dazzle, haze
ō	open, tone, go	d	dip, beadle, had	ch	chin, catcher, arch
ô	all, horn, law	f	fall, after, off	sh	she, cushion, dash
ōō	ooze, tool, crew	g	get, haggle, dog	th	thin, nothing, truth
oo	look, pull, moor	h	he, ahead, hotel	th	then, father, lathe
yōō	use, cute, few	j	joy, agile, badge	zh	azure, leisure
yoo	united, cure, globule	k	kill, tackle, bake	ŋ	ring, anger, drink
oi	oil, point, toy	l	let, yellow, ball	″	see p. 15.
ou	out, crowd, plow	m	met, camel, trim	✓	see p. 15.
u	up, cut, color	n	not, flannel, ton	+	see p. 14.
ur	urn, fur, deter	p	put, apple, tap	′	see p. 15.
†See p. 14.		†See p. 16.		○	see p. 14.

PHOTOGRAVURE
fō′ tə grə. vyoor′ 4*
fō′ tə grā′ vyər 1

PHOTON +
fō′ tän′ 2*
fō′ tän 2

PHOTOSTAT
fō′ tə stat′ 4

PHRASEOLOGY +
frā′ zē äl′ ə jē 4
frā′ zäl′ ə jē 1

PHRENOLOGY +
fri näl′ ə jē 4*
fre näl′ ə jē 1

PHYLACTERY
fə lak′ tə rē 2*
fi lak′ tə rē 2
fə lak′ trē 1

PHYLOGENY +
fī läj′ ə nē 4

PHYLUM
fī′ ləm 4

PHYSIOGNOMY +
fiz′ ē äg′ nə mē 4*
fiz′ ē än′ ə mē 3

PHYSIOTHERAPY
fiz′ ē ō ther′ ə pē 4

PHYSIQUE
fi zēk′ 3*
fə zēk′ 1

PIANISSIMO
pē′ ə nis′ ə mō′ 3
pē′ ə nis′ ə mō 1

PIANIST
pē an′ ist 3
pē′ ə nist 3
pyan′ ist 2*
pē an′ əst 1
pē′ ə nəst 1

PIANO (n)
pē an′ ō 4
pyan′ ō 2*
pē an′ ō′ 1
pe än′ ō 1
pē an′ ə 1

PIASTER
pē as′ tər 4*
pē äs′ tər 1

PIAZZA
pē az′ ə 4
pē at′ sə 2*
pē ä′ zə 2
pē ät′ sə 1

PICA
pī′ kə 4

PICADOR
pik′ ə dôr′ 4*
pik′ ə dôr′ 1

PICARESQUE
pik′ ə resk′ 4*
pē′ kə resk 1
pē′ kə resk′ 1

PICAYUNE
pik′ ə yo͞on′ 3*
pik′ ē yo͞on′ 2
pik′ ē o͞on′ 2

PICCOLO
pik′ ə lō′ 4

PICOT
pē′ kō 4*
pē kō′ 2
pē′ kō′ 1

PICTORIAL
pik tôr′ ē əl 4*
pik tōr′ ē əl 3

PICTURE
pik′ chər 4

PIDGIN
pij′ ən 3*
pij′ in 1

PIEBALD
pī′ bôld 4*
pī′ bôld′ 1

PIETÁ
pyā tä′ 4
pē ā′ tə 2*
pē ā tä′ 2

PIETISM
pī′ ə tiz′ əm 2*
pī′ i tiz′ əm 1
pī′ ə tiz′m 1

PIETY
pī′ ə tē 3*
pī′ i tē 1

PILAF
pi läf′ 4*
pē läf′ 3
pē′ läf 1

PILLAGE
pil′ ij 4

PILLORY
pil′ ə rē 4*
pil′ rē 1

PILULE
pil′ yo͞ol 4

PINAFORE
pin′ ə fôr′ 4*
pin′ ə fōr′ 3

PINCE NEZ
pans′ nā′ 2
pins′ nā′ 2
pans′ nā′ 1*
pans nā′ 1
pins′ nā′ 1

PINCERS
pin′ sərz 4*
pin′ chərz 1

PINION
pin′ yən 4

PINNACE
pin′ is 3*
pin′ əs 1

PINNACLE
pin′ ə kəl 2
pin′ ə k'l 1*
pin′ i kəl 1

PINOCHLE +
pē′ nuk′ əl 2
pē′ näk′ əl 1*
pē′ nuk əl 1
pē′ näk əl 1
pē′ nuk'l 1
pē′ näk'l 1

PIÑON +
pin′ yən 3*
pin′ yän′ 3
pēn′ yōn 1

PINTO
pin′ tō 4*
pēn′ tō 1
pin′ tō′ 1

PIOUS
pī′ əs 4

PIPETTE
pī pet′ 4*
pi pet′ 1

PIQUANT
pē′ kənt 4*
pē′ känt′ 2
pē′ känt 2
pē känt′ 1
pē′ kwənt 1
pik′ wənt 1

PIQUE
pēk 4

PIQUÉ
pi kā′ 3
pē kā′ 3*
pē′ kā 1

PIRACY
pī′ rə sē 4

PIRANHA
pi rän′ yə 4*
pi ran′ yə 4

PIROUETTE ○
pir′ ōō et′ 2*
pir′ oo wet′ 1
pir′ ə wet′ 1

PISCES
pī′ sēz 4*
pis′ ēz 2
pis′ ēz′ 1
pis′ kās′ 1

PISMIRE
pis′ mīr′ 4
piz′ mīr′ 3*

PISTACHIO
pi stash′ ē ō′ 4*
pi stä′ shē ō′ 3
pi stash′ ō 1

PRONUNCIATION KEY

Symbol	Key words	Symbol	Key words	Symbol	Key words
a	asp, fat, parrot	†ə	a in ago	r	red, port, dear
ā	ape, date, play		e in agent	s	sell, castle, pass
†ä	ah, car, father		i in sanity	t	top, cattle, hat
e	elf, ten, berry		o in comply	v	vat, hovel, have
ē	even, meet, money		u in focus	w	will, always, swear
i	is, hit, mirror	ər	perhaps, murder	y	yet, onion, yard
ī	ice, bite, high	b	bed, fable, dub	z	zebra, dazzle, haze
ō	open, tone, go	d	dip, beadle, had	ch	chin, catcher, arch
ô	all, horn, law	f	fall, after, off	sh	she, cushion, dash
ōō	ooze, tool, crew	g	get, haggle, dog	th	thin, nothing, truth
oo	look, pull, moor	h	he, ahead, hotel	th	then, father, lathe
yōo	use, cute, few	j	joy, agile, badge	zh	azure, leisure
yoo	united, cure, globule	k	kill, tackle, bake	ŋ	ring, anger, drink
oi	oil, point, toy	l	let, yellow, ball	″	see p. 15.
ou	out, crowd, plow	m	met, camel, trim	✓	see p. 15.
u	up, cut, color	n	not, flannel, ton	+	see p. 14.
ur	urn, fur, deter	p	put, apple, tap	′	see p. 15.
†See p. 14.		†See p. 16.		○	see p. 14.

PITHECANTHROPUS
pit*h*′ i kan′ t*h*rə pəs   2*
pit*h*′ i kan t*h*rō′ pəs   2
pit*h*′ ə kan′ t*h*rə pəs   2
pit*h*′ ə kən t*h*rō′ pəs   2
pit*h*′ i kant′ t*h*rə pəs   1

PITIFUL
pit′ i fəl   4

PITUITARY ✓
pi tōō′ ə ter′ ē   3*
pi tyōō′ ə ter′ ē   3
pi tōō′ i ter′ ē   1
pi tyōō′ i ter′ ē   1

PIVOTAL
piv′ ət ′l   3*
piv′ ət əl   1

PIZZA
pēt′ sə   4

PIZZERIA
pēt′ sə rē′ ə   4

PIZZICATO
pit′ sə kät′ ō   2*
pit′ si kät′ ō   2

PLACARD
plak′ ərd   4*
plak′ ärd′   2
plak′ ärd   2

PLACATE
plā′ kāt′   2*
plā′ kāt   2
plak′ āt′   2
plak′ āt   2

PLACEBO (medicine)
plə sē′ bō   4*

PLACENTA
plə sen′ tə   4

PLAGIARISM
plā′ jə riz′ əm   3*
plā′ jə riz′m   1
plā′ jē ə riz′ əm   1
plā′ jē ə riz′m   1

PLAGIARIZE
plā′ jə rīz′   4*
plā′ jē ə rīz′   3

PLAGUE
plāg   4

PLAID
plad   4

PLAIT
plāt   4*
plat   4

PLANETARIUM ✓
plan′ ə ter′ ē əm   3*
plan′ i ter′ ē əm   1

PLANGENT
plan′ jənt   4

PLANTAIN
plan′ tin   2*
plan′ t′n   2
plan′ tən   1

PLAQUE
plak   4

PLASMA
plaz′ mə   4

PLATEAU
pla tō′   4*
pla′ tō   1

PLATEN
plat′n   4

PLATINUM
plat′ ′n əm   3*
plat′ nəm   2

PLATITUDE
plat′ ə tōōd′   3*
plat′ ə tyōōd′   3
plat′ i tōōd′   1
plat′ i tyōōd′   1

PLATONIC   +
plə tän′ ik   4*
plā tän′ ik   4

PLATYPUS
plat′ i pəs   3*
plat′ ə pəs   1
plat′ i poos   1

PLAUDIT
plô′ dit   3*
plô′ dət   1

PLAUSIBLE
plô′ zə bəl   3*
plô′ zə b′l   1

PLAZA
plä′ zə   4*
plaz′ ə   4

PLEASANCE   .
plez′ əns   2*
plez′ ′ns   2
plez′ ′nts   1

PLEBE
plēb   4

PLEBEIAN
pli bē′ ən   4*
pli bē′ yən   1

PLEBISCITE
pleb′ ə sīt′   3*
pleb′ ə sit   2
pleb′ i sit′   1
pleb′ i sit   1
pleb′ ə sət   1

PLENARY ✓
plen′ ə rē   4*
plē′ nə rē   4

PLENIPOTENTIARY ✓
plen′ ē pə ten′ shē er′ ē   2
plen′ i pə ten′ shə rē   1*
plen′ i pə ten′ shē er′ ē   1
plen′ ə pə tench′ rē   1
plen′ ə pə tench′ ə rē   1
plen′ ə pə ten′ chē er′ ē   1

PLENITUDE
plen′ ə tōōd′   3*
plen′ ə tyōōd′   3
plen′ i tōōd′   1
plen′ i tyōōd′   1

PLEONASM
plē′ ə naz′ əm   3*
plē′ ə naz′m   1

PLENTEOUS
plen′ tē əs   4

PLENUM
plē′ nəm   4
plen′ əm   3*

PLETHORA
pleth′ ə rə   4

PLEURISY
ploor′ ə sē   3*
ploor′ i sē   1

PLIANT
plī′ ənt   4

PLOVER
pluv′ ər   4*
plō′ vər   4

PLUMAGE
plōō′ mij   4

PLURAL
ploor′ əl   4

PLURALITY
ploo ral′ ə tē   3
ploo ral′ i tē   1*

PLUTOCRACY   +
plōō täk′ rə sē   4

PLUTOCRAT
plōōt′ ə krat′   4

PLUTONIUM
plōō tō′ nē əm   4

PNEUMATIC
nōō mat′ ik   3*
nyōō mat′ ik   3
noo mat′ ik   1
nyoo mat′ ik   1

PNEUMONIA
noo mōn′ yə   3*
nyoo mōn′ yə   3
noo mō′ nē ə   3
nyoo mō′ nē ə   3

PODIATRIST
pə dī′ ə trist   3*
pō dī′ ə trist   2
pə dī′ ə trəst   1
pō dī′ ə trəst   1

PODIATRY
pə dī′ ə trē   4*
pō dī′ ə trē   3

PODIUM
pō′ dē əm   4

POEM
pō′ əm   4*
pō′ im   1
pō′ em   1

PRONUNCIATION KEY

Symbol	Key words	Symbol	Key words	Symbol	Key words
a	asp, fat, parrot	†ə	a in ago	r	red, port, dear
ā	ape, date, play		e in agent	s	sell, castle, pass
†ä	ah, car, father		i in sanity	t	top, cattle, hat
e	elf, ten, berry		o in comply	v	vat, hovel, have
ē	even, meet, money		u in focus	w	will, always, swear
i	is, hit, mirror	ər	perhaps, murder	y	yet, onion, yard
ī	ice, bite, high	b	bed, fable, dub	z	zebra, dazzle, haze
ō	open, tone, go	d	dip, beadle, had	ch	chin, catcher, arch
ô	all, horn, law	f	fall, after, off	sh	she, cushion, dash
ōō	ooze, tool, crew	g	get, haggle, dog	th	thin, nothing, truth
oo	look, pull, moor	h	he, ahead, hotel	th	then, father, lathe
yōō	use, cute, few	j	joy, agile, badge	zh	azure, leisure
yoo	united, cure, globule	k	kill, tackle, bake	ŋ	ring, anger, drink
oi	oil, point, toy	l	let, yellow, ball	″	see p. 15.
ou	out, crowd, plow	m	met, camel, trim	✓	see p. 15.
u	up, cut, color	n	not, flannel, ton	+	see p. 14.
ur	urn, fur, deter	p	put, apple, tap	′	see p. 15.
†See p. 14.		†See p. 16.		○	see p. 14.

POESY
pō′ ə zē 2*
pō′ ə sē 2
pō′ ə zē′ 1
pō′ ə sē′ 1
pō′ i sē 1
pō′ i zē 1

POETASTER
pō′ ə tas′ tər 2*
pō′ i tas′ tər 2

POETRY
pō′ ə trē 2*
pō′ i trē 2

POGROM +
pō gräm′ 4
pō′ grəm 3
pə grum′ 2*
pə gräm′ 1
pō grum′ 1

POIGNANT
poin′ yənt 4*
poin′ ənt 3

POINCIANA
poin′ sē an′ ə 4*
poin′ sē än′ ə 2
poin′ sē ä′ nə 2
point′ sē an′ ə 1
pän′ sē an′ ə 1
pwänt′ sē an′ ə 1

POINSETTIA
poin set′ ē ə 4*
poin set′ ə 3

POLARITY ✓
pō lar′ ə tē 3*
pō lar′ i tē 1
pō ler′ ə tē 1

POLARIZATION
pō′ lər i zā′ shən 3*
pō′ lər ə zā′ shən 2

POLEMIC
pə lem′ ik 4*
pō lem′ ik 2

POLIO
pō′ lē ō′ 4

POLIOMYELITIS
pō′ lē ō mī′ ə līt′ əs 4

POLITBURO +
pə lit′ byoor′ ō 4*
päl′ it byoor′ ō 3
pō′ lit byoor′ ō 1
päl′ ət byoor′ ō 1

POLITESSE +
päl′ i tes′ 2*
päl′ ə tes′ 2
pô li tes′ 1

POLITIC +
päl′ ə tik 3*
päl′ i tik 1

POLITICO
pə lit′ i kō′ 4

POLITY +
päl′ ə tē 3*
päl′ i tē 1

POLKA
pōl′ kə 4*
pō′ kə 2

POLL
pōl 4

POLLUTE
pə lōōt′ 4

POLONAISE +
päl′ ə nāz′ 4*
pō′ lə nāz′ 4

POLTERGEIST
pōl′ tər gīst′ 4

POLTROON +
päl trōōn′ 4

POLYANDRY +
päl′ ē an′ drē 4
päl′ ē an′ drē 2*

POLYGAMOUS
pə lig′ ə məs 4

POLYGAMY
pə lig′ ə mē 4

POLYGLOT +
päl′ ē glät′ 2*
päl′ i glät′ 2

POLYMER +
päl′ ə mər 3*
päl′ i mər 1

POLYP +
päl′ ip 3*
päl′ əp 1

POLYPHONIC +
päl′ ē fän′ ik 2*
päl′ i fän′ ik 2

POLYPHONY
pə lif′ ə nē 4

POLYSYLLABIC +
päl′ ē si lab′ ik 2*
päl′ i si lab′ ik 1
päl′ i sə lab′ ik 1

POLYTHEISM +
päl′ ē thē iz′ əm 2*
päl′ ē thē′ iz əm 1
päl′ i thē iz′m 1
päl′ i thē iz′ əm 1

POMADE +
pə mād′ 4*
pə mäd′ 4
pō mād′ 4
pō mäd′ 4
pä mād′ 1
pä mäd′ 1

POMANDER
pō man' dər   3
pō' man' dər   2
pō' man dər   2
pə man' dər   1*

POMEGRANATE   +
päm' gran' it   3
pum' gran' it   3
päm' ə gran' it   2*
päm' ə gran' it   1
pum' ə gran' it   1
päm' ə gran' ət   1
päm' gran' ət   1
pum' gran' ət   1

POMPADOUR   +
päm' pə dôr'   4*
päm' pə dōr'   3
päm' pə door'   1

POMPON   +
päm' pän'   3*
päm' pän   1

POMPOSITY   +✓
päm päs' ə tē   2*
päm päs' i tē   1
päm' päs' ə tē   1

POMPOUS   +
päm' pəs   4

PONCHO
pän' chō   4*
pän' chō'   1

PONGEE   +
pän jē'   4*
pän' jē   3

PONIARD   +
pän' yərd   4

PONTIFF   +
pän' tif   3*
pän' təf   1

PONTIFICAL   +
pän tif' i kəl   3*
pän tif' i k'l   1

PONTIFICATE (n)   +
pän tif' i kit   2*
pän tif' i kāt'   2
pän tif' i kāt   1
pän tif' i kət   1
pän tif' ə kit'   1
pän tif' ə kāt'   1

PONTIFICATE (v)   +
pän tif' i kāt'   4

PONTOON   +
pän tōōn'   4

POPULACE   +
päp' yə lis   2*
päp' yə ləs   2

PORCELAIN
pôrs' lin   3*
pōrs' lin   2
pôr' sə lin   2
pōr' sə lin   2
pôr' s'l in   1
pôr' slən   1
pōr' slən   1
pōr' sə lən   1

PORCINE
pôr' sīn'   3*
pôr' sin   2
pôr' sīn   1

PORGY
pôr' gē   4

PRONUNCIATION KEY

Symbol	Key words	Symbol	Key words	Symbol	Key words
a	asp, fat, parrot	†ə	a in ago	r	red, port, dear
ā	ape, date, play		e in agent	s	sell, castle, pass
†ä	ah, car, father		i in sanity	t	top, cattle, hat
e	elf, ten, berry		o in comply	v	vat, hovel, have
ē	even, meet, money		u in focus	w	will, always, swear
i	is, hit, mirror	ər	perhaps, murder	y	yet, onion, yard
ī	ice, bite, high	b	bed, fable, dub	z	zebra, dazzle, haze
ō	open, tone, go	d	dip, beadle, had	ch	chin, catcher, arch
ô	all, horn, law	f	fall, after, off	sh	she, cushion, dash
ōō	ooze, tool, crew	g	get, haggle, dog	th	thin, nothing, truth
oo	look, pull, moor	h	he, ahead, hotel	th	then, father, lathe
yōō	use, cute, few	j	joy, agile, badge	zh	azure, leisure
yoo	united, cure, globule	k	kill, tackle, bake	ŋ	ring, anger, drink
oi	oil, point, toy	l	let, yellow, ball	"	see p. 15.
ou	out, crowd, plow	m	met, camel, trim	✓	see p. 15.
u	up, cut, color	n	not, flannel, ton	+	see p. 14.
ur	urn, fur, deter	p	put, apple, tap	'	see p. 15.
†See p. 14.		†See p. 16.		○	see p. 14.

POROSITY +
pə räs′ ə tē 3*
pō räs′ ə tē 2
pô räs′ ə tē 2
pō räs′ i tē 1
pô räs′ i tē 1
pə räs′ i tē 1

PORPHYRY
pôr′ fər ē 4*
pôr′ frē 1

PORPOISE
pôr′ pəs 4

PORRIDGE +
pär′ ij 4*
pôr′ ij 4

PORRINGER +
pôr′ in jər 3
pär′ in jər 2*
pôr′ ən jər 1
pär′ ən jər 1

PORTAGE
pôr′ tij 4*
pōr′ tij 3
pôr täzh′ 2

PORTCULLIS
pôrt kul′ is 3*
pōrt kul′ is 2
pôrt kul′ əs 1
pōrt kul′ əs 1

PORTE-COCHÈRE ✓
pôrt′ kō sher′ 4*
pōrt′ kō sher′ 3
pōrt′ kə sher′ 1
pôrt′ kə sher′ 1

PORTEND
pôr tend′ 4*
pōr tend′ 3

PORTENT
pôr′ tent′ 3*
pōr′ tent′ 3
pôr′ tent 1
pōr′ tent 1

PORTFOLIO
pôrt fō′ lē ō′ 4*
pōrt fō′ lē ō′ 3

PORTICO
pôr′ tə kō′ 2*
pôr′ ti kō′ 2
pōr′ ti kō′ 2

PORTMANTEAU
pôrt man′ tō 4
pôrt′ man tō′ 3*
pōrt man′ tō 3
pōrt′ man tō′ 2

PORTRAIT
pôr′ trit 3*
pôr′ trāt′ 3
pōr′ trit 2
pōr′ trāt′ 1
pôr′ trət 1
pōr′ trət 1
pôr′ trāt 1

PORTRAITURE
pôr′ tri chər 2
pôr′ trə choor 1*
pôr′ tri choor 1
pōr′ tri choor 1
pōr′ tri chər 1
pōr′ trə choor 1
pôr′ trə chər 1
pōr′ trə chər 1
pôr′ trə tyoor′ 1
pōr′ trə toor′ 1

POSEUR
pō zʉr′ 3

POSIT +
päz′ it 3*
päz′ ət 1

POSSE +
päs′ ē 4

POSSET +
päs′ it 3*
päs′ ət 1

POSTERIOR + ○
päs tir′ ē ər 4
pōs tir′ ē ər 3*

POSTERITY +
päs ter′ ə tē 3*
päs ter′ i tē 1

POSTERN +
päs′ tərn 4*
pōs′ tərn 3

POST HOC +
pōst′ häk′ 2*
pōst häk′ 1

POSTHUMOUS +
päs′ choo məs 3
päs′ tyoo məs 2*
päs′ chə məs 2
päs′ tə məs 1
pōst hyoo′ məs 1

POSTILION +
pōs til′ yən 4*
päs til′ yən 3
pə stil′ yən 1

POST MORTEM
pōst môr′ təm 4

POSTPONE
pōst pōn′ 4*
pōs pōn′ 3

POST PRANDIAL
pōst pran′ dē əl 4*
pōs pran′ dē əl 1

POSTULANT +
päs′ chə lənt 3*
päs′ choo lənt 1

POSTULATE (n) +
päs′ chə lāt′ 2
päs′ chə lit 2*
päs′ choo lit 1
päs′ choo lāt 1
päs′ chə lat 1

POSTULATE (v) +
päs′ chə lāt′ 3*
päs′ choo lāt′ 1

POSTURE
päs′ chər 4

POTABLE
pōt′ ə bəl 3*
pōt′ ə b'l 1

POTASH +
pät′ ash′ 2*
pät′ ash 2

POTATO
pə tā′ tō 4*
pə tät′ ə 2

POTENT
pōt′ 'nt 3*
pōt′ ənt 1

POTENTATE
pōt′ 'n tāt′ 4

POTPOURRI +
pō′ poo rē′ 4*
pät poo′ rē 2

POTSHERD +
pät′ shurd′ 4

POULTICE
pōl′ tis 3*
pōl′ təs 1

POULTRY
pōl′ trē 4

PRAETORIAN
prē tôr′ ē ən 3*
prē tōr′ ē ən 3
pri tôr′ ē ən 1

PRAIRIE ✓
prer′ ē 4

PRALINE
prä′ lēn 4*
prā′ lēn 4

PREAMBLE
prē′ am′ bəl 3*
prē′ am′ b'l 1
prē am′ bəl 1
prē am′ b'l 1

PRECARIOUS ✓
pri ker′ ē əs 4*
pri kar′ ē əs 1

PRECEDE
pri sēd′ 4

PRECEDENCE
pri sēd′ 'ns 3*
pres′ ə dəns 3
pres′ i dəns 1

PRECEDENT
pres′ ə dənt 3*
pres′ i dənt 1

PRECEPT
prē′ sept′ 2*
prē′ sept 2

PRECINCT
prē′ siŋkt 4

PRONUNCIATION KEY

Symbol	Key words	Symbol	Key words	Symbol	Key words
a	asp, fat, parrot	†ə	a in ago	r	red, port, dear
ā	ape, date, play		e in agent	s	sell, castle, pass
†ä	ah, car, father		i in sanity	t	top, cattle, hat
e	elf, ten, berry		o in comply	v	vat, hovel, have
ē	even, meet, money		u in focus	w	will, always, swear
i	is, hit, mirror	ər	perhaps, murder	y	yet, onion, yard
ī	ice, bite, high	b	bed, fable, dub	z	zebra, dazzle, haze
ō	open, tone, go	d	dip, beadle, had	ch	chin, catcher, arch
ô	all, horn, law	f	fall, after, off	sh	she, cushion, dash
oo	ooze, tool, crew	g	get, haggle, dog	th	thin, nothing, truth
oo	look, pull, moor	h	he, ahead, hotel	th	then, father, lathe
yoo	use, cute, few	j	joy, agile, badge	zh	azure, leisure
yoo	united, cure, globule	k	kill, tackle, bake	ŋ	ring, anger, drink
oi	oil, point, toy	l	let, yellow, ball	"	see p. 15.
ou	out, crowd, plow	m	met, camel, trim	✓	see p. 15.
u	up, cut, color	n	not, flannel, ton	+	see p. 14.
ur	urn, fur, deter	p	put, apple, tap	'	see p. 15.
†See p. 14.		†See p. 16.		○	see p. 14.

PRECIOSITY   +
presh' ē äs' ə tē   3*
presh' ē äs' i tē   1
pres' ē äs' ə tē   1

PRECIPICE
pres' ə pis   3*
pres' ə pəs   1
pres' pəs   1

PRECIPITATE (v)
pri sip' ə tāt'   3*
pri sip' i tāt'   1

PRECIPITATE (n, adj)
pri sip' ə tāt'   3
pri sip' ə tit   2*
pri sip' i tit   1
pri sip' i tāt'   1

PRECIPITOUS
pri sip' ə təs   3*
pri sip' i təs   1

PRÉCIS
prā' sē   4*
prā sē'   4
prā' sē'   1

PRECISE
pri sīs'   4

PRECISION
pri sizh' ən   4

PRECOCITY   +
pri käs' ə tē   3*
pri käs' i tē   1

PRECOCIOUS
pri kō' shəs   4

PRECURSOR
pri kur' sər   4*
prē' kur' sər   2
prē' kur sər   1

PREDATOR
pred' ə tər   4
pred' ə tôr'   2*

PREDATORY
pred' ə tôr' ē   4*
pred' ə tōr' ē   3

PREDECESSOR
pred' ə ses' ər   3*
prē' də ses' ər   2
pred' ə ses' ər   2
prēd' ə ses' ər   2

PREDICAMENT
pri dik' ə mənt   4

PREDICATE (n, adj)
pred' ə kit   2*
pred' i kit   1
pred' i kət   1

PREDICATE (v)
pred' ə kāt'   4

PREDILECTION
pred' 'l ek' shən   3*
prēd' 'l ek' shən   3
pred' əl ek' shən   1
prēd' əl ek' shən   1

PREDOMINATE   +
pri däm' ə nāt'   4

PREEMINENT
prē em' ə nənt   4

PREEMPT
prē empt'   4

PREFACE
pref' is   3*
pref' əs   1

PREFATORY
pref' ə tôr' ē   4*
pref' ə tōr' ē   3

PREFECTURE
prē' fek chər   2*
prē' fek' chər   2

PREFERABLE
pref' ər ə bəl   3*
pref' rə bəl   2
pref' ər ə b'l   1
pref' rə b'l   1

PREFERENCE
pref' ər əns   4*
pref' ərns   1
pref' rəns   1

PREFERENTIAL
pref' ə ren' shəl   3*
pref' ə ren' chəl   1

PREFERMENT
pri fur' mənt   4

PREHENSILE
pri hen' sil   2
pri hen' səl   1*
pri hen' s'l   1
pri hen' sīl   1
prē hent' səl   1
prē hen' sīl'   1
prē hent' sīl'   1

PREJUDICE
prej' ə dis   3*
prej' ə dəs   1

PREJUDICIAL
prej' ə dish' əl   4

PRELATE
prel' it   3*
prel' ət   1
prē' lāt'   1

PRELUDE
prel' yōōd'   3*
prā' lōōd   3
prē' lōōd   2
prāl' yōōd   2
prel' yōōd   1
pre' lōōd'   1

PREMATURE
prē′ mə choor′ 4*
prē′ mə toor′ 4
prē′ mə tyoor′ 4
prē′ mə choor′ 1

PREMIER ○ (n)
pri mir′ 4
prē′ mē ər 3*
pri myir′ 3
prem′ ē ər 1

PREMIÈRE
pri mir′ 4
pri myer′ 3*
pri mē er′ 2
pri myir′ 1

PREMISE
prem′ is 3*
prem′ əs 1

PREMONITION
prem′ ə nish′ ən 4*
prē′ mə nish′ ən 4

PRENATAL
prē nāt′ ′l 4

PREPARATORY ✓
pri par′ ə tôr′ ē 4*
pri par′ ə tōr′ ē 3
pri per′ ə tôr′ ē 2
prep′ rə tōr′ ē 1
prep′ rə tôr′ ē 1
prep′ ə rə tôr′ ē 1
prep′ ə rə tōr′ ē 1

PREPONDERANT +
pri pän′ dər ənt 4*
pri pän′ drənt 1

PREPOSTEROUS +
pri päs′ tər əs 4*
pri päs′ trəs 2

PREPUCE
prē′ pyoos′ 2*
prē′ pyoos 2

PREREQUISITE
prē rek′ wə zit 1*
pri rek′ wi zit 1
pri rek′ wə zit 1
prē rek′ wə zət 1

PREROGATIVE +
pri räg′ ə tiv 4

PRESAGE (v)
pri sāj′ 4
pres′ ij 2*

PRESBYTER
prez′ bə tər 2*
pres′ bə tər 2
prez′ bi tər 1
pres′ bi tər 1

PRESCIENCE
prē′ shē əns 4
presh′ əns 3*
presh′ ē əns 3
prē′ shəns 2
prē′ sē əns 1
pres′ ē əns 1

PRESENT (n, adj)
prez′ ′nt 2*
prez′ ənt 2

PRESENT (v)
pri zent′ 4

PRESENTATION
prē′ zən tā′ shən 4*
prez′ ən tā′ shən 2
prez′ ′n tā′ shən 2

PRONUNCIATION KEY

Symbol	Key words	Symbol	Key words	Symbol	Key words
a	asp, fat, parrot	†ə	a in ago	r	red, port, dear
ā	ape, date, play		e in agent	s	sell, castle, pass
†ä	ah, car, father		i in sanity	t	top, cattle, hat
e	elf, ten, berry		o in comply	v	vat, hovel, have
ē	even, meet, money		u in focus	w	will, always, swear
i	is, hit, mirror	ər	perhaps, murder	y	yet, onion, yard
i	ice, bite, high	b	bed, fable, dub	z	zebra, dazzle, haze
ō	open, tone, go	d	dip, beadle, had	ch	chin, catcher, arch
ô	all, horn, law	f	fall, after, off	sh	she, cushion, dash
oo	ooze, tool, crew	g	get, haggle, dog	th	thin, nothing, truth
oo	look, pull, moor	h	he, ahead, hotel	th	then, father, lathe
yoo	use, cute, few	j	joy, agile, badge	zh	azure, leisure
yoo	united, cure, globule	k	kill, tackle, bake	ŋ	ring, anger, drink
oi	oil, point, toy	l	let, yellow, ball	″	see p. 15.
ou	out, crowd, plow	m	met, camel, trim	✓	see p. 15.
u	up, cut, color	n	not, flannel, ton	+	see p. 14.
ur	urn, fur, deter	p	put, apple, tap	′	see p. 15.
†See p. 14.		†See p. 16.		○	see p. 14.

PRESENTIMENT
pri zen′ tə mənt   4

PRESERVE
pri zʉrv′   4

PRESIDE
pri zīd′   4

PRESIDIO
pri sid′ ē ō′   4*
pri sēd′ ē ō′   2
pri zēd′ ē ō′   1
pri zid′ ē ō′   1

PRESIDIUM
pri sid′ ē əm   4*
pri zid′ ē əm   1
prī′ sid′ ē əm   1
prī zid′ ē əm   1

PRESTIDIGITATION
pres′ tə dij′ i tā′ shən   3*
pres′ ti dij′ i tā′ shən   1

PRESTIGE
pres tēzh′   4*
pres tēj′   3
pres′ tij   1

PRESTIGIOUS
pres tij′ əs   4*
pres tēj′ əs   4
pres tēj′ ē əs   2
pres tēzh′ əs   1
pres tēzh′ ē əs   1

PRESUME
pri zo͞om′   4*
pri zyo͞om′   1

PRESUMPTION
pri zump′ shən   4*
pri zum′ shən   1

PRESUMPTUOUS
pri zump′ cho͞o əs   2*
pri zump′ choo wəs   1
pri zum′ chə wəs   1
pri zump′ chə wəs   1
pri zum′ shəs   1
pri zump′ shəs   1
pri zum′ chəs   1
pri zump′ chəs   1

PRETENSE
pri tens′   4*
prē′ tens′   2
prē′ tens   2
prē′ tents′   1
pri tents′   1

PRETENTIOUS
pri ten′ shəs   3*
pri ten′ chəs   1

PRETERNATURAL
prēt′ ər nach′ ər əl   4*
prēt′ ər nach′ rəl   2

PRETEXT
prē′ tekst′   2*
prē′ tekst   2

PRETTIFY
prit′ ə fī′   2
prit′ i fī′   2
poort′ i fī′   1
proot′ i fī′   1

PREVALENT
prev′ ə lənt   4*
prev′ lənt   1

PREVARICATE
pri var′ ə kāt′   4

PRIAPISM
prī′ ə piz′ əm   2
prī′ ə piz′m   1

PRIMACY
prī′ mə sē   4

PRIMA DONNA   +
prim′ ə dän′ ə   4*
prē′ mə dän′ ə   4

PRIMA FACIE
prī′ mə fā′ shē   3
prī′ mə fā′ shə   2*
prī′ mə fā′ shē ē′   1
prī′ mə fā′ shi ē′   1
prī′ mə fā′ shə   1
prī′ mə fā′ sē   1
prī′ mə fā′ shē   1

PRIMAL
prī′ məl   3*
prī′ m′l   1

PRIMARILY   ✓
prī mer′ ə lē   4
prī′ mer′ ə lē   2*
prī′ mer ə l ē   1
prī′ mər ə lē   1

PRIMARY   ✓
prī′ mə rē   3*
prī′ mer′ ē   2
prī′ mer ē   2
′prīm′ rē   1

PRIMATE (bishop)
prī′ māt′   2*
prī′ mit   2
prī′ māt   2
prī′ mət   1

PRIMATE (monkey)
prī′ māt′   2*
prī′ māt   2

PRIMER
(elementary book)
prim′ ər   4

PRIMER
prī′ mər   4

PRIMEVAL
prī mē′ vəl   3*
prī mē′ v′l   1

PRIMITIVE
prim' ə tiv   3*
prim' i tiv   1

PRIMOGENITURE
prī' mō jen' ə choor'   2*
prī' mə jen' i chər   2
prī mō jen' ə chər   1
prī mō jen' ə toor   1
prī mō jen' ə tyoor   1

PRIMORDIAL
pri môr' dē əl   3*
prī môr' dē əl   1

PRIOR
prī' ər   4
prīr   1

PRIORITY   +
prī är' ə tē   4*
prī ôr' ə tē   4

PRISM
priz' əm   3
priz' 'm   1*

PRISTINE
pris tēn'   3*
pris' tēn'   2
pris' tēn   2
pris' tin   2
pris' tīn   1

PRIVACY
prī' və sē   4

PRIVATEER   ○
prī' və tir'   4

PRIVET
priv' it   3*
priv' ət   1

PRIVILEGE
priv' ə lij   3*
priv' lij   3
priv' 'l ij   1

PRIVY
priv' ē   4

PRIX FIXE
prē' fēks'   3*
prē' fiks'   2

PROBABLY   +
präb' ə blē   4*
präb' blē   1
präb' lē   1

PROBATE
prō' bāt'   2*
prō' bāt   2

PROBITY   +
prō' bə tē   3*
präb' ə tē   2
prō' bi tē   1
präb' i tē   1

PROBOSCIS   +
prō bäs' is   3*
prə bäs' əs   1

PROCEDURE
prə sē' jər   4*
prō sē' jər   1

PROCEED
prə sēd'   4
prō sēd'   3*

PRONUNCIATION KEY

Symbol	Key words	Symbol	Key words	Symbol	Key words
a	asp, fat, parrot	†ə	a in ago	r	red, port, dear
ā	ape, date, play		e in agent	s	sell, castle, pass
†ä	ah, car, father		i in sanity	t	top, cattle, hat
e	elf, ten, berry		o in comply	v	vat, hovel, have
ē	even, meet, money		u in focus	w	will, always, swear
i	is, hit, mirror	ər	perhaps, murder	y	yet, onion, yard
ī	ice, bite, high	b	bed, fable, dub	z	zebra, dazzle, haze
ō	open, tone, go	d	dip, beadle, had	ch	chin, catcher, arch
ô	all, horn, law	f	fall, after, off	sh	she, cushion, dash
o͞o	ooze, tool, crew	g	get, haggle, dog	th	thin, nothing, truth
oo	look, pull, moor	h	he, ahead, hotel	th	then, father, lathe
yo͞o	use, cute, few	j	joy, agile, badge	zh	azure, leisure
yoo	united, cure, globule	k	kill, tackle, bake	ŋ	ring, anger, drink
oi	oil, point, toy	l	let, yellow, ball	"	see p. 15.
ou	out, crowd, plow	m	met, camel, trim	✓	see p. 15.
u	up, cut, color	n	not, flannel, ton	+	see p. 14.
ur	urn, fur, deter	p	put, apple, tap	'	see p. 15.
†See p. 14.		†See p. 16.		○	see p. 14.

PROCEEDS (n)
prō′ sēdz 2*
prō′ sēdz′ 2

PROCEEDS (v)
prə sēdz′ 4*
prō sēdz′ 3

PROCESS +
präs′ es 3*
prōs′ es 1
präs′ əs 1
prōs′ əs 1

PROCESSION
prə sesh′ ən 4*
prō sesh′ ən 1

PROCLAMATION +
präk′ lə mā′ shən 3*
präk lə mā′ shən 1

PROCLIVITY
prō kliv′ ə tē 3*
prō kliv′ i tē 1

PROCRASTINATE
prō kras′ tə nāt′ 4*
prə kras′ tə nāt′ 4

PROCREATE
prō′ krē āt′ 4

PROCRUSTEAN
prō krus′ tē ən 4*
pə krus′ tē ən 1
prə krus′ tē ən 1

PROCURATOR +
präk′ yə rāt′ ər 4

PROCURER
prō kyoor′ ər 4*
prə kyoor′ ər 3

PRODIGAL +
präd′ i gəl 3*
präd′ ə gəl 1

PRODIGALITY +
präd′ i gal′ ə tē 2*
präd′ ə gal′ i tē 1
präd′ ə gal′ ə tē 1

PRODIGIOUS
prə dij′ əs 4

PRODIGY +
präd′ ə jē 3*
präd′ i jē 1

PRODUCE (n)
präd′ yōōs 4*
präd′ ōōs 4
prō′ dōōs 4
prō′ dyōōs 4

PRODUCE (v)
prə dōōs′ 4*
prə dyōōs′ 4
prō dōōs′ 2
prō dyōōs′ 2

PROFANE
prō fān′ 4*
prə fān′ 4

PROFANITY
prō fan′ ə tē 3*
prə fan′ ə tē 3
prō fan′ i tē 1
prə fan′ i tē 1

PROFFER +
präf′ ər 4

PROFILE
prō′ fīl 4

PROFLIGACY +
präf′ li gə sē 2*
präf′ lə gə sē 2

PROFLIGATE +
präf′ lə git 2*
präf′ lə gāt′ 2
präf′ li git 1
präf′ li gāt′ 1
präf′ li gət 1

PROFUSE
prə fyōōs′ 4*
prō fyōōs′ 2

PROGENITOR
prō jen′ ə tər 3*
prō jen′ i tər 1
prə jen′ ə tər 1

PROGENY +
präj′ ə nē 4*
präj′ nē 1

PROGNATHOUS +
präg′ nə thəs 4*
präg nā′ thəs 3

PROGNOSIS +
präg nō′ sis 4

PROGNOSTICATE +
präg′ näs′ tə kāt′ 3*
präg′ näs′ ti kāt′ 1

PROGRAM
prō′ grəm 4
prō′ gram′ 2*
prō′ gram 2

PROGRESS (n) +
präg′ rəs 3*
präg′ res 3
präg′ res′ 1

PROGRESS (v)
prə gres′ 4

PROHIBITION
prō′ ə bish′ ən 4*
prō′ hə bish′ ən 1

PROJECT (n) +
präj′ ikt 3*
präj′ ekt 3
präj′ ekt′ 1

PROJECT (v)
prə jekt′ 4

PROJECTILE
prə jek' t'l   2*
prə jek' tīl'   2
prə jek' tīl   2
prə jek' təl   1
prə jek' til   1

PROLETARIAN ✓
prō' lə ter' ē ən   3*
prō' li ter' ē ən   1

PROLETARIAT ✓
prō' lə ter' ē ət   2*
prō' lə ter' ē it   1
prō' li ter' ē ət   1
prōt' lə tar' ē ət   1

PROLIFERATE
prō lif' ə rāt'   3*
prə lif' ə rāt'   2

PROLIFIC
prō lif' ik   3*
prə lif' ik   2

PROLIX
prō liks'   4*
prō' liks   4

PROLOGUE   +
prō' läg   3*
prō' lôg'   2
prō' lôg   2
prō' läg'   1

PROMENADE   +
präm ə näd'   2*
präm ə nād'   2
präm' ə näd'   2
präm' ə nād'   2

PROMETHEAN
prə mē' thē ən   4

PROMISCUITY   +
präm is kyōō' ə tē   2*
prō' mis kyōō' ə tē   2
präm' is kyōō' ə tē   1
präm' is kyōō' i tē   1
prō' mis kyōō' i tē   1

PROMISCUOUS
prə mis' kyōō əs   2*
prə mis' kyoo wəs   1
prə mis' kyə wəs   1

PROMISSORY   +
präm' i sôr' ē   3*
präm' i sōr' ē   2
präm' ə sôr' ē   1
präm' ə sōr' ē   1

PROMONTORY   +
präm' ən tôr' ē   4*
präm' ən tōr' ē   3

PROMULGATE   +
präm' əl gāt'   4*
prō mul' gāt   2
prō' məl gāt'   1

PRONUNCIAMENTO
prō nun' sē ə men' tō   2*
prə nun' sē ə men' tō   2
prə nun' shē ə men' tō   1

PRONUNCIATION
prə nun' sē ā' shən   4*
prə nunt' sē ā' shən   1

PROPAGATE   +
präp' ə gāt'   4

PRONUNCIATION KEY

Symbol	Key words	Symbol	Key words	Symbol	Key words
a	asp, fat, parrot	†ə	a in ago	r	red, port, dear
ā	ape, date, play		e in agent	s	sell, castle, pass
†ä	ah, car, father		i in sanity	t	top, cattle, hat
e	elf, ten, berry		o in comply	v	vat, hovel, have
ē	even, meet, money		u in focus	w	will, always, swear
i	is, hit, mirror	ər	perhaps, murder	y	yet, onion, yard
ī	ice, bite, high	b	bed, fable, dub	z	zebra, dazzle, haze
ō	open, tone, go	d	dip, beadle, had	ch	chin, catcher, arch
ô	all, horn, law	f	fall, after, off	sh	she, cushion, dash
ōō	ooze, tool, crew	g	get, haggle, dog	th	thin, nothing, truth
oo	look, pull, moor	h	he, ahead, hotel	th	then, father, lathe
yōō	use, cute, few	j	joy, agile, badge	zh	azure, leisure
yoo	united, cure, globule	k	kill, tackle, bake	ŋ	ring, anger, drink
ɔi	oil, point, toy	l	let, yellow, ball	''	see p. 15.
ɔu	out, crowd, plow	m	met, camel, trim	✓	see p. 15.
u	up, cut, color	n	not, flannel, ton	+	see p. 14.
ʉr	urn, fur, deter	p	put, apple, tap	'	see p. 15.
†See p. 14.		†See p. 16.		○	see p. 14.

PROPAGANDA   +
präp' ə gan' də   4*
prō' pə gan' də   2

PROPHESY (n)   +
präf' ə sē   3*
präf' i sē   1

PROPHECY (v)   +
präf' ə sī'   3*
präf' i sī'   1

PROPHYLACTIC   +
prō' fə lak' tik   4*
präf' ə lak' tik   3

PROPINQUITY
prō piŋ' kwə tē   3*
prō piŋ' kwi tē   1

PROPITIATE
prō pish' ē āt'   3*
prə pish' ē āt'   2

PROPITIOUS
prə pish' əs   4*
prō pish' əs   1

PROPRIETARY   ✓
prə prī' ə ter' ē   3*
prə prī' i ter' ē   1
pə prī' ə ter' ē   1

PROPRIETY
prə prī' ə tē   3*
prə prī' i tē   1

PRO RATA
prō rät' ə   4*
prō rāt' ə   4
prō rat' ə   1

PROSAIC
prō zā' ik   4

PROSCENIUM
prō sē' nē əm   4

PROSCIUTTO
prō shoo' tō   2
prə shoo' tō   1*

PROSCRIBE
prō skrīb'   4

PROSECUTE   +
präs' ə kyoot'   3*
präs' i kyoot'   1

PROSELYTE   +
präs' ə līt'   4

PROSELYTIZE   +
präs' ə lə tīz'   2*
präs' ə li tīz'   2
präs' ə lī tīz'   1
präs' lə tīz'   1

PROSIT
prō' sit   3
prō' zət   1*
prōst   1
prō' sət   1

PROSODY   +
präs' ə dē   3

PROSPECTUS   +
prə spek' təs   4*
prä spek' təs   2

PROSTATE   +
präs' tāt   3*
präs' tāt'   1

PROSTHESIS   +
präs thē' sis   3*
präs thē' səs   1
präs' thə sis   1
präs' thə səs   1

PROSTITUTE   +
präs' tə toot'   3*
präs' tə tyoot'   3
präs' ti toot'   1
präs' ti tyoot'   1

PROSTRATE   +
präs' trāt   3*
präs' trāt'   1

PROSY
prō' zē   4

PROTEAN
prōt' ē ən   4*
prō tē' ən   3

PROTÉGÉ
prōt' ə zhā'   4*
prōt' ə zhā'   3

PROTEIN
prō' tēn   4*
prō' tē in   3

PRO TEMPORE
prō tem' pə rē   2*
prō tem' pə rē'   2

PROTEST (n)
prō' test'   2*
prō' test   2

PROTEST (v)
prə test'   4*
prō test'   2
prō' test'   2

PROTESTATION   +
prät' is tā' shən   3*
prō tes tā' shən   2
prō tis tā' shən   1
prō' tis tā' shən   1
prät' əs tā' shən   1
prō təs tā' shən   1

PROTOCOL   +
prōt' ə kôl'   4*
prōt' ə käl'   4
prōt' ə kōl'   4

PROTON   +
prō' tän   3*
prō' tän'   1

PROTOPLASM
prō′ tə plaz′ əm   3*
prō′ tə plaz′m   1

PROTOTYPE
prō′ tə tīp′   4

PROTOZOAN
prō′ tə zō′ ən   4

PROTUBERANCE
prō to͞o′ bər əns   4*
prō tyo͞o′ bər əns   4
prō to͞ob′ rəns   1
prō tyo͞ob′ rəns   1

PROVENANCE   +
präv′ ə nəns   4*
präv′ ə näns   2
präv′ nəns   1
präv′ näns   1

PROVENDER   +
präv′ ən dər   4

PROVERBIAL
prə vʉr′ bē əl   4

PROVIDENCE   +
präv′ ə dəns   3*
präv′ ə dens   1
präv′ i dəns   1

PROVIDENT   +
präv′ ə dənt   2*
präv′ ə dent′   1
präv′ ə dent   1
präv′ i dənt   1

PROVINCIAL
prə vin′ shəl   3*
prə vin′ chəl   1

PROVISO
prə vī′ zō   4*
prə vī′ zō′   1

PROVOCATION   +
präv′ ə kā′ shən   4

PROVOCATIVE   +
prə väk′ ə tiv   4

PROVOLONE
prō′ və lō′ nē   3

PROVOST   +
prō′ vōst′   4*
präv′ əst   4
prō′ vəst   2
prō′ vō   1

PROVOST (military)
prō′ vō   3

PROXIMITY   +
präk sim′ ə tē   3*
präk sim′ i tē   1

PRURIENT
proor′ ē ənt   4

PRURITUS
proo rī′ təs   4*
proo rē′ təs   1

PSALM
säm   4*
sälm   1

PSALMIST
sä′ mist   3*
sä′ məst   1
säl′ məst   1

PSALTERY
sôl′ tə rē 4
sôl′ trē 2*

PSEUDO
sōō′ dō 4*
syōō′ dō 1

PSEUDONYM
sōō′ də nim′ 2*
sōōd′ ′n im 2
syōō′ də nim 1

PSHAW
shô 4

PSITTACOSIS
sit′ ə kō′ sis 3*
sit′ ə kō′ səs 1

PSORIASIS
sə rī′ ə sis 3*
sə rī′ ə səs 1

PSYCHE
sī′ kē 4

PSYCHEDELIC
sī′ kə del′ ik 3*
sī′ ki del′ ik 1

PSYCHIATRIC
sī′ kē at′ rik 4

PSYCHIATRIST
sī′ kī′ ə trist 4*
sə kī′ ə trist 2
si kī′ ə trist 1

PSYCHIATRY
sī kī′ ə trē 4*
si kī′ ə trē 3

PSYCHIC
sī′ kik 4

PSYCHOANALYSIS
sī′ kō ə nal′ ə sis 3*
sī′ kō ə nal′ i sis 1
sī kə wə nal′ ə səs 1

PSYCHOANALYST
sī kō an′ əl ist 2
sī kō an′ ′l əst 1*
sī kō an′ ′l ist 1

PSYCHOLOGY +
sī käl′ ə jē 4

PSYCHOSIS
sī kō′ sis 3*
sī kō′ səs 1

PSYCHOSOMATIC
sī′ kō sō mat′ ik 3*
sī kə sə mat′ ik 1

PSYCHOTHERAPY
sī′ ko ther′ ə pē 4

PSYCHOTIC +
sī kät′ ik 4

PTARMIGAN
tär′ mi gən 2*
tär′ mə gən 2

PTERODACTYL
ter′ ə dak′ til 2*
ter′ ə dak′ t′l 2

PTOMAINE
tō mān′ 3
tō′ mān′ 2*
tō′ mān 2

PUBERTY
pyōō′ bər tē 4

PUBESCENT
pyōō bes′ ′nt 2*
pyōō bes′ ənt 2

PUBIC
pyōō′ bik 4

PUCE
pyōōs 4

PUEBLO
pweb′ lō 4*
pōō eb′ lō 1
pyōō eb′ lō 1

PUERILE
pyōō′ ər əl 2*
pyoor′ əl 2
pyōō′ ər il 2
pyōōr′ il 2
pyōō′ ər īl 1
pyōōr′ īl′ 1
pwer′ il 1
pwer′ īl′ 1

PUERPERAL
pyōō ʉr′ pər əl 4*
pyōō ʉr′ prəl 1

PUGILIST
pyōō′ jə list 3*
pyōō′ jə ləst 1

PUGNACIOUS
pug nā′ shəs 4

PUISSANT
pwis′ ′nt 2*
pwis′ ənt 2
pyōō′ ə sənt 2
pyōō is′ ənt 2
pyōō is′ ′nt 2
pyōō′ i sənt 2

PUKKA
puk′ ə 4

PULCHRITUDE
pul′ kri tōōd′ 2*
pul′ kri tyōōd′ 2
pul′ krə tōōd′ 2
pul′ krə tyōōd′ 2

PULLULATE
pul′ yə lāt′ 3*
pul′ yoo lāt′ 1

PULMONARY ✓
pool′ mə ner′ ē 4*
pul′ mə ner′ ē 4

PULPIT
pool′ pit   4*
pul′ pit   4
pool′ pət   1
pul′ pət   1

PULVERIZE
pul′ və rīz′   4

PUMA
pyōō′ mə   4*
pōō′ mə   2

PUMICE
pum′ is   3*
pum′ əs   1

PUMPKIN
pump′ kin   3*
puŋ′ kin   3
pum′ kin   2
puŋ′ kən   1
pum′ kən   1
pump′ kən   1

PUNCTILIO
puŋk til′ ē ō′   4*
puŋk til′ ē ō   1
puŋ til′ ē ō′   1
puŋ til′ ē ō   1

PUNCTILIOUS
puŋk til′ ē əs   4*
puŋ til′ ē əs   1

PUNCTUAL
puŋk′ chōō əl   2*
puŋk′ choo wəl   1
puŋk′ chə wəl   1
puŋ′ chəl   1

PUNCTUATE
puŋk′ chōō āt′   2*
puŋk′ choo wāt′   1
puŋk′ chə wāt′   1
puŋ′ chə wāt′   1

PUNCTURE
puŋk′ chər   4*
puŋ′ chər   1

PUNGENT
pun′ jənt   4

PUNITIVE
pyōō′ nə tiv   2*
pyōō′ ni tiv   2

PUNY
pyōō′ nē   4

PUPA
pyōō′ pə   4

PURDAH
pur′ də   4

PURÉE
pyoo rā′   4*
pyoor′ ā   3
pyoo rē′   1
pyoor′ ē   1

PURGATIVE
pur′ gə tiv   4

PURGATORY
pur′ gə tôr′ ē   4*
pur′ gə tōr′ ē   3

PURGE
purj   4

PRONUNCIATION KEY

Symbol	Key words	Symbol	Key words	Symbol	Key words
a	asp, fat, parrot	†ə	a in ago	r	red, port, dear
ā	ape, date, play		e in agent	s	sell, castle, pass
†ä	ah, car, father		i in sanity	t	top, cattle, hat
e	elf, ten, berry		o in comply	v	vat, hovel, have
ē	even, meet, money		u in focus	w	will, always, swear
i	is, hit, mirror	ər	perhaps, murder	y	yet, onion, yard
ī	ice, bite, high	b	bed, fable, dub	z	zebra, dazzle, haze
ō	open, tone, go	d	dip, beadle, had	ch	chin, catcher, arch
ô	all, horn, law	f	fall, after, off	sh	she, cushion, dash
ōō	ooze, tool, crew	g	get, haggle, dog	th	thin, nothing, truth
oo	look, pull, moor	h	he, ahead, hotel	th	then, father, lathe
yōō	use, cute, few	j	joy, agile, badge	zh	azure, leisure
yoo	united, cure, globule	k	kill, tackle, bake	ŋ	ring, anger, drink
oi	oil, point, toy	l	let, yellow, ball	″	see p. 15.
ou	out, crowd, plow	m	met, camel, trim	✓	see p. 15.
u	up, cut, color	n	not, flannel, ton	+	see p. 14.
ur	urn, fur, deter	p	put, apple, tap	′	see p. 15.
†See p. 14.		†See p. 16.		○	see p. 14.

PURITANICAL
pyoor′ ə tan′ i kəl   2*
pyoor′ i tan′ i kəl   1
pyoor′ ə tan′ i k'l   1

PURLIEU
purl′ yo͞o   4*
pur′ lo͞o   3
purl′ yo͞o′   1

PURLOIN
pər loin′   4*
pur′ loin′   2
pur′ loin   2
pur′ loin′   1

PURPORT (n)
pur′ pôrt′   2*
pur′ pōrt′   2
pur′ pôrt   2
pur′ pōrt   1

PURPORT (v)
pər pôrt′   4*
pər pōrt′   3
pur′ pôrt′   1
pur′ pōrt′   1
pur′ pôrt   1
pur′ pōrt   1

PURSUANT
pər so͞o′ ənt   4

PURULENCE
pyoor′ ə ləns   4
pyoor′ yə ləns   3*
pyoor′ yoo ləns   1
poor′ ə lənts   1
poor′ yə lənts   1

PURVEY
pər vā′   4*
pur′ vā′   2

PURVIEW
pur′ vyo͞o   4*
pur′ vyo͞o′   1

PUSILLANIMOUS
pyo͞o′ sə lan′ ə məs   3*
pyo͞o′ s'l an′ ə məs   1
pyo͞o′ zə lan′ ə məs   1

PUSTULE
pus′ cho͞ol   3*
pus′ tyo͞ol   2
pus′ chool   1
pus′ to͞ol   1

PUTATIVE
pyo͞o′ tə tiv   4

PUTREFACTION
pyo͞o′ trə fak′ shən   4

PUTREFY
pyo͞o′ trə fī′   4

PUTRESCENT
pyo͞o tres′ ənt   2*
pyo͞o tres′ 'nt   2

PUTRID
pyo͞o′ trid   3*
pyo͞o′ trəd   1

PUTSCH
pooch   4

PUTTEE
put′ ē   4
pu tē′   3*
poo tē′   1

PUTTY
put′ ē   4

PYORRHEA
pī′ ə rē′ ə   4

PYRAMID ○
pir′ ə mid   4

PYRAMIDAL
pi ram′ ə d'l   2*
pi ram′ i d'l   1
pi ram′ ə dəl   1

PYRE
pīr   3*
pī′ ər   1

PYROMANIA
pī′ rō mā′ nē ə   2*
pī′ rō mān′ yə   2
pī′ rə mā′ nē ə   2
pī′ rə mān′ yə   1

PYROTECHNICS
pī′ rə tek′ niks   4

PYRRHIC ○
pir′ ik   4

PYTHON +
pī′ thən   4
pī′ thän   3*
pī′ thän′   1

QUA
kwā   4
kwä   4*

QUACK
kwak   4

QUAD
kwäd   4

QUADRANT
kwäd′ rənt

QUADRILLE
kwä dril′   3*
kwə dril′   3
kə dril′   3

QUADROON
kwä dro͞on′   4

QUADRUPED
kwäd′ roo ped′   3*
kwäd′ rə ped′   1

QUADRUPLE
kwä dro͞o′ pəl   3*
kwä drup′ əl   2
kwäd′ roo pəl   2
kwä dro͞o′ p′l   1
kwä drup′ ′l   1
kwäd′ roo p′l   1

QUADRUPLET
kwä drup′ lit   3
kwäd′ ro͞o plit   3
kwä dro͞o′ plit   2*
kwä drup′ lət   1
kwä dro͞o′ plət   1
kwäd′ rə plət   1

QUAFF
kwäf   4*
kwaf   4
kwôf   2

QUAGMIRE
kwag′ mīr′   3*
kwäg′ mīr′   3
kwag mī ′r   1

QUALM
kwäm   4*
kwôm   3
kwälm   1

QUANDARY
kwän′ drē   4*
kwän′ də rē   3

QUANTITATIVE
kwän′ tə tāt′ iv   4*
kwän′ ti tāt′ iv   1
kwän′ ə tāt′ iv   1

QUANTITY
kwän′ tə tē   3*
kwän′ ti tē   1
kwän′ ə tē   1

QUANTUM
kwän′ təm   4

QUARANTINE
kwôr′ ən tēn′   4
kwär′ ən tēn′   4
kwär′ ən tēn′   1*
kwôr′ ən tēn′   1

QUARRY
kwôr′ ē   4
kwär′ ē   4*

QUARTILE
kwôr′ tīl′   2*
kwôr′ tīl   2
kwôr′ t′l   2
kwôr′ til′   1
kwôr′ til   1

QUARTO
kwôr′ tō   4

QUARTZ
kwôrts   4

QUASAR
kwā′ sər   3
kwā′ sär   2*
kwā′ zər   2
kwā′ zär′   1
kwā′ sär′   1

QUASI
kwä′ sē   4
kwä′ zē   4
kwā′ sī   2*
kwā′ zī   2
kwā′ zī′   2
kwā′ sī′   2
kwā′ zē   1

QUATERNARY ✓
kwät′ ər ner′ ē   4*
kwə tur′ nər ē   4

QUATRAIN
kwä′ trān′   2*
kwä′ trān   2
kwä trān′   2

QUAVER
kwā′ vər   4

QUAY
kē   4*
kā   1

QUEASY
kwē′ zē   4

QUERULOUS ○
kwer′ yə ləs   4*
kwer′ ə ləs   4
kwir′ ə ləs   1
kwir′ yə ləs   1

QUERY ○
kwir′ ē   4

QUESTION
kwes′ chən   4*
kwesh′ chən   2

QUESTIONNAIRE ✓
kwes′ chə ner′   4*
kwesh′ chə ner′   3
kwesh′ chə nar′   1

QUETZAL
ket säl′   4*
ket sal′   1

QUEUE
kyōō   4

QUICHE
kēsh   3

QUID PRO QUO
kwid′ prō kwō′   3*
kwid′ prō kwō′   1

QUIESCENT
kwī es′ ′nt   2*
kwē es′ ənt   2
kwī es′ ənt   1

QUIETUS
kwī ēt′ əs   4

QUININE
kwī′ nīn′   2*
kwī′ nīn   2

QUINSY
kwin′ zē   4

QUINTESSENCE
kwin tes′ əns   2*
kwin tes′ ′ns   2
kwin tes′ ′nts   1

QUINTESSENTIAL
kwin′ ti sen′ shəl   1*
kwin′ tə sen′ shəl   1
kwin′ tə sen′ shəl   1
kwin′ tə sen′ chəl   1

QUINTET
kwin tet′   4

QUINTUPLE
kwin tōō′ pəl   3*
kwin tyōō′ pəl   3
kwin tup′ əl   3
kwin′ too pəl   2
kwin tōō′ p′l   1
kwin tyōō′ p′l   1
kwin′ tyoo pəl   1
kwin tup′ ′l   1

QUINTUPLETS
kwin tup′ lits   3*
kwin tōō′ plits   3
kwin tyōō′ plits   3
kwin′ too plits   3
kwin′ tyoo plits   1
kwin tup′ ləts   1
kwin tōō′ pləts   1
kwin tyōō′ pləts   1

QUIRE
kwīr   3*
kwī′ ′r   1

QUISLING
kwiz′ liŋ   4

QUI VIVE
kē vēv′   4

QUIXOTIC   +
kwik sät′ ik   4

QUOIT
kwoit   4*
koit   2
kwāt   1

QUONDAM   +
kwän′ dəm   3*
kwän′ dam   3

QUONSET   +
kwän′ sit   3*
kwän′ sət   1
kwänt′ sət   1

QUORUM
kwôr′ əm   4*
kwōr′ əm   3

QUOTA
kwōt′ ə   4

QUOTIDIAN
kwō tid′ ē ən   4

QUOTIENT
kwō′ sнənt   4

QUOTH
kwōtн   4

PRONUNCIATION KEY

Symbol	Key words	Symbol	Key words	Symbol	Key words
a	asp, fat, parrot	†ə	a in ago	r	red, port, dear
ā	ape, date, play		e in agent	s	sell, castle, pass
†ä	ah, car, father		i in sanity	t	top, cattle, hat
e	elf, ten, berry		o in comply	v	vat, hovel, have
ē	even, meet, money		u in focus	w	will, always, swear
i	is, hit, mirror	ər	perhaps, murder	y	yet, onion, yard
i	ice, bite, high	b	bed, fable, dub	z	zebra, dazzle, haze
ō	open, tone, go	d	dip, beadle, had	ch	chin, catcher, arch
ô	all, horn, law	f	fall, after, off	sh	she, cushion, dash
o͞o	ooze, tool, crew	g	get, haggle, dog	th	thin, nothing, truth
oo	look, pull, moor	h	he, ahead, hotel	tн	then, father, lathe
yo͞o	use, cute, few	j	joy, agile, badge	zh	azure, leisure
yoo	united, cure, globule	k	kill, tackle, bake	ŋ	ring, anger, drink
oi	oil, point, toy	l	let, yellow, ball	′′	see p. 15.
ou	out, crowd, plow	m	met, camel, trim	✓	see p. 15.
u	up, cut, color	n	not, flannel, ton	+	see p. 14.
ʉr	urn, fur, deter	p	put, apple, tap	′	see p. 15.
†See p. 14.		†See p. 16.		○	see p. 14.

RABBI
rab′ ī 4

RABBINATE
rab′ i nāt′ 2
rab′ ə nit 1*
rab′ i nit 1
rab′ ə nət 1
rab′ ə nāt′ 1

RABBINICAL
rə bin′ i kəl 3*
rə bin′ i k'l 1

RABELAISIAN
rab′ ə lā′ zē ən 4*
rab′ ə lā′ zhən 4

RABID
rab′ id 3*
rab′ əd 1

RABIES
rā′ bēz 4*
rā′ bē ēz′ 1

RACHITIC
rə kit′ ik 4

RACISM
rā′ siz′ əm 2*
rā′ siz əm 1
rā′ siz ’m 1

RACONTEUR +
rak′ än tʉr′ 4

RACQUET
rak′ it 3*
rak′ ət 1

RADAR
rā′ där 3*
rā′ där′ 1

RADIATE
rā′ dē āt′ 4

RADIATION
rā′ dē ā′ shən 4

RADIATOR
rā′ dē āt′ ər 4

RADII
rā′ dē ī′ 4

RADISH
rad′ ish 4*
red′ ish 1

RADIUM
rā′ dē əm 4

RADIUS
rā′ dē əs 4

RAGA
rä′ gə 4

RAGGED (adj)
rag′ id 3*
rag′ əd 1

RAGLAN
rag′ lən 4

RAGOUT
ra gōō′ 4

RAILLERY
rāl′ ər ē 4

RAJAH
rä′ jə 4

RAKISH
rā′ kish 4

RAMBUNCTIOUS
ram buŋk′ shəs 4

RAMEKIN (RAMEQUIN)
ram′ ə kin   3*
ram′ i kən   1

RAMPAGE (n)
ram′ pāj   4

RAMPAGE (v)
ram pāj′   3*
ram′ pāj   2

RAMPANT
ram′ pənt   4*
ram′ pant′   1

RAMPART
ram′ pärt   4*
ram′ pərt   3

RANCHERO ✓
ran cher′ ō   4*
rän cher′ ō   1

RANCID
ran′ sid   3*
ran′ səd   1
rant′ səd   1

RANCOR
raŋ′ kər   4*
raŋ′ kôr   1

RANCOROUS
raŋ′ kər əs   4*
raŋ′ krəs   1

RANEE (RANI)
rä′ nē   4

RANGY
rān′ je   4

RAPACIOUS
rə pā′ shəs   4

RAPACITY
rə pas′ ə tē   3
rə pas′ i tē   1*

RAPIER
rā′ pē ər   4*
rāp′ yər   2

RAPINE
rap′ in   4*
rap′ ən   1

RAPPORT
rə pôr′   2*
rə pōr′   2
ra pôr′   2
ra pôrt′   1
ra pōr′   1

RAPSCALLION
rap skal′ yən   4

RAPTURE
rap′ chər   4

RAREBIT ✓
rer′ bit   4*
rar′ bət   1

RAREE ✓
rer′ ē   3
rar′ ē   1*

RAREFY ✓
rer′ ə fī′   3*
rar′ ə fī′   1

RARITY ✓
rer′ ə tē   3*
rer′ i tē   1
rar′ ə tē   1

RASPBERRY
raz′ ber′ ē   4*
raz′ bə rē   4
räz′ ber′ ē   2
räz′ bə rē   2
raz′ brē′   1

RATHER
rath′ ər   4*
räth′ ər   4
ruth′ ər   1

RATHSKELLER
rät′ skel′ ər   3*
rat′ skel′ ər   2
rath′ skel′ ər   2

RATIO
rā′ shō   4
rā′ shē ō′   4*

RATIOCINATE   +
rash′ ē äs′ ə nāt′   3*
rat′ ē äs′ ə nāt′   2
rash′ ē ō′ sə nāt′   1
rat′ ē ō′ sə nāt′   1

RATION
rash′ ən   4*
rā′ shən   4

RATIONAL
rash′ ən ′l   3*
rash′ ən əl   1
rash′ nəl   1

RATIONALE
rash′ ə nal′   4*
rash′ ə nā′ lē   2

RATTAN
ra tan′   4
rə tan′   1*

RAUCOUS
rô′ kəs   4

RAUNCHY
rän′ chē   4*
rôn′ chē   4
roun′ chē   1

RAVAGE
rav′ ij   4

RAVEN (n)
rā′ vən   4

RAVEN (v.)
rav′ ən   3
rav′ ′n   2*

RAVENOUS
rav′ ə nəs 4

RAVINE
rə vēn′ 4

RAVIOLI
rav′ ē ō′ lē 3*
räv ē ō′ lē 2

REAGENT
rē ā′ jənt 4

REALITY
rē al′ ə tē 3*
rē al′ i tē 1

REALIZATION
rē′ ə lə zā′ sʰən 2*
rē′ ə li zā′ sʰən 2
rē′ lə zā′ sʰən 1

REALIZE
rē′ ə līz′ 4*
rē′ līz′ 1

REALLY
rē′ lē 3
rē′ ə lē 3
rē′ ə lē′ 2*
ri′ lē 1

REALM
relm 4

REALPOLITIK
rā äl′ pō′ li tēk′ 2*
rē äl′ pō′ li tēk 1

REALTOR
rē′ əl tər 4
rē′ əl tôr′ 3*
rēl′ tər 1

REALTY
rē′ əl tē 4*
rēl′ tē 1

REBATE (n)
rē′ bāt′ 2*
rē′ bāt 2
ri bāt′ 1

REBATE (v)
ri bāt′ 4*
rē′ bāt′ 2
rē′ bāt 1

REBEC
rē′ bek′ 2*
rē′ bek 2

REBEL (n)
reb′ əl 3*
reb′ ′l 1

REBEL (v)
ri bel′ 4

REBOUND (n)
rē′ bound′ 4*
ri bound′ 4

REBOUND (v)
ri bound′ 4*
rē′ bound′ 1

REBUFF (n)
ri buf′ 4*
rē′ buf 1

PRONUNCIATION KEY

Symbol	Key words	Symbol	Key words	Symbol	Key words
a	asp, fat, parrot	†ə	a in ago	r	red, port, dear
ā	ape, date, play		e in agent	s	sell, castle, pass
†ä	ah, car, father		i in sanity	t	top, cattle, hat
e	elf, ten, berry		o in comply	v	vat, hovel, have
ē	even, meet, money		u in focus	w	will, always, swear
i	is, hit, mirror	ər	perhaps, murder	y	yet, onion, yard
ī	ice, bite, high	b	bed, fable, dub	z	zebra, dazzle, haze
ō	open, tone, go	d	dip, beadle, had	ch	chin, catcher, arch
ô	all, horn, law	f	fall, after, off	sh	she, cushion, dash
o͞o	ooze, tool, crew	g	get, haggle, dog	th	thin, nothing, truth
oo	look, pull, moor	h	he, ahead, hotel	th	then, father, lathe
yo͞o	use, cute, few	j	joy, agile, badge	zh	azure, leisure
yoo	united, cure, globule	k	kill, tackle, bake	ŋ	ring, anger, drink
oi	oil, point, toy	l	let, yellow, ball	″	see p. 15.
ou	out, crowd, plow	m	met, camel, trim	✓	see p. 15.
u	up, cut, color	n	not, flannel, ton	+	see p. 14.
ur	urn, fur, deter	p	put, apple, tap	′	see p. 15.
†See p. 14.		†See p. 16.		○	see p. 14.

REBUFF (v)
ri buf′ 4

REBUKE
ri by o͞ok′ 4

REBUS
rē′ bəs 4

RECALCITRANT
ri kal′ si trənt 2*
ri kal′ sə trənt 2

RECALL (n)
rē′ kôl′ 4*
ri kôl′ 4

RECALL (v)
ri kôl′ 4

RECAPITULATE
rē′ kə pich′ ə lāt′ 3*
rē′ kə pich′ oo lāt′ 1

RECEIPT
ri sēt′ 4

RECESS
ri ses′ 4*
rē′ ses′ 2
rē′ ses 2

RECHERCHÉ ✓
rə sher shā′ 4

RECIDIVIST
ri sid′ ə vist 3*
ri sid′ ə vəst 1

RECIPE
res′ ə pē′ 3*
res′ ə pē 2

RECIPIENT
ri sip′ ē ənt 4

RECIPROCAL
ri sip′ rə kəl 3*
ri sip′ rə k'l 1

RECIPROCATE
ri sip′ rə kāt′ 4

RECIPROCITY +
res′ ə präs′ ə tē 3*
res′ ə präs′ i tē 1
res′ ə präs′ tē 1

RECITATIVE
res′ ə tə tēv′ 3*
res′ i tə tēv′ 1
res′ tə tēv′ 1

RECLAMATION
rek′ lə mā′ shən 4

RECLUSE
ri klo͞os′ 4
rek′ lo͞os′ 2*
rek′ lo͞os 2
rek′ lo͞oz 1

RECOGNIZANCE +
ri käg′ nə zəns 2*
ri käg′ ni zəns 2
ri kän′ i zəns 2
ri kän′ ə zəns 2

RECOGNIZE
rek′ əg nīz′ 3*
rek′ ig nīz′ 1

RECOLLECT
rek′ ə lekt′ 4

RECOMMEND
rek′ ə mend′ 4

RECOMPENSE
rek′ əm pens′ 4*
rek′ əm pents′ 1

RECONCILE
rek′ ən sīl′ 4

RECONCILIATION
rek ən sil′ ē ā′ shən 4

RECONDITE +
rek′ ən dīt′ 4*
ri kän′ dīt′ 2
ri kän′ dit′ 2

RECONNAISANCE +
ri kän′ ə zəns 4
ri kän′ ə səns 3*
ri kän′ i səns 1

RECONNOITER
rē′ kə noit′ ər 4*
rek′ ə noit′ ər 4

RECORD (n, adj)
rek′ ərd 4

RECORD (v)
ri kôrd′ 4

RECOUNT (n)
rē′ kount′ 4*
rē kount′ 3

RECOUNT (v)
rē kount′ 3*
rē′ kount′ 1

RECOUP
ri ko͞op′ 4

RECOURSE
ri kôrs′ 4
ri kōrs′ 3
rē′ kôrs′ 2*
rē′ kōrs′ 2
rē′ kôrs 2
rē′ kōrs 1

RECREANT
rek′ rē ənt 4

RE-CREATE
rē′ krē āt′

RECREATION
rek′ rē ā′ shən 4

RECRUDESCENCE
rē' krōō des' 'ns   2*
rē' krōō des' əns   2

RECRUIT
ri krōōt'   4

RECTITUDE
rek' tə tōōd'   3*
rek' tə tyōōd'   3
rek' ti tōōd'   1
rek' ti tyōōd'   1

RECUMBENT
ri kum' bənt   4

RECUPERATE
ri kōō' pə rāt'   4*
ri kyōō' pə rāt'   4

RECUSANT
rek' yə zənt   3
ri kyōō' zənt   2*
rek' yoo zənt   1

REDOLENT
red' 'l ənt   3*
red' əl ənt   1

REDOUBT
ri dout'   4

REDOUBTABLE
ri dout' ə b'l   2*
ri dout' ə bəl   2

REDRESS (n)
rē' dres   4*
ri dres'   3

REDRESS (v)
ri dres'   4

REDUCE
ri dōōs'   4*
ri dyōōs'   4

REFECTORY
ri fek' tər ē   4*
ri fek' trē   1

REFERABLE
ref' ər ə bəl   2*
ri fur' ə bəl   2
ref' ər ə b'l   1
ri fur' ə b'l   1
ref' rə bəl   1

REFEREE
ref' ə rē'   4

REFERENDUM
ref' ə ren' dəm   4

REFERENT
ref' ər ənt   3*
ri fur' ənt   2
ref' rənt   1

REFERRAL
ri fur' əl   4

REFORMATION
ref' ər mā' shən   4

REFORMATORY
ri fôr' mə tôr' ē   3*
ri fôr' mə tōr' ē   3

REFRACTORY
ri frak' tə rē   4*
ri frak' trē   1

REFUGE
ref' yōōj   4

PRONUNCIATION KEY

Symbol	Key words	Symbol	Key words	Symbol	Key words
a	asp, fat, parrot	†ə	a in ago	r	red, port, dear
ā	ape, date, play		e in agent	s	sell, castle, pass
†ä	ah, car, father		i in sanity	t	top, cattle, hat
e	elf, ten, berry		o in comply	v	vat, hovel, have
ē	even, meet, money		u in focus	w	will, always, swear
i	is, hit, mirror	ər	perhaps, murder	y	yet, onion, yard
ī	ice, bite, high	b	bed, fable, dub	z	zebra, dazzle, haze
ō	open, tone, go	d	dip, beadle, had	ch	chin, catcher, arch
ô	all, horn, law	f	fall, after, off	sh	she, cushion, dash
ōō	ooze, tool, crew	g	get, haggle, dog	th	thin, nothing, truth
oo	look, pull, moor	h	he, ahead, hotel	th	then, father, lathe
yōō	use, cute, few	j	joy, agile, badge	zh	azure, leisure
yoo	united, cure, globule	k	kill, tackle, bake	ŋ	ring, anger, drink
oi	oil, point, toy	l	let, yellow, ball	''	see p. 15.
ou	out, crowd, plow	m	met, camel, trim	✓	see p. 15.
u	up, cut, color	n	not, flannel, ton	+	see p. 14.
ur	urn, fur, deter	p	put, apple, tap	'	see p. 15.
†See p. 14.		†See p. 16.		○	see p. 14.

REFUGEE
ref′ yo͞o jē′   2*
ref′ yoo jē′   2

REFULGENT
ri ful′ jənt   4*
ri fo͝ol′ jənt   1

REFUND (n)
rē′ fund′   3*
rē′ fund   1

REFUND (v)
ri fund′   4*
rē′ fund′   2

REFUSAL
ri fyo͞o′ zəl   3*
ri fyo͞o′ z′l   1

REFUSE (n)
ref′ yo͞os   4*
ref′ yo͞oz   2

REFUSE (v)
ri fyo͞oz′   4

REFUTE
ri fyo͞ot′   4

REGAL
rē′ gəl   4

REGALE
ri gāl′   4

REGALIA
ri gāl′ yə   4*
ri gā′ lē ə   3

REGATTA
ri gat′ ə   4*
ri gä′ tə   4

REGENCY
rē′ jən sē   4

REGENT
rē′ jənt   4

REGICIDE
rej′ ə sīd′   4

REGIME
rā zhēm′   4*
ri zhēm′   2
rə zhēm′   2

REGIMEN
rej′ ə men′   4
rej′ ə mən   3*

REGISTRAR
rej′ i strär′   3*
rej′ i strär′   3
rej′ ə strär′   1

REGRESS
ri gres′   4

REGULAR
reg′ yə lər   4

REGULATE
reg′ yə lāt′   4

REGULATORY
reg′ yə lə tôr′ ē   4*
reg′ yə lə tōr′ ē   3

REGURGITATE
rē gur′ jə tāt′   2*
ri gur′ ji tāt′   2

REHABILITATE
rē hə bil′ ə tāt′   3*
rē ə bil′ ə tāt′   2
rē hə bil′ i tāt′   1

REHASH (n)
rē′ hash′   4

REHASH (v)
rē hash′   4

REICHSMARK
rīks′ märk′   4

REITERATE
rē it′ ə rāt′   4

REJECT (n)
rē′ jekt   4

REJECT (v)
ri jekt′   4

REJUVENATE
ri jo͞o′ və nāt′   4

RELAPSE (n)
rē′ laps   4*
ri laps′   3

RELAPSE (v)
ri laps′   4

RELATIVE
rel′ ə tiv   4

RELATIVITY
rel′ ə tiv′ ə tē   3*
rel′ ə tiv′ i tē   1

RELAY (n)
rē′ lā   4*
ri lā′   1

RELAY (v)
ri lā′   3*
re′ lā   2
rē′ lā′   1

RELEASE
ri lēs′   4

RELEGATE
rel′ ə gāt′   4

RELEVANT
rel′ ə vənt   4

RELIC
rel′ ik   4

RELICT
rel′ ikt   4*
ri likt′   2

RELIGIOSITY   +
ri lij′ ē äs′ ə tē   3*
ri lij′ ē äs′ i tē   1

RELINQUISH
ri liŋ′ kwish   4*
ri lin′ kwish   1

RELIQUARY   ✓
rel′ ə kwer′ ē   4

REMAND
ri mand′   4*
ri mänd′   1

REMEDIABLE
ri mē′ dē ə bəl   3*
ri mē′ dē ə b'l   1

REMEDIAL
ri mē′ dē əl   4

REMEMBRANCE
ri mem′ brəns   4*
ri mem′ brənts   1
ri mem′ bə rəns   1

REMINISCE
rem′ ə nis′   4

REMINISCENCE
rem′ ə nis′ 'ns   2*
rem′ ə nis′ əns   2
rem′ ə nis′ 'nts   1

REMISS
ri mis′   4

REMONSTRANCE   +
ri män′ strəns   4

REMONSTRATE   +
ri män′ strāt   3*
ri män′ strāt′   1

REMORSE
ri môrs′   4

RÉMOULADE
rā′ mə läd′   2
rā′ mo͞o läd′   1*

REMUNERATE
ri myo͞o′ nə rāt′   4

REMUNERATION
ri myo͞o′ nə rā′ shən   4

RENAISSANCE
ren′ ə säns′   3*
ren′ ə zäns′   3
ren′ i säns′   1
ren′ i zäns′   1
ren′ ə säns′   1
ren′ ə zäns′   1
ri nā′ səns   1

RENAL
rē′ n'l   3*
rē′ nəl   1

RENASCENCE
ri nās′ 'ns   2*
ri nas′ əns   2
ri nās′ əns   2
ri nas′ 'ns   2

RENASCENT
ri nās′ 'nt   2*
ri nas′ 'nt   2
ri nas′ ənt   2
ri nās′ ənt   2

PRONUNCIATION KEY

Symbol	Key words	Symbol	Key words	Symbol	Key words
a	asp, fat, parrot	†ə	a in ago	r	red, port, dear
ā	ape, date, play		e in agent	s	sell, castle, pass
†ä	ah, car, father		i in sanity	t	top, cattle, hat
e	elf, ten, berry		o in comply	v	vat, hovel, have
ē	even, meet, money		u in focus	w	will, always, swear
i	is, hit, mirror	ər	perhaps, murder	y	yet, onion, yard
ī	ice, bite, high	b	bed, fable, dub	z	zebra, dazzle, haze
ō	open, tone, go	d	dip, beadle, had	ch	chin, catcher, arch
ô	all, horn, law	f	fall, after, off	sh	she, cushion, dash
o͞o	ooze, tool, crew	g	get, haggle, dog	th	thin, nothing, truth
oo	look, pull, moor	h	he, ahead, hotel	th	then, father, lathe
yo͞o	use, cute, few	j	joy, agile, badge	zh	azure, leisure
yoo	united, cure, globule	k	kill, tackle, bake	ŋ	ring, anger, drink
oi	oil, point, toy	l	let, yellow, ball	″	see p. 15.
ou	out, crowd, plow	m	met, camel, trim	✓	see p. 15.
u	up, cut, color	n	not, flannel, ton	+	see p. 14.
ʉr	urn, fur, deter	p	put, apple, tap	′	see p. 15.
†See p. 14.		†See p. 16.		○	see p. 14.

RENDEZVOUS
rän′ dā vōō′ 4*
rän′ də vōō′ 3
rän′ di vōō′ 1
rän′ dē vōō′ 1

RENEGADE
ren′ ə gād′ 3*
ren′ i gād′ 1

RENEGE
ri neg′ 4*
ri nig′ 4
ri nēg′ 4
ri nāg′ 1

RENEW
ri nōō′ 4*
ri nyōō′ 4

RENOVATE
ren′ ə vāt′ 4

RENOWN
ri noun′ 4

RENUNCIATION
ri nun′ sē ā′ shən 4*
ri nun′ shē ā′ shən 2
ri nunt′ sē ā′ shən 1

REPARATION
rep′ ə rā′ shən 4

REPARABLE
rep′ ər ə bəl 3*
rep′ ər ə b′l 1
rep′ rə bəl 1

REPARTEE
rep′ ər tē′ 4
rep′ ər tā′ 4
rep′ är tā′ 3*
rep′ är tē′ 3

REPAST
ri past′ 4*
ri päst′ 3
rē′ past 1

REPATRIATE
rē pā′ trē āt′ 4

REPERCUSSION
rē′ pər kush′ ən 4
rep′ ər kush′ ən 2*

REPERTOIRE
rep′ ər twär′ 2*
rep′ ər twär 2
rep′ ə twär′ 2
rep′ ər tôr 1
rep′ ər twôr′ 1

REPERTORY
rep′ ər tôr′ ē 4*
rep′ ər tōr′ ē 3
rep′ ə tôr′ ē 2

REPETITIOUS
rep′ ə tish′ əs 3*
rep′ i tish′ əs 1

REPETITIVE
ri pet′ ə tiv 3*
ri pet′ i tiv 1

REPLETE
ri plēt′ 4

REPLEVIN
ri plev′ in 3*
ri plev′ ən 1

REPLICA
rep′ lə kə 3*
rep′ li kə 2

REPORT
ri pôrt′ 4*
ri pōrt′ 2

REPOSE
ri pōz′ 4

REPOSITORY +
ri päz′ ə tôr′ ē 3*
ri päz′ ə tōr′ ē 2
ri päz′ i tôr′ ē 1
′ri päz′ i tōr′ ē 1

REPOUSSÉ
rə pōō sā′ 4

REPREHENSIBLE
rep′ ri hen′ sə bəl 3*
rep′ ri hen′ sə b′l 1

REPRIEVE
ri prēv′ 4

REPRIMAND
rep′ rə mand′ 4*
rep′ rə mänd′ 3

REPRINT (n)
rē′ print′ 4

REPRINT (v)
rē print′ 4

REPRISAL
ri prī′ zəl 3*
ri prī′ z′l 1

REPRISE
ri prēz 2*
ri prīz′ 2
rə prēz′ 1

REPROBATE
rep′ rə bāt′ 4

REPROOF
ri prōōf′ 4

REPTILE
rep′ tīl 3
rep′ t′l 2*
rep′ til 1

REPTILIAN
rep til′ ē ən 4*
rep til′ yən 4

REPUDIATE
ri pyōō′ dē āt′ 4

REPUGNANCE
ri pug′ nəns 4*
ri pug′ nənts 1

REPUTABLE
rep′ yə tə bəl   3*
rep′ yo͞o tə b′l   1

REPUTE
ri pyo͞ot′   4

REQUIEM
rek′ wē əm   4*
rē′ kwē əm   2
rāk′ wē əm   2

REQUISITE
rek′ wə zit   2*
rek′ wi zit   1
rek′ wə zət   1

REQUITAL
ri kwīt′ ′l   4

REQUITE
ri kwīt′   4

RESCIND
ri sind′   4

RESEARCH
ri sʉrch′   4*
rē′ sʉrch   3
rē′ sʉrch′   1

RESERVOIR
rez′ ər vwär′   4*
rez′ ər vôr′   4
rez′ ər vwôr′   2
rez′ ə vwär′   3
rez′ ə vôr′   3
rez′ ə vwôr′   3

RESIDUAL
ri zij′ o͞o əl   2*
ri zij′ oo wəl   1
ri zij′ wəl   1
ri zij′ ə wəl   1

RESIDUE
rez′ ə do͞o′   3*
rez′ ə dyo͞o′   3
rez′ i do͞o′   1
rez′ i dyo͞o′   1

RESIDUUM
ri zij′ o͞o əm   2*
ri zij′ oo wəm   1
ri zij′ ə wəm   1

RESILIENT
ri zil′ yənt   4*
ri zil′ ē ənt   2

RESIN
rez′ ′n   2*
rez′ in   2

RESOLUTE
rez′ ə lo͞ot′   4*
rez′ ə lət   1

RESOLUTION
rez′ ə lo͞o′ shən   4

RESOLVE   +
ri zälv′   4*
ri zôlv′   2

RESONANCE
rez′ ə nəns   4*
rez′ ′n əns   1
rez′ ′n ənts   1
rez′ nəns   1
rez′ nənts   1

RESORT
ri zôrt′   4

PRONUNCIATION KEY

Symbol	Key words	Symbol	Key words	Symbol	Key words
a	asp, fat, parrot	†ə	a in ago	r	red, port, dear
ā	ape, date, play		e in agent	s	sell, castle, pass
†ä	ah, car, father		i in sanity	t	top, cattle, hat
e	elf, ten, berry		o in comply	v	vat, hovel, have
ē	even, meet, money		u in focus	w	will, always, swear
i	is, hit, mirror	ər	perhaps, murder	y	yet, onion, yard
ī	ice, bite, high	b	bed, fable, dub	z	zebra, dazzle, haze
ō	open, tone, go	d	dip, beadle, had	ch	chin, catcher, arch
ô	all, horn, law	f	fall, after, off	sh	she, cushion, dash
o͞o	ooze, tool, crew	g	get, haggle, dog	th	thin, nothing, truth
oo	look, pull, moor	h	he, ahead, hotel	th	then, father, lathe
yo͞o	use, cute, few	j	joy, agile, badge	zh	azure, leisure
yoo	united, cure, globule	k	kill, tackle, bake	ŋ	ring, anger, drink
oi	oil, point, toy	l	let, yellow, ball	″	see p. 15.
ou	out, crowd, plow	m	met, camel, trim	⸌	see p. 15.
u	up, cut, color	n	not, flannel, ton	+	see p. 14.
ʉr	urn, fur, deter	p	put, apple, tap	′	see p. 15.
†See p. 14.		†See p. 16.		○	see p. 14.

RESOUND
ri zound′ 4*
ri sound′ 1

RESOURCE
ri sôrs′ 4*
ri sōrs′ 3
ri zôrs′ 3
ri zōrs′ 2
rē′ sôrs′ 2
rē′ sōrs′ 2
rē′ zôrs′ 2
rē′ zōrs′ 2

RESPIRATION
res′ pə rā′ shən 4

RESPIRATOR
res′ pə rāt′ ər 4

RESPIRATORY
res′ pər ə tôr′ ē 3
ri spīr′ ə tôr′ ē 2*
res′ pər ə tōr′ ē 2
ri spīr′ ə tōr′ ē 1
res′ prə tôr′ ē 1
res′ pə tōr′ ē 1
res′ pə tôr′ ē 1

RESPITE
res′ pit 3*
res′ pət 1
res′ pīt′ 1

RESTAURANT
res′ tə ränt′ 4*
res′ tə rənt 4
res′ tränt′ 1
res′ tərnt 1

RESTAURATEUR
res′ tər ə tur′ 4

RESTITUTION
res′ tə tōō′ shən 3*
res′ tə tyōō′ shən 3
res′ ti tōō′ shən 1
res′ ti tyōō′ shən 1

RESTIVE
res′ tiv 4

RESTORATIVE
ri stôr′ ə tiv 4*
ri stōr′ ə tiv 3

RÉSUMÉ
rez′ oo mā′ 3
rez′ oo mā′ 2
rā′ zoo mā′ 1*
rez′ ə mā′ 1
rā′ zoo mā′ 1
rez′ ə mā′ 1

RESURGENT
ri sur′ jənt 4

RESURRECT
rez′ ə rekt′ 4

RESURRECTION
rez′ ə rek′ shən 4

RESUSCITATE
ri sus′ ə tāt′ 3*
ri sus′ i tāt′ 1

RETAIL (n)
rē′ tāl 2
rē′ tāl′ 2*

RETARDATE
ri tär′ dāt′ 2*
ri tär′ dāt 2
ri tär′ dit 1
ri tär′ dət 1

RETICENT
ret′ ə sənt 2*
ret′ i sənt 1
ret′ ə s'nt 1

RETICULE
ret′ i kyōōl′ 2*
ret′ ə kyōōl′ 2

RETINA
ret′ 'nə 4*
ret′ nə 2

RETINUE
ret′ 'n yōō′ 3*
ret′ 'n ōō′ 3
ret′ ə nōō′ 1
ret′ ə nyōō′ 1

RETORT (n)
ri tôrt′ 4*
rē′ tôrt′ 2

RETORT (v)
ri tôrt′ 4

RETORT (v)
ri tôrt′ 4

RETRIBUTION
ret′ rə byōō′ shən 4

RETRIEVE
ri trēv′ 4

RETROACTIVE
ret′ rō ak′ tiv 4*
rē′ trō ak′ tiv 1

RETROGRADE
ret′ rə grād′ 4

RETROGRESS
ret′ rə gres′ 4*
ret′ rə gres′ 3

RETROSPECT
ret′ rə spekt′ 4*
rē′ trə spekt′ 1

RETROUSSÉ
ret′ rōō sā′ 3*
ret′ roo sā′ 1
rə trōō sā′ 1

REVEILLE
rev′ ə lē 4

REVEL
rev′ əl 3*
rev′ 'l 1

REVENANT
rev′ ə nənt   4

REVENUE
rev′ ə nyo͞o′   3*
rev′ ə no͞o′   3
rev′ ə no͞o   1
rev′ ə nyo͞o   1

REVERE ○
ri vir′   4

REVERIE
rev′ ər ē   4*
rev′ rē   1

REVETMENT
ri vet′ mənt   4

REVILE
ri vīl′   4

REVOCABLE
rev′ ə kə bəl   3*
rev′ ə kə b′l   1

REVUE
ri vyo͞o′   4

REVULSION
ri vul′ shən   4

RHAPSODIC +
rap säd′ ik   4

RHAPSODY
rap′ sə dē   4

RHESUS
rē′ səs   4

RHETORIC
ret′ ər ik   4

RHETORICAL +
ri tär′ i kəl   3*
ri tôr′ i kəl   3
ri tōr′ i kəl   1
ri tôr′ i k′l   1

RHEUM
ro͞om   4

RHEUMATIK
roo mat′ ik   3
ro͞o mat′ ik   1*

RHEUMATISM
ro͞o′ mə tiz′ əm   3*
ro͞o′ mə tiz′ ′m   1

RHINITIS
rī nī′ tis   2*
rī nī′ təs   2

RHINOCEROS +
rī näs′ ər əs   3*
rī näs′ rəs   1

RHODODENDRON
rō′ də den′ drən   4

RHUBARB
ro͞o′ bärb′   2*
ro͞om′ bärb   2

RHUMBA
rum′ bə   4*
room′ bə   2

RHYME
rīm   4

RHYTHM
ri*th*′ əm   4*
ri*th*′ ′m   1

PRONUNCIATION KEY

Symbol	Key words	Symbol	Key words	Symbol	Key words
a	asp, fat, parrot	†ə	a in ago	r	red, port, dear
ā	ape, date, play		e in agent	s	sell, castle, pass
†ä	ah, car, father		i in sanity	t	top, cattle, hat
e	elf, ten, berry		o in comply	v	vat, hovel, have
ē	even, meet, money		u in focus	w	will, always, swear
i	is, hit, mirror	ər	perhaps, murder	y	yet, onion, yard
ī	ice, bite, high	b	bed, fable, dub	z	zebra, dazzle, haze
ō	open, tone, go	d	dip, beadle, had	ch	chin, catcher, arch
ô	all, horn, law	f	fall, after, off	sh	she, cushion, dash
o͞o	ooze, tool, crew	g	get, haggle, dog	th	thin, nothing, truth
oo	look, pull, moor	h	he, ahead, hotel	*th*	then, father, lathe
yo͞o	use, cute, few	j	joy, agile, badge	zh	azure, leisure
yoo	united, cure, globule	k	kill, tackle, bake	ŋ	ring, anger, drink
oi	oil, point, toy	l	let, yellow, ball	″	see p. 15.
ou	out, crowd, plow	m	met, camel, trim	✓	see p. 15.
u	up, cut, color	n	not, flannel, ton	+	see p. 14.
ur	urn, fur, deter	p	put, apple, tap	′	see p. 15.
†See p. 14.		†See p. 16.		○	see p. 14.

RIATA
rē ä′ tə 4*
rē at ə 1

RIBALD
rib′ əld 4

RIBOFLAVIN
rī′ bō flā′ vin 2*
rī′ bō flā′ vin 1
rī′ bə flā′ vin 1
rī bə flā′ vin 1

RICKSHA
rik′ shô′ 2*
rik′ shô 2

RICOCHET
rik′ ə shā′ 4*
rik′ ə shā′ 2

RICOTTA +
ri kät′ ə 3*
ri kôt′ ə 1
rē kôt′ tä 1

RIDICULE
rid′ ə kyo͞ol′ 4

RIDICULOUS
ri dik′ yə ləs 3*
rə dik′ yə ləs 1

RIGATONI
rig′ ə tō′ nē 4

RIGHTEOUS
rī′ chəs 4

RIGOR
rig′ ər 4

RIGOR MORTIS
rig′ ər môr′ tis 3*
ri′ gôr môr′ tis 2
rig′ ər môr′ təs 1

RIND
rīnd 4

RINSE
rins 4*
rints 1

RIOTOUS
rī ət əs 4

RIPARIAN ✓
ri per′ ē ən 3*
rī per′ ē ən 3
rə per′ ē ən 1

RIPOSTE
ri pōst′ 4

RISIBILITY
riz′ ə bil′ ə tē 3*
riz′ ə bil′ i tē 1

RISIBLE
riz′ ə bəl 3*
riz′ ə b'l 1

RISQUÉ
ris kā′ 4

RITUAL
rich′ o͞o əl 2*
rich′ oo wəl 1
rich′ wəl 1

RIVET
riv′ it 3*
riv′ ət 1

ROBOT +
rō′ bət 4*
rō′ bät 2

ROBUST
rō bust′ 4*
rō′ bust 4

ROCOCO
rə kō′ kō 4*
rō′ kə kō′ 3

RODENT
rōd′ 'nt 3*
rōd′ ənt 1

RODEO
rō′ dē ō′ 4*
rō dā′ ō 3
rə dā′ ō 1

RODOMONTADE +
räd′ ə män täd′ 3
rō′ də män täd′ 2*
räd ə män tād′ 2
räd′ ə män tād′ 2
rō′ də män tād′ 2
rō də mən tād′ 2

ROENTGEN
rent′ gən 4*
runt′ gən 3
rent′ jen 2
ren′ chən 2

ROGUE
rōg 4

ROGUISH
rō′ gish 4

ROMAINE
rō mān′ 4*
rə mān′ 1
rō′ mān 1

ROMANCE
rō mans′ 4*
rō′ mans 4
rō mants′ 1

RONDEAU +
rän′ dō 4*
rän dō′ 3

ROOF
ro͞of 4*
roof 4

ROOK
rook 4

ROOM
ro͞om 4*
room 4

ROOT
ro͞ot 4*
ro‿ot 4

ROQUEFORT
rōk′ fərt 3

ROSÉ
rō zā′ 4

ROSEATE
rō′ zē āt′ 4
rō′ zē it 3*
rō′ zē ət 1

ROSETTE
rō zet′ 4

ROSIN +
räz′ 'n 2*
räz′ in 2
rôz′ 'n 1

ROSTER +
räs′ tər 4

ROSTRUM +
räs′ trəm 4

ROTARY
rō′ tə rē 4

ROTATE
rō′ tāt′ 2
rō′ tāt 2
rō tāt′ 1*

ROTISSERIE
rō tis′ ə rē 4*
rō tis′ rē 1

ROTOGRAVURE
rōt′ ə grə vyo‿or′ 4*
rōt′ ə grā′ vyər 2

ROTOR
rō′ tər 4

ROTUND
rō tund′ 4*
rō′ tund 1

ROTUNDA
rō tun′ də 4

ROUÉ
ro͞o ā′ 3*
ro͞o′ ā 2

ROUGE
ro͞ozh 4

ROULADE
ro͞o läd′ 4

ROULETTE
ro͞o let′ 4

ROUNDELAY
rou̇n′ də lā′ 4

ROUT
rou̇t 4

ROUTE
ro͞ot 4*
rou̇t 4

ROUTINE
ro͞o tēn′ 4

ROWAN
rou̇′ ən 4*
rō′ ən 3

RUBELLA
ro͞o bel′ ə 4

PRONUNCIATION KEY

Symbol	Key words	Symbol	Key words	Symbol	Key words
a	asp, fat, parrot	†ə a in ago		r	red, port, dear
ā	ape, date, play	e in agent		s	sell, castle, pass
†ä	ah, car, father	i in sanity		t	top, cattle, hat
e	elf, ten, berry	o in comply		v	vat, hovel, have
ē	even, meet, money	u in focus		w	will, always, swear
i	is, hit, mirror	ər	perhaps, murder	y	yet, onion, yard
ī	ice, bite, high	b	bed, fable, dub	z	zebra, dazzle, haze
ō	open, tone, go	d	dip, beadle, had	ch	chin, catcher, arch
ô	all, horn, law	f	fall, after, off	sh	she, cushion, dash
o͞o	ooze, tool, crew	g	get, haggle, dog	th	thin, nothing, truth
o‿o	look, pull, moor	h	he, ahead, hotel	th	then, father, lathe
yo͞o	use, cute, few	j	joy, agile, badge	zh	azure, leisure
yo‿o	united, cure, globule	k	kill, tackle, bake	ŋ	ring, anger, drink
ȯi	oil, point, toy	l	let, yellow, ball	″	see p. 15.
ou̇	out, crowd, plow	m	met, camel, trim	✓	see p. 15.
u	up, cut, color	n	not, flannel, ton	+	see p. 14.
ʉr	urn, fur, deter	p	put, apple, tap	′	see p. 15.
†See p. 14.		†See p. 16.		◯	see p. 14.

RUBICON +
ro͞o′ bi kän′ 2*
ro͞o′ bi kän 1
ro͞o′ bə kän′ 1

RUBICUND
ro͞o′ bi kund′ 2*
ro͞o′ bə kund 1
ro͞o′ bə kund′ 1

RUBLE
ro͞o′ bəl 3
ro͞o′ b'l 1

RUBRIC
ro͞o′ brik 3*
ro͞o′ brik′ 1

RUCHE
ro͞osh 4

RUCKSACK
ruk′ sak′ 4*
rook′ sak′ 4

RUCKUS
ruk′ əs 4*
ro͞ok′ əs 1
rook′ əs 1

RUDIMENT
ro͞o′ də mənt 4

RUFFIAN
ruf′ ē ən 4*
ruf′ yən 3

RUIN
ro͞o′ in 3*
ro͞o′ ən 1
ro͞o′ in′ 1

RUMINANT
ro͞o′ mə nənt 4

RUMINATE
ro͞o′ mə nāt′ 4

RUNIC
ro͞o′ nik 3

RUPEE
ro͞o pē′ 4
ro͞o′ pē 4*

RUPTURE
rup′ chər 4

RURAL
roor′ əl 4

RUSE
ro͞oz 4*
ro͞os 1

RUTABAGA
ro͞ot′ ə bā′ gə 4*
ro͞ot′ ə bā gə 1
root′ ə bā′ gə 1
ro͞ot′ ə beg′ ə 1
root′ ə beg′ ə 1

RUTHLESS
ro͞oth′ lis 3*
ro͞oth′ ləs 1
rooth′ ləs 1

SABER
sā′ bər 4

SABOTAGE
sab′ ə täzh′ 4*

SABOTEUR
sab′ ə tɹr′ 4*
sab′ ə toor′ 1
sab′ ə tyoor′ 1

SABRA
sä′ brə 3*
sä′ brä 2

SACCHARIN (n)
sak′ ə rin 3*
sak′ ə rən 1
sak′ rən 1

SACCHARINE (adj)
sak′ ə rīn′ 4
sak′ ə rin 3*
sak′ ə rēn′ 1
sak′ rən 1
sak′ ə rən 1

SACERDOTAL
sas′ ər dōt′ ′l 4*
sak′ ər dōt′ ′l 2

SACHEM
sā′ chəm 4

SACHET
sa shā′ 4

SACRAMENT
sak′ rə mənt 4

SACRIFICE
sak′ rə fīs′ 4*
sak′ rə fəs 1

SACRILEGE
sak′ rə lij 4

SACRILEGIOUS
sak′ rə lē′ jəs 4*
sak′ rə lij′ əs 3

SACROILIAC
sak′ rō il′ ē ak′ 4*
sā′ krō il′ ē ak′ 4

SACRISTAN
sak′ ris tən 3*
sak′ rəs tən 1

SACRISTY
sak′ ris tē 3*
sak′ rəs te 1

SACROSANCT
sak′ rō saŋkt′ 4

SADISM
sā′ diz′ əm 2*
sad′ iz′ əm 2
sā′ diz′m 1
sad′ iz′m 1

SADIST
sad′ ist 3
sā′ dist 2*
sā′ dəst 1
sad′ əst 1

SADISTIC
sə dis′ tik 4*
sa dis′ tik 2
sā dis′ tik 2

SAFARI
sə fär′ ē 4*
sə far′ ē 1

SAFFRON
saf′ rən 4

SAGA
sä′ gə 4*
sa′ gə 1

SAGACIOUS
sə gā′ shəs 4

SAGACITY
sə gas′ ə tē 3*
sə gas′ i tē 1

SAGITTARIUS ✓
saj′ ə ter′ ē əs 2*
saj′ i ter′ ē əs 2

SAHIB
sä′ hib 3
sä′ ib 3
sä′ ēb 2*
sä′ hēb 2

SAITH
seth 3*
sā′ əth 3

SAKE (drink)
sä′ kē 4

SALAAM
sə läm′ 4

SALACIOUS
sə lā′ shəs 4

SALAMANDER
sal′ ə man′ dər 4

SALAMI
sə lä′ mē 4

SALARY
sal′ ə rē 4*
sal′ rē 2

SALIENT
sā′ lē ənt 4
sāl′ yənt 2*

SALINE
sā′ līn′ 2*
sā′ lēn′ 2
sā′ lēn 2
sā′ līn 2

SALIVA
sə lī′ və 4

SALIVARY
sal′ ə ver′ ē 4

SALMON
sam′ ən 4

SALMONELLA
sal′ mə nel′ ə 4

SALON +
sə län′ 3
sa län′ 1*

SALUBRIOUS
sə loo′ brē əs 4

SALUTARY
sal′ yə ter′ ē 3*
sal′ yoo ter′ ē 1

SALUTATORIAN
sə loot′ ə tôr′ ē ən 4*
sə loot′ ə tōr′ ē ən 3

SALUTE
sə loot′ 4

SALVAGE
sal′ vij 4

SALVE (n)
sav 4*
säv 3

SALVE (v)
salv 3*
sav 3
säv 3

SALVER
sal′ vər 4

SALVO
sal′ vō 4

SAMARITAN ✓
sə mer′ ə t′n 2
sə mar′ ə t′n 1*
sə mar′ i t′n 1
sə mar′ i tən 1

SAMBA
sam′ bə 4
säm′ bə 3*
säm′ bä 1

SAMOVAR
sam′ ə vär′ 4
sam′ ə vär′ 3*
säm′ ə vär′ 1

SAMURAI
sam′ oo rī′ 2*
sam′ ə rī 1
sam′ ə rī′ 1

SANATORIUM
san′ ə tôr′ ē əm 4*
san′ ə tōr′ ē əm 3

SANCTIMONIOUS
saŋk′ tə mō′ nē əs 4*
saŋk′ tə mō′ nyəs 1

SANCTION
saŋk′ shən 4

SANCTUARY
saŋk′ choo er′ ē 2*
saŋk′ choo wer′ ē 1
saŋk′ chə wer′ ē 1

SANCTUM
saŋk′ təm 4

SANCTUM SANCTORUM
saŋk′ təm saŋk tôr′ əm 4*
saŋk′ təm saŋk tōr′ əm 3

SANDWICH
sand′ wich 4*
san′ wich 4

SANGUINARY
saŋ′ gwə ner′ ē 4

SANGUINE
saŋ' gwin   3*
saŋ' gwən   1

SANHEDRIN
san hed' rin   2*
sän hed' rin   2
san hēd' rən   1

SANITARIUM   ✓
san' ə ter' ē əm   4

SAPIENT
sā' pē ənt   4*
sap' ē ənt   1

SAPPHIRE
saf' īr   3*
saf' ī'r   2

SARAPE (see SERAPE)

SARCASM
sär' kaz' əm   3
sär' kaz'm   1*

SARCASTIC
sär kas' tik   4

SARCOMA
sär kō' mə   4

SARCOPHAGI   +
sär käf' ə jī'   4

SARCOPHAGUS   +
sär käf' ə gəs   4

SARDINE
sär dēn'   4

SARDONIC   +
sär dän' ik   4

SARGASSO
sär gas' ō   4

SARI
sär' ē   4

SARONG   +
sə rông'   4
sə räng'   4*

SARSAPARILLA
sas' pə ril' ə   4*
sär' sə pə ril' ə   3
särs' pə ril' ə   2
sas' pə rel' ə   1
särs' pə rel' ə   1

SARTORIAL
sär tôr' ē əl   4*
sär tōr' ē əl   3

SASHAY
sa shā'   4

SASSAFRAS
sas' ə fras'   4*
sas' fras'   1

SATAN
sāt' 'n   4

SATANIC
sə tan' ik   4*
sā tan' ik   3

SATIATE
sā' shē āt'   4

PRONUNCIATION KEY

Symbol	Key words	Symbol	Key words	Symbol	Key words
a	asp, fat, parrot	†ə	a in ago	r	red, port, dear
ā	ape, date, play		e in agent	s	sell, castle, pass
†ä	ah, car, father		i in sanity	t	top, cattle, hat
e	elf, ten, berry		o in comply	v	vat, hovel, have
ē	even, meet, money		u in focus	w	will, always, swear
i	is, hit, mirror	ər	perhaps, murder	y	yet, onion, yard
ī	ice, bite, high	b	bed, fable, dub	z	zebra, dazzle, haze
ō	open, tone, go	d	dip, beadle, had	ch	chin, catcher, arch
ô	all, horn, law	f	fall, after, off	sh	she, cushion, dash
ōō	ooze, tool, crew	g	get, haggle, dog	th	thin, nothing, truth
oo	look, pull, moor	h	he, ahead, hotel	th	then, father, lathe
yōō	use, cute, few	j	joy, agile, badge	zh	azure, leisure
yoo	united, cure, globule	k	kill, tackle, bake	ŋ	ring, anger, drink
oi	oil, point, toy	l	let, yellow, ball	"	see p. 15.
ou	out, crowd, plow	m	met, camel, trim	✓	see p. 15.
u	up, cut, color	n	not, flannel, ton	+	see p. 14.
ur	urn, fur, deter	p	put, apple, tap	'	see p. 15.
†See p. 14.		†See p. 16.		○	see p. 14.

SATIETY
sə tī′ ə tē   3*
sə tī′ i tē   1

SATIRE
sa′ tīr   3*
sa′ tī′r   1

SATIRICAL   ○
sə tir′ i kəl   3
sə tir′ i k′l   1*

SATRAP
sā′ trap   3*
sat′ rap   2
sā′ trap′   1

SATRAPY
sā′ trə pē   4*
sat′ rə pē   4

SATURATE
sacʰ′ ə rāt′   4

SATURNALIA
sat′ ər nā′ lē ə   4*
sat′ ər nāl′ yə   3

SATURNINE
sat′ ər nīn′   4

SATYR
sā′ tər   4*
sat′ ər   4

SATYRIASIS
sat′ ə rī′ ə sis   4

SAUCY
sô′ sē   4*
sas′ ē   1

SAUERBRATEN
sour′ brät ′n   4*
zou′ ər brät ′n   2

SAUERKRAUT
sour′ krout′   4
sou′ ər krout′   2*

SAUNA
sou′ nə   4
sô′ nə   2*
sou′ nä   1
sô′ nä   1

SAURIAN
sôr′ ē ən   4

SAUSAGE
sô′ sij   4

SAUTÉ
sô tā′   4*
sō tā′   4

SAUTERNE
sô tʉrn′   4*
sō tʉrn′   4

SAVANT
sav′ ənt   4
sə vänt′   3
sa vänt′   2*

SAVIOR
sāv′ yər   4*
sāv′ yôr   1

SAVOIR FAIRE   ✓
sav′ wär fer′   3*
sav′ wär far′   1

SAVOR
sā′ vər   4

SAVORY
sā′ vər ē   4*
sāv′ rē   1

SCABIES
skā′ bēz′   4*
skā′ bē ēz′   2

SCABROUS
skab′ rəs   4*
skā′ brəs   3

SCALD
skôld   4

SCALLION
skal′ yən   4

SCALLOP   +
skäl′ əp   4*
skal′ əp   4

SCALLOPINE
skäl′ ə pē′ nē   4*
skal′ ə pē′ nē   3

SCAMPI
skäm′ pē   3
skam′ pē   2*

SCARAB
skar′ əb   4

SCARIFY
skar′ ə fī′   4

SCATHE
skāth   4

SCATOLOGICAL   +
skat′ ′l äj′ i kəl   3*
skat′ əl äj′ i kəl   1

SCAVENGER
skav′ in jər   3*
skav′ ən jər   1

SCENARIO   ✓
si ner′ ē ō′   4*
si när′ ē ō′   2
sə nar′ ē ō′   1

SCENIC
sē′ nik   4*
sen′ ik   3

SCEPTER
sep′ tər   4

SCHEDULE
skej′ o͞o əl   3*
skej′ o͞ol   3
skej′ əl   3
skej′ ool   2

SCHEMA
kē′ mə

SCHEMATIC
skē mat′ ik 3*
ki mat′ ik 1
kə mat′ ik 1

SCHEME
skēm 4

SCHERZO
ker′ tzō 4

SCHISM
siz′ əm 4*
skiz′ əm 2
siz′ ′m 1

SCHISMATIC
siz mat′ ik 4*
skiz mat′ ik 3

SCHIST
shist 4

SCHIZOID
skit′ soid′ 2*
skit′ soid 2
skiz′ oid 2

SCHIZOPHRENIA
skit′ sə frē′ nē ə 4*
skit′ sə fren′ ē ə 2
skiz′ ə frē′ nē ə 2
skit′ sə frēn′ yə 1

SCHIZOPHRENIC
skit′ sə fren′ ik 4*
skiz′ ə fren′ ik 2
skit′ sə frē′ nik 2

SCHLEMIEL
shlə mēl′ 4

SCHMALTZ
shmälts 4*
shmôlts 2

SCHNAPPS
shnaps 4
shnäps 3*

SCHNAUZER
shnou′ zər 4*
shnout′ zər 1

SCHNITZEL
shnit′ səl 3
shnit′ s′l 1*

SCHNOOK
shnook 4

SCHNORRER
shnôr′ ər 4*
shnōr′ ər 2

SCHNOZZLE +
shnäz′ əl 2
shnäz′ ′l 1*

SCHOONER
skoo′ nər 4

SCHOTTISCHE +
shät′ ish 4*
shä tēsh′ 1

SCHUSS
shoos 4*
shoos 2

PRONUNCIATION KEY

Symbol	Key words	Symbol	Key words	Symbol	Key words
a	asp, fat, parrot	†ə	a in ago	r	red, port, dear
ā	ape, date, play		e in agent	s	sell, castle, pass
†ä	ah, car, father		i in sanity	t	top, cattle, hat
e	elf, ten, berry		o in comply	v	vat, hovel, have
ē	even, meet, money		u in focus	w	will, always, swear
i	is, hit, mirror	ər	perhaps, murder	y	yet, onion, yard
ī	ice, bite, high	b	bed, fable, dub	z	zebra, dazzle, haze
ō	open, tone, go	d	dip, beadle, had	ch	chin, catcher, arch
ô	all, horn, law	f	fall, after, off	sh	she, cushion, dash
oo	ooze, tool, crew	g	get, haggle, dog	th	thin, nothing, truth
oo	look, pull, moor	h	he, ahead, hotel	th	then, father, lathe
yoo	use, cute, few	j	joy, agile, badge	zh	azure, leisure
yoo	united, cure, globule	k	kill, tackle, bake	ŋ	ring, anger, drink
oi	oil, point, toy	l	let, yellow, ball	″	see p. 15.
ou	out, crowd, plow	m	met, camel, trim	✓	see p. 15.
u	up, cut, color	n	not, flannel, ton	+	see p. 14.
ur	urn, fur, deter	p	put, apple, tap	′	see p. 15.
†See p. 14.		†See p. 16.		◯	see p. 14.

SCHWA
sḥwä 4*
sḥvä 3

SCIATICA
sī at′ i kə 4

SCIMITAR
sim′ ə tər 3*
sim′ ə tär 2
sim′ i tər 1

SCINTILLA
sin til′ ə 4

SCINTILLATE
sin′ t′l āt′ 3*
sin′ təl āt′ 1

SCION
sī′ ən 4

SCLEROSIS
skli rō′ sis 2
sklə rō′ sis 1*
sklə rō′ səs 1

SCLEROTIC   +
sklə rät′ ik 3*
skli rät′ ik 1

SCONCE   +
skäns 4*
skänts 1

SCONE   +
skōn 4*
skän 3

SCORBUTIC
skôr byōō′ tik 4

SCORPIO
skôr′ pē ō′ 4

SCOURGE
skʉrj 4

SCRIMSHAW
skrim′ sḥô′ 4

SCRIVENER
skriv′ nər 4
skriv′ ə nər 1*

SCROFULA   +
skräf′ yə lə 4*
skrôf′ yə lə 1

SCROTUM
skrōt′ əm 4

SCROUNGE
skrounj 4

SCRUPLE
skrōō′ pəl 3
skrōō′ p′l 1*

SCRUPULOUS
skrōō′ pyə ləs 4

SCRUTINIZE
skrōōt′ ′n īz′ 3*
skrōōt′ ə nīz′ 1

SCUBA
skōō′ bə 4

SCURRILITY
skə ril′ ə tē 3*
skə ril′ i tē 1

SCURRILOUS
skʉr′ ə ləs 4

SCUTCHEON
skuch′ ən 4

SCYTHE
sī th 4

SÉANCE
sā′ äns′ 2*
sā′ äns 2

SEBACEOUS
si bā′ shəs 4

SECKEL
sek′ əl 2*
sik′ əl 2
sek′ ′l 1

SECRETARIAL ✓
sek′ rə ter′ ē əl 3*
sek′ ri ter′ ē əl 1

SECRETARIAT ✓
sek′ rə ter′ ē ət 3*
sek′ rə ter′ ē it 1

SECRETARY ✓
sek′ rə ter′ ē 3*
sek′ ri ter′ ē 1

SECRETE
si krēt′ 4

SECRETION
si krē′ shən 4

SECRETIVE
si krē′ tiv 4*
sē′ krə tiv 3
sē′ kri tiv 1

SECULAR
sek′ yə lər 4

SEDAN
si dan′ 4

SEDATE
si dāt′ 4

SEDATION
si dā′ shən 4

SEDATIVE
sed′ ə tiv 4

SEDENTARY ✓
sed′ ′n ter′ ē 4

SEDER
sā′ dər 4

SEDITIOUS
si dish′ əs   4

SEDUCE
si do͞os′   4*
si dyo͞os′   4

SEDULOUS
sej′ ə ləs   2*
sej′ oo ləs   2

SEETHE
sēth   4

SEGUE
seg′ wā   3*
sā′ gwā   3

SEIDEL
sīd′ ′l   4*
zīd′ ′l   4

SEINE
sān   4

SEISMIC
sīz′ mik   4*
sīs′ mik   4

SEISMOGRAPH
sīz′ mə graf′   4*
sīz′ mə gräf′   3
sīs′ mə graf′   1
sīs′ mə gräf′   1

SELAH
sē′ lə   3
se′ lə   2
se lä′   1*
sē′ lä   1

SELVAGE
sel′ vij   4

SEMAPHORE
sem′ ə fôr′   4*
sem′ ə fōr′   3

SEMEN
sē′ mən   4

SEMESTER
sə mes′ tər   3*
si mes′ tər   1

SEMINAL
sem′ ə n′l   3*
sem′ ə nəl   1

SEMINAR
sem′ ə närʹ   4

SEMINARY ✓
sem′ ə ner′ ē   4

SEMITE
sem′ īt   4

SEMITIC
sə mit′ ik   4

SENESCENT
si nes′ ənt   4

SENESCHAL
sen′ ə shəl   4

SENILE
sē′ nīl′   2*
sē′ nīl   2
sen′ īl   2
sen′ īl′   2
sē′ nil   1

SENILITY
si nil′ ə tē   3*
si nil′ i tē   1

PRONUNCIATION KEY

Symbol	Key words	Symbol	Key words	Symbol	Key words
a	asp, fat, parrot	†ə	a in ago	r	red, port, dear
ā	ape, date, play		e in agent	s	sell, castle, pass
†ä	ah, car, father		i in sanity	t	top, cattle, hat
e	elf, ten, berry		o in comply	v	vat, hovel, have
ē	even, meet, money		u in focus	w	will, always, swear
i	is, hit, mirror	ər	perhaps, murder	y	yet, onion, yard
ī	ice, bite, high	b	bed, fable, dub	z	zebra, dazzle, haze
ō	open, tone, go	d	dip, beadle, had	ch	chin, catcher, arch
ô	all, horn, law	f	fall, after, off	sh	she, cushion, dash
o͞o	ooze, tool, crew	g	get, haggle, dog	th	thin, nothing, truth
oo	look, pull, moor	h	he, ahead, hotel	th	then, father, lathe
yo͞o	use, cute, few	j	joy, agile, badge	zh	azure, leisure
yoo	united, cure, globule	k	kill, tackle, bake	ŋ	ring, anger, drink
oi	oil, point, toy	l	let, yellow, ball	″	see p. 15.
ou	out, crowd, plow	m	met, camel, trim	✓	see p. 15.
u	up, cut, color	n	not, flannel, ton	+	see p. 14.
ur	urn, fur, deter	p	put, apple, tap	′	see p. 15.
†See p. 14.		†See p. 16.		○	see p. 14.

SENIORITY +
sēn yôr′ ə tē 4
sēn yär′ ə tē 4*

SENSUAL
sen′ shoo wəl 2
sen′ shoo̅ əl 1*
sench′ wəl 1
sench′ ə wəl 1
sen′ shəl 1
sen′ shoo əl 1

SENSUOUS
sen′ shoo̅ əs 1*
sen′ shoo wəs 1
sench′ wəs 1
sench′ ə wəs 1
sen′ shoo əs 1

SENTENTIOUS
sen ten′ shəs 3*
sen ten′ chəs 1

SENTIENT
sen′ shənt 2*
sen′ chənt 1
sen′ chi ənt 1
sen′ shē ənt 1

SEPARABLE
sep′ rə bəl 4*
sep′ ər ə bəl 3
sep′ ər ə b′l 1

SEPARATE (n, adj)
sep′ ə rit 3
sep′ rit 2*
sep′ rət 1

SEPARATE (v)
sep′ ə rāt′ 4*
sep′ rāt′ 1

SEPIA
sē′ pē ə 4

SEPTICEMIA
sep′ ti sē′ mē ə 2*
sep′ tə sē′ mē ə 2

SEPTUAGENARIAN ✓
sep′ choo̅ ə jə ner′ ē ən 2*

sep′ too̅ ə jə ner′ ē ən 2
sep′ too̅ wə ji ner′ ē ən 1

sep′ tyoo̅ wə ji ner′ ē ən 1

sep′ choo wə ji ner′ ē ən 1

SEPULCHER
sep′ əl kər 3
sep′ ′l kər 1*

SEPULCHRAL
sə pul′ krəl 4

SEPULTURE
sep′ əl chər 2*
sep′ ′l chər 1
sep′ əl choor 1

SEQUEL
sē′ kwəl 4*
sē′ kwel 1

SEQUENCE
sē′ kwəns 4*
sē′ kwens 1
sē′ kwents 1

SEQUENTIAL
si kwen′ shəl 3*
si kwen′ chəl 1

SEQUESTER
si kwes′ tər 4

SEQUESTRATE
si kwes′ trāt′ 3*
si kwes′ trāt 1
sēk′ wəs trāt′ 1

SEQUIN
sē′ kwin 4

SEQUOIA
si kwoi′ ə 4

SERAGLIO
si ral′ yō 3*
si räl′ yō 3
sə ral′ yō 1
sə räl′ yō 1

SERAPE (SARAPE)
sə rä′ pē 4

SERAPH
ser′ əf 4

SERAPHIC
si raf′ ik 4

SERAPHIM
ser′ ə fim′ 2*
ser′ ə fim 2

SERE ○
sir 4

SERENADE
ser′ ə nād′ 4*
ser′ ə nād′ 1

SERENDIPITY
ser′ ən dip′ ə tē 3*
ser′ ən dip′ i tē 1

SERENE
sə rēn′ 3*
si rēn′ 1

SERENITY
sə ren′ i tē 2*
si ren′ ə tē 1
sə ren′ ə tē 1

SERGE
surj 4

SERGEANT
sär′ jənt 4

SERIATIM ○
sir' ē āt' əm   2*
sir' ē āt' im   2
sir' ē ät' əm   2
ser' ē āt' əm   1
ser' ē ät' əm   1

SERIF
ser' if   3*
ser' əf   1

SERPENTINE
sur' pən tīn'   4*
sur' pən tēn'   4

SERRIED
ser' ēd   3

SERUM ○
sir' əm   4

SERVIETTE
sur vē et'   4

SERVILE
sur' vīl'   3
sur' vəl   2*
sur' vil   1
sur' v'l   1

SERVITUDE
sur' və tyōōd'   3*
sur' və tōōd'   3
sur' vi tōōd'   1
sur' vi tyōōd'   1

SESAME
ses' ə mē   3*
ses' ə mē'   1

SESQUICENTENNIAL
ses' kwi sen ten' ē əl   3*
ses' kwə sen ten' ē əl   1

SESQUIPEDALIAN
ses' kwi pə dāl' yən   2*
ses' kwə pə dā' lē ən   1
ses' kwi pi dā' lē ən   1
ses' kwi pi dāl' yən   1
ses' kwi pə dā' lē ən   1

SETTEE
se tē'   4

SEVER
sev' ər   4

SEVERANCE
sev' ər əns   3*
sev' rəns   3
sev' rənts   1

SEVERE ○
sə vir'   4

SEVERITY
sə ver' ə tē   3*
sə ver' i tē   1

SEWAGE
sōō' ij   4*
syōō' ij   1

SEWER
sōō' ər   4*
syōō' ər   1

SEWERAGE
sōō' ər ij   4*
syōō' ər ij   1
soor' ij   1

PRONUNCIATION KEY

Symbol	Key words	Symbol	Key words	Symbol	Key words
a	asp, fat, parrot	†ə	a in ago	r	red, port, dear
ā	ape, date, play		e in agent	s	sell, castle, pass
†ä	ah, car, father		i in sanity	t	top, cattle, hat
e	elf, ten, berry		o in comply	v	vat, hovel, have
ē	even, meet, money		u in focus	w	will, always, swear
i	is, hit, mirror	ər	perhaps, murder	y	yet, onion, yard
ī	ice, bite, high	b	bed, fable, dub	z	zebra, dazzle, haze
ō	open, tone, go	d	dip, beadle, had	ch	chin, catcher, arch
ô	all, horn, law	f	fall, after, off	sh	she, cushion, dash
ōō	ooze, tool, crew	g	get, haggle, dog	th	thin, nothing, truth
oo	look, pull, moor	h	he, ahead, hotel	th	then, father, lathe
yōō	use, cute, few	j	joy, agile, badge	zh	azure, leisure
yoo	united, cure, globule	k	kill, tackle, bake	ŋ	ring, anger, drink
oi	oil, point, toy	l	let, yellow, ball	″	see p. 15.
ou	out, crowd, plow	m	met, camel, trim	✓	see p. 15.
u	up, cut, color	n	not, flannel, ton	+	see p. 14.
ur	urn, fur, deter	p	put, apple, tap	'	see p. 15.
†See p. 14.		†See p. 16.		○	see p. 14.

SEXTUPLET
seks' to͞o plit   3
seks tup' lit   2*
seks to͞o' plit   2
seks tyo͞o' plit   2
seks' tyo͞o plit   1
seks tup' lət   1
seks to͞o' plət   1
seks tyo͞o' plət   1

SEXUAL
sek' sho͞o əl   2*
sek' sho͞o wəl   1
seksh' wəl   1
sek' shəl   1

SEXUALITY
sek' sho͞o al' ə tē   1*
sek' sho͞o al' i tē   1
sek' sho͞o wal' ə tē   1
sek' shə wal' ə tē   1

SHAH
shä   4*
shô   1

SHAKO
shak' ō   4
shā' kō   2*
shäk' ō   1

SHALLOT   +
shə lät'   4

SHALOM
shä lōm'   3
shə lōm'   1*

SHAMAN
shā' mən   4*
shä' mən   4
sham' ən   3

SHAMPOO
sham po͞o'   4

SHAMUS
shā' məs   4*
shä' məs   4

SHANGHAI
shaŋ hī'   4*
shaŋ' hī   2

SHANGRI LA
shaŋ' gri lä'   2*
shaŋ' grə lä'   1
shaŋ' grə lä'   1
shaŋ' grə lä'   1

SHASHLIK
shäsh' lik   4*
shäsh lik'   2

SHEATH
shēth   4

SHEATHE
shēth   4

SHEIK
shēk   3*
shāk   2

SHEKEL
shek' əl   3
shek' 'l   1*

SHELLAC
shə lak'   4

SHERBET
shur' bət   2*
shur' bit   2

SHIBBOLETH
shib' ə leth'   3
shib' ə lith   2
shib' ə ləth   2*

SHILLELAGH
shə lā' lē   4*
shə lā' lə   3

SHIRR
shur   4

SHISH KEBAB   +
shish' kə bäb'   4

SHIVAREE
shiv ə rē'   2*
shiv' ə rē   2

SHOFAR
shō' fər   4*
shō' fär   1

SHOGUN
shō' go͞on'   3
shō' gun'   3*
shō' gən   1

SHORT-LIVED
shôrt' līvd'   4*
shôrt' livd'   3
shôrt' livd'   1

SHOVE
shuv   4

SHRIVEL
shriv' əl   3
shriv' 'l   1*

SIBYL
sib' əl   2
sib' 'l   1*
sib' il   1

SIBYLLINE
sib' ə līn'   3*
sib' ə lēn'   3
sib' ə lin   1
sib' 'l īn   1
sib' 'l ēn   1

SIC
sik   4*
sēk   2

SIDDUR
sid' ər   3*
sid' oor'   3
si door'   1

SIDEREAL   ○
sī dir' ē əl   4

SIDLE
sīd' 'l 4

SIENNA
sē en' ə 4

SIERRA
sē er' ə 4

SIESTA
sē es' tə 4

SIEVE
siv 4

SIGIL
sig' il 3
sij' əl 2*
sij' il 2

SIGNATORY
sig' nə tôr' ē 4*
sig' nə tōr' ē 3

SIGNATURE
sig' nə chər 3*
sig' nə choor' 2
sig' nə toor 1
sig' nə tyoor 1

SIGNET
sig' nit 3*
sig' nət 1

SIGNIFICANT
sig nif' ə kənt 3
sig nif' i kənt 1*

SIGNOR
sēn yôr' 4*
sēn yōr' 3

SIGNORA
sēn yôr' ə 3*
sēn yōr' ə 2
sin yōr' ə 1
sin yôr' ə 1

SIKH
sēk 4

SILAGE
sī' lij 4

SILHOUETTE
sil' ōo et' 2*
sil' oo wet' 1
sil' ə wet' 1

SILICA
sil' i kə 3*
sil' ə kə 1

SILICONE
sil' i kōn' 2*
sil' ə kōn' 2

SILICOSIS
sil' ə kō' sis 2*
sil' ə kō' səs 1
sil' i kō' sis 1

SILO
sī' lō 4

SIMIAN
sim' ē ən 4

SIMILE
sim' ə lē 3*
sim' ə lē' 2

PRONUNCIATION KEY

Symbol	Key words	Symbol	Key words	Symbol	Key words
a	asp, fat, parrot	†ə	a in ago	r	red, port, dear
ā	ape, date, play		e in agent	s	sell, castle, pass
†ä	ah, car, father		i in sanity	t	top, cattle, hat
e	elf, ten, berry		o in comply	v	vat, hovel, have
ē	even, meet, money		u in focus	w	will, always, swear
i	is, hit, mirror	ər	perhaps, murder	y	yet, onion, yard
ī	ice, bite, high	b	bed, fable, dub	z	zebra, dazzle, haze
ō	open, tone, go	d	dip, beadle, had	ch	chin, catcher, arch
ô	all, horn, law	f	fall, after, off	sh	she, cushion, dash
ōo	ooze, tool, crew	g	get, haggle, dog	th	thin, nothing, truth
oo	look, pull, moor	h	he, ahead, hotel	th	then, father, lathe
yōo	use, cute, few	j	joy, agile, badge	zh	azure, leisure
yoo	united, cure, globule	k	kill, tackle, bake	ŋ	ring, anger, drink
oi	oil, point, toy	l	let, yellow, ball	"	see p. 15.
ou	out, crowd, plow	m	met, camel, trim	✓	see p. 15.
u	up, cut, color	n	not, flannel, ton	+	see p. 14.
ur	urn, fur, deter	p	put, apple, tap	'	see p. 15.
†See p. 14.		†See p. 16.		○	see p. 14.

SIMILITUDE
si mil′ ə to͞od′ 2*
si mil′ ə tyo͞od′ 2
si mil′ i to͞od′ 1
si mil′ i tyo͞od′ 1
sə mil′ ə to͞od′ 1
sə mil′ ə tyo͞od′ 1

SIMONY
sī′ mə nē 4*
sim′ ə nē 4

SIMOOM
si mo͞om′ 4*
sī mo͞om′ 1

SIMPATICO
sim pä′ ti kō′ 4*
sim pa′ ti kō′ 4

SIMULACRUM
sim′ yə lā′ krəm 3*
sim′ yoo lā′ krəm 1
sim′ yə lak′ rəm 1

SIMULATE
sim′ yə lāt′ 3*
sim′ yoo lāt′ 1

SIMULTANEOUS
sī′ məl tā′ nē əs 3
sim′ əl tā′ nē əs 2
sī′ m'l tā′ nē əs 1*

SINCERITY ○
sin ser′ ə tē 3*
sin sir′ ə tē 2
sin ser′ i tē 1

SINECURE
sī′ nə kyoor′ 3*
sin′ ə kyoor′ 3
sī′ ni kyoor′ 1

SINEW
sin′ yo͞o 4

SINGE
sinj 4

SINGULAR
siŋ′ gyə lər 4

SINISTER
sin′ i stər 3*
sin′ ə stər 1

SINUOUS
sin′ yo͞o əs 2*
sin′ yoo wəs 1
sin′ yə wəs 1

SINUS
sī′ nəs 4

SINUSITIS
sī nə sīt′ əs 4

SIPHON
sī′ fən 4

SIREN
sī′ rən 4*
sī rēn′ 1

SIRLOIN
sur′ loin′ 2*
sur′ loin 2

SIROCCO +
sə räk′ ō 4

SISAL
sī′ səl 3*
sī′ zəl 2
sī′ s'l 1
si′ səl 1

SITAR
si tär′ 4*
sə tär′ 1

SITUATION
sich′ o͞o ā′ shən 2*
sich′ oo wā′ shən 1
sich′ ə wā′ shən 1

SIZING
sī′ zing 4

SKALD
skôld 2*
skäld 2

SKEIN
skān 4

SKEWER
skyo͞o′ ər 4*
skyo͞or 1

SKIRL
skurl 4

SKOAL
skōl 4

SLALOM
slä′ ləm 4*
slä′ lōm 1

SLAUGHTER
slô′ tər 4

SLAVER (v)
slav′ ər 4*
slä′ vər 3
slā′ vər 2

SLAVER (n)
slā′ vər 4

SLAVISH
slā′ vish 4

SLEAZY
slē′ zē 4*
slā′ zē 2

SLEIGH
slā 4

SLEIGHT
slīt 4

SLEUTH
slo͞oth 4

SLIMY
slī′ mē 4

SLITHER
sli*th*′ ər   4

SLIVER
sliv′ ər   4

SLOE
slō   4

SLOTH   +
slō*th*   4*
slô*th*   4
slä*th*   3

SLOUGH (n)
slo͞o   4
slou   3*

SLOUGH (v)
sluf   4

SLOVENLY
sluv′ ən lē   4

SLUICE
slo͞os   4

SMIDGEON
smij′ ən   4

SMITHEREENS
smi*th*′ ə rēnz′   4

SMITHY
smit*h*′ ē   4*
smi*th*′ ē   4

SMOOTH
smo͞o*th*   4

SMORGASBORD
smôr′ gəs bôrd′   4*
smôr′ gəs bōrd′   3

SNIVEL
sniv′ əl   3
sniv′ ′l   1*

SNOOD
sno͞od   4

SNOOKER
snook′ ər   4

SNORKEL
snôr′ kəl   3
snôr′ k′l   1*

SNOUT
snout   4

SOBRIETY
sō brī′ ə tē   3*
sə brī′ ə tē   2
sə brī′ i tē   1
sō brī′ i tē   1

SOBRIQUET
sō′ bri ket′   2
sō′ bri kā′   2
sō′ bri kā′   2
sō′ bri ket′   2*
sō′ brə kā′   1

SOCIETAL
sə sī′ ə t′l   2*
sə sī′ i t′l   1
sə sī′ ə təl   1

SOCIOLOGY   +
sō′ sē äl′ ə jē   4*
sō′ shē äl′ ə jē   4

SOCRATIC
sō krat′ ik   4
sə krat′ ik   3*

PRONUNCIATION KEY

Symbol	Key words	Symbol	Key words	Symbol	Key words
a	asp, fat, parrot	†ə	a in ago	r	red, port, dear
ā	ape, date, play		e in agent	s	sell, castle, pass
†ä	ah, car, father		i in sanity	t	top, cattle, hat
e	elf, ten, berry		o in comply	v	vat, hovel, have
ē	even, meet, money		u in focus	w	will, always, swear
i	is, hit, mirror	ər	perhaps, murder	y	yet, onion, yard
ī	ice, bite, high	b	bed, fable, dub	z	zebra, dazzle, haze
ō	open, tone, go	d	dip, beadle, had	ch	chin, catcher, arch
ô	all, horn, law	f	fall, after, off	sh	she, cushion, dash
o͞o	ooze, tool, crew	g	get, haggle, dog	th	thin, nothing, truth
oo	look, pull, moor	h	he, ahead, hotel	*th*	then, father, lathe
yo͞o	use, cute, few	j	joy, agile, badge	zh	azure, leisure
yoo	united, cure, globule	k	kill, tackle, bake	ŋ	ring, anger, drink
oi	oil, point, toy	l	let, yellow, ball	″	see p. 15.
ou	out, crowd, plow	m	met, camel, trim	✓	see p. 15.
u	up, cut, color	n	not, flannel, ton	+	see p. 14.
ur	urn, fur, deter	p	put, apple, tap	′	see p. 15.
†See p. 14.		†See p. 16.		○	see p. 14.

SODALITY
sō dal′ ə tē 3*
sō dal′ i tē 1
sə dal′ i tē 1

SODOMITE +
säd′ əm it′ 4

SODOMY +
säd′ əm ē 4

SOFTEN
sôf′ ən 3*
säf′ ən 1
sôf′ 'n 1
säf′ 'n 1

SOIRÉE
swä rā′ 4

SOJOURN (n)
sō′ jurn 4*
sō jʉrn′ 2

SOJOURN (v)
sō jʉrn′ 4*
sō′ jʉrn 3

SOLACE +
säl′ is 3
säl′ əs 1*
sōl′ əs 1

SOLAR
sō′ lər 4

SOLARIUM ✓
sō ler′ ē əm 4
sə ler′ ē əm 2*
sō lar′ ē əm 1
sə lar′ ē əm 1

SOLDER +
säd′ ər 4*
sôd′ ər 2

SOLECISM +
säl′ ə siz′ 'm 2*
sō′ lə siz′ əm 2
säl′ ə siz′ əm 1
säl′ i siz′ əm 1

SOLEMN +
säl′ əm 4

SOLEMNITY
sə lem′ nə tē 3*
sə lem′ ni tē 1

SOLICITOUS
sə lis′ ə təs 3*
sə lis′ i təs 1
sə lis′ təs 1

SOLICITUDE
sə lis′ ə tōōd′ 3*
sə lis′ ə tyōōd′ 2
sə lis′ i tōōd′ 1
sə lis′ i tyōōd′ 1

SOLILOQUIZE
sə lil′ ə kwīz′ 4

SOLILOQUY
sə lil′ ə kwē 4

SOLIPSISM +
säl′ əp siz′ əm 2*
sō′ ləp siz′ əm 2
säl′ ip siz′ əm 1
säl′ ip siz′ 'm 1

SOLITAIRE +✓
säl′ ə ter′ 3*
säl′ i ter′ 1
säl′ ə tar 1

SOLITARY +✓
säl′ ə ter′ ē 3*
säl′ i ter′ ē 1

SOLITUDE +
säl′ ə tōōd′ 3
säl′ ə tyōōd′ 3
säl′ i tōōd′ 1*
säl′ i tyōōd′ 1

SOLON +
sō′ lən 4*
sō′ län 2

SOLUBILITY +
säl′ yə bil′ ə tē 2
säl′ yə bil′ i tē 1*
säl′ yoo bil′ ə tē 1

SOLUBLE +
säl′ yə bəl 3*
säl′ yōō b′l 1

SOMATIC
sə mat′ ik 3*
sō mat′ ik 2

SOMBER +
säm′ bər 4

SOMBRERO ✓ +
säm brer′ ō 4*
səm brer′ ō 1

SOMERSAULT
sum′ ər sôlt′ 4

SOMMELIER
sum′ əl yā′ 3*
sôm′ əl yā′ 1

SOMNAMBULIST +
säm nam′ byə list 2*
säm nam′ byoo list 1
säm nam′ byə ləst 1

SONAR
sō′ när′ 2*
sō′ när 2

SONATA
sə nät′ ə 2*
sō nät′ ä 2

SONIC +
sän′ ik 4

SONOROUS   +
sän' ər əs   4*
sə nôr' əs   4
sə nōr' əs   3

SOOT
soot   4*
so͞ot   3
sut   2

SOOTHE
so͞oth   4

SOOTHSAYER
so͞oth' sā' ər   4

SOOTY
soot' ē   4*
so͞ot' ē   4
sut' ē   2

SOPHISM   +
säf' iz' əm   2
säf' iz' 'm   1*
säf' iz əm   1

SOPHISTICATE
sə fis' tə kāt'   3
sə fis' tə kit   2
sə fis' ti kit   1*

SOPHISTICATED
sə fis' tə kāt' id   2
sə fis' tə kāt' əd   1
sə fis' ti kāt' id   1*

SOPHISTRY   +
säf' əs trē   2*
säf' is trē   2

SOPHOMORE   +
säf' ə môr'   3*
säf' ə mōr'   1
säf' 'm ōr'   1
säf' mōr   1
säf' môr   1
säf' mōr'   1
säf' môr'   1

SOPHOMORIC   +
säf' ə môr' ik   4*
säf' ə mär' ik   2
säf' ə mōr' ik   1

SOMNOLENCE   +
säm' nə ləns   4*
säm' nə lənts   1

SOPORIFIC   +
säp' ə rif' ik   4*
sō' pə rif' ik   2

SOPRANO
sə pran' ō   4
sə prän' ō   2*

SORCERER
sôr' sər ər   3*
sôrs' rər   1

SORGHUM
sôr' gəm   4*
sōr' gəm   1

SORORITY   +
sə rôr' ə tē   3
sə rär' i tē   1*
sə rär' ə tē   1
sə rōr' ə tē   1
sə rôr' i tē   1

PRONUNCIATION KEY

Symbol	Key words	Symbol	Key words	Symbol	Key words
a	asp, fat, parrot	†ə	a in ago	r	red, port, dear
ā	ape, date, play		e in agent	s	sell, castle, pass
†ä	ah, car, father		i in sanity	t	top, cattle, hat
e	elf, ten, berry		o in comply	v	vat, hovel, have
ē	even, meet, money		u in focus	w	will, always, swear
i	is, hit, mirror	ər	perhaps, murder	y	yet, onion, yard
ī	ice, bite, high	b	bed, fable, dub	z	zebra, dazzle, haze
ō	open, tone, go	d	dip, beadle, had	ch	chin, catcher, arch
ô	all, horn, law	f	fall, after, off	sh	she, cushion, dash
o͞o	ooze, tool, crew	g	get, haggle, dog	th	thin, nothing, truth
oo	look, pull, moor	h	he, ahead, hotel	th	then, father, lathe
yo͞o	use, cute, few	j	joy, agile, badge	zh	azure, leisure
yoo	united, cure, globule	k	kill, tackle, bake	ŋ	ring, anger, drink
oi	oil, point, toy	l	let, yellow, ball	"	see p. 15.
ou	out, crowd, plow	m	met, camel, trim	✓	see p. 15.
u	up, cut, color	n	not, flannel, ton	+	see p. 14.
ur	urn, fur, deter	p	put, apple, tap	'	see p. 15.
†See p. 14.		†See p. 16.		○	see p. 14.

SORREL +
sôr′ əl 4
sär′ əl 3*

SORTIE
sôr′ tē 3*
sôr tē′ 1

SORTILEGE
sôrt′ ′l ij 2*
sôr′ tə lij 1
sôr′ ti lij 1

SOTTO VOCE +
sät′ ō vō′ chē 4

SOU
sōō 4

SOUBRETTE
sōō bret′ 4

SOUFFLÉ
sōō flā′ 4*
sōō′ flā 2

SOUGH
sou 4*
suf 4

SOUPÇON +
sōōp sôn′ 1*
sōōp sän′ 1
sōōp sōn′ 1

SOUSAPHONE
sōō′ zə fōn′ 4*
sōō′ sə fōn′ 4

SOUSE
sous 4

SOUTANE
sōō tän′ 4
sōō tan′ 2*

SOUTHERLY
suth′ ər lē 4

SOUTHERN
suth′ ərn 4

SOUVENIR ○
sōō′ və nir′ 4*
sōō′ və nir′ 3

SOVEREIGN +
säv′ ər in 2*
säv′ rin 2
säv′ ər ən 1
suv′ rin 1

SOVIET +
sō′ vē et′ 3*
sō′ vē it 2
sä′ vē et′ 2
sō vyet′ 1
sä′ vē et 1
sä′ vē ət 1
sō′ vē ət 1

SOW (n)
sou 4

SOW (v)
sō 4

SPA
spä 4*
spô 1

SPANIEL
span′ yəl 4

SPARSE
spärs 4

SPARTAN
spär′ t′n 4

SPASM
spaz′ əm 3
spaz′ ′m 1*

SPASMODIC +
spaz mäd′ ik 4

SPATULA
spach′ ə lə 4*
spach′ lə 1

SPAVIN
spav′ ən 2*
spav′ in 2

SPECIALTY
spesh′ əl tē 4

SPECIE
spē′ shē 4*
spē′ sē 4

SPECIES
spē′ shēz 4*
spē′ sēz 4

SPECIOUS
spē′ shəs 4

SPECTATOR
spek′ tāt ər 4*
spek tāt′ ər 3

SPECTRAL
spek′ trəl 4

SPECTRUM
spek′ trəm 4

SPECULUM
spek′ yə ləm 4

SPELEOLOGY +
spē′ lē äl′ ə jē 4

SPELUNKING
spi luŋ′ kiŋ 4*
spē luŋ′ kiŋ 1

SPHERE ○
sfir 4

SPHERICAL ○
sfir′ i k′l 2
sfer′ i kəl 2*
sfir′ i kəl 1
sfer′ i k′l 1

SPHEROID ○
sfir′ oid′   2*
sfir′ oid   2
sfer′ oid′   2

SPHINCTER
sfiŋk′ tər   4*
sfiŋ′ tər   1

SPHINX
sfiŋks   3*
sfinks   1
sfiŋs   1

SPIEL
spēl   4*
s/hpēl   1

SPIGOT
spig′ ət   4*
spik′ ət   2

SPIKENARD
spīk′ närd′   2*
spīk′ närd   2
spīk′ nərd   2

SPINAL
spī′ n′l   3*
spī′ nəl   1

SPINET
spin′ it   3*
spin′ ət   1

SPINNAKER
spin′ ə kər   3*
spin′ i kər   1

SPINY
spī′ nē   4

SPIRAL
spī′ rəl   4

SPIRITUAL
spir′ i choo əl   2*
spir′ i choo wəl   1
spir′ i chool   1
spir′ ich wəl   1

SPIRITUOUS
spir′ i choo əs   2*
spir′ i choo wəs   1
spir′ ich wəs   1

SPIROCHETE
spī′ rə kēt′   4

SPITTOON
spi toon′   4*
spə toon′   1

SPLENETIC
spli net′ ik   4

SPOLIATION
spō′ lē ā′ s/hən   4

SPONGY
spun′ jē   4

SPONTANEITY   +
spän′ tə nē′ ə tē   3*
spän′ tə nā′ ə tē   2
spän′ tə nē′ i tē   1
spän′ tə nā′ i tē   1

SPONTANEOUS   +
spän tā′ nē əs   4

SPOOR
spoor   4*
spôr   3
spōr   2

SPORADIC
spə rad′ ik   3*
spô rad′ ik   3
spō rad′ ik   2

SPORRAN   +
spär′ ən   4
spôr′ ən   2*

SPOUSE
spous   4*
spouz   4

SPUME
spyōom   4

SPUMONI
spə mō′ nē   3*
spoo mō′ nē   1

SPURIOUS
spyoor′ ē əs   2*
spyōor′ ē əs   2

SPUTNIK
spoot′ nik   4*
sput′ nik   4
spōot′ nik   1

SPUTUM
spyōot′ əm   4*
spōot′ əm   1

SQUAB
skwäb   3*
skwôb   2

SQUALID
skwôl′ id   3
skwäl′ id   2*
skwäl′ əd   1

SQUALL
skwôl   4

SQUALOR
skwäl′ ər   4*
skwôl′ ər   2
skwāl′ ər   1

SQUANDER
skwän′ dər   4*
skwôn′ dər   1

SQUASH
skwäsh   4*
skwôsh   3

STABILE (n)
stā′ bēl′   2*
stā′ bēl   2

STABILE (adj)
stā′ bil   4
stā′ bīl′   3
stā′ bəl   1*

STABILIZE
stā′ bə līz   3*
stā′ bə līz′   2

STACCATO
stə kä′ tō   4

STADIUM
stā′ dē əm   4

STAGY
stā′ jē   4

STAID
stād   4

STALACTITE
stə lak′ tīt′   2*
stə lak′ tīt   2
stal′ ək tīt′   2

STALAG
stal′ ag   2*
stal′ əg   1
stäl′ äg   1

STALAGMITE
stə lag′ mīt′   2*
stə lag′ mīt   2
stal′ əg mīt′   2

STALLION
stal′ yən   4

STALWART
stôl′ wərt   4

STAMEN
stā′ mən   4

STAMINA
stam′ ə nə   4

STAMPEDE
stam pēd′   4

STANCH
stänch   4
stanch   3*
stônch   3

STANCHION
stan′ chən   4
stan′ shən   3*

STANZA
stan′ zə   4

STAPES
stā′ pēz′   2*
stā′ pēz   2

STAPHYLOCOCCI   +
staf′ ə lō käk′ sī   2*
staf′ ə lō käk′ sī′   2
staf′ ə lō käk′ sē′   1
staf′ ə lō käk′ ī′   1
staf′ ə lō käk′ ē′   1

STAPHYLOCOCCUS   +
staf′ ə lō käk′ əs   2*
staf′ ə lō käk′ əs   1
staf′ ə lə käk′ əs   1
staf′ lō käk′ əs   1

STARBOARD
stär′ bərd   4*
stär′ bôrd   1

STATISTICIAN
stat əs tish′ ən   2*
stat′ is tish′ ən   2

STATISTICS
stə tis′ tiks   4

STATUARY ✓
stach′ ͞o͞o er′ ē   2*
stach′ oo wer′ ē   1
stach′ ə wer′ ē   1

STATUE
stach′ ͞o͞o   4

STATUESQUE
stach′ ͞o͞o esk′   3*
stach′ oo wesk   1
stach′ ə wesk   1

STATURE
stach′ ər   4

STATUS
stat′ əs   4
stā′ təs   3*

STATUS QUO
stā′ təs kwō′   3*
stat′ əs kwō′   3
stā′ təs kwō′   1
stat′ əs kwō′   1

STATUTE
stach′ ͞o͞ot   4*
stach′ oot   2

STATUTORY
stach′ oo tôr′ ē   2*
stach′ ə tôr′ ē   2
stach′ ə tōr′ ē   2
stach′ oo tōr′ ē   1

STAUNCH
stônch   4*
stänch   4

STEAD
sted   4

STEALTH
stelth   4

STEIN
stīn   4

STELE
stē′ lē   4*
stēl   2

STENTORIAN
sten tôr′ ē ən   4*
sten tōr′ ē ən   3

STEPPE
step   4

STEREO ○
ster′ ē ō′   4
stir′ ē ō′   4*

STEREOPTICON   + ○
ster′ ē äp′ ti kän   3
stir′ ē äp′ ti kən   2*
ster′ ē äp′ tə kən   1

STEREOPHONIC   + ○
stir′ ē ə fän′ ik   3*
ster′ ē ə fän′ ik   3
ster′ ē ō fän′ ik   1
ster′ ē ō fōn′ ik   1
stir′ ē ō fän′ ik   1
stir′ ē ō fōn′ ik   1

STEREOTYPE ○
stir′ ē ə tīp′   3*
ster′ ē ə tīp′   3

PRONUNCIATION KEY

Symbol	Key words	Symbol	Key words	Symbol	Key words
a	asp, fat, parrot	†ə	a in ago	r	red, port, dear
ā	ape, date, play		e in agent	s	sell, castle, pass
†ä	ah, car, father		i in sanity	t	top, cattle, hat
e	elf, ten, berry		o in comply	v	vat, hovel, have
ē	even, meet, money		u in focus	w	will, always, swear
i	is, hit, mirror	ər	perhaps, murder	y	yet, onion, yard
ī	ice, bite, high	b	bed, fable, dub	z	zebra, dazzle, haze
ō	open, tone, go	d	dip, beadle, had	ch	chin, catcher, arch
ô	all, horn, law	f	fall, after, off	sh	she, cushion, dash
͞o͞o	ooze, tool, crew	g	get, haggle, dog	th	thin, nothing, truth
oo	look, pull, moor	h	he, ahead, hotel	th	then, father, lathe
y͞o͞o	use, cute, few	j	joy, agile, badge	zh	azure, leisure
yoo	united, cure, globule	k	kill, tackle, bake	ŋ	ring, anger, drink
oi	oil, point, toy	l	let, yellow, ball	″	see p. 15.
ou	out, crowd, plow	m	met, camel, trim	✓	see p. 15.
u	up, cut, color	n	not, flannel, ton	+	see p. 14.
ur	urn, fur, deter	p	put, apple, tap	′	see p. 15.
†See p. 14.		†See p. 16.		○	see p. 14.

STERILE
ster′ əl 2*
ster′ il 1
ster′ ’l 1

STERILITY
stə ril′ ə tē 3*
stə ril′ i tē 1

STEROID ○
stir′ oid 3*
ster′ oid 3

STETHOSCOPE
steth′ ə skōp′ 4*
steth′ ə skōp′ 1

STEVEDORE
stē′ və dôr′ 3*
stē′ və dōr′ 2
stē′ vi dôr′ 1
stē′ vi dōr′ 1

STEW
stōō 4*
styōō 4

STEWARD
stōō′ ərd 4*
styōō′ ərd 4

STIFLE
stī′ fəl 3
stī′ f’l 1*

STIGMATA
stig mät′ ə 4*
stig′ mə tə 4
stig mat′ ə 1

STILETTO
sti let′ ō 3*
stə let′ ō 1

STIMULANT
stim′ yə lənt 4

STIMULI
stim′ yə lī′ 4*
stim′ yə lē′ 2

STIMULUS
stim′ yə ləs 4

STINGY
stin′ jē 4

STIPEND
stī′ pənd 4*
stī′ pend′ 3

STIRRUP
stir′ əp 4*
stʉr′ əp 4
stur′ əp 2

STODGY +
stäj′ ē 4

STOGY (stogie)
stō′ gē 4

STOIC
stō′ ik 4

STOICISM
stō′ i siz′ əm 2
stō′ ə siz′ əm 1*
stō′ i siz′ ’m 1

STOLLEN
stō′ lən 4*
shtō′ lən 1
stô′ lən 1
shtô′ lən 1

STOMACH
stum′ ək 4*
stum′ ik 1

STOMACHER
stum′ ək ər 3*
stum′ ik ər 1
stum′ ich ər 1

STOOGE
stōōj 4

STOUP
stōōp 4

STOWAWAY
stō′ ə wā′ 4

STRAFE
strāf 4*
sträf 2

STRAIT
strāt 4

STRATA
strat′ ə 4
strā′ tə 2*
strä′ tə 2

STRATAGEM
strat′ ə jəm 4

STRATEGIC
strə tē′ jik 4

STRATEGIST
strat′ ə jist 2*
strat′ i jist 1
strat′ ə jəst 1

STRATEGY
strat′ ə jē 3*
strat′ i jē 1

STRATOSPHERE ○
strat′ ə sfir 2
strat′ ə sfir′ 2

STRATUM
strā′ təm 4*
strat′ əm 4
strä′ təm 2

STRENGTH
streŋkth 4*
streŋth 4

STRENUOUS
stren′ yōō əs 2*
stren′ yoo wəs 1
stren′ yə wəs 1

STREPTOCOCCI   +
strep′ tə käk′ sī   3*
strep′ tə käk′ sē   1
strep′ tə käk′ ē   1
strep′ tə käk′ ī   1

STREPTOCOCCUS   +
strep′ tə käk′ əs   4

STREPTOMYCIN
strep′ tə mī′ sən   3*
strep′ tō mī′ sin   1

STRICTURE
strik′ chər   4

STRIDENT
strīd′ ′nt   3*
strīd′ ənt   1

STRINGENT
strin′ jənt   4

STROBOSCOPE   +
strō′ bə skōp′   4*
sträb′ ə skōp′   2

STRONTIUM   +
strän′ tē əm   3
strän′ shəm   2*
strän′ shē əm   2
strän′ chəm   1
strän′ chē əm   1

STRUCTURE
struk′ chər   4

STRUDEL
stro͞od′ ′l   4*
shtro͞od′ ′l   1

STRYCHNINE
strik′ nin   2*
strik′ nīn   2
strik′ nēn   2
strik′ nən   2

STUCCO
stuk′ ō   4

STUDENT
sto͞od′ ′nt   3*
styo͞od′ ′nt   3
sto͞od′ ənt   1
styo͞od′ ənt   1

STUDIO
sto͞o′ dē ō′   3
styo͞o′ dē ō′   3
sto͞o′ dē ō   1*
styo͞o′ dē ō   1

STUDIOUS
sto͞o′ dē əs   4*
styo͞o′ dē əs   4

STUPEFACTION
sto͞o′ pə fak′ shən   4*
styo͞o′ pə fak′ shən   4

STUPEFY
sto͞o′ pə fī′   4*
styo͞o′ pə fī′   4

STUPENDOUS
sto͞o pen′ dəs   2*
styo͞o pen′ dəs   2
stoo pen′ dəs   2
styoo pen′ dəs   2

STUPID
sto͞o′ pid   3*
styo͞o′ pid   3
sto͞o′ pəd   1
styo͞o′ pəd   1

STUPIDITY
stoo pid′ ə tē   2
styoo pid′ ə tē   2
sto͞o pid′ ə tē   1*
sty o͞o pid′ ə tē   1
sto͞o pid′ i tē   1
sty o͞o pid′ i tē   1

STUPOR
sto͞o′ pər   4*
sty o͞o′ pər   4

STURGEON
stɐr′ jən   4

STYGIAN
stij′ ē ən   4*
stij′ ən   2

STYLUS
stī′ ləs   4

STYMIE
stī′ mē   4

STYPTIC
stip′ tik   4

SUAVE
swäv   4*
swāv   1

SUBALTERN
səb ôl′ tərn   2
sub ôl′ tərn   1*
sub′ ôl′ tərn   1

SUBDUE
səb do͞o′   4*
səb dyo͞o′   4

SUBJECT (n, adj)
sub′ jikt   4

SUBJECT (v)
səb jekt′   2*
sub jekt′   2

SUBJUGATE
sub′ jə gāt′   4

SUBLIMATE (v)
sub′ lə māt′   4

SUBLIMINAL
sub lim′ ə n′l   3*
sub lī′ mə nəl   1
səb lim′ ə n′l   1
sub′ lim′ ə n′l   1

SUBLIMITY
sə blim′ ə tē   3*
sə blim′ i tē   1

SUBLUNARY ✓
sub lo͞on′ ər ē   3*
sub′ loo ner′ ē   3

SUBORDINATE (adj, n)
sə bôr′ də nit   2
sə bôrd′ ′n it   1*
sə bôrd′ ′n ət   1
sə bôrd′ nət   1

SUBORDINATE (v)
sə bôrd′ ′n āt′   2*
sə bôr′ də nāt′   2

SUBORN
sə bôrn   4

SUBORNATION
sub′ ôr nā′ shən   3*
sub′ ər nā′ shən   1

SUBPOENA
sə pē′ nə   4*
səb pē′ nə   1

SUB ROSA
sub rō′ zə   4

SUBSEQUENT
sub′ sə kwənt   3*
sub′ si kwənt   1

SUBSERVIENT
səb sɐr′ vē ənt   4

SUBSIDIARY ✓
səb sid′ ē er′ ē   3*
səb sid′ ē ar′ ē   1
səb sid′ ə rē   1

SUBSIDY
sub′ sə dē   3*
sub′ si dē   1
sub′ zə dē   1

SUBSTANTIATE
səb stan′ shē āt′   3*
səb stan′ chē āt′   1

SUBSTANTIVE
sub′ stən tiv   4*

SUBSTITUTE
sub′ stə to͞ot′   3*
sub′ stə tyo͞ot′   3
sub′ sti to͞ot′   1
sub′ sti tyo͞ot′   1

SUBSTRATUM
sub′ strāt′ əm   4*
sub′ strat′ əm   4

SUBSUME
səb so͞om′   3*
sub so͞om′   1
sub syo͞om′   1

SUBTERFUGE
sub′ tər fyo͞oj′   4

SUBTERRANEAN
sub′ tə rā′ nē ən   4*
sub′ tə rā′ nyən   1

SUBTLE
sut′ ′l   4

SUBTLETY
sut′ ′l tē   4

SUBURB
sub′ ərb   3*
sub′ ɐrb   1

SUBURBAN
sə bur′ bən   4

SUBURBIA
sə bur′ bē ə   4

SUBVERSION
səb vur′ zhən   4*
səb vur′ shən   4

SUCCINCT
sək siŋkt′   4

SUCCOR
suk′ ər   4

SUCCUBUS
suk′ yə bəs   3*
suk′ yoo bəs   1

SUCCULENT
suk′ yə lənt   3*
suk′ yoo lənt   1

SUCCUMB
sə kum′   4

SUEDE
swād   4

SUET
soo′ it   3*
syoo′ it   1
soo′ ət   1

SUFFICE
sə fīs′   4*
sə fīz′   3

SUFFRAGE
suf′ rij   4

SUFFRAGETTE
suf′ rə jet′   3*
suf′ ri jet′   1

SUFFUSE
sə fyooz′   4

SUGGEST
səg jest′   4*
sə jest′   4

SUICIDAL
soo′ i sīd′ ′l   2*
soo′ ə sīd′ ′l   2
syoo′ ə sīd′ ′l   2

SUICIDE
soo′ ə sīd′   3*
syoo′ ə sīd′   2
soo′ i sīd′   1

SUITE
swēt   4*
soot (furniture set)   4

SUKIYAKI
soo′ kē yä′ kē   2*
soo′ kē yä′ kē   1
skē äk′ ē   1

SULFUR (SULPHUR)
sul′ fər   4

SULFURIC (SULPHURIC)
sul fyoor′ ik   2*
sul′ fyoor′ ik   2

SULTAN
sul′ t'n   3*
sul′ tən   1
sul′ tan′   1
sool tän′   1

PRONUNCIATION KEY

Symbol	Key words	Symbol	Key words	Symbol	Key words
a	asp, fat, parrot	†ə	a in ago	r	red, port, dear
ā	ape, date, play		e in agent	s	sell, castle, pass
†ä	ah, car, father		i in sanity	t	top, cattle, hat
e	elf, ten, berry		o in comply	v	vat, hovel, have
ē	even, meet, money		u in focus	w	will, always, swear
i	is, hit, mirror	ər	perhaps, murder	y	yet, onion, yard
ī	ice, bite, high	b	bed, fable, dub	z	zebra, dazzle, haze
ō	open, tone, go	d	dip, beadle, had	ch	chin, catcher, arch
ô	all, horn, law	f	fall, after, off	sh	she, cushion, dash
oo	ooze, tool, crew	g	get, haggle, dog	th	thin, nothing, truth
oo	look, pull, moor	h	he, ahead, hotel	th	then, father, lathe
yoo	use, cute, few	j	joy, agile, badge	zh	azure, leisure
yoo	united, cure, globule	k	kill, tackle, bake	ŋ	ring, anger, drink
oi	oil, point, toy	l	let, yellow, ball	″	see p. 15.
ou	out, crowd, plow	m	met, camel, trim	✓	see p. 15.
u	up, cut, color	n	not, flannel, ton	+	see p. 14.
ur	urn, fur, deter	p	put, apple, tap	′	see p. 15.
†See p. 14.		†See p. 16.		○	see p. 14.

SULTANA
sul tan′ ə 4*
sul tän′ ə 3
sool tän′ ə 1

SULTANATE
sul′ t′n āt′ 3*
sul′ t′n it 1
sul′ tən āt′ 1
sul′ tən it 1
sul tan′ ət 1
sool tän′ ət 1

SUMAC
so͞o′ mak′ 2*
sho͞o′ mak′ 2
sho͞o′ mak 2
so͞o′ mak 2

SUMMARILY ✓
sum′ ər ə lē 3*
sə mer′ ə lē 3
sə mar′ ə lē 1
sum′ rə lē 1

SUMPTUOUS
sump′ cho͞o əs 2*
sump′ choo wəs 1
sump′ chəs 1
sump′ chə wəs 1
sumpsh′ wəs 1
sumsh′ wəs 1

SUNDAE
sun′ dē 4*
sun′ dā 4

SUPERANNUATED
so͞o′ pər an′ yə wāt əd 1*
so͞o′ pər an′ yo͞o wāt′ id 1
so͞o′ pər an′ yo͞o ā′ tid 2

SUPERB
soo purb′ 4*
sə purb′ 2
so͞o purb′ 2

SUPERCILIOUS
so͞o′ pər sil′ ē əs 4*
so͞o′ pər sil′ yəs 1

SUPEREROGATION
so͞o′ pər er′ ə gā′ shən 4

SUPEREROGATORY +
so͞o′ pər ə räg′ ə tôr′ ē 2*
so͞o′ pər ə räg′ ə tōr′ ē 2
so͞o′ pər i räg′ ə tôr′ ē 2
so͞o′ pər i räg′ ə tōr′ ē 1

SUPERFICIAL
so͞o′ pər fish′ əl 4

SUPERFLUITY
so͞o′ pər flo͞o′ ə tē 3*
so͞o′ pər flo͞o′ i tē 1

SUPERFLUOUS
soo pur′ flo͞o əs 1*
soo pur′ flə wəs 1
soo pur′ floo wəs 1
soo pur′ floo əs 1

SUPERINTENDENT
so͞o′ pər in ten′ dənt 3*
so͞o′ prin ten′ dənt 2

SUPERLATIVE
soo pur′ lə tiv 4*
sə pur′ lə tiv 2

SUPERNUMERARY ✓
so͞o′ pər no͞o′ mə rer′ ē 3*
so͞o′ pər nyo͞o′ mə rer′ ē 2
so͞o′ pər no͞o′ mə rar′ ē 1
so͞o′ pər nyo͞o′ mə rar′ ē 1
so͞o′ pər no͞om′ rē 1
so͞o′ pər nyo͞om′ rē 1

SUPERSTITION
so͞o′ pər stish′ ən 4

SUPINE
soo pīn′ 2
so͞o′ pīn′ 1*
so͞o′ pīn′ 1
so͞o pīn′ 1

SUPPLANT
sə plant′ 4*
sə plänt′ 2

SUPPLE
sup′ əl 3
sup′ ′l 1*

SUPPLEMENT (n)
sup′ lə mənt 4

SUPPLEMENT (v)
sup′ lə ment′ 4

SUPPLEMENTARY
sup′ lə men′ tər ē 4*
sup′ lə men′ trē 2

SUPPLIANT
sup′ lē ənt 3*
sup′ li ənt 1

SUPPLICANT
sup′ li kənt 2*
sup′ lə kənt 2

SUPPOSITORY +
sə päz′ ə tôr′ ē 2*
sə päz′ ə tōr′ ē 1
sə päz′ i tōr′ ē 1
sə päz′ i tôr′ ē 1
sə pôz′ ə tôr′ ē 1
sə pôz′ ə tōr′ ē 1

SUPPURATE
sup′ yə rāt′ 3
sup′ yoo rāt′ 1

SUPREMACIST
sə prem′ ə sist 3*
soo prem′ ə sist 2
soo prem′ ə səst 1

SUPREMACY
sə prem′ ə sē   3*
soo prem′ ə sē   3

SUPREME
sə prēm′   3*
soo prēm′   3

SURAH
soor′ ə   4

SURCEASE
sur′ sēs   3*
sər sēs′   2

SURCINGLE
sur′ siŋ′ gəl   3
sur′ siŋ′ g'l   1*

SURETY
shoor′ ə tē   3*
shoor′ tē   3
shoor′ i tē   1

SURFEIT
sur′ fit   3*
sur′ fət   1

SURMISE (n)
sər mīz′   4*
sur′ mīz   3

SURMISE (v)
sər mīz′   4

SURPLICE
sur′ plis   3*
sur′ pləs   1

SURPLUS
sur′ pləs   4
sur′ plus   3*

SURPRISE
sər prīz′   4*
sə prīz   1

SURREALISM
sə rē′ ə liz′ əm   3*
sə rē′ ə liz′m   1

SURREPTITIOUS
sur′ əp tish′ əs   4*
sə rep′ tish′ əs   1

SURREY
sur′ ē   4

SURROGATE (n, adj)
sur′ ə gāt′   4
sur′ ə git   2*

SURVEILLANCE
sər vā′ ləns   4*
sər vāl′ yəns   3
sər vā′ lənts   1

SURVEY (n)
sur′ vā′   2*
sər vā   2

SURVEY (v)
sər vā′   4*
sur′ vā′   2

SUSCEPTIBLE
sə sep′ tə bəl   3
sə sep′ tə b'l   1*

SUSPECT (n, adj)
sus′ pekt   3
sus′ pekt′   2*

SUSPECT (v)
sə spekt′   4

PRONUNCIATION KEY

Symbol	Key words	Symbol	Key words	Symbol	Key words
a	asp, fat, parrot	†ə	a in ago	r	red, port, dear
ā	ape, date, play		e in agent	s	sell, castle, pass
†ä	ah, car, father		i in sanity	t	top, cattle, hat
e	elf, ten, berry		o in comply	v	vat, hovel, have
ē	even, meet, money		u in focus	w	will, always, swear
i	is, hit, mirror	ər	perhaps, murder	y	yet, onion, yard
ī	ice, bite, high	b	bed, fable, dub	z	zebra, dazzle, haze
ō	open, tone, go	d	dip, beadle, had	ch	chin, catcher, arch
ô	all, horn, law	f	fall, after, off	sh	she, cushion, dash
o͞o	ooze, tool, crew	g	get, haggle, dog	th	thin, nothing, truth
oo	look, pull, moor	h	he, ahead, hotel	th	then, father, lathe
yo͞o	use, cute, few	j	joy, agile, badge	zh	azure, leisure
yoo	united, cure, globule	k	kill, tackle, bake	ŋ	ring, anger, drink
oi	oil, point, toy	l	let, yellow, ball	′′	see p. 15.
ou	out, crowd, plow	m	met, camel, trim	✓	see p. 15.
u	up, cut, color	n	not, flannel, ton	+	see p. 14.
ur	urn, fur, deter	p	put, apple, tap	′	see p. 15.
†See p. 14.		†See p. 16.		○	see p. 14.

SUSURRUS
soo sur' əs   4

SUTTEE
su' tē'   2*
su tē'   2
su' tē   2
su' tē'   2

SUTURE
soo' chər   4

SVELTE
svelt   3*
sfelt   3

SWAMI
swä' mē

SWARD
swôrd   4

SWARTHY
swôr' t͟hē   4*
swôr' t͟hē   3

SWASTIKA   +
swäs' ti kə   4*
swä stē' kə   2

SWATH
swôt͟h   4
swät͟h   3*

SWATHE
swät͟h   3*
swāt͟h   3
swôt͟h   1

SWINISH
swīn' ish   4

SWIVEL
swiv' əl   3
swiv' 'l   1*

SYBARITE
sib' ə rīt'   3*
sib' ə rīt   1

SYCAMORE
sik' ə môr'   4*
sik' ə mōr'   3

SYCOPHANCY
sik' ə fən sē   4

SYCOPHANT
sik' ə fənt   4

SYLLABLE
sil' ə bəl   3
sil' ə b'l   1*

SYLLABUS
sil' ə bəs   4

SYLLOGISM
sil' ə jiz' əm   3*
sil' ə jiz' 'm   1

SYLPH
silf   4

SYMBIOSIS
sim' bī ō' sis   3*
sim' bē ō' sis   3
sim' bī' ō' səs   1
sim' bi ō' sis   1

SYMBIOTIC   +
sim' bī ät' ik   4*
sim' bē ät' ik   3
sim' bi ät' ik   1

SYMBOLIC   +
sim bäl' ik   4

SYMMETRICAL
sə met' ri kəl   2
si met' ri k'l   1*
si met' ri kəl   1

SYMMETRY
sim' ə trē   3
sim' i trē   1*

SYMPHONIC   +
sim fän' ik   4

SYMPOSIUM
sim pō' zē əm   4*
sim pō' z͟həm   1

SYNAGOGUE   +
sin' ə gäg'   3*
sin' ə gôg'   1
sin' i gäg'   1

SYNAPSE
sin' aps   2
si naps'   2
sin' aps'   1*
sə naps'   1

SYNCHRONIZE
siŋ' krə nīz'   4*
sin' krə nīz'   2

SYNCOPATE
siŋ' kə pāt'   4*
sin' kə pāt'   3

SYNDICALISM
sin' di kə liz' əm   3*
sin' di k'l iz'm   1

SYNDICATE (n)
sin' də kit   2*
sin' di kit   1
sin' di kət   1

SYNDICATE (v)
sin' də kāt'   3*
sin' di kāt'   1

SYNDROME
sin' drōm'   2*
sin' drōm   2
sin' drə mē   1
sin' drəm   1

SYNOD
sin' əd   4

SYNONYM
sin' ə nim   2*
sin' ə nim'   2

SYNONYMOUS +
si nän' ə məs 4

SYNOPSIS +
si näp' sis 3*
si näp' səs 1

SYNTHESIS
sin' thə sis 2*
sin' thi sis 1
sin' thə səs 1
sint' thə səs 1

SYNTHETIC
sin thet' ik 4

SYPHILIS
sif' ə lis 3*
sif' ə ləs 1
sif' ləs 1

SYRINGE ○
sə rinj' 4*
sir' inj 3

SYRUP
sir' əp 4*
sur' əp 4

SYSTEMIC
si stem' ik 4

SYSTOLE
sis' tə lē 3*
sis' tə lē' 3

SYSTOLIC +
sis täl' ik 4

PRONUNCIATION KEY

Symbol	Key words	Symbol	Key words	Symbol	Key words
a	asp, fat, parrot	†ə	a in ago	r	red, port, dear
ā	ape, date, play		e in agent	s	sell, castle, pass
†ä	ah, car, father		i in sanity	t	top, cattle, hat
e	elf, ten, berry		o in comply	v	vat, hovel, have
ē	even, meet, money		u in focus	w	will, always, swear
i	is, hit, mirror	ər	perhaps, murder	y	yet, onion, yard
ī	ice, bite, high	b	bed, fable, dub	z	zebra, dazzle, haze
ō	open, tone, go	d	dip, beadle, had	ch	chin, catcher, arch
ô	all, horn, law	f	fall, after, off	sh	she, cushion, dash
oo	ooze, tool, crew	g	get, haggle, dog	th	thin, nothing, truth
oo	look, pull, moor	h	he, ahead, hotel	th	then, father, lathe
yoo	use, cute, few	j	joy, agile, badge	zh	azure, leisure
yoo	united, cure, globule	k	kill, tackle, bake	ŋ	ring, anger, drink
oi	oil, point, toy	l	let, yellow, ball	''	see p. 15.
ou	out, crowd, plow	m	met, camel, trim	✓	see p. 15.
u	up, cut, color	n	not, flannel, ton	+	see p. 14.
ur	urn, fur, deter	p	put, apple, tap	'	see p. 15.
†See p. 14.		†See p. 16.		○	see p. 14.

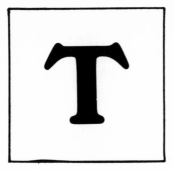

TABERNACLE
tab′ ər nak′ əl   3
tab′ ər nak″l   1*

TABLATURE
tab′ lə chər   3*
tab′ lə choor′   2
tab′ lə toor′   1
tab′ lə tyoor′   1
tab′ lə tər   1

TABLEAU
ta blō′   4*
tab′ lō   2

TABLEAUX
ta blōz′   4*
tab′ lōz   2

TABLE D'HÔTE
tä′ bəl dōt′   3*
tab′ əl dōt   1
tab əl dōt′   1
tab′ əl dōt′   1
tä′ b'l dōt′   1
tab′ 'l dōt′   1

TABOO
ta bo͞o′   4*
tə bo͞o′   4

TABOR
tā′ bər   4

TABORET
tab′ ə ret′   4*
tab′ ə rā′   2
tab′ ə rit   2

TABULAR
tab′ yə lər   4

TACHISTOSCOPE
tə kis′ tə skōp′   4

TACHOMETER   +
tə käm′ ə tər   3
ta käm′ ə tər   2*
tə käm′ i tər   1

TACHYCARDIA
tak′ i kär′ dē ə   3*
tak′ ə kär′ dē ə   1

TACIT
tas′ it   3*
tas′ ət   1

TACITURN
tas′ ə tərn   3*
tas′ i turn′   1

TACO
tä′ kō   4

TACTILE
tak′ t'l   2*
tak′ tīl′   2
tak′ təl   1
tak′ til   1
tak′ tīl   1

TAFFETA
taf′ ə tə   2*
taf′ i tə   2

TAFFRAIL
taf′ rāl′   4*
taf′ rəl   2

TALER (THALER)
tä′ lər   4

TALESMAN
tālz′ mən   4*
tā′ lēz mən   4

TALISMAN
tal′ iz mən   3*
tal′ is mən   3
tal′ əs mən   1
tal′ əz mən   1

TALLYHO
tal′ ē hō′   4

TALMUD
tal′ məd   4
täl′ mood′   3
täl′ məd   2*
tal′ mood   2
täl′ mood   1

TALON
tal′ ən   4

TAMALE
tə mä′ lē   4

TAMARACK
tam′ ə rak′   4

TAMARIND
tam′ ə rind   2
tam′ ə rind′   2*
tam′ ə rənd   1

TAMARISK
tam′ ə risk   2
tam′ ə risk′   2*

TAMBOUR
tam′ boor′   3
tam boor′   2*
tam′ boor   1

TAMBOURINE
tam′ bə rēn′   4

TAMPON   +
tam′ pän′   2*
tam′ pän   2

TANDEM
tan′ dəm   4

TANAGER
tan′ ə jər   2*
tan′ i jər   2

TANGENT
tan′ jənt   4

TANGENTIAL
tan jen′ shəl   3*
tan jen′ chəl   1

TANGERINE
tan′ jə rēn′   4*
tan′ jə rēn′   2

TANGIBLE
tan′ jə bəl   3
tan′ jə b'l   1*

TANGO
taŋ′ gō   4*
taŋ′ gō′   1

TANTAMOUNT
tan′ tə mount′   4

TANTIVY
tan tiv′ ē   4

TANTRUM
tan′ trəm   4

TAPER
tā pər   4

TAPESTRY
tap′ i strē   3*
tap′ ə strē   1

TAPIOCA
tap′ ē ō′ kə   4

TAPIR   ○
tā′ pər   4*
tə pir′   2

TARANTELLA
tar ən tel′ ə   4

TARANTULA
tə ran′ chə lə   2*
tə ran′ choo lə   2
tə ranch′ lə   1
tə ran′ t'l ə   1

TAROT
tar′ ō   2*
ta rō′   2
tar′ ət   1

TARPAULIN
tär′ pə lin   4*
tär pô′ lin   3
tär pô′ lən   1

TARPON   +
tär′ pən   4*
tär′ pän   1

TARRAGON   +
tar′ ə gən   3*
tar′ ə gän′   2
tar′ ə gän   2

TARTAN
tär′ t'n   4

TARTAR
tär′ tər   4

TASSEL
tas′ əl   3*
tas′ 'l   1

TATTERDEMALION
tat′ ər di māl′ yən   3*
tat′ ər di mal′ yən   3
tat′ ər di māl′ ē ən   2
tat′ ər di mal′ ē ən   2

TATTERSALL
tat′ ər sôl′   4*
tat′ ər səl   2

TATTOO
ta tōō′   4

TAUNT
tônt   4*
tänt   3

TAUPE
tōp   4

TAURUS
tôr′ əs   4

TAUT
tôt   4

TAUTOLOGY   +
tô täl′ ə jē   4

TAXIDERMIST
tak′ si dʉr′ mist   2*
tak′ sə dʉr′ mist   2

TAXIDERMY
tak′ si dʉr′ mē   2*
tak′ sə dʉr′ mē   2

TAXONOMY   +
tak sän′ ə mē   4

TAWDRY
tô′ drē   4

TEAR (weep)   ○
tir   4

TEAR (rend)   ✓
ter   4*
tar   1

TEAT
tēt   4*
tit   4

TECHNICIAN
tek′ nish′ ən   3*
tek nish′ ən   1

TECHNIQUE
tek nēk′   4

TECHNOCRACY   +
tek näk′ rə sē   4

TEDIOUS
tē′ dē əs   4*
tē′ jəs   2

TEDIUM
tē dē əm   4

TEETHE
tee*th*   4

TEETOTALER
tē′ tōt′ ′l ər   4*
tē′ tōt ′l ər   1

TEGUMENT
teg′ yə mənt   3*
teg′ yoo mənt   1

TELEGRAPHER
tə leg′ rə fər   4

TELEGRAPHY
tə leg′ rə fē   4

TELEOLOGY   +
tel′ ē äl′ ə jē   4
tē′ lē äl′ ə jē   2*
tē lē äl′ ə jē   2

TELEPATHIC
tel′ ə path′ ik   4

TELEPATHY
tə lep′ ə th*ē*   4

TELEPHONIC   +
tel′ ə fän′ ik   4

TELEPHOTO
tel′ ə fōt′ ō   3*
tel′ ə fōt′ ō   1

PRONUNCIATION KEY

Symbol	Key words	Symbol	Key words	Symbol	Key words
a	asp, fat, parrot	†ə	a in ago	r	red, port, dear
ā	ape, date, play		e in agent	s	sell, castle, pass
†ä	ah, car, father		i in sanity	t	top, cattle, hat
e	elf, ten, berry		o in comply	v	vat, hovel, have
ē	even, meet, money		u in focus	w	will, always, swear
i	is, hit, mirror	ər	perhaps, murder	y	yet, onion, yard
ī	ice, bite, high	b	bed, fable, dub	z	zebra, dazzle, haze
ō	open, tone, go	d	dip, beadle, had	ch	chin, catcher, arch
ô	all, horn, law	f	fall, after, off	sh	she, cushion, dash
o͞o	ooze, tool, crew	g	get, haggle, dog	th	thin, nothing, truth
oo	look, pull, moor	h	he, ahead, hotel	*th*	then, father, lathe
yo͞o	use, cute, few	j	joy, agile, badge	zh	azure, leisure
yoo	united, cure, globule	k	kill, tackle, bake	ŋ	ring, anger, drink
oi	oil, point, toy	l	let, yellow, ball	′′	see p. 15.
ou	out, crowd, plow	m	met, camel, trim	✓	see p. 15.
u	up, cut, color	n	not, flannel, ton	+	see p. 14.
ʉr	urn, fur, deter	p	put, apple, tap	′	see p. 15.
†See p. 14.		†See p. 16.		○	see p. 14.

TELESCOPIC   +
tel′ ə skäp′ ik   3*
tel′ i skäp′ ik   1

TELEVISE
tel′ ə vīz′   4

TEMBLOR
tem′ blər   4
tem′ blôr′   2*
tem′ blôr   2
tem′ blōr   1
tem blôr′   1
tem blōr′   1

TEMERARIOUS   ✓
tem′ ə rer′ ē əs   4*
tem′ ə rar′ ē əs   1

TEMERITY
tə mer′ ə tē   3*
tə mer′ i tē   1

TEMPERA
tem′ pər ə   4

TEMPERAMENT
tem′ prə mənt   4*
tem′ pər ə mənt   3
tem′ pər mənt   2

TEMPERAMENTAL
tem′ prə men′ t′l   4*
tem′ pər ə men′ t′l   4
tem′ pər men′ t′l   1

TEMPERANCE
tem′ pər əns   4*
tem′ prəns   4
tem′ prənts   1
tem′ pərns   1
tem′ pərnts   1

TEMPERATE
tem′ pər it   3*
tem′ prit   3
tem′ prət   1

TEMPERATURE
tem′ pər ə chər   2*
tem′ pər ə choor′   2
tem′ prə choor′   2
tem′ prə chər   2
tem′ pər choor   1
tem′ pər chər   1
tem′ pər tyoor′   1
temp′ ə chər   1

TEMPESTUOUS
tem pes′ choo əs   2*
tem pes′ choo wəs   1
tem pes′ chə wəs   1
tem pesh′ chə wəs   1

TEMPI
tem′ pē   3*
tem′ pē′   1

TEMPLATE
tem′ plit   3*
tem′ plət   1

TEMPO
tem′ pō   4*
tem′ pō′   1

TEMPORAL
tem′ pər əl   4*
tem′ prəl   4

TEMPORIZE
tem′ pə rīz′   4

TENABLE
ten′ ə bəl   3
ten′ ə b′l   1*

TENACITY
tə nas′ ə tē   3*
tə nas′ i tē   1

TENACIOUS
tə nā′ shəs   4

TENDENTIOUS
ten den′ shəs   3*
ten den′ chəs   1

TENDON
ten′ dən   4

TENEBROUS
ten′ ə brəs   4

TENET
ten′ it   3*
ten′ ət   1
tē′ nit   1

TENON
ten′ ən   4

TENOR
ten′ ər   4

TENSILE
ten′ səl   3*
ten′ sīl   2
ten′ sil   1
ten′ s′l   1
tent′ səl   1

TENSION
ten′ shən   3*
ten′ chən   1

TENSOR
ten′ sər   4*
ten′ sôr′   2
ten′ sôr   2
tent′ sər   1

TENTACLE
ten′ tə kəl   2
ten′ tə k′l   1*
ten′ ti kəl   1

TENTATIVE
ten′ tə tiv   4

TENUOUS
ten′ yoo əs   2*
ten′ yoo wəs   1
ten′ yə wəs   1

TENURE
ten′ yər   4*
ten′ yoor   3

TEPEE
tē′ pē   4*
tē′ pē′   1

TEPID
tep′ id   3*
tep′ əd   1

TEQUILA
tə kē′ lə   4

TERCENTENARY
tʉr′ sen ten′ ə rē   3
tʉr sen′ tə ner′ ē   2*
tʉr sen′ t′ner′ ē   1
tʉr′ sen′ ten′ ə rē   1

TERCET
tʉr′ sit   3*
tər set′   1
tʉr′ sət   1
tʉr set′   1

TERGIVERSATE
tʉr′ ji vər sāt′   3*
tʉr′ jə vʉr′ sāt′   1
tʉr′ jiv′ ər sāt′   1
tʉr′ giv′ ər sāt′   1

TERGIVERSATION
tʉr′ ji vər sā′ shən   3*
tʉr′ ji′ vər sā′ shən   1
tʉr′ gi′ vər sā′ shən   1

TERIYAKI
ter′ ē yä′ kē   3*
ter′ ē ä kē   1

TERMAGANT
tʉr′ mə gənt   4

TERMINATE
tʉr′ mə nāt′   4

TERMINOLOGY   +
tʉr′ mə näl′ ə jē   4

TERMINUS
tʉr′ mə nəs   4

TERPSICHOREAN
tʉrp′ sə kôr′ ē ən   3*
tʉrp′ si kə rē′ ən   3
tʉrp′ sə kōr′ ē ən   3
tʉrp′ sə kə rē′ ən   1

TERRACE
ter′ əs   3*
ter′ is   1

TERRA COTTA   +
ter′ ə kät′ ə   4

TERRA FIRMA
ter′ ə fʉr′ mə   4

TERRAIN
tə rān′   4*
te rān′   4

TERRAMYCIN
ter′ ə mī′ sən   2*
ter′ ə mī′ s′n   2

TERRAPIN
ter′ ə pin   2*
ter′ ə pən   2
tar′ ə pən   1

TERRARIUM   ✓
tə rer′ ē əm   4*
tə rar′ ē əm   1

PRONUNCIATION KEY

Symbol	Key words	Symbol	Key words	Symbol	Key words
a	asp, fat, parrot	†ə	a in ago	r	red, port, dear
ā	ape, date, play		e in agent	s	sell, castle, pass
†ä	ah, car, father		i in sanity	t	top, cattle, hat
e	elf, ten, berry		o in comply	v	vat, hovel, have
ē	even, meet, money		u in focus	w	will, always, swear
i	is, hit, mirror	ər	perhaps, murder	y	yet, onion, yard
ī	ice, bite, high	b	bed, fable, dub	z	zebra, dazzle, haze
ō	open, tone, go	d	dip, beadle, had	ch	chin, catcher, arch
ô	all, horn, law	f	fall, after, off	sh	she, cushion, dash
o͞o	ooze, tool, crew	g	get, haggle, dog	th	thin, nothing, truth
oo	look, pull, moor	h	he, ahead, hotel	th	then, father, lathe
yo͞o	use, cute, few	j	joy, agile, badge	zh	azure, leisure
yoo	united, cure, globule	k	kill, tackle, bake	ŋ	ring, anger, drink
oi	oil, point, toy	l	let, yellow, ball	″	see p. 15.
ou	out, crowd, plow	m	met, camel, trim	✓	see p. 15.
u	up, cut, color	n	not, flannel, ton	+	see p. 14.
ʉr	urn, fur, deter	p	put, apple, tap	′	see p. 15.
†See p. 14.		†See p. 16.		○	see p. 14.

TERRAZZO
tə rät′ sō   3*
tə raz′ ō   3
tə rä′ zō   1
te rät′ sō   1
te raz′ ō   1

TERRESTRIAL
tə res′ trē əl   4*
tə res′ chəl   1
tə resh′ chəl   1
tə res′ tē əl   1

TERTIARY
tur′ shē er′ ē   4*
tur′ shə rē   2

TESTICLE
tes′ ti kəl   3
tes′ ti k'l   1*

TESTES
tes′ tēz   3*
tes′ tēz′   1

TESTOSTERONE   +
tes täs′ tə rōn′   4

TETANUS
tet′ n əs   4*
tet′ nəs   1

TETANY
tet′ 'n ē   4*
tet′ nē   1

TETHER
te*th*′ ər   4

TETRALOGY
te tral′ ə jē   4*
te träl′ ə jē   2

TETRAMETER
te tram′ ə tər   3*
te tram′ i tər   1

TÊTE À TÊTE
tāt′ ə tāt′   4

TEXTILE
teks′ til   2*
teks′ tīl   2
teks′ t'l   2

TEXTUAL
teks′ choo əl   2*
teks′ choo wəl   1
teks′ chəl   1
teks′ chə wəl   1

TEXTURE
teks′ chər   4

THALAMUS
thal′ ə məs   4

THALIDOMIDE
thə lid′ ə mīd′   3*
tha lid′ ə mīd′   1

THANATOPSIS   +
than′ ə täp′ sis   3

THAUMATURGY
thô′ mə tur′ jē   4

THEATER (RE)
thē′ ə tər   4

THEATRICAL
thē at′ ri kəl   3
thē at′ ri k'l   1*

THEISM
thē′ iz′ əm   2
thē′ iz'm   1*
thē′ iz əm   1

THEMATIC
thē mat′ ik   2*
thi mat′ ik   2

THENCE
*th*ens   4*
thens   3
thents   1

THEOCRACY   +
thē äk′ rə sē   4

THEOLOGIAN
thē′ ə lō′ jən   4*
thē′ ə lō′ jē ən   2

THEOLOGY   +
thē äl′ ə jē   4

THEOREM   ○
thē′ ə rəm   4*
thir′ əm   3

THEORETICIAN
thē′ ər ə tish′ ən   3*
thē′ ər i tish′ ən   1
thēr i tish′ ən   1

THEORY   ○
thē′ ə rē   4*
thir′ ē   3

THEOSOPHY   +
thē äs′ ə fē   4

THERAPIST
ther′ ə pist   3*
ther′ ə pəst   1

THERAPEUTIC
ther′ ə pyoot′ ik   4

THERAPY
ther′ ə pē   4

THERMAL
thur′ məl   3*
thur′ m'l   1

THERMODYNAMICS
thur′ mō dī nam′ iks   3
thur′ mō di nam′ iks   1*
thur′ mə di nam′ iks   1

THERMOMETER   +
thər mäm′ ə tər   3*
thər mäm′ i tər   1
thə mäm′ ə tər   1

THERMONUCLEAR
thur′ mō noo′ klē ər   4*
thur′ mō nyoo′ klē ər   4

THERMOS
thur' məs   4

THERMOSTAT
thur' mə stat'   4

THESAURUS
thi sôr' əs   4

THESIS
thē' sis   3*
thē' səs   1

THESPIAN
thes' pē ən   4

THEW
thyōo   4*
thōo   1

THETA
thāt' ə   4*
thēt' ə   4

THIAMINE
thī' ə mēn'   4
thī' ə min   3*
thī' ə mən   1

THINE
thīn   4

THISTLE
this' əl   3
this'l   1*

THITHER
thith' ər   4*
thith' ər   4

THORACIC
thə ras' ik   3*
thô ras' ik   2
thō ras' ik   1

THORAX
thôr' aks'   2*
thōr' aks'   2
thôr' aks   2
thōr' aks   1

THOUGH
thō   4

THRALL
thrôl   4

THREAT
thret   4

THRESHOLD
thresh' hōld'   2*
thresh' ōld'   2
thresh' ōld   2
thresh' hōld   2

THRENODY
thren' ə dē   4

THROMBOSIS   +
thräm bō' sis   4*
thräm bō' səs   1
thrəm bō' səs   1

THRONG   +
thrôŋ   3
thräŋ   2*

THROUGH
throo   4

THUS
thus   4

THY
thī   4

PRONUNCIATION KEY

Symbol	Key words	Symbol	Key words	Symbol	Key words
a	asp, fat, parrot	†ə	a in ago	r	red, port, dear
ā	ape, date, play		e in agent	s	sell, castle, pass
†ä	ah, car, father		i in sanity	t	top, cattle, hat
e	elf, ten, berry		o in comply	v	vat, hovel, have
ē	even, meet, money		u in focus	w	will, always, swear
i	is, hit, mirror	ər	perhaps, murder	y	yet, onion, yard
ī	ice, bite, high	b	bed, fable, dub	z	zebra, dazzle, haze
ō	open, tone, go	d	dip, beadle, had	ch	chin, catcher, arch
ô	all, horn, law	f	fall, after, off	sh	she, cushion, dash
ōo	ooze, tool, crew	g	get, haggle, dog	th	thin, nothing, truth
oo	look, pull, moor	h	he, ahead, hotel	th	then, father, lathe
yōo	use, cute, few	j	joy, agile, badge	zh	azure, leisure
yoo	united, cure, globule	k	kill, tackle, bake	ŋ	ring, anger, drink
oi	oil, point, toy	l	let, yellow, ball	"	see p. 15.
ou	out, crowd, plow	m	met, camel, trim	✓	see p. 15.
u	up, cut, color	n	not, flannel, ton	+	see p. 14.
ʉr	urn, fur, deter	p	put, apple, tap	'	see p. 15.
†See p. 14.		†See p. 16.		○	see p. 14.

THYME
tīm 4*
t<i>h</i>īm 1

THYMUS
t<i>h</i>ī′ məs 4

THYROID
t<i>h</i>ī′ roid 3*
t<i>h</i>ī′ roid′ 1

TIARA ✓
tē ar′ ə 4*
tē är′ ə 4
tē er′ ə 4
tī er′ ə 1
tī ar′ ə 1

TIC DOULOUREUX
tik′ doo′ lə roo′ 1*
tik′ doo′ loo roo′ 1
tik′ doo′ loo roo′ 1
tik′ doo′ loo roo′ 1

TICKLISH
tik′ lis<i>h</i> 4*
tik′ ə lis<i>h</i> 1

TIDAL
tīd ′l 4

TIER ○
tir 4

TIDY
tī′ dē 4

TIGRESS
tī′ gris 3*
tī′ grəs 1

TIMBALE
tim′ bəl 3*
tim′ b′l 1

TIMBER
tim′ bər 4

TIMBRE
tim′ bər 4
tam′ bər 3*

TIMOROUS
tim′ ər əs 4*
tim′ rəs 1

TIMPANI (TYMPANI)
tim′ pə nē 4

TINCTURE
tiŋk′ c<i>h</i>ər 4*
tiŋ c<i>h</i>ər 1

TINGE
tinj 4

TINSEL
tin′ səl 3*
tin′ s′l 1
tin′ z′l 1
tin′ zəl 1
tint′ səl 1

TINTINNABULATION
tin′ ti nab′ yə lā′ s<i>h</i>ən 2*
tin′ ti nab′ yoo lā′ s<i>h</i>ən 1
tin′ tə nab′ yə lā′ s<i>h</i>ən 1

TINY
tī′ nē 4

TIRADE
tī rād′ 4
tī′ rād 3*

TISANE
ti zan′ 4*
ti zän′ 2

TISSUE
tis<i>h</i>′ oo 4*
tis<i>h</i>′ oo′ 1

TITAN
tīt′ ′n 4

TITANIC
tī tan′ ik 4*
ti tan′ ik 2
tə tan′ ik 1

TITHE
tī<i>th</i> 4

TITIAN
tis<i>h</i>′ ən 4

TITILLATE
tit′ ′lāt′ 3*
tit′ ə lāt′ 1

TITIVATE
tit′ ə vāt′ 4

TITULAR
tic<i>h</i>′ ə lər 3*
tic<i>h</i>′ oo lər 1
tit′ yə lər 1
tic<i>h</i>′ lər 1

TOADY
tōd′ ē 4

TOBACCONIST
tə bak′ ə nist 3*
tə bak′ ə nəst 1

TOBOGGAN +
tə bäg′ ən 4

TOCCATA
tə kät′ ə 4

TOCSIN +
täk′ sin 3*
täk′ sən 1

TOFFEE +
täf′ ē 4*
tôf′ ē 3

TOGA
tō′ gə 4

TOILETTE
twä let′   3*
toi let′   2

TOLERABLE   +
täl′ ər ə bəl   3
täl′ ər ə b'l   1*
täl′ ər bəl   1
täl′ rə bəl   1

TOLERANT   +
täl′ ər ənt   4*
täl′ rənt   1

TOLL
tōl   4

TOMAHAWK   +
täm′ ə hôk′   3*
täm′ i hôk′   1

TOMATO
tə māt′ ō   4*
tə mät′ ō   4
tə māt′ ə   1
tə mät′ ə   1

TOMB
tōōm   4

TOME
tōm   4

TONAL
tō′ nəl   2*
tō′ n'l   2

TONICITY
tō nis′ ə tē   3*
tō nis′ i tē   1

TONNEAU   +
tu nō′   3*
tə nō′   1
tä′ nō   1

TONSIL   +
tän′ səl   3
tän′ s'l   1*
tänt′ səl   1

TONSILLECTOMY   +
tän′ sə lek′ tə mē   4*
tänt′ sə lek′ tə mē   1

TONSILLITIS   +
tän′ sə līt′ əs   2
tän′ sə līt′ is   2*

TONSORIAL   +
tän sôr′ ē əl   4*
tän sōr′ ē əl   3

TONSURE   +
tän′ sнər   3*
tän′ chər   1

TONTINE   +
tän tēn′   4*
tän′ tēn   3
tän′ tēn′   1

TOPAZ
tō′ paz   3*
tō′ paz′   1

TOPER
tō′ pər   4

TOPIARY
tō′ pē er′ ē   4

TOPOGRAPHY   +
tə päg′ rə fē   4

PRONUNCIATION KEY

Symbol	Key words	Symbol	Key words	Symbol	Key words
a	asp, fat, parrot	†ə	a in ago	r	red, port, dear
ā	ape, date, play		e in agent	s	sell, castle, pass
†ä	ah, car, father		i in sanity	t	top, cattle, hat
e	elf, ten, berry		o in comply	v	vat, hovel, have
ē	even, meet, money		u in focus	w	will, always, swear
i	is, hit, mirror	ər	perhaps, murder	y	yet, onion, yard
ī	ice, bite, high	b	bed, fable, dub	z	zebra, dazzle, haze
ō	open, tone, go	d	dip, beadle, had	ch	chin, catcher, arch
ô	all, horn, law	f	fall, after, off	sh	she, cushion, dash
ōō	ooze, tool, crew	g	get, haggle, dog	th	thin, nothing, truth
oo	look, pull, moor	h	he, ahead, hotel	th	then, father, lathe
yōō	use, cute, few	j	joy, agile, badge	zh	azure, leisure
yoo	united, cure, globule	k	kill, tackle, bake	ŋ	ring, anger, drink
oi	oil, point, toy	l	let, yellow, ball	″	see p. 15.
ou	out, crowd, plow	m	met, camel, trim	✓	see p. 15.
u	up, cut, color	n	not, flannel, ton	+	see p. 14.
ur	urn, fur, deter	p	put, apple, tap	′	see p. 15.
†See p. 14.		†See p. 16.		○	see p. 14.

TOPSAIL   +
täp′ sāl′   4
täp′ səl   3*
täp′ s'l   1

TOQUE
tōk   4

TOR
tôr   4

TORAH
tō′ rə   4*
tôr′ ə   3

TORERO   ✓
tə rer′ ō   4

TOREADOR   +
tôr′ ē ə dôr′   4*
tōr′ ē ə dôr′   1
tär′ ē ə dôr′   1

TORMENT (n)
tôr′ ment′   2*
tôr′ ment   2

TORMENT (v)
tôr ment′   4*
tôr′ ment′   1

TORNADO
tôr nā′ dō   4

TORPEDO
tôr pē′ dō   4

TORPOR
tôr′ pər   4

TORQUE
tôrk   4

TORRENT   +
tôr′ ənt   4
tär′ ənt   4*

TORRENTIAL   +
tə ren′ shəl   3*
tô ren′ shəl   3
tä ren′ shəl   1
tô ren′ chəl   1
tə ren′ chəl   1

TORRID   +
tär′ id   3*
tôr′ id   3
tôr′ əd   1
tär′ əd   1

TORSO
tôr′ sō   4*
tôr′ sō′   1

TORTE
tôrt   4*
tôrt′ ə   1

TORTILLA
tôr tē′ ə   3
tôr tē′ yə   2*

TORTOISE
tôr′ təs   4

TORTUOUS
tôr′ chŌō əs   2*
tôr′ choo wəs   1
tôr′ chə wəs   1
tôrch′ wəs   1

TORTURE
tôr′ chər   4

TOTALITARIAN   ✓
tō tal′ ə ter′ ē ən   3
tō tal′ i ter′ ē ən   1*
tō′ tal ə ter′ ē ən   1

TOTALITY
tō tal′ ə tē   3
tō tal′ i tē   1*

TOTEM
tō′ təm   4

TOUCAN
tŌō′ kan′   2*
tŌō′ kän′   2
tŌō′ kan   2
tŌō kän′   2

TOUCHÉ
tŌō shā′   4

TOUCHY
tuch′ ē   4

TOUPEE
tŌō pā′   4

TOUR
toor   4

TOUR DE FORCE
toor′ də fôrs′   2*
toor′ də fōrs′   2
tŌōr′ də fôrs′   1

TOURNAMENT
toor′ nə mənt   4*
tʉr′ nə mənt   4

TOURNEY
tʉr′ nē   4*
toor′ nē   4

TOURNIQUET
tʉr′ nə kit   2*
toor′ nə kit   2
toor′ ni kit   1
toor′ ni kā′   1
tʉr′ ni kit   1
tʉr′ ni kā′   1
tʉr′ nə kā′   1
toor′ ni kət   1
tʉr′ ni kət   1

TOUSLED
tou′ zəld   3
tou′ z'ld   1*

TOUT
tout   4

TOVARISCH (TOVARICH)
tǝ vär' ish 2*
tō vär' ish 2
tǝ vär' ishch 1

TOW
tō 4

TOWARD
tôrd 4*
tǝ wôrd' 4
tōrd 3
tō' ǝrd 2
twôrd 1
twōrd 1

TOWHEAD
tō' hed' 4

TOWHEE
tō' hē 4
tō hē' 3
tou' hē 2
tō' ē 1*

TOWLINE
tō' līn' 4

TOXEMIA +
täk sē' mē ǝ 4

TOXIC +
täk' sik 4

TOXICITY +
täk sis' ǝ tē 3*
täk sis' i tē 1

TOXICOLOGY +
täk' sǝ käl' ǝ jē 2*
täk' si käl' ǝ jē 2

TOXIN +
täk' sin 3
täk' sǝn 1*

TRACHEA
trā' kē ǝ 4

TRACHEOTOMY +
trā' kē ät' ǝ mē 4

TRACHOMA
trǝ kō' mǝ 4

TRADUCE
trǝ dōōs' 4*
trǝ dyōōs' 4

TRAGEDIAN
trǝ jē' dē ǝn 4

TRAGEDIENNE
trǝ jē' dē en' 4

TRAIPSE
trāps 4

TRAIT
trāt 4

TRAJECTORY
trǝ jek' tǝ rē 4*
trǝ jek' trē 1

TRAMPOLINE
tram' pǝ lēn' 4
tram' pǝ lēn' 3*
tram' pǝ lin 2

TRANCE
trans 4*
träns 2
trants 1

PRONUNCIATION KEY

Symbol	Key words	Symbol	Key words	Symbol	Key words
a	asp, fat, parrot	†ǝ	a in ago	r	red, port, dear
ā	ape, date, play		e in agent	s	sell, castle, pass
†ä	ah, car, father		i in sanity	t	top, cattle, hat
e	elf, ten, berry		o in comply	v	vat, hovel, have
ē	even, meet, money		u in focus	w	will, always, swear
i	is, hit, mirror	ǝr	perhaps, murder	y	yet, onion, yard
ī	ice, bite, high	b	bed, fable, dub	z	zebra, dazzle, haze
ō	open, tone, go	d	dip, beadle, had	ch	chin, catcher, arch
ô	all, horn, law	f	fall, after, off	sh	she, cushion, dash
ōō	ooze, tool, crew	g	get, haggle, dog	th	thin, nothing, truth
oo	look, pull, moor	h	he, ahead, hotel	th	then, father, lathe
yōō	use, cute, few	j	joy, agile, badge	zh	azure, leisure
yoo	united, cure, globule	k	kill, tackle, bake	ŋ	ring, anger, drink
oi	oil, point, toy	l	let, yellow, ball	′′	see p. 15.
ou	out, crowd, plow	m	met, camel, trim	╱	see p. 15.
u	up, cut, color	n	not, flannel, ton	+	see p. 14.
ur	urn, fur, deter	p	put, apple, tap	′	see p. 15.
†See p. 14.		†See p. 16.		◯	see p. 14.

TRANQUIL
tran′ kwil 3
traŋ′ kwil 2*
traŋ′ kwəl 1

TRANQUILIZER
traŋ′ kwə lī′ zər 3*
tran′ kwə lī′ zər 3

TRANQUILLITY
tran′ kwil′ ə tē 3
traŋ′ kwil′ ə tē 2*
traŋ′ kwil′ i tē 1

TRANSACT
tran zakt′ 4*
tran sakt′ 4

TRANSCEND
tran send′ 4*
trant send′ 1

TRANSCENDENTAL
tran′ sen den′ t′l 4*
trant′ sen den′ t′l 1

TRANSEPT
tran′ sept′ 2*
tran′ sept 2
trant′ sept′ 1

TRANSFER (n)
trans′ fər 3*
trans′ fər′ 1
trants′ fər 1

TRANSFER (v)
trans fʉr′ 4*
trans′ fər 4
trants fʉr′ 1

TRANSFERENCE
trans fʉr′ əns 4*
trans′ fər əns 4
trants fʉr′ əns 1
trants′ fər əns 1

TRANSFORM
trans fôrm′ 4*
trants fôrm′ 1

TRANSFUSION
trans fyōō′ zhən 4*
trants fyōō′ zhən 1

TRANSGRESS
tranz gres′ 4*
trans gres′ 4
trants gres′ 1

TRANSIENT
tran′ shənt 3*
tran′ zhənt 2
tran′ zē ənt 2
tran′ chənt 1
tranch′ ē ənt 1
trants′ ē ənt 1

TRANSISTOR
tran zis′ tər 4*
tran sis′ tər 3

TRANSIT
tran′ sit 3*
tran′ zit 3
tran′ sət 1
tran′ zət 1
trant′ sət 1

TRANSITION
tran zish′ ən 4*
tran sish′ ən 4

TRANSITIVE
tran′ sə tiv 3*
tran′ zə tiv 3
tran′ si tiv 1
tran′ zi tiv 1
trans′ tiv 1

TRANSITORY
tran′ sə tôr′ ē 2*
tran′ zə tôr′ ē 2
tran′ sə tōr′ ē 1
tran′ zə tōr′ ē 1
tran′ si tōr′ ē 1
tran′ zi tōr′ ē 1
tran′ si tōr′ ē 1
tran′ zi tōr′ ē 1

TRANSLATE
trans lāt′ 4*
tranz lāt′ 4
tranz′ lāt 2
trans′ lāt 2
trans′ lāt′ 1
tranz′ lāt′ 1
trants lāt′ 1

TRANSLITERATE
tranz lit′ ə rāt′ 4*
trans lit′ ə rāt′ 4
trants lit′ ə rāt′ 1

TRANSLUCENT
trans lōō′ s′nt 2*
trans lōō′ sənt 2
tranz lōō′ sənt 2
tranz lōō′ s′nt 2

TRANSMIGRATION
tranz′ mī grā′ shən 4*
trans′ mī grā′ shən 4
trants′ mī grā′ shən 1

TRANSMOGRIFY +
tranz mäg′ rə fī′ 4*
trans mäg′ rə fī′ 4
trants mäg′ rə fī′ 1

TRANSOM
tran′ səm 4*
trant′ səm 1

TRANSPARENT ✓
trans par′ ənt 4*
trans per′ ənt 4
trants per′ ənt 1
trants par′ ənt 1

TRANSPLANT (n)
trans′ plant′ 4*
trans′ plänt′ 3
trants′ plant′ 1

TRANSPLANT (v)
trans plant′ 4*
trans plänt′ 3
trants plant′ 1

TRANSPORT (n)
trans′ pôrt′ 4*
trans′ pōrt′ 3

TRANSPORT (v)
trans pôrt′ 4*
trans pōrt′ 3

TRANSUBSTANTIATION
tran′ səb stan′ shē ā′ shən
4

TRANSVERSE
trans vʉrs′ 4*
tranz vʉrs′ 4
trans′ vʉrs′ 2
tranz′ vʉrs′ 2

TRANSVESTITE
tranz ves′ tīt 2*
trans ves′ tīt′ 2
tranz ves′ tīt′ 2
trans ves′ tīt 2
trants ves′ tīt 1

TRAPEZE
tra pēz′ 4
trə pēz′ 2*

TRAPUNTO
trə poon′ tō 3*
trə po͞on′ tō 1
trə po͞on′ tō′ 1

TRAUMA
trou′ mə 4*
trô′ mə 4

TRAUMATIC
trou mat′ ik 4*
trô mat′ ik 4
trə mat′ ik 1

TRAVAIL
trə vāl′ 4*
trav′ āl′ 2
trav′ āl 2
trə vā′ əl 1
trav′ əl 1

TRAVERSE
trə vʉrs′ 4*
trav′ ərs 3
tra vʉrs′ 1

TRAVERTINE
trav′ ər tēn′ 4*
trav′ ər tin 3
trav′ ər tən 1

TRAVESTY
trav′ i stē 3*
trav′ ə stē 1

TREACHEROUS
trech′ ər əs 4*
trech′ rəs 1

TREACHERY
trech′ ə rē 4*
trech′ rē 1

TREACLE
trē′ kəl 3
trē′ k'l 1*

TREADLE
tred′ 'l 4

TREASON
trē′ z'n 2*
trē′ zən 2

PRONUNCIATION KEY

Symbol	Key words	Symbol	Key words	Symbol	Key words
a	asp, fat, parrot	†ə	a in ago	r	red, port, dear
ā	ape, date, play		e in agent	s	sell, castle, pass
†ä	ah, car, father		i in sanity	t	top, cattle, hat
e	elf, ten, berry		o in comply	v	vat, hovel, have
ē	even, meet, money		u in focus	w	will, always, swear
i	is, hit, mirror	ər	perhaps, murder	y	yet, onion, yard
ī	ice, bite, high	b	bed, fable, dub	z	zebra, dazzle, haze
ō	open, tone, go	d	dip, beadle, had	ch	chin, catcher, arch
ô	all, horn, law	f	fall, after, off	sh	she, cushion, dash
o͞o	ooze, tool, crew	g	get, haggle, dog	th	thin, nothing, truth
o͝o	look, pull, moor	h	he, ahead, hotel	th	then, father, lathe
yo͞o	use, cute, few	j	joy, agile, badge	zh	azure, leisure
yo͝o	united, cure, globule	k	kill, tackle, bake	ŋ	ring, anger, drink
oi	oil, point, toy	l	let, yellow, ball	″	see p. 15.
ou	out, crowd, plow	m	met, camel, trim	✓	see p. 15.
u	up, cut, color	n	not, flannel, ton	+	see p. 14.
ʉr	urn, fur, deter	p	put, apple, tap	′	see p. 15.
†See p. 14.		†See p. 16.		○	see p. 14.

TREASURE
trezh' ər 4*
trā' zhər 2

TREASURY
trezh' ə rē 4*
trāzh' ə rē 2
trezh' rē 1
trāzh' rē 1

TREATISE
trē' tis 4

TREBLE
treb' əl 3
treb' 'l 1*

TREFOIL
trē' foil' 2*
trē' foil 2
tref' oil' 2

TREMENDOUS
tri men' dəs 4

TREMOLO
trem' ə lō' 4

TREMOR
trem' ər 4
trē' mər 2*

TREMULOUS
trem' yə ləs 3*
trem' yoo ləs 1

TRENCHANT
tren' chənt 4

TREPHINE
tri fīn' 3*
tri fēn' 3
trē' fīn' 1

TREPIDATION
trep' ə dā' shən 3
trep' i dā' shən 1*

TRESPASS
tres' pəs 4*
tres' pas' 4

TRESTLE
tres' əl 3
tres' 'l 1*

TREY
trā 4

TRIAD
trī' ad' 2*
trī' ad 2
trī' əd 2

TRIAGE
trē äzh' 2

TRIBUNAL
trī byoo' n'l 3*
tri byoo' n'l 3
trī byoo' nəl 1
tri byoo' nəl 1

TRIBUNE
trib' yoon 2*
trib' yoon' 2
tri byoon' 2

TRIBUTARY
trib' yə ter' ē 3*
trib' yoo ter' ē 1

TRIBUTE
trib' yoot 4*
trib' yoot' 1
trib' yət 1

TRICHINA
tri kī' nə 4

TRICHINOSIS
trik' ə nō' sis 3*
trik' ə nō' səs 1

TRICOLOR
trī' kul' ər 4*

TRICOT
trē' kō 4*
trē' kō' 1
trī' kət 1

TRIDENT
trīd' 'nt 3*
trīd' ənt 1

TRIGLYPH
trī' glif 3*
trī' glif' 1

TRILOBITE
trī' lə bīt' 4

TRILOGY
tril' ə jē 4

TRIMESTER
trī mes' tər 4
trī' mes tər 2*
trī' mes' tər 1

TRINITROTOLUENE +
trī' nī' trō täl' yoo ēn' 2*
trī' nī' trō täl' yoo wēn 1
trī' nī' trō täl' yə wēn' 1

TRIO
trē' ō 4*
trē' ō' 1

TRIOLET
trī' ə lit 3
trē' ə lət 1*
trē' ə lā 1
trī' ə lət 1
trē' ə let' 1

TRIPARTITE
trī pär' tīt' 3*
trī pär' tīt 1
trī' pär' tīt 1

TRIPLICATE
trip′ lə kit   2*
trip′ li kit   1
trip′ lə kāt′   1
trip′ lə kət   1

TRIPOD   +
trī′ päd   3*
trī′ päd′   1

TRIPTYCH
trip′ tik   4*
trip′ tik′   1

TRIREME
trī′ rēm′   2*
trī′ rēm   2

TRIUMVIR
trī um′ vər   4

TRIUMVIRATE
trī um′ vər it   3*
trī um′ və rāt′   1
trī um′ və rət   1

TRIUNE
trī′ yo͞on′   2*
trī′ yo͞on   2
trī′ o͞on   1

TRIVET
triv′ it   3*
triv′ ət   1

TRIVIA
triv′ ē ə   4

TRIVIAL
triv′ ē əl   4*
triv′ yəl   1

TROCHEE
trō′ kē   4*
trō′ kē′   1

TROGLODYTE   +
träg′ lə dīt′   4

TROIKA
troi′ kə   4

TROLL
trōl   4

TROLLOP   +
träl′ əp   4

TROMBONE   +
träm bōn′   4*
trəm bōn′   2
träm′ bōn   2
träm′ bōn′   1
trum bōn′   1

TROPISM   +
trō′ piz′ əm   3*
trō′ piz′m   1
träp′ iz′ əm   1

TROTH   +
trōth   4
trôth   4*
träth   3

TROUBADOUR
tro͞o′ bə dôr′   4*
tro͞o′ bə dōr′   3
tro͞o′ bə door   3

TROUBLOUS
trub′ ləs   4*
trub′ ə ləs   1

PRONUNCIATION KEY

Symbol	Key words	Symbol	Key words	Symbol	Key words
a	asp, fat, parrot	†ə	a in ago	r	red, port, dear
ā	ape, date, play		e in agent	s	sell, castle, pass
†ä	ah, car, father		i in sanity	t	top, cattle, hat
e	elf, ten, berry		o in comply	v	vat, hovel, have
ē	even, meet, money		u in focus	w	will, always, swear
i	is, hit, mirror	ər	perhaps, murder	y	yet, onion, yard
ī	ice, bite, high	b	bed, fable, dub	z	zebra, dazzle, haze
ō	open, tone, go	d	dip, beadle, had	ch	chin, catcher, arch
ô	all, horn, law	f	fall, after, off	sh	she, cushion, dash
o͞o	ooze, tool, crew	g	get, haggle, dog	th	thin, nothing, truth
oo	look, pull, moor	h	he, ahead, hotel	th	then, father, lathe
yo͞o	use, cute, few	j	joy, agile, badge	zh	azure, leisure
yoo	united, cure, globule	k	kill, tackle, bake	ŋ	ring, anger, drink
oi	oil, point, toy	l	let, yellow, ball	″	see p. 15.
ou	out, crowd, plow	m	met, camel, trim	✓	see p. 15.
u	up, cut, color	n	not, flannel, ton	+	see p. 14.
ur	urn, fur, deter	p	put, apple, tap	′	see p. 15.
†See p. 14.		†See p. 16.		○	see p. 14.

TROUGH
trôf 4*
träf 2

TROUSSEAU
trōō' sō 4*
trōō sō' 4
trōō' sō' 1

TROUPE
trōōp 4

TROWEL
trou' əl 4*
troul 1

TRUANT
trōō' ənt 4

TRUCULENT
truk' yə lənt 3*
trōō' kyə lənt 1
truk' yoo lənt 1

TRUFFLE
truf' əl 3
trōō' fəl 2
truf' 'l 1*
trōō' f'l 1

TRUSTEE
trus tē' 4

TRUISM
trōō' iz əm 2*
trōō' iz' əm 1
trōō' iz'm 1

TRUNCHEON
trun' chən 4

TRUTHS
trōō thz 4*
trōōths 3

TRYST
trist 4*
trīst 3

TSAR (see CZAR)

TSETSE
tset' sē 4
tsēt' sē 3*
set' sē 1
sēt' sē 1
tet' sē 1
tēt' sē 1

TUBA
tōō' bə 3*
tyōō' bə 3

TUBE
tōōb 4*
tyōōb 4

TUBER
tōō' bər 4*
tyōō' bər 4

TUBERCLE
tōō' bər kəl 3*
tyōō' bər kəl 3
tōō' bər k'l 1
tyōō' bər k'l 1

TUBERCULAR
too bur' kyə lər 4*
tyoo bur' kyə lər 4

TUBERCULOSIS
too bur' kyə lō' sis 4*
tyoo bur' kyə lō' sis 4

TUBULAR
tōō' byə lər 4*
tyōō' byə lər 4

TUESDAY
tōōz' dē 4
tyōōz' dē 4
tōōz' dā 2*
tyōōz' dā 2
tōōz' dā' 1
tyōōz' dā' 1

TUITION
tōō ish' ən 2*
tyōō ish' ən 2
too wish' ən 1
tyoo wish' ən 1
too ish' ən 1
tyoo ish' ən 1

TULAREMIA
tōō' lə rē' mē ə 4*
tyōō' lə rē' mē ə 2

TULIP
tōō' lip 3*
tyōō' lip 3
tōō' ləp 1
tyōō' ləp 1

TULLE
tōōl 4

TUMBREL
tum' brəl 4

TUMESCENT
tōō mes' ənt 2*
tōō mes' 'nt 2
tyōō mes' 'nt 2
tyōō mes' ənt 1

TUMOR
tōō' mər 4*
tyōō' mər 4

TUMULT
tōō' mult 2*
tōō' məlt 2
tyōō' məlt 2
tyōō' mult 2

TUMULTUOUS
tə mul' choo əs 1*
too mul' choo wəs 1
too mulch' wəs 1
tyoo mulch' wəs 1
too mulch' ə wəs 1
tyoo mulch' ə wəs 1
tōō mul' chōō əs 1
tyōō mul' chōō əs 1

TUMULUS
to͞o′ myə ləs   4*
tyo͞o′ myə ləs   4

TUNA
to͞o′ nə   4*
tyo͞o′ nə   4

TUNDRA
tun′ drə   4*
toon′ drə   3

TUNE
to͞on   4*
tyo͞on   4

TUNGSTEN
tuŋ′ stən   4*
tuŋk′ stən   1

TUNIC
tyo͞o′ nik   4
to͞o′ nik   4*

TURBID
tʉr′ bid   4

TURPENTINE
tʉr′ pən tīn′   4

TURBINE
tʉr′ bīn   4*
tʉr′ bin   4

TURBOJET
tʉr′ bō jet′   4

TURBOT
tʉr′ bət   4

TURBULENT
tʉr′ byə lənt   4

TUREEN
too rēn′   3*
tyoo rēn′   3
tə rēn′   1

TURGID
tʉr′ jid   4

TURMERIC
tʉr′ mər ik   3*
to͞om′ ə rik   1

TURMOIL
tʉr′ moil   4

TURNVEREIN
tʉrn′ və rīn′   3*
toorn′ və rīn′   2
tʉrn′ fə rīn′   1

TURPITUDE
tʉr′ pə to͞od′   3*
tʉr′ pə tyo͞od′   3
tʉr′ pi to͞od′   1
tʉr′ pi tyo͞od′   1

TURQUOISE
tʉr′ kwoiz′   2*
tʉr′ koiz′   2
tʉr′ kwoiz   2
tʉr′ koiz   2

TUTELAGE
tyo͞ot′ ′l ij   3*
to͞ot′ ′l ij   3
to͞ot′ əl ij   1
tyo͞ot′ əl ij   1

TUTELARY ✓
tyo͞ot′ ′l er′ ē   3*
to͞ot′ ′l er′ ē   3
to͞ot′ əl er′ ē   1
tyo͞ot′ əl er′ ē   1

PRONUNCIATION KEY

Symbol	Key words	Symbol	Key words	Symbol	Key words
a	asp, fat, parrot	†ə	a in ago	r	red, port, dear
ā	ape, date, play		e in agent	s	sell, castle, pass
†ä	ah, car, father		i in sanity	t	top, cattle, hat
e	elf, ten, berry		o in comply	v	vat, hovel, have
ē	even, meet, money		u in focus	w	will, always, swear
i	is, hit, mirror	ər	perhaps, murder	y	yet, onion, yard
ī	ice, bite, high	b	bed, fable, dub	z	zebra, dazzle, haze
ō	open, tone, go	d	dip, beadle, had	ch	chin, catcher, arch
ô	all, horn, law	f	fall, after, off	sh	she, cushion, dash
o͞o	ooze, tool, crew	g	get, haggle, dog	th	thin, nothing, truth
oo	look, pull, moor	h	he, ahead, hotel	th	then, father, lathe
yo͞o	use, cute, few	j	joy, agile, badge	zh	azure, leisure
yoo	united, cure, globule	k	kill, tackle, bake	ŋ	ring, anger, drink
oi	oil, point, toy	l	let, yellow, ball	″	see p. 15.
ou	out, crowd, plow	m	met, camel, trim	✓	see p. 15.
u	up, cut, color	n	not, flannel, ton	+	see p. 14.
ʉr	urn, fur, deter	p	put, apple, tap	′	see p. 15.
†See p. 14.		†See p. 16.		○	see p. 14.

TUTOR
to͞ot' ər 4
tyo͞ot' ər 4*

TUTORIAL
to͞o tôr' ē əl 4
to͞o tōr' ē əl 3
tyo͞o tôr' ē əl 3*
tyo͞o tōr' ē əl 2

TUTTI-FRUTTI
to͞ot' ē fro͞ot' ē 4

TUTU
to͞o' to͞o 4*
to͞o' to͞o' 1

TWINGE
twinj 4

TWOPENCE
tup' əns 3*
tup' 'ns 1
tup' ənts 1
to͞o' pens 1
to͞o' pents 1

TYCOON
tī ko͞on' 4

TYKE
tīk 4

TYMPANI (see TIMPANI)

TYPHOID
tī' foid' 2*
tī' foid 2
tī foid' 1

TYPHOON
tī fo͞on' 4

TYPHUS
tī' fəs 4

TYPICAL
tip' i kəl 3*
tip' i k'l 1

TYPOGRAPHY +
tī päg' rə fē 4

TYRANNICAL
tī ran' i kəl 3
ti ran' i kəl 2
ti ran' i k'l 1*
tī ran' i k'l 1
tə ran' i kəl 1

TYRANNIZE
tir' ə nīz' 4

TYRANNOSAUR
ti ran' ə sôr' 4*
tī ran' ə sôr' 4

TYRANNY
tir' ə nē 4

TYRANT
tī' rənt 4

TYRO
tī' rō 4

U

UBIQUITOUS
yo͞o bik′ wə təs   2*
yoo bik′ wə təs   1
yo͞o bik′ wi təs   1

UKASE
yo͞o kās′   3*
yo͞o kāz′   3
yo͞o′ kas′   2
yo͞o′ kāz′   2
o͞o käz′   1

UKULELE
yo͞o′ kə lā′ lē   4

ULCER
ul′ sər   4

ULTERIOR ○
ul tir′ ē ər   4

ULTIMATUM
ul′ tə mā′ təm   3*
ul′ tə mä′ təm   3

ULTRAMONTANE +
ul′ trə män′ tān′   4*
ul′ trə män tān′   2

ULULATE
yo͞ol′ yə lāt′   3*
ul′ yə lāt′   3
yo͞ol yoo lāt′   1
o͞ol′ yə lāt′   1

UMBILICAL
um′ bil′ i kəl   2
um bil′ i k'l   1*
um bil′ i kəl   1

UMBILICUS
um′ bə lī′ kəs   4
um′ bil′ i kəs   3*
um′ bil′ ə kəs   1

UMBRAGE
um′ brij   4

UMLAUT
oom′ lout′   2*
oom′ lout   2
o͞om′ lout′   1

UMPIRE
um′ pīr   2*
um′ pī′r   2

UNANIMITY
yoo′ nə nim′ ə tē   2
yo͞o′ nə nim′ i tē   1*
yo͞o′ nə nim′ ə tē   1

UNANIMOUS
yoo nan′ ə məs   2*
yo͞o nan′ ə məs   2

UNBRIDLED
un brī′ d'ld   3*
un brī′ dəld   1

UNCONSCIONABLE +
un kän′ shən ə b'l   1*
un′ kän′ shən ə bəl   1
un kän′ shən ə bəl   1
un känch′ nə bəl   1
un kän′ chən ə bəl   1

UNCOUTH
un′ ko͞oth   4

UNCTION
uŋk′ shən   4*
uŋ′ shən   1

UNCTUOUS
uŋk′ cho͞o əs   2*
uŋk′ choo wəs   1
uŋ′ chəs   1
uŋ′ chə wəs   1

UNDUE
un′ do͞o′   4*
un′ dyo͞o′   4

UNDULATE
un' joo lāt' 4
un' dyə lāt' 2*
un' də lāt' 1
un' jə lət 1

UNDULY
un' do͞o' lē 2*
un' dyo͞o' lē 2
un do͞o' lē 2
un dyo͞o' lē 2

UNEQUIVOCAL
un' i kwiv' ə kəl 4

UNERRING
un' ʉr' iŋ 2*
un' er' iŋ 2
un ʉr' iŋ 2
un er' iŋ 2

UNFEIGNED
un' fānd' 2*
un fānd' 2

UNGUENT
uŋ' gwənt 4*
un' gwənt 1
un' jənt 1

UNICAMERAL
yo͞o' nə kam' ər əl 2*
yo͞o' ni kam' ər əl 1
yo͞o' ni kam' rəl 1

UNICELLULAR
yo͞o ni sel' yə lər 3*
yo͞o' nə sel' yə lər 1

UNICORN
yo͞o' nə kôrn' 4

UNISON
yo͞o' nə zən 3
yo͞o' nə sən 3*
yo͞o' ni sən 1
yo͞o' ni zən 1

UNLEAVENED
un lev' ənd 3

UNPRECEDENTED
un' pres' ə den' tid 1*
un pres' ə den' tid 1
un pres' i den' tid 1
un' pres' ə den' təd 1

UNSATURATED
un sach' ə rā' tid 2
un' sach' ə rā' tid 1*
un' sach' ə rā' təd 1

UNSAVORY
un sā' vər ē 3*
un' sā' vər ē 1
un sāv' rē 1

UNSCATHED
un' skāthd' 2*
un skāthd' 2

UNSHEATHE
un' shēth' 2*
un shēth' 2

UNTOWARD
un' tôrd' 2*
un' tōrd' 2
un tôrd' 2
un tōrd' 1
un tō' ərd 1
un tô' ərd 1

UNTUTORED
un to͞ot' ərd 3
un tyo͞ot' ərd 3
un' to͞ot' ərd 1*
un' tyo͞ot' ərd 1

UNWARY ✓
un wer' ē 3*
un war' ē 1
un' wer' ē 1

UNWONTED
un' wôn' tid 2*
un' wōn' tid 2
un' wun' tid 2
un wôn' tid 2
un wun' tid 2

UPHEAVAL
up' hē' vəl 2*
up hē' vəl 1
up hē' v'l 1
ə pē' vəl 1

UPSET (n)
up' set' 4

UPSET (adj, v)
up set' 4

URANIUM
yoo rā' nē əm 4

URBAN
ʉr' bən 4

URBANE
ʉr' bān' 2*
ʉr bān' 2

URBANITY
ʉr' ban' ə tē 2*
ʉr ban' ə tē 1
ʉr ban' i tē 1

URCHIN
ʉr' chin 3*
ʉr' chən 1

UREMIA
yoo rē' mē ə 4*
yoo rēm' yə 1

URETER
yoo rē' tər 3*
yoor' ə tər 1

URETHRA
yoo rē' thrə 4

URINAL
yoor' ə n'l 3*
yoor' ə nəl 1

URINE
yoor' in 3*
yoor' ən 1

URN
ʉrn   4

URSINE
ʉr′ sīn′   2*
ʉr′ sīn   2
ʉr′ sin   2

USAGE
yo͞o′ zij   4*
yo͞o′ sij   4

USE (n)
yo͞os   4

USE (v)
yo͞oz   4

USED
yo͞ozd   4

USURER
yo͞o′ zhər ər   4*
yo͞ozh′ rər   1

USURIOUS
yo͞o zhoor′ ē əs   3*
yoo zhoor′ ē əs   1
yoo zoor′ ē əs   1

USURP
yo͞o sʉrp′   4*
yo͞o zʉrp′   4

USURPATION
yo͞o′ sər pā′ shən   4*
yo͞o′ zər pā′ shən   4

USURY
yo͞o′ zhə rē   2*
yo͞o′ zho͞o rē   1
yo͞ozh′ rē   1

UTENSIL
yo͞o ten′ səl   3*
yo͞o ten′ s′l   1
yoo ten′ səl   1
yoo tent′ səl   1

UTERUS
yo͞o′ tər əs   4*
yo͞o′ trəs   1

UTERINE
yoot′ ər īn′   4
yo͞ot′ ər in   3*
yoot′ ər ən   1

UTILITARIAN ✓
yo͞o til′ ə ter′ ē ən   4

UTILITY
yoo til′ ə tē   2
yo͞o til′ ə tē   1*
yo͞o til′ i tē   1

UTOPIAN
yo͞o tō′ pē ən   3*
yoo tō′ pē ən   1

UXORIOUS
ug zôr′ ē əs   3
ug zōr′ ē əs   3
uk′ sôr′ ē əs   2*
uk′ sōr′ ē əs   2
ək sôr′ ē əs   1
əg zôr′ ē əs   1

PRONUNCIATION KEY

Symbol	Key words	Symbol	Key words	Symbol	Key words
a	asp, fat, parrot	†ə	a in ago	r	red, port, dear
ā	ape, date, play		e in agent	s	sell, castle, pass
†ä	ah, car, father		i in sanity	t	top, cattle, hat
e	elf, ten, berry		o in comply	v	vat, hovel, have
ē	even, meet, money		u in focus	w	will, always, swear
i	is, hit, mirror	ər	perhaps, murder	y	yet, onion, yard
ī	ice, bite, high	b	bed, fable, dub	z	zebra, dazzle, haze
ō	open, tone, go	d	dip, beadle, had	ch	chin, catcher, arch
ô	all, horn, law	f	fall, after, off	sh	she, cushion, dash
o͞o	ooze, tool, crew	g	get, haggle, dog	th	thin, nothing, truth
o͝o	look, pull, moor	h	he, ahead, hotel	t͟h	then, father, lathe
yo͞o	use, cute, few	j	joy, agile, badge	zh	azure, leisure
yo͝o	united, cure, globule	k	kill, tackle, bake	ŋ	ring, anger, drink
oi	oil, point, toy	l	let, yellow, ball	″	see p. 15.
ou	out, crowd, plow	m	met, camel, trim	✓	see p. 15.
u	up, cut, color	n	not, flannel, ton	+	see p. 14.
ʉr	urn, fur, deter	p	put, apple, tap	′	see p. 15.
†See p. 14.		†See p. 16.		○	see p. 14.

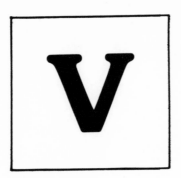

VACCILATE
vas′ ə lāt′ 4

VACCINATE
vak′ sə nāt′ 4

VACCINE
vak sēn′ 4*
vak′ sēn 3
vak′ sin 2

VACUITY
va kyōō′ ə tē 3*
və kyōō′ ə tē 1
va kyōō′ i tē 1

VACUOUS
vak′ yōō əs 2*
vak′ yoo wəs 1
vak′ yə wəs 1

VACUUM
vak′ yōōm 3
vak′ yōō əm 2*
vak′ yoo wəm 1
vak′ yəm 1

VAGARY ✓
və ger′ ē 4*
vā′ gə rē 3

VAGINA
və jī′ nə 4

VAGINAL
vaj′ ə n′l 3
vaj′ ə nəl 1*
və jī′ n′l 1

VAGRANCY
vā′ grən sē 4

VAGRANT
vā′ grənt 4

VAGUE
vāg 4

VALANCE
val′ əns 4*
vāl′ əns 2

VALEDICTORIAN
val′ ə dik tôr′ ē ən 2*
val′ ə dik tōr′ ē ən 1
val′ i dik tōr′ ē ən 1
val′ i dik tôr′ ē ən 1

VALEDICTORY
val′ ə dik′ tər ē 3*
val′ i dik′ tər ē 1
val′ ə dik′ trē 1

VALET
val′ it 3*
va lā′ 3
val′ ā 3
val′ ət 1

VALETUDINARIAN ✓
val′ ə tōō də ner′ ē ən 2*
val′ ə tyōō də ner′ ē ən 1
val′ ə tōō d′n er′ ē ən 1
val′ ə tyōō d′n er′ ē ən 1
val′ i tōō d′n er′ ē ən 1
val′ i tyōō d′n er′ ē ən 1

VALIANT
val′ yənt 4

VALID
val′ id 3*
val′ əd 1

VALIDITY
və lid′ ə tē 3*
və lid′ i tē 1

VALISE
və lēs′ 4

VALUABLE
val′ yə bəl 3
val′ yo͞o ə bəl 2*
val′ yoo b′l 1
val′ yoo wə b′l 1

VANILLA
və nil′ ə 4*
və nel′ ə 2

VAPID
vap′ id 3*
vap′ əd 1
vāp′ əd 1

VAPOR
vā′ pər 4

VAQUERO ✓
vä ker′ ō 4

VARIABLE ✓
ver′ ē ə b′l 2*
ver′ ē ə bəl 2
var′ ē ə b′l 2

VARICOSE
var′ ə kōs′ 4

VARIEGATED ✓
ver′ ē ə gāt′ id 3*
var′ ə gāt′ id 2
ver′ ē ə gāt′ əd 1
var′ ē ə gāt′ id 1
var′ ē ə gāt′ əd 1
ver′ ə gāt′ id 1
ver′ i gāt′ əd 1
var′ i gāt′ əd 1

VARIORUM ✓
ver′ ē ôr′ əm 4*
ver′ ē ōr′ əm 3
var′ ē ôr′ əm 2

VARIOUS ✓
ver′ ē əs 4*
var′ ē əs 2

VARY ✓
very 4*
vary 2

VASE
vāz 4*
vās 4
väz 2

VASECTOMY
vas ek′ tə mē 4

VASELINE
vas′ ə lēn′ 4
vas′ ə lēn′ 2*
vas′ ə lin 1

VASSAL
vas′ əl 3*
vas′ ′l 1

VAUDEVILLE
vôd′ vil 4*
vōd′ vil 3
vô′ də vil′ 2
vôd′ vəl 1

VAULT
vôlt 4

VAUNT
vônt 4*
vänt 4

VEGETABLE
vej′ tə bəl 3*
vej′ ə tə bəl 1
vej′ i tə bəl 1
vej′ tə b′l 1

VEHEMENT
vē′ ə mənt 4*
vē′ hi mənt 1

VEHICLE
vē′ i kəl 3*
vē′ ə k′l 1
vē′ hi k′l 1
vē′ hi kəl 1

VEHICULAR
vē hik′ yə lər 3*
vē hik′ yoo lər 1

VELDT
velt 4*
felt 3

VELOCIPEDE +
və läs′ ə pēd′ 4

VELOCITY +
və läs′ ə tē 3*
və läs′ i tē 1
və läs′ tē 1

VELOUR
və lo͞or′ 2*
və loor′ 2

VENAL
vē′ n′l 3
vē′ nəl 1*

VENALITY
vē nal′ ə tē 2*
vi nal′ ə tē 2
və nal′ i tē 1
vē nal′ i tē 1

VENDETTA
ven det′ ə 4

VENDOR
ven′ dər 4*
ven′ dôr 1

VENEER ○
və nir′ 4

VENERATE
ven′ ə rāt′ 4

VENEREAL ○
və nir′ ē əl 4

VENERY
ven′ ər ē 4

VENGEANCE
ven' jəns 4*
ven' jənts 1

VENIAL
vēn' yəl 4*
vē' nē əl 4

VENIREMAN ○
və nī' rē mən 3*
vi nī' rē mən 1
və nir' ē mən 1

VENISON
ven' ə sən 2
ven' ə zən 2
ven' i sən 1*
ven' i zən 1
ven' i s'n 1
ven' i z'n 1

VENOM
ven' əm

VENOUS
vē' nəs

VENTRICLE
ven' tri kəl 3
ven' tri k'l 1*

VENTRILOQUIST
ven tril' ə kwist 3*
ven tril' ə kwəst 1

VENTURE
ven' chər 4

VENUE
ven' yo͞o 4*
ven' o͞o 2

VERACITY
və ras' ə tē 3*
və ras' i tē 1

VERANDA (VERANDAH)
və ran' də 4

VERBATIM
vər bāt' im 1*
vər bāt' əm 1
vur bāt' əm 1
vur bāt' im 1

VERBIAGE
vur' bē ij 4

VERBOSE
vər bōs' 4

VERBOSITY +
vər bäs' ə tē 3*
vər bäs' i tē 1

VERDANT
vur' d'nt 3*
vur dənt 1

VERDIGRIS
vur' də grēs' 2
vur' də gris 2
vur' də grē' 1*
vur' di grēs' 1
vur' di gris' 1
vur' də grēs 1

VERDURE
vur' jər 4

PRONUNCIATION KEY

Symbol	Key words	Symbol	Key words	Symbol	Key words
a	asp, fat, parrot	†ə	a in ago	r	red, port, dear
ā	ape, date, play		e in agent	s	sell, castle, pass
†ä	ah, car, father		i in sanity	t	top, cattle, hat
e	elf, ten, berry		o in comply	v	vat, hovel, have
ē	even, meet, money		u in focus	w	will, always, swear
i	is, hit, mirror	ər	perhaps, murder	y	yet, onion, yard
ī	ice, bite, high	b	bed, fable, dub	z	zebra, dazzle, haze
ō	open, tone, go	d	dip, beadle, had	ch	chin, catcher, arch
ô	all, horn, law	f	fall, after, off	sh	she, cushion, dash
o͞o	ooze, tool, crew	g	get, haggle, dog	th	thin, nothing, truth
o͝o	look, pull, moor	h	he, ahead, hotel	th	then, father, lathe
yo͞o	use, cute, few	j	joy, agile, badge	zh	azure, leisure
yo͝o	united, cure, globule	k	kill, tackle, bake	ŋ	ring, anger, drink
oi	oil, point, toy	l	let, yellow, ball	"	see p. 15.
ou	out, crowd, plow	m	met, camel, trim	✓	see p. 15.
u	up, cut, color	n	not, flannel, ton	+	see p. 14.
ur	urn, fur, deter	p	put, apple, tap	'	see p. 15.
†See p. 14.		†See p. 16.		○	see p. 14.

VERISIMILITUDE
ver′ i si mil′ i ty$\overline{oo}$d′   2*
ver′ i si mil′ i t$\overline{oo}$d′   2
ver′ ə si mil′ ə t$\overline{oo}$d′   1
ver′ ə si mil′ ə ty$\overline{oo}$d′   1
ver′ ə sə mil′ ə t$\overline{oo}$d′   1
ver′ ə sə mil′ ə ty$\overline{oo}$d′   1

VERITABLE
ver′ ə tə bəl   2
ver′ i tə b′l   1*
ver′ i tə bəl   1

VERMICELLI
vʉr′ mə chel′ $\overline{e}$ 3*
vʉr′ mə sel′ $\overline{e}$ 3
vʉr′ mi chel′ $\overline{e}$ 1
vʉr′ mi sel′ $\overline{e}$ 1

VERMIFUGE
vʉr′ mə fyooj′   4

VERMILION
vər mil′ yən   4

VERMOUTH
vər m$\overline{oo}$th′   4

VERNACULAR
vər nak′ yə lər   4*
və nak′ yə lər   1

VERSATILE
vʉr′ sə t′l   2*
vʉr′ sə təl   1
vʉr′ sə til   1

VERSION
vʉr′ zhən   4*
vʉr′ shən   4

VERTEBRA
vʉr′ tə brə   4

VERTIGINOUS
vər tij′ ə nəs   4

VERTIGO
vʉr′ ti g$\overline{o}$′   3*
vʉr′ tə g$\overline{o}$′   1

VESTIBULE
ves′ tə by$\overline{oo}$l′   4

VESTIGE
ves′ tij   4

VESTIGIAL
ves tij′ $\overline{e}$ əl   2*
vəs tij′ $\overline{e}$ əl   2
ves tij′ əl   2

VETERAN
vet′ ər ən   4*
vet′ rən   3

VETERINARIAN ✓
vet′ rə ner′ $\overline{e}$ ən   4
vet′ ər ə ner′ $\overline{e}$ ən   3*
vet ər ə ner′ $\overline{e}$ ən   1

VEXED
vekst   4

VIA
v$\overline{i}$′ ə   4*
v$\overline{e}$′ ə   4

VIABLE
v$\overline{i}$′ ə bəl   3
v$\overline{i}$′ ə b′l   1*

VIADUCT
v$\overline{i}$′ ə dukt′   4

VIAL
v$\overline{i}$′ əl   4*
v$\overline{i}$l   2

VIAND
v$\overline{i}$′ ənd   4

VIATICUM
v$\overline{i}$ at′ i kəm   3*
v$\overline{e}$ at′ i kəm   2
v$\overline{i}$ at′ ə kəm   1

VIBRANT
v$\overline{i}$′ brənt   4

VIBRATE
v$\overline{i}$′ brāt′   2*
v$\overline{i}$′ brāt   2

VIBRATO
vi brät′ $\overline{o}$ 3*
v$\overline{e}$ brät′ $\overline{o}$ 3
v$\overline{i}$ brät′ $\overline{o}$ 1

VIBURNUM
v$\overline{i}$ bʉr′ nəm   4

VICAR
vik′ ər   4

VICARIOUS ✓
vi ker′ $\overline{e}$ əs   3*
v$\overline{i}$ ker′ $\overline{e}$ əs   3
v$\overline{i}$ kar′ $\overline{e}$ əs   1

VICEGERENT ○
v$\overline{i}$s jir′ ənt   4

VICEROY
v$\overline{i}$s′ roi   2*
v$\overline{i}$s′ roi′   2

VICE VERSA
v$\overline{i}$s′ vʉr′ sə   4
v$\overline{i}$′ sə vʉr′ sə   3*
v$\overline{i}$′ s$\overline{e}$ vʉr′ sə   3
v$\overline{i}$ si vʉr′ sə   1

VICHYOISSE
vish′ $\overline{e}$ swäz′   4
v$\overline{e}$′ sh$\overline{e}$ swäz′   3*

VICINAGE
vis′ ə nij   3*
vis′ ′n ij   1
vis′ nij   1

VICINITY
vi sin′ ə t$\overline{e}$ 2*
vi sin′ i t$\overline{e}$ 1
və sin′ ə t$\overline{e}$ 1

VICIOUS
vish′ əs   4

VICISSITUDE
vi sis′ ə tyood′   2*
vi sis′ ə tood′   2
i sis′ i tood′   1
i sis′ i tyood′   1
ə sis′ ə tood′   1
ə sis′ ə tyood′   1
ī sis′ ə tyood′   1
ī sis′ ə tood′   1

VICTUAL
vit′ ′l   4

VICUNA
vī koon′ yə   4
vī koon′ ə   4
vī kyoon′ ə   3*
və koon′ ə   3
və kyoon′ ə   3
və koon′ yə   2
vi koon′ yə   1
vi koon′ ə   1

VIDEO
vid′ ē ō′   4

VIE
vī   4

VIGIL
vij′ əl   4

VIGILANT
vij′ ə lənt   4

VIGILANTE
vij′ ə lan′ tē   2*
vij ə lan′ tē   2

VIGNETTE
vin yet′   4*
vēn yet′   1

VILIFY
vil′ ə fī′   4

VILLANELLE
vil′ ə nel′   4

VINAIGRETTE
vin′ ə gret′   3*
vin′ i gret′   1

VINEYARD
vin′ yərd   4

VINOUS
vī′ nəs   4

VINYL
vī′ nəl   2*
vī′ n′l   2
vī′ nil   2

VIOL
vī′ əl   4
vī′ ōl   1*

VIOLA
vē ō lə   4*
vī ō′ lə   3
vī′ ə lə   1

VIOLET
vī′ ə lit   3
vī′ ə lət   1

VIOLIN
vī′ ə lin′   4

VIOLONCELLO   +
vē′ ə lən chel′ ō   3*
vē′ ə län chel′ ō   2
vī′ ə lən chel′ ō   1

VIRAGO ○
vi rā' gō 3
vī rā' gō 3
vī rä' gō 3
vi rä' gō 2*
və rä' gō 1
vir' ə gō' 1

VIRAL
vī' rəl

VIRELAY ○
vir' ə lā' 4

VIRGO ○
vʉr' gō 4*
vir' gō 1

VIRGULE
vʉr' gyo͞ol 4

VIRILE
vir' əl 4

VIRILITY
və ril' ə tē 3*
və ril' i tē 1

VIRTUE
vʉr' cho͞o 4

VIRTUOSITY +
vʉr' cho͞o äs' ə tē 1*
vʉr' choo wäs' ə tē 1
vʉr' cho͞o' äs' i tē 1
vʉr' chə wäs' ə tē 1

VIRTUOSO
vʉr' cho͞o ō' sō 2*
vʉr' choo wō' sō 1
vʉr' chə wō' sō 1

VIRTUOUS
vʉr' cho͞o əs 2*
vʉr' choo wəs • 1
vʉrch' wəs 1

VIRULENT ○
vir' yə lənt 3*
vir' ə lənt 3
vir' yoo lənt 1
vir' oo lənt 1

VIRUS
vī' rəs 4

VISA
vē' zə 4

VISAGE
viz' ij 4

VIS-À-VIS
vē' zə vē' 4*
vē' zä vē' 1

VISCERA
vis' ər ə 4

VISCID
vis' id 3*
vis' əd 1

VISCOSITY +
vis käs' ə tē 3*
vis käs' i tē 1

VISCOUNT
vī' kount' 4

VISCOUS
vis' kəs 4

VISE
vīs 4

VISOR
vī' zər 4*
viz' ər 2

VITIATE
vish' ē āt' 4

VITREOUS
vit' rē əs 4

VITRIOL
vit' rē əl 3*
vit' rē ōl' 2

VITRIOLIC +
vit' rē äl' ik 4

VITUPERATION
vī to͞o' pə rā' shən 4*
vī tyo͞o' pə rā' shan 4
vi to͞o' pə rā' shan 3
vi tyo͞o' pə rā' shən 3

VIVACIOUS
vī vā' shəs 4
vi vā' shəs 3*
və vā' shəs 1

VIVACITY
vī vas' ə tē 3
vi vas' ə tē 2*
vi vas' i tē 1
və vas' ə tē 1
vī vas' i tē 1

VIVA VOCE
vī' və vō' sē 3*
vī' və vō' sē 1

VIVIPAROUS
vī vip' ər əs 3*
vī vip' rəs 1

VIXEN
vik' sən 3*
vik' s'n 1

VIZIER ○
viz' yər 4
vi zir' 3*
və zir' 1

VOCIFEROUS
vō sif' ər əs 3*
vō sif' rəs 1

VODKA +
väd' kə 4

VOGUE
vōg 4

VOILE
voil 4

VOLATILE +
väl′ ə t′l 3*
väl′ ə til 2

VOLCANIC +
väl kan′ ik 4*
vôl kan′ ik 1

VOLCANO +
väl kā′ nō 4*
vôl kā′ nō 1

VOLITION
və lish′ ən 3*
vō lish′ ən 3

VOLUBLE +
väl′ yə bəl 3*
väl′ yoo b′l 1

VOLUME +
väl′ yəm 4*
väl′ yo͞om 2
väl′ yoom 2

VOLUMINOUS
və lo͞o′ mə nəs 4

VOLUNTARY ✓
väl′ ən ter′ ē 4

VOLUPTUARY
və lup′ cho͞o er′ ē 2*
və lup′ choo wer′ ē 1
və lup′ chə wer′ ē 1

VOLUPTUOUS
və lup′ cho͞o əs 2*
və lup′ choo wəs 1
və lup′ chə wəs 1

VOMIT +
väm′ it 3*
väm′ ət 1

VORACIOUS
vô rā′ shəs 4
və rā′ shəs 4*
vō rā′ shəs 2

VOTARY
vō′ tə rē 4

VOUCHSAFE
vouch′ sāf′ 4*
vouch′ sāf′ 1

VOYEUR
vwä yur′ 4*
voi yur′ 2

VULCANIZE
vul′ kə nīz′ 4

VULGATE
vul′ gāt′ 2*
vul′ gāt 2
vul′ git 2
vul′ git′ 1
vul′ gət 1

VULPINE
vul′ pin 3
vul′ pīn′ 2*
vul′ pīn 2

VULTURE
vul′ chər

PRONUNCIATION KEY

Symbol	Key words	Symbol	Key words	Symbol	Key words
a	asp, fat, parrot	†ə	a in ago	r	red, port, dear
ā	ape, date, play		e in agent	s	sell, castle, pass
†ä	ah, car, father		i in sanity	t	top, cattle, hat
e	elf, ten, berry		o in comply	v	vat, hovel, have
ē	even, meet, money		u in focus	w	will, always, swear
i	is, hit, mirror	ər	perhaps, murder	y	yet, onion, yard
ī	ice, bite, high	b	bed, fable, dub	z	zebra, dazzle, haze
ō	open, tone, go	d	dip, beadle, had	ch	chin, catcher, arch
ô	all, horn, law	f	fall, after, off	sh	she, cushion, dash
o͞o	ooze, tool, crew	g	get, haggle, dog	th	thin, nothing, truth
oo	look, pull, moor	h	he, ahead, hotel	th	then, father, lathe
yo͞o	use, cute, few	j	joy, agile, badge	zh	azure, leisure
yoo	united, cure, globule	k	kill, tackle, bake	ŋ	ring, anger, drink
oi	oil, point, toy	l	let, yellow, ball	″	see p. 15.
ou	out, crowd, plow	m	met, camel, trim	✓	see p. 15.
u	up, cut, color	n	not, flannel, ton	+	see p. 14.
ur	urn, fur, deter	p	put, apple, tap	′	see p. 15.
†See p. 14.		†See p. 16.		○	see p. 14.

WAFER
wā′ fər 4

WAFFLE
wäf′ ′l 2*
wôf′ ′l 2
wôf′ əl 1

WAFT
wäft 4*
waft 4

WAINSCOT +
wān′ skət 4
wān′ skät′ 3*
wān′ skōt′ 2

WAISTCOAT
wāst′ kōt′ 4
wes′ kət 3*
wes′ kit 1

WAIVE
wāv 4

WAIVER
wā′ vər 4

WALLABY
wäl′ ə bē 3*
wôl′ ə bē 1

WALLOP
wäl′ əp 3*
wôl′ əp 2

WAMPUM
wäm′ pəm 4*
wôm′ pəm 2

WAN
wän 4*
wôn 1

WANDERLUST
wän′ dər lust′ 4*
wôn′ dər lust′ 1

WANTON
wän′ t′n 3
wôn′ t′n 2
wän′ tən 1*

WAPITI
wäp′ ə tē 3
wə pet′ ē 1*
wäp′ i tē 1

WARMONGER +
wôr′ muŋ′ gər 4
wôr′ mäŋ′ gər 2*

WARRANT
wär′ ənt 4*
wôr′ ənt 4

WARRANTY
wär′ ən tē 4*
wôr′ ən tē 4

WARRIOR
wôr′ ē ər 4*
wär′ ē ər 4
wär′ yər 4
wôr′ yər 3

WARY ✓
wer′ ē 4*
war′ ē 1

WASSAIL
was′ əl 4
wäs′ āl 3*
wäs′ əl 2
wäs′ ′l 1

WASTREL
wā′ strəl 4

WATER
wô′ tər 4*
wä′ tər 4

WAYLAY
wā′ lā′ 3*
wā lā′ 1
wā′ lā′ 1

WEAL
wēl 4

WEAN
wēn 4

WEAPON
wep′ ən 4

WEDNESDAY
wenz′ dē 4*
wenz′ dā 2

WEIR ○
wir 4*
war 1
wer 1

WEIRD ○
wird 4

WELSH
welsh 4*
welch 4

WELTSCHMERZ
velt′ shmerts 4

WEREWOLF ○ ✓
wer′ woolf′ 4
wir′ woolf′ 4*
wur′ woolf′ 4

WHARF
hwôrf 4
wôrf 3*

WHARVES
hwôrvz 4
wôrvz 3*

WHAT
hwut 4
wät 3
wut 3
hwät 3*

WHELK
hwelk 4
welk 3*

WHET
hwet 4*
wet 2

WHELP
hwelp 4
welp 3*

WHEN
hwen 4*
wen 3

WHERE ✓
hwer 4*
wer 3
hwar 1
war 1

WHEY
hwā 4*
wā 3

WHICH
hwich 4*
wich 3

WHILE
hwīl 4*
wīl 3

WHIMSICAL
hwim′ zi kəl 3
wim′ zi kəl 2
wim′ zi k′l 2
hwim′ zi k′l 1*

WHIMSY
hwim′ zē 4*
wim′ zē 3

WHINNY
hwin′ ē 4*
win′ ē 3

WHIP
hwip 4*
wip 3

WHIPPOORWILL
hwip′ ər wil′ 4*
hwip′ ər wil′ 3
wip′ ər wil′ 3
wip′ ər wil′ 2

WHIR
hwur 4*
wur 3

WHIRL
hwurl 4*
wurl 3

WHISPER
hwis′ pər 4*
wis′ pər 3

WHISTLE
hwis′ əl 3*
wis′ əl 2
hwis′ ′l 1
wis′ ′l 1

WHIT
hwit 4*
wit 3

WHITE
hwīt 4*
wīt 3

WHITHER
hwith′ ər 4
with′ ər 3*

WHOLLY
hōl′ lē 4*
hō′ lē 4

WHOOP
ho͞op 4*
hwo͞op 4
wo͞op 2
woop 1

WHORE
hôr 4*
hōr 3
hoor 1

WHORL
hwôrl 4*
hwurl 4
wôrl 3
wurl 3

WIDTH
width 4*
with 3
witth 2

WIENER
wē' nər 4*
wē' nē 1

WIENER SCHNITZEL
vē' nər shnit' səl 2
wē' nər shnit' səl 1*
vē' nər shnit' zəl 1
wē' nər snit' səl 1

WIGWAM
wig' wäm 3*
wig' wôm 2

WILDEBEEST
wil' də bēst' 2*
vil' də bēst' 2

WILY
wī' lē 4

WINCE
wins 4*
wints 1

WIRY
wīr' ē 3*
wī'r' ē 2

WISEACRE
wīz' ā' kər 4

WISTERIA ○
wi stir' ē ə 4

WITHE
wit͟h 4*
with 4
wit͟h 4

WITHHOLD
with hōld' 4
wit͟h hōld' 3*

WITTICISM
wit' i siz' əm 2*
wit' ə siz'm 1
wit' ə siz əm 1

WIZENED
wiz' 'nd 2*
wiz' ənd 2
wēz' 'nd 1

WOEBEGONE +
wō' bi gän' 4*
wō' bi gôn' 4

WOLVERINE
wool' və rēn' 4*
wool' və rēn' 2

PRONUNCIATION KEY

Symbol	Key words	Symbol	Key words	Symbol	Key words
a	asp, fat, parrot	†ə	a in ago	r	red, port, dear
ā	ape, date, play		e in agent	s	sell, castle, pass
†ä	ah, car, father		i in sanity	t	top, cattle, hat
e	elf, ten, berry		o in comply	v	vat, hovel, have
ē	even, meet, money		u in focus	w	will, always, swear
i	is, hit, mirror	ər	perhaps, murder	y	yet, onion, yard
ī	ice, bite, high	b	bed, fable, dub	z	zebra, dazzle, haze
ō	open, tone, go	d	dip, beadle, had	ch	chin, catcher, arch
ô	all, horn, law	f	fall, after, off	sh	she, cushion, dash
o͞o	ooze, tool, crew	g	get, haggle, dog	th	thin, nothing, truth
oo	look, pull, moor	h	he, ahead, hotel	th	then, father, lathe
yo͞o	use, cute, few	j	joy, agile, badge	zh	azure, leisure
yoo	united, cure, globule	k	kill, tackle, bake	ŋ	ring, anger, drink
oi	oil, point, toy	l	let, yellow, ball	"	see p. 15.
ou	out, crowd, plow	m	met, camel, trim	✓	see p. 15.
u	up, cut, color	n	not, flannel, ton	+	see p. 14.
ur	urn, fur, deter	p	put, apple, tap	'	see p. 15.
†See p. 14.		†See p. 16.		○	see p. 14.

WOMB
wo͞om 4

WOMBAT +
wäm′ bat′ 2*
wäm′ bat 2

WONT (used to)
wōnt 4*
wunt 4
wônt 4

WON'T
wōnt 4*
wunt 2

WOOF
woof 4*
wo͞of 4

WORSHIP
wʉr′ ship 3
wʉr′ shəp 1*

WORSTED (n)
woos′ tid 4*
wʉr′ stid 3
wʉr′ stəd 1

WOUND (n v)
wo͞ond 4

WOUND (past of wind v)
wound 4

WRAITH
rāth 4

WREAK
rēk 4

WREATH
rēth 4

WREATHE
rēth 4

WRESTLE
res′ əl 3*
res′ ′l 1
ras′ əl 1

WRITHE
rīth 4

WROTH
rôth 4

WROUGHT
rôt 4

WRY
rī 4

XENOPHOBE
zen' ə fōb' 4

XENOPHOBIA
zen' ə fō' bē ə 4

XEROGRAPHY +
zi räg' rə fē 3*
zə räg' rə fē 1

XEROX + ○
zir' äks 3

XYLOPHONE
zī' lə fōn' 4

YACHT +
yät 4

YAHOO
yä' hōō 4*
yā' hōō 3
yä hōō' 2

YAHWE
yä' we 3*
yä' wā 1

YARMULKE
yär' məl kə 3*
yä' məl kə 2

YEARN
yurn 4

YEAST
yēst 4

YEOMAN
yō' mən 4

YESHIVAH
yə shē' və 3

YEW
yōō 4

YIDDISH
yid' ish 4

YODEL
yōd"l 4

YOGA
yō' gə 4

YOGI
yō' gē 4

YOGHURT (YOGURT)
yō' gərt 4

YOKEL
yō' kəl 3
yō' k'l 1*

YOLK
yōk 4*
yōlk 2

YOM KIPPUR +
yäm kip' ər 3
yum kip' ər 1
yōm kip' ər 1*

YOUR
yôr 4*
yoor 4
yər (unstressed) 4
yōr 3

YOUTHS
yōōthz 4*
yōōths 4

YUCCA
yuk' ə 4

YULETIDE
yōōl' tīd' 4

ZABAGLIONE
zäb′ əl yō′ nē   3*
zab′ əl yō′ nē   1

ZANY
zā′ nē   4

ZEAL
zēl   4

ZEALOT
zel′ ət   4

ZEALOUS
zel′ əs   4

ZEITGEIST
tzīt′ gīst′   4*
zīt′ gīst′   1

ZENITH
zē′ nith   3*
zē′ nəth   1

ZEPHYR
zef′ ər   4

ZEPPELIN
zep′ ə lin   4*
zep′ lin   1

ZERO ○
zē′ rō   4*
zir′ ō   2
zē′ rō′   1

ZIONISM
zī′ ən iz′ əm   3*
zī′ ən iz ′m   1

ZIRCON +
zʉr′ kän   3*
zʉr′ kän′   1

ZITHER
zith′ ər   4*
zith′ ər   2

ZODIAC
zō′ dē ak′   4

ZOMBIE +
zäm′ bē   4

ZOOLOGY +
zō äl′ ə jē   4

ZOOLOGICAL +
zō′ ə läj′ i kəl   3
zō′ ə läj′ i k′l   1*

ZUCCHINI
zoo kē′ nē   3*
zōō kē′ nē   1
tsōō kē′ nē   1